FUNDAMENTALS

Second Edition

OF GUIDANCE

Bruce Shertzer

and

Shelley C. Stone

PURDUE UNIVERSITY

Houghton Mifflin Company · Boston

New York · Atlanta · Geneva, Illinois · Dallas · Palo Alto

Printed in the U.S.A.

Library of Congress Catalog Card Number: 72–129680

ISBN: 0–395–05403–6

To Our Fathers

Edwin F. Shertzer and Shelley C. Stone, Sr.

who taught us the dignity
and value of work
within a context of
appreciation for others

EDITOR'S
INTRODUCTION

Upon occasion an editor's introduction should focus entirely upon the book being considered. The editor should eschew all temptations to provide a matrix of his own thoughts and observations within which the book can be read. This second edition of Shertzer and Stone's *Fundamentals of Guidance* provides just such an occasion. One reviewer of the first edition dwelt upon the encyclopedic nature of the book—its coverage of the entire field of guidance, including both its historical development and a thoroughly comprehensive view of the contemporary scene. Whatever I might write to provide historical or social perspective has probably already been covered by the authors!

In my introduction to the first edition I wrote:

> This book commends itself as a thorough and scholarly analysis of both over-all concepts and specific roles and procedures. In controversial areas the authors are impartial and objective, often presenting both the pros and cons of a point of view and leaving to the reader a considerable element of free choice. In spite of the author's modest claim to the contrary in their preface, the book is so thorough in many areas that it may be considered a handbook of both concepts and practices that will be found useful in daily practice by any functioning counselor.

The present edition is even more scholarly and comprehensive. There is, for example, a new section on the "Adolescent in the 1970's" in Chapter 1. This is a penetrating but cautious analysis of what is happening and what might happen in student protest and dissent, drug abuse, sexual behavior, concern for minorities, political activity, distrust of adults, and demands for a voice in decision making.

These are not only crucial contemporary issues for students but they are concerns that are likely to remain with us throughout much of the next decade. Shertzer and Stone are noted for providing reading references that are current and this edition is no exception.

There are to me some exciting new sections in other chapters. There is, for example, a new review of the philosophical and operating principles of guidance—accompanied by a "don't-spare-the-whip" listing of current criticism of guidance. There are two additional models of guidance in the "models" chapter and an analysis of the career patterns of counselors which tells us that we don't know enough about counselors' careers! There is new discussion of computer-based and simulation-based guidance and, in the final chapter, new statements on both simulation materials and behavior-modification techniques.

I haven't yet mentioned a completely new chapter on guidance in non–high school settings (Chapter 4). For those who think of guidance, and particularly of counseling, as a school-based field of work, there will be some surprises in this chapter. The reader may even stop to wonder about the placement of *his* counseling career.

As one who has worked in this field since 1926, I have become very weary of the overworked and overgeneralized term "guidance." Shertzer and Stone have put some new boundaries around the field for me and some new substance into its meaning. As a "counselor" I have come to appreciate "guidance!"

C. GILBERT WRENN

PREFACE

This second edition of *Fundamentals of Guidance,* like the original one, was designed for use in introductory guidance courses. The authors undertook the revision because they felt obliged to keep the content current so that students would be well served in such courses. Consequently, a major objective of this revision was to incorporate literature and ideas that had appeared since the book's original publication in 1966. While the format remains the same, a new chapter which describes guidance in a variety of settings has been added and new material has been included in many chapters. In addition to these modifications, parts of the earlier edition have been rewritten and the annotated bibliography and selected references have been made current.

Students who enroll in introductory courses are often individuals who have diverse yet related professional objectives. Among others, these objectives often include teaching, educational administration, psychology, and social work as well as school counseling. Because of these wide-ranging objectives, the usual approach in introductory courses is to present a broad overview of the field of guidance. Thus, depth in specialized areas, e.g., counseling or testing, will not be found in this volume. Such treatment is found more appropriately in courses designed especially for thorough coverage of narrower, specialized topics.

The objectives of this edition of *Fundamentals of Guidance* remain the same as those set forth in the original edition:

1. To acquaint students with the fundamental subject matter of guidance— the individual, his development and needs.

2. To provide students with a framework of knowledge from which they may gain a perspective of what guidance has been, what it is now, and what it may become in the future.

3. To provide students with an orientation to the services of guidance— their purposes, their make-up, and their strengths and limitations.

4. To help students understand the problems and issues confronting present-day guidance practitioners as well as the rationale behind the patterns of behavior ascribed to professional guidance personnel.

5. To clarify for students existing issues and emerging trends in the field of guidance.

6. To help students develop some appreciation of the field, its practitioners, its aspirations, and its problems.

Much effort has gone into documentation of content and the stipulation of sources that can be pursued by the serious student. Hopefully, this effort underscores the fact that there is content and substance to be mastered by those who seriously entertain the notion of entering the field. The truly professional counselor is thoroughly familiar with the disciplines and subject matter upon which he bases his actions. Good intentions and a predisposition to be helpful to students are insufficient. In short, the counselor must be thoroughly conversant with the history of his field, the setting in which he practices, the individuals with whom he works and, insofar as possible, contemporary and future developments in his field of interest. The authors hope that the material presented is a comprehensive integration of fact and interpretation which clarifies and make salient the basic principles in the aforementioned areas.

Any author of a general introductory text naturally and necessarily draws on the thoughts and labors of a multitude of coworkers and predecessors. The present authors are no exception. The footnotes throughout the text indicate the many sources of factual data incorporated into the book. Yet the most influential sources of thinking and knowledge that have entered into the book's development cannot always be cited. In this category are the contributions—both written and verbal—of former students, clients, teachers, and colleagues.

The authors again wish to acknowledge the assistance of many individuals. Special recognition is due to Dr. H. Allan Dye who graciously assisted in the preparation of Chapter 16 and to Dr. Dorothy Johnson who was very helpful in the preparation of part of Chapter 6 and provided the material presented in the Appendix. We express our continuing gratitude to the publisher and especially to its consulting editor, C. Gilbert Wrenn. Help and assistance from these sources did much to improve and expedite the revision. We have attempted to incorporate in this edition the constructive criticisms and thoughtful commentary of numerous students and colleagues who used the original edition. One thing is certain: this invaluable source of assistance continues to be sought.

BRUCE SHERTZER

SHELLEY C. STONE

CONTENTS

FUNDAMENTALS OF GUIDANCE

PART ONE
THE ADOLESCENT, EDUCATION, AND GUIDANCE

T HE OBJECT of Part One is to present an overview of the adolescent, the meaning and purpose of guidance in education, past and current guidance models, and the status and responsibilities of school counselors. This overview should enable students to gain greater familiarity with the past and present character of the guidance function. Such a perspective should lead to a critical, meaningful examination of guidance services, teacher responsibilities, and counselor roles, as well as the issues and trends presented in the final chapters of this book.

Since the pupil is the recipient of guidance, it is appropriate that the volume open with a consideration of the adolescent. Chapter 1 describes the adolescent in today's society: his characteristics and concerns, the character of a separate adolescent society, major youth problems with which the school must cope, and projections for the 1970's.

Chapter 2 attempts to place guidance in the total educational enterprise. Attention is given to the historical development of guidance services. A brief statement of guidance principles is set forth. In addition, a short statement directs attention to current criticisms of guidance and its practitioners.

The models upon which guidance services have been patterned are described in Chapter 3. The description given of each model should enable students to discern its form, content, and intent. Examination of these various approaches to guidance strategy may help students reach some understanding of what guidance has been and may become. Reflection upon such proposals may lead to the single conclusion, if no other,

1

that great diversity exists in viewpoints and practices. But the more appropriate conclusion would be that the sweep of guidance has increased, especially in recent years.

Chapter 4 presents an overview of guidance in settings other than public secondary schools. Attention is directed to the nature of the service in these settings, and points of variability and commonality among settings are set forth.

The changing responsibilities of the person most directly charged with school guidance—the counselor—constitute the focus of Chapters 5 and 6. The increase in the number of school counselors is briefly traced. Chapter 5 reviews the content and character of counselor education and state counselor certification requirements. Chapter 6 delineates the characteristics and functions of school counselors. Finally, the reader is directed to the evolving nature of the counselor's work in present-day schools.

1

THE ADOLESCENT IN TODAY'S SOCIETY

What characteristics describe adolescents?
What are the main characteristics of the adolescent society?
What perennial youth concerns and problems presently confront the schools?
What may the world of the adolescent of the 1970's be like?
What implications for guidance personnel stem from existing and impending change?

The vast majority of guidance services in public schools currently exist at the junior and senior high school levels. Therefore, they exist for adolescents. Adolescent psychology and development are not the major focus of this book, but in a fundamental sense the adolescent age group is the book's reason for being. It is appropriate, therefore, that the presentation begin with a chapter which, while not exhaustive, has as its major purpose extending the reader's range of understandings about adolescents. This involves focusing attention upon the characteristics of adolescents, the concerns they have, and the network of relationships that depict their society.

An effort has been made to incorporate views of adolescence derived from social science literature and the popular press. The recent attitudinal and behavioral changes among some within this age group have been presented vividly by the mass communications media. In truth, the authors were faced with the danger of discounting existing knowledge that we believe to be relevant and valuable in understanding most adolescents or overemphasizing observations and speculations about teenage behavior that have emerged within the past five years. Our approach has been to include material from both sources.

Educators, psychologists, and sociologists have long been concerned with the significance of the physical, social, and psychological dimensions of adolescence. This broad interest in the adolescent period is markedly evident;

How about spiritual?

3

the necessity for understanding adolescence, obvious. Despite the fact that much has appeared in both professional and lay literature about the age group, there are numerous indications that adolescents are not well understood by those who are dedicated to helping them—parents, teachers, and counselors. In everyday, interpersonal relations with teenage boys and girls, many adults seem to lack awareness of their psychological and physical needs, as well as a general appreciation of the changes and adjustments which adolescents undergo.

The term "adolescence" as used in this context refers to the transitional period between childhood and maturity. It is also used to denote the physical, psychological, and social development and maturation that take place. The time span in years is roughly from twelve to twenty. Theoreticians have tended to define adolescence as the total of all adjustments to changes and conditions beginning with puberty. They have stressed that puberty is a part of adolescence but not synonymous with it, since adolescence encompasses more than physical or sexual development. The necessity to cope with the conditions of puberty brings forth a variety of modes of tension release, gratification, and defenses in the individual which are responsible for the sometimes "unusual" behavior all too frequently cited by adults as the major characteristic of this age.

THE CHARACTERISTICS OF ADOLESCENTS

Adolescence is most frequently described and discussed from an external frame of reference in which the criteria are adult standards and expectations. More helpful to those who work with the adolescent are perceptions based upon a frame of reference using criteria from the world of the adolescent.

G. Stanley Hall, often called the Father of Child Study in America, collected extensive data and wrote many descriptions of adolescent behavior. His views of the adolescent were from an external framework, emphasizing the differences between adolescent behavior and that which precedes and follows it. In brief, Hall and other early psychologists believed the adolescent period to be a metamorphic one for an individual. Typical of this view was the outcome of Meek's research during the 1930's. She described in great detail the adult view of the adolescent. Meek noted the following changes which occur during the transition from childhood to adolescence:

1. From that period of body contour having very little shape to body contour and stature resembling an adult.
2. From that period of many fleeting interests to greater stability of interests that are fewer in number but vastly more meaningful.
3. From that period of little regard for peer standards and status among peers to that marked by a large concern about them in relation to the adult pattern of culture to which he aspires.

4. From that period when activity is engaged in for its own sake to that marked by much modified adult behavior.
5. From that period in which all social activities are informal to that in which social activities are by choice more formal.
6. From that period marked by temporary and transient friendships to one marked by friendships that are more sustained and steady.[1]

The storm, stress, and conflict associated with adolescence often give rise to rather flowery, subjective analysis in descriptions of teenagers. For example, consider the following:

> With the advent of puberty the sleeping lion awakens, stretches, and as though fortified and rejuvenated by his long rest, proceeds to tear apart the elaborate structure which has apparently kept him so satisfactorily under control in the preceding six or seven years. This new strength of the instincts, as we know, derives from the enormous accession of energy as the gonads begin to function at puberty. The former peace no longer prevails.[2]

> The most striking characteristic of this mysterious period in human existence is the simultaneous presence of contradictory, mutually exclusive trends. Adolescence is both unproductive and yet strangely creative and fertile. Useless and irresponsible centering of all interest on the self occurs together with an almost unlimited capacity for idealistic self-sacrifice.[3]

> The adolescent is altruistic and egocentric, devoted and unfaithful, gregarious and solitary, blindly submissive to a leader and defiant of authority, idealistic and cynical, sensitive and callous, ascetic and libertine, optimistic and pessimistic, enthusiastic and indifferent.[4]

Most authorities would agree with the following generalizations about adolescence:

1. Adolescence is a transition period between childhood and adulthood. It refers to the physiological and psychological characteristics dominant between puberty and maturity. The use of chronological age to denote the period is virtually meaningless because the onset of puberty varies fairly widely and researchers agree on no specific age as the termination for adolescence. The most frequently cited age span is twelve to twenty.
2. Physical and sexual maturation as evidenced by changes in both the primary and secondary sex characteristics results in shifts in attitude to-

[1] L. H. Meek, *The Personal-Social Development of Boys and Girls, with Implications for Secondary Education* (New York: Progressive Education Association Committee on Workshops, 1940).

[2] Joseph Lander, "The Pubertal Struggle Against the Instincts," *American Journal of Orthopsychiatry* Vol. 12 (July 1942), p. 457.

[3] Frederick J. Hacker and Elizabeth R. Geleerd, "Freedom and Authority in Adolescence," *American Journal of Orthopsychiatry* Vol. 15 (October 1945), p. 625.

[4] Maxwell Gitelson, "Character Synthesis: The Psychotherapeutic Problems of Adolescence," *American Journal of Orthopsychiatry* Vol. 18 (July 1948), p. 425.

ward the proper masculine and feminine sex role. This period of development includes the acceptance of one's own physical self and its potential reproductive processes.

3. Adolescence also includes searching for emotional, social, and economic independence. It is a time for the individual to utilize at a more mature and complex level the ability to give as well as get, to communicate with others and to trust them, and to learn what is harmful and what is good for himself and others.

During the 1950's, some authors sought to define adolescence in concepts associated with psychological identity. For example, it has been defined as "a social process through which a clear and stable self-identification is established";[5] or as "the process of identification completed if and when the adolescent loses childhood identifications to a new kind of identification, achieved in absorbing sociability and in competitive apprenticeship with and among his age-mates."[6]

George Gallup and Evan Hill, basing their conclusion on interviews with three thousand American young people between the ages of fourteen and twenty-two, presented the following composite portrait at the beginning of the 1960's:

> No one can say that the American youth is going to hell. He's not. But he is a pampered hothouse plant and likes it that way. The beatnik is a rarity; the delinquent is a minority.
>
> Our typical youth will settle for low success rather than risk high failure. He has little spirit of adventure. He wants to marry early—at twenty-three or twenty-four—after a college education. He wants two or three children and a spouse who is "affectionate, sympathetic, considerate and moral"; rarely does he want a mate with intelligence, curiosity or ambition. He wants a little ranch house, an inexpensive new car, a job with a large company, and a chance to watch TV each evening after the smiling children are asleep in bed.
>
> He is a reluctant patriot who expects nuclear war in his time and would rather compromise than risk an all-out war. He is highly religious yet winks at dishonesty. He wants very little because he has so much and is unwilling to risk what he has. Essentially he is quite conservative and cautious. He is old before his time; almost middle-aged in his teens.[7]

Many boys and girls of the present generation have been reared and educated in child-centered homes and schools. Parents, like educators, have made genuine efforts to understand their children rather than impose arbitrary standards of parental authority which might be detrimental to the

[5] E. Z. Friedenberg, *The Vanishing Adolescent* (Boston: Beacon Press, 1959), pp. 8–12.

[6] Erik H. Erikson. *Childhood and Society* (New York: W. W. Norton & Company, Inc., 1950), p. 269.

[7] George Gallup and Evan Hill, "Youth—The Cool Generation," *Saturday Evening Post* Vol. 234 (December 23, 1961), p. 64.

growth of character. Taylor, a former university president, sees two results from such attitudes and actions:

> Two things have happened. One is that the young have already learned to practice in their own way what there is to know about the social life and customs of adult society. The other is that the younger generation has separated itself from the older by a shift in attitude toward parental authority, a shift that has come about largely through the modern attitude of parents toward their children. The young have now established their own quasi-adult society with its own vocabulary, emotions, heroes, attitudes, and customs. They have become self-sufficient and independent as a group, but in a curious way less identifiable as individuals, more easily classified as groups with common customs and ideas. They take their cues from their own kind, rather than from individual models provided by their parents.[8]

Taylor further believes that it is difficult for the "understood" adolescent to rebel, and since he is understood rather than suppressed, he has nothing to fight.

The views presented by Gallup and Hill and by Taylor were written in the early 1960's and based upon observations of adolescent behavior and attitudes existing in the late 1950's. While the reader will want to compare these views with those presented in the section dealing with the adolescent in the 1970's, it is important to recognize the degree to which the observations from these two older sources still hold for the majority of today's teenagers.

Adult views of this age group are usually colored by adult value judgments which often tend to emphasize negative qualities. Because of this it is easy to overlook the many positive qualities of the adolescent. The description that follows attempts to minimize the usual adult bias and to stress the positive aspects of this age group. What does research reveal about the characteristics of this so-called half-child/half adult? The literature[9, 10, 11, 12, 13] indicates that he possesses some or all of the following traits.

The adolescent youth is in an age marked by disruption, particularly in the eyes of adults. Adult descriptions emphasize such factors as resistance to family authority, hypercriticalness toward parents and other adults, over-

[8] Harold Taylor, "The Understood Child," *Saturday Review* Vol. 44 (May 20, 1961), p. 47.

[9] Peter Blos, *On Adolescence* (New York: Free Press of Glencoe, Inc., 1962).

[10] David P. Ausubel, *Theory and Problems of Adolescent Development* (New York: Grune & Stratton, Inc., 1954).

[11] Laurence K. and Mary Frank, *Your Adolescent* (New York: New American Library of World Literature, 1956).

[12] Raymond K. Kuhlen, *The Psychology of Adolescent Development* (New York: Harper & Brothers, 1952).

[13] Texas Study of Secondary Education, *Criteria for Evaluating Junior High Schools*, Research Study No. 15 (Austin, Tex.: State Department of Education, 1954).

sensitivity to adult suggestions regarding hours, friends, and appropriate use of time. Particularly disruptive at this age is an almost infantile selfishness regarding the use of family possessions such as radio, telephone, television, and bathrooms. Adults tend to become particularly alarmed about the adolescent's compelling drive to conform to the mannerism, speech, and dress of his age group, and his fierce loyalties in retaining and defending his friends.

In contrast to the regressive and aggressive characteristics cited above, the adolescent frequently shows an increasingly mature curiosity about himself and his environment. This is evident in his experiments to discover where his special abilities, strengths, and endurances lie; in his attempts to project himself into many imaginary roles; in his questioning effort to reconcile the realities of life with the idealism that frequently characterizes the instruction he receives; in his attempts to succeed by rationalizing situations in which he feels inadequate; in his labile feelings of superiority and inferiority; and in his intense overreactions to successes and failures. Changes in such behaviors always accompany changes in attitudes and interests.

He is concerned about his adjustment to rapid body changes. This characteristic is revealed in many ways—such as assuming a body posture to disguise whatever he thinks is too great a deviation from the normal, overzealous dieting to correct rapid weight changes, emotional reaction to the awkwardness that results from sudden disproportionate body changes. This concern is also noticeable in his constant attempt to meet the needs of a seemingly insatiable appetite and in his strange feelings toward the opposite sex which he can neither understand nor adequately manage.

The adolescent strives to attain independence while simultaneously maintaining a base of security. This may be seen in his emerging interest in vocational pursuits, in his desire for work experience and financial independence, and in his insistence on the right to manage as well as to mismanage this independence without questions from parents. It is expressed through his desire to select his own clothes, friends, and schedules; through his impulsive but rare manifestation of love for his parents; through his stressing and distorting of what he sees as symbols of adulthood such as smoking pot, drinking, or whatever form of self-assertion is admired by his contemporaries.

The adolescent critically re-examines the personal values he blindly incorporated as a child. This reassessment of fundamental beliefs is marked by an apparent search for new values and an active test of both old and new ideals. The search for the new is most evident in his rapidly shifting identification with and mimicry of the person most admired at the time, coupled with contradictory feelings of loyalty to former identification figures. Preoccupation with fundamental beliefs is revealed through the adolescent's deep concern about right and wrong; through his rigid adherence to the code of behavior accepted by his age group; through his naive belief in the form, symbol, and ritual of organization; and through actively challenging adults when their idealistic preachments do not "square" with the reality of adult behavior.

The adolescent begins to recognize that the independence he seeks must be justified by the acquisition of skills and knowledge. He demonstrates this in a desire for a better understanding of his own abilities, skills, interests, and knowledge. He is disturbed about being too different from the group and therefore frequently refuses to take advantage of the activities that would give him knowledge and skill because such activities point up his deficiencies. Paradoxically, he will enthusiastically, but often disastrously, take advantage of opportunities to display the special abilities he has as yet not mastered.

These characteristics may strike one as the usual biased adult view from which most individuals abstract only the negative, forgetting the crucial point that most of the described behaviors reflect exaggerations of desirable adult behavior and efforts at self-mastery. Embedded within what is frequently viewed as misbehavior is a testing of that which adults strive to teach children at an earlier age. Recognition of this fact would help those adults attempting to cope with this age group—whether as parents, teachers, or counselors—attain a more constructive approach by avoiding some of the obvious misunderstandings.

THE ADOLESCENT SOCIETY

The social development of an individual is a continuous and cumulative process. With puberty comes increasing social awareness. The adolescent becomes more aware of his attitudes toward himself, which in turn are reflected in his social behavior. He strives to attain approval from those of the same sex as well as from the opposite sex. The emotional tensions that attend these adjustments often cause the adolescent to be anxious, insecure, fearful, and suspicious of others.

The social group with which the adolescent most closely associates determines to a considerable extent the sort of individual into which he will develop. As the adolescent's social horizons broaden, the degree of influence of each group upon him depends upon the degree of intimacy existing among the members of the group. The greatest influence comes from primary groups such as family, close friends, and the like.

Because of his feelings of insecurity, the adolescent is often slavishly conforming in his behavior. He desires to appear and behave like the group with which he associates. This conformity is often a means of escape from embarrassment and self-consciousness. Often one of the greatest tragedies of the adolescent years is for an individual to perceive himself as "different" from others in his age group. In a desperate attempt to achieve peer acceptance, an adolescent may resort to deviant behavior, which can result in the very rejection he sought to avoid.

Adolescents look increasingly to each other rather than to parents, teachers, and other adults for social rewards and social recognition. Horrocks succinctly summarizes this concern for group reactions in the case of adolescents who deviate from the group because of differences in body development:

> Adolescents are particularly prone to ridicule or reject those among their age mates who possess physical anomalies or who deviate in some way from the physical norm. Such ridicule or rejection only serves to accentuate the difficulties of an adolescent who may already be worrying as to whether or not he is normal.[14]

Horrocks points up that the important thing is not so much what actually is happening to the body of the person at this time but rather what he thinks about it. His attitudes make the difference, and these attitudes have a developmental history, just as physical growth does.

It has long been asserted that adolescence is a period of emotional turmoil because of the stresses and strains attendant upon achieving sexual and physical maturity. Recent research has modified this view. Storm and stress are not inevitably direct products of puberty as has long been contended but instead appear to originate in cultural and societal expectations. Elkin and Westley, studying the patterns of socialization among forty adolescents living in an upper-class suburb of Montreal, believed they had substantial evidence to challenge at least three commonly held assumptions:

1. Adolescents suffer from "storm and stress" which results from their peculiar age-grade position in the American social structure.
2. A "youth culture" is a widespread and dominant pattern among adolescents in America.
3. The youth culture of the adolescent is etiologically and functionally linked to the storm and stress of the individual.[15]

Although Elkin and Westley attack the notion of a distinctive youth culture, a considerable body of descriptive and analytical materials relating to a society of adolescents in the United States is now available. Smith,[16] Coleman,[17] and others hold that an emerging adolescent society exists in America. They maintain that there is a distinctive system of social relationships engaged in and maintained by adolescents as "their world." The existence of such a society does not mean that it is the only world to which adolescents are responsive, but it does mean that they alone "live in it." Not all adolescents participate actively, but enough of them do in enough different ways to provide evidence that such a society exists. Coleman states:

> This setting-apart of our children in schools—which take on ever more functions, ever more "extracurricular activities"—for an ever longer period of training has a singular impact on the child of high-school age. He is "cut-

[14] John A. Horrocks, *The Psychology of Adolescence* (Boston: Houghton Mifflin Company, 1951), p. 300.

[15] F. Elkin and William A. Westley, "The Myth of Adolescent Culture," *American Sociological Review* Vol. 20 (December 1955), pp. 680–684.

[16] Ernest A. Smith, *American Youth Culture* (Glencoe, Ill.: The Free Press, 1962).

[17] James S. Coleman, *The Adolescent Society* (Glencoe, Ill.: The Free Press, 1961).

off" from the rest of society, forced inward toward his own age group, made to carry out his whole social life with others his own age. With his fellows he comes to constitute a small society, one that has most of its important interactions *within* itself, and maintains only a few threads of connection with the outside adult society.[18]

And again:

In sum, then, the general point is this: our adolescents today are cut off, probably more than ever before, from the adult society. They are still oriented toward fulfilling their parents' desires, but they look very much to their peers for approval as well. Consequently, our society has within its midst a set of small teen-age societies, which focus teen-age interests and attitudes on things far removed from adult responsibilities, and which may develop standards that lead away from those goals established by the larger society.[19]

Some of the reasons why an independent adolescent society has emerged may lie in the discontinuities so markedly evident in the transition from childhood to adulthood. One such discontinuity is that even though children are taught that sexual expression is dangerous, they become biologically ready for and psychologically attracted to sexual experience with no socially approved outlets. Another discontinuity lies in the fact that children are financially and economically dependent and consequently alienate adults because they do not contribute to the family income at a time when they are making increasing demands upon it.

The adolescent's relationships with his peers are, for all practical purposes, determined by whether he is enrolled in school and, if so, by the relationships he has in the school. Bernard points out that participation in the adolescent society is largely proscribed by leaving school and going to work. She states:

Not all teenagers participate in the teen-age culture. Those who are in the civilian labor force, who are in the armed services, or who are married . . . are chronologically, but not necessarily culturally teenagers. They are neophytes in the adult culture of our society.[20]

Smith has identified and discussed the characteristics distinctive of this American youth culture. The following characteristics are abstracted from his book, *American Youth Culture,* and represent modifications or adaptations of adult values and behavior:

[18] *Ibid.,* p. 3. Reprinted with permission of The Macmillan Co. from *The Adolescent Society* by James S. Coleman. Copyright © 1961 by The Free Press, a corporation.

[19] *Ibid.,* p. 9. Reprinted with permission of The Macmillan Co. from *The Adolescent Society* by James S. Coleman. Copyright © 1961 by The Free Press, a corporation.

[20] Jessie Bernard, "Teen-Age Culture: An Overview," *Annals of the American Academy of Political and Social Science* Vol. 338 (November 1961), p. 2.

1. The values inherent in the Judeo-Christian religious tradition—respect for private property, upward occupational aspiration, thrift, self-denial, etc.—are not a dominant influence in youth culture except in the areas of competitive and individual success.

2. Although the family serves as a primary field of socialization and ascribes social-class position to youth, youth modify adult norms by muting economic differences. Their associations cover a wide socio-economic class spread.

3. Secrecy and concealment characterize youth culture. Secrecy protects youth from adult sanctions, especially in matters in which adolescent behavior violates adult norms. However, adult sex taboos on premarital sex relations are reinforced in the youth culture, particularly among middle-class youth.

4. Dating, a major institution of youth culture, has been initiated and perpetuated by youth. Adolescents elaborate dating norms and sentiments independent of, and even conflicting with, dominant adult norms. Youth dating norms emphasize sequential dating partners, no mutual emotional commitment, mutual exploitation, and petting as a sexual release.

5. The clique within the youth culture sets norms that are often the highest authority for its members and may take precedence over both family and other adult norms. The clique acts as a protective structure against adult authority and sanctions and may even discipline youth who accept or practice disapproved adult norms.

6. A compulsive conformity is required of the members of the youth culture. This conformity is revealed in appearance and dress, in which distinctive clothing and hair styles are sought.

7. Youth have developed a language that identifies and unifies its members as well as sets them apart. This language is directed toward making invidious distinctions among people and events. It also serves as a means for approving conformists or unmasking deviants.

8. The youth culture is perpetuated and transmitted through succeeding generations through the process of the younger individuals looking up to and emulating those in the age-grade immediately above them.

9. Parent-youth conflicts and disputes are the end products of a process of opposition which begins in early infancy and comes to fruition in adolescence. Tension points are frequently such things as the use of the family car, diet, school grades, money, and personal habits. An absence of transitional rituals and the prolongation of dependence of American youth lead to parent-youth conflicts.

10. The technology of the youth culture—its money, cars, telephones, food —is controlled and manipulated by adults.

11. Youth tend to withdraw socially rather than physically from their families. The conspiracy of silence or secrecy that separates youth from adults leads to a significant lack of communication between them. Overt and covert deception is a natural mode of adjustive behavior used by adolescents when conflict arises with adults.[21]

---

[21] Abstracted from Smith, *American Youth Culture,* pp. 4–39.

A great deal of interest has been directed to studying the attraction that groups have for adolescents. The pull toward contemporaries, the need for group activities, and the need to be a part of a group explain why the teenager's peers are important, just as adult peers are important to adults. Bossard, analyzing peer groups, sees them as meeting needs through the following functions: (1) developing a recognition of the rights of others; serving as a control over behavior; (2) giving security at a needed stage of development; (3) providing a source of cultural identification; and (4) determining behavioral roles.[22] The peer group may well help the teenager to escape from many destructive feelings or desires. He learns not to demand from age-mates what he expects or demands from parents and siblings. This self-limiting aspect of the group is important and helpful to him.

On the other hand, the peer group may provide something that children seek but do so in ways that are not constructive. Coleman describes the high school setting as a "cruel jungle" of dating and rating with tightly knit crowds and cliques. Summarizing the responses of some nine thousand pupils in ten different schools, he reported the shared-peer activities and interests of boys (outdoor games) and girls (dating and dancing). An overwhelming importance was attached to car ownership as well as to the remodeling of cars to produce customized models. Of prime importance to popularity was athletic participation by boys and leadership in activities by girls. According to Coleman, boys value athletics and car ownership; girls value social success, physical beauty, enticing manners, and clothes; academic success is not as important to teenagers as adults would like to think; and boys and girls tend to look "upward" for those they would most like to be like—socially upward to those among them whose backgrounds were more privileged than their own. However, they choose as leaders those who are most like themselves.[23]

Types of Peer Groupings

McGovern points out that *peer groups* differ from *gangs* by these features: (1) the peer group has from three to fifteen members compared to the gang's large (sometimes hundreds) interlocking membership; (2) the peer group has informal processes of selection, induction, leadership, and withdrawal, while gangs are more formally organized; (3) peer group members reflect middle-class society, but gangs reflect lower-class culture; (4) social and recreational activities predominate in peer groups, but gangs engage in predatory activities; (5) gangs use physical coercion and force as sanctions, while peer groups use manipulation, control, avoidance, and rejection. McGovern also describes the component parts and developmental phases of the peer group. He views its first phase as the clique. The *clique*

[22] James Bossard, *The Sociology of Child Development* (New York: Harper & Brothers, 1954), pp. 502–515.

[23] Coleman, *The Adolescent Society*, pp. 11–141.

begins in childhood, is one-sexed in membership, is class selective, links childhood and adolescent periods, and either coexists with or is absorbed by the crowd. The *crowd* is the second phase of the peer group. The crowd may contain many cliques, and it serves as a transitional structure from puberty to courtship. As such, it enables the individual to move from monosexual to heterosexual relationships.[24]

Social Class and Participation

Systematic study of social class in American society was initiated by Warner and his associates in 1941.[25] Hollingshead's *Elmstown's Youth* was the first analysis that dealt specifically with the impact of class status on teenage behavior.[26] Mounting evidence makes it clear that ready acceptance into, and active participation in, teenage affairs are influenced by the adolescent's socioeconomic status. Large and consistent differences in "attitude" or ideology exist among students of different family income and occupational circumstances.

It is not the purpose here to describe sociological views of the social classes but rather to indicate that they exist and that teachers and counselors must realize their existence and act accordingly if they are to perform their functions effectively. From a combination of several studies, Havighurst and Neugarten summarize the population distribution by social class as follows:[27]

Class	Percentage of Population
I—upper upper	1–3
II—lower upper	
III—upper middle	7–12
IV—lower middle	20–35
V—upper lower	25–40
VI—lower lower	15–25

It should be noted that the lines between the classes are not clear cut; for instance, an individual may have three characteristics of Class III and three of Class IV. The public school staff member usually does not encounter the Class I individual since the latter most often attends a private school. The other classes of pupils, however, are frequently encountered in the public

[24] Joseph W. McGovern, "The Adolescent and His Peer Group," in Alexander A. Schneiders (ed.), *Counseling the Adolescent* (San Francisco: Chandler Publishing Company, 1967), pp. 15–16.

[25] W. Lloyd Warner and Paul S. Lunt, *The Social System of a Modern Community* (New Haven, Conn.: Yale University Press, 1941).

[26] A. B. Hollingshead, *Elmstown's Youth: The Impact of Social Class on Adolescents* (New York: John Wiley & Sons, Inc., 1949).

[27] Robert J. Havighurst and Bernice L. Neugarten, *Society and Education* (Boston: Allyn and Bacon, Inc., 1962), p. 21.

schools. Therefore, a generalized characterization of these classes as provided by Bernard may be useful at this point:

> Class II, III, and IV children (especially III) work hard, are obedient, and respect the teacher and counselor. They have, though with great variability, a background for education through the example of their parents, the moral support of their families, and the presence of books and magazines in the home. Homework typically takes priority over designated household duties. Class II parents and pupils are said to have an "education compulsion."
>
> Class V and VI pupils are found most frequently in the primary and intermediate grades, before dropouts occur. They are usually not so likeable as those just described. They are not so clean (some in grade schools are sent to the shower before attending class), not so conforming (they have been instructed "not to take nuthin' off nobody," and teachers represent authority), not so serious about school as those from the "right side of the tracks." Their average test intelligence is not so high as the average of those in the higher classes, but it must be remembered that their tested IQ's are subject to question because of differences in reading skills, motivation, and the cultural bias of the testing instruments. There are many who are brighter than the average of those in the higher classes—*many* simply because these two classes comprise approximately half of the total population.[28]

Study after study has shown that in American communities (1) income and occupational strata consistently differ in behavior and attitudes; (2) different occupational positions are given different social evaluations; (3) awareness of stratification is highly variable but is universally important. In what ways does social stratification influence teenage participation in their society? One way, as pointed out previously, is that dropping out of school normally removes the teenager from participation in adolescent society. Dropout studies make it abundantly clear that early school leavers are overwhelmingly from the lower strata rather than from middle- or upper-class families. Hollingshead reported that some 93 percent of the youth from the upper-class and upper-middle-class families were in school, whereas 41 percent from Class IV (upper-lower) families and 89 percent from Class V (lower-lower) families had left school.[29] Havighurst and his associates point out that nine out of ten students from the upper two (of four) strata remained in school, but 38 percent of those from the next lower and 66 percent of those from the lowest had withdrawn.[30]

A second influence of social-class membership on participation in teenage society is the domination of the adolescent society by upper- and middle-class youth. Youth from the upper strata tend to fill the leadership

[28] Harold Bernard, "Socio-Economic Class and the School Counselor," *Theory into Practice* Vol. 2 (February 1963), p. 19.

[29] Hollingshead, *Elmtown's Youth;* see Chapters 6 and 8.

[30] Robert J. Havighurst, *et al., Growing Up in River City* (New York: John Wiley & Sons, Inc., 1962), pp. 57–64.

roles in school and community activities operated for them. Such youth control student activities and acquire leadership experiences while youth from other strata do not. A third influence cited by Hollingshead is that the system of school discipline is often adjusted to favor the upper-class child.[31] Finally, students from the middle class participate more actively in the academic work of the school and receive a disproportionate share of "A's" and "B's," while "D's" and "F's" are disproportionately received by lower-class youngsters.[32] It is, of course, true that many factors contribute to the generally higher grades among the upper-class youth—a higher incidence of academic aptitude, possession of background information which predisposes upper-class youth to acceptable accomplishment, and family emphasis on academic achievement. However, such factors probably do not fully explain the differences in grade distributions associated with social-class phenomena.

Harold Taylor summarized the impact the present social order has upon teenagers with these words:

> There is accordingly a general type of "American high school student," identified by foreign visitors and others who look at our educational system from the outside. He has absorbed the influence of an extroverted community in his home town, particularly in the urban and suburban areas, and models his conduct to a large extent on a young American type, itself a product of the movies, the television, the radio, and phonograph records. The boys and girls have a coeducational attitude to teenage life and a complicated ritual of dating, pledging, riding in cars, attending sports events, along with a common vocabulary of popular phrases. . . . The values are for the most part accepted uncritically. The model for the boy is of a star athlete who has a straight A record, is popular with girls and elected to student office by popular acclaim. The model for the girl is one who is pretty, popular, having a B plus record so that it will not be a threat to her popularity with boys, who likes sports, popular records, movies, has a well-knit social life, and is neither arty nor too brainy nor too intense about anything.[33]

PERENNIAL PERSONAL CONCERNS AND SCHOOL PROBLEMS

An extensive body of literature dating from the 1940's has sought to describe adolescent concerns identified by adolescents themselves. The categories of preoccupations expressed vary in specificity, but a relatively consistent pattern of personal concerns is present. Findings reported in the 1940's, 1950's and early 1960's do not, however, include many factors at work in adolescent society today, e.g., drugs and more open sexual behavior.

[31] Hollingshead, *Elmstown's Youth,* p. 38.

[32] *Ibid.,* pp. 172–175.

[33] Taylor, "The Understood Child," p. 48.

Teenagers responding to questionnaires through the years have said that they are most concerned about changes in physical development, such as breast size, body size and skin conditions; interpersonal relationships, such as friendships and popularity; school activities, such as homework, grades and study habits; family situations; relationships with the opposite sex, including dating, petting, and other sexual behavior. The insecurities arising from these personal concerns generate anxiety which may lead to great lability in mood and extreme fluctuations in behavior. Overactivity, withdrawal, loneliness and preoccupation with fantasy may result. Some of the adolescent's desires are: "I want to like myself; I want others to like me; I want to like others; I want to develop into what can really be me." Bettelheim has put the adolescent's dilemma in perspective:

> It is not his physiological development alone which reduces the adolescent to a state of insecurity. He also lives in a continuous, anxiety evoking dilemma —biologically, emotionally, and culturally. His biological dilemma originates in the conflict between the reawakening of his sex drives and his inability to gratify them because of inhibitions and social pressure. His emotional dilemma centers in the fact that, though he is no longer a child, he is not yet grown up; that, though he desires to free himself from his ties to his parents, he cannot afford to give them up. His cultural dilemma is highlighted by the many new grown-up duties and responsibilities which he is expected to fulfill although he does not yet enjoy adult rights.[34]

American schools, like all formal educational organizations, seek to induct the young into membership in society by giving its pupils a common language and a common set of ideas, beliefs, and values. Nevertheless, American schools tend to exhibit variety, experimentation, improvisation, eclecticism, and aversion to total planning. Critics of American education have commented on the outstanding lack of agreement concerning the ends that schools should serve. But such an agreement would require a virtually static society, and such a society does not and probably never will exist. The impact of massive international and national events upon American life during the last three decades has produced a number of problems with which the schools must cope. The characteristic of American schools noted above—willingness to experiment, to improvise, to try out—will undoubtedly aid the schools' efforts to find solutions to youth problems.

What are some of the youth problems that confront the educational enterprise? To respond fully to this question is beyond the scope of this chapter, but six major problems which teachers, counselors, parents, and administrators are now facing will be briefly outlined. It should be noted that the major problems outlined here are not simply school problems. Their origin lies in the complex social discontinuities that exist in America, and their solution lies in a multi-institutional approach.

[34] Bruno Bettelheim, "The Social-Studies Teacher and Emotional Needs of Adolescents," *The School Review* Vol. 56 (December 1948), p. 586. Reprinted by permission of the publisher, The University of Chicago Press.

The School Dropout

Although the percentage of students dropping out of school is smaller than ever before, dropouts pose a major problem to school personnel. Conant referred to this problem as "... a serious threat to our free society" and as "social dynamite."[35] In recent years numerous studies of dropouts as a group and as individuals have been made locally, statewide, and nationally to learn more about why such students leave school.[36] These studies have, with remarkable consistency, arrived at similar conclusions. Some of the findings fly in the face of reason; others confirm our predetermined thoughts concerning the "why" of the dropout problem. School dropouts are largely a social-class phenomenon. Typical analyses of dropouts indicate reasons such as work, early marriage, grade failures, inability to get along with teachers, dislike of social relationships in the school, and the belief that school course work is unrelated to individual needs.

The number of youth who drop out each year is estimated at almost one million. This impressive statistic dramatizes a monumental problem. While statistics vary somewhat according to source and, of course, vary for different subsections of society, they agree in essence. Regardless of variation in numbers, the dropout problem is of such magnitude that one need not be concerned with a difference of a few percentage points: the fact remains that 30 to 40 percent of all students who begin high school fail to complete it. Each year four hundred thousand students in high school in June (excepting from this figure those who graduate) fail to return in September to complete their education. Each year between the opening date for schools and the end of the school year, another seven hundred thousand students fail to complete the academic year. This means that approximately one million boys and girls annually fail to take advantage of the relatively limited time in their lives which society allots for the completion of what is considered in this day a minimum education. The dropout rate in the larger American cities has been estimated to be 50 percent, particularly in the blighted, gray areas, where there is a concentration of migrant, culturally disadvantaged families. In a study of seven communities, the dropout rate was the highest at age sixteen (34 percent) and seventeen (27 percent).[37] In a report on talent losses before high school graduation, Stice found that 90 percent of the most able third of students graduated, but that only 80 percent of the middle third and 69 percent of the least able third graduated.[38]

[35] James B. Conant, *Slums and Suburbs* (New York: McGraw-Hill Book Co., Inc., 1961), p. 2.

[36] Daniel Schreiber (ed.), *Guidance and the School Dropout* (Washington: National Education Association and American Personnel and Guidance Association, 1964).

[37] U.S. Department of Health, Education and Welfare, *High School Dropouts in a Rural Community: Their Problems and Adjustments* (Washington: Government Printing Office, 1956).

[38] Glen Stice, *Research Memorandum* (Princeton, N.J.: Educational Testing Service, January, 1960).

Jacques reports that the Hastings, Nebraska, Public Schools successfully used the following list of characteristics to identify potential dropouts.

Excessive absence
Low placement on mental tests
Broken homes
Failure in school subjects
Minimal family education
Low family income status
Male sex
Lack of participation in school activities
School retardation
Low scores on standardized reading tests[39]

Bernard has suggested four fundamental causes for the high rate of dropouts among lower social classes:

1. Lower class students do not participate in student activities, except football, in proportion to their representation in the school population. They are not an integral part of the school.
2. Lower class students are not likely to be able to afford the cashmere sweaters, the currently in-vogue shoes, the approved trousers that they believe are expected by others. Thus they are unable, or think they are unable, to gain peer approval so important to adolescents.
3. The hidden costs of attending school (books, laboratory fees, student-body tickets, club dues, yearbooks, class rings, etc.) prevent them from feeling that they are part of the student body.
4. The cliquishness of youngsters is a formidable barrier to becoming an enthusiastic participant in school life.[40]

Williams, basing his remarks upon data collected from 13,715 dropouts in Maryland schools during the 1960–61 school year, reported that four reasons accounted for 77.6 percent of school leavers: (1) lack of interest in school, (2) lack of success in school, (3) economic necessity, and (4) marriage and pregnancy.[41]

Many of the factors mentioned above which contribute to students' leaving school early can be remedied in the school—providing, of course, that efforts by the school are given adequate support. However, some of the factors cannot be directly remedied by the schools unless schools reach heavily into areas that are normally outside the province of usual school functions. There are encouraging signs that national support is forthcoming in the form of increased concern over not only the size of the dropout problem but also the ultimate harmful effects of premature school leaving for

[39] William T. Jacques, "Hastings High School Works on the Dropout Problem," *Personnel and Guidance Journal* Vol. 35 (September 1956), pp. 39–40.

[40] Harold W. Bernard, "Socio-Economic Class and the School Counselor," p. 21.

[41] Percy V. Williams, "Dropouts," *NEA Journal* Vol. 52 (February 1963), p. 11.

the individual and for society. For example, in August 1963, President Kennedy allotted $250,000 from the President's Emergency Fund to finance the early return of school counselors to their schools so that they might work with potential dropouts and their families. While the authors have not seen any documentation of the results of this effort, informal reports are that 1,374 counselors in some sixty-three communities contacted 59,301 "potential dropouts." Approximately 51 percent of these returned to school in September 1963, but over half of them dropped out before school terminated in June 1964. If these informal reports were accurate, it could be inferred that these students left school because changes had not been made in curricular offerings and in teacher and peer expectations.

Many schools, especially those in metropolitan areas, have either increased their commitment to programs specifically designed for potential school dropouts or have taken the initiative in instigating new programs to counteract early school leaving. These programs, as well as efforts to go beyond the usual school confines, are efforts to cope with the latter group of reasons mentioned, such as dissatisfaction with curricula, family attitudes toward education, and the like.

The prospect for the school dropout is bleak. His future of marginal employment, his proneness to delinquency and, perhaps most important of all, his almost certain inability to live his life as a fully developed person strongly argue for the support and involvement of all who are responsible for youth.

The reasons for dropping out of school are not simple. Membership in a given social class is not an all-inclusive explanation. Nevertheless, teachers, counselors, and administrators would do well to examine their perceptions of potential dropouts. But awareness and introspection are not enough. Leadership will have to be exerted to broaden and deepen the educational goals of the school so that hundreds of thousands of teenagers will be saved from a lifetime of economic and social unproductiveness.

Pregnancies of Unmarried Teenagers

Of all the woes in America's much troubled society, few evoke more misery or remorse than pregnancies among unmarried high school girls. Each year some 84,000 unmarried teenage girls bear a child, according to estimates of the Department of Health, Education, and Welfare. Many such individuals are automatically forced out of school, and almost all face intense hostility within their communities. Few have adequate prenatal care.

The pattern for many unmarried, pregnant girls is simple and tragic: they are forced out of school; give birth to the baby; are unwilling or unable to return to school; are unable to get a job; are ostracized by friends (and sometimes family members); are driven by loneliness, poverty, and frustration to seek the companionship of other men; become pregnant again. In 1964 the Children's Bureau began a demonstration project which sought to break up this repeated pattern. It offered continuing education during and after pregnancy, social work assistance for girls and their families, and health care that included birth control advice. The success of the initial demonstration project paved the way for others, and now similar projects exist in fifty-four cities. While these projects are of unquestioned value, the number of girls reached by them falls far short of the existing need.

Youthful Marriages

The rate of high school marriages is rapidly rising in the United States today. Teenage marriages pose not only a major social, legal, and educational challenge to our country but also flash signals of grim economic problems. The stark fact is that an overwhelming percentage of the youth who marry in high school drop out of school and only a few re-enter.

The extent to which high school marriages have been increasing in the United States is startling. A twenty-six-state survey by the Population Reference Bureau disclosed that in 1958, 39 percent of all brides and 12 percent of all grooms were under 20, compared with 32 and 7 percent, respectively, in 1950. In 1960, half of the bridegrooms were under the age of 22.8 and half of the brides were under 20.3. The chance of a teenage marriage ending in divorce is three times as great as that of a marriage between older persons. That teenage marriage interferes with educational attainment has been revealed by Burchinal, who reported that nine out of ten teenagers who married were girls, that of the girls who married in high school, 80 percent dropped out, and that of those who dropped out, only 8 percent re-entered. Of the boys, 43 percent dropped out and 9 percent re-entered. From many studies of teenage marriages, Burchinal concluded that these youth (1) had known each other less than a year, (2) had very short engagements, if any, (3) had low incomes and had to accept help from their parents, and (4) had babies before they built a sound husband-wife relationship.[42]

Although the curtailment of education is serious in itself, the social and legal aspects of early marriage are also disturbing, since annulment and divorce rates are highest among those who marry in their teens. Not only is there a strong feeling against permitting married students to continue in high school, but many schools bar them from taking part in extracurricular activities. Many expel or suspend pregnant wives.

Juvenile Delinquency

Juvenile delinquency is now recognized as a pervasive social problem, although little is known empirically about the origins of delinquent behavior. Wirth postulated the theory of culture conflict, which states that delinquency arises either (1) as a way of managing personality conflicts that result when

[42] Lee G. Burchinal, "Can Teen-agers Make a Go of Marriage?" *PTA* Vol. 55 (February 1961), pp. 4–7.

an individual simultaneously internalizes two divergent cultural codes or (2) as a consequence of internalizing a cultural code which so deviates from the prevailing middle-class code that conformity with it is officially defined as delinquent.[43] Another theory holds that delinquent gangs develop in response to tensions created in the transition from adolescence to adulthood. American society, according to this theory, encourages the young to want to achieve adult status but places obstacles in their way when they attempt to attain this goal. Gangs arise, then, to perform the functions served by *rites de passage* in more ordered societies.[44]

More recently, Cloward and Ohlin theorized (1) that delinquency is not simply an asocial reaction, (2) that delinquent behavior results from lack of opportunities for conforming behavior, and (3) that delinquency represents a search for solutions to problems of adjustment.[45]

Available evidence indicates that delinquent behavior appears to be more frequent in economically depressed sectors of urban areas. It is true that delinquent patterns can be found in all parts of American society, but most observers indicate that such behavior is most prevalent in impoverished areas.

A publication of Mobilization for Youth cites the following causes of delinquent behavior in youth living in disadvantaged areas:

1. Discrepancies between social and economic aspirations and opportunities to achieve these aspirations by legitimate means.
2. Emphasis on upward mobility causes dissatisfaction and discontent with present positions.
3. Traditional channels to higher positions, such as through education, are restricted for large categories of people.
4. Self-defeating attitudes and behavior adaptations that become "functionally autonomous"—that is, once they come into existence, they tend to persist quite independent of the forces to which they were originally a response.
5. A feeling of alienation from the social order, conventional rules, and ideologies.[46]

As was pointed out, a delinquent act frequently represents a solution to a child. At the same time, it creates another problem because the child's solution now brings him into conflict with his parents, teachers, police, and others, who have more conventional solutions in mind for him. Statistics that record how many children have been given the label "delinquent

[43] Louis Wirth, "Culture Conflict and Misconduct," *Social Forces* Vol. 9 (June 1931), pp. 484–492.

[44] Herbert Block and Arthur Neiderhoffer, *The Gang: A Study in Adolescent Behavior* (New York: Philosophical Library, 1958).

[45] Richard A. Cloward and Lloyd Ohlin, *Delinquency and Opportunity: A Theory of Delinquent Gangs* (Glencoe, Ill.: The Free Press, 1960).

[46] *A Proposal for the Prevention and Control of Delinquency by Expanding Opportunities* (New York: Mobilization for Youth, December 9, 1961), pp. 46–66.

youth" are inaccurate. The most reliable figures (based on cases reported to the Children's Bureau, Department of Health, Education, and Welfare) indicate that in 1961 some 750,000 were seen in the juvenile courts of the country. Three times this number had some police contacts. Concealed delinquent behavior is even more prevalent at all social-class levels and especially among middle- and upper-class children, who tend not to appear as statistics in police records. The cost of combating juvenile delinquency— detection, study, diagnosis, treatment—is big business. The real tragedy however, lies in the human suffering, misery, and waste of human lives.

School personnel are in a strategic position to help the delinquent-prone find more positive direction for themselves. Through guidance and social services, they can help to provide diagnosis and treatment. School personnel can be leaders in initiating and maintaining community understanding and support for the massive program needed to curb delinquency.

Youth Unemployment

The importance of work is self-evident. Gainful employment is the accepted means of attaining monetary rewards in our money-oriented culture. The extent of unemployment among youth today has been amply documented: As of April 1970, the unemployment rate for youth from sixteen to twenty years was 13.1 percent as compared to an overall unemployment rate of 4.3 percent. During the 1970's the problem of youthful unemployment will be aggravated by the entry of 26,000,000 new workers into the labor market, or an increase of 30 percent over the entries during the preceding decade. The percentage of unemployment among unskilled workers is twice as high as among all other job categories, and the percentage among persons with less than a high school education is nearly double that among high school graduates and triple that among persons with some college education.[47]

The pattern of the future is obvious even now. During the spring of 1969, only one out of fifty professional and technical workers was out of a job, while one of every eight semi-skilled and factory workers was unemployed. Projecting this ratio to the 1970's, imagine what will happen if, as is officially anticipated, some 30 percent of the young people entering the labor force will not have completed a high school education and cannot enter the labor market at more than the semi-skilled or unskilled levels.

Although creating new jobs and employment opportunities for young people is in part a responsibility of local, state, and national agencies and organizations and will rest heavily on the national economy, schools have a most important obligation to young people looking for employment. School personnel can carry out a program of publicizing the existing opportunities and the ways to take advantage of these opportunities. Sensitive vocational counseling can aid youth in developing career plans and can

[47] U.S. Department of Labor, "Labor Force Facts," April, 1970.

clarify what preparation is needed for careers. Placement services that will increase contact between youth and community institutions and adults will aid in solving this problem. Further, school programs closely integrated with the tasks and training requisites of the work world are crucial.

Designing Appropriate Educational Programs

Another problem that confronts educators is that of designing appropriate educational programs to fit a diversity of pupil abilities, interests, and needs. The principle in American education of equality of opportunity commensurate with ability has been taken to mean not only that all children have the right to a public school education but also that individual differences in learning must be taken into account. Between 1950 and 1960 public school enrollment in this country increased by nearly half, which inevitably implies increased diversity in student-body characteristics. How to develop an educational program that is closely related to the unique abilities, interests, and experiences of those whom it is designed to serve has become an even greater challenge to teachers, counselors, and administrators because of the expanding numbers of youth who attend school.

The adolescent's future depends in a large part on the adequacy of the educational experience made available to him. The school's responsibility is to design a program and provide services that will enable students to learn to live in the world in such a way that they will leave their mark upon it.

By presenting these recurring personal concerns and school problems, the authors do not wish to imply that all teenagers are unhappy, emotionally disturbed, or "delinquency prone." Many are not overly confused or unduly tortured by internal physiological or psychological changes or by the conflicts they experience in today's society. Nor are drug use, overt rebellion and other current problems to be discussed in the next section necessarily characteristic of all contemporary teenagers.

Most adolescents cope constructively with the torment as well as the wonder and beauty associated with their age. But mere survival does not mean that the majority are untouched by psychological, social or intellectual problems. Virtually all have problems and concerns for which they frequently seek or desire help. These problems and concerns often stem from the frustration of normal developmental processes, such as the growth of a need for independence and identity.

THE ADOLESCENT OF THE 1970'S

The foregoing description of the characteristics and problems of adolescents may not apply, at least to the same degree, to adolescents of the 1970's. Many astute observers have asserted that American teenagers' attitudes and behavior have changed substantially during the years 1960–1970. These changes—their nature and magnitude—are not easy to document accurately or to describe with precision because they are constantly in flux and are still evolving. *Time* (January 5, 1970) notes that it is impossible to rationalize the condition of contemporary youth; rather, one "feels" the changes.

The standard sources of information about today's adolescents may be relatively useless as source material in understanding contemporary youth. Carefully documented investigations, professional journal articles and textbook descriptions become dated rapidly. One cannot enjoy the luxury of a solid historical perspective in studying today's adolescent. If one stops to collect data, the very nature of that which is studied changes. Today's observer of the adolescent's world frequently finds that his information must come from the less "scientific" or "authoritative" sources such as newspapers, popular magazines, television documentaries and the like. Often one of his best sources of information is the systematic observation of those adolescents around him.

While non-verified sources often leave one uneasy and doubtful of their authenticity, they nevertheless constitute a major portion of the current data available to those who work with today's teenager. The intention here is not to deprecate these sources, for in truth they provide the contemporary data which eventually form the foundation of the history of mankind. The problem lies in dealing with a mass of diverse, sometimes conflicting, observations without the luxury of time to sort and cross-validate information.

These next few pages represent an attempt to project the adolescent's behavior and some of the social factors effecting it. This description attempts to take into account the turmoil of the latter half of the 1960's. Descriptions often permit only fleeting glimpses of mass behavior and the observer is confronted constantly with two crucial questions: How characteristic is such behavior of all adolescents or of a single adolescent? Does such behavior represent individual change or merely a new, different and certainly more noticeable way of expressing that which is present in all individuals?

As stated at the outset of this chapter, we chose to present views distilled from both the traditional literature on adolescence and current observations about this age group. This approach was taken because of our inability to respond adequately to the two foregoing questions. Only time will provide the complex answers to these questions.

The conditions described in the following commentary are related to: (1) a transitional phase in American society, (2) economic affluence and (3) radical college student behaviors. The authors are unable to specify at this time whether the transition will lead to profound and pervasive change among the majority of adolescents, whether the conditions will hold but for a few adolescents or whether the conditions will be washed away completely. Nor are we able to predict the impact of future economic conditions upon adolescents. A major contraction in the economy could alter, if not wipe out, many of the conditions which appear to have facilitated behavioral change among this age group. For example, according to the press, the tighter job market for some college graduates in the spring of 1970 contributed to the reappearance of "low profile" hair styles and more conventional dress. Finally, we are unable to predict the degree to which the more radical behavior of older adolescents will filter down and influence the younger members of this group. While things may never be the same again, it is not possible to know how different they will be for the majority of teenagers in the immediate future.

Protest and Dissent

The latter half of the 1960 decade, without question, has been marked by protest and dissent among American youth, particularly those in their late adolescent years. Their protests were aimed against adult values that seemed irrelevant or outmoded, against impediments to the eradication of poverty and segregation, against living in impersonal, indifferent large organizations. Painfully sensitive to these and other wrongs, youth denounced them, sometimes violently. It is difficult to disapprove of the issues chosen to protest, the institutions attacked, or the social values challenged. To disapprove places one squarely on the side of social injustice, war and gross economic inequities in society—aspects of life which humane persons have struggled against since the beginning of history.

To those whose primary concern is the individual, attempts to capture the motivation behind the dissent of large masses of individuals become an exercise in futility. Gross generalizations—about alienation and feelings of impotence, search for identity, frustrated altruism and developmental rebellion—while true for some and perhaps for many, are often an inadequate basis for understanding an individual. For most counselors whose very work is dependent upon values and a perception of the world which focuses upon the person, the overriding concern is with the unique mix of the social and humane motives. Beyond that, the counselor's concern is necessarily with the interaction of a complex of motives within the individual.

Many predict that adolescent dissent will continue and intensify during the 70's. Older adolescents during this period are likely to be even more alienated, politicized and willing to do battle with the "establishment" than are present-day individuals of a comparable age. The reasons for this are fairly obvious. First, the social conditions that have been protested—injustice, materialism, hypocrisy, air and water pollution among others—are complex and difficult to change. Most of these problems are still with us and may always be present to some degree. Presumably those who predict more dissent do so from the safety of an old psychological truism: The best predictor of future behavior is past behavior. An often overlooked factor which may modify this prediction is that society probably will not permit extremism which threatens its total destruction. Extremist behavior may result in severe repressive measures which could drive underground or nullify dissent. It is doubtful that the majority of dissenters seek to destroy completely the structure of society. If it is true that dissenters seek meaningful modifications, some equilibrium between revolutionary and reactionary forces will undoubtedly emerge.

Second, a common perspective attributed to youth across the ages by observers of all kinds—philosophers, psychologists, social historians, sociologists—is that of a present-time orientation and a demand for immediate gratification. Youth's impatience demands action now. Words and promises, unless swiftly implemented, are insufficient; indeed, if they remain unimplemented, they serve only to confirm the fact that adults are untrustworthy. To a generation which has lived with such phrases as "with all deliberate speed" since the 1954 desegregation decision and which knows the facts about the continuation of segregated schools, both North and South, even the law of the land becomes suspect.

Third, the spreading affluence (particularly among white Americans) and the need for a technological society to hold large numbers of the young out of the labor market liberate ever more young people to reject the materialism of their elders and to search for meaning in their lives in humanitarian and aesthetic terms. Many of today's youth come from family environments where abundance, economic security and political freedom are facts of life, not goals to be striven for as they were in their father's time. Their disengagement from work responsibilities produces gaps in attitudes between them and previous generations that went directly from adolescence to work and marital responsibilities. Because the young regard the psychological imperatives, the social institutions and the cultural values of the industrial ethic as outdated, they also tend to regard the establishment's requests for loyalty, restraint or conformity as a moral outrage, as authoritarian repression or as an effort at manipulation.

Adolescent dissent during the 1970's, like its counterpart during the 1960's, will be accompanied by much emotion. The dissenter's behavior not only is highly emotional but is intended to evoke an emotional response from those he challenges. In a sense this is the political strategy of dissent. Unless the dissenter can evoke a charged reaction he cannot hope to dramatize or to jar loose the thinking of those who subscribe to the status quo, let alone achieve any modification of time-honored and comfortable social structures, no matter how wrong they may seem.

Protest and dissent are not to be equated with the violence that reportedly has been sweeping through U.S. classrooms. *Time* (November 14, 1969) reports that Chicago teachers were attacked 1,065 times in 1968 and that this represented an eight-fold rise in five years. Many ascribe school violence (much of it centered in junior high schools) to racial desegregation, to overcrowded classrooms, to the volatility of ghetto students, and to administrators who underplay it out of fear that it will reflect upon their ability to maintain control.

Drug Abuse

Drug usage has become an increasingly serious problem at all levels and at all ages in our society. Broadly speaking, the American public has used and increasingly depends upon a broad array of chemical substances— aspirin, alcohol, tranquilizers, etc.—to allay anxiety and insecurity stemming from the pressure of contemporary life. The new element in the nation's drug problem is the rather sudden spread of drugs that induce fantasies or hallucinations or that "expand the mind." The spread of these types of drugs is especially disturbing because little is known of the effects of these compounds and because usage has apparently spread into new and larger segments of society.

Estimates of drug use among youth vary widely. Some authorities claim that school officials minimize and discount estimates to protect their institutions. High school and college administrators cite estimates ranging from 5 to 35 percent usage. Students report that from 50 to 90 percent of their friends smoke pot. Younger and younger teenagers, along with many 11- and 12-year-olds, are inhaling, ingesting and injecting an astonishing array of chemical substances. Of particular concern to adults are the facts that (1) the age of drug users appears to be dropping rapidly, sometimes reaching down into elementary schools, and (2) as drugs become more and more widespread, the young seem to build a culture and a self-perpetuating, self-approving rationale of their own around drug use.

A major concern is the use of so-called hard drugs by youth. It is beyond the scope of this discussion to deal with the complexities and controversies surrounding the various available drugs and narcotics. For in truth, drug use and abuse (the use of a drug for non-medical or non-scientific purposes with potentiality of harm to the user or society) have social, legal, medical and psychological implications. The kinds of student drug users include those who conform to peer group pressure, thrill seekers, and hard-core addicts. Most authorities agree that there is little to assist in identifying those who will or will not use drugs or for that matter, those who will try them and then move on to become hard-core users. An answer to questions of who will use drugs and why they are used lies in the mix of such variables as the drug effect itself, the environmental pressures, and the individual personality.

Some direct evidence of adolescents' views on drugs is available. For example, according to the Purdue Opinion Poll, high school students (1) did not believe the sale of marijuana should be legalized (79 percent); (2) rejected a proposal that it was all right to experiment with illegal drugs (81 percent); (3) said that they would not experiment with drugs even if the danger of arrest or addiction were removed (69 percent); and (4) believed that if they discovered a friend using drugs it would change their relationship (65 percent). The Poll reported that high school students tended to believe that while marijuana use was widespread in other schools, such was not the case in their own high school.[48] These data were collected in 1968 and therefore may already be outdated, given the fluid condition of society and the reported further spread of drug use.

Potentially, usage of any drugs can lead to psychological addiction and, for some unfortunates, to eventual reliance upon narcotics and to physiological addiction. Since drug usage is becoming such a pressing social problem, it is probable that the next few years will see the continuation of heavy investment in research efforts to clarify the psychology and effects of drug use. Severe punitive measures applied to possession and strict control of supply have been less than effective as deterrents. Many of today's schools are accepting the responsibility for presenting drug education programs. The more successful of these programs appear to be those which have stressed a straightforward factual presentation and discussion and which have recognized that the ultimate decision as to whether one takes drugs is the individual's responsibility.

For the adolescent of the 1970's drugs will continue to be a matter for decision. Without doubt, he will continue to run a variety of tremendous risks should he decide to participate in a drug culture. These risks exist primarily at a personal level, i.e., potential physiological and psychological disasters; but they are significant at the social level as well because of the unsystematic legal penalties attached to arrest and conviction for drug use. Legal penalties vary from state to state and are often applied capriciously. While some legal changes appear to be under consideration, it is very unlikely that society will totally alter its position or that any nationwide uniform legal restrictions in penalties will emerge suddenly.

The welter of legal implications and practices leaves school personnel, especially counselors, in an ambiguous position that can be clarified only by carefully developed school policies. Even with such policies available, the counselor who has knowledge of drug use among his clients is confronted with difficult ethical problems similar to those he faces in any instance involving illegal acts. The struggle to determine a course of action remains each counselor's responsibility in line with the appropriate ethical stipulations of his profession.

Sexual Behavior

Millions of words have been written about sexual behavior but it has yet to go away! Current concern is over what many describe as a relaxation in standards of sexual behavior. Alterations in these standards have been well documented by many sources across many years. Clearly the standards in this vital area of life are being influenced by the behavior of the young. Rockefeller reported that many young people were exploring human rela-

[48] Purdue Opinion Panel. *Current Views of High School Students Toward the Use of Tobacco, Alcohol and Drugs and Narcotics.* Report of Poll Number Eighty-six. Lafayette, Ind.: Measurement and Research Center, Purdue University, March 1969.

tionships with a new kind of freedom and that their approach to sex was basically open and positive. This, of course, contrasts sharply with the approach of society in general where the practice has been to try to control sexual behavior by taboos and inhibitions, by silence, and by limiting knowledge which could stimulate interest and participation. Rockefeller sought to illuminate why the confusing range of problems associated with sex exists today in our society. It is his contention that the beginning of a basic understanding lies in recognizing the relationship between puritanism and pornography. Seemingly at opposite poles, one begets the other. That is, because puritanism generally regards sex as dirty and illicit and to be guarded against by the imposition of rigid moral codes, this attitude opens the way for exploitation of the excitement of that which is forbidden. The more that sex is exploited, the more pressure is generated to reaffirm and reinforce the puritan ethic; the more this happens the more the appetite for the forbidden is whetted.[49]

Two major contributors to modified sexual mores are to be found in the medical advances which have helped to eradicate fear of the sex act. The first is found in the cheap and effective treatment of venereal disease and the second lies in improved contraceptive devices and procedures. While neither of these advances is totally effective in eradicating venereal disease or preventing pregnancy, they have measurably reduced the traditional constraints placed upon sexual behavior. There are conflicting opinions about how much more sexual activity may be occurring as a result of these advances.

Despite the medical advances and, in truth, because of them, increasing problems related to sexual involvement continue to confront the young. Venereal disease and illegitimate pregnancies continue to increase among this age group. A physician friend of the authors once remarked that teenagers seem to know enough to get into bed but not enough to stay out of trouble! It may be that removal of the fears created a vacuum that has yet to be filled with any healthy form of individual control based upon adequate knowledge and personal codes of conduct.

Massive changes in the structure of the public's attitudes toward sexual behavior are reflected in most if not all of the mass communications media, dress, the openness of sex discussion between the sexes, equality between sexes and so on. No one fully understands why there has been a sexual revolution. While no one doubts that such changes have occurred, the specific attitudes are literally impossible to explicate briefly. Their relevance here lies in the fact that they have had and will continue to have a profound impact upon youth.

For school personnel, the fact remains that contemporary youth live in a society which appears to condone through its attitudes and behavior a more relaxed and casual attitude toward sex (some would say a more healthy

---

[49] John D. Rockefeller, III. "Youth, Love and Sex: The New Chivalry," *Look* (October 7, 1969), pp. 32–42.

attitude because that which was hushed up and ridden with guilt has been brought out into the open) and one in which complete control of undesirable outcome is, in theory, medically possible. Presumably this is the world the adolescent of the 1970's will live in and the one with which he must cope. The majority of school personnel are fully aware that adequate and appropriate sex education for all youth is badly needed and, moreover, even wanted by most adolescents. The question that remains unanswered is whether schools will exercise leadership in this area and whether certain segments of society will permit them to do so. Indeed, it is amazing that, in an area of human behavior common to all and where so much ignorance and secrecy abound, some people seek to destroy any honest effort to bring more understanding and rationality.

To most who work directly with youth the fact is obvious that participation in sexual activities is ultimately a choice of the individual. For them it would suffice that such decisions be made upon as informed a basis as possible, with full knowledge of the risks and dangers involved. They are also aware that the decision to abstain will not always be made because there are many emotional and physical contingencies which push strongly for expression. Sex is a powerful force and as such must be handled wisely and with self-restraint if its true meaning is to be realized. For the adolescent there will be difficult personal decisions to be made all along the way if his course of action is to be one that he can live with over the years.

Concern for Culturally Unassimilated Groups

For many people, social injustice remains an abstraction because they lack the direct experience that would let them see it as a reality. But at least the vicarious experience has been thrust upon society during the past decade, particularly in respect to the plight of black Americans. Idealistic individuals and especially the younger generation, coupled with increasingly militant Negro groups, have cast this problem in bold relief. The past decade has seen an evolution in demands to correct social inequity, an evolution that has moved from relatively passive protests to angry and, in some cases, destructive actions.

Most observers are not surprised that many young people have been in the vanguard of this social movement and will continue to be there. It is not new to find that young people are highly sensitive to injustice and are altruistic in their intentions. To them, evil is not an irreducible component of life but is most often committed by the older generation, the "establishment," and can be eradicated through love and action. What does appear to be different is the involvement of youth in attempts to remedy undesirable conditions through direct personal action. Few of them are so naïve as to believe that their individual actions will greatly alter long-standing ills, but most appear aware that by their collective personal actions they create pressure that may foster social change.

Adolescents of the 1960's were touched by the glaring inequities that existed between the more affluent American society and clearly visible segments such as the blacks, the American Indians, Spanish-speaking Americans, impoverished whites and other groups. They participated in many positive ways, such as tutoring programs and VISTA, as well as in ways that many would view as less constructive. The adolescent of the 1970's will, no doubt, follow the same pattern.

Political Activity

The 1968 national political campaign saw the emergence of a massive involvement of youth in politics. Perhaps for the first time in American politics they became a force with which to be reckoned. Many young people may have emerged from this experience discouraged and disenchanted but others who took a longer view cannot fail to recognize that they exerted considerable influence upon existing political machinery. Action has been taken to lower the voting age (in June, 1970, President Nixon signed legislation that enables 18-year-olds to vote and asked for a quick court test of the law) and serious consideration has been given to the direct selection of political candidates by the public. Youth, no doubt, will be a potent force in future politics.

The average age of the population is becoming younger; this fact, coupled with the decision by many young people to try to change the status quo through political party participation, will inevitably result in political change. For most adolescents of the 1970's, being politically uninformed will not be fashionable, being politically uncommitted will not be acceptable, and being politically active will be highly desirable. This combination of attitudes is the essence of a democratic, knowledgeable, active electorate.

Distrust of Adults

It is very probable that youth have always distrusted adults. The difference today is that they appear willing and ready to say so openly. Presumably this heightened distrust of adults is, in large measure, based upon youth's perception of adult behavior. Discrepancies between the ideals verbalized by adults and their actual behavior often loom large to the young. Lip service to ideals and an apparent inability to modify radically or to resolve the problems confronting society make up a large part of adults' shortcomings.

Generations of adolescents have, of course, claimed that adults did not understand their interests and problems. But today's parents, teachers and other adults find themselves baffled by the indifference manifested by youth when adults seek to discuss the problems and interests of young people with them. Seemingly, the adult is viewed as not worth listening to, but rather is suspect and fraudulent, and perhaps even dishonest. In the eyes of youth, adult models frequently leave much to be desired, particularly when the adult model condemns marijuana but frequently overindulges in alcohol, rails against casual sexual practices but overflows the courts with divorces and engages in serial marriages, verbalizes a concern for the unfortunate yet supports the expenditure of the nation's resources upon military hardware and nonhuman technology. Perhaps the greatest reason of all for such distrust is to be found in the older generation's predilection to make a phony acknowledgment of young people's views and ideas. All too often adults encourage token communication from young people and comfort themselves that they have listened. The experience of most teenagers in this process is that it frequently results in a two-fold outcome: what little adults do hear is ignored; and perhaps even more hurtful, their opinions are twisted and used as ammunition against them. If youth had the upper hand, one might hear adults saying, "You can't trust anyone under thirty!"

Parents, of course, feel uncertain and helpless in communicating with their children because they believe that there should be "clear-cut answers" for their children's dilemmas. Because pat or prescribed solutions are so ineffective and elusive in a rapidly changing world, parents are often reduced to the uncomfortable position of saying "this is something you must work out for yourself" or "how have your friends solved this?" The latter question is particularly discomforting to parents because they believe that their child's friends are moving in ways that are unsafe for their child. Adult behavior, according to Margaret Mead, must be altered. She suggests that "We must, in fact, teach ourselves how to alter adult behavior; we must create new models for adults who can teach their children not what to learn, but how to learn, and not what they should be committed to, but the value of commitment."[50]

A Voice in Decision Making

The adolescent of the 1970's will continue to press for a stake in the decisions that affect him. It should be recognized that this matter, on a mass level, is inextricably bound to increased participation in political activity and the issue of protest and dissent.

Adolescents realize that the fulfillment of this goal for themselves depends on its being satisfied for others in their age group. Many observers have noted that this question of self-determination is, particularly in educational institutions, one in which tremendous gains have been won by young people. At many colleges, students now have a voice in a range of matters, including curriculum revision, instructor and course evaluations, housing arrangements, disciplinary policies and the like. At the high school level they have been consulted in establishing dress codes, disciplinary policies and special programs such as drug and sex education.

While these gains are potentially positive they depend upon the good

[50] Margaret Mead, "Youth Revolt: The Future is Now," *Saturday Review* (January 10, 1970), p. 113.

faith of all involved. It would be naïve not to recognize that mere involvement without influence is insufficient for most adolescents. It will be very unfortunate if gains are merely nominal and are made only to undercut the influence of dissident students. Such an outcome could only confirm suspicion of the adult world and create additional conflict. Only time will permit judgment as to how meaningful and enduring such gains will be.

IMPLICATIONS FOR GUIDANCE PERSONNEL

If the description of the adolescent and his world in the 70's is reasonably accurate, what implications may be suggested that are relevant for guidance personnel?

1. The implication that is most fundamental is that guidance personnel, to the best of their abilities, must be thoroughly aware of and sensitive to the facts of the specific population and the setting they serve. While this is not a novel suggestion, the press and importance of the issues discussed previously demand more than the mere recognition of this principle. Without detailed knowledge gained through personal concern and constant examination of the best factual data available, school personnel have no sure foundation upon which to base their actions. Counselors who do engage in this process will be viewed as more valuable by students, school staff, and parents. Indeed, fulfillment of this principle is basic to coping with the remaining implications that follow.
2. To work and live in a school will no longer be a sheltered existence (if indeed it ever was). Throughout the preceding and somewhat frightening description of the change and turmoil that will characterize the adolescent of the 1970's runs a thread of deep concern about losing control of highly volatile situations. For some, the sheer magnitude and rapidity of change occurring in what was once seen as a relatively placid and predictable age group will be overwhelming. Withdrawal or attempts to maintain the conditions of yesteryear will provide no solution. A parallel and equally nonproductive reaction which may appear attractive to some is to overrespond by indiscriminately joining one or the other opposing camp. Guidance personnel cannot afford to be seen by adolescents as the "establishment" or by the adult population as the champion of the youthful militant. This is not to suggest mealy-mouthed fence straddling or noninvolvement. Rather, a stance must be adopted by guidance personnel which recognizes the desirability and inevitability of change while simultaneously avoiding the pitfall of chaos that accompanies the destruction of society's restraints and values. Prudence, historical perspective, experience, self-discipline—while admittedly somewhat unfashionable qualities—remain the counselor's best hope for the 1970's.

3. The work of guidance personnel in a period of time marked by turmoil may shift to an emphasis upon mediation between subpopulations found in their work setting. In this role the counselor interposes himself between factions as an equal friend to each. Much of his activity will involve interpretation of the behavior of each side to the other. This, of course, involves accurate knowledge of the values, attitudes and motives of each faction with which he works. The mediating role, while highly complex and little understood, is not totally foreign to most counselors who have intervened in conflict situations arising between students and teachers, between children and parents, or between various adult factions within and without the school.

4. The life style attributed to adolescents not only expresses that which they are and want to be but that which they seek to avoid. It contains the very ingredients which form their attitudes and eventually shapes their beliefs and behavior. The adolescent's feelings, dress, heroes, villains, talk, music, films—all that appeals to him—serve as models from which a life style is derived. If young people are able to fashion and follow that life style, according to Max Lerner,[51] they accomplish the crucial youth experience. From this perspective, identity and style, rather than power and revolution, are the things that are sought by contemporary youth. In seeking a style and an identity, they rebel against a way of life they reject and become zealots for a way of life whose outlines are only dimly perceived.

5. A final overriding observation concerns the attitude with which one approaches change in this age group. The initial reaction of many adults is confusion followed by anger and/or despair. The more productive view takes into account two frequently overlooked factors. One of these involves faith in the management of life by adolescents themselves. Most are indeed highly flexible and resilient and will sort out and make positive use of their experiences. Damage may occur to a part of the adolescent group and serious damage to some. While this has been true throughout the history of mankind, it also is a large part of the reason why counselors are present in the school, for the possibility of damage provides the rationale for the remedial view of counseling. The second factor concerns the frequently overlooked fact that the behavioral changes that have occurred among this age group are predominantly healthy. One has only to contrast descriptions of the inactive, uninspired, uninvolved youth of the 1950's to the dynamism of today's youth to have this forcibly brought home.

If Guid. & Counselling principles have truth, they should be equally palatable to both parties!

[51] Max Lerner, "Identity, Style Concern Youth Far More Than Causes, Revolutions," Lafayette, Ind.: *The Journal Courier* (January 30, 1970).

ANNOTATED BIBLIOGRAPHY

COLEMAN, JAMES S. *The Adolescent Society*. Glencoe, Ill.: The Free Press, 1961. 368 pp.

This volume reports the results of a sociological study of ten selected high schools in the United States. Documenting his belief that an adolescent sub-culture exists in the United States, Coleman treats the value climates, the heroes, leaders, success patterns, and the psychological effects of such a society. Certainly this book is mandatory reading for teachers and counselors.

ROSENBERG, MORRIS. *Society and the Adolescent Self-Image*. Princeton, N.J.: Princeton University Press, 1965. 328 pp.

This book reports the findings of a large-scale, systematic survey of adoles-cents' self perceptions and feelings. Some five thousand students were studied to ascertain the impact of family, neighborhood, and minority-group mem-bership on self-image.

SCHNEIDERS, ALEXANDER A. *Counseling the Adolescent*. San Francisco: Chand-ler Publishing Company, 1967. 489 pp.

Part One (pp. 3–65) is composed of five selections which examine the adolescent's needs, problems, and peer group. Special aspects of adolescent problems such as early dating, a case study of an obsessive-compulsive adoles-cent, and a case study centered upon academic difficulty will interest the be-ginning student in guidance.

SMITH, ERNEST A. *American Youth Culture*. Glencoe, Ill.: The Free Press, 1962. 264 pp.

Smith summarizes the body of descriptive and analytical studies that bear upon an independent American youth culture. Attention is given to the ap-pearance, dress, language, technology, ideology, family orientation, cliques, dating patterns, and courtship processes of adolescents.

SELECTED REFERENCES

ASPY, DAVID N. "Elephants in the Living Room." *Personnel and Guidance Journal* Vol. 48 (December 1969), pp. 287–293.

BAIRD, LEONARD. "The Undecided Student—How Different Is He?" *Personnel and Guidance Journal* Vol. 47 (January 1969), pp. 429–434.

BANKS, WILLIAM M. "The Changing Attitudes of Black Students." *Personnel and Guidance Journal* Vol. 48 (May 1970), pp. 739–746.

"The Battering Parent," *Time* (November 7, 1969), pp. 77–80.

BRONFENBRENNER, URIE. "The Split-Level American Family." *Saturday Review* (October 7, 1967), pp. 60–66.

BROUGH, JAMES R., AND REEVES, MARTHA L. "Activities of Suburban and In-ner-City Youth." *Personnel and Guidance Journal* Vol. 47 (November 1968), pp. 209–212.

BUNDA, RICHARD, AND MEZZANO, JOSEPH. "A Study of the Effects of a Work Experience Program on Performance of Potential Dropouts." *The School Counselor* Vol. 15 (March 1968), pp. 272–274.

CAREY, RICHARD W. "Student Protest and the Counselor." *Personnel and Guidance Journal* Vol. 48 (November 1969), pp. 185–191.

DIEDRICH, RICHARD C., AND JACKSON, PHILIP W. "Satisfied and Dissatisfied Students." *Personnel and Guidance Journal* Vol. 47 (March 1969), pp. 641–649.

ECKERSON, LOUISE O. "The Teen Age Problem Is the Adult." *Personnel and Guidance Journal* Vol. 47 (May 1969), pp. 849–854.

GAETANO, CARL R. "The Rural School Dropout." *The School Counselor* Vol. 15 (March 1968), pp. 286–289.

GOTTLIEB, DAVID. "Poor Youth Do Want to Be Middle-Class, but It's Not Easy." *Personnel and Guidance Journal* Vol. 46 (October 1967), pp. 116–122.

HALPERN, GERALD, AND NORRIS, LILA. "Student Curriculum Decisions." *Personnel and Guidance Journal* Vol. 47 (November 1968), pp. 240–243.

HASCALL, EDWARD O. "Campus Unrest: Worldwide Challenge for Student Affairs." *Personnel and Guidance Journal* Vol. 48 (April 1970), pp. 619–628.

HOTT, IRVING. "The School Counselor and Drugs." *The School Counselor* Vol. 17 (September 1969), pp. 14–16.

JONES, JOHN E. "Components of the High School Environment." *Personnel and Guidance Journal* Vol. 47 (September 1968), pp. 40–43.

KELLY, HARRY. "Adolescents: A Suppressed Minority Group." *Personnel and Guidance Journal* Vol. 47 (March 1969), pp. 634–640.

KETTERMAN, CLARK S. "A Drug Abuse Workshop." *The School Counselor* Vol. 17 (November 1969), pp. 99–100.

MEAD, MARGARET. "Youth Revolt: The Future is Now." *Saturday Review* (January 10, 1970), pp. 23–25; 113.

NEVERS, ANN M. "Counseling the Unwed Mother at School." *The School Counselor* Vol. 17 (September 1969), pp. 30–33.

"The New Feminists: Revolt Against 'Sexism.'" *Time* (November 21, 1969), pp. 53–56.

POWELL, ROBERT S., JR. "Participation is Learning." *Saturday Review* (January 10, 1970), pp. 56–58; 82.

ROCKEFELLER, JOHN D., III. "Youth, Love and Sex: The New Chivalry." *Look* (October 7, 1969), pp. 32–42.

SEGAL, STANLEY J., AND TIEDEMAN, DAVID V. "The Case for Delay in College Entry: High School Seniors Need Time, Guidance, in Identity Search." *The School Counselor* Vol. 15 (January 1968), pp. 167–171.

SEXTON, PATRICIA. "How the American Boy is Feminized." *Psychology Today* Vol. 3 (January 1970), pp. 23–29; 66–67.

SMITH, LOUISE. "A Statistic Strikes Back." *Personnel and Guidance Journal* Vol. 45 (May 1967), pp. 872–877.

VONTRESS, CLEMMONT E. "Counseling Blacks." *Personnel and Guidance Journal* Vol. 48 (May 1970), pp. 713–720.

WARNER, RICHARD W., JR. "Alienated Youth: The Counselor's Task." *Personnel and Guidance Journal* Vol. 48 (February 1970), pp. 443–448.

WEINBERG, CARL. "Sociological Explanations for Student Problems." *Personnel and Guidance Journal* Vol. 46 (May 1968), pp. 852–857.

WILLIAMS, ROBERT L., AND BYARS, HARRY. "Negro Self-Esteem in a Transitional Society." *Personnel and Guidance Journal* Vol. 47 (October 1968), pp. 120–125.

WILLIAMS, ROBERT L., AND COLE, SPURGEON. "Self-Concept and School Adjustment." *Personnel and Guidance Journal* Vol. 46 (January 1968), pp. 478–481.

WILLIAMSON, E. G. "Youth's Dilemma: To Be or To Become." *Personnel and Guidance Journal* Vol. 46 (October 1967), pp. 173–177.

WRENN, ROBERT L. "The Authority Controversy and Today's Student." *Personnel and Guidance Journal* Vol. 46 (June 1968), pp. 949–953.

YAMAMOTO, KAORU. "The 'Healthy Person': A Review." *Personnel and Guidance Journal* Vol. 44 (February 1966), pp. 596–603.

————. "Healthy Students in the College Environment." *Personnel and Guidance Journal* Vol. 48 (June 1970), pp. 809–816.

2

GUIDANCE IN THE EDUCATIONAL SETTING

What is guidance?
How is guidance related to education?
What factors influenced the development of guidance?
What basic principles undergird guidance?
What criticisms of guidance programs and personnel have been made?

The questions cited above, while admittedly broad in scope, serve as focal points for a discussion of the guidance function as it operates in today's schools. They also indicate the major subdivisions of this chapter, just as other questions do in later chapters.

WHAT IS GUIDANCE?

Guidance has been defined in many ways. An examination of the plethora of books and articles written on the topic indicates that the word most often has been used to convey each author's opinions and biases. Indeed, a major criticism, past and present, is that the word "guidance" has been rendered relatively meaningless by the variety of ways in which it is used. This and other criticisms will be discussed in greater detail in the last section of this chapter.

Guidance Defined

How is guidance defined? What does it mean? For individuals who do not claim it as part of their occupational titles, its meaning seems at face value to derive from its root word, "guide," which means to direct, pilot, manage, or steer. Parents and other lay persons basically view the counselor as one who directs or steers children into or away from certain occupational or educational endeavors.

Arbuckle,[1] Peters and Farwell,[2] and others have attempted to clarify the usage of the term by pointing out the distinctions implicit in the word "guidance" used as a concept (mental image), as an educational construct (intellectual synthesis), and as an educational service (actions taken to meet a demand). Conceptually, guidance denotes the utilization of a point of view in order to help an individual; as an educational construct, it refers to the provision of experiences that help pupils to understand themselves; and as a service, it refers to procedures and processes organized to achieve a helping relationship.

Graduate students in a recent introductory class in guidance conducted by one of the authors collected over one hundred definitions of guidance from the literature available at the time. Needless to say, there was much overlap among the definitions; substantial agreement (at least among those who write about guidance) was evident.

No attempt will be made here to supply a new definition or to play on words in order to create one superficially. Guidance, as used throughout this volume, is the process of helping an individual to understand himself and his world.

As is true with all definitions, there immediately come to mind questions that call for clarification and qualification of key words in the definition. *First,* what is meant by process? A process is any phenomenon that shows continuous change over time, and the use of the word here denotes that guidance is not a single event but involves a series of actions or steps progressing toward a goal. *Second,* what is meant by helping? Helping is defined as aiding, assisting, or availing. Many "helping occupations" such as psychiatry, psychology, social work, and the like have as their major purpose the prevention, remediation, and amelioration of human difficulties by the provision of specialized help. *Third,* the word "individual" in the above definition refers to pupils in the school setting. More specifically, guidance is seen here as the assistance given to "normal" students—those who need help with the events and concerns that occur during normal development. *Fourth,* what does the phrase "to understand himself and his world" mean? It means that the individual comes to know who he is as an individual; he becomes aware of his personal identity; he perceives clearly the nature of his person; he experiences his world, the aggregate of surroundings and the people with whom he comes into contact, more deeply and completely.

[1] Dugald S. Arbuckle, *Pupil Personnel Services in the Modern School* (Boston: Allyn and Bacon, Inc., 1966), pp. 96–108.

[2] Herman J. Peters and Gail Farwell, *Guidance: A Developmental Approach,* 2nd Ed. (Chicago: Rand McNally, 1967), pp. 3–11.

Purpose of Guidance

An additional word needs to be said about the purpose of guidance. For instance, what is the goal of the helping process that leads to understanding of self and world? The assumption is that the individual who understands himself and his world will become a more effective, more productive, and happier human being. He will become more fully functioning as a person in the sense described by Rogers.[3] Through guidance the individual achieves greater awareness not only of who he is but of who he can become. Rogers maintains, "The purpose of most of the helping professions, including guidance counseling, is to enhance the personal development, the psychological growth toward a socialized maturity, of its clients."[4]

Guidance Services

Guidance services are the formalized actions taken by the school to make guidance operational and available to students. These services have been delimited by common agreement to provide unique actions which overlap minimally with other familiar school functions. The guidance most frequently found in modern secondary schools is organized around the following services:

1. The *appraisal service,* which is designed to collect, analyze, and use a variety of objective and subjective personal, psychological, and social data about each pupil for the purpose of better understanding him as well as assisting him to understand himself.
2. An *informational service,* which is designed to provide students with a greater knowledge of educational, vocational, and personal-social opportunities so that they may make better informed choices and decisions in an increasingly complex society.
3. The *counseling service,* which is designed to facilitate self-understanding and development through dyadic or small-group relationships. The major focus of such relationships tends to be upon personal development and decision-making that is based on self-understanding and knowledge of the environment.
4. A *planning, placement, and followup service,* designed to enhance the vocational development of the student by helping him select and utilize job opportunities within the school and in the outside labor market.

[3] Carl R. Rogers, "A Therapist's View of the Good Life: The Fully Functioning Person," Chapter 9 in *On Becoming a Person* (Boston: Houghton Mifflin Company, 1961), pp. 183–196.

[4] Carl R. Rogers, "The Interpersonal Relationship: The Core of Guidance," *Harvard Educational Review* Vol. 32 (Fall 1962), p. 428.

These services are directly focused upon the student. A fifth service, *evaluation,* is often added by authors to the four cited above; however, evaluation is not a direct service to school youth; it is performed largely for the benefit of school officials and the community. Consequently, in this book the evaluation function will be treated separately from the guidance services provided to youth.

GUIDANCE WITHIN EDUCATION

Education is a priceless asset of fundamental importance to the individual and to society. It can never be adequately described merely by citing the number of pupils served and the personnel involved, the value of buildings or equipment, or the research performed—despite the fact that such readily available facts are frequently used as measures of growth and quality. Education is all these things but more. It is a process essential to the achievement of personal goals and individual aspirations. Philosophically and historically it represents perhaps more than any other factor the means of attaining the American ideal.

Expectations for Education

Pupils look to the school to help them realize their aspirations. Parents expect the school to provide for the intellectual development of their children. The American people anticipate that education will provide a continuing supply of increasingly capable citizens.

Schools must be wisely used lest they be exploited and their value diminished. As the last quarter of the twentieth century approaches, it is clear that elementary and secondary schools are being subjected to pressures which could weaken them or divert them from their major purpose. For example, some have urged that schools ought to be the agency to provide greater child-welfare programs; others have called for schools to turn away from universal education and instead educate a chosen few. Though it remains the prerogative of the public to define by common consent the goals of their institution, appropriate leadership to prevent a weakening of the educational enterprise must be provided by individual citizens and alert professional educators.

The phenomenal growth of American education is apparent to all who have even a general familiarity with it. This growth has involved an increase in the proportion of youth enrolled in schools, the retention in school of greater numbers of youth for an ever-increasing number of years, and, since World War II, a marked expansion of school facilities and educational offerings. This growth may be accounted for by two widely different factors: (1) the belief and faith of the American people in education, and (2) an economic system able to provide the basic resources and leisure time for formal schooling. In fact, the advanced technological system in which we live demands education. Our technology depends on an extensive and highly varied educational program for its existence; it also makes such an education possible.

The value of education is increasingly being cast in economic terms which are indeed impressive. A Chase Manhattan Bank publication summarized one economic study as indicating that 24 percent of the increase in gross national product between 1929 and 1957 and 44 percent of the advance in the increase per worker could be attributed to the higher level of education in the labor force. But the value of education lies in more than economic returns. Its chief worth is that it makes individuals more valuable—to both themselves and the community. Through education a person has a better chance to achieve that which is quite proper to him as an individual living in a free democratic society. It aids him in bringing the kind of strength and quality needed to meet the vicissitudes confronting him in our society. Horace Mann, the Father of Public Education, once observed that the great equalizer in our culture is education. The opportunity for equality, for social mobility, for the choice of an occupation regardless of birth, depends upon it. Former President Johnson pointed up the value of education in the following way:

> The noblest search of today is the search for excellence. In every endeavor, there simply cannot be allowed any lessening in this search.
>
> In every challenge we face, the very best that we can do is the only thing we must do. For these problems, these challenges, will not go away untended by superior effort.[5]

An article of educational faith in this country has been that a maximum degree of equality of opportunity should be extended to every man. No man or group of men is wise enough to judge the heights to which an individual may rise, the contributions he can make, if given the chance. Gradually the guaranteed equal educational opportunities in the United States have been raised to include the high school. The forces compelling the raising of opportunity to this level have been the increasing complexity of the world and the public need for more intellectual preparation of youth before the individual enters the work force. Because the world continues to grow more complex, the educational levels that meant intellectual maturity yesterday do not go far enough today. Consequently, extension of opportunity to include two-year colleges as well as other kinds of post–high school education is rapidly becoming a reality.

Functions of Education

That education has a number of important functions to perform is accepted without question by most individuals. Yet these functions remain in many cases vaguely defined. If education is to have orientation and direction, its major functions need careful definition. What does the school

[5] Lyndon B. Johnson, "The Challenge We Face," *This Week* (April 26, 1964), p. 2.

do? Three primary functions of education are clearly visible and will be discussed briefly here.

THE DEVELOPMENTAL FUNCTION OF EDUCATION

Education has a responsibility to develop the unique qualities of each individual. More specifically, it should enhance the individual's skills in the arts, sciences, social adjustment, and personal philosophy, as well as his skills in vocational endeavors. The uniqueness of an individual often finds its ultimate expression in highly personal activities outside his occupational endeavor. Through education he has the opportunity to enlarge his special interests, abilities, and talents.

THE DIFFERENTIATING FUNCTION OF EDUCATION

Differences in abilities, interests, and purposes of students crystallize into markedly different patterns as the individual matures. These differences make it imperative that educators, recognizing that education cannot and should not reduce the range of human differences, provide within the general educational framework different systematically organized programs appropriate to the needs of youth. Classroom techniques or educational programs of any kind cannot miraculously cause individual differences to disappear or enable all students to achieve specific goals with equal success. There can be no single, uniform program for all students, no defined body of content for all, nor even any body of skills in which all will achieve with uniform excellence.

THE INTEGRATING FUNCTION OF EDUCATION

A major function of education is to contribute insofar as possible to the cultural integration of students. Social stability and the ability to act cooperatively as a nation fundamentally depend upon everyone possessing a measure of common understandings, attitudes, beliefs, skills, and purposes. Society depends in part upon education to develop in children a common core of shared beliefs, attitudes, values, and underlying knowledge.

It should be understood that formal education does not perform this function alone. Other institutions—the home, church, etc.—have equal if not greater responsibility.

The Function of Guidance

The impact of education upon an individual depends upon the effectiveness and the wisdom with which he isolates and determines his life purposes and goals. It should be recognized that schools are preparing pupils not just for life today but also for the problems they will face twenty years from now. Yet who in the school exhibits interest and responsibility for engaging pupils in a process by which their life goals and purposes may be clarified and understood? How well boys and girls meet change—social, economic, industrial, political—depends not only upon their skills but also upon their attitudes and personal resources.

Guidance both as a concept and as a service focuses upon youth and their future. Operating within education, guidance has as its context the individual and the decisions that ultimately only he can make. While every teacher is implored to see each pupil as a distinct individual, guidance personnel are education's insurance that the individual will not be submerged in the group. Their purpose is to make sure that the pupil, the teacher, and the parent understand the various phases of the individual's development and their impact upon his growth, adjustment, and the decision-making process.

Guidance within education represents society's expression of concern for the individual. In no other country has guidance developed to the extent that it has in American schools. Its contributions include bringing to the student increased understanding of the educational, vocational, and social information needed to make wise choices; utilizing psychological and sociological data for teacher and counselor understanding of each pupil as an individual; clarifying and assisting in learning tasks; and helping the individual understand himself and his world. Basic to these contributions is (1) a point of view which encourages individual differences and respect for the individual; (2) careful study of each pupil; (3) the establishment and maintenance of helping relationships; and (4) the coordination and management of school and community resources.

Within education, guidance personnel are individuals who are not expected to act as judges or evaluators. They differ from teachers and administrators as well as from parents in this respect. They are not responsible, as are teachers, for seeing that children meet standards of achievement in given areas. Consequently, those directly responsible for guidance can establish relationships free from threat and unrestricted in scope, relationships which will facilitate individual growth and development.

In summary, guidance exists to aid students in understanding the variety, depth, and breadth of personal experiences, the opportunities available, and the choices open to them by helping them recognize, interpret, and act upon their personal strengths and resources.

THE DEVELOPMENT OF GUIDANCE

It has been stated that in no other country has guidance developed to the point it has in America. Why should guidance have evolved here? It may have taken root because of the emphasis our society places upon the individual. Brewer has advanced four conditions in our society that were responsible: division of labor, growth of technology, democratic government, and extension of vocational education.[6]

[6] J. M. Brewer, *History of Vocational Guidance* (New York: Harper & Brothers, 1942), p. 3.

Historical Events

Uncertainty marks any attempt to designate "firsts" in guidance. Guidance seems to have begun in a number of schools and other agencies somewhat simultaneously. Its beginnings go back to the early 1900's and to the cities where industry was fast developing. In such cities as Detroit, Boston, New York, and Chicago, the industrial expansion brought social problems and abuses. Mathewson points out that Jesse B. Davis, while serving as eleventh-grade principal (1898–1907), spent most of his time actively counseling boys and girls. When Davis became principal of the Grand Rapids, Michigan, High School in 1907, he added a weekly period in English composition devoted to "vocational and moral guidance."[7] In Boston in 1908 Frank Parsons founded a vocational bureau to advise young men seeking jobs. Parsons, often referred to as the Father of Guidance, was concerned that each individual understand his strengths and weaknesses and use this knowledge in choosing among his vocational opportunities. At approximately the time that Davis and Parsons were beginning their work, Eli Weaver sought to assist the great army of child laborers who were leaving the schools in New York City under unfavorable conditions. Simultaneously, other pioneer programs and organizations were beginning operations in Salt Lake City; Lincoln, Nebraska; and Oakland, California. So the guidance movement spread.

Contributing to its extension was the founding of the National Vocational Guidance Association. In 1910 a conference was conducted in Boston for those responsible for guidance services. The year 1913 marks the official founding of a permanent national organization at Grand Rapids, Michigan. Its publication, the *Vocational Guidance Bulletin,* which spotlighted the emerging profession's problems and aspirations, was established in 1915.

In 1951 the increase in NVGA's membership, the diversity of the members' interests, and the increased psychological understanding of the individual led to the combining of NVGA with other personnel organizations. From this polygamous marriage, the present national organization, the American Personnel and Guidance Association, was established in July 1952. In 1970 the APGA had a membership of approximately twenty-seven thousand. Its members belong to one or more of the following eight divisions: the American College Personnel Association (ACPA), the Association for Counselor Education and Supervision (ACES), the National Vocational Guidance Association (NVGA), the Student Personnel Association for Teacher Education (SPATE), the American School Counselor Association (ASCA), the American Rehabilitation Counseling Association (ARCA), the National Employment Counselors Association (NECA), and the Association for Measurement and Evaluation of Guidance

---

[7] Robert Hendry Mathewson, *Guidance Policy and Practice* (New York: Harper & Row, Publishers, 1962), p. 72.

(AMEG). The executive secretary of the APGA, Willis Dugan, and his staff may be contacted at the headquarters building, 1605 New Hampshire Avenue, N.W., Washington, D.C. 20009.

Membership in the APGA includes a subscription to the *Personnel and Guidance Journal* and to the official publication of the divisions to which a member belongs. The *Personnel and Guidance Journal* (now published ten times yearly) is currently under the editorship of Leo Goldman, City University of New York. *Elementary School Guidance and Counseling,* edited by Donald Dinkmeyer, was started in 1967 and is also published by the APGA. The ACPA publishes the *Journal of College Student Personnel;* the ACES, *Counselor Education and Supervision;* the NVGA, the *Vocational Guidance Quarterly;* the SPATE, the *Student Personnel Association for Teacher Education Journal;* the ASCA, the *School Counselor;* and the ARCA, the *Rehabilitation Counseling Bulletin.*

The events cited briefly above simply mark the chronology of the guidance movement. A more complete history may be found in Chapter 3 of a volume commemorating the NVGA's fiftieth anniversary.[8] A briefer recent statement by E. G. Williamson may be found in the *Personnel and Guidance Journal.*[9] The same author's most recent book, *Vocational Counseling,* presents a detailed historical review of how the counseling profession has developed. His book traces the philosophical foundations of the guidance movement and describes innovations in the practice of vocational counseling.[10] A greater understanding of why and how guidance developed may be obtained by examining the cultural, social, and philosophical context in which guidance was born, developed, and matured. Without an appreciation of the prevailing social and cultural temper of the times, the episodes are incomprehensible.

Major Influences

Traxler[11] has identified five divergent factors contributing to the gestation of guidance. Some of the following comments are drawn from his discussion of these factors.

PHILANTHROPY AND HUMANITARIANISM

The guidance movement was encouraged by the humanitarian movements of the late 1800's and early 1900's in the United States. Immigrants, who came primarily to the cities, were forced into slums and usually kept

[8] Henry Borow (ed.), *Man in a World at Work* (Boston: Houghton Mifflin Company, 1964), pp. 45–64.

[9] E. G. Williamson, "An Historical Prospective of the Vocational Guidance Movement," *Personnel and Guidance Journal* Vol. 41 (May 1964), pp. 854–859.

[10] E. G. Williamson, *Vocational Counseling* (New York: McGraw-Hill Book Co., Inc., 1965).

[11] Arthur B. Traxler, *Techniques of Guidance* (New York: Harper & Brothers, 1957), pp. 3–4.

there by low wages. The humanitarian spirit, which stressed regard for the welfare of man, was evidenced in the assistance given by many to help those less fortunate. Philanthropists were active in promoting improved conditions and in providing money for the establishment of Parsons' Vocational Bureau in Boston in 1908. Traxler points out that philanthropists and humanitarians believed our society could be improved if the misfits, particularly vocational misfits, were helped. They viewed the schools as the logical place to start such improvement.

RELIGION

Traxler reasoned that the religious man often interpreted the world as a constant struggle between the forces of good and evil, and as a result he sought the help of the school to work with youth so that they would be prepared to lead the moral life. Thus another group added its influence and in turn stimulated the guidance movement.

MENTAL HYGIENE

Awakened by Clifford Beers' book, *A Mind that Found Itself* (1908), a group of citizens concerned with mental hygiene established the National Committee for Mental Health in 1909. The work of the National Committee has been broad in scope and far reaching in effect. Beginning as a humanitarian program designed to ameliorate the living conditions of those who already had succumbed to serious mental disorders, it endeavored to ensure humane treatment, adequate living quarters, intelligent commitment laws, and a tolerant public attitude toward these unfortunates. It also sought to promote the psychological viewpoint in the treatment of such individuals. Later the Committee turned its attention to the study, treatment, and rehabilitation of persons suffering from less serious mental disorders. It recognized that a variety of symptoms of maladjustment might appear as a result of social restrictions and that maladjustment in individuals calls for therapy. Because such illnesses can be better treated when identified early, mental hygienists encouraged educators to become more sensitive to the deep insecurities and loss of identity prevalent among youth.

SOCIAL CHANGE

The impact of two world wars, unemployment, depression, technological advances, child-labor laws, compulsory school attendance, and similar forces drove thousands of young people into school who had no marked desire to be there and few clear ideas regarding why they were there or what they wanted. These social changes led to increased enrollments, which in turn led to an expansion of curricular offerings. It was soon seen that increased personal attention was needed to help each individual marshal his assets in order to find his way through the school and the complex environment outside the school. Counselors are still expected to provide this kind of help to students who might otherwise be overwhelmed during their years in school.

THE MOVEMENT TO KNOW PUPILS AS INDIVIDUALS

Traxler points out that this movement is closely associated with the history of testing and measurement. Guidance was facilitated by the recognition that it is the duty of the school to know its pupils as individuals, to perceive the essential dignity and worth of each one, and to study each student through every resource of the school. Because it is virtually impossible for any one person to know more than a few pupils well enough to provide guidance on the basis of personal acquaintanceship, each school should make a systematic attempt to collect information about each pupil and to pool its essential knowledge year after year.

Other factors not cited by Traxler which were conducive to the development of guidance are briefly cited below.

MEASUREMENT MOVEMENT

In 1890 James McKeen Cattell published an article in *Mind* in which the term "mental tests" was used for the first time in the history of psychological literature. In 1896 Alfred Binet and V. Henri published an article in *L'Année Psychologique* describing tests measuring complex mental functions. In 1905 these testing concepts were incorporated in the first Binet Simon Intelligence Scale. Eleven years later L. M. Terman published a revision of Binet's scale, which he had standardized on a population of American children. However, the testing movement of the 1920's did not get its impetus from individual scales such as the Stanford-Binet as much as it did from the Army Alpha Test—the first group intelligence test to be administered on a mass basis. During the period following World War I, objective testing grew rapidly in popularity.

The measurement movement was helpful to guidance because it stressed that if one is to work with an individual, information about him must be gathered systematically and used intelligently.

FEDERAL GOVERNMENT SUPPORT

Federal government support has helped the guidance movement. The George-Reed (1929), George-Ellzey (1934), George-Dean (1936), and George-Barden (1946) Acts, all dealing with vocational education, paved the way for the establishment of occupational information and guidance divisions within state departments of education. A 1936 ruling which permitted vocational funds from these acts to be used for supervision in the states produced slow progress in the number of states providing such supervision.

In 1938, the U.S. Office of Education created the Occupational Information and Guidance Services Bureau with Harry Jaeger as director. Its publications and research efforts consistently stressed school guidance needs.

The passage of the National Defense Education Act of 1958 and its subsequent extensions probably has been the greatest stimulation the field of guidance has ever experienced. Originally, Title Va provided fifteen million dollars yearly to be used by local schools for strengthening guidance services, and Title Vb provided approximately seven million dollars per year for the conduct of counselor training institutes by universities. The 1968 Amendments to the Vocational Education Act of 1963 and the Education Professions Development Act of 1968 provided federal funds for the preparation and employment of counselors but reduced amounts earmarked specifically for guidance from those provided in NDEA legislation.

CLIENT-CENTERED THERAPY

Finally, a most important influence upon the development of guidance has been that of nondirective or client-centered therapy. Through the leadership, research, and publications of Carl R. Rogers, the highly directive, paternalistic methods and authoritarian attitudes characterizing earlier guidance efforts have been greatly modified. Rogerian therapy has made counselors more aware of the unity of personality, of the fact that a counselor counsels people rather than problems, of the fact that problems of adjustment in one segment of life have effects in other sectors. It has pointed up the complexity of the process of counseling concerning any type of individual adjustment, whether in the field of occupations, living with others, or personal values. Of even greater importance, it has done much to enable all types of counselors to better understand counseling processes and techniques.

EFFECTS OF THESE INFLUENCES

What has been the result of these many influences? Although confusion and uncertainty cloud the progress of guidance, change is observable. It can be seen most clearly in numbers. For example, in 1917 it was estimated that there were some fifty school counselors; in 1958 their numbers had grown to approximately twelve thousand; and in 1970 there were some forty thousand. Growth has also come in federal support for guidance. The George-Dean Act of 1936 provided some $2,500,000 to states for occupational information and guidance, while federal funding to support state and local counseling and guidance services from 1959 through 1969 amounts to approximately $187,000,000. Growth can also be seen in the number of counselor training institutions. In 1910 there was one, the Vocational Bureau in Boston; in 1957 there were 212 universities providing such training. In 1968 it was estimated that there were some 450 institutions involved in greater or lesser degree in counselor training. State certification of counselors is another indication of professional growth. In 1920 no state provided for the certification of counselors; in 1952 thirty-seven states had such a provision; and in 1968 fifty-three out of fifty-five states and territories had established minimum certification standards.

But the effect of all these factors is not in numbers alone. Guidance concepts and functions have changed. Guidance is no longer regarded as concerned purely with vocational pursuits but rather with all the developmental problems of youth. Change has also occurred in the programing of guidance services; the specialized service added to the regular school program has been replaced by a guidance service which functions as an integral part of the total school program.

Another new development is the recognition that essential guidance services are conducted by every professional staff member, instead of only by the school counselor. And more recently the province of guidance has ceased to be restricted to the latter years of secondary school; guidance is now being provided for pupils at all educational levels, from kindergarten through higher education.

BASIC PRINCIPLES OF GUIDANCE

Most textbooks used in introductory guidance courses typically carry a statement of the basic principles that undergird the guidance function. In many cases these include statements of assumptions, aims and practices, and principles. The authors of this book seek to present a statement of basic principles (fundamental truths or doctrine) accepted by most authorities as characteristic of the guidance function. Sources from which these principles were drawn include Miller,[12] Cribbon,[13] Beck,[14] Wrenn,[15] and especially Kehas.[16]

Principle I. Guidance is concerned primarily and systematically with the personal development of the individual. Kehas explains that the thrust of "personal development" is for the individual to marshal intelligence about the "self" through systematic, personal inquiry. Usually the effort of the school centers upon "intellectual learning," and only when interference with intellectual development occurs do the personal and emotional components of human development receive attention. Kehas urges that education be defined as "involvement with learning." Further, the *primary* nature of guidance practitioners' work would be the personal development, while the *primary* nature of teachers' involvement would be the intellectual development of the individual. The character of guidance programs, then, exists in helping students acquire knowledge of the self, to understand their experiences. Kehas states, "This concept of personal development assumes that it

---

[12] Carroll H. Miller, *Foundations of Guidance* (New York: Harper & Brothers, 1961), pp. 449–451.

[13] James J. Cribbin, "A Critique of the Philosophy of Modern Guidance," *Catholic Education Review* Vol. 53 (February 1955), pp. 73–91.

[14] Carlton E. Beck, *Philosophical Foundations of Guidance* (Englewood Cliffs, N.J.: Prentice-Hall, Inc., 1963), pp. 145–147.

[15] C. Gilbert Wrenn, "Philosophical and Psychological Bases of Personnel Services in Education," in *Personnel Services in Education,* Fifty-Eighth Yearbook of the National Society for the Study of Education [Chicago: The Society (distributed by the University of Chicago Press), 1959], pp. 41–81.

[16] See Chris Kehas, "Education and Personal Development" in Bruce Shertzer and S. C. Stone (eds.), *Introduction to Guidance: Selected Readings* (Boston: Houghton Mifflin, 1970), pp. 59–71.

it desirable for individuals to have opportunity both to think about the kind of self they are building and have built and to confront themselves with the meanings they attribute to their experiencing and the consequences such attributions will have on their future self."[17] Therefore guidance could be conceptualized as the school's provision for enabling the student to create meaning in his life.

Principle II. The primary mode by which guidance is conducted lies in individual behavioral processes. Since guidance is concerned with personal development, its practitioners' subject matter is the personal world of each student. Guidance practitioners utilize personal interviews, counseling relationships, test interpretation sessions and the like to advance a student's understanding of his own internal structure. Through these methods the individual can examine the world he creates for himself and the meanings to be derived from his personal experiences. Miller points out that guidance operates in the zone in which the individual's own unique world of perceptions interacts with the external order of events in his life context.[18] Therefore, the processes and practices employed by guidance personnel are designed to assist the individual to understand better his subjective states and external social conditions. The intent of the practitioners' operations is that the individual master his experiences, attitudes and meanings in order to exert control over his development.

Principle III. Guidance is oriented toward cooperation, not compulsion. Students cannot be compelled to submit to guidance. Guidance takes place by the mutual consent of the individuals involved. Consent is given either explicitly or implicitly. The absence of coercion or pressure is the hallmark of guidance. When unwilling students are referred to guidance personnel, the resentment and resistance usually present must be taken into account and resolved. Guidance depends upon releasing the internal motivation, and/or willingness to change, rather than upon external coercion or threat. Duress creates mistrust rather than improvement.

Principle IV. Guidance is based upon recognizing the dignity and worth of the individual as well as his right to choose. Respect is accorded a person because he is an individual, possessing worth and dignity and because he is human. Guidance rests on a belief in the fundamental dignity and importance of the *individual,* in the essential *equality* of human beings and in their need to exercise *freedom.* This emphasis on the supreme worth and central position of the individual has been an unbroken thread in democratic thought. Its fundamental proposition lies in the integrity of the individual—he has the right to be treated as a unique and inviolable person.

[17] *Ibid.,* p. 61.

[18] Miller, *Foundations of Guidance,* p. 450.

Further, each individual should have the maximum opportunity to select his own purposes in life and to choose the means to accomplish these purposes. The core of freedom is self-determination. It involves the power to act positively toward those goals that an individual chooses. Certainly, the freedom to make choices and to act upon them is essential to personal development. By using his freedom the individual develops a sense of responsibility and self-restraint.

Principle V. Guidance is a continuous, sequential, educational process. It should begin with the elementary school and continue throughout education; it should be united by a single theme; and it should be integrated with the total school program.

Perhaps Wrenn has best summarized these principles when he asks what is important in student personnel work and responds by citing the following from the personnel point of view in education:

1. Above all else, personnel service in education is predicated upon seeing the learner *totally*.
2. We are dedicated to treat the student with dignity, to respect his integrity and his right to self-fulfillment.
3. Personnel work is concerned with the student's plans for the future as well as optimum living in the present.
4. We are the prime advocates of individual differences in the school.
5. Personnel work depends upon a varied methodology, one that is fitted to the ends to be served.
6. Just as the best conception of counseling is that of a creative relationship between counselor and student, so the important element in all personnel work is the quality of the relationship established between worker and learner, between worker and colleague.
7. Finally, personnel services must remain in the central stream of educational effort.[19]

CRITICISMS OF GUIDANCE

A survey of guidance would be incomplete without some examination of the criticisms at issue in the field. This section attempts to bring together some of the more conspicuous ones. As these were being set down, the authors were at a loss as to whether to indicate their own biases in these matters or simply to narrate the criticisms. The position finally observed was that the criticisms would be reported but that some indication of the authors' attitudes, opinions, and convictions about these and other matters would be given in Chapter 18, "Issues in Guidance" and in Chapter 19, "Trends in Guidance." It should be noted that these criticisms have been made not only by people outside the field of guidance but also by those who are employed in the field. Only a few of the major criticisms of guidance

[19] Wrenn, "Philosophical and Psychological Bases", pp. 41–44.

will be dealt with here since the issues confronting the field will be detailed in greater length in Chapter 17.

A consistent criticism, past and present, has been that the word "guidance" is meaningless. Wrenn is among those who have been most critical of the term. He states, "The term 'guidance workers,' already in disfavor, will disappear from our vocabulary as a vague and ambiguous term involving a person whose time may be spread so thinly over such a variety of activities that no one of them can be performed adequately."[20] On the other hand, Hoyt has argued for retention of the term because it "is essential if the role of the counselor in education and in pupil personnel work is to be placed in proper perspective." Hoyt sees it as a symbol of the share all educators must have in the process.[21]

Critics point out that the term conveys direction, authoritarianism, and paternalism which is just the opposite of that which people in the field claim that they practice. Defenders of the term claim that from a historical sense guidance has meaning in education and furthermore, no better term has yet been advanced that is acceptable.

In view of these difficulties Hobbs has facetiously suggested:

> One way out of this semantic quandary would be to invent some new words. We might take a cue from government and world organizations and get some words that stand for the person engaged in guidance work. A few samples are supplied, without much self investment in their perpetuation: COOSSD, AIPP, and WANTAPICU. These stand, respectively, for: "Coordinator of Opportunities for Student Self Development," "Assistant to Individuals in Personal Planning," and "Wheedler and Needler of Teachers and Principals in the Interest of the Child Undivided." A person could get an M.A. in AIPP or accept a position as COOSSD in his home town high school. On further thought, maybe we had better stick to the word guidance, limp as it is.[22]

Another criticism is that guidance and counseling have lost their identity to psychology. In his 1950 presidential address to the National Vocational Guidance Association, Hoppock reviewed some of the accomplishments of vocational guidance and then stated:

> Massive as this program has been and still is, the foundations upon which it rests are beginning to crumble. . . . Client-centered counseling now challenges the basic assumption underlying the whole concept of testing and diagnosis as the indispensable preliminary to clinical counseling.[23]

[20] C. Gilbert Wrenn, *The Counselor in a Changing World* (Washington: American Personnel and Guidance Association, 1962), p. 111.

[21] Kenneth B. Hoyt, "Guidance: A Constellation of Services," *Personnel and Guidance Journal* Vol. 40 (April 1962), pp. 690–697.

[22] Nicholas Hobbs, "Some Notions About Guidance," *Peabody Journal of Education* Vol. 29 (January 1962), p. 229.

[23] Robert Hoppock, "NVGA Presidential Address," *Occupations* Vol. 28 (May 1950), p. 498.

Tyler, in an editorial comment entitled "What Do You Mean, Routine?" described the tendency of many to consider educational and vocational counseling routine and to prefer clients with therapeutic needs.[24] Tooker criticized school counselors because of their tendency to cling to the coattails of clinical psychology.[25] At issue is whether personnel in guidance, by virtue of using concepts and techniques from developmental, personality, and clinical psychology, have denigrated themselves and lost their distinguishing professional features.

Another criticism is that guidance personnel are inadequately trained to perform the functions which originally served as the basis for their employment. Wolfle, in the preface to Wrenn's report, *The Counselor in a Changing World,* very forcefully makes clear that

> The current reality is that most school counselors are inadequately prepared to meet these rigorous standards. They are largely recruited from among persons who originally prepared themselves for one career—for example, teaching history—and who later, on the basis of meager additional training, became "counselors." The hard truth is that many school counselors have not been trained to give a student much help in finding his way in an increasingly complex world.[26]

Over time, perhaps this criticism will be blunted when the APGA Counselor Education Standards are fully implemented. These standards call for two years of graduate preparation of school counselors.

Another criticism is that counselors spend all their time with college-bound students and neglect the large numbers of the youth who enter the labor market. In many cases this criticism can be reduced to the fact that counselors spend too much time with bright students, and consequently students of average and low ability cannot receive their fair share of the counselor's time, skills, and knowledge. Walton has stated that ". . . a real danger lies in a tendency on the part of school guidance workers to stress that with which they are most familiar, curricular and college guidance areas, and to neglect that which is not their 'natural' interest, the vocational area . . ."[27] Many have implied and others have forthrightly stated that the counselor's lack of work experience in business and industry commits his attention, loyalty, and practices to those students who will remain in school.

Many have criticized the counselor's use of his time. Hitting hard at the counselor's overinvolvement in such tasks as clerical work, substitute teaching, discipline, activity-club supervision, and other quasi-administrative

[24] Leona E. Tyler, "What Do You Mean, Routine?" *Journal of Counseling Psychology* Vol. 6 (Fall 1959), p. 174.

[25] Ellis D. Tooker, "Counselor Role: Counselor Training," *Personnel and Guidance Journal* Vol. 36 (December 1957), pp. 263–267.

[26] Dael Wolfle, Preface to Wrenn, *The Counselor in a Changing World* (Washington: American Personnel and Guidance Association, 1962), p. i.

[27] L. G. Walton, "The Scope and Function of Vocational Guidance, *Educational Outlook* Vol. 31 (May 1957), pp. 119–128.

tasks, Arnold,[28] Goldstein,[29] Martyn,[30] Hitchcock,[31] Purcell,[32] Hollis and Isaacson,[33] and others urge the counselor to spend more time in counseling. This situation has led Tennyson[34] to cry for "time" and relief from administrative duties; Stewart to draft a "bill of rights" seeking time, space, and support for concentration on counseling and related activities,[35] and Novak to plead, "Let the counselor counsel!"[36]

Still others are critical of the fact that titles assigned guidance personnel do not convey functions, and that all too often counselors serve dual roles in the school when they should be assigned full time to their responsibilities. All kinds of titles abound for those who work in the schools: educational counselor, adviser, guidance counselor, vocational counselor, school counselor, psychological counselor, guidance director, staff adviser, staff assistant, and the like. Critics claim the titles obscure rather than clarify roles. Arbuckle's statement is illustrative of those who decry part-time assignments. Arbuckle reasons:

> It is interesting to note that of these groups (teachers, administrators, and specialized service personnel) it is only the school counselor who is willing to accept the part-time, dual-role status. Other professional workers may spend only part of their time in the service of the school, but they are not part-time doctors, or part-time nurses, or part-time psychologists, or psychiatrists. Like pregnancy, "they are or they ain't," and there is no in-between status. We have no doctor-teacher, or nurse-principal, or psychologist-janitor, but we have thousands of teacher-counselors, or even more absurd, principal-counselors, and even, horror added upon horror, superintendent-counselors. Even worse, this schizophrenic fellow doesn't seem to mind this dual or triple status, and goes blithely walking off in several directions at the same time, quite unaware that one set of feet is falling over the others.[37]

[28] Dwight L. Arnold, "Time Spent by Counselors and Deans on Various Activities," *Occupations* Vol. 27 (March 1949), pp. 391–393.

[29] H. A. Goldstein, "Job Analysis of Junior and Senior High School Counselors," *Industrial Arts and Vocational Education* Vol. 39 (December 1950), pp. 386–388.

[30] K. A. Martyn, "Counselors Revealed as Clerical Workers," *Occupations* Vol. 29 (January 1951), p. 294.

[31] W. L. Hitchcock, "Counselors Feel They Should," *Personnel and Guidance Journal* Vol. 32 (October 1953), pp. 72–74.

[32] Florence E. Purcell, "Counselor Duties—A Survey," *School Counselor* Vol. 4 (December 1957), pp. 35–38.

[33] Joseph Hollis and Lee Isaacson, "How School Counselors Spend Their Time," *School Counselor* Vol. 9 (March 1962), pp. 89–95.

[34] W. W. Tennyson, "Time, The Counselor's Dilemma," *Personnel and Guidance Journal* Vol. 37 (October 1958), pp. 129–135.

[35] C. C. Stewart, "A Bill of Rights for School Counselors," *Personnel and Guidance Journal* Vol. 37 (March 1959), pp. 500–503.

[36] B. J. Novak, "Let the Counselor Counsel!" *Phi Delta Kappan* Vol. 43 (January 1962), pp. 171–173.

[37] Dugald S. Arbuckle, "The Conflicting Functions of the School Counselor," *Counselor Education and Supervision* Vol. 1 (Winter 1961), p. 56.

A final criticism is that guidance is atheoretical. That is, that present-day guidance practice is not and cannot be based upon any theory. The contention is that attention has been directed to providing a service to students —to the detriment of building theories that explain the behavior of individuals involved in guidance processes. Closely associated with this criticism is the view that "borrowed" psychotherapy models have been misapplied to school guidance. These critics assert that self theory counseling, psychoanalytic, behavioristic and other models do not fit that which is done in school helping relationships because of the brevity of counselor-student contacts and for other reasons. Few school counselors would dispute that much more work in theory building is sorely needed.

Super has written the words which serve well to end this section:

> That the school counselor has been organizing to improve himself, and insisting on having a greater voice in deciding where and how, is good. It is to be hoped that he will not let criticism lead him to overact, to imagine threats which do not exist, to reject assistance which he needs, wants and knows how to use effectively. It is to be hoped, too, that those who want to help him will find ways of making their help available which are both acceptable and effective.[38]

ANNOTATED BIBLIOGRAPHY

BREWER, JOHN M. *History of Vocational Guidance.* New York: Harper & Brothers, 1942. 344 pp.

This is the original study of the history of vocational guidance, with emphasis on guidance in the schools.

MILLER, CARROLL H. *Foundations of Guidance.* New York: Harper & Brothers, 1961. 464 pp.

Discusses the sources that have been instrumental in the development of guidance. Chapter 1 (pp. 1–17) presents past and present emphases in the concepts of guidance, and Chapter 6 (pp. 144–173) documents the guidance movement in the United States.

BECK, CARLTON E. *Philosophical Foundations of Guidance.* Englewood Cliffs, N.J.: Prentice-Hall, Inc., 1963. 171 pp.

Traces the major philosophical foundations upon which guidance has been built. Beck sees five stages of development—the amorphous, the prescriptive, the nondirective, the phenomenological, and the existential.

SELECTED REFERENCES

AUBREY, ROGER F. "Misapplication of Therapy Models to School Counseling." *Personnel and Guidance Journal* Vol. 48 (December 1969), pp. 273–278.

[38] Donald E. Super, "The Professional Status and Affiliations of Vocational Counselors," in Henry Borow (ed.), *Man in a World at Work* (Boston: Houghton Mifflin Company, 1964), p. 571.

BOROW, HENRY. "Milestones: A Chronology of Notable Events in the History of Vocational Guidance." In Henry Borow (ed). *Man In a World at Work.* Boston: Houghton Mifflin Company, 1964, pp. 45–64.

DALDRUP, ROGER J. "Counselor's Time: A Persisting Problem." *Counselor Education and Supervision* Vol. 6 (Spring 1967), pp. 179–184.

FARSON, RICHARD E. "The Education of Jeremy Farson." *The School Counselor* Vol. 16 (May 1969), pp. 328–342.

HARRIS, PHILIP R. "Guidance and Counseling: Where It's Been—Where It's Going." *The School Counselor* Vol. 15 (September 1967), pp. 10–15.

LORIMER, JOHN, AND HADDAD, JOSEPH. "Pupil Personnel Services in the Elementary Schools." *Personnel and Guidance Journal* Vol. 47 (June 1969), pp. 975–978.

McDANIELS, CARL. "The Impact of Federal Aid on Counselor Education." *Counselor Education and Supervision* Vol. 6 (Spring 1967), pp. 263–274.

MITCHELL, JOYCE SLAYTON. "High School: Relevant?" *The School Counselor* Vol. 17 (May 1970), pp. 345–349.

MOORE, GILBERT D., AND CRAMER, STANLEY H. "Toward More Effective Use of Counselor Time." *The School Counselor* Vol. 16 (March 1969), pp. 261–262.

PATTERSON, C. H. "Pupil Personnel Services in the Automated School." *Personnel and Guidance Journal* Vol. 48 (October 1969), pp. 101–108.

QUINN, PAUL F. "Rapprochement—The Teachers and the Counselor." *The School Counselor* Vol. 16 (January 1969), pp. 170–173.

ROUSSEVE, RONALD J. "The Role of the Counselor in a Free Society." *The School Counselor* Vol. 16 (September 1968), pp. 6–10.

VAN HOOSE, WILLIAM H., AND VAFAKAS, CATHERINE M. "Status of Guidance and Counseling in the Elementary School." *Personnel and Guidance Journal* Vol. 46 (February 1968), pp. 536–539.

WALZ, GARRY, AND MILLER, JULIET. "School Climates and Student Behavior: Implications for Counselor Role." *Personnel and Guidance Journal* Vol. 47 (May 1969), pp. 859–867.

3

MODELS FOR GUIDANCE

How was guidance first conceptualized?
What guidance models were later established?
What models are now being proposed?
How is guidance organized in contemporary education?

One way of understanding present-day guidance is to study the historical events and the personal goals possessed by individuals who were the decision makers since the inception of organized guidance services. Another approach is through the study of the major social institutions which constitute the means by which educational change occurs. Schools not only adapt to our culture but also shape our culture, turning it into means to reach ends. Both approaches to understanding must be taken into account, for neither provides sufficient understanding by itself. Borow stresses that the history of vocational guidance teaches at least two lessons: "(1) The growth of the movement must be evaluated against the *Zeitgeist*. Without an appreciation of the prevailing social and intellectual temper of the times, the interpretation of episodes in the sweep of the professional history remains incomplete and often distorted. (2) Progress flows from seemingly small beginnings."[1]

The purpose of this chapter is to examine some of the models that have been proposed for guidance by considering both the historical events and the institutions of society which forced change. For each model, the description will take into account (1) historical context; (2) rationale and/or

[1] Henry Borow (ed.), *Man in a World at Work* (Boston: Houghton Mifflin Company, 1964), p. 47.

basic assumptions; (3) advantages and disadvantages; and (4) outcomes and/or implications. As used here, "model" refers to the representation from which a final product is abstracted because of its inherent worth.

EARLY GUIDANCE MODELS

The Parsonian Model

HISTORICAL CONTEXT

As noted in Chapter 2, Frank Parsons, a civic-minded writer and lecturer, founded the Vocational Bureau in Boston in 1908. He coined the term "vocational guidance" in his book, *Choosing A Vocation,* which was published posthumously.[2] Historically, humanitarian and philanthropic movements were in full swing during this period of the nation's history. At the same time, serious study was being given to the educational problems of the mentally retarded, as well as to industrial turnover (resignations, unemployment). Freudian psychology was beginning to gain acceptance both in Europe and in this country through Sigmund Freud's series of lectures on psychoanalysis at Clark University in 1909. Individual differences became the focus of much psychological research and study in Europe and the United States.

Some of the individuals who adopted Parsons' model were Meyer Bloomfield, who succeeded to Parsons' position as head of the Vocational Bureau and taught the first vocational course at the university level at Harvard in 1911, and Hugo Munsterberg, who published *Psychology and Industrial Efficiency* in Germany (American edition, 1913) in which experimental psychology was applied to vocational choice.[3, 4]

RATIONALE

Parsons' methods consisted of matching the characteristics of the individual to the requirements of the occupation. He believed that if individuals were employed in the line of work to which they could best adapt because of compatibility between the characteristics of the person and the job, both the individual and society would profit. His observations of young people at the Vocational Bureau led him to the conclusion that they needed careful and systematic help from experienced individuals in choosing a vocation. He reasoned that three major factors were operative in selecting a vocation and that these factors suggested methods by which experienced individuals

[2] Frank Parsons, *Choosing a Vocation* (Boston: Houghton Mifflin Company, 1909).

[3] Meyer Bloomfield, *The Vocational Guidance of Youth* (Boston: Houghton Mifflin Company, 1911).

[4] Hugo Munsterberg, *Psychology and Industrial Efficiency* (Boston: Houghton Mifflin Company, 1913).

or counselors could help the young person. The three major factors may be summarized as follows:

1. *Man Analysis.* The counselor and counselee together analyze the counselee's capabilities, interests, and temperament.
2. *Job Analysis.* Student study of occupational opportunities, requirements, and employment prospects in various lines of work.
3. *Joint and Cooperative Comparison of These Two Sets of Analyses.* The counselor and student reason out the relationships between these two sets of data.

Unique at that time was Parsons' first step; i.e., the diagnosis of the individual's capabilities prior to choice. Parsons emphasized that special efforts should be made to develop the analytic powers of the individual to aid him in choice-making. Samples of work were analyzed by the student as well as books describing analytical powers. The young person was advised to visit industries and to talk with workers and management.

Parsons urged counselors to gather biographical information on the characteristics of leading men in given fields of work, particularly during their youth. This was to be done in an effort to determine the relationship between youthful characteristics and their later vocational development.

ADVANTAGES AND DISADVANTAGES

The advantages of Parsons' model seem rather obvious. It appealed to logic and common sense; it recognized that many individuals having problems in the area of vocational choice could be helped by a more mature, experienced person; and it could be programed into the schools because of its definitiveness. The criticisms of Parsons' model which incorporate its disadvantages have been cited by Barry and Wolf and are summarized briefly below:

1. The theory became practice before adequate evaluation could take place.
2. The original assumptions were based on only three and a half months' work with fewer than one hundred immigrants of all ages who sought Parsons' help.
3. The training for vocational counselors started before anyone could be sure what their training should be or what the counselors should do.
4. The vocational guidance methodology is predicated upon the outmoded assumption that information teaches, that advice and information-giving are functions of the counselor, and that vocational guidance can exist apart from "personal" guidance.
5. Some believe that it has limited counselors by causing them to feel that occupational information can only be presented in the classic pamphlet or brochure.
6. Formal information can never be totally factual, realistic, and authentic.
7. The brief informational tract proposed by Parsons was developed on the basis of experience in only one city, yet the same outline has been used

to develop brochures and monographs that have national coverage, which has increased problems.

8. Anthropological and sociological investigations of social class, status, and structure did not appear until the latter half of the 1920's; thus few of these findings have been combined with psychological contributions to stress the importance of motivations, class, origins, culture, values, and the wholeness of human personality. Parsons' work stressed occupational choice based on "reasoning" about the relations of only two groups of facts.[5]

OUTCOMES AND IMPLICATIONS

Several writers have suggested that Parsons' major contribution was the degree of emphasis placed upon individual analysis before one's choice of an occupation. In this approach, he was inventive in calling for the use of psychological techniques for diagnosing the individual's characteristics. Parsons' theory encouraged test development to facilitate "man analysis," because for him, observation should be objective. Another implication of his work was that guidance was seen as a one-step operation that occurred before employment. This concept was held for a long period of time, and only much later, with Super's adaptation of Buehler's concepts of life stages, gave way to the realization that guidance is usually needed repeatedly at successive stages in life.[6, 7] Another outcome of Parsons' approach was that guidance was focused upon vocational aspects. Many tried to restrict guidance exclusively to a vocational emphasis.

Guidance as Identical with Education

HISTORICAL CONTEXT

The concept of guidance as identical with education has been attributed to Brewer, whose book *Education as Guidance* was published in 1932.[8] However, Super[9] and others have objected to identifying Brewer with this point of view. Brewer studied at Harvard under Paul Hanus, the original Chairman of the Executive Committee of Parsons' Boston Vocational Bureau. Brewer taught at Harvard in 1916 and 1917 and then went to what is now the University of California at Los Angeles and taught courses in vocational guidance and vocational education. In 1919 he returned to Harvard to teach and serve as director of the Bureau of Vocational Guidance. The original Vocational Bureau had been made over into the Harvard

[5] Abstracted from Ruth Barry and Beverly Wolf, *Epitaph for Vocational Guidance* (New York: Bureau of Publications, Teachers College, Columbia University, 1961), pp. 8–10.

[6] Donald E. Super, *The Dynamics of Vocational Adjustment* (New York: Harper & Brothers, 1942).

[7] Charlotte Buehler, *From Birth to Maturity* (London: Kegan and Paul, 1935).

[8] John M. Brewer, *Education as Guidance* (New York: The Macmillan Co., 1932).

[9] Super, *Dynamics of Vocational Adjustment,* p. 5.

Division of Education in 1917. Brewer emphasized working with secondary schools and organized a series of courses for preparing counselors.

The term "educational guidance" was first used by Truman L. Kelley in his doctoral dissertation at Teachers College, Columbia University in 1914. He used it to describe the help given to students who had questions about choice of studies and school adjustment. The following year, Meyer Bloomfield, addressing a group of teachers at Tacoma, Washington, was quoted as saying, "all education is now recognized as guidance." Hawkes stated that "education is guidance and guidance is education."[10] Hildreth also maintained that no valid distinction was possible between education and guidance in purpose, method, or results.[11]

The historical context of guidance as identical with education would be incomplete without mentioning the impact of a pamphlet of the Bureau of Education (now the U.S. Office of Education), *Cardinal Principles of Secondary Education,* upon the educational movement in the United States in the 1920's and 1930's.[12] This pamphlet, first issued in 1918, declared that the goal of education was effective living in several areas of human activity: health, fundamental mental processes, home membership, vocation, citizenship, worthy use of leisure time, and ethical character. Guidance as identical with education grew out of an attempt by Brewer and others to describe vocational guidance as a means for implementing the seven cardinal principles.

Brewer suggested the following definitions of guidance:

> Guidance is frequently misconceived; it is best understood through the concept of self guidance, its ultimate aim. . . . Guidance is neither adjusting nor suggesting, neither conditioning nor controlling, neither directing nor taking responsibility for anybody.
>
> . . . the work we do in schools may be described as helping children to understand, organize, extend and improve their individual and cooperative activities. . . . [This] means guidance.[13]

RATIONALE

Brewer, concerned over the fact that schools were pre-occupied with knowledge and rarely concerned about action, drew heavily upon the seven cardinal principles. He advanced the thesis that the goal of education is to prepare students to engage in meaningful life activities, with knowledge and wisdom as the means to acquire this end. He believed that schools exist

---

[10] Herbert E. Hawkes and Anna L. Rose Hawkes, *Through a Dean's Open Door* (New York: McGraw-Hill Book Co., Inc., 1945), p. 37.

[11] Gertrude H. Hildreth, "Guidance in the Lincoln School," *Teachers College Record* Vol. 37 (February 1936), p. 432.

[12] *Cardinal Principles of Secondary Education,* Department of the Interior, Bureau of Education, Bulletin No. 35, 1918 (Washington: Government Printing Office, 1918).

[13] Brewer, *Education as Guidance,* p. 2.

to guide children in their individual and cooperative activities, and that these activities should be defined in terms of the cardinal principles. Guidance and education were used almost interchangeably by Brewer, with both concepts having as their function the guidance of young people in living. Brewer cites the following as criteria of guidance: (1) the person is guided in solving a problem, performing a task, or moving towards some objective; (2) the person being guided usually takes the initiative and asks for guidance; (3) the guide is sympathetic, friendly, and understanding; (4) the guide should have experience, knowledge, and wisdom; (5) the method of guidance is to offer opportunities for new experiences and enlightenment; (6) the person guided progressively consents to receive guidance, reserves the right to use the guidance offered, and makes his own decisions; (7) the guidance offered helps the individual receiving it to become better able to guide himself.[14] Guidance as identical with education was seen as a series of activities and actions permeating all educational activity.

ADVANTAGES AND DISADVANTAGES

Guidance in its inception had been unduly limited by the use of the descriptive adjective "vocational." Guidance as identical with education deserves some credit for broadening the concept of guidance to encompass a wider range of areas. Guidance as education emphasized the individual and life situations in relation to the total educational process. Although the attempt to get teachers to teach "children" rather than "subjects" still goes on today, this model should receive recognition for its contribution to this goal. Guidance as identical with education pointed up that the individual has a right to his own individuality and to an education tailored to his needs.

One disadvantage which may be pointed out is that the broadening of guidance to include education carried with it the effect of introducing a multitude of descriptive adjectives: educational, ethical, personal, moral, *ad infinitum*. Certainly, viewing guidance as identical with education has certain disadvantages. For one, the concept was interpreted to mean that information could be provided efficiently and economically through the various activities and classes within the school. This often led to inadequate provision for the assessment and application of information. Most present-day educational authorities identify three inseparable aspects of the total educational process: (1) instructional, (2) administrative, and (3) guidance or pupil personnel.

OUTCOMES AND IMPLICATIONS

One of the outcomes of the model of guidance as education is still haunting today's counselors; this carryover is the concept that guidance is some-

[14] Brewer, *Education as Guidance,* p. 22.

thing that can be "taught" in the same manner as an academic subject. This is evident in the fact that many high schools still offer formal courses in occupations, health, citizenship, and the like. Another variation of this same theme can be seen in the regularly scheduled group guidance classes that are a part of many guidance programs. While guidance as education was never a concept widely implemented, it left its mark upon counseling and guidance as it is known today.

LATER GUIDANCE MODELS

Guidance as Distribution and Adjustment

HISTORICAL CONTEXT

During the middle 1920's, William M. Proctor pointed out that American high schools needed more guidance programs.[15] He conceptualized guidance as a mediating force that helps the student cope with school and life forces. It was his opinion that the needs of high school students extend far beyond occupational considerations. He believed that students need help in the selection of school subjects, extracurricular activities, colleges, and vocational schools. By 1930 the concept of "educational and vocational guidance" was well on its way to general acceptance. During the period 1925–1937, Proctor shifted the emphasis in his definition of the proper guidance function from the concept of the mediating force to the concept that guidance deals with the processes of distribution and adjustment of pupils. Other individuals were also instrumental in defining this model. In the early 1930's, Koos and Kefauver enlarged upon Proctor's philosophy, from which the model of guidance as distribution and adjustment was derived.[16, 17]

Hand was also an active individual in viewing guidance as distribution and adjustment.[18] His work with Kefauver stressed that guidance must incorporate two major functions:

1. *Distribution.* The counselor seeks to aid the pupil in formulating his goals in vocational, social, civic, and recreational as well as other pursuits. This requires assisting the student to know himself in his environment. In the distributive function, students are helped in the most effec-

[15] William M. Proctor, *Educational and Vocational Guidance* (Boston: Houghton Mifflin Company, 1925).

[16] Leonard V. Koos, "The Interpretation of Guidance," *The Clearing House* Vol. 8 (September 1933), p. 8.

[17] Leonard V. Koos and Grayson N. Kefauver, *Guidance in the Secondary Schools* (New York: The Macmillan Co., 1932), pp. 15–17.

[18] Grayson N. Kefauver and Harold C. Hand, *Appraising Guidance in Secondary Schools* (New York: The Macmillan Co., 1941).

tive manner possible to find suitable educational-vocational opportunities.

2. *Adjustment.* The counselor helps the pupil to adjust when he has been unable to integrate knowledge about himself and his environment in accordance with his goals.

RATIONALE

Guidance as distribution and adjustment seeks to help students match their selection of school subjects, extra-class activities, colleges, trade schools, and vocations with their own abilities, interests, and purposes. The objectives of guidance as perceived by the distribution and adjustment school of thought can be stated as follows: (1) to help students attain a high level of efficiency and satisfaction in the appropriate activities in which they will engage; (2) to help students engage in appropriate out-of-school activities in the manner that will contribute most to social welfare and individual happiness; (3) to help students formulate appropriate goals and plans for participation in life activities and appropriate plans for education in harmony with these goals; (4) to help students secure information concerning (a) the factors which should be considered in defining those plans, (b) the probabilities of success and satisfaction in various types of school and out-of-school activities, (c) their personal abilities and interests, (d) the life activities from which choices will be made, (e) programs of the school in which they are now enrolled and in which they will be enrolled later, (f) the training opportunities afforded by nonschool agencies in the community, and (g) suitable or false guidance.

ADVANTAGES AND DISADVANTAGES

Some of the advantages cited for guidance as distribution and adjustment include the fact that emphasis is placed upon helping students to understand themselves in their environment. The model proposes help to students in finding suitable vocational opportunities as well as in adjusting to these situations. Another advantage is that the model stresses that the individual has the opportunity to make choices compatible with his concept of self and environment.

A disadvantage of this view is that very often precisely those high school courses that are suited to the purposes and capabilities of the student are missing in the curriculum. But the major disadvantage lies in the fact that guidance is seen as being offered only at crisis points.

OUTCOMES AND IMPLICATIONS

When the functions of the distributive and adjustive conception of guidance are successfully carried out, they serve to help educators and parents to become more conscious of the abilities, interests, and educational needs of students. This would lead to modifications of the educational program in order to serve the different needs of students. Another outcome is the encouragement of student motivation by the formulation of goals and the interpretation of the significance of the different activities that students anticipate. The extent to which the student achieves successful adjustment is one indication of the effectiveness of the distribution and adjustment process of guidance.

Guidance as a Clinical Process

It should be noted by the reader that this model should not be viewed strictly as a guidance model, since it pertains more directly to one facet of guidance services; namely, counseling.

HISTORICAL CONTEXT

The beginning of psychology as a science is usually associated with the founding in 1879 of the first psychological laboratory by Wilhelm Wundt. One of his students, James M. Cattell brought to America the use of mental measurement to study individual differences. At that time psychological measurement consisted primarily of evaluating simple motor and sensory tasks such as number-checking and memory for numbers heard. In addition, in 1905 another type of test of man's capabilities was developed by Binet and Simon, which led to the modern intelligence test.

Guidance as a clinical process was first introduced by M. S. Viteles, Donald G. Paterson,[19] E. G. Williamson,[20] and others. The development of the clinical method rests heavily upon measurement research efforts by applied psychologists who, for the most part, were not concerned with the guidance movement as such. These men addressed themselves primarily to the task of developing ways and means for measuring vocationally significant mental traits. The development of group intelligence testing before and during World War I together with the widespread application of this technique in schools and colleges therefore represents a major contribution.

Many persons recognized the desirability of a more scientific approach to guidance work. However, others raised objections to utilizing scientific techniques in actual guidance situations because they feared science when it touched the individual.

RATIONALE

Cribbin stated that as a model the clinical approach to guidance was characterized as (1) representing a protest against shoddy methods which frequently masquerade as guidance; (2) seeking to develop techniques to provide comprehensive analysis of the individual; (3) constituting the means by which educators' professed interest in individualizing education

---

[19] Donald G. Paterson, "The Genesis of Modern Guidance," *The Educational Record* Vol. 16 (January 1938), p. 41.

[20] E. G. Williamson, *How to Counsel Students* (New York: McGraw-Hill Book Co., Inc., 1939), p. 37.

could be translated into practice; (4) introducing order through a sub-division of labor among instructional, advisory, administrative, and clinical groups, all of whom work cooperatively to benefit the student, while retaining their own spheres of independent action; (5) stressing the role of professionally trained counselors whose task it is to help students with their more difficult problems of adjustment; and (6) following an orderly, but not necessarily mechanical, procedure in terms of analysis, synthesis, diagnosis, prognosis, counseling, and followup.[21]

Guidance as a clinical process stresses the use of psychological tests, clinical techniques and analytical diagnostic studies so that the clinician can better understand his client and determine the client's problems sooner and more accurately. This permits the most suitable form of treatment to begin sooner. The clinical process involves uncovering the person's inner problems through external techniques. The clinician is not concerned with making decisions for the client but rather seeks to organize learning situations in such a manner that the client secures enough insight into the related causes of his trouble to permit him to select appropriate alternatives of behavior and action suited to his own best long- or short-term interests or desires.

ADVANTAGES AND DISADVANTAGES

One advantage of this model is that, because the process is directive in its approach, its application frequently results in efficiency and economy by allowing the counselor to work with more individuals. The clinical process is scientific in its approach to problem-solving and uses objective tools which supply the individual with concrete data. Some of its disadvantages include the fact that, since the clinical process is directive, it places a tremendous burden of responsibility on the diagnostician. It places considerable emphasis on external techniques and may dissect the individual into small, perhaps unrelated segments through scientific investigation and then assume that the problems of the individual are unrelated rather than intimately related.

OUTCOMES AND APPLICATIONS

Guidance as a clinical process requires extensive gathering of scientific data and calls for more objective data than approaches which do not stress detailed assessment of the individual. Its emphasis upon research and followup has been helpful to the field's development. Another outcome was that guidance as a clinical process generated the idea of a qualification card as the basic personnel technique. This technique has since been developed into the cumulative record card as a basic guidance tool in education. Another outcome was that it forced the professionalization of the guidance worker. Mere knowledge of occupations obtained from books and pamphlets was not enough. The approach emphasized that guidance workers

---

[21] James J. Cribbin, "A Critique of the Philosophy of Modern Guidance," *The Catholic Educational Review* Vol. 53 (February 1955), p. 87.

should possess knowledge of psychology, research, statistics, and clinical procedures.

Guidance as Decision-Making

HISTORICAL CONTEXT

Two authorities, Jones and Myers, were among those who earlier perceived guidance as decision-making.[22, 23] Jones' six editions between 1949 and 1970 have portrayed guidance as assistance in making choices. More recently, Katz has formulated such a model.[24]

As has previously been pointed out, guidance in its infancy was strictly vocationally focused; it was directed mainly toward assisting the individual to make vocational choices in industry, training, and employment. Attempts to assist youth to make wise vocational choices revealed the interdependence of vocational choice with other needs: health, leisure, and/or educational needs. Gradually, but surely, came the realization that guidance was not something that concerns only a part of the individual and consequently should not deal solely with a part of his life.

RATIONALE

Both Jones and Myers stress that the guidance situation exists only when the student needs help in making choices, interpretations, or adjustments. For Jones, guidance is the help given in making wise choices and adjustments and in solving problems in critical situations in such a way as to ensure continual development of the ability for self-direction. Myers maintained that guidance must relate only to decision-making and that decision-making involves situations in which two sets of differences exist, namely, differences among individuals and differences among possible choices. With this as his criterion, Myers excluded from the purview of guidance all such concepts as recreational guidance, social guidance, health guidance, and the fifty-seven other varieties. His point was that these were matters for instruction, not guidance. The fundamental guidance areas were educational and vocational.

Katz defines guidance as ". . . professional intervention in the choices an individual makes among the educational and occupational options our society allows him."[25] Noting that "career" represents a sequence of choices as well as outcomes for each choice, Katz stated that decision-making is characterized by an individual's social and psychological transaction with

---

[22] Arthur J. Jones, *Principles of Guidance,* 6th ed. Revised and updated by Buford Stefflre and Norman Stewart. (New York: McGraw-Hill Book Co., Inc., 1970), p. 7.

[23] George Myers, *Principles and Techniques of Vocational Guidance* (New York: McGraw-Hill Book Co., Inc., 1941), pp. 15–16.

[24] Martin Katz, *Decisions and Values: A Rationale for Secondary School Guidance* (New York: College Entrance Examination Board, 1963), 67 pp.

[25] *Ibid.,* p. 2.

the environment. Social and cultural factors determine the timing of choice points and thereby initiate decision-making at each point. Since values are a major synthesizing element in decision-making—in that they order, arrange, and unify the student's perceptions of traits and social forces—then examination of values must be of prime concern for guidance. The counselor does not champion one set of values over another, but advocates a full examination of each set of values.

According to Katz, two major choice points exist for pupils—at the beginning of secondary school and near its end. Decision-making at each stage is seen as a strategy for acquiring and processing information. True decision-making exists when the person (1) does not know what information he needs, (2) does not have what information he wants, or (3) cannot use what information he has. At each stage (Grades 8–9 and Grades 11–12) some decision will be made if only by drift or default. A first task of guidance personnel in this model is to encourage the student to take cognizance of the range of values and to bring his own choice of values into full consciousness when he is making decisions. In a later publication, Katz stated:

> For in order to identify and define his values, the student needs to know not only what they are but also what they are not, where they appear and where they do not appear. Helping the student to work through these perceptions in a rational way, helping him to choose among them (perhaps by a process of successive approximations), and helping him to implement his choices are the primary concerns of guidance for career decision-making.[26]

A second task in the process is to provide the student with information about the opportunities available in each option he has, and the third task is to mobilize predictive data to show how the three tasks can be combined in a rational process.

Those who stress guidance as decision-making assume that differences among individuals in abilities and interests are significant. Further, it is assumed that important crises cannot be met successfully by young people without assistance. The school is in the most advantageous position to give the assistance needed, not in prescription-like fashion but in a way that will aid the progressive development of the individual's ability for self-direction.

ADVANTAGES AND DISADVANTAGES

Guidance as decision-making involves the individual in a process which attains great importance in a democratic society. For the individual, it provides participation in decision-making and provides a foundation for future life needs. Some of the disadvantages are that individuals are frequently reluctant to make decisions and that the process of decision-making does not necessarily result in action. However, perhaps the most critical limitation is that guidance is seen as occurring only at specific points or times, which could lead to the view that such assistance is for crisis situations only.

[26] Martin Katz, "A Model of Guidance for Career Decision-Making," *Vocational Guidance Quarterly* Vol. 15, No. 1 (September 1966), p. 4.

OUTCOMES AND IMPLICATIONS

Choice confronts all individuals, especially in a democratic society. The process of choosing leads to personal development. This model is consistent with democratic beliefs and objectives. Democracy stresses the fact that the individual is capable of self-improvement and that he should actively work toward attaining maximum fulfillment.

Guidance as an Eclectic System

As in the case of the clinical process, it should be noted that "eclecticism" is more correctly used to refer to a counseling approach rather than to a guidance model.

HISTORICAL CONTEXT

During the 1940's and the 1950's, guidance materials and professional literature stressed the procedures to be employed and focused upon the pragmatics of the guidance function. Publications tended to emphasize technique. The vast majority of practitioners tried to combine into a workable system many elements from different sources which had proved their usefulness. The emphasis in guidance shifted from the purely vocational concept to one which included educational and personal concerns; this shift necessitated an expansion of techniques and understanding. As a result, clinical psychology, sociology, and personality theory were all used as sources in an effort to develop an eclectic model for guidance. Wilkens and Perlmutter,[27] in reviewing the literature of guidance in the 1950's, state that most of the books failed to present a consistent philosophy of guidance. Ennis[28] likewise found a plethora of information about methodology but a paucity of material relating to philosophic or theoretical foundations.

Guidance as an eclectic system cannot be identified with a single originator but is represented in the views of Strang,[29] Traxler,[30] Erickson,[31] Froehlich and Darley,[32] Thorne,[33] and others. The word "eclectic" means selecting; choosing appropriate doctrines or methods from various sources or

---

[27] W. D. Wilkens and B. J. Perlmutter, "The Philosophical Foundations of Guidance and Personnel Work," *Review of Educational Research* Vol. 30 (April 1960), pp. 97–104.

[28] Mae Ennis, "The Need for a Philosophy of Guidance Still Haunts Us," *Vocational Guidance Quarterly* Vol. 9 (Winter 1960–61), pp. 138–140.

[29] Ruth Strang, *Counseling Techniques in College and Secondary Schools* (New York: Harper & Brothers, 1964).

[30] Arthur E. Traxler, *Techniques of Guidance* (New York: Harper & Brothers, 1957).

[31] Clifford Erickson, *The Counseling Interview* (New York: Prentice-Hall, Inc., 1950).

[32] Clifford Froehlich and John Darley, *Studying Students* (Chicago: Science Research Associates, 1952).

[33] Frederick Thorne, *Principles of Personality Counseling* (Brandon, Vt.: Journal of Clinical Psychology, 1950).

systems. Strang, one proponent of guidance as an eclectic system, has authored several influential publications since 1932.

RATIONALE

Strang sees guidance as positive in nature and believes that school experiences should be selected and incorporated into total life experiences. The core of guidance to her is (1) to know the individual, (2) to know educational opportunities, and (3) to help the individual to make appropriate choices through group work and counseling. It is her belief that in practice all techniques are interrelated and that these techniques should be used for appraisal and adjustment, which are the main processes of guidance.

The eclectic system's basic assumptions are that the individual requires special professional help periodically in understanding himself and his situation and in dealing with his problems. This special help should be educative in nature; it supplies information about individual personality and social reality which the individual can get in no other way except perhaps through wasteful trial and error. Guidance can in part eliminate or prevent this wasted effort. The eclectic believes that, to the extent that human nature can be understood and predicted and information about the environment assembled, individuals can learn and can make plans. To this extent, the eclectic professional can aid the individual in learning about himself. All this can be achieved through methods that depend upon the ability of the individual to learn purposefully and to decide and act for himself.

The eclectic believes that a single orientation is limiting and that procedures, techniques, and points of view from many sources should be utilized to best serve the needs of the person seeking help. He maintains that he has a consistent philosophy and purpose in his work, and he employs techniques for reasons that are as well verified as possible rather than completely trial and error. From his knowledge of perception, development, learning, and personality, the eclectic counselor develops a repertoire of methods and selects those most appropriate for the particular problem and the specific individual.

ADVANTAGES AND DISADVANTAGES

The eclectic system gives the counselor methodological freedom to employ whatever particular skills he possesses by the means he chooses in what he judges to be the best interests of the client. It emphasizes the importance of diagnosis as a cornerstone to understanding the individual. Counselors following this model must know the indications and contraindications of many methods and be able to utilize them without bias. Its comprehensive nature makes the eclectic approach acceptable to many individuals and its broad scope squares with such democratic ideals as providing for the individual needs of all students.

Disadvantages include the fact that many believe that the eclectic system does not yet possess a consistent philosophy of guidance. That is, choosing bits and pieces from a wide spectrum of theories and methods results in a hodge-podge of contradictory assumptions and incompatible techniques. Few quantitative measures to evaluate this system exist. Some would quarrel with such a model in that it would be more difficult to establish standards for the functions and duties of counselors. Eclecticism is not effective in situations in which students are trained in only one orientation and are either oblivious to other methods or insecure in their applications. Frequently, the objection is raised that a counselor cannot function equally well using many divergent approaches, nor can he function in an unbiased way using approaches that he may not completely understand or accept.

OUTCOMES AND IMPLICATIONS

Some of the implications of this model are that guidance services must be accepted as an essential part of the school program. Cooperation among teachers, administrators, and specialists is essential. The eclectic recognizes the classroom teacher as sharing in the guidance function while acknowledging the need for qualified guidance specialists. Eclecticism as a model presupposes that counselors be broadly trained and that there be effective articulation between the work of teachers, counselors, and other specialists.

Eclectic guidance has been visualized by some as a compromise to reduce the polarization on a continuum—with Williamson at the pole of directive counseling, and Rogers at the other pole, representing nondirective methods. This view is outmoded because of modifications in the positions of Rogers and Williamson over the years. However, because of the sheer range of problems facing school counselors, acceptance of either extreme appears to be unwarranted, even if such polarization existed.

CONTEMPORARY GUIDANCE MODELS

Guidance as a Constellation of Services

HISTORICAL CONTEXT

Currently the most prevalent model of guidance found in American elementary and secondary schools is that of a constellation of services. Hoyt,[34] who described the model in 1962, was in reality using the model to justify the maintenance of the status quo against reforms and changes then being proposed. It may be remembered that in the early 1960's not only were federal funds (NDEA of 1958) available, but many authorities were suggesting, among other things, that counselors needed to counsel more; that the word "guidance" should be abandoned; that a counseling practicum should be required in the preparation of counselors; that the counselor's role and functions should be clarified; and that teacher education and teaching experience were not necessarily the only route to becoming a school

---

[34] Kenneth B. Hoyt, "Guidance: A Constellation of Services," *Personnel and Guidance Journal* Vol. 40 (April 1962), pp. 690–697.

counselor. Hoyt argued against most of these proposals. For example, he sought to retain the word "guidance" because he believed that (1) it permitted the program to be seen as "school-wide assistance to youth" (everyone in the school has guidance responsibilities, not just the school counselor); (2) it provided a rationale for viewing the counselor as a key figure who has major—but not exclusive—responsibility for the complete guidance program (not just counseling); and (3) it permitted the counselor's primary working relationships to remain with teachers rather than with school psychologists, social workers and the like.

RATIONALE

Hoyt describes guidance as ". . . that part of pupil personnel services—and therefore of elementary and secondary education—aimed at maximum development of individual potentialities through devoting schoolwide assistance to youth in the personal problems, choices and decisions each must face as he moves toward maturity."[35] He emphasizes the opportunities that classroom teachers have for guidance and does not want them relegated to passive or minor roles in school guidance programs.

Hoyt believes that the counseling service will be successful only if its goals are integrated within the context of the educational objectives set forth by the school. For this reason he argues that counselors should exhibit a career commitment to education and that they should consider themselves educators rather than professionals who work with educators. Further, counselors should have teaching certificates because this (1) confirms their commitment to education and (2) wins them acceptance by teachers and administrators.

Hoyt proposed that school counselors engage in three main activities and he estimated the time to be devoted to each activity: "(1) relating directly with pupils—one half time; (2) relating with others contributing to the total complex of activities called guidance—one third time; and (3) assembling, studying and interpreting data required for successful accomplishment of Activities One and Two—one sixth time."[36] According to Hoyt, counselors could be distinguished from other pupil personnel specialists because counselors emphasize developmental objectives. Counselors differ from teachers and administrators by their concentration upon counseling and their knowledge of students and their opportunities. In an earlier paper, Hoyt had specified that counselors were more knowledgeable than any other school staff member on these topics: "(1) student appraisal procedures and dynamics involved in *understanding* student behavior; (2) educational and occupational information including both college and noncollege opportunities for youth; (3) counseling methods and procedures; (4) referral procedures and skills in recognizing the need for referral; (5) group procedures in guidance; and (6) methods and procedures in con-

[35] *Ibid.*, p. 692.
[36] *Ibid.*, p. 695.

ducting local research studies in the areas of student needs and opportunities."[37]

Hoyt proposed that the counselor function with other school professionals "both as a consultant and as a recipient of consultative services." That is, the counselor helps teachers by interpreting student data to them, by giving teachers environmental data to pass on to students and by serving as a referral source for teachers and as a liaison person with other referral sources. The counselor is to encourage teachers to work directly with students. In turn, he receives help from teachers in collecting student data and in following through with those individuals whom he has counseled. The counselor is to regard other pupil personnel specialists primarily as referral sources to help those whose needs demand their specialized kinds of service. The counselor is knowledgeable as well about the referral agencies that exist outside the school.

Finally, Hoyt argues that the counselor ". . . regards himself as a member of the principal's staff in the school in which he is employed."[38] The principal is his administrative superior and is regarded as the one person who is responsible for the direction of the guidance program. The counselor, on the other hand, determines the means by which desired objectives are to be achieved.

ADVANTAGES AND DISADVANTAGES

Unquestionably, Hoyt has described the model of guidance employed in most schools, not only in 1962 but in 1970. The advantages of this model are that (1) it recognizes that more than counseling is involved in the helping relationships maintained by school counselors, especially if the word "counseling" is defined in a narrow, highly technical sense; (2) it recognizes that the responsibility for the mental health of the school cannot be ascribed to a few individuals called counselors but necessarily remains the obligation of all who work in the school; (3) it is a model that is understood by teachers and administrators and one that appeals to them. The disadvantages of the model are that (1) the word "guidance" tends to be construed by the public in directive and prescriptive ways; (2) commitment to education is viewed as being achieved only through teaching; (3) assessment and evaluation of the program outcomes are extremely difficult, especially if Hoyt's view prevails that guidance is but a part of the pupil personnel complex and the goals of counseling are the same as (he states, "integrated with") school objectives; (4) consultation with other specialists, such as psychologists and psychometrists, only as referral sources for difficult cases seems to downgrade their competencies and undercuts their true contributions to the school; (5) counseling is de-emphasized, while special attention is given to supporting services (testing, informational

---

[37] Kenneth B. Hoyt, "What the School Has a Right to Expect of Its Counselor," *Personnel and Guidance Journal* Vol. 40 (October 1961) p. 130.

[38] Hoyt, "Guidance: A Constellation of Services," p. 698.

services, etc.); and (6) the concept of guidance as a constellation of services is atheoretical.

OUTCOMES AND IMPLICATIONS

Advocates of guidance as a constellation of services usually assert that it exists in schools to support the work of teachers. That is, guidance services are needed because students encounter learning difficulties due to emotional and environmental factors which must be remedied if students are to be successful in classroom (intellectual learning) situations. This view considers teachers to be the primary professionals in the school. As a supporting service, guidance is by definition auxiliary. It does not have any goals in its own right; rather, its objectives are tied to or bound up in achieving teaching-learning objectives.

Several authorities (see the next few pages) have observed that this model relegates counselors to the level of technicians who are subservient to teachers. Others question Hoyt's contention that the principal should necessarily be responsible for the direction of the guidance program— because they contend that principals should no longer be autonomous in their buildings. Rather, they feel that responsibility for guidance should be lodged with those whose expertise is guidance.

Developmental Guidance

HISTORICAL CONTEXT

The concept of guidance as a developmental process stresses help to all students in all areas of their vocational, educational, and personal-social experiences at all stages of their lives; this concept is a relatively new one. Certainly the attempt to put such a broad model into action is now only beginning to garner active support. Proponents of the developmental approach include Wilson Little and A. L. Chapman, whose work includes *Developmental Guidance in the Secondary School*;[39] Herman J. Peters and Gail Farwell, who authored *Guidance: A Developmental Approach*;[40] and Robert Mathewson, who delineated many of its principles in his volume, *Guidance Policy and Practice*.[41] Mathewson sees the adjustive and distributive approaches to guidance merging because counselors desire to achieve professional status and seek a clearly defined role. This merger entails a combination of therapeutic and casework approaches to adjustment problems with utilization of the trait-and-factor approach to match students and occupations. Mathewson recognizes that the developmental

[39] Wilson Little and A. L. Chapman, *Developmental Guidance in the Secondary School* (New York: McGraw-Hill Book Co., Inc., 1955).

[40] Herman J. Peters and Gail F. Farwell, *Guidance: A Developmental Approach,* 2nd ed. (Chicago: Rand McNally and Company, 1967).

[41] Robert H. Mathewson, *Guidance Policy and Practice* (New York: Harper & Row, Publishers, 1962).

approach identifies and stresses the centrality of choice-making in educational-vocational and personal areas. Developmental guidance has been defined as having as its prime concern the positive growth of all maturing boys and girls. This involves teamwork among classroom teachers, school counselors, and administrators.

RATIONALE

Mathewson cites four process areas that correspond to guidance needs: (1) the need for appraisal and self-understanding; (2) the need for adjustment to self as well as to environmental demands and realities; (3) the need for orientation toward present and future conditions; and (4) the need for development of personal potentialities.[42] Adjustive guidance is problem centered and deals with a specific issue at a point in time, usually with a "problem individual"; developmental guidance, on the other hand, attempts to "get inside" the pupil and focus attention on ego function and self-concept. Developmental guidance is cumulative or concerned with long-term growth, comprehensive rather than limited to either the vocational or educational area, and interpretive rather than deterministic.

Philosophically, developmental guidance is directed toward the achievement of personal adequacy and effectiveness through self-knowledge, the awareness of one's surroundings and a thorough mastery of the relationship between self and environment, and a thorough understanding of personal and social values. It is seen as a comprehensive process with its foundation in the school as well as the community and involving all school personnel, pupils, parents, and community resources. Individuality is accentuated and the individual's power to judge, act, and evaluate the links between self and situation becomes the basic credo of developmental guidance. Emphasis is given to the dynamic (changing) nature of the person and his potentiality for change. The way an individual defines his situation and relates it to his needs, interests, and values affects his personal performance. Through the process of guidance, the individual exercises his potentiality for growth and forms a more mature view of himself in relation to his opportunities. Guidance enhances the individual by (1) supplying him with information about the situation, about himself and/or the two in relationship; (2) helping the individual to think developmentally (over longer periods of time); and (3) mobilizing his capacities and dispositions. Organizationally, a developmental guidance program depends upon classroom teachers, counseling specialists, administrators, and other personnel workers. Each teacher, counselor, administrator, and specialist, is expected to function as a team member. Each is expected to have a thorough understanding of students. Developmental guidance is seen as continuous from the kindergarten through adult education, comprehensive in the sense that it encompasses every school activity, and definitive in that there is a specific set of activities and procedures which are employed. It is also coordinative in that

---

[42] *Ibid.*, pp. 16–17.

a team approach is utilized which centers upon the needs and problems of the individual student.

ADVANTAGES AND DISADVANTAGES

Developmental guidance as a concept enlists the active support of all school staff as well as community resources. It strives to help the individual attain his maximum development. There is particular emphasis on the point that the individual realize his development through time. The disadvantage of developmental guidance lies in the fact that not all teachers, administrators, and specialists are equipped by training or disposition to provide the kind of aid it specifies. Establishing and truly maintaining such an all-inclusive service are complex endeavors.

OUTCOMES AND IMPLICATIONS

As a model, developmental guidance provides a base on which the pupil can build with experience an understanding of self, environment, and the interrelationship of the two. Attention is centered upon what is happening inside the pupil to help him alter and control his own motivation and direction. The focus of the developmental process lies in assisting the individual to evaluate self and personal experiences through contact with the counselor. The counselor provides the helping relationship and this relationship enables the individual to review consciously his unique self-situational relationships under permissive conditions. It relies upon the development of ego function in the individual and upon long-term results, and it strives for self-direction as opposed to external solutions to given problems at single points in time.

The developmental approach to guidance is based upon the premises that all individuals need guidance throughout their lives, that guidance should be cumulative, and that it should be directed toward the individual's ability to see himself accurately so that he can develop his capacities to the fullest extent for his own benefit and that of society.

Guidance as the Science of Purposeful Action

HISTORICAL CONTEXT

Guidance as the science of purposeful action was proposed in 1962 by Tiedeman and Field.[43] They believe that the current practice of guidance reflects traditional desires to make teaching more effective without limiting the influence of teachers. Because of the nature of the educational system, the teacher is in a position superior to that of the counselor. Further, this relationship implies that the counselor is a technician and that his theory and practices are a kind of technology. They point out that current guidance practices take place *beside* rather than *within* education, and because

[43] David V. Tiedeman and Frank L. Field, "Guidance: The Science of Purposeful Action Applied Through Education," *Harvard Educational Review* Vol. 32 (Fall 1963), pp. 483–501.

of this, full and effective application of guidance is blocked. Tiedeman and Field cite two reasons for this situation:

1. It is impossible either to marshal or develop the resources—scholarship, basic research, rigorous training, and occupational opportunity—necessary to outgrow our status as technicians and/or trainers of technicians. Because we lack a valid professional identity, we are still neither expected nor invited *creatively* to develop the science of education. Rather, we are hired to *apply borrowed principles* from current behavioral sciences in order to assist teachers in pursuing their own "established" educational goals. In essence, we believe that our ancillary role has derived from the position of the teacher as the central figure, rather than a partner, in American education.
2. Those of us who do manage to achieve professional status (but usually as psychologists or sociologists, scientists or professors rather than as guidance personnel) are nevertheless employed to enhance the practice of teachers, to operate under the management of persons representing different occupations, i.e., teachers or psychotherapists, principals or deans, superintendents or presidents.[44]

Tiedeman and Field cite three recent efforts to make guidance a profession: (1) the views of professional organizations such as the American Personnel and Guidance Association and the American Psychological Association; (2) the influence of money and of law which includes the National Defense Education Act of 1958 and its subsequent extensions; and (3) the view of theorists such as Robert H. Mathewson, Donald Super, and C. Gilbert Wrenn. However, they believe these efforts have fallen short because guidance has not attained professional status and lacks any unifying theory that takes into account setting, purpose, and techniques.

RATIONALE

Tiedeman and Field define guidance as the professional use of a science of purposeful action within the specific structure of education. They emphasize that it should exist within an educational process which liberates; i.e., wherein the student is freed from overt conditioning or indoctrination, ignorance, and bias. In this process, students are viewed as being capable of choosing their own ends or goals with a minimum of external intervention. This approach may be contrasted to "conditioning education," wherein students achieve goals chosen for them in advance.

Tiedeman and Field define teaching as communication of others' experiences while guidance involves an examination of the individual student's experiences and the process of forming conclusions about them. Teaching continually creates discontinuities while guidance deals with the individualized reduction of discontinuities by (1) pointing out where discontinuities have come to exist, or may come to exist, (2) making them seem not undesirable or overwhelming but useful, and (3) making them a possible

[44] *Ibid.*, pp. 484–485.

base from which the individual can choose actions designed to reduce (or establish and then reduce) discontinuity.

The model that these authors propose for the maintenance of purpose in guidance involves the establishment of ends before or simultaneously with means. Although goals are by definition "desired future states," an idea of this "future state" can exist in the present. Students experience discontinuity which results from internal developmental aspirations contrasted with external situations. The task of guidance is to provide the student with information about new situations; criteria for evaluating them; knowledge regarding available sources of information; and help in establishing or modifying their purpose or awareness of internal and/or external changes.

The term "purposeful action" is used to describe (1) behavior to be encouraged on the part of individual student, (2) behavior that is practical for the individual guidance professional, and (3) behavior that is not random; i.e., action likely to achieve the currently desired by acting upon the currently observed. A crucial factor is the student's assumption of responsibility for his life. This responsibility is facilitated by his "catching on to the process of change." The focus in helping students to meet discontinuities is upon *purposing* through choosing *or* knowing how to choose or select. The practitioner of such a model would (1) serve to bring together student and information, pupil and teacher, client and counselor, patient and therapist; (2) hold a concept of the "ideal student making ideal progress through or within an ideal system," (3) possess the ability to see where the individual fell short of the ideal, and (4) possess the necessary knowledge to marshal the special skills and/or information most relevant to an individual's problems.

Advantages and Disadvantages

One disadvantage of this model as set forth by Tiedeman and Field is that no ready-made body of relevant basic theory exists which encompasses both behavioral change and independence on the part of the individual in the process of change. Second, few if any educational programs are available to prepare counselors to operate as required by this model. The advantages of the model lie in the facts that (1) guidance would be an operational part of education, (2) it would attain the status of a profession, and (3) it would be equal to teaching and administration.

In reviewing the model by Tiedeman and Field, Kehas has asked the following questions:

(a) Does guidance share with teaching in the development of individual purpose in the educational process? Or does this function of developing individual purpose differentiate guidance from other functions? The latter question touches on how teacher autonomy is to be preserved and on the interrelations of the roles of guidance and teaching. (b) The assumption that behavior is *normally* random—to be made purposeful, i.e., rational, through individual action—conflicts with the premise of most psychologies, if not of all social science, that behavior is normally guided by principles and there- fore is already purposeful. (c) Must responsibility for one's life be deliber- ately or consciously assumed, i.e., learned, by an individual? Or is individual responsibility a given, as in existential thought in present day guidance? What is the relationship among these differing premises?[45]

Outcomes and Implications

Tiedeman and Field's model would necessitate more than a single year of training for the master counselor. Their contention that today's counselor is a technician because he exists to make teaching more powerful may be questioned. Is this the only dimension or the major one on which to decide the issue? In actuality (in school settings) are school counselors viewed as inferior to teachers?

Guidance as Social Reconstruction

Historical Context

This model for guidance was proposed in 1962 by Edward J. Shoben, Jr.,[46] who believes that in spite of its great expansion, guidance shows little in the way of solid research to demonstrate its merits or accomplishments and that its basic techniques of counseling and testing evoke mistrust. Acknowledging that guidance aspires to professional status and presumably has its roots in the behavioral sciences, Shoben believes that its very am- bitions leave it vulnerable and that a considerable gap exists between its successes and pretensions.

Shoben believes that guidance is the unwitting smuggler of certain values. The teacher's function is to draw students into the traditions of society. The counselor's function is to furnish the information, the recommendations, and the impetus likely to move particular children into distinctive directions on the basis of their special characteristics and potentialities. Shoben asserts that guidance remains an effort to influence particular youngsters in par- ticular directions and that these directions are not given by scientific data or principles that may in other ways be relevant to the enterprise. In short, the guidance worker appeals to science (test data, psychological development, prediction in performance) to support the movement of children toward the values of the middle class which tend to reduce indi- viduality and autonomy. For example, by accepting as referrals those chil- dren perceived by teachers as disruptive or disorderly in a classroom group, the counselor accepts, to a degree, the definition of his job as fitting chil- dren to the prevailing behavior pattern of the school.

[45] Chris D. Kehas, "Theoretical Formulations and Related Research," *Review of Educational Research* Vol. 36, No. 2 (April 1966), p. 211.

[46] Edward J. Shoben, Jr., "Guidance: Remedial Function or Social Reconstruction?" *Harvard Educational Review* Vol. 32 (Fall 1962), pp. 430–443.

RATIONALE

At the present time many guidance workers tend to think of themselves as specialists in specific areas; e.g., testing, counseling, occupational information. However, the guidance movement was started to combat the less desirable effects of mass education, including specialization and impersonality. The major task of guidance is to emphasize individual growth and help students find socially appropriate ways for expressing their distinctiveness. Guidance should systematically encourage students to search for values and to live the "examined life."

Shoben's central point is that the process of self-exploration and the cultivation of the examined life are facilitated by intimate exposure to a variety of human models. He points out that some schools are more "potent institutions" in this respect because they provide more opportunity for the child to identify with several different persons and thus to develop more distinctive personal characteristics. The counselor's traditional roles (college advisor, test administrator, and vocational planner) are to be replaced by two major new ones: (1) a human feedback function by which the impact of the school is assessed and made available for the consideration of its official personnel, and (2) a catalyst for the clarification of the character of the school as a community and source of appropriate models for developing youngsters. The counselor is to assist each individual to re-evaluate constantly each segment of his life and reformulate his goals. Shoben believes that counselors can fulfill the feedback function because they have opportunities to hear from children themselves far more than do teachers or administrators. They can carry out the catalyst role in reconstructing the school culture because of their grounding in behavioral science and their orientation toward the individual pupil.

ADVANTAGES AND DISADVANTAGES

A disadvantage of such a model at the present time is that there is probably an insufficient number of counselors who have themselves achieved the degree of self-actualization needed to assist students to attain their autonomy. Massive reconstruction of the school and radically different training of its personnel would be a prerequisite. The values of the social reconstruction model lie in the fact that the ideal of guidance—to facilitate individuality—would move closer to becoming an actuality. The school would have greater cogency for individual students.

IMPLICATIONS AND OUTCOMES

Guidance as social reconstruction would require creative leadership of counselors in such areas as the grouping of pupils, diversification of teacher load, specifying contributions of the curriculum to encourage the "examined life," and the like. If this model were accepted and implemented, if counselors were in fact to become leaders in social reconstruction in schools, what would be the function of school administrators? Theoretically and traditionally, school administrators exercise leadership of the nature implied in Shoben's model. Are counselors to replace them?

Guidance as Personal Development

HISTORICAL CONTEXT

This model, proposed in the late 1960's by Chris D. Kehas[47] of the Claremont Graduate School, is viewed by its author as a first step in establishing a framework for counseling in education. Concern for the individual is given a prominent place when the goals of education are discussed, but Kehas believes that all too often school personnel translate this concern solely into how well the individual does intellectually. He observes that only when there is interference with intellectual development do personal and emotional components of human development receive attention in schools. Consequently, he believes that personal development has not been institutionalized as a function of the public schools. Further, Kehas believes that no facet or portion of present-day education is "primarily and systematically concerned with the personal development of the individual."

RATIONALE

Kehas states that professionals, other than teachers, are only reluctantly accepted in education. Moreover, other professionals—counselors, psychometrists, psychologists—do not participate in an integral way in the basic processes of education. This attitude of school personnel toward other professionals is illustrated when teachers ask other professionals "What can you bring us that will help us in our current work?" Other professionals have little to say about what the work of the school is to be; they are expected to accommodate their positions to the teacher's existing educational functions.

The basic premises characteristic of the assumptive structure in education, according to Kehas, include that (1) education *is* teaching; (2) the primary concern in education is with the *teaching-learning* situation; (3) the primary relationship is that of *teacher to student*. A fourth premise implicit in the three given is that there is only one type of educator, the teacher. Kehas believes that these premises highlight the centrality of the teacher and teaching. Learning is viewed as taking place only in teacher-student relationships. As a direct consequence of defining education as teaching, individuals who now serve as school counselors, social workers or psychologists can contribute only ancillary services of which the primary purpose is to make instructional functions more effective. Needless to say, Kehas contends that today's existing definition of guidance is restricted by this definition of education.

As a solution to the present dilemma, Kehas proposes that education be redefined as "involvement with learning." Separate functions and separate roles could be established along the dimensions of "involvement with

[47] Chris D. Kehas, "Education and Personal Development" in Bruce Shertzer and Shelley C. Stone (eds.), *Introduction to Guidance: Selected Readings* (Boston: Houghton Mifflin, 1970), pp. 59–71.

learning." Various types of "educators" could become involved with different aspects of development (or dimensions of learning) using different modes of relationships. Counselors would no longer be viewed as auxiliary personnel who exist only to support teachers, rather they would be seen as educators whose primary responsibility is that of personal development.

The nature of the teacher's "involvement with learning," according to Kehas, is fundamentally that of developing the intellect. The teacher's focus is upon bringing the student into a good academic relationship with the established knowledge of the teacher's academic discipline. His responsibilities are to help the student experience the ways in which knowledge is developed within a discipline. Further, the student learns "to experience what it means to 'think mathematically'; to come to know the consequences of so conceiving that portion of reality in those ways." Opportunity is available for the student to "make that knowledge and those ways of knowing personally relevant; i.e., relevant to him as an individual."[48] Kehas maintains that teachers intend students to incorporate established knowledge so that it will influence their behavior, but established knowledge (the continuity, sequential organization, configuration of the known) is external to the individual. Kehas reasons that teachers, consequently, are concerned ". . . with the personal meaning system of an individual *only as* and *because* it affects and is affected by its relationship to the configuration and structure of the knowledge which is his discipline and which he has been given responsibility to teach." Therefore teachers are not, cannot and should not be involved systematically with personal development.

The nature of "personal development" is defined by Kehas as

> . . . concerned with the continuing *development of intelligence about self,* with the development of self-knowledge through systematic, personal inquiry (as distinguished, perhaps, from scientific inquiry and social inquiry). It is concerned with methodical, ordered consideration of the *personal meaning systems* of individuals, of the idiosyncratic world of each person. It is concerned with that aspect of human experiencing which has been variously characterized as self-concept system, personal construct system, ego identity, self-evaluation, self attitudes. This concept of personal development assumes that it is desirable for individuals to have opportunity both to think about the kind of self they are building and have built and to confront themselves with the meanings they attribute to their experiencing and the consequences such attributions will have on their future self.[49]

The anticipated outcome, according to Kehas, is that the individual would develop and establish purpose and meaning for his life. He would thus be able to exert the control which he has over his own development.

Above all, Kehas has sought to convey that teaching and counseling are two ways of relating with students and that the two modes are complementary and collaborative. Further, both teaching and counseling are

---

[48] *Ibid.,* p. 62.

[49] *Ibid.,* p. 61.

equally important, indeed, necessary if the school is to meet its goals. But neither is sufficient unto itself. Redefining education, he points out, does not ensure the development of guidance as an integral part of the school. It merely creates an opportunity for guidance to develop in a way that is now not possible.

ADVANTAGES AND DISADVANTAGES

One advantage of the model presented by Kehas is that it represents an effort to make explicit that which is guidance. It defines guidance as being essentially concerned with personal development. As such, the role formulations of teachers and counselors can be more precisely described, defined, and articulated. At present, a shortcoming of the model proposed by Kehas is that little is known about the nature of the complementary relationship that ought to exist between teachers and counselors. The parameters of that complementarity and the processes by which collaboration takes place between individuals who are in the two positions are not understood, let alone developed. Another disadvantage is that it tends to divide the child into compartments with teachers responsible for intellectual development and counselors for personal development.

OUTCOMES AND IMPLICATIONS

Kehas has pointed out that the proposed model would undoubtedly influence present conceptions of the role of the teacher. Further, he believes that the requirement of teacher education and teaching experience for counselors should be removed. The counselor envisioned by Kehas would be grounded in the sciences of man since his work centers upon individual behavioral processes. Above all, he would be psychologically sophisticated and expert in helping individuals to create and develop intelligence about themselves. Much research would need to be pursued to understand better the processes of teaching and counseling, and of the relationship of teaching to counseling in education.

Summary

Naturally, one must eventually face the awkward question of what can be made of these "models" of guidance. It is highly doubtful that the reader who goes to the schools will find these models in operation. Instead, he will find that guidance as practiced in the school is atheoretical; that it has simply evolved haphazardly and is beyond characterization. Primarily, guidance practitioners believe that what they do is to provide a service to students. Consequently, practices do not follow theory. Rather, the search is for a rationale to justify a practice. Many authors have pointed out that this condition impedes systematic inquiry, which in turn retards the development of guidance.

Kehas presents a penetrating examination of theoretical formulations in the guidance field. He cites and discusses seven factors that have served as barriers to theory building. Six of the seven are summarized here: (1) theoretical considerations become somewhat irrelevant when guidance is viewed as a clinical service; (2) the professional organizations to which guidance practitioners belong have focused narrowly upon counseling rather than upon guidance; (3) conceptual distinctions between teaching and guidance are lacking; (4) guidance in today's schools is viewed structurally and conceptually as an aspect of either teaching or administration; (5) much guidance theory building has restricted itself to either career development or counseling theories; and (6) the belief prevails that those who produce theory are a different group from those who practice guidance.[50]

ORGANIZATIONAL PATTERNS OF GUIDANCE

General Organizational Structures

No matter which guidance model is accepted, it must find expression in the operational structure of the school. The formal organization of the school becomes manifest as the school performs its functions. There is assignment of responsibility and authority to achieve meaningful objectives. Four types of formal organizational structure are often described in the general literature on administration.

1. *Line and Staff.* Enterprises organized according to this concept are such that at any given level of authority, individuals and/or departments may be classified by function into line or staff. Line structure involves the division of an organization according to authority from top to bottom and vice versa while staff organization is division according to functions performed. Traditionally, only line personnel have given commands or orders while staff personnel have been concerned with service, quality control, coordination, fiscal control, and the like.

2. *Scalar.* Organizations that employ scalar or *hierarchical* structure grade the duties to be performed according to degrees of authority and responsibility. All individuals and/or positions are arranged in a hierarchy according to the degree of responsibility and authority they possess and use. For example, in an educational organizational chart, the board of education is placed at the top, indicating ultimate authority, followed by the superintendent of schools, indicating executive authority.

3. *Spatial.* This form of organization deals more with the "geography"— the degree of centralization of functions in a main office—of an organization. For example, many argue about the merits of centralizing control in federal governmental agencies compared to decentralizing func-

[50] Chris D. Kehas, "Theoretical Formulations and Related Research," *Review of Educational Research* Vol. 36, No. 2 (April 1966) pp. 214–216.

tions in the various state governmental agencies. The question revolves around the efficiency with which functions can be carried out. Usually the central office retains general supervisory and administrative responsibility, while special services are decentralized into branch offices. Keeping lines of communication open to achieve articulation among decentralized coordinates is a problem in this form of organization.

4. *Radial.* This type of structure is often called "spherical" or "circular." Here, the chief executive occupies the center position or hub, with all departments having equal authority and similar responsibility. Administrative fiat is to be avoided with dependence placed upon recommendations and departmental concensus. If conflicting views emerge, the central executive often makes the decision (reverting to vertical authority).

While none of these four types of organizational structure may be found intact in a given educational enterprise, elements of all may exist. It may be speculated that educational organizations, as public institutions, typically follow line and staff and scalar structures because of the necessity for legal and fiscal authority. Within such institutions, guidance services may best be organized on a radial basis, since professional judgment and competence usually must be balanced against legal and fiscal authority.

Many have commented upon the patchwork organization of guidance services and the chance-determined character of guidance in American schools. Lloyd-Jones has described general educational programs as being divided into three patterns: classical, neo-classical, and instrumental. Guidance has been similarly characterized. Proponents of the classical point of view generally have refused to recognize guidance as a professional endeavor, assigning guidance duties to the academic and administrative faculty; administrators of neo-classical institutions have generally accepted guidance services; and those administering instrumental institutions not only have accepted guidance but have stressed the creation of an environment for experimenting with and testing guidance patterns and functions.[51]

Glanz cites four approaches to guidance programing in the schools. These four approaches are summarized below:

1. *Centralized Specialism.* This approach utilizes professionally prepared counselors, test administrators, social workers and other highly qualified personnel in specific, defined, coordinated positions to help solve pupil problems.

2. *Decentralized Generalism.* This approach depends upon all personnel— teachers and administrators—to perform the guidance function within the roles historically assigned them. Specialists are usually avoided or are used only in a supporting role. "Every teacher a counselor" is the watchword and defense of those who employ this approach.

[51] Esther Lloyd-Jones, "Personnel Work and General Education," in *General Education,* Fifty-First Yearbook of the National Society for the Study of Education, Part I (Chicago: The Society (distributed by the University of Chicago Press), 1952), pp. 214–229.

3. *Curricular Counseling and Guidance.* This approach seeks to integrate guidance within curricular activities. The application of a group approach in orientation programs, curricular units, and occupational classes is meant to encourage in pupils an interest in self-study and educational and vocational planning.
4. *Human Relations and Group Work.* This approach focuses upon broad aspects of mental health including adjustment, mature thinking, and effective interpersonal skills.[52]

Mathewson states that guidance programs as organized in schools reflect differing strategies of practice which can be represented as patterns scaled according to seven bi-polar dimensions. These dimensions are summarized as follows:

1. *Educative—Directive.* At one end of the axis, guidance is conceived as a learning process in which the individual is educated to make his own choices. At the other end, guidance practices are conceived as diagnosis of individual problems by an expert followed by recommendations for the consideration of the individual and his mentors.
2. *Cumulative—Problem-Point.* Guidance is seen either as a continuous, cumulative process of a special educative type for all pupils or as assistance rendered only at problem points or decision points by a few pupils who need special help.
3. *Self-Evaluative—Mentor-Evaluative.* The dimension here consists of the following: (1) Personal precepts and constructs can be formed into an integrative self-identity with little or no outside help. (2) The individual needs extrinsic motivations and interpretations from others to achieve self-definition.
4. *Personal Value—Social Value.* The opposing points here are concern for the satisfaction of unique individual needs contrasted to concern for social or institutional needs, demands, or consequences.
5. *Subjective Focus—Objective Focus.* Attention on the subjective side is directed toward psychological states and events concerned with the self-defining and self-conceptualizing process. The objective focus is directed toward the evaluation and interpretation of objective data, i.e., tests, ratings, and the like.
6. *Multiphasic—Uniphasic.* In the multiphasic interpretation, guidance is programed as a comprehensive process in which all normal needs and problems may be handled by an adequately trained general practitioner. At the other extreme, concentration is given to only one phase, such as educational, vocational, or personal.
7. *Coordinative—Specialized.* At one pole of this dimension, guidance is dependent on cooperative endeavors, while at the other end it is performed by specialists with only supplementary help from teachers and others.[53]

[52] Abstracted from Edward C. Glanz, "Emerging Concepts and Patterns of Guidance in American Education," *Personnel and Guidance Journal* Vol. 40 (November 1961), pp. 259–265.

[53] Abstracted from Mathewson, *Guidance Policy and Practice*, pp. 97–117.

Any comparison of guidance programs from school to school reveals considerable communality as well as diversity of organization. Diversity exists because of historical antecedents in institutions as well as differences in the leadership and personalities of those charged with the responsibility for controlling the institution. Fundamentally those who seek to implement a program of guidance have three basic questions to which they must address themselves. These questions, raised by Shaw and Tuel, center on and include:

Timing. At what point is intervention to take place?
Scope. Is guidance for all students or is it for but a segment of the student body?
Focus. Is intervention to be direct (made directly with the individual student) or indirect (made with significant others, who, in turn, influence the individual)?[54]

Adaptation is characteristic of most schools' guidance organizations. Since no one type of administrative structure serves each and every type of school, perhaps the best that can be accomplished here is to enumerate the advantages and disadvantages of centralization and decentralization.

ADVANTAGES OF CENTRALIZED ORGANIZATION
(1) More economical and efficient administration of staff is possible. (2) There is greater opportunity to avoid duplication of efforts. (3) Usually better qualified and professionally prepared guidance staff members are employed. (4) Personnel who administer and staff the program are more likely to treat students from a guidance point of view rather than from an institutional point of view. (5) Referral resources are more likely to be identified and used.

DISADVANTAGES OF CENTRALIZED ORGANIZATION
(1) Specialists are often more expensive to employ and shortages often exist; thus it is more difficult to obtain a full staff. (2) There may be a tendency to de-emphasize the teacher's role in guidance with the result that teachers look to counselors to perform all guidance functions. (3) Particular problems of students may be emphasized, leading to compartmentalization of the student.

ADVANTAGES OF DECENTRALIZED GUIDANCE SERVICES
(1) Support is given to the guidance efforts and contributions of the classroom teacher. (2) There is concern for the total learning situation.

---

[54] Merville C. Shaw and John K. Tuel, "A Focus for Public School Guidance Programs: A Model and a Proposal," *Personnel and Guidance Journal* Vol. 44 (April 1966), pp. 824–830.

DISADVANTAGES OF DECENTRALIZED GUIDANCE SERVICES

(1) Too often, poorly trained personnel who lack adequate preparation in counseling, testing, and group work are utilized. (2) There is a de-emphasis of the guidance function because it is seen as "everyone's business" but no one's specific responsibility. Usually the teacher sees youth problems only in the context of classroom or academic experiences. (3) Teachers have to be all things to all people and often give only incidental and episodic attention to the more complicated problems of children.

Schools are increasingly centralizing their guidance services. The guidance organization is usually headed by a director who is responsible for communicating to the staff, central administration, and the public regarding (1) guidance definition and goals; (2) personnel needs; (3) needs for physical facilities and budget; (4) selection, assignment, and supervision of guidance personnel; (5) evaluation of the guidance program; and (6) the necessity and program for staff inservice education in guidance. Within the typical school guidance organization a counselor is assigned four to six hundred students for whom he is responsible for such things as (1) counseling, (2) group work, (3) program planning, and (4) test interpretation. Such individuals strive to occupy "staff roles" to serve as consultants to teachers, administrators, and parents in addition to performing their "counseling roles" with pupils.

Guidance practice in schools will continue to be determined by the educational philosophy that prevails in a particular place at a particular time. Farsighted guidance leaders favor developmental forms of guidance which stress the maximization of individual potentiality. It seems sufficient to end this chapter with the observation that guidance personnel suffer an embarrassment of riches in the realm of "how-to," but a vast confusion of voices in the realm of "know-why" or "what-for." Rational and responsible planning is essential if guidance personnel are to meet the increasingly complex problems of the future and broaden the opportunities for individual youth. Responsible progress in the conceptualization and design of guidance programs is certain to come about. It is clear that impatience with the lack of a unified theory of guidance is spreading daily among practitioners and students of the field.

ANNOTATED BIBLIOGRAPHY

BECK, CARLTON. *Philosophical Foundations of Guidance.* Englewood Cliffs, N.J.: Prentice Hall, Inc., 1963. Chapters 1–4.

Beck provides an overview of the changing presuppositions in the guidance function in Chapter 1. In Chapter 2, he reviews the literature dealing with the philosophy of guidance. Chapter 3 includes a discussion of the major presuppositions drawn from the guidance literature. Chapter 4 discusses the *daseinanalyse* point of view.

LANDY, EDWARD, AND KROLL, ARTHUR M. (eds.). *Guidance in American Education III: Needs and Influencing Forces,* Vol. 3. Cambridge, Mass.: Harvard University Press, 1966, 261 pp.

Section V, "Contemporary Observations of Guidance Practices" (pp. 173–223), and Section VI, "Policies and Practices in Pupil Personnel Services" (pp. 227–257), are helpful. Bud B. Khleif identifies some sociocultural assumptions and relates them to the work of school counselors and school administrators. Harold B. Pepinsky advances two theses about help-giving in America. Walter B. Waetjen describes policies and practices in pupil personnel services and Bruce Shear traces the historical development of pupil personnel services and identifies some of the current problem areas.

WILLIAMSON, E. G. "An Historical Perspective of the Vocational Guidance Movement," *Personnel and Guidance Journal* Vol. 42 (May 1964), pp. 854–859.

Williamson discusses Parsons' contributions to guidance as well as those of his precursors. He cites seven dimensions of the vocational guidance movement.

SELECTED REFERENCES

ALLPORT, GORDON W. "Psychological Models for Guidance." *Harvard Educational Review* Vol. 32 (Fall 1962), pp. 373–381.

AUBREY, ROGER F. "Misapplication of Therapy Models to School Counseling." *Personnel and Guidance Journal* Vol. 48 (December 1969), pp. 273–278.

BLOCHER, DONALD H. "Wanted: A Science of Human Effectiveness." *Personnel and Guidance Journal* Vol. 44 (March 1966), pp. 824–830.

BRAMMER, LAWRENCE M. "Eclecticism Revisited." *Personnel and Guidance Journal* Vol. 48 (November 1969), pp. 192–200.

COTTINGHAM, HAROLD. "National-Level Projection for Elementary School Guidance." *Personnel and Guidance Journal* Vol. 44 (January 1966), pp. 499–502.

DANSKIN, DAVID G., KENNEDY, C. E., JR., and FRIESEN, WALTER S. "Guidance: The Ecology of Students." *Personnel and Guidance Journal* Vol. 44 (October 1965), pp. 130–135.

DOUGLAS, NORMAN, and FLANDERS, JOHN N. "A Model Counseling Program in Appalachia?" *The School Counselor* Vol. 16 (May 1969) pp. 370–374.

DREYFUS, EDWARD A. "Counseling and Existentialism." *Journal of Counseling Psychology* Vol. 9 (Summer 1962), pp. 128–132.

GELATT, H. B. "Decision-Making: A Conceptual Frame of Reference for Counseling." *Journal of Counseling Psychology* Vol. 9 (Fall 1962), pp. 240–245.

GLANZ, EDWARD C. "Emerging Concepts and Patterns of Guidance in American Education." *Personnel and Guidance Journal* Vol. 40 (November 1961), pp. 259–265.

HIPPLE, JOHN. "Development of a Personal Philosophy and Theory of Counseling." *The School Counselor* Vol. 16 (November 1968), pp. 86–89.

HOYT, KENNETH B. "Guidance: A Constellation of Services." *Personnel and Guidance Journal* Vol. 40 (April 1962), pp. 690–697.

ISAKSEN, HENRY L. "Emerging Models of Secondary School Counseling as Viewed from the Context of Practice." *The School Counselor* Vol. 14 (May 1967), pp. 273–280.

KALDOR, DONALD R., and ZYTOWSKI, DONALD G. "A Maximizing Model of Occupational Decision-Making." *Personnel and Guidance Journal* Vol. 47 (April 1969), pp. 781–788.

KATZ, MARTIN. "A Model of Guidance for Career Decision-Making." *The Vocational Guidance Quarterly* Vol. 15 (September 1966), pp. 2–10.

KEHAS, CHRIS D. "Toward the Development of Theory in the Administration and Organization of Guidance Services." *Counselor Education and Supervision* Vol. 1 (Winter 1961) pp. 96–101.

————. "Guidance in Education: An Examination of the Interplay between Definition and Structure." In V. F. Calia and B. D. Wall (eds.), *Pupil Personnel Administration: New Perspectives and Foundations.* Springfield, Ill.: Charles C Thomas, Publisher, 1968.

KREMER, BRUCE J., and EMMET, THOMAS A. "Counseling and Guidance in Non-Public Schools." *Personnel and Guidance Journal* Vol. 45 (April 1967), pp. 781–784.

LISTER, JAMES L. "The Counselor's Personal Theory." *Counselor Education and Supervision* Vol. 3 (Summer 1964), pp. 207–213.

————. "The Eclectic Counselor: An Explorer." *The School Counselor* Vol. 14 (May 1967), pp. 287–293.

LOCKWOOD, OZELMA, SMITH, DAVID B. and TREZISE, ROBERT. "Four Worlds: An Approach to Occupational Guidance." *Personnel and Guidance Journal* Vol. 47 (January 1969), pp. 440–445.

MEYERSON, LEE, and MICHAEL, JACK. "A Behavioral Approach to Counseling and Guidance." *Harvard Educational Review* Vol. 32 (Fall 1962), pp. 382–402.

MOORE, GILBERT D., and GAIER, EUGENE L. "Social Forces and Counselor Role." *Counselor Education and Supervision* Vol. 2 (Fall 1963), pp. 29–36.

PATERSON, DONALD G. "The Genesis of Modern Guidance." In A. H. Brayfield (ed.), *Readings in Modern Methods of Counseling.* New York: Appleton-Century-Crofts, Inc., 1950, pp. 13–21.

PATTERSON, CECIL H. "The Counselor in the Elementary School." *Personnel and Guidance Journal* Vol. 47 (June 1969), pp. 979–986.

PENNEY, JAMES F. "Student Personnel: A Profession Stillborn." *Personnel and Guidance Journal* Vol. 47 (June 1969), pp. 958–962.

SHAW, MERVILLE C., and TUEL, JOHN K., "A Focus for Public School Guidance Programs: A Model and a Proposal." *Personnel and Guidance Journal* Vol. 44 (April 1966), pp. 824–830.

STILLER, ALFRED. "Social Pressures and the Guidance Function." *The School Counselor* Vol. 11 (May 1964), pp. 233–237.

STUBBINS, JOSEPH. "The Politics of Counseling." *Personnel and Guidance Journal* Vol. 48 (April 1970), pp. 611–618.

WILLIAMSON, EDWARD G. "An Historical Prospective of the Vocational Guidance Movement." *Personnel and Guidance Journal* Vol. 42 (May 1964), pp. 854–859.

WOOD, BENJAMIN D. "The Major Strategy of Guidance." *Educational Record* Vol. 15 (October 1934), pp. 419–444.

ZACCARIA, JOSEPH S. "Developmental Tasks: Implications for the Goals of Guidance." *Personnel and Guidance Journal* Vol. 44 (December 1965), pp. 372–375.

————. "Some Aspects of Developmental Guidance within an Existential Context." *Personnel and Guidance Journal* Vol. 47 (January 1969), pp. 440–445.

4

GUIDANCE IN SETTINGS OTHER THAN THE PUBLIC SECONDARY SCHOOL

What are the settings in which guidance is provided? What is the nature of guidance as practiced in these settings?

This chapter is concerned with guidance services provided in a variety of settings. The inclusion of a descriptive overview of these services in an introductory textbook is appropriate on several grounds. First, the types of helping relationships provided in many agencies embody activities and techniques highly similar to those employed in the public secondary school setting. Second, the preparation of personnel for employment in such settings differs more in emphasis than in kind from the preparation of high school counselors. Third, both during and after formal counselor education, individuals sometimes shift from one setting to another. Fourth, knowledge that these settings exist and of the nature of the service provided are essential to all professionals who engage in helping relationships, if for no other reason than for referral requirements. Perhaps the most significant reason for providing an overview of guidance services in these varied settings arises from the generally accepted conceptualization of guidance as a process that should be available in a variety of forms at a number of points during an individual's life span and for a variety of purposes. Undoubtedly, guidance-like services exist in settings not cited here; however, this chapter does cover the major services available in settings other than the public secondary school with the exceptions of post–high school technical schools and institutions of higher learning. Little literature is available about the first exception, while the second is treated extensively by texts devoted to student personnel work.

ELEMENTARY SCHOOLS

During the past decade, programs in elementary school guidance have emerged and experienced rapid growth. And some would say, "Rightfully so," for they believe that the elementary school is where guidance should have been established and nurtured. In any case, elementary school guidance is very much in evidence today.

Van Hoose and Kurtz surveyed state directors of guidance about the provisions for elementary school guidance in the 50 states and 4 territories. They reported that some 6,041 counselors were employed in elementary schools (K–6 grades) in 50 states (and two territories) and that approximately 70 percent of these counselors were employed full time. Over half (57 percent) of the counselors were supported by state and federal funds. Some 23 states had developed certification requirements for elementary school counselors that differed in some respect from those for secondary school counselors. Van Hoose and Kurtz suggested that, while a definite upsurge in elementary school guidance programs was taking place, much confusion remained. One example they cited was that the term "counselor" was applied to any specialist who worked in the elementary school, regardless of what he did. Another illustration of the confusion was the lack of a discernible direction of elementary school guidance programs.[1]

Two observations may be drawn, in part from the work of Van Hoose and Kurtz and in part from the authors' experience, about the current scene in elementary school guidance. First, many elementary school guidance programs have been supported, either fully or partially, by federal funds. If these funds were withdrawn, some programs would undoubtedly disappear or be greatly scaled down. Second, the definitive characteristics of elementary school guidance have yet to be revealed, either in practice or in expository works.

Nature of Service

Not many educators question the need for elementary school guidance. The pervasive hope is that early treatment and prevention of problems will result in pupil behavioral disorders that are less serious and shorter lived; and further, early treatment might facilitate the development of responsibility, decision-making skills, and personal development. Those few educators who do question the need for elementary school guidance often do so on the basis that teachers are close to pupils and that children in grades kindergarten through six do not have to make educational or vocational choices. Presumably, these critics' view of guidance emphasizes decision-making.

Many counselor educators and elementary school counselors are fond

[1] William Van Hoose and Sister Marie Kurtz, "Status of Guidance in the Elementary School," *Personnel and Guidance Journal* Vol. 48 (January 1970), pp. 381–384.

of saying that elementary school guidance is different from its secondary school counterpart. But, when pressed to describe the differences, usually their only response is that the elementary school counselor counsels more than the typical secondary school counselor. No one, of course, will deny that that is important. However, the distinguishing characteristics that differentiate elementary school guidance programs from those in the secondary schools have yet to be clearly set forth. It may be that time and experience are needed for elementary school guidance to create an identity of its own. Certainly, all who are interested and informed hope that those working in the elementary schools do not make the same mistakes that have been made in secondary school guidance.

For some unspecified reason (perhaps because of the closer teacher-pupil relationship) the counselor-student ratio in elementary schools has tended to be established at two to three times that of secondary schools. For many years the ratio of 600 or 1,000 elementary school pupils to one full-time counselor was reported in the professional literature.[2] During the past five years, this figure has been scaled down, and most authorities now assert that it should be one full-time counselor for 250–300 pupils.

Elementary school counselors, like their secondary school counterparts, engage in (1) counseling individuals and small groups (six to eight) of pupils; (2) consulting with teachers, parents and administrators; and (3) performing supporting guidance services such as testing, working with teachers on the use of vocational guidance materials with pupils, referring pupils who need special help, and conducting parent study groups. Most counselor educators involved in preparing elementary school counselors stress the counseling and consultant functions, but not necessarily in that order, and sometimes they stress one function to the exclusion of the other. It should be recognized that the nature of guidance services in many schools places at least equal emphasis upon services that support counseling, i.e., appraisal, informational services.

Considerable debate has taken place as to whether counseling or consulting is the pivotal function in the elementary school counselor's work. Patouillet was one of the first to advocate that the elementary school counselor function primarily as a consultant to teachers and the principal.[3] Smith and Eckerson reported that elementary school principals listed consultation with parents and teachers foremost among many counselor activities.[4]

Patterson is one of several who question the desirability of the elementary school counselor devoting full time to consultant activities. He believes that if the counselor becomes "nothing but a consultant," he becomes

[2] See, for example, *Review of Progress Under Title V-A, National Defense Education Act of 1958, As Amended* (Washington, D.C.: Office of Education, 1969), p. 35.

[3] Raymond Patouillet, "Organizing for Guidance in the Elementary School." *Teachers College Record* Vol. 58 (May 1957), p. 435.

[4] H. Smith and Louise Eckerson. *Guidance Services in Elementary Schools: A National Survey* (Washington, D.C.: U.S. Government Printing Office, 1963), pp. 1–22.

remote from and uninvolved with children—with the outcome that the counselor's observations become evaluative and his viewpoint external. Patterson charges that it is ". . . those who are not closely involved in schools or with children, including some counselor educators and U.S. Office of Education officials, who would de-emphasize counseling and replace it by consulting or coordinating functions."[5]

Elementary school guidance programs which were launched with the support of federal or state funds were most often located in a single school building (one housing kindergarten through grade 6). However, some programs were initiated with a full-time counselor serving more than one building in a school district.

Elementary School Counselors

The demand for elementary school counselors has exceeded the supply since 1964 when the National Defense Education Act was amended to permit state education departments to extend financial support to guidance programs in elementary schools. Amendments in 1968 authorized short-term training programs to prepare counselors for elementary schools.

The demand for elementary school counselors is unlikely to abate. In 1965–66, some 2,500 counselors were working in elementary schools; but given the elementary school enrollment, more than 88,000 would have been required to meet the recommended ratio of 1 : 300. Further, in 1969–70, about 90,000 counselors were needed to meet this recommended ratio.

NONPUBLIC SCHOOLS

Factual information about the extent and nature of guidance services in nonpublic schools is almost nonexistent, despite the fact that approximately one out of ten high school students is enrolled in this type of school. The largest number of children attending nonpublic schools are going to church-related or parochial schools. During 1965–66, Kremer and Emmet[6] examined the guidance services in the 103 secondary schools of the Catholic Archdiocese of Detroit. They received reports from 91 of the 103 schools. Their investigation concentrated upon secondary school guidance services since they could find only one elementary school in that archdiocese which had a formally organized guidance program staffed by qualified personnel. A school counselor was named as the person primarily responsible for student counseling in only 14 of the 91 schools. The counselor–pupil ratio in the 14 schools was one counselor for every 635 pupils. Those schools with larger enrollments tended to provide guidance services.

[5] C. H. Patterson, "The Counselor in the Elementary School," *Personnel and Guidance Journal* Vol. 47 (June 1969), pp. 979–986.

[6] Bruce J. Kremer and Thomas A. Emmet. "Counseling and Guidance in Non-Public Schools." *Personnel and Guidance Journal* Vol. 45 (April 1967), pp. 781–784.

Even fewer data are available about guidance services in secular private schools. Sporadic contacts with individuals in nonpublic schools and the scant literature available have permitted the authors to make the following observations about nonpublic school guidance services:

1. The nature of guidance services provided in nonpublic schools tends to be quite similar to that found in public schools. Presumably the religious and moral education stressed in parochial school instructional programs is also a part of the basic attitude behind the guidance efforts provided to students. Nonpublic schools tend to emphasize traditional academic programs. Consequently, long-established private secular schools are generally known for their college preparatory programs, although large numbers of private schools exist for specialized student populations and are more therapeutically than educationally oriented. Examples of these specialized programs exist in schools for emotionally disturbed children, for mentally retarded children, and the like.

2. Counselors employed in nonpublic schools frequently have less formal preparation than public school counselors. More counselors are employed on a part-time basis in non-public schools than in public schools. Often faculty members of such schools who have little or no counselor preparation are "designated" as counselors for one or two periods a day.

3. Guidance services tend to be more prevalent and extensive in so-called laboratory schools or private schools affiliated with colleges and universities. These types of schools tend to serve educational personnel in training, attempt to provide model educational services and therefore involve a full array of educational specialists. Emphasis in such guidance programs tends to be placed on educational guidance with services focusing upon counseling of the college-bound students who constitute the majority of their enrollment.

4. On the average, the counselor-pupil ratio appears to be higher in non-public schools than in public schools.

5. Larger nonpublic schools are more apt to provide formally organized guidance services than are smaller schools. This observation, of course, holds true for public schools as well as for nonpublic schools.

Many nonpublic school officials are concerned about the provision of school guidance services. They are actively involved in strengthening the guidance services offered to students and in encouraging their personnel to secure preparation as counselors.

U.S. EMPLOYMENT SERVICE

Public employment services designed to help individuals secure jobs have long been in existence. The federal government created placement services in 1907 with the formation of the United States Employment Service (USES) whose original purpose was to help immigrants find employment. During the depression, the Wagner-Peyser Act of 1933 established a national system of employment offices for "men, women and juniors." Large numbers of youth applied and since many had little idea about their capabilities, counselors were appointed in employment offices, particularly those located in the larger cities. However, the critical labor shortages which accompanied World War II brought a curtailment of the counseling services. Emphasis was placed upon the recruitment, utilization and allocation of manpower for the war effort. However, 1939 through 1946 were productive years, for during these years the Employment Service developed the use of job analysis, interviewing guides, the General Aptitude Test Battery, the *Dictionary of Occupational Titles* and other aids for their work. Currently some 2,000 local employment offices scattered across the United States seek out employment opportunities, place job applicants and select individuals for training and retraining programs.

Nature of Service

The nature of the service provided by the state offices of the U.S. Employment Service is shaped by the ultimate goal of placing individuals in jobs. The fundamental characteristics of the service are to be found in testing, training and retraining, counseling and placement. Therefore, essentially it stresses vocational guidance. Some of the major vocational guidance tasks which the Employment Service local offices undertake include:

1. *Collection of labor market information.* Needs, changes and trends in the local employment situation are assessed regularly. This information is collected and pooled at state and national levels and returned to the local offices to be made available to those who seek jobs.
2. *Screening, Evaluation and Classification.* Where appropriate, applicants are provided information about themselves through aptitude testing, interest inventories, trade, proficiency and other tests and inventories. Employment counselors use such data along with data collected through interviews to classify individuals occupationally so that appropriate employment referrals can be made and so that applicants can understand themselves and their vocational possibilities. Testing is used only when the counselor believes that it will facilitate this process. General Aptitude Test Battery data enable the individual's aptitudes in nine areas to be compared with those required in numerous occupations.
3. *Counseling.* Applicants without previous work experience or those who have difficulty in securing and holding employment are offered the service of counseling. So, too, are individuals who have career decision-making problems, or who need to acquire suitable work patterns and attitudes, or whose impoverished environment produces work-adjustment problems, or who need help in establishing vocational objectives and the means to achieve them.

4. *Placement.* Those individuals who wish to enter the labor market are registered, classified occupationally, and referred to prospective employers. Employers submit their needs for workers to the Employment Service office and applicants' qualifications are matched to the employers' specifications.
5. *Service to veterans and to handicapped applicants.* Each office provides special placement assistance to veterans who seek employment and to individuals who are handicapped.

The state employment service clients are (1) those who are entering the labor market with little or limited work experience, (2) those who need information about employment opportunities and their own qualifications, (3) those who want or need to shift to new occupations, (4) older persons who enter or re-enter the labor market, (5) applicants who are physically or mentally handicapped, and (6) those who experience vocational maladjustment or who have personal problems which limit their ability to work. An employment service counselor, in his initial interview, verifies the applicant's need for counseling. Counseling is extended if the individual is receptive, is about to enter the labor force and/or is uncertain about his vocational goals. Essentially, the employment service counselor helps a client define his employment problem, understand occupational life and opportunities, understand his own characteristics, determine the barriers in locating and holding a job, and formulate and carry out a vocational plan.

Gellman characterizes the employment counseling process as a patterned sequential approach based upon five phases: (1) identification and delimitation of the problem, (2) vocational appraisal and analysis, (3) assistance through counseling, information, or services, (4) decision-making, and (5) implementation of the vocational plan.[7]

The nature of the vocational guidance service provided by the state employment service in many ways parallels guidance in schools. There is an *informational* service which provides information about occupations and jobs on local, state and national levels as well as information about training opportunities. The testing and assessment conducted by the state service finds its counterpart in the school's *appraisal service,* and *counseling* is provided in both situations. Gellman, who has described vocational guidance services extended by certain nonschool agencies, concluded that state employment services generally (1) consider job placement their primary objective and relegate vocational counseling to a secondary role, (2) subordinate personal-social and long-range vocational problems to employment needs, (3) exhibit wide variation in the training and qualification of their counselors, and (4) tend in their counseling services to be problem centered, cross-sectional, short-term and technique oriented.[8] Many ob-

[7] William Gellman. "Government and Community Setting for Vocation Guidance." In Henry Borrow (ed.), *Man in a World at Work* (Boston: Houghton Mifflin Company, 1964), p. 515.

[8] *Ibid.,* p. 515.

servers believe that this description parallels a large number of present-day school guidance services.

Employment Service Counselors

The 1970–1971 edition of the *Occupational Outlook Handbook* estimates that some 4,400 full-time and 900 part-time counselors were employed in state employment service offices. In general, the minimal educational requirements for employment are that the counselor hold a bachelor's degree, preferably with a major area of concentration in one of the social sciences and that he have been credited with 15 semester hours in counseling or related course work. Many states have adopted a three-level counselor classification system. The first level is *employment counselor intern* or *trainee* (minimum qualifications are those stated above). The second level is employment *counselor* which requires 30 graduate hours in counseling and related courses, and the third level is *master counselor* which requires a master's degree and three years of experience, at least one of which is in employment counseling.

Salaries for the employment counselor trainee are approximately $600 to $750 a month, while those for the employment counselor are $630 to $785 a month. Highly experienced master counselors may earn up to $11,000 a year. Individuals who apply to become employment counselor trainees are given a written test which covers vocational guidance, interviewing, occupational testing, the psychology of occupations, community resources and the like. Candidates for employment counselor (second level) are also examined. The written portion (70 percent) of the examination covers techniques of registering, interviewing, placement, state industries, federal, state and local regulations of employment, vocational guidance, testing, supervision and the like. The remaining portion (30 percent) of the examination involves an evaluation of the applicant's previous experience and training.

State employment counselors have certain hardships to endure, though conditions are improving constantly. In some local employment offices counselors are sometimes taken away from counseling work at seasonal peaks of unemployment and are assigned to the relatively routinized tasks of handling unemployment compensation claims. Some local offices have been unable to provide counselors with offices which ensure auditory and visual privacy. In some offices, counselors are expected to conduct as many as 12 or 13 interviews during an eight-hour day, with the result that their work tends to be hurried and limited.

The outlook for state employment counselors is bright. Employment opportunities during the 1970's are expected to increase rapidly because of federal legislation that extends help to out-of-school youth, older persons, and disadvantaged individuals; and provides training and retraining opportunities to the unemployable. Most counselors work a 40-hour week and are eligible for various employee benefits, including retirement plans and vacations.

VOCATIONAL REHABILITATION

The Vocational Rehabilitation Administration, a federal agency within the Department of Health, Education and Welfare, provides leadership and coordination and sponsors research and demonstration projects. In addition it provides and administers matching funds for its affiliated divisional offices in the various states. Rehabilitation programs, initiated in 1918 for veterans and extended in 1920 to civilians, were characterized by modest growth until after World War II when the nation began to recognize its obligation to disabled veterans. A public rehabilitation program, financed cooperatively with federal and state funds, is available in every state. As of 1970, there were 90 of these agencies.

Nature of Service

The Vocational Rehabilitation Administration estimates that over two million persons in the U.S. need rehabilitation counseling. Rehabilitation has long been defined as the restoration of the handicapped to the fullest physical, mental, social, vocational and economic usefulness of which they are capable. DiMichael points out that

> Rehabilitation is a combination of philosophy, a body of knowledge contributed by many disciplines which work together, and the methods and techniques applicable to those who will have to learn to live with residual impairments as fully as modern knowledge and skills permit and to overcome the obstacles standing in the way of a full and productive life.[9]

Disabled individuals want and need to work. Vocational rehabilitation services exist to translate this need and will into the *ability* to work. Essentially, the vocational rehabilitation service consists of identifying the handicap; correcting or modifying the handicap through physical therapy, surgery, prosthetic limbs or training; and providing placement in an appropriate occupation. Individuals with disabilities resulting from birth, accident, disease or emotional causes are eligible for services. Typical disabilities include arm and leg deformities, amputations, heart and lung ailments, defects of hearing, speech, and vision, etc. In general, to be eligible for services from a state office of vocational rehabilitation one must (1) have a disability that substantially interferes with employment, (2) have a reasonable possibility of becoming suitably employed within a reasonable time period and (3) be within an employable age range.

The vocational rehabilitation services available may be outlined as follows:

1. *Medical examinations.* These are conducted for all who apply in order to determine the extent of disability, to discover hidden disabilities, and

---

[9] Salvatore G. DiMichael, "Vocational Rehabilitation: A Major Social Force." In Henry Borow (ed.), *Man in A World At Work* (Boston: Houghton Mifflin Company, 1964), p. 536.

to ascertain work capacity. Medical examination is essential to determine eligibility.

2. *Assessment and counseling.* Assessment includes a survey of education, mental ability, interests, recreational pursuits, work history, achievements, personality patterns, social adjustment, family relationships and the like. Applicants are extended personal and vocational counseling where necessary. Emphasis is given to the dynamic forces influencing vocational choice and adjustment and the psychological factors involved in implementation of training and/or vocational goals. Psychological testing for personality diagnosis is conducted to determine interests and aptitudes as well as to help the disabled person establish occupational objectives. Counseling is viewed as a means of modifying counselee attitudes and behavior so that he can progress toward vocational planning, choice, or adjustment in training or employment.

3. *Surgical, psychiatric and/or hospital treatment.* These services are provided where needed by the disabled. Public funds are used if the individual is unable to pay part or all of the costs.

4. *Education and/or training.* This includes education or training in schools, colleges, on the job, tutoring, or correspondence courses. Maintenance and transportation costs, fees, books, tuition and supplies may be supplied, depending upon the state plan.

5. *Artificial limbs, hearing aids and braces.* Various prosthetic devices are provided where appropriate.

6. *Tools, licenses and occupational equipment.* These are available when needed for the occupation.

7. *Placement and followup.* Individuals are placed and followed up to make sure they are in appropriate positions and that they are adjusting to the job demands.

The rehabilitation counselor is responsible for locating clientele, determining their eligibility, collecting data on them, working with them to develop vocational goals and helping them to establish a rehabilitation plan. While counseling is a major function of rehabilitation counselors, other functions are performed that complement counseling. Chief among these is the counselor's effort to reach out and influence prospective clients, the community and placement possibilities.

Gellman[10] describes the transition stages which have marked the development of vocational rehabilitation services and these are summarized here. First, Vocational Rehabilitation counseling services were similar to those of the Employment Service model but the traditional vocational guidance prototype was extended for the VRA by the inclusion of a provision for systematic rehabilitation of the disabled. Second, in 1951 when its caseload decreased, Vocational Rehabilitation began to place greater stress upon vocational counseling by emphasizing the dynamic forces influencing vocational choice and adjustment. Third, in 1961, personal-adjustment

[10] Gellman, "Government and Community Setting," pp. 520–522.

counseling was integrated with vocational counseling to help the client achieve resolution or amelioration of emotional difficulties. Present methodology includes counseling, interviewing, testing, individual appraisal, case analysis, observation of performance in training or schooling, environmental modification, and referral for medical, psychiatric or social casework services—for job placement or for workshop services.

Vocational Rehabilitation Counselors

The 1970–71 *Occupational Outlook Handbook* estimates that some 12,000 vocational rehabilitation counselors were employed in 1968 and that four-fifths were full-time counselors. Approximately 75 percent were employed in state and local agencies financed cooperatively with federal and state funds. Others were employed by hospitals, labor unions, sheltered workshops and other settings. Estimates are that approximately 3,000 new vocational rehabilitation counselors will be needed each year for the next 10 years. Graduate training programs produce about 400 counselors a year with about 60 percent of the graduates actually going into rehabilitation agencies.

Generally, vocational rehabilitation counselors are at least college or university graduates with course credits in counseling, psychology and related fields. Uniform requirements have yet to be established. Two years are usually required to complete the master's degree in rehabilitation counseling offered by some 60 universities through training grants provided by the Vocational Rehabilitation Administration. In 1968, beginning salaries for rehabilitation counselors ranged from $6000 to $8500 a year. Counselors usually work a 40-hour week. In approximately three-fourths of the state rehabilitation agencies, applicants are required to comply with state civil service and merit system rules.

Vigorous study has been given to the role of vocational rehabilitation counselors. For example, Berry, Keil and Robin note that patients in state psychiatric hospitals typically receive vocational counseling away from the therapeutic environment and in government employment offices or the hospital's placement services department. These three investigators sought to determine whether the vocational rehabilitation counselor would engage in more functions if he were integrated within the therapeutic milieu. The traditional functions of placement and vocational counseling were expanded to include the roles of consultant to the therapeutic team, subordinate of the team, and integrated member of the team. Typically, conflict existed between the counselor and his team members on account of different perceptions of the counselor role with psychotic patients. Counselors were found to be somewhat reluctant to assume new role behavior with psychotics.[11]

[11] K. L. Berry, E. C. Keil, and Stanley Robin, "Role Expectations of the Vocational Rehabilitation Counselor In a Therapeutic Milieu." *Journal of Counseling Psychology* Vol. 16 (May 1969), pp. 203–208.

Keil and Berry investigated the role expectancies held for the vocational rehabilitation counselor by treatment staff and administrators in a state mental health center for the emotionally ill. They reported that disagreement existed between treatment staff and counselors over counselor role expectations and that the condition of the patient was a significant mediating variable. Counselors wanted to enact more therapeutic and vocational counseling roles and be less of a subordinate member of the team and less required to serve in an employer contact role. The treatment team, on the other hand, expected the counselor to conduct more placement-related activities when dealing with the more disturbed patient.[12]

Jacques and Linkowski compared three national samples of rehabilitation counselors to examine the changes in prevalent characteristics during the period 1957–1965. Rehabilitation counseling provided an avenue for upward social mobility for approximately four-fifths of the employed counselors and for two-thirds of the rehabilitation counseling student sample. More women were being employed in the last sample, and approximately twenty-five percent of rehabilitation counselors reported that they possessed some type of personal disability.[13]

The shortage of vocational rehabilitation counselors has led to the employment of college graduates who do not have preparation in counseling. Designated as counselors, counselor aides or trainees, these individuals are usually given inservice training and close supervision. Patterson questions whether they are, in fact, counselors. Further, he believes that if college graduates are able to perform all functions assigned to counselors, then vocational rehabilitation counseling is not a profession but a trade. He suggests that vocational rehabilitation service centers need professionals who serve as *counselors* and other individuals who serve as *coordinators* or as case managers.[14]

VETERANS ADMINISTRATION

The magnitude of the Veterans Administration has led some to refer to it as a "quiet giant." It reaches into virtually every area where Americans live and work.

The counseling program of the Veterans Administration was established in 1943 in association with the vocational rehabilitation, education and training of veterans. Reviewing the history of veterans counseling, McCully commented that between 1943 and 1957 some two and one-half million

[12] E. C. Keil and K. L. Berry, "The Vocational Rehabilitation Counselor on Mental Patient Treatment Teams." *Personnel and Guidance Journal* Vol. 47 (February 1969), pp. 531–536.

[13] Marceline E. Jacques and Donald C. Linkowski, "Social Mobility Patterns and Other Characteristics of Rehabilitation Counselors." *Journal of Counseling Psychology* Vol. 15 (May 1968), pp. 245–249.

[14] C. H. Patterson, "Rehabilitation Counseling: A Profession or a Trade," *Personnel and Guidance Journal* Vol. 46 (February 1968) pp. 567–571.

veterans were given counseling to enable them to select educational and vocational objectives or to receive help with problems of personal adjustment.[15] Further, Gellman reports that some form of vocational guidance was given to approximately 11,000,000 veterans who undertook vocational training and that vocational counseling as a prelude to college or university preparation was given to some 3,500,000 veterans through 400 Veterans Administration guidance centers.[16]

Legal authorization for veterans counseling services derives from an assortment of federal laws designed to aid veterans, including Public Law 16, which provided vocational rehabilitation benefits for disabled World War II veterans; Public Law 346, popularly known as the "G.I. Bill" (Public Law 894 extended similar benefits to Korean War veterans); Public Law 634, The War Orphans Educational Assistance Act of 1956; and Public Law 89–358, The Veterans Readjustment Benefits Act of 1966 which provided various VA benefits and services to post-Korean conflict veterans.

The Veterans Administration employs counselors in two different departments: the Department of Veterans Benefits and the Department of Medicine and Surgery. The latter department maintains a psychological division which employs over 800 psychologists in the approximately 165 VA hospitals and 202 outpatient clinics scattered across the nation. Counselors employed are generally Ph.D.-trained experimental, clinical or counseling psychologists (approximately 125–150 are counseling psychologists) who work in medical settings. The Department of Veterans Benefits maintains 56 regional offices and contracts for 183 VA Guidance Centers. The latter are located mostly in universities and colleges.

Nature of Service

The VA psychologists in the Department of Medicine and Surgery serve as consultants in all segments of VA health care units. Fundamentally their emphasis is upon modification of maladaptive behavior patterns which interfere with rehabilitation, restoration or care of veteran patients. They are involved in therapy, rehabilitation, training and research roles. The 1968 *Annual Report*[17] cites their work in developing screening procedures for Vietnam veterans so that vocational counseling services can be provided quickly and so that hospitalization can be shorter and readmissions decreased. Currently much attention is being given by VA psychologists to behavior therapy methods which give promise to reduce treatment time of a wide spectrum of emotional and physical disorders. The VA psychologists have developed programs for deconditioning patients suffering from

[15] C. Harold McCully, "Developments of a Decade of VA Counseling." *Personnel and Guidance Journal* Vol. 36 (September 1957), pp. 21–27.

[16] Gellman, "Government and Community Setting," p. 520.

[17] Administrator of Veteran Affairs. *Annual Report* (Washington, D.C.: U.S. Government Printing Office, 1968), pp. 35–38.

alcoholism and heavy smoking as well as a special "reality orientation" training program for confused geriatric patients.

Counselors employed in the Department of Veterans Benefits provide vocational counseling and educational assistance to: (1) veterans and servicemen with service after January 31, 1955; (2) sons and daughters of deceased veterans or of permanently or totally disabled veterans; and (3) veterans with service-connected disabilities who wish to pursue a course of training to prepare for suitable occupations. Eligible veterans are entitled to one month of educational assistance allowance for each month of active duty after January 31, 1955, up to a maximum of 36 months.

Counseling is available for veterans who desire assistance in making vocational choices and in selecting a program of education or training. During the fiscal year, 1968, counseling was provided to 23,256 veterans in connection with their plans for education or training and to 28,900 disabled veterans. Special counseling programs have been developed for educationally disadvantaged veterans.

The 183 Guidance Centers provide counseling assistance to approximately 40,000 veterans. These centers, operated on a fee-basis contract with the VA, provide testing and counseling services without cost to the veteran.

The counseling model and procedures employed by Veterans Counseling were originally set forth in the *Manual of Advisement and Guidance* (April 1945). Essentially the concepts and practices were those of vocational guidance. Emphasis was placed upon the use of occupational information, individual analysis through interviews, review and study of school and work histories, psychological tests for evaluation, and the synthesis of data with vocational opportunities and vocational exploration.

In 1951, the model was modified and emphasis was placed upon combining personal counseling with vocational counseling. The necessity of taking into account counselee perceptions and motivation was stressed. Veterans counseling records were revised in such a way that fact-finding during the interview was reduced and the importance of counselee perceptions and attitudes was stressed. Additionally, an attempt was made to stimulate the counselor to formulate tentative hypotheses to be tested in the counseling relationship.

The Veterans Administration specifies in detail the duties of its counselors. Administrative control is maintained over the size of the caseload so that the quality of the work will remain high.

Veterans Counselors

Counselors employed by the Veterans Administration were originally called "Vocational Advisors." Later, the position of "Personal Counselor" was established. In 1952, the U.S. Civil Service approved the position "Counseling Psychologist." Educational requirements for the latter include a doctorate in psychology or counseling or two years of graduate work with a specified distribution of courses and work experience including therapeutic counseling. Counselors employed in the Department of Medicine and Surgery must have completed 60 graduate hours in counseling or psychology as a minimum (the doctorate is preferred but not always required of applicants). For positions in the VA Department of Veterans Benefits, qualified individuals are those whose background of experience and education enables them to use educational, vocational rehabilitation, or therapeutic counseling techniques to help clients select educational and vocational goals. For most positions at the federal level of GS-11, experience must have been in vocational counseling along with either personal adjustment or rehabilitation counseling, for most positions at the GS-12 grade level, experience has to be in all three areas.

Estimates are that some 750 to 1,000 counselors are employed by the Veterans Administration Services. More extended training brings higher salaries. Counselors with at least one year of qualifying counseling experience may be employed at the GS-9 through GS-12 levels (the latter pays approximately $11,000). The Veterans Administration is one of the few counseling agencies that does not have a shortage of counselors and has little difficulty in recruiting counselors.

PROGRAMS FOR THE DISADVANTAGED

Federal legislation enabling counseling services, along with other aids, to be established in a variety of settings has proliferated during the past few years. This legislation not only has heightened the demand for counselors but also has identified specific populations which may benefit from counseling services. Much recent legislation has been aimed at segments of the population commonly referred to as the culturally deprived or culturally unassimilated. Terms such as "chronically poor," "poverty stricken," "socially and culturally disadvantaged" have been employed to describe individuals handicapped by depressed social and/or economic conditions. Central to these programs has been the employment of counselors whose goals have been expressed by Gross, as follows: (1) to increase the accuracy of the individual's self percepts; (2) to increase the accuracy of the individual's environmental perceptions; (3) to integrate the individual's self percepts with environmental realities and perceptions; (4) to present relevant information; and (5) to improve the individual's ability to make plans and execute them.[18] Silverstein adds to this list a most important one: to refer individuals to a job or to a training program.[19]

The magnitude of these federally supported counseling services is exceedingly broad. Authority for many of the programs was given originally

[18] Edward Gross, "Counselors Under Fire: Youth Opportunity Centers." *Personnel and Guidance Journal* Vol. 47 (January 1969), pp. 405.

[19] Gerson Silverstein, "Authors Under Fire." *Personnel and Guidance Journal* Vol. 47 (June 1969), pp. 1029–1031.

to the Department of Labor but subsequent legislation and/or executive decree has shifted the programs to other federal departments and offices, mainly within the Department of Health, Education and Welfare.

Examples of programs utilizing counselors which were instigated by the federal government are those established under the authority of the Area Redevelopment Act of 1961 and the Manpower Development and Training Act of 1962 (to identify those to be trained and to help them enter training programs for which they are best suited) and the Economic Opportunity Act of 1964 (to provide job corps centers for disadvantaged high school dropouts).

Gross points out that justification for such programs has been based upon economic, humanitarian and educational grounds. The *economic* justification is that a jobless man put to work is a man no longer on the welfare rolls. The *humanitarian* justification is that help ought to be given to those who cannot help themselves. The *educational* justification lies in the belief that it is through education and training that men change and can join and participate fully in our society.[20]

The stress upon guidance services in such programs led Gross to question whether the faith in counselors was justified. He interviewed counselors, supervisors and community workers associated with Youth Opportunity Centers and his findings led him to conclude that many basic assumptions about the work of the counselor were untenable. The untenable assumptions included: (1) that clients come voluntarily; (2) that the client wants help; (3) that the client accepts the counselor's authority; (4) that the client is viewed as an individual rather than as a case or that the counselor accept the client. Gross believes that these assumptions were not operative because of (1) the bureaucratic conditions that exist in government programs, (2) client poverty and demoralization, and (3) the client's race. He suggested that highly directive counseling was perhaps more appropriate for the population and further, that a self-help group approach that builds upon the client's informal and quasi-public life structure would be even better.[21]

As the nation's priorities turn increasingly to that which most needs attention—the disadvantaged among us—the demand for counselors to serve in such programs will become more urgent. For many counselors, the work to be done with such groups will enable them to express, in a dramatic but not easy way, that to which all are committed: the advancement of the individual.

COMMUNITY AGENCIES

The general expansion of school guidance services has been paralleled by support for such services among state, county and municipal govern-

[20] Gross, "Counselors Under Fire," p. 404.

[21] Gross, "Counselors Under Fire," pp. 404–409.

ments and the voluntary and private sectors of our society. Community agencies that offer counseling and guidance services differ by types of services offered, by client population or problems treated, and by source of financial support. Many agencies are supported by taxes and are under the administration of governmental agencies while others are supported by community funds and various other combinations of financial resources (see Chapter 17).

Nature of Service

CLINICS FOR CHILD GUIDANCE AND MENTAL HEALTH

Many communities have established child guidance centers and community mental health clinics which offer assistance directly to children and their parents. Community mental health centers seek to make available several forms of care—individual and group therapy, day-care programs, halfway houses, emergency or "walk-in" services—for the disturbed individual to help him and the social system of which he is a member to function together as harmoniously as possible. Basic to comprehensive mental health programs is the belief that mental disorder is neither the private misery of the individual nor a personal problem solely of his making. Further, emotional disorder has its roots, as well as its effects, in the social relationships and settings of which the individual is a part.

Many, if not most, of the child cases coming to guidance clinics and mental health clinics reflect problem behavior in the school setting. Frequently the school has suggested to parents that they seek specialized help for their child outside the school. The major focus of these agencies is on mental health and on learning problems, particularly those bound up in emotional difficulties. The professional staff members, such as psychiatrists, psychologists, and psychiatric social workers employed in such settings are usually able to diagnose and treat emotional, learning, reading, and study difficulties. Clients who have problems involving educational and vocational choices and planning may also receive help at some of these centers or clinics.

SPECIAL CLINICS

Some communities have established separate clinics where problems such as alcoholism, drug abuse and addiction, epilepsy or the like, are treated in settings especially instituted for these disorders. Individuals who exhibit antisocial behavior and who are minors are often treated in juvenile houses or prisons. Others may request help or their parents or relatives may do so for them from child guidance and mental health clinics.

MARRIAGE AND/OR FAMILY COUNSELORS

Changes often attributed to a more equalitarian family life, to the shifting roles of fathers and to the rapidly evolving role of women have produced stresses and problems within modern family relationships and have led many individuals to seek help from marriage and family counselors. The range of problems treated by marriage and family counselors is wide and includes: getting married, staying married, getting divorced, sexual problems, concerns about appropriate masculine role (functioning as a husband, lover, father) or appropriate feminine role (functioning as a wife, lover, mother). In most marriage counseling cases, both the husband and wife are seen because to work with one marriage partner alone often merely serves to widen the breach in the relationship.

Attorneys, clergymen and physicians are particularly active in referring couples who need premarital or marital counseling. In some situations, the giving of factual information (for example in regard to sexual matters, family planning, budgeting, etc.) is all that may be needed. Other situations call for counseling or short-term psychotherapy which seeks to facilitate better understanding of self, the mate and the relationship. In providing assistance, the marriage counselor must attend not only to the psychological makeup of each partner but also to the sociopsychological factors involved. He concentrates upon the interaction that exists between husband and wife and the nature of the relationship they have established or seek to establish.

Many marriage counselors were trained as psychologists or social workers. Kimber[22] reports that as of 1964 the American Association of Marriage Counselors membership numbered 476. The AAMC adopted a code of ethics in 1962 and has a full-time paid executive secretary.

PASTORAL COUNSELING

The term "pastoral counseling" originally referred to the helping service established by the minister with some of his parishioners. Currently, many ministerial associations, church organizations, community associations of churches and individual churches have established counseling centers for their parishioners and others. Most of these centers accept as clients any community resident, but some restrict their services to church members or those who attend their particular church. Some centers employ trained counselors and ministers who serve part-time, while others are staffed entirely by ministers. Many such centers contract for psychiatric and psychological consultation.

The problems brought to pastoral counselors are legion and include for example: (1) marital problems, (2) parent-child problems, (3) disturbing love affairs, (4) adolescent conflicts, (5) emotional problems of young adults. When the pastoral counselor is unable to treat the situation, he still helps by making appropriate referrals to other available services or agencies.

---

[22] J. A. Morris Kimber, "Psychologists and Marriage Counselors in the United States." in Ben A. Ard, Jr., and Constance C. Ard (eds.), *Handbook of Marriage Counseling.* (Palo Alto: Science and Behavior Books, Inc., 1969), p. 19.

Community Agency Counselors

Little disagreement exists as to the minimum requirement for employment as a counselor in a private or community agency. Most agencies prefer, and many require, that counselors possess at least a master's degree in psychology, guidance, social work, or the like. Most such agencies have at least one or more staff members who have completed the doctor's degree in counseling or clinical psychology.

More and more community agencies are seeking approval of their services from the American Board on Counseling Services. Inservice training is being increasingly stressed since agencies are unable currently to recruit staff members at the level of preparation and experience they hope to attract. Intensive supervision is given, and attendance at professional meetings is encouraged strongly as is involvement in research activities.

Salaries vary widely ($5,000 to $20,000 a year) for those employed as counselors in clinics supported by governmental units and philanthropic organizations. Variance in salary is due to the size, location, and the source and amount of budget of the particular agency.

Currently, many community agencies have enlarged their services and improved their facilities because of the availability of certain federal and state funds. The use of these funds came at a highly appropriate time inasmuch as the competition for private and community funds has become increasingly competitive. It must also be kept in mind that progress in construction and staffing originally stimulated by the Community Mental Health Centers Act of 1963 (Public Law 88–164), while startling in some locations, has been slow and painful in some areas—and nonexistent in others. Curtailment of the amount of money available for construction and staffing in the late 1960's also negatively influenced the potential impact of the original legislation.

PRIVATE PRACTICE

The term "private" counseling practitioner refers to those individuals whose work is not supported by an institution. They are unsalaried and depend upon fees from their clients to support themselves and their offices. Harrower[23] points out that private practice differs in two essential respects from other forms of employment. The first is the way that financial returns are secured and the second is the way in which clients are secured. The ethical codes of professional organizations specify the conditions governing methods of obtaining and expanding the private practitioner's clientele.

While the exact number of counselors engaged in full-time private practice is unknown, it is believed to be very small. Some estimates are that

[23] Molly Harrower, "Psychologists in Independent Practice." In Welse B. Webb (ed.), *The Profession of Psychology* (New York: Holt, Rinehart and Winston, 1962), pp. 128–159.

the number does not exceed 500 in full-time practice. Many more are engaged in part-time private practice. Accurate data are difficult to come by since few surveys of such individuals have been made.

Yamamoto[24] reported in 1963 that less than five percent of 1,016 counseling psychologists who were members of APA Division 17 were engaged in private practice. In 1962, Peterson and Featherstone reported that only 2 of the 337 graduates of thirty APA-approved counseling psychology programs were engaged in full-time private practice.[25] Duncan[26] surveyed private-practice counselors in Florida by mailing a questionnaire to every marriage counselor, child guidance specialist and psychologist listed in the yellow pages of Florida telephone directories. The telephone directories did not list counselors separately, and clergy and psychiatry listings were excluded from his survey. Some 142 individuals were mailed a questionnaire and cover letter, and 87 usable returns were received from persons engaged in either full- or part-time private practice. About 60 percent of those who responded had a full-time private practice, and 32 percent were involved in agency work in addition to their own private practice. Nearly 57 percent called themselves clinical psychologists and 70 percent used the word "psychologist" in their titles. While 21 percent used the word "counseling" in their titles, only six persons specifically called themselves "counselors." About 4 percent were affiliated with the APGA, while 49 percent reported APA affiliations and 14 percent reported affiliation with the National Association of Social Workers. All but two held advanced degrees, with 74 percent holding doctorates.

Duncan noted that his investigation was based upon a small number and that only tentative conclusions could be drawn since one-third of the population did not reply. He concluded (1) that an identifiable profession of counselors engaged in private practice had yet to emerge, and (2) that most private practitioners identified with psychology even though their academic preparation may have come from a different area of study.

Nature of Service

Generally, counselors in private practice engage in diagnostic, counseling and research activities. While the magnitude of the activities engaged in tends to be small, variations do exist—determined by the individual's preparation and interest. The clients referred to private practitioners come from a variety of sources including schools, physicians, attorneys, social agency personnel, others engaged in private practice and so on.

[24] Kaoru Yamamoto, "Counseling Psychologists–Who Are They?" *Journal of Counseling Psychologists* Vol. 10 (Fall 1963), pp. 211–221.

[25] Ron Peterson and Fred Featherstone, "Occupations of Counseling Psychologists." *Journal of Counseling Psychology* Vol. 9 (Fall 1962), pp. 221–224.

[26] C. W. Duncan, "Counselors in Private Practice: A Survey Report." *Personnel and Guidance Journal* Vol. 47 (December 1968), pp. 337–340.

The APGA has established the American Board on Counseling Services to combat quackery and fraud among those who offer counseling and guidance services to the public. Unsavory as the thought may be, it is true that there are any number of "counselors," completely or relatively untrained, often unscrupulous, who "counsel" people for a fee. The Board's directory notes that some individuals employed in private practice offer counseling by mail, "blind" analysis based on tests alone, "memory" courses designed to improve or ensure personal adjustment or vocational success, etc. Further, quacks and frauds who prey upon the public, often offering "guarantees" to those who use their services, appear to be proliferating at an alarming rate.

The American Board on Counseling Services evaluates the standards and practices of individuals and agencies and determines whether they are qualified to provide counseling services. Individuals and agencies that seek this approval and meet the Board's standards are listed in the *Directory of Approved Counseling Agencies,* a biennial publication. The counseling functions evaluated include (1) counseling about educational progress, (2) counseling about occupations and careers, and (3) counseling about other personal concerns that do not require prolonged and intensive psychotherapy. The Board evaluates vocational guidance but not sheltered workshops (unless counseling were offered as a service in the workshop); placement services where counseling is given; and marriage counseling, "life-adjustment" counseling, rehabilitation counseling and "clinical" counseling (as long as the criteria of professional training, experience and practices are met by the agency or individual). Agencies or individuals who receive approval of the Board receive a certificate which gives the expiration date of the Board's approval.

Private Practice Counselors

Most counselors engaged in private practice are to be found in large cities or university towns. The length of their working day varies but many maintain early-morning office hours. Counselors in private practice have to work out procedures for accepting cases and must spend time in knowing the community in which they practice. The unpredictable work schedules, the unpredictable incomes, and the isolation from other counselors demand that those who engage in private practice possess considerable emotional maturity.

SUMMARY

Examination of the foregoing material leads to a number of observations about the similarities and differences found in the guidance services as provided in a variety of settings. Observations can be made only in the form of generalities because of the many contingencies operating within such a broad spectrum of settings. Any generalization pertaining to the several settings described may not hold true for a specific setting and certainly is not applicable to all in the same degree. To further complicate attempts at generalization, a given type of service may vary geographically as well as from office to office in a given region.

Points of Variation

1. In the case of most agencies considerable difference is to be found in the reasons for the existence of the service. The nationwide public services—for example, Veterans Administration, Vocational Rehabilitation, Employment Security—were instigated and fostered by the federal government to assist specific groups. Presumably, a social need existed which required their establishment and stimulated their expansion. Community agencies too, appear to have emerged from social need and enlightment to serve various segments of the population not otherwise served. Private practice, on the other hand, developed, at least in part from a general public acceptance of the value of counseling services and it provides a setting for those who want and can afford to pay for the help they need.
2. A source of variation highly related to the rationale for the service may be found in the clientele served. Some differences are visible in regard to type of client served, kinds of problems treated, age of clients, qualifications necessary for being a client (e.g., veteran, handicapped) as well as many other criteria. Frequently in government supported operations these factors are related to the mission of the agency and most often such restrictions are set by law and/or regulations.
3. The kind and quality of service may vary considerably from brief contacts leading to immediate employment placement to extensive assistance that is complex and has several specialties. Public agencies in particular tend to stress evaluation and short-term counseling that is followed by placement in suitable gainful employment. Ideally these same agencies, when appropriate, are able to, and will, make full use of all available techniques and special services (psychological, medical, etc.). Clearly contributing to the variety and quality of service are two other factors. First, partly because of the type of service offered and partly because of administrative necessity, the personnel employed within various settings differ to some degree in their training background. Second, while the foregoing condition is attributable in part to specific skills required for specific services peculiar to a given agency, it remains regrettably true that many entry-level employees may be inappropriately and inadequately prepared for their responsibilities.

Points of Similarity

1. No matter what the setting, the helping relationships extended to clients have much in common. In effect, the very provision of helping relation-

ships cuts across all settings. Certainly that which is done in all settings appears to rest upon similar, if not identical, philosophical bases.

2. As with the philosophical basis for providing assistance to individuals, the educational and training experiences of professional staff tend to overlap considerably. This is not to say that differences among sub-groups of specialists are unimportant or nonexistent. Rather, it is to stress that a large amount of commonality exists across both specialties and settings. The closer the individual in any setting comes to achiev-ing full preparation and competency, the more mutual background he shares with other persons in related settings.

3. Assessment and evaluation of the individual to be helped, coupled with the use of these data to assist the individual in decision-making tend to characterize all of the settings discussed above. Wide variation may exist in the emphasis placed upon assessment techniques but client as-sessment nevertheless exists as an essential component of the kind of assistance provided in these settings.

These observations about variations and similarities are incomplete at best. The knowledgeable reader or the novice who will in the future become more familiar with a variety of counseling settings could undoubtedly identify numerous others which may be of equal or greater importance. Particularly, differences loom larger when a specific setting is matched against another. As was mentioned at the outset of this section, the effort here was to present a few tentative generalizations that appear to apply across settings.

ANNOTATED BIBLIOGRAPHY

GELLMAN, WILLIAM. "Government and Community Settings for Vocational Guidance," in Henry Borow (ed.) *Man In A World at Work.* Boston: Houghton Mifflin Company, 1964, pp. 510–533.

The author provides an insightful commentary upon vocational guidance practices and programs in a variety of settings. The characteristics and the broad scope of the services in these settings are identified and compared.

MUTHARD, J. E., AND SALOMONE, P. R. "The Roles and Functions of the Re-habilitation Counselor," *Rehabilitation Counseling Bulletin* Vol. 13, No. 1–SP (October 1969), pp. 81–168.

The two authors report the research findings associated with 10 hypotheses formulated about rehabilitation counselors, roles, and functions. Among the major findings is that these counselors spend only about one-third of their time in counseling and guidance activities.

PETERSON, JAMES A. (ed.) *Marriage and Family Counseling: Perspective and Prospect.* New York: Association Press, 1968, 188 pp.

This volume commemorates the twenty-fifth anniversary of the American Association of Marriage Counselors and is composed of seven papers pre-pared originally for presentation at the Association's anniversary meeting.

The papers, written by experts in the field, treat the research practices and trends in marriage counseling.

SARASON, SEYMOUR; LEVINE, MURRAY; GOLDENBERG, I. IRA; CHERLIN, DENNIS L.; and BENNETT, EDWARD M. *Psychology in Community Settings.* New York: John Wiley and Sons, Inc., 1966, 714 pp.

The book reports the activities of the Psycho-Educational Clinic in Yale's Psychology Department. The authors' novel approach to schools and their treatment practices are well worth reading.

THOROMAN, E. C. *The Vocational Counseling of Adults and Young Adults.* Boston: Houghton Mifflin Company, 1968, 195 pp.

The author presents a philosophy, principles, techniques and tools for counseling adults. The concerns and problems of different types of clients—veterans, disabled individuals, women, senior citizens, junior college students—are treated. Attention is given to the future of adult counseling.

SELECTED REFERENCES

BERRY, K. L., KEIL, ELLSWORTH C., and ROBIN, STANLEY S. "Role Expectations of the Vocational Counselor in a Therapeutic Milieu." *Journal of Counseling Psychology* Vol. 16 (May 1969), pp. 203–208.

CHENAULT, JOANN. "Help Giving and Morality." *Personnel and Guidance Journal* Vol. 48 (October 1969), pp. 89–96.

DUNCAN, C. W. "Counselors in Private Practice: A Survey Report." *Personnel and Guidance Journal* Vol. 47 (December 1968), pp. 337–340.

GROSS, EDWARD. "Counselors Under Fire: Youth Opportunity Centers." *Personnel and Guidance Journal* Vol. 47 (January 1969), pp. 404–409.

HEILBRUN, A. B., JR., and JORDAN, BRIAN T. "Vocational Rehabilitation of the Socially Disadvantaged: Demographic and Intellectual Correlates of Outcome." *Personnel and Guidance Journal* Vol. 47 (November 1968), pp. 213–217.

HOFFNUNG, ROBERT J., and MILLS, ROBERT B. "Situational Group Counseling with Disadvantaged Youth." *Personnel and Guidance Journal* Vol. 48 (February 1970), pp. 458–464.

JAFFE, ARTHUR, and REED, ALICE. "Involving the Turned-On Generation Through Structured 'Rapping.'" *Personnel and Guidance Journal* Vol. 48 (December 1969), pp. 311–315.

JOHNSON, R. PAUL. "Job Corps: Information for School Counselors." *The School Counselor* Vol. 16 (March 1969), pp. 291–295.

KRANZLER, GERALD D. "The Elementary School Counselor as Consultant: An Evaluation." *Elementary School Guidance and Counseling* Vol. 3 (May 1969), pp. 285–288.

MOORE, LAMIRE H. "Elementary School Guidance: The Search for Identity." *Counselor Education and Supervision* Vol. 8 (Spring 1969), pp. 213–219.

NELSON, RICHARD C., and FREY, DAVID H. "Issues and Dialogue: The Elementary School Counselor and Testing." *Elementary School Guidance and Counseling* Vol. 4 (October 1969), pp. 59–63.

NISSMAN, BLOSSOM, and STAMM, MARTIN. "The Case for Elementary Guidance." *The School Counselor* Vol. 17 (January 1970), pp. 165–166.

PATTERSON, C. H. "The Counselor in the Elementary School." *Personnel and Guidance Journal* Vol. 47 (June 1969), pp. 979–986.

RUSSELL, R. D. "Black Perceptions of Guidance." *Personnel and Guidance Journal* Vol. 48 (May 1970), pp. 721–728.

VONTRESS, CLEMMONT E. "Cultural Barriers in the Counseling Relationship." *Personnel and Guidance Journal* Vol. 48 (September 1969), pp. 11–17.

5

THE SCHOOL COUNSELOR: NEED, PREPARATION, AND CERTIFICATION

How many school counselors are currently employed?
What is the current status of counselor supply and de-mand?
What is the nature of counselor preparation programs?
What is the nature of state certification requirements for school counselors?

SCHOOL COUNSELORS: NUMBER AND NEED

Employment of school counselors has accelerated rapidly since 1957, the year the Russians launched Sputnik I. It is to be hoped that the increase results from public insistence on an improved educational enterprise consistent with full development of human resources.

Expansion in Numbers

In 1954, Jones and Miller[1] published a survey of school guidance services and personnel. In thirty-nine states, three territories, and the District of Columbia they found that 23,000 schools employed a total of 7000 counselors who were assigned half-time or more to guidance responsibilities. In 1958, the number of full-time equivalent persons with the title, School Counselor, had risen to 12,000; and in 1970, to approximately 40,000. Table I shows the rapid expansion in numbers of personnel employed in guidance nationally and the corollary decrease in counselor-pupil ratio.

State by state, the number of persons employed as school counselors shows marked variability. Since limitations of space prevent a review of

[1] A. J. Jones and L. M. Miller, "The National Picture of Pupil Personnel and Guidance Services in 1953," *National Association of Secondary School Principals Bulletin* Vol. 38 (February 1954), pp. 105–156.

TABLE I
Number of Secondary School Guidance Personnel
Employed and Counselor–Pupil Ratio, 1958–1968

YEAR	TOTAL FULL-TIME EQUIVALENTS	COUNSELOR- PUPIL RATIO
1958–59	12,000	1–960
1959–60	18,739	1–640
1960–61	21,828	1–570
1961–62	24,492	1–550
1962–63	27,180	1–530
1963–64	29,206	1–525
1964–65	33,000	1–475
1965–66	34,500	1–460
1966–67	36,200	1–450
1967–68	38,000	1–440
1968–69	39,600	1–430

Based upon data from U.S. Department of Health, Education, and Welfare, Office of Education, *Commitment to Youth* (Washington: Government Printing Office, 1964) and other U.S. Office of Education reports.

each state, a few representative states have been selected as illustrative of the increase in the number of school counselors. In Ohio in 1956–57 according to Farwell and Vehick, 51 percent of the secondary schools did not employ a counselor.[2] But Peters and his associates[3] found that by 1960, based upon a 90 percent response from some 1,079 Ohio schools, 1,839 persons were assigned guidance duties in Ohio.

H. V. Davis[4] reported that in 1958–59 some 1,245 personnel workers were employed in Illinois. Pruett, Shertzer, and Stone[5] surveyed Indiana school guidance personnel during the 1961–62 school year and reported a total of 574 full-time and 1,088 part-time personnel workers. Doi, Hyman, and Young reported a 1961 survey of 342 assigned guidance personnel who served one-half time or more in Colorado public secondary schools.[6]

These and other studies of the quantity of school guidance personnel indicate that the absolute number of guidance personnel has increased and

[2] Gail F. Farwell and Anne M. Vehick, "Status and Certification of Counselors in Ohio Schools," *Personnel and Guidance Journal* Vol. 38 (December 1959), pp. 285–289.

[3] Herman J. Peters, *et al., Guidance in Ohio* (Columbus, Ohio: Division of Guidance, Ohio State Department of Education, 1961).

[4] H. V. Davis, "Who Are Public School Pupil Personnel Workers?" *Vocational Guidance Quarterly* Vol. 8 (Spring 1960), pp. 165–167.

[5] Rolla F. Pruett, Bruce Shertzer, and Shelley C. Stone, *A Survey of Indiana Guidance Programs and Personnel,* Bulletin 258 (Indianapolis: Indiana State Department of Public Instruction, 1964), pp. 8–9.

[6] Edith Doi, Bernard Hyman, and Earl Young, "A Survey of Colorado Counselors," *Counselor Education and Supervision* Vol. 2 (Fall 1962), pp. 14–16.

will continue to increase because of expansion in school enrollment at un-precedented rates. Dugan has identified other factors that account for the demand for school counselors:

1. National concern for the early identification and development of talent.
2. Increasing professional and public acceptance of guidance services as normal and expected functions of the schools.
3. Support of educational leaders and professional organizations for an adequate ratio of counselors to students (ranging from 1 to 250 to 1 to 500).
4. Marked increase in total school population, forecasting, in turn, the need for as many as 100,000 new teachers and 5,000 new counselors each year through 1970.
5. Federal subsidies for the development of state-wide testing programs, development of school counseling services and the preparation of a larger supply of secondary school counselors under Title V of the National Defense Education Act.
6. Recognition that much wastage of talent might be counteracted by guidance services through which teachers and counselors work more effectively together on such youth problems as: underachievement, uncorrected deficiencies, drop-outs, unrealistic objectives, lack of motivation, economic and cultural deprivation.[7]

Counselor Supply and Demand

Various estimates have been made of the supply as well as the need for additional school counselors. Irwin, writing in 1960, estimated a counselor shortage of twenty thousand.[8] In 1961, Dugan stated:

To keep pace with the enlarging school population and replacement requirements, at least 5,000 well-qualified, new counselors will be required each year through 1970. Currently, 475 colleges and universities have listed course offerings and/or programs of counselor preparation. Not more than one-fourth of these institutions represent clearly recognized, well established graduate programs of counselor preparation. Their productivity rate, based on a regional sample of degree candidates, suggest an average of twenty to twenty-two new master's level counselors per institution each year for an annual production of 2500 counselors eligible for certification.[9]

Table II presents an estimate by the U.S. Office of Education of the school counselors employed, state by state, in 1959 compared to 1967. Examination of these data reveals that the gains achieved have been dramatic in certain states or territories.

Figure 1 presents the portrayal of the U.S. Office of Education's Guidance Services Division of the present school-counselor-student ratio, the

[7] Willis E. Dugan, "Critical Concerns of Counselor Education," *Counselor Education and Supervision* Vol. 0 (Spring 1961), pp. 5–6.

[8] Theodore Irwin, "We Need 20,000 Guidance Counselors," *Coronet* (October 1960), p. 52.

[9] Dugan, "Critical Concerns," p. 7.

TABLE II
Number of Full-Time Equivalent Public Secondary-School Counselors, by State, Fiscal Year (FY) 1959 and FY 1967

State	FY 1959	FY 1967	State	FY 1959	FY 1967
Alabama	45	468	Nebraska	139	161
Alaska	18	48	Nevada	46	105
Arizona	—	273	New Hampshire	55	150
Arkansas	—	299	New Jersey	483	1,490
California	2,211	4,032	New Mexico	—	294
Colorado	149	518	New York	1,841	4,319
Connecticut	247	657	North Carolina	55	678
Delaware	30	120	North Dakota	39	74
District of Columbia	52	150	Ohio	715	1,846
Florida	294	1,203	Oklahoma	97	355
Georgia	322	648	Oregon	53	526
Hawaii	38	144	Pennsylvania	1,380	1,964
Idaho	31	180	Rhode Island	—	233
Illinois	—	1,760	South Carolina	127	520
Indiana	—	1,024	South Dakota	9	100
Iowa	242	576	Tennessee	23	521
Kansas	81	392	Texas	823	1,315
Kentucky	389	347	Utah	149	357
Louisiana	131	462	Vermont	50	82
Maine	58	165	Virginia	438	970
Maryland	361	809	Washington	538	900
Massachusetts	516	1,226	West Virginia	19	229
Michigan	—	2,095	Wisconsin	—	770
Minnesota	132	750	Wyoming	—	72
Mississippi	35	312	Guam	—	19
Missouri	385	786	Puerto Rico	106	256
Montana	39	153	Virgin Islands	—	12
Total, All States				12,991	37,915

Source: *Review of Progress*. Washington, D.C.: Office of Education, 1969, p. 114.

number of full-time equivalent counselors, and the need in 1963 for full-time counselors to achieve a counselor-student ratio of 1:300 by geographic regions used by regional accrediting associations. California, a regional accrediting association in and of itself, possesses the "best" counselor-pupil ratio comparatively and is less in need of full-time counselors. The geographic area composed of the Southern States Association has the highest counselor-pupil ratio (1:856) and the greatest need for more full-time counselors (8,659) to achieve a ratio of one full-time counselor for three hundred students. It should be noted that these data are based upon secondary school enrollments only.

Hilsinger, a former program specialist in the Counseling and Guidance Institutes, U.S. Office of Education, has written a provocative article on

FIGURE 1

Counselor Supply and Demand in the United States, Fiscal Year 1963, Grouped According to Regional Accrediting Associations

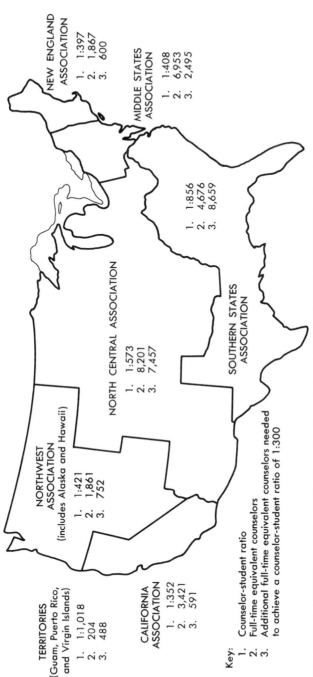

NEW ENGLAND ASSOCIATION
1. 1:397
2. 1,867
3. 600

MIDDLE STATES ASSOCIATION
1. 1:408
2. 6,953
3. 2,495

SOUTHERN STATES ASSOCIATION
1:856
4,676
8,659

NORTH CENTRAL ASSOCIATION
1. 1:573
2. 8,201
3. 7,457

NORTHWEST ASSOCIATION (includes Alaska and Hawaii)
1. 1:421
2. 1,861
3. 752

TERRITORIES (Guam, Puerto Rico, and Virgin Islands)
1. 1:1,018
2. 204
3. 488

CALIFORNIA ASSOCIATION
1. 1:352
2. 3,421
3. 591

Key:
1. Counselor-student ratio
2. Full-time equivalent counselors
3. Additional full-time equivalent counselors needed to achieve a counselor-student ratio of 1:300

NEW ENGLAND ASSOCIATION: Me., N. H., Mass., Vt., Conn., R. I.   MIDDLE ATLANTIC ASSOCIATION: N. J., Penn., N. Y., Md., Wash. D. C., Del. NORTH CENTRAL ASSOCIATION: N. D., S. D., Minn., Wis., Mich., Ind., Ill., Ohio, Iowa, Kans., Mo., Ark., Okla., N. M., Ariz., Colo., Wyo., Neb., W. Va. SOUTHERN STATES ASSOCIATION: Ala., Texas, La., Fla., Ga., Miss., N. C., S. C., Va., Ken., Tenn.   NORTHWEST ASSOCIATION; Alaska, Hawaii, Wash.,Mont., Nev., Oregon, Idaho, Utah.

counselor-student ratio.[10] The counselor-student ratio which is commonly defined as the number of students served by a single counselor, has been used to illustrate the relative proportion of counselors to students in a given situation and to estimate the number of counselors who may be needed. Hilsinger points out that various interpretations attributable to this simple ratio are extremely confusing. He cites five logical ways in which the number of counselors in a population may be tabulated:

1. The number of persons employed in some guidance capacity, part and full-time. This might represent the total number of persons providing guidance services.
2. The number of persons employed in at least a half-time guidance position. This may be used to count the number of persons whose primary responsibility is guidance.
3. The number of persons employed in full-time guidance positions. This might indicate the number of persons whose sole responsibility is guidance.
4. The number of full-time counselor equivalents. (This is a proportional addition of guidance time assignments: less than half-time, half-time, more than half but less than full-time, and full-time.) This might represent the average number of persons providing guidance services and is the most frequently used figure in assessing counselor-student ratios.
5. The number of adjusted full-time counselor equivalents, excluding those persons who are assigned less than half-time guidance positions. This is an average similar to (4) above, but includes only those persons whose primary responsibility is guidance.[11]

Hilsinger presents two tables (reproduced here as Table III and Table IV) which reflect the confusion that can arise when the computations are approached in these various ways. Close scrutiny of these data clearly indicate that a useful and frequently employed index can be easily reduced to a numbers game of counselor-student ratio and counselor supply.

Severity of Counselor Shortage and Suggestions for Its Reduction

The severe shortage of counselors has been increasing in intensity during the past five years. An estimated shortage of 19,800 secondary school counselors, 1,840 junior college counselors and 85,550 elementary school counselors existed during the 1965–66 school year. This estimate was based upon the total elementary, secondary, and college populations, using ratios of one full-time counselor per 750 college students, one to 300 secondary school students, and one to 600 elementary school students. Further, the U.S. Office of Education has stated that by 1969–1970, 153,220 coun-

---

[10] Roderick A. Hilsinger, "Variations on a Theme: The Counselor-Student Ratio," *Counselor Education and Supervision* Vol. 3 (Spring 1964), pp. 132–136.

[11] *Ibid.*, p. 133. Reprinted by permission.

TABLE III
Counselors and Secondary Students in the U.S. in 1962

a. THE NUMBER OF PUBLIC SECONDARY SCHOOL COUNSELORS MEETING STATE
QUALIFICATION STANDARDS IN THE FISCAL YEAR 1962[a]

Counselor Accounting Classification	*No. of Counselors*
1. The number of persons employed in some guidance capacity, part- and full-time	36,386
2. The number of persons employed in at least a one half-time guidance position	25,391
3. The number of persons employed in a full-time guidance position	15,675
4. The number of full-time equivalent counselors (a proportional addition of ¼, ½, ¾ and full-time counselors)	24,497
5. The number of adjusted full-time equivalent counselors (a proportional addition of ½, ¾ and full-time counselors)	21,687

b. THE NUMBER OF PUPILS ENROLLED IN FULL-TIME LOCAL, PUBLIC, "SECON-
DARY" DAY SCHOOLS IN THE FALL OF 1962

1. Total U.S. secondary school enrollment as defined and reported by states[b]	13,484,024
2. Total U.S. actual enrollment in grades 7 through 12[c]	16,127,429

[a] Data taken from the reports of state educational agencies for NDEA Title Va, courtesy of Drs. Frank Sievers and Frank Wellman, U.S. Office of Education.
[b] Carol Joy Hobson and Samuel Schloss, *Fall 1962 Statistics on Enrollment, Teachers, and Schoolhousing,* U.S. Department of Health, Education and Welfare, publication number OE–20007–62, Circular number 703 (Washington: Government Printing Office, 1963), pp. 14–15.
[c] *Ibid.,* pp. 16–17. The U.S. totals in the following columns were combined: "7th grade," "8th grade," "total 9–12, including post-graduate and secondary ungraded."
Source: Roderick A. Hilsinger, "Variations on a Theme: The Counselor-Student Ratio," *Counselor Education and Supervision,* Vol. 3 (Spring, 1964), Table 1, p. 134. Reprinted by permission.

selors were needed to meet the above ratios at a total cost of approximately $1,300 million.[12]

Many factors contribute to the shortage: expanding school enrollments, the extension of guidance programs to elementary schools and to junior colleges and higher education, the number of counselors trained each year by counselor education programs, the number of counselor educators available for staffing programs, attrition rates (roughly 5 percent annually) among counselors and counselor educators, entry of trained personnel into other nonschool counselor employment settings, the amount of government financial support for counselor preparation, and the like.

[12] *Notes and Working Papers Concerning the Administration of Programs Authorized Under Title V of The National Defense Education Act, as amended* (Washington, D.C.: U.S. Government Printing Office, October 1967), p. 10.

TABLE IV

Local, Public, Secondary, Day School Counselor–Student Ratios Based on U.S. Totals for Fiscal 1962 (Counselors) and Fall Enrollment 1962 (Students)

Description	Figures	Counselor–Student Ratio
1. Secondary school enrollment	13,484,024	
No. persons in guidance positions	36,386	1:371
2. Secondary school enrollment	13,484,024	
No. persons in at least ½ time		
guidance positions	25,391	1:531
3. Secondary school enrollment	13,484,024	
No. persons in full-time guidance		
positions	15,675	1:860
4. Secondary school enrollment	13,484,024	
Total No. full-time equivalent coun-		
selors	24,497	1:550
5. Secondary school enrollment	13,484,024	
No. adjusted full-time equivalent		
counselors, omitting persons in less		
than ½ time guidance positions	21,687	1:622
6. Enrollment in grades 7–12	16,127,429	
No. persons in guidance positions	36,386	1:443
7. Enrollment in grades 7–12	16,127,429	
No. persons in at least ½ time		
guidance positions	25,391	1:635
8. Enrollment in grades 7–12	16,127,429	
No. persons in full-time guidance		
positions	15,675	1:1029
9. Enrollment in grades 7–12	16,127,429	
Total no. full-time equivalent coun-		
selors	24,497	1:658
10. Enrollment in grades 7–12	16,127,429	
No. adjusted full-time equivalent		
counselors, omitting persons in less		
than ½ time guidance positions	21,687	1:744

Source: Roderick A. Hilsinger, "Variations on a Theme: The Counselor-Student Ratio," *Counselor Education and Supervision,* Vol. 3 (Spring, 1964), Table 2, p. 135. Reprinted by permission.

Suggested solutions for alleviating the shortage have been few in number. But one suggestion is that individuals other than teachers be permitted to enter counselor education programs. A second suggestion is that more paraprofessionals or support personnel be utilized. Another suggestion is that federal funds be devoted to increasing the number of institutions capable of offering counselor education programs of satisfactory professional quality. These suggestions undoubtedly would help, but are they sufficient? With respect to the last suggestion, two questions come quickly to mind: Should federal monies be used to develop counselor education programs or should they be used to secure more candidates to be placed in existing quality counselor education programs? How many quality counselor education programs are needed and how many can be maintained with the resources available?

An important factor to be borne in mind in estimating counselor shortages is that such estimates are based on attaining a ratio of counselors to students deemed desirable by the profession. Whether schools and communities, individually and collectively, see a need equal to the profession's statement and will make the efforts to attain that ratio is open to question. In short, estimates of shortages based upon actual demands (i.e., actual openings) for school counselors may differ markedly from the number desired or thought necessary by professional groups.

COUNSELOR PREPARATION

Selection for Program

Essential to an effective program of counselor education is a selection process that identifies for training those individuals with the greatest potential for effective counseling. Should it be assumed that the needs which motivate an individual to enter counselor training are related to: (1) the aspects of the profession which he will emphasize, and (2) the type of counseling relationship he establishes? Stone and Shertzer[13] illustrate how counselors with either a need for a structured work setting and a low tolerance for ambiguity or a need for status coupled with a high degree of deference to authority tend to emphasize the administrative rather than the counseling aspect of the profession. Studies in a therapy setting by Ashby, *et al.,*[14] Karmiol,[15] and Luborsky[16] provide data relevant to the relationship between counselors' personality characteristics and needs and their behavior in the counseling setting. Ashby, *et al.,* found that counselors who seemed to have a strong need for approval and acceptance cultivated their client's affection while tending to avoid discussing material which was up-

[13] Shelley C. Stone and Bruce Shertzer, "The Militant Counselor," *Personnel and Guidance Journal* Vol. 43 (December 1963), pp. 342–347.

[14] J. D. Ashby, D. H. Ford, B. G. Guerney, Jr., and Louise F. Guerney, "Effects of a Reflective and a Leading Type of Psychotherapy," *Psychological Monograph* Vol. 71, No. 24 (1957), pp. 1–32.

[15] E. Karmiol, "The Effect of the Therapist's Acceptance of Therapeutic Role on Client-Therapist Relationship in a Reflective and Leading Type of Psychotherapy," unpublished doctoral dissertation, Pennsylvania State University, University Park, Pa., 1961.

[16] L. Luborsky, "The Personalities of Successful and Less Successful Psychotherapists," *American Psychologist* Vol. 7 (July 1952), p. 337.

setting or potentially threatening to the client. Since it is reasonable to assume that an individual's needs not only attract him toward particular vocations but are related to the aspect of the vocation he emphasizes and the type of interpersonal relationships he cultivates, studies of counselor patterns of need satisfaction as related to counselor personality and to judgments of counselor effectiveness would seem to be a fruitful area for research relevant to counselor characteristics.

Satisfactory selection procedures require adequate selection criteria. Mathewson points out that the process of selection is limited by the instruments available.[17] Recent surveys of selection procedures (Santavicca,[18] Hill and Green,[19] Hill,[20] Patterson,[21] and Stripling and Lister[22]) indicate that the undergraduate record, personal recommendations, teaching experience, and standardized tests of academic aptitude, personality, attitudes, and values are currently employed to screen applicants for admission to counselor education programs.

Counselor educators agree that present procedures are inadequate. Particularly lacking in effectiveness are instruments to measure nonintellective variables. Brams[23] notes that available objective instruments for measuring personality are not adequate for test-sophisticated graduate students. It has been suggested that the devices presently employed will more likely screen out misfits than identify potentially effective counselors.[24] To improve selection procedures, counselor education staffs have been encouraged to develop their own assessment techniques.[25]

The selection process, whether in counselor education or other fields, depends heavily upon clear, unambiguous conceptions of the ultimate role

[17] Robert Hendry Mathewson, *Guidance Policy and Practice,* Third Edition (New York: Harper & Row, 1962), pp. 322–334, 361–375.

[18] G. Gene Santavicca, "Supervised Experience and Selection of Counselor Trainees," *Personnel and Guidance Journal* Vol. 38 (November 1959), pp. 195–197.

[19] George E. Hill and Donald A. Green, "The Selection, Preparation, and Professionalization of Guidance and Personnel Workers," *Review of Educational Research* Vol. 30 (April 1960), pp. 115–130.

[20] George E. Hill, "The Selection of School Counselors," *Personnel and Guidance Journal* Vol. 39 (Januray 1961), pp. 355–360.

[21] C. H. Patterson, "Selection of Rehabilitation Counseling Students," *Personnel and Guidance Journal* Vol. 41 (December 1962), pp. 318–324.

[22] Robert O. Stripling and James L. Lister, "Selection, Preparation, and Professionalization of Specialists," *Review of Educational Research* Vol. 33 (April 1963), pp. 171–178.

[23] Jerome M. Brams, "Counselor Characteristics and Effective Communication in Counseling," *Journal of Counseling Psychology* Vol. 8 (Spring 1961), pp. 25–30.

[24] American Personnel and Guidance Association, Committee Report on Professional Training, Licensing and Certification, "Counselor Preparation: Recommendation for Minimum Standards," *Personnel and Guidance Journal* Vol. 37 (October 1958), pp. 162–166.

[25] Stripling and Lister, "Selection, Preparation, and Professionalization," pp. 171–178.

of the individual in the eventual employment setting or settings. Lack of success in selection and retention of candidates is not due entirely to the relatively crude instruments employed. Rather, the less-than-ideal results obtained, and indeed the uneasiness often experienced by those responsible for selection and retention procedures, may stem from uncertainty about what final product should be turned out to meet the job demands found in various counseling work settings. The instrumentation and procedures employed for selection can only be efficient and accurate when they relate relatively precisely and specifically to the demands of the setting in which the individual's work is ultimately evaluated.

Recent years have witnessed increased efforts to assess counselor personality characteristics as they influence the counseling relationship. In some instances, special evaluative instruments have been devised for the particular study, with the preponderance of the instruments being Q-sorts, checklists, and rating scales. Layton[26] was concerned with counselor-client constructs, of themselves and of each other, as they related to communication in the counseling situation. Pohlman and Robinson[27] studied the counselee's image of the counselor and his reactions to counseling. Heilbrun[28] reported on interaction of client and counselor personality variables as they related to continuation or termination of counseling. Lesser,[29] using the Q-technique, an Empathic Understanding Scale, and a Felt Similarity Scale, found that correct awareness on the part of the counselor of similarity between himself and the client was positively related to counseling progress. Grigg and Goodstein,[30] using as subjects students who had attended the State University of Iowa Counseling Service, sent questionnaires to former counselees to judge their counselors' performance. Results suggested that clients of the type who see counselors as taking an active role in counseling are more likely to report favorable outcomes for counseling than are those who see counselors as passive listeners. Moreover, it was shown that counselees who feel comfortable in the counseling situation tended to regard their experience as having favorable results.

Thus, the last decade has witnessed a growing body of research concerned with the counseling relationship and nonintellective variables as-

[26] Wilbur L. Layton, "Constructs and Communication in Counseling: A Limited Theory," *Journal of Counseling Psychology* Vol. 8 (Spring 1961), pp. 3–17.

[27] Edward Pohlman and Francis P. Robinson, "Client Reaction to Some Aspects of the Counseling Situation," *Personnel and Guidance Journal* Vol. 38 (March 1960), pp. 546–551.

[28] Alfred B. Heilbrun, Jr., "Male and Female Personality Correlates of Early Termination in Counseling," *Journal of Counseling Psychology* Vol. 8 (Spring 1961), pp. 31–36.

[29] William M. Lesser, "The Relationship Between Counseling Progress and Empathic Understanding," *Journal of Counseling Psychology* Vol. 8 (Winter 1961), pp. 330–336.

[30] A. E. Grigg and L. D. Goodstein, "The Use of Clients as Judges of the Counselor's Performance," *Journal of Counseling Psychology* Vol. 4 (Spring 1957), pp. 31–36.

sociated with it. The studies mentioned here are simply representative of the directions research has taken and the techniques employed. Little research is available which attempts to relate outcomes to selection procedures. Rather, the emphasis has tended to be directed toward the counseling relationship *per se,* and to contribute to the selection process by providing *a posteriori* descriptive information only.

Selection for counselor training is viewed as a continuous process which may take place not only at the point of admission to a counselor education program but throughout the entire preparation period. Thus selection is a concept that has equal applicability to admission, didactic course enrollment, practicum enrollment, and job placement. In view of the need for improved selection criteria related to nonintellective variables, investigation is needed which studies the relationship between measured counselor personality and judged counseling effectiveness to ascertain whether certain personality characteristics are associated with criteria for counselor effectiveness.

School counselors are in short supply, despite the impetus for training provided by the release of U.S. Office of Education funds for counselor education. It was estimated that approximately five thousand new counselors were required annually during the 1960's, but Dugan also warned against emphasis on quantity alone as ". . . representing a threat to standards of excellence in recruitment and continuing selection standards for counselor candidates."[31] It seems desirable, therefore, that counselor education institutions realize maximum return from the use of their training resources without compromising standards of excellence. Maximum return, while maintaining excellence, demands that individuals selected for counselor education possess definite potential for the work of the school counselor. The initial selection of counselor candidates and the selective retention of the most able, then, become crucial to the success of any program of counselor education.

Evidence of potential for graduate work as measured by the commonly used standardized instruments of scholastic aptitude remains the first requirement for admission to graduate school. Valid measures of nonintellective variables find a second-place position when essentials for satisfactory counselor candidate selection procedures are considered. Recent research suggests that nonintellective variables are of critical significance in counseling effectiveness, and counselor educators agree concerning the inadequacy of available instruments to measure these characteristics.

Numerous research efforts have been directed toward the study of personality variables, the counseling relationship, and client satisfaction. Most of these investigations have been of limited value for selection purposes, however, since many were restricted in scope and concerned solely with factors internal to the counseling interview. Counseling effectiveness tends to be evaluated by observer-judges, supervisors, or peers, rather than by

[31] Dugan, "Critical Concerns," p. 7.

recipients of the counseling experience. Furthermore, interrelationships among these measures have been largely neglected. Investigation should be given over to studying the relationship between counselor personality characteristics and counseling effectiveness through subjective as well as objective measures that are both internal and external to the counseling relationship.

Program Content

Professional guidance organizations,[32] national[33] and state[34] offices, and the authors of various books[35] in the guidance field have emphasized that counselors should be trained in the following areas: counseling techniques; testing; the use of educational, occupational and personal-social information with individuals and groups; statistics; organization and administration of guidance programs; practicum and supervised field work; group processes; and related psychological and sociological subject matter.

Harmon and Arnold surveyed 150 members of the American School Counselors Association in the Northern, Western, and Eastern sections of the United States to ascertain their opinion of their counselor preparation. One of the most significant suggestions they received from those surveyed was that supervised counseling and group techniques should be required in the preparation of counselors. It was found that 53 percent of the respondents had no supervised practicum, and 42 percent had not taken group guidance in their preparation for a counseling job.[36] Santavicca queried college and university counselor educators as to whether they included supervised practice and/or internship for counselor candidates: 16 percent (21 of 129) of the schools reported having neither of these activities, but the remainder offered one or both.[37] Polmantier and Schmidt, in a report of the extent to which 54 state universities offered courses in

[32] For example, see the American Personnel and Guidance Association, *Standards for the Preparation of Secondary School Counselors—1967* (Washington: The Association, 1967) and the National Vocational Guidance Association, *Counselor Preparation* (Washington: The Association, 1949).

[33] For example, see "The National Defense Education Act," *School Life* Vol. 41 (January 1959), pp. 24–31.

[34] For example, see Indiana Department of Public Instruction, *The Education of Indiana Teachers* (Indianapolis: The Department, 1963).

[35] See Milton E. Hahn and Malcolm S. MacLean, *Counseling Psychology*, Second Edition (New York: McGraw-Hill Book Co., Inc., 1955); Merle Ohlsen, *Guidance Services in the Modern School* (New York: Harcourt, Brace & World, Inc., 1964); and Leona E. Tyler, *The Work of the Counselor*, Second Edition (New York: Appleton-Century-Crofts, Inc., 1961).

[36] Donald Harmon and D. L. Arnold, "High School Counselors Evaluate Their Formal Preparation," *Personnel and Guidance Journal* Vol. 39 (December 1960), pp. 303–316.

[37] Santavicca, "Supervised Experience and Selection," pp. 195–197.

guidance, found that the following seven areas were presented by more than half of the state universities: (1) basic course in guidance; (2) methods and techniques of counseling; (3) occupational and educational information; (4) supervised practicum and/or internship; (5) tests and measurements; (6) individual inventory; and (7) organization and administration of guidance.[38]

In 1960, the United States Office of Education convened a representative group of counselor-educators to discuss the content of counselor education programs. The report of the conference stressed that (1) counselor candidates should have a deep commitment and orientation to education; (2) traditional emphasis on techniques, materials and methods is insufficient; (3) counselor skills and competencies should be based on a foundation of theory and research in the social and behavioral sciences; (4) preparation for counseling requires a multidisciplinary approach; (5) the trend is toward an integration of theory and practice; (6) emphasis should be placed on the counselor as a person—his self-understanding, his values, and his attitudes; (7) part-time counselors require more than partial preparation; (8) candidates should complete supervised practicum experience; and (9) emphasis in counselor preparation should be placed on the responsibilities of the entire educational profession for counselor education.[39]

The number of colleges and universities offering training programs in guidance is increasing. According to a United States Office of Education publication, 206 institutions were providing such work in 1954; 444, in 1958; and 475 in 1960.[40] This increase in institutions offering counselor preparation has led to an increasing concern over the quality of training programs and has directly contributed to the development of counselor preparation standards.

A cooperative national study of counselor education was launched in April 1960 by the Association for Counselor Education and Supervision. A regional chairman for each of the five geographic areas of the country was appointed and many grassroots committees worked to develop criteria to serve as guidelines for colleges and universities in the organization, staffing, and curricular planning of counselor education programs. Several position papers were subsequently written and presented at the national conventions of the American Personnel and Guidance Association. In March 1964, at the APGA San Francisco convention, *Standards for Coun-*

[38] Paul C. Polmantier and Lyle D. Schmidt, "Areas of Preparation for School Guidance Workers," *Personnel and Guidance Journal* Vol. 39 (September 1960), pp. 45–46.

[39] National Association of Guidance Supervisors and Counselor Trainers, *Report of the Conference on Counselor Education* (Washington: American Personnel and Guidance Association, March 27, 1961).

[40] Office of Education, U.S. Department of Health, Education, and Welfare, *Preparation Programs and Course Offerings in School and College Personnel Work, 1959–60* (Washington: Government Printing Office, 1961).

selor Education in the Preparation of Secondary School Counselors were adopted on an experimental basis for a three-year period. The 1964 edition of the Standards was tried out by some 100 institutions. The Standards were revised in 1967, submitted to (by mail poll), and endorsed almost unanimously by members of the Association for Counselor Education and Supervision.[41] The program of studies specified that opportunities should exist to develop understanding and competencies in the following areas:

a. The foundations and dynamics of human behavior and of the individual in his culture.
b. The educational enterprise and processes of education.
c. Professional studies in school counseling and related guidance activities:
   (1) Philosophy and principles underlying guidance and other pupil personnel services.
   (2) The nature and range of human characteristics and methods of measuring them in individual appraisal.
   (3) Vocational development theory.
   (4) Educational and occupational information, its nature and uses.
   (5) Counseling theory and practice.
   (6) Statistics and research methodology, independent research and familiarization with data processing and programming techniques.
   (7) Group procedures in counseling and guidance.
   (8) Professional relationships and ethics in keeping with the APGA Ethical Standards.
   (9) Administration and coordination of guidance and pupil personnel services.
   (10) Supervised experience (laboratory, practicum, and internship)[42]

Preparation Programs for Elementary School Counselors

Hill and Nitzschke, in 1961, reported the results of a status survey of preparation programs in elementary school guidance. At that time they concluded that preparation programs for such personnel were not well defined, that little differentiation was being made between counselor preparation for elementary and secondary schools, and that few universities had clearly planned definitive programs for elementary guidance workers.[43]

In a followup of their survey, Nitzschke[44] sought to identify, among other things, the universities offering counselor preparation for elementary schools and the content and scope of such programs. Of the 527 institutions responding to his survey questionnaire (from a total of 575 questioned),

[41] "Standards for the Preparation of Secondary School Counselors—1967," *Personnel and Guidance Journal* Vol. 46 (September 1967), pp. 95–106.

[42] Ibid., pp. 99–100.

[43] George E. Hill and Dale Nitzschke, "Preparation Programs in Elementary School Guidance," *Personnel and Guidance Journal* Vol. 40 (October 1961), pp. 155–159.

[44] Dale Nitzschke, "Preparation Programs in Elementary School Guidance—A Status Study," *Personnel and Guidance Journal* Vol. 43 (April 1965), pp. 751–756.

only 45 indicated that they offered a preparation program for elementary school guidance personnel which they considered to be "significantly" different from that offered secondary school personnel. These 45 institutions were asked for more complete information on their program, and 36 responded. Nitzschke reported that "required" courses which were specific to elementary guidance personnel included (numbers following indicate number of institutions so reporting): Guidance in the Elementary School (21); Guidance and Counseling Practicum (16); Seminar in Child Development (13); Elementary School Counseling Techniques (10); Child Psychology (9); Supervised Counseling and Field Experience (9); Exceptional and Atypical Child (8); and Individual Testing and Analysis (7).

The major objectives of counselor education for elementary school personnel cited by the institutions included (1) to encourage counselors to discover creative and imaginative ways of identifying needs of children and to grow personally and professionally; (2) to prepare diagnosticians and counselors who can practice preventive guidance; (3) to prepare counselors to serve as consultants to parents and teachers; and (4) to prepare counselors who can coordinate services.

Merle M. Ohlsen, Chairman of the ACES committee charged with formulating standards for the preparation of elementary school counselors, reported that standards for these individuals could be readily adapted from the secondary school counselor education standards. The report by his committee stated that "Though elementary school counselors can be taught some of the core courses with other counselors, those counselors polled by the committee strongly recommend that certain courses in individual counseling techniques, group counseling and guidance techniques, and the practicum be taught in separate sections designed especially for elementary school counselors."[45] The program of studies cited the following topics as professional studies in elementary school counseling: "(1) Counseling theories and techniques, (2) Group procedures in guidance and counseling, (3) Professional identification, the profession, and its ethics, (4) Role Definition, program development and coordination of elementary school guidance services, (5) The consultation process (6) Individual appraisal, (7) Vocational development theory, including the use of appropriate materials for elementary school children, (8) Research skills to enable the elementary school counselor to understand the relevant research and to approve the outcomes of his services."[46]

Character of Counselor Training

The character of counselor education programs is rapidly undergoing change. Much diversity exists in content, techniques, and organization of

[45] Merle M. Ohlsen, "Standards for the Preparation of Elementary School Counselors," *Counselor Education and Supervision* Vol. 7 (Spring 1968), p. 174.

[46] *Ibid.,* pp. 45–46.

programs. Change has come principally because of the funds available for training counselors from the National Defense Education Act of 1958 and its later amendments and extensions. But even the NDEA training programs have been criticized. Patterson questioned whether NDEA Counseling Institute students should be taught separately from students in the regular existing counselor education program, citing the following reasons: (1) NDEA trainees do not consider themselves a part of the college or university as do other students and are often deprived of exposure to varying points of view; (2) institute instructors tend to be isolated from the rest of the staff; and (3) institute programs are detrimental to the development of permanent counselor education programs because universities will not increase regular permanent staff since temporary staffing of institutes decreases the need.[47] A most marked change in counselor education is the movement to lengthen the program from one year to a minimum of two years of graduate study. Chenault states that philosophical differences exist in counselor education in that counselor educators have humanistic views, while the preparation programs reflect mechanistic operations. She charges that

> Unentitled to examine his own conscience openly, denied the freedom to make his own aims, and perhaps misled by our tones of confidence and assurance, our product (the counselor) enters the professional world all smiling and happy, clutching his diploma with the certain knowledge that his goal is to become (as defined by his mentors) *more* accepting, *more* research oriented, etc. From the eager desire to be a good counselor, from the placid adoption of the stereotyped ideal, from the necessity of playing the role—emerges the phony counselor.[48]

Hunt identified five different types of attitudes among enrollees in an academic-year institute. He pointed out that these attitudes blended gradually from one phase to the next. But chronology of change among enrollees was described and is summarized as follows:

1. *Initial Period.* In this period trainees undergo threat, and present a facade of knowledge to cover inadequacies.
2. *Mechanical Period.* The influence of measurements, tests, and test interpretation causes counselors in training to perceive the counselee as an object for giving tests, posing questions, and relating test findings.
3. *Discovery Period.* Because of the impact of the different views and methods of their fellow trainees and instructors, the academic course work, and the opportunity to do a fuller type of counseling, the counselor in training arrives at a point where he begins to be confused as to what he is doing and what he is trying to accomplish.

[47] C. H. Patterson, "The NDEA and Counselor Education," *Counselor Education and Supervision* Vol. 3 (Fall 1963), pp. 4–7.

[48] Joann Chenault, "The Education of the Phony Counselor," *Phi Delta Kappan* Vol. 45 (June 1964), p. 452.

4. *Fuller Realization of Self.* This fourth period in the chronology of change is a period of self-reflection and exploration of philosophical outlook. Self-examination of prejudices, biases, fears, opinions, and incomplete thoughts is part of the period.
5. *Transcending the Former View of Self.* The new enlightenments from the fourth period are reflected in a broader concept of the role and utilization of self. The counselor has greater faith in his ability to overcome his shortcomings.[49]

Hilsinger[50] compared the selected characteristics of twenty-five counselor education programs whose proposals for NDEA Counselor and Guidance Institutes had been rated favorably by a panel of consultants to twenty-five institutions whose proposals had been rated by consultants as not possessing the capability to conduct institutes satisfactorily. The .20 level of significance was set because of the subjective nature of the rating procedure and the small number of proposals involved. Significance was found in thirty-five of the sixty-two tests conducted; thus the null hypothesis of no difference was rejected in 56 percent of the items. Differences were such that the faculty of the recommended group (1) completed their doctorates before 1960; (2) had been secondary school counselors; (3) maintained private counseling practice; and (4) devoted more than half of their time to teaching required counselor education courses.

The instructional programs of recommended institutions revealed a higher ratio of degree programs existing beyond the first graduate year, and courses taught by faculties whose primary commitment was to the education of counselors. In addition, a larger percentage initiated a supervised counseling practicum before the second half of the first graduate year and relegated field experiences to the second graduate year.

Of equal interest are those items which did not differentiate. Both groups reported similar ratios of full- to part-time students, faculty to graduates, faculty to departmental graduate assistants, faculty to departmental secretaries, day to evening and Saturday classes, and academic-year day classes to evening, Saturday and summer session classes. Similarly, it was not possible to discriminate between the groups on the basis of reported faculty teaching loads, the proportion of faculty with elementary or secondary school teaching experience, the proportion of faculty holding permanent appointments, and the uniformly light emphasis on group procedures as a separate course.

Hilsinger noted that twenty-six (or 74 percent) of the thirty-five items yielding significance were primarily reflections of differences in program size (institute proposals rated satisfactorily were larger).

[49] Clifford M. Hunt, "Developmental Phases of Counselor Growth," *Counselor Education and Supervision* Vol. 2 (Fall 1962), pp. 45–48.

[50] Roderick A. Hilsinger, "Selected Characteristics of Fifty Counselor Education Programs," Paper delivered at the American Personnel and Guidance Association Convention, April 1965.

Bixler has indicated that he believes that a forward-looking training program would place less faith in current academic and counseling fads, stressing instead methods of evaluation and the basic science of psychology. Six components of such a program include: (1) identification with education; (2) courses in psychology; (3) training in counseling; (4) research training; (5) milieu therapy or environmental manipulation; and (6) educational and occupational information.[51] Atkins and Poppendieck have addressed themselves to a rationale for preparation programs, identifying three significant concepts which, in their opinion, were permeating and directional for counselor preparation: (1) counseling is meant to improve the quality of living for the client; (2) the acceleration of culture change and the segregating effect of specialization make it imperative that the counselor have a broad orientation as well as technical competence; (3) the educative process is a complex of the stimulation, endowment, and release of the developmental energies of the student.[52]

Wrenn sees four major emphases in the professional education of the future counselor: psychological preparation which includes knowledge and skill in understanding and dealing with individual behavior dynamics and with groups; study of the immediate culture of the community, the larger culture of the nation, and the various cultures of the world; up-to-date understanding of school purpose, organization, curriculum, and instructional procedures; and minimal understanding of research procedures and cautions. Wrenn proposes a two-year graduate program that includes a major core in psychology and concentration in sociology, anthropology, economics, and international relations.[53]

The 1967 edition of the standards of the Association for Counselor Education and Supervision lists as general program characteristics the following seven points.

1. The institution provides a graduate program in counselor education, based primarily on the program of studies and supervised practice. . . . The institution provides a minimum of one year of graduate counselor education. In order to fulfill the requirements of the studies and supervised practice . . . , the institution provides at least one additional year of graduate study in counselor education either through its own staff and facilities or through cooperative working relationships with other institutions which do have at least a two-year program of counselor education.
2. There is evidence of quality instruction in all aspects of the counselor education program.
3. Planned sequences of educational experiences are provided.

---

[51] Ray H. Bixler, "The Changing World of the Counselor, II: Training for the Unknown," *Counselor Education and Supervision* Vol. 2 (Summer 1963), pp. 168–175.

[52] William H. Atkins and Robert Poppendieck, "A Rationale for Programs in the Preparation of Guidance Specialists," *Counselor Education and Supervision* Vol. 1 (Summer 1962), pp. 181–183.

[53] C. Gilbert Wrenn, *The Counselor in a Changing World* (Washington: American Personnel and Guidance Association, 1962), pp. 166–168.

4. Cooperation exists among staff members directly responsible for the professional education of counselors and representatives of departments or schools offering courses in related fields.
5. Within the framework of the total counselor education program, there are available curricular resources as well as procedures that make it possible for the counselor candidate to develop understandings and skills beyond the minimum requirements of the program.
6. The counselor education program encourages the spirit of inquiry and the production and use of research data.
7. Opportunities for self-evaluation and the further development of self-understanding are provided for the counselor candidate.[54]

In summary, the character of counselor education programs now emphasizes: (1) a minimum of two years of planned, sequential graduate preparation for counseling; (2) a larger core of work in the behavioral sciences, including psychology, sociology, and anthropology; (3) a block of supervised experiences, including on-campus practicum and an internship in a local school; and (4) opportunities for self-development and understanding.

STATE CERTIFICATION

Preparation programs for school counselors and state certification are, of course, highly related. State certification is seen as providing a floor of minimum standards for educating school counselors. State requirements necessarily follow professional standards and often lag some ten to fifteen years behind new training concepts and developments.

However, studying the counselor certification requirements in the states and territories that have such requirements gives some minimal level of expectation. In 1966, 53 out of 55 states and territories had certification requirements for school counselors. The state of Washington required only teacher certification and Michigan did not have any requirements. Fifty-one states required teacher certification eligibility. Forty-five states required from one to five years of teaching experience for permanent school counselor certification. Forty-eight states required a master's degree or a definite number of semester or quarter hours of graduate education (ranging from six to sixty hours) for permanent certification as a school counselor.[55]

Typically, state certification for school counselors requires from one to five years of experience as a teacher, a valid teaching certificate, a master's degree, and a varying number of hours in professional guidance courses. Many states are moving to a two- or three-step plan of certification for school counselors. Step 1, which is often a provisional certificate, may require the applicant to have from 6 to 12 hours of graduate credit in guidance; Step 2

[54] "Standards for the Preparation of Secondary School Counselors—1967," *Personnel and Guidance Journal* Vol. 46 (September 1967), pp. 98–99.

[55] Hubert W. Houghton, *Guidance Workers Certification Requirements* (Washington: Government Printing Office, 1967), pp. 142–144.

requires the applicant to have completed 12 to 24 hours; and Step 3 often requires 24 to 40 hours or more, or a specialist degree or certificate. In addition, varying years of counseling experience may be required.

Most colleges and universities with counselor education programs have certain requirements that candidates must meet before they will be recommended for state certification in guidance. These requirements are often more demanding than the certification requirements of the state departments of education. For example, many of the counselor education programs will not recommend candidates who have not taken the supervised practicum work, which too often is listed as an optional requirement by state standards.

Professional requirements at the state level have been and are in the process of being steadily raised. However, most of the required courses tend to be "technique" oriented—counseling techniques, individual analysis, organization and administration of guidance. One long-sought change that may be realized even more in the future is reciprocity among state departments of education in certifying school counselors. Dudley and Ruff reported that 5 states will grant certification to fully certified counselors from all other states and that 15 states will do so for those counselors with a master's degree in guidance from an accredited university.[56] Certainly, those counselors prepared in approved counselor education institutions in one state should not experience difficulty in being certified as school counselors in another state.

ANNOTATED BIBLIOGRAPHY

HILL, GEORGE E., AND MUNGER, PAUL F. (eds.). Up-Grading Guidance Practice. *Counselor Education and Supervision.* Vol. 7, No. 35P (Spring 1968) pp. 161–236.

    This special issue contains nine articles grouped into three major categories: The Standards Movement, The Accrediting Movement and Areas of Counselor Education Needing Attention. Emeliza Swain's article (pp. 164–171) is particularly useful in helping an individual gain an understanding of the problems, people, and the professional issues involved in improving counselor education.

PATTERSON, C. H. (ed). *The Counselor in the School.* New York: McGraw-Hill, Inc., 1967, 495 pp.

    Part IV, "Selection and Preparation" (pp. 163–219), is helpful in understanding some of the issues in counselor education. One article focuses upon selection of counselors, three articles deal with the matter of teaching as a prerequisite to counseling and the remaining three articles present policy statements on counselor preparation by the American Psychological Association and the American Personnel and Guidance Association.

---

[56] Gerald Dudley and Eldon E. Ruff, "School Counselor Certification: A Study of Current Requirements," *The School Counselor* Vol. 17 (March 1970), pp. 304–311.

STEWART, LAWRENCE H., AND WARNATH, CHARLES F. *The Counselor and Society: A Cultural Approach.* Boston: Houghton Mifflin Company, 1965. 400 pp.

Stewart and Warnath's first six chapters are especially appropriate because of their treatment of factors such as cultural impact, psychological dynamics, and school climate. The remaining chapters reflect a more traditional treatment of school guidance services.

SELECTED REFERENCES

CARKHUFF, ROBERT R. "A 'Non-Traditional' Assessment of Graduate Education in the Helping Professions." *Counselor Education and Supervision* Vol. 7 (Spring 1968), pp. 252–261.

———. "Critical Variables in Effective Counselor Training." *Journal of Counseling Psychology* Vol. 16 (May 1969), pp. 238–245.

CARROLL, MARY ANN, AND TYSON, JAMES C. "Is the Counselor–Teacher the Answer After All?" *The School Counselor* Vol. 8 (Summer 1969), pp. 303–307.

CHENAULT, JOANN. "A Proposed Model for a Humanistic Counselor Education Program." *Counselor Education and Supervision* Vol. 8 (Fall 1968), pp. 4–11.

DANIELSON, HARRY A. "Personality of Prospective Elementary School Counselors: Implications for Preparation?" *Counselor Education and Supervision* Vol. 8 (Winter 1969), pp. 99–103.

DELANEY, DANIEL J. "Simulation Techniques in Counselor Education: Proposal of a Unique Approach." *Counselor Education and Supervision* Vol. 8 (Spring 1969), pp. 183–188.

DOLE, ARTHUR A., NOTTINGHAM, JACK, AND WRIGHTSMAN, LAWRENCE S., JR. "Beliefs About Human Nature Held by Counseling, Clinical and Rehabilitation Students." *Journal of Counseling Psychology* Vol. 16 (May 1969), pp. 197–202.

DONNAN, HUGH H., AND HARLAN, GRADY. "Personality of Counselors and Administrators." *Personnel and Guidance Journal* Vol. 47 (November 1968), pp. 228–232.

DUDLEY, GERALD, AND RUFF, ELDON E. "School Counselor Certification: A Study of Current Requirements." *The School Counselor* Vol. 17 (March 1970) pp. 304–311.

GEOFFROY, KEVIN E. "The Verbal Behavior of Counseling Trainees in an Observational Setting." *Personnel and Guidance Journal* Vol. 47 (February 1969), pp. 552–556.

GRUBERG, RONALD. "A Significant Counselor Personality Characteristic: Tolerance of Ambiguity." *Counselor Education and Supervision* Vol. 8 (Winter 1969), pp. 119–124.

HANSEN, JAMES C., AND MOORE, GILBERT D. "The Full-time—Part-Time Debate: A Research Contribution." *Counselor Education and Supervision* Vol. 8 (Fall 1968), pp. 18–22.

HOYT, DONALD P., AND RHATIGAN, JAMES J. "Professional Preparation of Junior and Senior College Student Personnel Administrators," *Personnel and Guidance Journal* Vol. 4 (November 1968), pp. 263–270.

KAPLAN, BERNARD A. "The New Counselor and His Professional Problems." *Personnel and Guidance Journal* Vol. 43 (January 1964), pp. 473–478.

MCDANIELS, CARL. "The Impact of Federal Aid on Counselor Education." *Counselor Education and Supervision* Vol. 6 (Spring 1967), pp. 263–274.

NELSON, RICHARD C. "The Preparation of Elementary School Counselors: A Model." *Counselor Education and Supervision* Vol. 6 (Spring 1967), pp. 197–200.

RICHARDSON, H. D. "Preparation for Counseling as a Profession." *Counselor Education and Supervision* Vol. 7 (Winter 1968), pp. 124–131.

SCHROEDER, PEARL, AND DOWSE, EUNICE. "Selection, Function and Assessment of Residence Hall Counselors." *Personnel and Guidance Journal* Vol. 42 (October 1968), pp. 151–156.

SCOTT, C. WINFIELD. "The Introductory Guidance Course." *Counselor Education and Supervision* Vol. 7 (Winter 1968), pp. 83–101.

STRIPLING, ROBERT. "The Role of Professional Associations in Counselor Education." *Counselor Education and Supervision* Vol. 6 (Spring 1967), pp. 255–262.

WASHINGTON, K. S. "What Counselors Must Know About Black Power." *Personnel and Guidance Journal* Vol. 47 (November 1968), pp. 204–208.

6

THE SCHOOL COUNSELOR: CHARACTERISTICS, FUNCTIONS, AND CAREER PATTERNS

What are counselors like?
What characteristics distinguish the effective from the ineffective counselor?
What do school counselors do?
What career patterns do counselors tend to follow?

The characteristics that distinguish counselors have increasingly become the focus of much investigation. This search has intensified since study of counselor role and function was initiated in 1960 by the American Personnel and Guidance Association.

In 1949, the National Vocational Guidance Association issued a statement that counselors, ideally, were characterized by such personal characteristics as interest in people, patience, sensitivity to others' attitudes and reactions, and emotional stability and objectivity, and that they respected facts and were trusted by others.[1] In 1951, Mowrer wrote that personal maturity was the most important characteristic for counselors, but that there was no valid way to assess it.[2] Hamrin and Paulson reported a study in which ninety-one counselors listed traits which, in their opinion, facilitated counseling. In order of frequency these traits were (1) understanding, (2) sympathetic attitude; (3) friendliness; (4) sense of humor; (5) stability; (6) patience; (7) objectivity; (8) sincerity; (9) tact; (10) fairness; (11) tolerance; (12) neatness; (13) calmness; (14) broadminded-

---

[1] National Vocational Guidance Association, *Counselor Preparation* (Washington: The Association, 1949).

[2] O. H. Mowrer, "Training in Psychotherapy," *Journal of Consulting Psychology* Vol. 15 (August 1951), pp. 274–277.

ness; (15) kindliness; (16) pleasantness; (17) social intelligence; and (18) poise.[3] Another listing of traits deemed desirable in individuals in college personnel work has been provided by the Council of Student Personnel Associations in Higher Education. This group recommended as desirable attributes for personnel workers: abiding interest in students, faith in students' capabilities, understanding of students' aspirations, interest in educational process, good physical and emotional health, willingness to serve others, ability to function at irregular hours, respect for others, patience, sense of humor.[4] Another group, the Association for Counselor Education and Supervision has said that counselors should have six basic qualities: (1) belief in each individual; (2) commitment to individual human values; (3) alertness to the world; (4) open-mindedness; (5) understanding of self, and (6) professional commitment.[5] Such listings have been of doubtful value and have sometimes led to the facetious accusation that those who endorse them endorse a reincarnation phenomenon.

In a more serious vein, such lists of personal characteristics led Cottle, in 1953, to state that although listings were helpful, they were unsatisfactory because (1) they represent merely the opinions of the people who make them; (2) they fail to distinguish between the counselor and other school personnel; (3) the traits of successful counselors vary so widely that it is difficult to select one list as being satisfactory; and (4) it is the interrelation or pattern of characteristics that is important.[6]

As the number of traits reached unwieldy proportions and as such speculations continued to be unrevealing of any unique concept of the counselor, researchers turned to the investigation of personality patterns for a more acceptable solution. The literature relating to counselor characteristics appears to fall into two general categories: (1) identification of counselor characteristics, and (2) measurement of characteristics that might distinguish effective counselors from ineffective counselors.

IDENTIFICATION OF COUNSELOR CHARACTERISTICS[7]

One approach to the identification of counselor characteristics has been to look at scores on standardized personality instruments to differentiate

[3] S. A. Hamrin and B. P. Paulson, *Counseling Adolescence* (Chicago: Science Research Associates, Inc., 1950), p. 323.

[4] Commission on Professional Development, *Careers in College Student Personnel Work* (Council on Student Personnel Associations in Higher Education, undated), pp. 9–10.

[5] Association for Counselor Education and Supervision, "The Counselor: Professional Preparational Role," *Personnel and Guidance Journal* Vol. 42 (December 1964), pp. 536–541.

[6] William C. Cottle, "Personal Characteristics of Counselors: I," *Personnel and Guidance Journal* Vol. 31 (April 1953), pp. 445–450.

[7] The authors gratefully acknowledge the assistance of Dr. Dorothy Johnson in the preparation of this section and the following one.

between counselors and non-counselors. Cottle and Lewis found that, as a group, male college counselors scored significantly higher on the Restraint, Sociability, Emotional Stability, Objectivity, Friendliness, Personal Relations, and Masculinity scales of the Guilford-Zimmerman Temperament Survey (GZTS) than did a regular college sample.[8] In the same study, these researchers reported that counselors scored significantly lower on the Lie and Ma (Hypomania) scales of the Minnesota Multiphasic Personality Inventory (MMPI) and higher on the K and Si (Social Introversion) scales than did the undifferentiated college group.

Cottle, Lewis, and Penny extended this study.[9] Combining selected items from the GZTS, the MMPI, and the Counseling Psychologist scale from the Strong Vocational Interest Blank (SVIB), they concluded that male teachers were markedly different from male counselors and male counselor candidates, as measured by this experimental attitude scale.

Kemp demonstrated significant differences between the psychological needs of principals and counselors as measured by the Edwards Personal Preference Scale (EPPS).[10] Principals exhibited significantly greater need for Achievement, Endurance, Deference, Order, and Aggression, whereas counselors scored significantly higher on the Intraception, Exhibitionism, and Affiliation scales.

Chenault and Seegars found that principals wished counselors were more forceful, more dominating, and more advice-giving, and that they would play more of a decision-making, leadership role.[11] Filbeck's findings[12] suggest that counselors and principals are in general argeement as to counseling approach. Clear disagreement occurred, however, on factors relating to the dimension of control. Principals are responsible for the effective management of the school as an institution. In situations which threaten his success, the principal, in contrast to the counselor, favors a highly controlling approach designed to reduce disruption by students.

Sweeney's study led him to report that the principal viewed the counselor as a quasi-administrator and that he (the principal) preferred more ad-

[8] W. C. Cottle and W. W. Lewis, Jr., "Personality Characteristics of Counselors, II: Male Counselor Responses to MMPI and GZTS," *Journal of Counseling Psychology* Vol. 1 (February 1954), pp. 27–30.

[9] W. C. Cottle, W. W. Lewis, Jr., and M. M. Penny, "Personal Characteristics of Counselors, III: An Experimental Scale," *Journal of Counseling Psychology* Vol. 1 (Summer 1954), pp. 74–77.

[10] C. G. Kemp, "Counseling Responses and Need Structures of High School Principals and Counselors," *Journal of Counseling Psychology* Vol. 9 (Winter 1962), pp. 326–328.

[11] Joann Chenault and James E. Seegars, Jr., "The Interpersonal Diagnosis of Principals and Counselors," *Personnel and Guidance Journal* Vol. 41 (October 1962), pp. 118–122.

[12] Robert W. Filbeck, "Perceptions of Appropriateness of Counselor Behavior: A Comparison of Counselors and Principals," *Personnel and Guidance Journal* Vol. 43 (May 1965), pp. 891–896.

ministrative-type leadership from counselors.[13] Knock and Cody, in a study of counselor candidates, practicing teachers and administrators, reported that individuals who were preparing for school counseling were more student centered than were practicing school teachers or administrators.[14]

Ordinarily, descriptions of counselors include expressions such as friendliness, understanding, respect for and belief in the worth of the individual, attitudes of acceptance, permissiveness, empathy, sense of humor, common sense, objectivity, freedom from prejudice. Measurement of many of these qualities is made difficult at the outset by semantic obstacles (Arbuckle[15]) and vagueness of concepts (Gage and Cronbach[16]). Nevertheless, Fiedler's now classic studies (Fiedler, 1950a,[17] 1950b,[18] and 1953[19]) suggest that the therapist himself, and not his adherence to a given school of counseling theory, is the key to the therapeutic relationship. Fiedler's work provided new impetus for investigations into the personal qualities of the counselor and the nature of the counseling relationship.

Grater, Kell, and Morse saw nurturance as the fundamental characteristic in counseling, and they contended that counselors choose counseling because they possess the need to nurture.[20] In their work, however, counselors develop patterns of relationships that tend to produce a certain amount of isolation, emotional distance, and loneliness. Thus both nurturance and emotional distance are considered to be counselor qualities. Fiedler concluded that one of the factors differentiating the expert therapist from the nonexpert was the former's ability to maintain appropriate emotional distance in the therapeutic relationship.[21]

[13] Thomas J. Sweeney, "The School Counselor as Perceived by School Counselors and Their Principals," *Personnel and Guidance Journal* Vol. 44 (April 1966), pp. 844–849.

[14] Gary H. Knock and John J. Cody, "Student-Centeredness: A Comparison of Counselor Candidates, Teachers and Administrators," *Counselor Education and Supervision* Vol. 6 (Winter 1967), pp. 114–119.

[15] D. S. Arbuckle, "Client Perception of Counselor Personality," *Journal of Counseling Psychology* Vol. 3 (Summer 1956), pp. 93–96.

[16] N. L. Gage and L. J. Cronbach, "Conceptual and Methodological Problems in Interpersonal Perception," *Psychological Review* Vol. 62 (November 1955), pp. 411–422.

[17] F. E. Fiedler, "A Comparison of Therapeutic Relationships in Psychoanalytic, Nondirective, and Adlerian Therapy," *Journal of Consulting Psychology* Vol. 14 (December 1950), pp. 436–445.

[18] F. E. Fiedler, "The Concept of an Ideal Therapeutic Relationship," *Journal of Consulting Psychology* Vol. 14 (August 1950), pp. 239–245.

[19] F. E. Fiedler, "Quantitative Studies on the Role of Therapists' Feelings Toward Their Patients," in O. Hobart Mowrer (ed.), *Psychotherapy: Theory and Research* (New York: The Ronald Press Company, 1953), pp. 296–315.

[20] H. A. Grater, B. L. Kell, and J. Morse, "The Social Service Interest: Roadblock and Road to Creativity," *Journal of Counseling Psychology* Vol. 8 (Spring 1961), pp. 9–12.

[21] Fiedler, "Comparison of Therapeutic Relationships," p. 314.

Lesser[22] hypothesized that (1) counseling progress is positively related to the counselor's empathic understanding of his client, and (2) counseling progress and empathic understanding are each positively related to the degree of similarity between the client's and counselor's self-concepts. Three devices were employed: a Q-sort, the Empathic Understanding Scale, and the Felt Similarity Scale. Counselors on the staff of Michigan State University's Counseling Center and their clients were the subjects. Counseling progress was measured by comparing client pre- and post-sorts, with twelve hours of counseling intervening. Each counselor was asked to describe himself by sorting the one hundred self-referent items, and each client was asked to sort the same items according to the way he (1) saw himself and (2) would most like to be. At the termination of the twelve hours of counseling, each client re-sorted the items, describing himself the way he then saw himself and the way he would most like to be. In addition, each client was asked to rate his counselor on the Empathic Understanding Scale. Counselors were asked to rate themselves on both the Empathic Understanding Scale and on the Felt Similarity Scale. Findings revealed the following: counselor empathic understanding as measured was unrelated to counseling progress; similarity between client and counselor self-perceptions was negatively related to counseling progress; correct awareness by the counselor of similarity between client and counselor was positively related to counseling progress; and empathic understanding was not related to similarity or to correct awareness of similarity or to overestimation of similarity.

According to Carl R. Rogers:

The purpose of most of the helping professions, including guidance counseling, is to enhance the personal development, the psychological growth toward a socialized maturity, of its clients.

. . .

The effectiveness of any member of the profession is most adequately measured in terms of the degree to which, in his work with clients, he achieves this goal.[23]

Rogers maintained that the qualities to be desired in the counselor are congruence, empathy, and unconditional positive regard for the client, and that the communication of these attitudes to the client is of utmost importance. Discussing a series of studies undertaken within the past few years, he described procedures employing various techniques, including ratings by expert judges of taped interviews, client ratings of interviews, and coun-

[22] W. M. Lesser, "The Relationship Between Counseling Progress and Empathic Understanding," *Journal of Counseling Psychology* Vol. 8 (Winter 1961), pp. 330–336.

[23] Carl R. Rogers, "The Interpersonal Relationship: The Core of Guidance," *Harvard Educational Review* Vol. 32 (Fall 1962), p. 428.

selor ratings; and devices, such as the MMPI, the Q-sort technique, and projective tests. Some of the findings of these studies have pertinence here and are presented in Rogers' words:

> The counselor is the most significant factor in setting the level of conditions in the relationship, though the client, too, has some influence on the quality of the relationship.
>
> .   .   .
>
> Clients who will later show more change perceive more of these attitudinal conditions early in the relationship with their counselor or therapist.
>
> .   .   .
>
> Counselors or therapists tend to be quite consistent in the level of the attitudinal conditions which they offer to each client.
>
> .   .   .
>
> The major finding from all of the studies is that those clients in relationships marked by a high level of counselor congruence, empathy, and unconditional positive regard, show constructive personality change and development.
>
> .   .   .
>
> A finding which seems to lend validity to the studies is that, as might be expected, more experienced counselors, when compared with inexperienced counselors, offer a higher level of these conditions, and are more successful in communicating these to their clients. Thus they are perceived as offering higher conditions, and their clients show more change over the course of the interviews.[24]

In his study of counselor characteristics, Brams' purpose was (1) to study the relationship between personality characteristics of counselor trainees and their ability to communicate effectively with clients in counseling interviews, and (2) to obtain a description of these trainees as measured by a series of objective instruments.[25] The following instruments were administered to twenty-seven counselor trainees (twenty-two males and five females) during the first half of the two-semester counseling practicum course at the University of Missouri: the MMPI, the Taylor Manifest Anxiety Scale (MAS), the Index of Adjustment and Values (IAV), and the Berkeley Public Opinion Questionnaire (POQ). Scores on the fifty-item scale developed by Anderson and Anderson served as a measure of effective communication. Trainees rated themselves and other trainees (having listened to each other's recorded interviews) on the Communication Rating Scale. In addition, each trainee was rated independently by two judges, individuals who had supervised the trainees during the practicum course. The mean of the total scores from these two ratings was the criterion of effective communication. The correlations between judges' ratings and those

---

[24] *Ibid.*, pp. 425–426.

[25] J. M. Brams, "Counselor Characteristics and Effective Communication in Counseling," *Journal of Counseling Psychology* Vol. 8 (Spring 1961), pp. 25–30.

of the trainee ranged from .81 to .95; peer ratings and judges' ratings correlated .73, also significant. Thus there was no significant difference in the perception of the effectiveness of communication as measured by judges' and peer ratings. Correlation between self-ratings and peer ratings, however, was .21, and between self-ratings and judges' ratings, it was .22, neither being significant. Trainees, it was observed, tended to rate themselves high. Correlations between the criterion and scale scores on the MMPI, the MAS and the IAV were too low to show a conclusive relationship. The exception was a significant negative correlation between judges' ratings and the Berkeley POQ, which Brams interpreted as ". . . tentatively supporting the hypothesis that counselors who create successful communicative counseling relationships are more tolerant of ambiguous material in the counseling interview than are less successful counselors."[26] Of the lack of significant relationships between effective communication and scores on the other objective instruments used in the study, Brams suggested that ". . . the available objective instruments are not suitable for personality measurement of test-sophisticated students in the area of counseling psychology."[27]

Brams compared the mean MMPI profile of the twenty-two males with that obtained by Cottle and Lewis (1954) for the sixty-five male college counselors and found them to be highly similar. Brams noted:

> Both groups appear to exert themselves to make good impressions on others, they are somewhat defensive in their behavior, they are sensitive in their dealings with others, and they appear relatively outgoing in their interpersonal relationships.[28]

Studies focusing on client-counselor similarity and its effect on the counseling relationship have employed various methods and devices and have produced conflicting results.

Tuma and Gustad assessed the effects on client learning of similarities and differences between personality traits of counselors and clients (all males) as measured by the Taylor MAS, the California F-Scale (for authoritarianism), and the California Psychological Inventory (CPI).[29] They suggested that client learning was best when client and counselor scored alike on the Sociability, Social Presence, and Self-Acceptance scales of the CPI and on Anxiety as measured by the MAS. Also, counselors were found to be above average on Dominance, Sociability, and Social Presence, and the closer the client and the counselor were on these variables, concluded Tuma and Gustad, the better the client's learning.

[26] *Ibid.,* p. 29.

[27] *Ibid.,* pp. 29–30.

[28] *Ibid.,* pp. 28–29.

[29] A. H. Tuma and J. W. Gustad, "The Effects of Client and Counselor Personality Characteristics on Client Learning in Counseling," *Journal of Counseling Psychology* Vol. 4 (Summer 1957), pp. 136–141.

Gerler used the Ewing Personal Rating Form and found that some medium degree of client-counselor similarity was more conducive to a favorable outcome than was a high degree of similarity.[30]

Lesser noted that correct counselor perception of the degree of client–counselor similarity was the important factor, since it enabled the counselor to ". . . perceive more correctly what the client is saying and feeling than when he merely feels similar to the client, or further, overestimates their similarity."[31]

Snyder and Snyder reported a study in which the Edwards Personal Preference Scale was used to ascertain client-counselor similarity and which employed counselor self-ratings to evaluate the cases.[32] This was the finding:

> It is interesting to note that three of the four clients whose Edwards PPS scores at the beginning of therapy were the most similar to those of the therapist were among the most difficult and unsuccessful of the cases rated by the therapist. Also, the four clients least like the therapist in PPS need structure at the beginning of therapy were the four cases ranked as most successful and possessing the best rapport with the therapist during therapy.[33]

Mendelsohn and Geller looked at client-counselor similarity and its relationship to continuation in counseling.[34] They suggested that continuation in counseling for three, four, or five sessions might be interpreted as an indication of the client's willingness to let himself become involved in counseling and thus might be a "limited indicator of success." They found that the greater the client-counselor similarity, the larger the number of counseling sessions.

Polmantier did a survey of the literature of counselor characteristics and has summed up the counselor's personality in ten statements. Abstracts of six of the ten statements serve to close this section.

1. The counselor is an intelligent person who possesses verbal and quantitative abilities sufficient to think, reason, and solve problems with logic and perception.
2. The counselor's measured interests reveal a desire to work with people but are scientific enough to consider and utilize the science of individual and social behavior.

[30] W. Gerler, "Outcome of Psychotherapy as a Function of Client–Counselor Similarity," unpublished doctoral dissertation, University of Illinois, Urbana, 1958.

[31] Lesser, "Counseling Progress and Empathic Understanding," p. 334.

[32] W. U. Snyder and B. J. Snyder, *The Psychotherapy Relationship* (New York: The Macmillan Co., 1961).

[33] *Ibid.,* p. 160.

[34] G. A. Mendelsohn and M. H. Geller, "Effects of Counselor–Client Similarity on the Outcome of Counseling," *Journal of Counseling Psychology* Vol. 10 (Spring 1963), pp. 71–77.

3. The counselor manifests an acceptance of self. He does not use clients to satisfy his personal needs beyond the limits imposed by his professional role.
4. The counselor possesses value commitments which he understands and recognizes since they influence his counseling behavior and his behavior in general.
5. The counselor exhibits a tolerance for ambiguity and has the ability to face ambiguity without letting it disorganize his work and life.
6. The counselor is flexible enough to understand and deal psychologically with all kinds of human behavior without mustering authority or social pressures to force the client to conform.[35]

COUNSELOR CHARACTERISTICS AND EFFECTIVENESS

Studies and Reports

Inquiries into characteristics associated with counseling effectiveness as contrasted with ineffectiveness frequently have been approached through sociometric techniques, often with class or group members selecting from among their peers those whom they would most like to have as counselors.

Arbuckle investigated the qualities of counselor trainees who had been selected by their classmates as individuals they would seek out when they wanted a counselor, as compared with those who were rejected.[36] The subjects, a group of counselor trainees who had had an opportunity to get to know each other rather well, were asked to list in order of preference (1) the three people in the group they would be most likely to go to for counseling; (2) the three people they would be least likely to go to for counseling; (3) the three traits they would most like to find in counselors; and (4) the three traits they would least like to find in counselors. Results showed that counselor trainees most frequently chosen by their classmates had a higher degree of confidence as measured by the Heston Personality Inventory, were more normal as measured by the MMPI, and displayed a high degree of interest in social service, persuasive, literary, and scientific activities as measured by the Kuder Preference Record (Vocational Form), although there was no significant difference in the interest areas between those chosen and those not chosen. Preferred traits were tolerance, warmth, interest, patience, and sincerity. The least desirable traits were lack of understanding, lack of interest, aggressiveness, probing, moralizing, insincerity, bias, authoritarianism, and a superior manner.

As part of a larger study to assess the personality characteristics of twenty-nine summer NDEA Institute members (twenty-five males and four females), Brown included a sociogram to determine which counselor

---

[35] Paul C. Polmantier, "The Personality of the Counselor," *Vocational Guidance Quarterly* Vol. 15 (December 1966), pp. 95–100.

[36] Arbuckle, "Client Perception of Counselor Personality," pp. 93–96.

trainees would be chosen by their own group members to counsel them.[37] Placing the four trainees most frequently chosen in the "selected" group, the investigator compared the personality characteristics of those in each group as measured by certain scales of given objective instruments. He found that the selected group could not be considered more normal than the rejected group as measured by the MMPI. Nor was there any difference between the groups on the Nurturance scale of the EPPS, and there was a little, though not a significant, difference between those selected and those rejected on the Friendliness scale of the GZTS. On the SVIB, however, the selected group scored significantly higher on the Psychologist and Public Administrator scales than did the rejected group.

Coutts administered the Kuder Preference Record, Personal, and the Study of Values to 214 male counselor candidates enrolled in the practicum course in twenty-seven institutions throughout the country.[38] Competence was judged by the practicum supervisor's ratings. Those rated high, as compared with those rated low, were distinguished in the following ways: (1) they were less prone to want to manipulate others; (2) they were more kindly, sympathetic, and demonstrative of love for their fellowmen; and (3) they tended to have higher religious motives, but not extremely high.

Kazienko and Neidt surveyed male enrollees (females were eliminated because there were so few) in twenty-five summer NDEA Counseling and Guidance Training Institutes throughout the United States.[39] They chose as their subjects the top and bottom 25 percent of the groups as ranked by the professional staffs in charge of the Institutes in the participating colleges and universities. As a result, 124 counselor trainees were placed in the "good counselors" category, and 115 were placed in the "poor counselors" category. The subjects were administered the Bennett Polydiagnostic Index, in which the trainees described themselves in terms of self-concepts, motivating forces, values, and feelings about others. Perhaps one of the most comprehensive descriptions of the "good counselor" to be found in recent literature appears in the report of this research:

> *Self-Concept:* intelligent, but not brilliant, or creative; professionally competent and administratively efficient; serious, empathetic, soft-voiced, reserved of judgment, dependable, democratic; not precise or orderly; emotionally stable though apprehensive; self-centered and not particularly generous; not daring, assertive, or active; friendly, kind, and not hostile; lonely and staid;

[37] D. J. Brown, "An Investigation of the Relationships Between Certain Personal Characteristics of Guidance Counselors and Performance in Supervised Counseling Interviews," unpublished doctoral dissertation, The Ohio State University, Columbus, 1960.

[38] R. L. Coutts, "Selected Characteristics of Counselor Candidates in Relation to Levels and Types of Competency in the Counseling Practicum," unpublished Doctoral Dissertation, Florida State University, Tallahassee, 1962.

[39] L. W. Kazienko and C. O. Neidt, "Self-Descriptions of Good and Poor Counselor Trainees," *Counselor Education and Supervision* Vol. 1 (Spring 1962), pp. 106–123.

moral though not devout; socially acceptable though preferring domesticity; not especially strong or masculine.

Personal Motivation: desires success, independence, and love; wants good health but is not concerned about physical attractiveness; does not crave personal recognition or advantageous economic status beyond a measure of security.

Values Leading to Happiness: intellectual initiative but not craftiness; personal freedom; humanitarianism; definite and direct truth; progressive; suppresses emotional experiences; values tolerance over strict and severe measures; values energy of youth.

Feelings About Other People: intelligent but without depth; understanding but short on patience and tenderness; sincere and honest; lacking in precision and orderliness; nervous and anxious; cheerful though not calm; self-centered but generous; lacking in courage and indolent; friendly, not hostile; moral though not especially religious; socially acceptable, and tending to weariness; lacking strength.[40]

As is to be expected, many characteristics were found to be common to both good and poor counselors, though differences in intensity of feeling, belief, or perception appeared to a significant degree. Pronounced differences between the two groups occurred in some instances:[41]

Good Counselor Group

Self Concept

Serious, earnest, patient, soft-spoken; aware of personal self-centeredness; more domestic than social; not mechanical[ly] or industrial[ly] [minded].

Motivation

Concerned about possessing a measure of security but rejects need for wealth.

Values

Rejects cunning . . . and shrewdness as leading to personal contentment; feels person should have right to be different; does not value severity and strictness.

Feelings About Others

Views people as possessing adequate measure of intellectual ability though self-centered.

Poor Counselor Group

Self Concept

Does not recognize qualities of seriousness, patience in self; tends toward loudness of voice; not aware of any personal self-centeredness; sees self as normal domestically and socially; mechanical[ly] and industrial[ly] [minded].

Motivation

Neither moved nor unmoved by prospects of security and riches.

Values

Places average value here; feels happiness lies in conformity; tends toward strict adherence to rules.

Feelings About Others

Gives others no particular credit for intellectual behavior.

[40] *Ibid.*, pp. 121–122. Reprinted by permission.

[41] *Ibid.*, p. 122.

Observing that judgment of counseling effectiveness may be approached in three ways, that is, by expert ratings, client ratings, and peer ratings, Stefflre, King, and Leafgren[42] described their investigation:

> This study is an exploration of the use of peer judgment as a criterion for the identification of differences between those who are chosen by their peers as effective counselors and those who are rejected as not being effective.[43]

At the conclusion of the program, the researchers asked the forty members of a one-semester NDEA Counseling and Guidance Training Institute (thirty-six males and four females) to complete a Q-sort to register the "extent to which you would go to various Institute members if you were a student in the school." The nine most often preferred were considered to be the effective group; the nine least often preferred were designated the ineffective group. Each trainee was then requested to re-sort the group, this time including himself (whereas he had excluded himself the first time), in the way he thought the *group* would rate each member. Effective and ineffective counselors were compared on the following bases:

1. Academic aptitude and performance as measured by MAT, pre- and post-tests of Knowledge of Guidance, Grade Point Average on undergraduate and graduate pre-Institute work, Institute field and class work.
2. Interest and values as measured by the Educational Interest Inventory, and the Social Welfare and Sales and Business Contact scales of the SVIB.
3. Personality characteristics as measured by the Taylor MAS, the Rokeach Dogmatism scale, and the EPPS.
4. Self concept as measured by Bills Index of Adjustment and Values and a discrepancy score obtained from the difference between the position each trainee thought the group average would give him and the position he was actually assigned.[44]

Stefflre and his colleagues found correlations of .96 and .97 on the first and second Q-sorts, respectively. These results led the authors to observe that ". . . group opinion is both stable and widely known. The individual not only *knows* who would be a good counselor, he *knows* the opinions of the others in the group on this matter."[45] Of the four areas in which effective and ineffective counselor candidates were compared, the first was academic aptitude and performance; a significant difference on this criterion was found between the groups, a result not anticipated by the investigators. From the evidence yielded by the Q-sorts and from differences in academic performances, the investigators suggested that possibly the trainees tended to equate "good counselor" with "good student," having not so much

[42] B. Stefflre, P. King, and F. Leafgren, "Characteristics of Counselors Judged Effective by Their Peers," *Journal of Counseling Psychology* Vol. 9 (Winter 1962), pp. 335–340.

[43] *Ibid.*, p. 335.

[44] *Ibid.*, pp. 336–337.

[45] *Ibid.*, p. 339.

"formed" opinions of other group members as "caught" evaluations from the staff.

In the area of interests and values, differences between the two groups were observed on the Social Welfare scales of the SVIB, the effective group having significantly higher ratings. Scores on the EPPS suggested significantly higher Deference and Order needs for the effective than for the ineffective group and significantly lower Abasement and Aggression needs. Results concerning the self-concept obtained from the Q-sorts showed that effective counselors underestimated themselves, whereas ineffective counselors overestimated themselves. This outcome was contrary to the investigators' expectations, for they had hypothesized that individuals in the effective group would perceive themselves more accurately than would the others. In summing up, Stefflre and his colleagues noted: "The basic method of identifying chosen and rejected counselors would seem to be a good one, but the nature of the differences between them is still largely hidden."[46]

In contrast to Stefflre and his colleagues and in agreement with several other research efforts, Joslin found no significant relationship between counselor candidates' knowledge of counseling and their competence in conducting counseling interviews.[47]

Combs and Soper attempted to distinguish good counselors from poor by ascertaining how twenty-nine members of a year-long NDEA Counseling and Guidance Training Institute perceived themselves and their surroundings.[48] A seven-point scale was employed in a blind rating by counselor educators of counselor trainees' "ways of perceiving" as indicated by four human-relations incidents written by the counselor candidates. Separation into groups of good and poor counselors was accomplished by having the faculty members who taught and supervised them rank the Institute members from best to worst at the conclusion of the year's program. Good counselors were found to differ significantly from the poor counselors on all twelve aspects of "perceptual organization" investigated. The twelve aspects supported by the data were hypothesized as follows:

With respect to their general perceptual orientations, good counselors will be more likely to perceive
  1. From an internal rather than from an external frame of reference.
  2. In terms of people rather than things.

With respect to their perceptions of other people, good counselors will perceive others as
  1. Able, rather than unable.
  2. Dependable rather than undependable.

---

[46] *Ibid.*, p. 340.

[47] Leeman C. Joslin, Jr., "Knowledge and Counseling Competence," *Personnel and Guidance Journal* Vol. 43 (April 1965), pp. 790–795.

[48] A. W. Combs and D. W. Soper, "The Perceptual Organization of Effective Counselors," *Journal of Counseling Psychology* Vol. 10 (Fall 1963), pp. 222–226.

3. Friendly rather than unfriendly. [Good counselors do not regard other people as being threatening.]
4. Worthy rather than unworthy.

Good counselors will perceive themselves as
1. Identified with people rather than apart from them.
2. Enough [sufficient] rather than wanting.
3. Self-revealing rather than self-concealing.

Good counselors will perceive their purposes as
1. Freeing rather than controlling.
2. Altruistic rather than narcissistic. [Good counselors are concerned about others, not merely about themselves.]
3. Concerned with larger rather than smaller meanings.[49]

In a study mentioned earlier in this chapter, Brown explored the relationship between personal qualities of twenty-nine counselor candidates (twenty-five males and four females) enrolled in a one-year NDEA Counseling and Guidance Training Institute and performance in the counseling relationship. Personal characteristics were measured by the Ohio State University Psychological Examination (OSPE), the EPPS, the GZTS, the MMPI, the SVIB, and a sociogram. The Performance Rating Scale, the criterion, was employed by two counseling and guidance doctoral candidates in judging the counselor trainees' performance in counseling practicum interviews on the following dimensions: division of responsibility, core of client's remarks, lead in counseling, statements of insight (made by client), planning (readiness for effective, self-directing behavior), participation, and acceptance of client. The trainees' ages ranged from twenty-three to fifty-three, and teaching experience, from one year to twenty. Because their number was so small, the females were sometimes dropped from the analyses. Results suggested that performance in counseling practicum is related to verbal ability and that outgoing social behavior helps counselor trainees to perform effectively. No relationship was found between personality characteristics as measured by the standardized instruments and performance, except for the Si (social introversion) and Ma (hypomania) scales on the MMPI and the General Activity, Ascendance, Sociability, and Thoughtfulness scales on the GZTS. No significant relationship was found between the criterion and the SVIB. Performance did not seem to be dependent upon age or teaching experience, and finally, there was no significant difference on criterion ratings between the selected and rejected groups. Brown observed that "it was thought that trainees' sophistication with some of the measures used in this study had an effect upon the obtained results."[50]

Moore also employed, among other instruments, the EPPS, the GZTS, the MMPI, and the SVIB in her study, which involved 447 enrollees (349 males and 98 females) in fifteen full-year NDEA Counseling and Guidance

[49] *Ibid.,* p. 223.

[50] D. J. Brown, "Relationships Between Personal Characteristics and Performance."

Training Institutes throughout the country.[51] Those candidates rated potentially the most successful by the counselor educators of their respective Institutes constituted Group I, the top 27 percent of the total number. Those rated potentially least successful, the bottom 27 percent, were compared with the counselor candidates in the top group. Age appeared to have no bearing on the perception of a counselor's potential for success. Twenty-three predictor variables were found as a result of an analysis of all the instruments. The relationship between these variables and the rating of potential counselor success was, however, too low for prediction. The investigator concluded that ". . . the findings of this study will support the statement that counselor educators were unable to rate the potential of a school counselor relative to personality characteristics with any great degree of reliability."[52] Moore suggests that characteristics of the rater may enter into the rating to contaminate it.

Concern regarding the cost, in terms of both staff time and facilities, of advanced counselor training, particularly the practicum course, led Blocher to investigate the problem of selective retention of counselor candidates.[53] The subjects were thirty counselor trainees in the University of Minnesota's NDEA Counseling and Guidance Training Institute for the year 1961–62. From information available at the end of the first quarter of the year's residence, Blocher attempted to arrive at a means for predicting which of the thirty counselor trainees might best profit from advanced training.

At the end of the first quarter, four members of the counselor education staff ranked the thirty counselor trainees on the basis of performance in both academic courses and practicum situations in relation to predicted performance as school counselors. Inter-rater correlations ranged from .64 to .83. Rankings were combined into a single criterion score. The following measures were used as predictors: (1) Peer rankings of predicted counselor effectiveness; (2) the NDEA Comprehensive Examination, administered at the beginning of the program; (3) the Counselor scale of the Kuder Preference Record, Form D, administered at the beginning of the program; and (4) an average of the fall quarter grades. Blocher found that the four measures predicted the criterion, staff rankings, .77. Further, he found that staff rankings and peer rankings correlated .62 and that there was a correlation of .66 between fall quarter grades and scores on the NDEA Comprehensive Examination. A high positive relationship was found to exist between the Kuder scale and staff rankings, though the Kuder scale was negatively related to the other factors. These findings suggest possibilities

---

[51] V. R. Moore, "A Critical Analysis of Objective Measures and Subjective Evaluations on a Select Group of School Counselor Candidates," unpublished doctoral dissertation, University of Illinois, Urbana, 1963.

[52] *Ibid.*, p. 110.

[53] D. H. Blocher, "A Multiple Regression Approach to Predicting Success in a Counselor Education Program," *Counselor Education and Supervision* Vol. 3 (Fall 1963), pp. 19–22.

for the development of selective retention procedures relatively early in the training program.

Summary

The research suggests that counselors can be differentiated from non-counselors in terms of nonintellective variables by means of some standardized instruments now available, but that these instruments have been frequently found to lack efficiency in discriminating between effective and ineffective counselors. The need structure of counselors, for example, consisted of need for intraception, exhibition, and affiliation, whereas, in comparison, noncounselors had high achievement and aggression needs and showed a need to manipulate others. The studies suggested that counselors are understanding, sensitive, and friendly, and that they value others and have a tolerance for ambiguity in interpersonal relationships.

Arbuckle, Brown, and Stefflre and his colleagues found that the effective and ineffective groups could be differentiated to a limited degree on the basis of a few SVIB scales, namely, the Psychologist scale and the Social Welfare scales. One researcher stated that effective counselors value the right to be different, whereas ineffective counselors tend to adhere strictly to the rules and view happiness as deriving from conformity. Generally, however, the distinction between the effective and the ineffective counselor seems to be largely attributable to difference in intensity of characteristics, as the studies by Kazienko and Neidt and by Stefflre, King, and Leafgren suggested. In the two investigations in which the age of the counselor was a variable (those by Brown and Moore), it appeared to be unrelated to the degree of effectiveness.

Findings relating to counselor perceptiveness and degree of client-counselor similarity, in terms of counseling effectiveness, have been largely conflicting and often contrary to expectations.

The diversity of methods employed in the studies surveyed attests to the lack of satisfaction with existing devices for measuring nonintellective characteristics. Even so, instruments such as the EPPS, some scales on the GZTS, the MMPI, and the SVIB have been used with limited success. Failure to find expected relationships between measured interests and personality variables and criterion measures was attributed by two investigators to the trainees' test sophistication, but another researcher blamed the criteria.

Underlying any study involving interests and personality characteristics and effectiveness in interpersonal relationships is the criterion problem—a problem which figured in many of the studies surveyed in this chapter. This problem is elaborated upon in Chapter 16 of this volume.

Shoben pointed out that some criteria are more promising than others,[54]

---

[54] E. J. Shoben, "Some Problems in Establishing Criteria of Effectiveness," *Personnel and Guidance Journal* Vol. 31 (February 1953), pp. 287–294.

and the research reported here appeared to support this contention in that users of sociometrics and the Q-technique, for example, felt that they were fruitful methods worthy of further investigation.

Ratings by expert judges, supervisors, and/or peers were frequently employed as criteria. In only one of the studies reported was client rating used, despite recommendations by such investigators as Shoben (1953) and Goodstein and Grigg (1957, 1959), and Pohlman and Robinson (1960)[55] concerning the value of clients' reactions in determining counseling effectiveness. Of the four studies employing both peer and supervisors' ratings, three found a highly significant relationship between the ratings of these groups.

An overriding conclusion to be drawn from a review of the literature pertaining to interests and personality characteristics and counseling effectiveness is that the findings so far have been inconclusive and often conflicting and that additional research is needed.

COUNSELOR ROLE AND FUNCTION

What do school counselors do? What is the character of their occupational identity or role definition? By definition, at least in Parsonian theory, role is viewed as a set of complementary expectations which result in behavior.[56] Individual behavior within a role is determined by the expectations or demands of the role. The concept of role has been used with repeated frequency in recent guidance literature. As Bentley points out, however, the concept of role has not been precisely used.[57] Many individuals have used the term loosely in its generic form rather than as a complex social science concept. One way of identifying the role of the school counselor is to examine the perceptions of him held by those whom he serves: pupils, teachers, administrators, parents.

Perceptions of Counselor Role

PUPIL PERCEPTIONS OF COUNSELORS

What perceptions do pupils—the direct recipients of counseling services —hold of counselors? When questioned, most students indicate that they believe a guidance program adds something of value to their school. Tyler notes that many inadequately controlled surveys reveal from 80 to 90 percent satisfaction with counseling because ". . . there are certain social

---

55 E. Pohlman and F. P. Robinson, "Client Reactions to Some Aspects of the Counseling Situation," *Personnel and Guidance Journal* Vol. 39 (March 1960), pp. 546–551.

56 Talcott Parsons and Edward Shills (eds.), *Toward a General Theory of Action* (Cambridge: Harvard University Press, 1954).

57 Joseph C. Bentley, "Role Theory in Counseling: A Problem in Definition of Role," *Personnel and Guidance Journal* Vol. 44 (September 1965), pp. 11–17.

conventions that make for positive findings in studies planned this way."[58] Gibson's study of guidance services in twelve secondary schools within a three-state area is pertinent here. He found that more than one-fourth of the students indicated that counselors had not assisted them personally in any way; that 56 percent reported that they were not sure what constituted the activities of their school guidance program; that one-third of them reported that the program had not been described, explained, or outlined to them during their three or four years in high school; and that many felt shortchanged because test results were not interpreted to them.[59]

Brough queried 631 eighth graders in a junior high school as to the origin of their views of the counselor and his functions.[60] As expected, their perceptions developed from multiple and diverse sources. Three frequent sources included counselors' discussions of their role with students, actual interviews, and descriptions of the counselor in student handbooks. The single most important source was actually talking with the counselor. Rippee and his associates developed a fifty-item questionnaire which they administered to students and teachers of three small secondary schools.[61] They concluded that a counseling program, established where one had not existed before, changed students' perceptions of the counselor role significantly. The direction of change was determined by what counselors do.

Grant studied the help given to students by counselors in educational planning, vocational planning, and personal-emotional problems. His analysis revealed that counselors were preferred as the students' first source of help in educational and vocational planning, but not with personal-emotional problems. Students at best perceived the counselor as playing a minor role in assisting them with problems of a personal-emotional nature.[62]

Heilfron, using an adaptation of Robinson's case descriptions, asked high school students to indicate the degree of counseling needed by individuals with various kinds of problems. High school students felt that those who were bright and performing well in school did not need counseling, and that it should be reserved for those who displayed marked character disorders.[63]

[58] Leona E. Tyler, *The Work of the Counselor* Third Edition (New York: Appleton-Century-Crofts, Inc., 1969), p. 218.

[59] Robert L. Gibson, "Pupil Opinions of High School Guidance Programs," *Personnel and Guidance Journal* Vol. 40 (January 1962), pp. 453–457.

[60] James R. Brough, "Sources of Student Perceptions of the Role of the Counselor," *Personnel and Guidance Journal* Vol. 43 (February 1965), pp. 597–599.

[61] Billy D. Rippee, William E. Hanvey, and Clyde Parker, "The Influence of Counseling on the Perception of Counselor Role," *Personnel and Guidance Journal* Vol. 43 (March 1965), pp. 696–701.

[62] Claude W. Grant, "The Counselor's Role," *Personnel and Guidance Journal* Vol. 33 (October 1954), pp. 74–77.

[63] Marilyn Heilfron, "The Function of Counseling as Perceived by High School Students," *Personnel and Guidance Journal* Vol. 39 (October 1960), pp. 133–136.

Jensen's study of pupil reactions toward the guidance program in Phoenix, Arizona, high schools showed that while counselors generally were preferred by high school students over teachers, parents, and friends as sources of educational and vocational help, students preferred to discuss personal problems with parents and peers.[64]

Studies such as these lead to the conclusion that students do not view the counselor as an effective source of help except in the area of educational-vocational decision-making. Students say that others who are in critical situations should have the benefit of the counselor's skills, despite the fact that they themselves would not seek the assistance of a counselor. Why is it for others? The readily available glib generalization that this tendency merely represents a student's reluctance to admit to his problems is inadequate. The painful, but more profitable, view might be that students are willing to see others risk themselves to this service, but that they are reluctant to place themselves in an obviously risky situation. Why? Perhaps it is because counselors have failed to convey to students feelings of acceptance and understanding.

TEACHERS' OPINIONS OF COUNSELORS

How do teachers view counselors? Darley's forthright presentation of the attitudes of teachers provides a cutting, five-fold description: (1) Counselors are administrators and the nicest thing you can say about administrators is that they are a necessary evil which may be tolerated but better yet eradicated; (2) counselors provide ancillary services and are therefore expendable; (3) counselors coddle and pamper those who would, and perhaps should, flunk out; (4) the counselor's pseudo-Freudian, pseudo-psychometric jargon is the purest nonsense; and (5) his pretense of confidentiality is merely a shield to hide behind when the welfare of the institution is involved or his activities challenged.[65]

Though it is tempting not to soften the edges of Darley's conclusions, most school counselors come from the ranks of teachers and therefore carry with them some residual feelings from their own teaching days which make the above particularly harsh. A quote from Pierson reveals one possible motive for such hostile opinions:

> . . . it is difficult for the classroom teacher to accept the need for specialists in human relations in the school. For to admit that specialists are necessary is to imply that teachers have certain limitations which they are reluctant to face.[66]

[64] Ralph E. Jensen, "Student Feeling About Counseling Help," *Personnel and Guidance Journal* Vol. 33 (May 1955), pp. 498–503.

[65] John G. Darley, "The Faculty Is Human, Too," *Personnel and Guidance Journal* Vol. 35 (December 1956), pp. 225–230.

[66] George A. Pierson, "Aesop and the School Counselor," *Personnel and Guidance Journal* Vol. 32 (February 1954), pp. 326–329.

However, the concern is with the seeds of truth within Darley's caricature, not with Pierson's hypothetical explanation of the dynamics behind such attitudes.

Possibly, teachers are largely correct in these negative assessments of the role of the counselor. If so, it then follows that: (1) to the degree that the counselor functions as an administrator, he will be seen as an administrator; (2) to the degree that the counselor provides only an ancillary service, rather than an integrated, valuable service to students and teachers, he will be expendable; (3) to the degree that the counselor's acceptance and understanding of pupils is purposeless coddling and pampering of academic incompetents, teachers are justified in their misperceptions; (4) to the degree that counselors rely on jargon rather than clear, understandable communications to the staff, they risk the brand "charlatan" in its purest sense —"one who pretends to knowledge"; (5) to the degree that confidentiality is used as a self-protective device rather than as an indispensable part of ethical conduct, the counselor's activities are suspect. In all fairness, could any respectable teacher tolerate, let alone relate to, the individual occupying such a role?

ADMINISTRATORS' OPINIONS OF COUNSELORS

What impressions do administrators have of the school counselor? Grant reported that administrators believed that counselors were not particularly competent to handle students' personal-emotional problems.[67] In relation to this perception, an article in *Look*[68] quotes one anonymous principal to the effect that he had failed to see any value in the counseling services to which dropouts were referred. Furthermore, this particular principal thought that counselors were second rate, in both their preparation and their personal characteristics. And perhaps even more telling was his criticism that counselors failed to get "close" to students and that the counselor's jargon "bored" students, was unrelated to their concerns, and made them distrustful.

Another and better documented index to the amount of confidence placed in counselors exists in the assignments made by school administrators. A number of studies, such as those by Martyn,[69] Purcell,[70] Vassallo and Kindred,[71] report that counselors frequently function as clerks or as quasi-administrators. Many administrators expect the counselor to be active in cer-

---

[67] Grant, "The Counselor's Role," pp. 74–77.

[68] Chandler Brossard, "Teenager Without a Job," *Look* Vol. 26 (February 27, 1962), p. 33.

[69] Kenneth A. Martyn, "We Are Wasting the Counselor's Time," *California Journal of Secondary Education* Vol. 32 (November 1957), pp. 439–441.

[70] Florence Purcell, "Counselor Duties—A Survey," *School Counselor* Vol. 4 (May 1957), pp. 35–38.

[71] Theodore Vassallo and Leslie Kindred, "How Counseling Can Be Improved," *Nations Schools* Vol. 59 (April 1957), pp. 58–60.

tain administrative and instructional areas such as curriculum planning, pupil attendance, schedule-making, discipline, substitute teaching, and the like.

The caricature created by opinions such as those expressed by the anonymous principal in the *Look* article is patently clear. Counselors are ineffective, if not incompetent, at any level one chooses to examine. It is implied that they do not earn their keep by producing the requisite number of "cures." The consensus of the other studies cited above is that the administrator views the counselor as a "jack-of-all-trades." Although seemingly unrelated, these views are intimately intertwined. To view the counselor's job in terms of a favorite administrative criterion, that of "efficiency," seems particularly inappropriate in the light of the disparate and mutually incompatible expectations of administrators. To relegate an employee to the position of jack-of-all-trades and then condemn him for his failure to perform the unique service for which he was originally employed is grossly unfair and possibly represents deceitful hiring practice. Clearly, if an individual is hired to do one thing, and then is loaded down with a second and a third and a fourth set of tasks, he is unable to perform his presumed original assignment very competently.

The fundamental issue is why the counselor permits this sequence of events to occur. An even more disturbing thought is that perhaps in a subtle and shrewd way counselors avoid facing the issue of a real test of their skills and services by tacit acceptance of inappropriate assignments or passive tolerance of such assignments.

PARENTS' OPINIONS OF COUNSELORS

What perceptual sets do parents have toward the role of the school counselor? Evraiff reports that parents ranked counselor duties in the following order: (1) programming, (2) handling school problems, (3) counseling pupils on future careers, and (4) counseling pupils with personal problems.[72] Bergstein and Grant completed a study of parents' expectations of school counselors based on interviews with 187 mothers and 179 fathers of students in Grades 6 through 12. The school was located in a small, compact community with an established guidance program that had maintained good public relations. They found, at a statistically significant level, that counselors were rated as more helpful in the areas of educational-vocational-personal problems than were the family's best friend or the school principal. Parents thought counselors were least helpful with personal-emotional-social problems.[73]

Two issues are suggested by the rather skimpy material cited. Evraiff's study indicates that parents seem to view counseling in an outdated way,

[72] William Evraiff, "Perceptions of the Counselor," *School Counselor* Vol. 8 (March 1961), pp. 78–82.

[73] Harry B. Bergstein and Claude W. Grant, "How Parents Perceive the Counselor's Role," *Personnel and Guidance Journal* Vol. 39 (May 1961), pp. 698–703.

since they rate program planning as the first duty of the counselor. The contention here is not that program planning is unworthy of the counselor's time but that it is no longer considered the major task of the counselor. Priority certainly should be given to other duties. And it seems a little saddening that counselors, who ostensibly devote the major portion of their energy to the so-called "helping relationship," are rated only a little more helpful than the family's best friend.

Although it is difficult to find published statements related to parents' expectations of counselors, there is no dearth of opinion among professional workers regarding what parents often do expect. There is little to be gained by belaboring the point that parents often wish the counselor to perform a persuasive function in the areas of educational and occupational choice or to somehow set right their child-rearing errors, which often have accumulated for years. Needless to say, the serving up of "instant aspiration" and the facile repair of long-standing parent-child conflicts are unrealistic expectations. The question is, should counselors permit themselves to be used to persuade adolescents to make "right" choices and decisions, especially when "right" is often synonymous with agreement or submission to parental demands?

CURRENT EMERGING OPINIONS AFFECTING THE GENERAL PUBLIC'S VIEW OF COUNSELORS

What does the public-at-large expect of the counselor, and why? Since the Russians launched Sputnik in October 1957, educators and counselors have been inundated with constant pleas to direct, pressure, channel, and put youngsters into careers demanded by America's manpower shortages. Counselors are seen as responsible for providing the appropriate number of workers to fill the jobs society needs. They are expected to coerce and seduce students into taking mathematics, science, and foreign languages. Especially pervasive has been the view that counselors should identify, cultivate, and place students with exceptional talent in critically needed professions.

Thus, the mental health and welfare of the individual are relegated to a lesser position than manpower needs. Such expectations apparently ignore or minimize the well-documented relationship of personal adjustment and mental health to job satisfaction and productivity. Efficient manpower utilization is as dependent on the former as on the latter.

Appropriate counseling, from the economist's point of view, stems from the pressures of society and the shape of the nation's economy. The National Manpower Commission has stated:

> School officials use their guidance and counseling staffs primarily for vocational guidance purposes and, when expanded resources of staff and funds permit, also for counseling students with personal adjustment problems.[74]

[74] Quoted in Douglas W. Bray, "Vocational Guidance in National Manpower Policy," *Personnel and Guidance Journal* Vol. 34 (December 1955), p. 197.

This statement declares openly that only when sufficient funds are available can schools legitimately be concerned with a full-fledged guidance program.

Weitz, in commenting on the results of some of these manpower pressures, has pointed out:

> The youth who is channeled into science or language study or engineering because he is "best suited" to this has been robbed of a chance to learn how this major life decision was made. He may be successful, he may be well adjusted, he may even be happy, but he has not learned the sense of responsibility which comes from making decisions *and accepting the consequences of that choice.*[75]

Is there not danger in the imposition of the counselor's conception of social needs upon the planning of an individual client's career? Manpower trends are pertinent information for both counselor and client. The objection is to the effect of such suggestions by manpower experts on public opinion. Will their statements eventually result in the ultimate public impression that counselors are "hidden persuaders" or "flesh peddlers," whose primary aim is to fill empty cells in the Bureau of Labor Statistics' manpower matrix?

Statements of Counselor Functions

The preceding conflicting and dissatisfying viewpoints of the school counselor's role have contributed to a movement by professional organizations and school counselors to define role and function more clearly. The need for clarification of school counselors' functions has been clear and pressing. In 1962, the American School Counselors Association initiated a formal study of counselor role and function. Many conditions militate against role clarification. Hill cites some of these, which are summarized here: (1) The school counselor is a member of a new profession, and all new professions experience a lack of understanding and acceptance; (2) the school counselor belongs to a public-service profession, which includes teachers, supervisors, and administrators, who are involved in defining the counselor's functions; (3) the school counselor's work, however defined, is a complicated, demanding job which is difficult to simplify; (4) the school counselor's work requires that he help young people predict both their own future and the general future of society; thus clarification of his functions is complicated by the immature character of his tools of prediction and the rapidity of social and economic change; (5) the counselor's profession is built upon a comparatively new ideal in human society, the ideal of the dignity, worth, and independence of each person, and the counselor not only has to practice this ideal but to defend it.[76]

---

[75] Henry Weitz, "Creating a Climate for Accepting Guidance Services," *Personnel and Guidance Journal,* Vol. 38 (November 1959), p. 191.

[76] George E. Hill, "How to Define the Functions of the School Counselor," *Counselor Education and Supervision* Vol. 3 (Winter 1964), pp. 56–61.

Moore and Gaier also point out that certain social forces affect the school counselor's role. They cite such social factors as (1) belief in equal opportunities and social mobility for all, (2) pressures from national manpower demands, and (3) pressures to seek out and encourage members of minority groups to achieve.[77] Arbuckle cites the following as reasons for the conflicting functions of school counselors: (1) the counselor is either unable or lacks the desire to articulate to himself or to anyone else just who he is and what he's supposed to do; (2) state department certification requirements equate professionalism with several semester hours of doubtful study in questionable institutions from instructors whose lack of understanding is surpassed only by their courage in teaching something about which they know nothing; and (3) the "part-timedness" devoted to performing counselor functions inherent in teacher-counselor positions is detrimental.[78]

Wasson and Strowig[79] investigated whether professionally isolated counselors (counselors who were relatively isolated from other counselors) were more satisfied with their positions than nonisolated counselors. They found that isolated counselors rated their positions as more satisfying and perceived administrators and teachers as more supportive of guidance programs than did nonisolates. The latter tended to do more professional reading while isolated counselors more often cited the counseling profession as a source of leadership in their work.

Some of the more recent statements of counselor function will be reviewed here. Wrenn, noting that a distinction exists between performing a function directly and seeing that it is done, proposes that the school counselor be directly responsible for:

1. *Counseling with students* on matters of self-understanding, decision-making, and planning, using both the interview and group situations.
2. *Consulting with staff and parents* on questions of student understanding and management.
3. *Studying changes in the character of the student population* and making a continuing interpretation of this information to the school administration and to curriculum-development committees.
4. *Performing a liaison function* between other school and community counseling resources and facilitating their use by teachers and students.[80]

The American School Counselors Association have set forth a Policy for Secondary School Counselors, a statement in which they list the func-

[77] Gilbert D. Moore and Eugene L. Gaier, "Social Forces and Counselor Role," *Counselor Education and Supervision* Vol. 3 (Fall 1963), pp. 29–36.

[78] Dugald S. Arbuckle, "The Conflicting Functions of the School Counselor," *Counselor Education and Supervision* Vol. 1 (Winter 1961), pp. 54–59.

[79] Robert M. Wasson and R. Wray Strowig, "Professional Isolation and Counselor Role," *Personnel and Guidance Journal* Vol. 43 (January 1965), pp. 457–460.

[80] C. Gilbert Wrenn, *The Counselor in a Changing World* (Washington: American Personnel and Guidance Association, 1962), p. 141.

tions of the school counselor. In presenting guidelines for implementing the counselor role and function, the ASCA cites the following basic and distinct counselor functions which help develop effective counseling programs:

1. *Planning and Development of the Guidance Program.* An effective guidance program in a school results from cooperative effort of the entire staff in planning and developing the program. Parents, pupils, and community agencies and organizations can also contribute toward these efforts. It is essential that the objectives of the program and procedures for meeting those objectives be clearly formulated.

   In planning and development of the guidance program, the school counselor—
   a. Assists in defining objectives of the program.
   b. Identifies the guidance needs of pupils.
   c. Assists in developing plans of action.
   d. Coordinates various aspects of the program in a meaningful sequence of guidance services.
   e. Assists in continued guidance program planning and curriculum development.
   f. Evaluates the program and assists other members of the school staff in evaluating their contributions to guidance services.

2. *Counseling.* It is essential that the majority of a school counselor's time be devoted to individual or small-group counseling. In a counseling relationship the counselor—
   a. Assists the pupil to understand and accept himself as an individual, thereby making it possible for the pupil to express and develop an awareness of his own ideas, feelings, values, and needs.
   b. Furnishes personal and environmental information to the pupil, as required, regarding his plans, choices, or problems.
   c. Seeks to develop in the pupil a greater ability to cope with and solve problems and an increased competence in making decisions and plans for which he and his parents are responsible.

3. *Pupil Appraisal.* The school counselor assumes the roles of leader and consultant in the school's program of pupil appraisal. In pupil appraisal the school counselor—
   a. Coordinates the accumulation of meaningful information concerning pupils as needed, through such means as interviews, standardized test scores, academic records, anecdotal records, personal data forms, records of past experiences, inventories, and rating scales.
   b. Coordinates the organization and maintenance of confidential files of pupil data.
   c. Interprets pupil information to pupils, parents, teachers, administrators, and others professionally concerned with the pupil.
   d. Identifies pupils with special abilities or needs.
   e. Takes advantage of available data-processing equipment for facilitating the processing and transmission of pupil data.

4. *Educational and Occupational Planning.* In efforts to provide pupils and parents with an understanding of the pupil as an individual in relation

to educational and occupational opportunities for his optimal growth and development and to promote self-direction of the pupil, the counselor—

a. Assists the pupil and his parents in relating the pupil's interests, aptitudes, and abilities to current and future educational and occupational opportunities and requirements, long-range educational plans, and choices.

b. Collects and disseminates to pupils and parents information concerning careers, opportunities for further education and training, and school curricular offerings. These activities should be provided through a carefully planned sequence and may include group and individual sessions with pupils and parents, special programs, provision of up-to-date educational and occupational files readily accessible to pupils, bulletin boards, guidance newsletters, and visits by pupils to educational institutions and industry.

c. Assists pupils and parents in understanding procedures for making applications and planning for financing the pupil's educational goals beyond high school.

d. Assists pupils in obtaining information about educational and occupational opportunities in the military service.

e. Consults with school administrators and members of the school faculty relative to the curricular offerings which will meet the abilities, interest, and needs of pupils.

f. Assists in the educational and occupational planning of pupils who have withdrawn or who have been graduated from the school.

5. *Referral Work.* The counselor is the principal person on the school staff who makes and coordinates referrals both to other specialists in pupil personnel services and to public and private agencies in the community. Recognizing his own limitations to provide total service, the counselor—

a. Assists pupils and parents who need such services to be aware of and to accept referral to other specialists in pupil personnel services and community agencies.

b. Maintains a close working relationship in referrals to other specialists in pupil personnel services.

c. Identifies pupils with special needs which require the services of referral sources.

d. Identifies community referral agencies and their services.

e. Assists in the development of referral procedures and in the maintenance of liaison and cooperative working relationships with community resources.

f. Provides a follow-up referral agency recommendations to help the pupil and/or his family work through the problems.

g. Encourages the development and/or extension of community agencies for handling pupil referrals.

6. *Placement.* The counselor's role in providing placement services for individual pupils involves assisting them in making appropriate choices of school subjects and courses of study and in making transitions from one school level to another, one school to another, and from school to employment. Placement thereby involves the informational services of educational and occupational planning, pupil appraisal, and counseling

assistance appropriate to the pupil's choices and progress in school subjects, extracurricular and community activities, and employment. In addition to these other types of assistance which aid effective placement, the counselor—

a. Helps pupils and parents to make a long-range plan of study for the high school years and assumes responsibility for periodic review and revision of such plans according to need as shown by such factors as changes in the curriculum, pupil appraisal data, school achievement, the pupil's maturity, and new goals.

b. Plans with administrators and teachers (1) to provide appropriate classroom placement for pupils with special abilities or disabilities and (2) to establish procedures for course selection by pupils and grouping of pupils.

c. Furnishes pupil data to the receiving school when a pupil transfers, obtains pupil data for new pupils, and gives individual pupil data to educational and training institutions, prospective employers, and employment agencies.

d. Assists in giving pupils and parents an understanding of procedures for making applications and financial plans for attending educational or training institutions and for making application for employment.

e. Confers with admissions personnel and personnel directors and visits educational and training institutions as well as businesses and industries applicable to pupils in his school.

7. *Parent Help.* The counselor holds conferences with parents and acts as a resource person on the growth and development of their children. Through individual or group conferences the counselor—

a. Interprets the guidance and counseling services of the school.

b. Assists parents in developing realistic perceptions of their children's aptitudes, abilities, interests, attitudes, and development as related to educational and occupational planning, school progress, and personal-social development.

c. Provides parents with information about school policies and procedures, school course offerings, educational and occupational opportunities and requirements, and resources that can contribute to the fullest development of their children.

8. *Staff Consulting.* The school counselor works closely with members of the administrative and teaching staffs to the end that all of the school's resources are directed toward meeting the needs of individual pupils. In staff consulting the counselor—

a. Shares appropriate individual pupil data with staff members, with due regard to confidentiality.

b. Helps teachers to identify pupils with special needs or problems and keeps teachers informed of developments concerning individual pupils which might have a bearing upon the classroom situation.

c. Participates in in-service training programs, staff meetings, and case conferences through which he discusses his own role, interprets a child-centered point of view, and encourages effective use of pupil data in teaching activities and guidance services given by teachers.

    d. Assists teachers in providing group guidance experiences for pupils.

    e. Provides materials and information concerning such matters as the characteristics and needs of the pupil population, follow-up studies, and employment trends for use in curriculum study and revision.

9. *Local Research.* Research in guidance is concerned with the study of pupil needs and how well school services and activities are meeting those needs. The school counselor plays a role of leadership in determining the need for research, conducting or cooperating in research studies, and interpreting research findings to members of the school staff.

    The counselor conducts or cooperates with others in conducting studies in areas such as the following:

    a. Follow-up of graduates or pupils who have withdrawn.

    b. Relationship of scholastic aptitude and achievement to selection of courses of study, class placement, and post high school educational and occupational placement.

    c. Characteristics, as well as educational and guidance needs, of the pupils.

    d. The use of records and pupil personnel data.

    e. Occupational trends in the community.

    f. Evaluation of the school's counseling and guidance services.

10. *Public Relations.* The school counselor has a responsibility for interpreting counseling and guidance services of the school to members of the school staff, parents, and the community. All of his efforts at giving service to individuals in the guidance and counseling program have potential value in public relations. In discharging his responsibility in public relations, the school counselor—

    a. Participates in programs of civic organizations and other community groups.

    b. Prepares or furnishes information for articles in school and community publications.

    c. Assists in programs for presentation by radio or television.[81]

Administrators of the Lexington, Massachusetts, public schools have prepared descriptions of the philosophy and role of professional workers employed in the Division of Pupil Personnel Services. Figure 2 cites the functions they expect of the school counselor as well as the functions which they consider to be outside his role.

In summary, although considerable evidence that clarification of the school counselor's role exists and more is emerging, much remains to be done. Homogeneity in regard to role and function will come when professional training becomes substantial, unified, and sequential. This kind of training would do much to generate a professional identity. It will come when school counseling becomes a career rather than a stepping stone to administration or an escape from the classroom.

[81] American School Counselors Association, *Policy for Secondary School Counselors* (Washington: American Personnel and Guidance Association, 1964). Reprinted by permission.

FIGURE 2
Functions of the School Counselor

School Counselor's Proper Functions	Functions Outside Counselor's Role
1. Engage in professional counseling with individuals and groups of pupils who have problems of any nature which inhibit their ability to learn. The school counselor provides an atmosphere in which pupils can deal with these problems openly and effectively, thereby improving their ability to profit from the instructional program.	1. Performing administrative duties. For example: providing parents with academic reports, issuing failure reports to parents, arranging for bus transportation, planning and conducting field trips (except those of a vocational information nature), establishing honor rolls, determining membership in honor societies, providing orientation to pupils regarding the physical plant and administrative policies, orienting new teachers to instructional and administrative procedures, approving or disapproving course transfers of pupils, and the routine interviewing of pupils who are failing in their academic studies.
2. Motivate pupils to seek counseling of their own volition through a creative and continuous program of orientation to counseling. In order for pupils to make the best use of the counseling service, the counselor must develop a positive image in their minds concerning his role as a professional counselor.	2. Performing instructional, tutorial, proctorial, or supervisory duties such as substitute teaching, remedial tutoring, study hall supervision, cafeteria supervision, or hall patrol.
3. Conduct research designed to measure the effectiveness of individual and group counseling and other guidance services in promoting the maturity and educational development of pupils.	3. The disciplining of pupils.
4. Provide informational services to pupils designed to meet their need for educational, vocational and personal-social information.	4. Clerical tasks which prevent him from devoting his full effort to professional activities. For example: screening incoming phone calls, recording routine information on accumulative records, punching McBee Keysort cards, preparing transcripts, scoring tests and recording test data, providing homework assignments for absentee students, preparing transfer forms, filing, scheduling parent-teacher conferences, and registering new pupils.
5. Function as a resource consultant to school and non-school personnel in providing services in the community to meet the needs of each individual pupil.	
6. Assist in providing testing services designed to help each pupil appraise his capabilities, achievements, interests and adjustment.	5. The scheduling of classes or the arrangement of academic programs.
7. Assist in the placement and grouping of pupils in order to provide a learning situation of maximum benefit to each. This would include helping new pupils select courses of study.	6. Checking attendance or serving as a truant officer.
8. Provide in-service training programs for teachers, administrators, and other school personnel designed to help them become better acquainted with the philosophical and empirical considerations which influence the work of the school counselor.	

From Committee on Philosophy and Role Descriptions, Lexington Public Schools, *Philosophy and Role Descriptions, Division of Pupil Personnel Services* (Lexington, Mass.: The Public Schools, March 10, 1962). (Mimeographed.)

CAREER PATTERNS OF COUNSELORS

The career patterns of school counselors have been the subject of much discussion but little research. Curiously, career development is studied extensively by counselors-in-preparation and it is a phenomenon about which they claim competency. But few of them have shown much interest in applying knowledge of career development patterns to their own occupational group.

An American School Counselor Association survey (*ASCA Newsletter,* September 1968), based upon a 20 percent sample of its membership in 1966–67, reveals the following career data:

1. The percentage of male counselors employed increases as the grade level of the pupils being served increases.
2. Female counselors are slightly older (mean age, 47) than male counselors (mean age, 41 years).
3. A shortage of counseling services exists in rural areas. Some 35 percent of the total population live in rural areas, but only 17 percent of the counselors in the survey work in rural areas.
4. Male counselors reported a mean salary of $9,000, while that of female counselors was $8,000. Some two-thirds of the sample reported that they were on a 10-month-or-less salary schedule.
5. Some four out of five of the respondents entered counseling directly from a teaching position. The mean age for entry into the field was 34 years, with a range from 26 to 43 years. Men entered the field earlier than women.
6. Seventy percent of the ASCA respondents reported that they were counseling full time. This same proportion were employed at the secondary school level.
7. All respondents held a bachelor's degree and 96 percent held additional degrees. The average educational level was the master's degree plus 30 semester hours of graduate study.
8. Nine reasons were listed for entering the field of counseling. The first four included "to get out of the classroom," "wanted to counsel," "need for a counselor in the school" and "opportunity for NDEA Counseling and Guidance Institute financial support to pursue education."
9. Nineteen percent of the counselors reported that they were counseling 10 years ago. Less than half expected to be counseling 10 years later (by 1976).

The career line most often described for school counselors is well known: teacher to counselor to principal. This sequence has led many counselor educators to decry the loss of counselors to the field of school administration. While this form of loss undoubtedly does occur, little is known about the reasons for it; for example, does it occur because of natural advancement, economic gain, status striving, or the use of counselor preparation as a "backdoor" entry into administration. Also unknown, at least with any great degree of accuracy, is the magnitude of the attrition. Some speculation exists that the career line (teacher to counselor to administrator) was representative of the field during the years before 1960 but no longer holds true.

Estimates of Attrition

Best estimates are that nationwide some 4,500 to 5,500 counselors (master's degree level) are prepared annually. The attrition rate, for any reasons, among individuals who have been prepared in NDEA Counseling and Guidance Institutes has been estimated at about five percent.[82] Presumably, these individuals did not enter school counseling positions immediately after completing an academic year of counselor preparation. The number of institute-trained counselors who enter and leave practice after a period of time is also unknown. It should also be noted that a higher loss-rate may exist among counselors who completed their preparation on a part-time basis.

Hitchcock further reported that estimates of annual attrition among teachers exceeds 20 percent while annual attrition among counselors varies from 15 percent for employment service counselors to 9 percent for rehabilitation counselors. Finally, the Bureau of Labor Statistics estimates that annual attrition among school counselors is approximately 10 percent.

Relatively little is known with any degree of accuracy about the rate of attrition among those trained as counselors. To be sure, estimates of loss exist, and logical explanations can be advanced, but definitive information is notably absent. Longitudinal study, across time, would add much in an important area where little is known. Such information would be of great value to those preparing counselors and to those seeking to enter the field since the costs both to the institution and to the individual are often high when errors are made involving human endeavor and time.

Typical Patterns

Observations, based upon experience, give some indication of the career patterns of those who complete school counselor preparation. After teacher preparation and usually one or more years of teaching experience, the individual enters counselor preparation. He completes preparation, often on a part-time basis, and is employed as a school counselor. After training, the following career patterns are often pursued:

1. The individual remains as a counselor, usually moving from small or rural schools to larger, city or suburban schools.

[82] Arthur A. Hitchcock, "Counselors: Supply, Demand, and Need," in John F. McGowan (ed.), *Counselor Development in American Society* (Washington: U.S. Department of Labor and U.S. Office of Education, June 1965), pp. 93–94.

2. The individual serves as a counselor for one or more years and then becomes a guidance administrator (director or supervisor of guidance). He remains in this capacity (sometimes until retirement), often making lateral career shifts achieved by moving into better financed school districts or pursuing vertical career shifts achieved by administering a schoolwide pupil personnel program.
3. The individual serves as a counselor for one or more years and then becomes a school administrator (assistant principal or principal), thereby leaving the counseling field.
4. The individual serves as a counselor for one or more years and then enters an advanced preparation program and becomes a college counselor, counselor educator, educational psychologist, school psychologist or the like.

These patterns appear to exist for those who actually enter the field. Other individuals enter counselor preparation but never enter practice for one reason or another.

Factors Influencing Career Patterns

The counselor's career development must be viewed as occurring within a situational context as the result of interaction over time between the personality of the counselor and the demands of the employment setting. Career development in counseling, just as in other occupations, is subject to many variables. Some of the variables acting upon counselors are identified here.

ENTRY MOTIVES

Why individuals enter counselor preparation has been the object of some investigation. Norris[83] collected biographical and other data to assess the characteristics of those who entered counseling and guidance at Michigan State University between the years 1945 and 1957. The five top motives of those who sought counselor preparation were desire to work with people (65 percent); influence of a particular person (41 percent); courses sounded interesting (31 percent); liked the first course in guidance (25 percent); hoped to become a better teacher (23 percent). Frey and Shertzer,[84] investigating the validity of the scored life history as a predictor index of counselor career commitment, reported that counselors who entered and remained in the field tended to move toward people, situations, and procedures necessary for goal attainment. This tendency contrasts with the prevalent attitude of individuals who remained as full-time classroom teachers after completing a year of counselor preparation. Frey reported that the life

[83] Willa Norris, "More Than a Decade of Training Guidance and Personnel Workers," *Personnel and Guidance Journal* Vol. 39 (December 1960), pp. 287–291.

[84] David H. Frey and Bruce Shertzer, "Life History Correlates of a Career Commitment to School Counseling," *Personnel and Guidance Journal* Vol. 47 (June 1969), pp. 951–957.

history responses of teachers indicated that they appeared to withdraw from social interaction and were unable to enter easily into approach behavior.

Schutz and Mazer[85] applied factor analytic procedures to the occupational choice motives of 153 graduate students in counseling. Among the adient or positive approach factors found in the data were a search for personal meaning, a wish to help others, and a search for opportunities for research; aversive factors included such motives as avoidance of personal threat, avoidance of the business world, avoidance of competition, and dislike of physical labor.

Clearly evident from these investigations is the fact that heterogeneity exists in the entry motives of those who begin counselor preparation. That some individuals may enter counselor preparation without any intent of becoming practicing school counselors should also be noted. Whether these individuals account for all who do not initially enter the field after training is very questionable. Surely some of the initial loss is composed of those who change their minds during or after training.

ECONOMIC CONSIDERATIONS

Economic necessity has undoubtedly forced some male counselors to leave the field. Many who enter the field do so at the time a growing family begins to exert a tremendous financial drain. Even though some school districts try to cope with these financial pressures by giving school counselors salary increments and/or extended school contracts, the lure of higher salaries associated with school administration, business, and industry is too great for some. It may be noted that the currently increasing percentage of school counselors who remain in the field (as counselors or guidance administrators) occurs at a time when teachers' (and therefore counselors') salaries have become more competitive with those of other salaried personnel.

Dunlop investigated counselor employment and compensation practices in 100 public school districts, selected because of relatively high salaries. He reported that counselors in these districts had high levels of training; that these counselors held full-time assignments; that hiring only individuals who had been employed in such districts was rare; that teacher training and/or experience were not necessarily prerequisite to employment in one-third of the districts; and that most counselors selected were experienced.[86]

STATUS FACTORS

The prestige attached to an occupation presumably has impact upon

---

[85] R. E. Schutz and G. E. Mazer, "A Factor Analysis of the Occupational Choice Motives of Counselors," *Journal of Counseling Psychology* Vol. 11 (Fall 1964), pp. 267–271.

[86] Richard S. Dunlop, "Employment and Compensation Practices for Counselors," *Personnel and Guidance Journal*, Vol. 47 (June 1969), pp. 944–950.

whether individuals enter and continue in it. Granger's[87] study of the prestige rankings of individuals in psychological professions placed the school counselor near the bottom of the psychologists' hierarchy. But observation of the counselor's status among those who hold positions in the school setting—school administrators, teachers, and the like—would probably place him in a more prestigious position. Those who seek high status (the reactions sought from others are those of deference, reverence, submission and subordination on the part of those of lower status) translate prestige into power—the capacity to influence or direct the behavior of others. If status, a subjective variable, is sought and found lacking in a counseling position, the resulting insecurity, frustration and anxiety may cause an individual to move to a different position.

WORKING CONDITIONS

In far too many situations, counselors are expected to practice in inadequate physical facilities. Moreover, most counseling staffs are not given adequate secretarial and clerical assistance. Finally, counseling—the function for which counselors are presumably employed—is often displaced by quasi-administrative tasks and demands. The net effect of working conditions can either encourage practitioners to continue or discourage even the most competent and cause them to seek employment outside the field.

FITTING AND BINDING ROLE BEHAVIOR

Many sources document the commonalities and differences existing among conceptions of the school counselor's role. Much of this literature indicates that conflict can occur because of differences in expectations, in personality attributes, in role demands, and the like. Undoubtedly individuals who have prepared as school counselors either find that the role they are expected to enact is binding or that it fits them. If it is binding and produces personal stress and strain, they may well seek to leave the profession. If it is congruent with their expectations and personality, then they are more apt to remain in the field.

ANNOTATED BIBLIOGRAPHY

LOUGHARY, JOHN W., *et al.* (eds.). *Counseling, A Growing Profession.* Washington, D.C.: American Personnel and Guidance Association, 1965, 106 pp.

This volume presents the problems and issues involved in APGA's attempt to formulate counseling policy. The basic policy statements issued by the APGA are reproduced; Paul W. Fitzgerald, John W. Loughary, and C. Gilbert Wrenn offer some thoughtful insights about the future of counseling and counselors.

WHITELEY, JOHN M. (ed). *Research in Counseling: Evaluation and Refocus.* Columbus, Ohio: Charles E. Merrill Publishing Company, 1967, 297 pp.

[87] Stephen G. Granger, "Psychologists' Prestige Rankings of 20 Psychological Occupations," *Journal of Counseling Psychology* Vol. 6. (Fall 1959) pp. 183–188.

Chapter Three, "The Selection of Counselors," by C. H. Patterson, presents an exhaustative review of the research on counselor characteristics and the selection of counselors. Patterson then examines counseling and the nature of the counseling and therapeutic relationship. He suggests some next steps for research. Patterson's work is reviewed and discussed by Martin J. Bohn, Jr., and Francis Robinson.

WRENN, C. GILBERT. *The Counselor in a Changing World.* Washington: American Personnel and Guidance Association, 1962. Pp. 137–185.

This report on the changing guidance program and the school counselor as a professional and as a person is necessary reading for all educators.

SELECTED REFERENCES

ARBUCKLE, DUGALD S. "The School Counselor—Reality or Illusion?" *Counselor Education and Supervision* Vol. 2 (Winter 1963), pp. 54–65.

————. "Counseling Effectiveness and Related Issues," *Journal of Counseling Psychology* Vol. 15 (September 1968), pp. 430–435.

————. "A Question of Counselor Function and Responsibility," *Personnel and Guidance Journal* Vol. 47 (December 1968), pp. 341–345.

————. "Does the School Really Need Counselors?" *The School Counselor* Vol. 17 (May 1970), pp. 325–331.

BAUER, GEORGE. "Counselor Role: A Proposal," *The School Counselor* Vol. 15 (May 1968), pp. 403–405.

BROUGH, JAMES R. "Sources of Student Perceptions of the Role of the Counselor," *Personnel and Guidance Journal* Vol. 43 (February 1965), pp. 597–599.

BROWN, DUANE, AND CANNADAY, MERILYNN. "Counselor, Counselee, and Supervisor Ratings of Counselor Effectiveness" *Counselor Education and Supervision* Vol. 8 (Winter 1969), pp. 113–118.

CARKHUFF, ROBERT R. AND BERENSON, BERNARD G. "The Counselor Is a Man and a Woman." *Personnel and Guidance Journal* Vol. 48 (September 1969), pp. 24–28.

CHENAULT, JOANN. "A Proposed Model for a Humanistic Counselor Education Program," *Counselor Education and Supervision* Vol. 8 (Fall 1968), pp. 4–11.

DONNAN, HUGH H., AND HARLAN, GRADY. "Personality of Counselors and Administrators," *Personnel and Guidance Journal* Vol. 47 (November 1968), pp. 228–232.

DONNAN, HUGH H., HARLAN, GRADY E., AND THOMPSON, SEABORN A. "Counselor Personality and Level of Functioning as Perceived by Counselees," *Journal of Counseling Psychology* Vol. 16 (November 1969), pp. 482–485.

GLADSTEIN, GERALD A. "Client Expectations, Counseling Experiences, and Satisfaction," *Journal of Counseling Psychology* Vol. 16 (November 1969), pp. 476–481.

GRANDE, PETER P. "Attitudes of Counselors and Disadvantaged Students Toward School Guidance," *Personnel and Guidance Journal* Vol. 46 (May 1968), pp. 889–892.

HART, DARRELL H., AND PRINCE, DONALD J. "Role Conflict for School Counselors: Training Versus Job Demands," *Personnel and Guidance Journal* Vol. 48 (January 1970), pp. 374–380.

HURST, JAMES C., AND JENSEN, VERNE H. "Personal Growth: An Ingredient in Counselor Education Programs?" *Counselor Education and Supervision* Vol. 8 (Fall 1968), pp. 12–17.

KETTERMAN, CLARK S. "The Opinion of Selected Publics Concerning the School Counselor's Functions," *The School Counselor* Vol. 16 (September 1968), pp. 41–45.

KRATOCHVIL, DANIEL W. "Changes in Values and in Interpersonal Functioning of Counselor Candidates," *Counselor Education and Supervision* Vol. 8. (Winter 1969), pp. 104–107.

LYTTON, HUGH. "School Counseling—An Outside View," *Personnel and Guidance Journal* Vol. 47 (September 1968), pp. 12–17.

McCLAIN, EDWIN W. "Sixteen Personality Factor Questionnaire Scores and Success in Counseling," *Journal of Counseling Psychology* Vol. 15 (November 1968), pp. 492–496.

PATTERSON, C. H. "What is Counseling Psychology?" *Journal of Counseling Psychology* Vol. 16 (January 1969), pp. 23–29.

PAYNE, J. WIN. "Impact of the ASCA Statement of Counselor Role," *The School Counselor* Vol. 12 (March 1965), pp. 136–139.

PAYNE, PAUL A., AND GRALINSKI, DENNIS M. "Effects of Supervisor Style and Empathy upon Counselor Learning," *Journal of Counseling Psychology* Vol. 15 (November 1968), pp. 517–521.

PRICE, LEAH Z., AND IVERSON, MARVIN A. "Students' Perceptions of Counselors with Varying Statuses and Role Behaviors in the Initial Interview," *Journal of Counseling Psychology* Vol. 16 (November 1969), pp. 469–475.

RIESE, HARLAN C., AND STONER, WILLIAM G. "Perceptions of the Functions and Role of the School Counselor," *The School Counselor* Vol. 17 (November 1969), pp. 126–130.

RIPPEE, BILLY D., HANVEY, WILLIAM E., AND PARKER, CLYDE. "The Influence of Counseling on the Perception of Counselor Role," *Personnel and Guidance Journal* Vol. 43 (March 1965), pp. 696–701.

WHETSTONE, BOBBY D. "Personality Differences Between Selected Counselors and Effective Teachers," *Personnel and Guidance Journal* Vol. 43 (May 1965), pp. 886–890.

WYNE, MARVIN D., AND SKJE, PRISCILLA. "The Counselor and Exceptional Pupils: A Critical Review," *Personnel and Guidance Journal* Vol. 48 (June 1970), pp. 828–835.

YAMAMOTO, KAORU. "Counseling Psychologists—Who Are They?" *Journal of Counseling Psychology* Vol. 10 (Fall 1963), pp. 211–221.

PART TWO
GUIDANCE
SERVICES

T HE MAJOR purpose of Part Two is to describe guidance services that exist in most contemporary schools.
Such services make guidance operational and permit
it to be conducted expeditiously. In Chapter 2, four
such services were briefly identified: pupil appraisal;
informational; counseling; and planning, placement, and
followup. A more detailed study of each of these is
presented in this section. From such study, it is hoped
that the student will gain (1) a familiarity with the
nature of each service, (2) a knowledge of the basic
methods used in the conduct of each service as well as
their more glaring inadequacies, and (3) an understanding of the purposes of such services.

Chapters 7 and 8 discuss the counseling service,
Chapter 7 focuses upon counseling with individuals
and Chapter 8 upon counseling in groups.

The pupil appraisal service constitutes the topic for
Chapters 9 and 10. Chapter 9 examines the purpose
and use of test data, and Chapter 10 is devoted to
non-test appraisal techniques.

Chapter 11 is devoted to the information service.
Attention is directed to the purposes of such a service,
the kinds of data dealt with, the materials in which
such data are to be found, and the methods employed
to help students use such materials.

Chapter 12 discusses the dynamic factors involved
in career planning, and Chapter 13 describes the career
planning, placement, and followup service. Career
planning is discussed extensively, with placement and
followup seen as a natural outgrowth of such planning.

Students are urged to make use of Appendix A,
"Profile of a Guidance Program," following the last

chapter of the book. The profile forms covering cumu-lative records, appraisal techniques, interviewing and counseling, and informational service are especially helpful in gaining an understanding of the guidance services.

7

COUNSELING WITH INDIVIDUALS

How is counseling distinguished from guidance and psychotherapy?
What are the purposes of counseling?
What basic approaches to counseling exist?
What is the nature of counseling?
What are some of the guidelines fundamental to successful interviewing?

GUIDANCE, COUNSELING, AND PSYCHOTHERAPY

Definitions

Most counselors know exactly what they mean by the terms "guidance," "counseling," and "psychotherapy"—until they try to distinguish among them for others. In part, this difficulty arises because of the personal relationship necessary and common to all. Other personal relationships—teacher-student, parent-child, friend-friend—also incorporate many of the elements found in the three terms. Another reason for confusion is the similarity in definitions of the three terms. Often the definitions are too general in nature and therefore require additional explanations or modifications before specific meanings can be made clear.

Guidance was defined as the process of helping an individual to understand himself and his world (see Chapter 2). The term "counseling" has also been applied to a wide range of activities designed to aid individuals in solving their problems. Most simply defined, counseling is a learning process in which the individual learns about himself and his interpersonal relationships. Although precise, inclusive definitions are elusive, Gustad[1]

[1] J. W. Gustad, "The Definition of Counseling," in Ralph F. Berdie (ed.), *Roles and Relationships in Counseling* (Minneapolis: University of Minnesota Press, 1953).

181

points out that published definitions contain three common characteristics: *participants,* generally two in number, one of whom has a specified role or affiliation, such as a minister or a psychologist; *goals,* usually improved adjustment, higher functioning, greater happiness; and *learning* which is emphasized in the relationship. Gustad, from his survey of definitions of counseling arrived at the following composite definition:

> Counseling is a learning-oriented process, carried on in a simple, one-to-one social environment, in which a counselor, professionally competent in relevant psychological skills and knowledge, seeks to assist the client by methods appropriate to the latter's needs . . . to learn more about himself, to learn how to put such understanding into effect in relation to more clearly perceived, realistically defined goals to the end that the client may become a happier and more productive member of his society.[2]

A much valued and frequently used definition is that given by the consulting editor of this book, C. Gilbert Wrenn, who says that ". . . counseling is a dynamic and purposeful relationship between two people in which procedures vary with the nature of the student's need, but in which there is always mutual participation by the counselor and the student with the focus upon self-clarification and self-determination by the student."[3]

Lehner has facetiously defined psychotherapy as an ". . . undefined technique which is applied to unspecified problems with nonpredictable outcomes." Nevertheless, he recommends rigorous training for those who seek to become therapists![4] Despite Lehner's humor, psychotherapy may be defined as the "treatment, by psychological means, of problems of an emotional nature in which a trained person deliberately establishes a professional relationship with the patient with the object of removing, modifying or retarding existing symptoms, of mediating disturbed patterns of behavior, and of promoting positive personality growth and development."[5]

Distinctions

Attempts to differentiate among guidance, counseling, and psychotherapy have not met with any notable degree of success. Many counseling practitioners and many psychotherapists believe that distinctions among the terms, particularly between counseling and psychotherapy, are artificial, and that the terms should be used interchangeably. Others think distinc-

[2] *Ibid.,* p. 17.

[3] C. Gilbert Wrenn, *Student Personnel Work in College* (New York: The Ronald Press Company, 1951), p. 57.

[4] George F. J. Lehner, "Defining Psychotherapy," *American Psychologist* Vol. 7 (September 1952), p. 457.

[5] L. R. Wolberg, *The Technique of Psychotherapy,* 2nd Ed. (New York: Grune and Stratton, 1967), p. 3.

tions must be made because the preparation programs are different, if for no other reason.

Although guidance, counseling, and psychotherapy have more common elements than differences, the possible, agreed-upon distinctions among the terms should be known. All three have as their basis a helping relationship which seeks to assist the individual in attaining self-direction. The distinctions among the three terms frequently tend to appear forced or contrived, and theoretical rather than qualitative and practical in nature. Yet it is important that these distinctions be known and understood by school personnel so that communications about them will be as clear as possible.

Detailed comparisons of distinctions can be found in Lewis,[6] Bordin,[7] Buchheimer and Balogh,[8] McGowan and Schmidt,[9] and Arbuckle.[10] Some common distinctions frequently made among guidance, counseling, and psychotherapy will be summarized here, but it should be noted that these distinctions are based largely upon emphasis of differences. In effect, they are based upon setting up "straw men" to establish the distinctions more clearly. *It should also be kept in mind that the distinctions tend to be generalizations that would not necessarily be agreed to by all and will not apply in all cases.*

1. Guidance is a broad term usually applied to a total school program of activities and services aimed at assisting pupils to make and carry out adequate plans and to achieve satisfactory adjustment in life. Counseling is usually viewed as one part of guidance services; it is subsumed by the general term, guidance, in that it is one service within guidance rather than a synonym.

2. Psychotherapy usually implies deeper involvement with the individual's personality and is more concerned with the amelioration of more serious behavior conditions. Guidance programs and the counseling service within them, usually deal with situational, environmental conditions. Counseling, as well as the total guidance program, stresses rational planning, problem solving and support in the face of situational pressures. The counseling relationship is usually characterized by much less intensity of emotional expression than that found in the therapeutic relationship.

[6] Edwin C. Lewis, *The Psychology of Counseling* (New York: Holt, Rinehart & Winston, 1970), pp. 16–23.

[7] Edward S. Bordin, *Psychological Counseling* (New York: Appleton-Century-Crofts, Inc., 1955), pp. 6–17.

[8] Arnold Buchheimer and Sara C. Balogh, *The Counseling Relationship* (Chicago: Science Research Associates, Inc., 1961), pp. ix-xii.

[9] John F. McGowan and Lyle D. Schmidt, *Counseling: Readings in Theory and Practice* (New York: Holt, Rinehart & Winston, Inc., 1962), pp. 163–240.

[10] Dugald S. Arbuckle, *Counseling: Philosophy, Theory and Practice*, 2nd Ed. (Boston: Allyn and Bacon, Inc., 1970), pp. 259–264.

3. The recipients of counseling are "normal" individuals rather than those who exhibit abnormal or extreme modes of adjustment. Psychotherapy exists for individuals with psychological disorders. Counseling helps the essentially normal individual remove frustrations and obstacles which interfere with development, while psychotherapy attempts to deal with disabling or disintegrating personality conflicts.

4. Counseling approaches are based more upon emphasizing present, conscious material (material available within the individual's awareness) while psychotherapeutic approaches tend to emphasize historic and symbolic material, relying heavily upon reactivation and consideration of unconscious materials.

5. Counseling services are usually located in schools, universities, community service agencies, and pastoral organizations, while psychotherapeutic services are usually found in clinics, hospitals, and private practice.

6. Counselors tend to stress positive individual strengths and their use in personal and social situations, while therapists stress diagnosis and remediation. Counselors employ normative data to a greater extent than do therapists who rely more on idiographic data.

7. Psychotherapy usually takes a longer period of time to achieve its goals than does counseling. Counseling is usually conducted during shorter, more limited contacts.

8. Counseling is often seen as assistance given individuals to attain a clear sense of identity while psychotherapy deals with intrapersonal conflict. Counseling focuses upon helping the individual to cope with developmental tasks such as self-definition, independence, and the like. Attention is given to clarifying the individual's assets, skills, strengths, and personal resources in terms of role development.

Figure 3 is an attempt to graphically portray the relationship among counseling, guidance, psychotherapy, and instruction. Although theoretical distinctions have been emphasized, the four are intimately related and share a common ultimate purpose; i.e., helping individuals achieve direction.

Figure 4 attempts to show that human problems could be placed on a continuum (see Row III). It also presents graphically the type of professional usually responsible for handling certain kinds of problems (see Row IV), the locale in which these individuals are usually employed (see Row I), and the nature of the helping relationship (see Row II). As may be seen by an examination of Figure 4, considerable overlap exists in the locale in which guidance, counseling, and psychotherapy are practiced.

As suggested by the overlap shown in Rows II and IV of this figure, referral for specialized assistance in two directions is indicated, depending upon the nature of the help needed. That is, the school counselor who is confronted with a student's serious emotional problem probably would refer the student to one of the specialists listed below him in Row IV. The

FIGURE 3

Model Relating Guidance and Counseling to Psychotherapy and Instruction

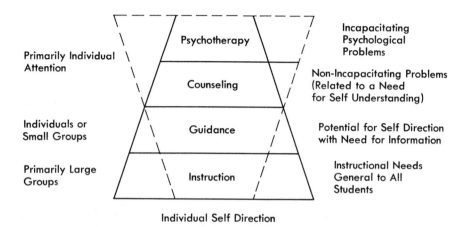

Adapted from Charles A. Curran, *Counseling in Catholic Life and Education* (New York: The Macmillan Co., 1952), p. 18.

psychiatrist, faced with a request for vocational or educational assistance by a patient, would often refer the individual to a counseling psychologist or school counselor who is better equipped to serve the patient in these matters.

Row III of Figure 4, "Classification of Problem," requires some explanation. The problem classes are listed in order of severity. The size of the shaded areas is meant only to imply that the problems occur in decreasing frequency in the population as one moves from right to left. The reader should *not* conclude that the shaded areas are scaled to the proportion of problems found in the general population, even though it is appropriate to infer that the bulk of the population may face situational problems at some time in their lives while very few suffer from chronic psychoses.

PURPOSES OF COUNSELING

The counseling service has been described by many as the keystone or heart of the guidance program. This is a rightful emphasis in that through counseling true meaning is given to individualized attention. It is in counseling that students are accepted without conditional restrictions. Though the purposes of counseling may be inferred from reviewing the distinctions made among counseling, guidance, and psychotherapy, a brief restatement is in order.

It is doubtful that a statement of specific counseling purposes could be set forth which would be universally acceptable to all counselors. For each counselor, the purpose of counseling undoubtedly reflects his training, value system, perception of role, and the needs of the individual being helped.

FIGURE 4
The Helping Relationships

I
Usual
Locale
	Hospital Setting
	      Clinic Setting
	            School Setting

II
Type of
Helping
Relationship
	Advising
	      Counseling
	Psychotherapy
	   Medical Therapy

III
Classification
of
Problem
	Chronic Acute
	Psychoses Psychoses Mild
	                Psychoses Neuroses Transient Educa-
	Organic Moderate tional Situational
	Psychoses [Character] to Severe Voca- Temporary
	                       Disorders Personal tional Problems
	                                    Problems Problems

IV Usual Professional Worker	.... School Counselors .... Counseling Psychologists .... Clinical Psychologists .... Psychiatrists .... Psychoanalysts ....

But agreement on the general purposes of counseling can be obtained. Almost all who counsel agree that the goal of counseling is to effect change in behavior which in turn will permit the recipient to live a more productive and self-satisfying life.

The central purpose of school counseling is to assist pupils to explore and understand themselves so that they can become self-directing individuals. In the security of the counseling relationship, the individual is able to explore the interrelationship among his feelings, his values, his perceptions of others, his interpersonal relationships, his fears, and his life choices. From this exploration comes role clarification and self-understanding. Most individuals in the field agree that the desired outcome of counseling is self-direction and self-realization on the part of the counselee or client.

The focus of school counseling is often seen as decision-making. Loughary has stated that the ". . . problems of secondary school students which the counselor encounters can in large part be reduced to decision-making problems."[11] In this context, counselors help counselees obtain information to make decisions and gain acceptance or clarification of certain personal characteristics that may interfere with, or be related to, making decisions. This does not mean that counselors tell students what is wrong and what they should do. Students are helped through counseling to achieve their own educational and vocational adjustment and fulfillment. Counseling, then, is focused upon the individual problems and needs of pupils and helps them learn what is needed to solve these problems. In this way the student becomes independently able to handle future difficulties. More recently, Fullmer and Bernard have stated that ". . . the central problem in counseling seems to be to find ways for the individual to relate outside knowledge to himself in such a way that this knowledge becomes part of him and can be utilized in his problem solving behavior."[12]

Byrne[13] examines counseling goals under three headings: ultimate, intermediate, and immediate. He points out that the counselor's ultimate goals derive their substance from his philosophical views of man, that his intermediate goals hinge on reasons why students seek counseling help, and that his immediate goals are his moment-by-moment intentions during counseling. Byrne evaluates many ultimate goals and finally synthesizes the following ultimate counseling goal:

> The counselor's goal, firmly based on the human worth of the individual, regardless of education, intelligence, color, or background, is to use his technical skills (a) to help each counselee attain and maintain an awareness of self so that he can be responsible for himself, (b) to help each counselee confront threats to his being, and thus to open further the way for the counselee to increase his concern for others' well-being, (c) to help each counselee bring into full operation his unique potential in compatability with his own life style and within the ethical limits of society.[14]

Rogers believes that the basic purpose of counseling is ". . . a more broadly based structure of self, an inclusion of a greater proportion of experience as a part of self, and a more comfortable and realistic adjustment to life."[15] Most pupils, at some time or another, experience discontinuities and uncertainties in their lives. Modern life has been characterized by many as an age of conflict, turmoil, and uncertainty. As a result many of the bases upon which decisions could be worked out have been removed from the

[11] John Loughary, *Counseling in Secondary Schools* (New York: Harper & Row, Publishers, 1961), p. 15.

[12] Daniel W. Fullmer and Harold W. Bernard, *Counseling: Content and Process* (Chicago: Science Research Associates, Inc., 1964), p. 157.

[13] Richard Hill Byrne, *The School Counselor* (Boston: Houghton Mifflin Company, 1963), pp. 6–20.

[14] *Ibid.,* pp. 19–20.

[15] Carl R. Rogers, *Client-Centered Therapy* (Boston: Houghton Mifflin Company, 1951), p. 195.

experiences of pupils. When an individual is troubled or uncertain he may want the help that counseling may bring. Tyler states that "It is in the relatively calm, non-threatening counseling atmosphere that such a person is most likely to be able to face confusions courageously, to sort out from the ideals and values he has been exposed to, the ones which are valid for him and thus to come out with a workable philosophy of life."[16]

But, Thompson and Zimmerman ask "Whose goals? and When?" These two investigators administered a goal checklist to 315 clients and their 27 counselors at several points during the counseling process to determine (a) the relationship between client goals and counselor goals and (b) whether this relationship changed over time. Clients were asked to check the goals they had for themselves and their counselors were asked to check the goals they viewed as appropriate for their clients. Thompson and Zimmerman reported that correspondence of clients with themselves over time averaged a correlation of .50; that of counselors with themselves over time, around the mid .30's; and that of clients with their counselors, in the mid .20's. Since convergence of goals over time did not take place to any appreciable degree, the two investigators suggest that outcomes in counseling (particularly research on outcomes) would be improved if client and counselor determined first what constitutes mutually desirable outcomes. Finally, they point out that it is doubtful whether there are goals which are appropriate to all clients.[17]

Some have given attention to what counseling *is not*. In doing so they provide a contrasting background which many find makes the legitimate goals of counseling stand out in bold relief. Walker and Peiffer listed the following as repudiated goals of counseling: (1) adjustment on a completely individual basis; (2) counselee contentment or happiness; (3) psychological autonomy without regard to social responsibilities; (4) adjustment solely in terms of social conformity; and (5) counselee emotional health as synonymous with the counselor's emotional health.[18] And Arbuckle has described four purposes or goals of the counselor which are unacceptable as counseling objectives: (1) solving the client's problems; (2) making the client happy or satisfied (this is a byproduct, rather than an objective); (3) making society happy and satisfied with the client; and (4) persuading the client to give up certain decisions and choices in favor of those that are "right." Arbuckle believes counseling should be based on the following principles: (1) man is basically a self-determining creature; (2) helping the client move toward a greater level of self-acceptance and

[16] Leona E. Tyler, *The Work of the Counselor,* 3rd Ed. (New York: Appleton-Century-Crofts, Inc., 1969), p. 8.

[17] Andrew Thompson and Robert Zimmerman, "Goals of Counseling: Whose? When?" *Journal of Counseling Psychology* Vol. 16 (March 1969), pp. 121–125.

[18] Donald E. Walker and Herbert C. Peiffer, "The Goals of Counseling," *Journal of Counseling Psychology* Vol. 4 (Fall 1957), pp. 204–209.

self-understanding; (3) helping the client develop a greater level of honesty, particularly honesty toward self; and (4) objectives should be based on client need, not counselor need.[19]

Included in the purposes of counseling is that of helping the individual achieve integration, adjustment, and identification with others. Many youngsters, sensitive to their surroundings and the pressures of the times, are searching for answers, for anchors for their beliefs and convictions. The increased use of inanimate teaching aids—television, programed learning, language laboratories, etc.—depersonalizes the learning process. Counseling seeks to enhance personal growth and development, to achieve harmony with the environment and recognition of individuality.

BASIC COUNSELING ORIENTATIONS

Perhaps unfortunately for the beginning student in guidance, professional opinion is not unanimous about counseling theory or approach. Wide reading reveals great diversity. Each approach can teach something, however, if one examines and evaluates the facts and opinions upon which it is based. Basic issues cut across all approaches and differences often appear to exist largely in emphasis and convictions.

Theory is a practical means or a framework for making systematic observations and explaining phenomena. Theory in counseling attempts to explain and provide understanding of what happens in the counseling relationship. Efforts to explain, predict, or evaluate events in counseling are based on theories of human behavior. Some years ago, Shoben and his associates stated that those who deal directly with clients use theoretical ideas, and that "their choice is not one of theory versus no theory, but between notions of human conduct that are explicit and formalized against those that are implicit and the inarticulate product of experience."[20] More recently, Stefflre, in his book *Theories of Counseling,* has said:

> The real question then is not whether we shall operate from theory since we have no choice in this matter, but rather what theories shall we use and how shall we use theories. Specifically, in a counseling situation when a client says "I hate my mother," the counselor's reactions are limited only by his biological status. He can slap the client, he can run out of the room, he can jump up on his chair, he can reply "It makes you bitter just thinking about her," or he can do any of a number of things. When he makes a choice among the responses open to him, he must act from theory. That is, he must act from some notion as to what the client means by his statement, what his statement means in the life of the client, what the proper goals of counseling are, what the function of the counselor is, what techniques are success-

[19] Dugald S. Arbuckle, *Counseling: Philosophy, Theory and Practice,* 2nd Ed. (Boston: Allyn and Bacon, Inc., 1970), pp. 195–203.

[20] Edward J. Shoben, Jr., *et al.,* "Behavior Theories and a Counseling Case: A Symposium," *Journal of Counseling Psychology* Vol. 3 (Summer 1956), pp. 107–124.

ful in moving toward the determined goals, and the other elements which taken together constitute for him a theory of counseling.[21]

Stefflre's book is recommended for those who want to explore further such questions as, What is a theory? Why is theory needed? What are the underlying bases of theories? What do theories do? How is a good theory known? How is theory to be used?

Although little or no compelling evidence exists that counseling success depends definitely upon the extent and explicitness of a counselor's theoretical orientation, or that one theory is superior to another, extensive effort within recent years has gone into theory construction. It is to be hoped that some day soon unification of the multiplicity of theories will take place. However it may be, as Black has stated, the resolution of theoretical differences will come through critical analysis of the process rather than the promotion of a particular point of view.[22]

Michael and Meyerson[23] and Strong[24] discuss a behavioristic approach to counseling; Phillips[25] provides a learning-theory approach called "interference theory" which Loughary[26] applies to school counseling; Kaam[27] describes counseling from the viewpoint of existential psychology; Hummel[28] sets forth a concept of counseling based upon ego functioning. These are but a few of the recent statements of counseling theory and methodology. Extensive discussion and examination of counseling theory are not possible within the confines of this book, but must, of necessity, come within courses designed explicitly for such purposes. Since this text serves a survey function, however, it appears useful here to identify a few counseling theories in chronological order. Treatment is given to four broad systems with little attention to the deviations within each or to the details or refinements.

Psychoanalytical Adaptations

Psychoanalysis refers to the original body of doctrine set forth by Sigmund Freud between approximately 1890 and 1939. The term also in-

[21] From *Theories of Counseling* by Buford Stefflre (ed.). Copyright 1965. McGraw-Hill Book Co. Used by permission. P. 3.

[22] J. D. Black, "Common Factors of the Patient-Therapist Relationship in Diverse Psychotherapies," *Journal of Clinical Psychology* Vol. 8 (July 1952), pp. 302–306.

[23] Jack Michael and Lee Meyerson, "A Behavioral Approach to Counseling and Guidance," *Harvard Educational Review* Vol. 32 (Fall 1963), pp. 382–402.

[24] Stanley R. Strong, "Verbal Conditioning and Counseling Research," *Personnel and Guidance Journal* Vol. 42 (March 1964), pp. 660–669.

[25] E. Lakin Phillips, *Psychotherapy, A Modern Theory and Practice* (Englewood Cliffs, N.J.: Prentice-Hall, Inc., 1956).

[26] Loughary, *Counseling in Secondary Schools*, pp. 21–22.

[27] Adrian van Kaam, "Counseling from the Viewpoint of Existential Psychology," *Harvard Educational Review* Vol. 32 (Fall 1962), pp. 403–415.

[28] Raymond C. Hummel, "Ego-Counseling in Guidance: Concept and Method," *Harvard Educational Review* Vol. 32 (Fall 1962), pp. 463–482.

cludes various modifications propounded by Freud's pupils. Individuals who accepted basic Freudian principles and simultaneously sought modifications in the form of modernization by attempting to incorporate the findings of contemporary psychology are usually referred to as neo-Freudians. Psychoanalysis, taken at its broadest meaning, according to English and English,[29] includes not only analytic psychology, individual psychology, and other departures from orthodox Freudianism, but also the literary, political, and social ideologies which have been influenced by Freud. The fundamental influence attributed to Freud is that of antirationalism which stresses unconscious motivation, conflict, and symbolism as its basic concepts.

Freud, over a considerable span of time, advanced a theory of personality which, in its simplest terms, is based on three fundamental premises. The *economic premise* postulated that certain amounts of psychic energy were available for utilization to the organism. The *genetic premise* relied upon the belief that an orderly sequence of steps are involved in the psychological development of an individual. The *structural premise* under which Freud variously postulated "psychic entities" as explanatory concepts, such as conscious, preconscious, unconscious, "superego," "ego," and "id" were useful to a theoretical understanding of mental structure.

No pretense can be made at summarizing the tremendous contributions Freud has made to the understanding of human behavior. His own works, irrespective of those of his students and followers, require twenty-three volumes[30] to reproduce and cover a time span of forty to fifty years. Freud's thinking, recognized and unrecognized, permeates many contemporary theories of personality.

It is a fundamental error to think of Freudian theory solely as a basis of treatment. Because it has permeated most if not all present-day personality theories, it has become the basis of much psychotherapeutic and counseling practice.

King has summarized the analytically trained counselor's beliefs and actions toward his clients in these words:

> Principally, he would view his client as having psychological processes of which he is unconscious as well as those of which he is conscious. He would feel that behavior is shaped in every moment of existence by an interaction of conscious and unconscious processes. He would pay particular attention to whether the unconscious factors in the personality were dominating or interfering with the client's behavior. He would feel that behavior could not be materially changed without ascertaining what these factors were. He would anticipate meeting resistance in the client that might require certain

[29] Horace B. English and Ava Champney English, *A Comprehensive Dictionary of Psychological and Psychoanalytical Terms* (New York: Longmans, Green and Company, 1958), p. 417.

[30] James Strachey (ed.), *The Standard Edition of the Complete Psychological Works of Sigmund Freud* (London: Hogarth Press, 1964).

techniques to overcome. His aim would be to bring these unconscious conflicts under the domain of conscious control.[31]

Trait-and-Factor Theory

Trait-and-factor approaches are less formally called directive or counselor-centered approaches. Most often cited for his application to counseling of this point of view has been E. G. Williamson.[32] Donald Paterson, Walter Bingham, and John Darley, along with Williamson, were among those who saw counseling as an objective measurement-centered process.

Directive counselors explain personality as a system of interdependent traits or factors such as abilities (memory, spatial, verbal), interests, attitudes, and temperament. Development of the individual progresses from infancy to adulthood with respect to the energizing and maturing of these factors. Attempts have been made to classify people into categories and to describe them by the use of various trait dimensions. Scientific study of the individual has included (1) assessing his traits by psychological tests and other means; (2) defining or portraying the individual; (3) helping him to know and understand himself and his environment; and (4) predicting probable success in certain ventures. Woolf and Woolf cite three assumptions which underlie trait-and-factor counseling: (1) It is essentially an intellectual process; (2) maladjustments in normal persons leave a large proportion of the mind intact and therefore the mind can be used in learning or relearning; (3) the counselor has superior information and experience and is competent to give advice about how a problem can be solved.[33]

The trait-and-factor counselor is often seen as a "teaching assistant" who directs the learning process of the counselee. The counselor is responsible for deciding what data are needed, collecting them and presenting them to the counselee. He also presents his points of view with definiteness and enlightens the counselee through expository statements.

Directive counselors stress diagnosis as a fundamental counselor function. Diagnosis is necessary to determine what issues and conditions are involved before efforts to help the individual can be successful.

Self-Theory Counseling

Other labels applied to self-theory counseling are client-centered, nondirective, and Rogerian counseling. Carl Rogers and his associates have de-

[31] From "Psychoanalytic Adaptations," by Paul T. King, in *Theories of Counseling* by Buford Stefflre (ed.). Copyright 1965. McGraw-Hill Book Co. Used by permission. P. 103.

[32] See E. G. Williamson, *Counseling Adolescents* (New York: McGraw-Hill Book Co., Inc., 1950), and "Vocational Counseling: Trait Factor Theory," in Buford Stefflre (ed.), *Theories of Counseling* (New York: McGraw-Hill Book Co., Inc., 1965), pp. 193–214.

[33] Maurice D. Woolf and Jeanne A. Woolf, *Student Personnel Programs* (New York: McGraw-Hill Book Co., Inc., 1953), p. 22.

veloped, described, and tested many of the theoretical formulations of self theory. Undoubtedly, client-centered counseling has been researched more than any other system.

This counseling approach stresses the counselee's ability to determine the issues discussed and to solve his own problems. Counselor intervention in this process is minimal. The most important quality of the counseling relationship is the establishment of a warm, permissive, and accepting climate which permits the client to explore his self-structure in relation to his unique experience. He is thus able to face his unacceptable characteristics without feeling threatened and anxious; he moves toward acceptance of himself and his values and is able to modify or change those aspects of himself which he thinks need modification.

According to Rogers, the central construct of self-theory counseling is the concept of self, or the self as a perceived object in a phenomenal field. He defines the self-concept as follows:

> The self-concept, or self-structure, may be thought of as an organized configuration of perceptions of the self which are admissible to awareness. It is composed of such elements as the perceptions of one's characteristics and abilities; the precepts and concepts of the self in relation to others and the environment; the value qualities which are perceived as associated with experiences and objects; and goals and ideals which are perceived as having positive and negative valence.[34]

A key concept in self theory is that all individuals strive for enhancement of self by moving in the direction of wholeness, integration, completeness, autonomy. The individual's capacities to solve his problems are taken for granted; the counselor, by his attitudes and techniques, helps the client to free these capacities. Rogers postulates that "self-actualization" tendencies are biologically determined, but that the direction of the growth potential is culturally determined by parents, teachers, peers and other significant individuals. Growth forces sometimes become distorted in the developmental process when the individual denies or rejects perceptions that conflict with his self-concept.

Another major hypothesis of self theory is that reality is that which the individual perceives. Events are significant only insofar as he experiences them as meaningful. Counselors understand the individual by inferring his phenomenological field from his behavior. The counselor must be able to integrate himself with the counselee and to learn how the individual views himself and his world. Rogers presents the major propositions of self theory counseling in a series of nineteen statements.[35]

Self-theory counseling has as its focus the experiencing individual. Change in behavior comes through releasing the individual's potentiality to evaluate his experiences, permitting him to clarify and gain insight into his feelings, which will presumably lead to positive planning and growth. Through

[34] Carl R. Rogers, *Client-Centered Therapy*, p. 136.

[35] *Ibid.*, pp. 483–524.

acceptance of the individual, the counselor enables him to express, examine, and incorporate previously consistent and inconsistent experiences into his self-concept. This leads the individual to accept others and to move toward becoming a more fully functioning individual.

McDaniel and Shaftel have cited three major contributions of client-centered counseling, which are summarized here:

1. The concept of "acceptance" has been clarified and has been given substance and meaning.
2. Clear expression has been given to the meaning of learning in the counseling process. Learning is a product of the relationship and of the client's development during the course of counseling.
3. The non-directive counseling group deserves much credit for initiating evaluation of counseling and suggesting research methodology of the dynamic nature of counseling.[36]

Behavioral Theories

The behavioral and learning theories of counseling are essentially synonymous. Behavioral theories stem from behavioristic psychology with its concomitant emphasis on learned behavior. Most of the basic research in behavioral theory derives from the efforts of experimental psychologists. The phenomenon of learning has long interested psychologists. Although he was preceded by many who were investigating the general problems of learning, J. B. Watson is generally recognized as the father of behavioristic psychology. A basic contention of behaviorism is that only objectively observable behavior can be the data of science. This view excludes virtually all hypothetical constructs such as those found in self theory and in Freudian theory.

Wide divergences exist in the specifics of behavioral theory. However, fundamental agreement exists regarding the fact that most human behavior is learned. If such is the case, behavior is modifiable by manipulation and creation of learning conditions. Basically the counseling process becomes the judicious and expert arrangement of learning or relearning experiences.

For a more complete description of the current status of behavioral theory applied to counseling, see Goodstein[37] and Krumboltz and Thoresen.[38]

THE NATURE OF COUNSELING

For the unsophisticated, counseling may seem no different from any conversation between two people. For graduate students preparing to become

[36] Henry B. McDaniel and G. A. Shaftel, *Guidance in the Modern School* (New York: Holt, Rinehart & Winston, Inc., 1956), pp. 128–129.

[37] Leonard D. Goodstein, "Behavior Theoretical Views of Counseling," in Buford Steffire (ed.), *Theories of Counseling* (New York: McGraw-Hill Book Co., Inc., 1965), pp. 140–192.

[38] John D. Krumboltz and Carl E. Thoresen, *Behavioral Counseling* (New York: Holt, Rinehart & Winston, 1969), 515 pp.

counselors, it may appear to be a mysteriously complex endeavor. In the past, researchers have given a great deal of attention to the nature of counseling—earlier, in the form of analyzing the content of counseling interviews, and more recently, in the form of investigating counseling as a process.

General Characteristics

Ford and Urban cite four general characteristics of psychotherapy. These four major elements also appropriately describe the nature of counseling:

1. Counseling involves two people in interaction, a generic term for the exchange of meanings between people which includes the direct communication of talking and listening as well as gestures, glances, nods or shakes of the head, frowns and other nonverbal features by which meaning is transmitted from one person to another.

   The interaction is highly confidential, and since the counselee discusses himself in an intimate fashion, it is highly private and unobserved by others.
2. The mode of interaction is usually limited to the verbal realm, i.e., the counselor and counselee talk with one another. The counselee talks about himself, his thoughts, feelings, and actions. He describes events in his life and the way he responds to these events. The counselor listens and responds in some fashion to what the counselee says to provoke further responses. The two think, talk, and share their ideas.
3. The interaction is relatively prolonged since alteration of behavior takes time. In contrast to a brief conversation with a friend in which distortions or unconscious desires are usually maintained and usually only temporary relief is gained, counseling has as its goal the change of behavior. It is assumed that through the counseling interaction the counselee will in time revise his distortions and alter his behavior.
4. The purpose of the relationship is change in the behavior of the counselee. The counselor focuses the interaction upon the counselee. The counselee need not be concerned about the happiness of the counselor but must devote his energies to changing himself.[39]

Ford and Urban's four major points highlight the fact that counseling is a collaborative relationship which permits the counselee to freely express and explore himself and the issues which are of concern to him. Unless he can bring himself to do this, there is little probability that he will achieve the goals he seeks. Counseling is an intimate, trusting relationship. Dinkmeyer cites four phases of counseling—the relationship, investigation of dynamics, interpretation, and reorientation—which are summarized here:

1. The *relationship* sought is a cooperative one. Counselor and client establish common goals and common purposes. The relationship implies collaboration.

[39] Abstracted from Donald H. Ford and Hugh B. Urban, *Systems of Psychotherapy* (New York: John Wiley & Sons, Inc., 1963), pp. 16–17.

2. An *investigation* is conducted to explore the current life situation as it is viewed by the counselee. The counselor investigates the client's complaints, problems and symptoms.
3. The counselor's *interpretations* put an emphasis on goals. Interpretations confront the client not only with his feelings, but with the purpose of these feelings. The individual's purposes, intentions, and private logic are pointed out.
4. A *reorientation* phase takes place in which the client gives up his mistaken concepts and beliefs in favor of more accurate ones.[40]

Patterson approached a description of the nature of counseling by first describing what it was not. Among those things excluded by Patterson were:

1. Giving information, though information may be given in counseling.
2. Giving advice, suggestions or recommendations (advice should be recognized as such and not camouflaged as counseling).
3. Influencing attitudes, beliefs or behavior by means of persuasion, leading or convincing, no matter how directly, subtly or painlessly.
4. Influencing behavior by admonishing, warning, threatening or compelling with or without the use of physical force or coercion (discipline is not counseling).
5. Selection for and/or assignment of individuals to various jobs or activities (personnel work is not counseling).
6. Interviewing (while interviewing is involved, it is not synonymous with counseling).

The nature of counseling, according to Patterson, is to be found in the following characteristics:

1. Counseling is concerned with influencing voluntary behavior change on the part of the client (client wants to change and seeks counselor's help to change).
2. The purpose of counseling is to provide conditions which facilitate voluntary change (conditions such as the individual's right to make choices, to be independent and autonomous).
3. As in all relationships, limits are imposed upon the counselee (limits are determined by counseling goals which in turn are influenced by the counselor's values and philosophy).
4. Conditions facilitating behavioral change are provided through interviews (not all interviewing is counseling but counseling always involves interviewing).
5. Listening is present in counseling but not all listening is counseling.
6. The counselor understands his client.
7. Counseling is conducted in privacy and the discussion is confidential.
8. The client has a psychological problem and the counselor is skilled in working with clients who have psychological problems.[41]

[40] Don Dinkmeyer, "Conceptual Foundations of Counseling: Adlerian Theory and Practice," *The School Counselor* Vol. 11 (March 1964), pp. 174–178.

[41] C. H. Patterson (ed.), *The Counselor in the School* (New York: McGraw-Hill Book Company, 1967), pp. 219–227.

The Counselor's Attitudes and Skills

How the counselor reacts to a counselee and how he communicates these feelings is important in counseling. Pupils come to the counselor for help and understanding. They bring to the counselor confused feelings, ideas, fears, and hopes with which they are struggling. The counselor's attitudes toward them determine in large measure the extent to which they will attempt to cope constructively with their problems and undertake positive actions. If the counselor demonstrates a genuine acceptance of the counselee, he will feel, as Rogers puts it, that he is *received*.

Fundamentally, acceptance means that the counselor is willing to permit the individual to be himself. He does not explicitly or implicitly hold forth conditions or qualifications that the counselee must meet to gain the counselor's respect. This nonjudgmental role permits the counselee to reveal himself so that he can obtain a true look at himself. Brammer and Shostrom cite four factors that are basic to acceptance: (1) acceptance is based on the idea that the individual has *infinite worth and dignity,* (2) it is the person's right to make his own decisions, (3) the client has the potential to choose wisely and to live a full, self-directed, socially useful life, (4) each person is responsible for his own life.[42]

Understanding marks the counselor's behavior toward the counselee. Understanding means that the counselor grasps clearly and completely, intellectually and emotionally, what the individual is attempting to convey. It is a sharing process in which the counselor obtains from the counselee's expressions the sense of meaning which he communicates. The counselee's words do not always convey clearly his meanings. Meanings are sometimes hidden, either intentionally or unintentionally, and it is the counselor's responsibility to understand the feelings and ideas beneath the surface of the words. Responding to the counselee with empathy is fundamental to understanding.

Communication is the main skill a counselor must develop to facilitate the counseling relationship. He must not only understand what the counselee is expressing but also be able to communicate this understanding to the individual. The counselor's communication techniques are selected to respond to the counselee's attitudes and internal frame of reference, which means that the counselor thinks *with* rather than *for* or *about* the counselee. The counselor's communication skills—reflection of feeling, silence, leads, and reassurance—help the individual discover for himself the various aspects of his problem and facilitate the assumption of responsibility by the counselee for his own decisions. His techniques help the counselee recall relevant aspects of his problem and open up new avenues to explore.

Sensitivity is often cited as a trait or skill necessarily possessed by counselors. It is often defined as the capacity to be aware of what is happening in the counseling process from the client's verbal and nonverbal behavior. The sensitive counselor perceives, responds to, and communicates the emotional

---

[42] Lawrence M. Brammer and Everett L. Shostrom, *Therapeutic Psychology,* 2nd Ed. (Englewood Cliffs, N.J.: Prentice-Hall, Inc., 1968), p. 175.

tones, the moods, and the conflicts of the counselee. He perceives and responds not just to the counselee's verbal content but to his underlying feelings and attitudes.

O'Hern and Arbuckle,[43] using a tape consisting of thirty different role-played client problems and counselor responses, sought to determine if age, education, intelligence, personal security, occupation, religion, sex and other variables influenced one's measured degree of sensitivity. Of these variables, only religion was significantly related to measured sensitivity. Students (N = 5) who identified themselves as Jewish or undeclared as to religion scored higher than Catholics or Protestants on the sensitivity scale.

Rogers has postulated six conditions that are necessary and sufficient to establish and maintain an effective counseling relationship:

1. Two persons are in psychological contact.
2. The first, whom we shall term the client, is in a state of incongruence, being vulnerable or anxious.
3. The second person, whom we shall term the therapist, is congruent or integrated in the relationship.
4. The therapist experiences unconditional positive regard for the client.
5. The therapist experiences an empathic understanding of the client's internal frame of reference and endeavors to communicate this experience to the client.
6. The communication to the client of the therapist's empathic understanding and unconditional positive regard is to a minimal degree achieved.[44]

Rogers' conditions emphasize the importance of sensitively and accurately understanding the counselee. The six conditions cited place in bold relief the fact that the counselor must empathically know the counselee's being and respond in a manner to communicate this understanding. The six conditions stress the importance of nonpossessive warmth and acceptance in the counseling relationship.

Truax and Carkhuff[45] have also stated that an essential condition in counseling is that of concreteness or specificity of the counselor's responses. In an analysis of sixteen different counseling variables, concreteness or specificity of counselor expression was the variable they found most highly related to criteria measures of therapeutic progress. Truax and Carkhuff cite three important functions served by concreteness:

. . . first, by ensuring that the therapist response does not become abstract and intellectual, and thus, more emotionally removed from the patient's feelings and experiences; secondly, by forcing the therapist to be more precisely

[43] Jane S. O'Hern and Dugald S. Arbuckle, "Sensitivity: A Measurable Concept?" *Personnel and Guidance Journal* Vol. 42 (February 1964), pp. 572–576.

[44] Carl R. Rogers, "The Necessary and Sufficient Conditions of Therapeutic Personality Change," *Journal of Consulting Psychology* Vol. 21 (April 1957), pp. 95–103.

[45] Charles B. Truax and Robert R. Carkhuff, "The Old and the New: Theory and Research in Counseling and Psychotherapy," *Personnel and Guidance Journal* Vol. 42 (May 1964), pp. 860–866.

accurate in his understanding of the client (thus even small misunderstand-ings become quite clear when the feelings and experiences are stated in specific terms and corrections can be immediately made); and thirdly, the client is directly influenced to attend with specificity to problem areas and emotional conflicts.[46]

Truax and Carkhuff emphasize that the counselor's verbal behavior is aimed at encouraging a language that is clear, relevant, and valid. If the coun-selor's responses impede the progress of communication or distort reality more for the counselee, his problems will be increased rather than de-creased.

Counselee Responsibility

It is hoped that the preceding comments do not convey the impression that a counselee need only bring himself physically to the counselor's office for relief to occur. The counselee has responsibilities in the counseling rela-tionship. Most of all, he has to be himself and to accept his past and an-ticipated behavior. Effective counseling does not nurture counselee depen-dence upon the counselor to solve his problems or make his decisions for him. Roskens has stated that:

> Some counselors have apparently been seduced into the belief that respon-sibility for alleviating the problems of school children is primarily theirs. Counselors are sometimes overheard to remark, "Oh, if I just had the time, I could reduce the number of 'problems' in this school." Again, the impli-cation that the client bears little responsibility for improving the climate should be noted.[47]

Privacy and Confidentiality

The necessity for confidentiality in the counseling relationship was im-plied in the discussion on the characteristics of the counseling relationship. Because of its importance, a few more brief words need to be said. A coun-seling relationship requires privacy—both auditory and visual—and con-fidentiality, because of the self-revealing and intimate experiences related by the counselee to the counselor. Unless the counselee trusts the coun-selor's integrity in the relationship, he will present nothing more than su-perficial problems to him.

Both the American Personnel and Guidance Association and the Amer-ican Psychological Association have adopted codes of ethics which govern the ethical responsibilities of their members. These codes point out that personal material imparted in counseling is an entrusted communication and that the nature of the counseling relationship imposes an obligation of

[46] *Ibid.*, p. 863.

[47] Ronald W. Roskens, "Memorandum to Counselors: 'Pry Loose Old Walls,' " *The School Counselor*, Vol. 11 (December 1963), p. 82.

confidentiality. At the same time, it is recognized that there are limits to the confidentiality of the relationship since the counselor also owes allegiance to the institution that employs him as well as to society at large. The right to hold communications privileged is not absolute for the school counselor and the limits of confidentiality he can give are influenced by factors such as the kind of material involved, the rights of parents to certain information, and the like. Schneiders has cited seven principles which apply to the limits of confidentiality:

1. The obligation of confidentiality is relative rather than absolute since there are conditions which can alter it.
2. Confidentiality depends on the nature of the material so that material which is already public or can easily become so is not bound by confidentiality in the same way as is the entrusted secret.
3. Material that is harmless does not bind the counselor to confidentiality.
4. The material that is necessary for a counselor or an agency to function effectively is often released from the bonds of confidentiality.
5. Confidentiality is often conditioned by the intrinsic rights of the counselee to his integrity and reputation, to the secret, and to resist unjust aggression. Such rights can be protected by the counselor even against the law.
6. Confidentiality is limited also by the rights of the counselor to preserve his own reputation and integrity, to resist harm or aggression, and to preserve privileged communication.
7. Confidentiality is determined and limited by the rights of an innocent third party and by the rights of the community.[48]

Matters of confidentiality and of counselor ethics in general are extremely complex and frequently can only be resolved in reference to the unique circumstances of the specific situation. All counselors should be thoroughly familiar with the ethical codes available as guides to their professional conduct. Sources for both the American Personnel and Guidance Association's and the American Psychological Association's codes of ethics can be found in the selected references at the end of this chapter.

INITIAL INTERVIEWING GUIDELINES

Although counseling is conducted in an interview situation, most counselors rightly believe that the word "interview" does not convey accurately and completely all that is counseling. Most counselors are quick to point out that interviewing implies interrogation to gain information while counseling obviously involves far more than the collection of information by one individual from another.

More counselors would agree that the initial contact between counselor and student might, in many cases, be labeled as an interview since often its purpose is to obtain background information. Such counselors regard this

[48] Abstracted from Alexander A. Schneiders, "The Limits of Confidentiality," *Personnel and Guidance Journal* Vol. 42 (November 1963), pp. 252–254.

initial interview as a sensitive inquiry directed toward learning more about the pupil and enabling him to unfold personal meanings related to his problems and goals. Viewing the initial contact as a sensitive inquiry to discover what he thinks, what he wants to do, and what he considers his problems to be means that the counselee is given an opportunity to make explicit his view of himself and his life. Tyler states that initial interviews have three objectives: (1) getting a sound counseling relationship started, (2) opening up the psychological realms of feeling and attitude within the person, and (3) clarifying the structure of the helping process.[49] Some guidelines for conducting interviews with students are presented below.

1. *Establish rapport with the student.* Rapport refers to a condition of mutual understanding, respect, and sustained interest between individuals. An expenditure of some time is necessary so that feelings of ease, confidence, and freedom may be developed between strangers. Rapport is generated by the counselor's conscious acts which enable the student to feel comfortable, and rapport is facilitated by the physical setting in which the interview takes place. Rapport is not something which, once established, can be forgotten about, nor is it turned off and on. It is a quality that is characterized by responsiveness to another and constant consideration of his attitudes and feelings. It is a quality that is essential to a successful initial interview and indispensable to the success of future interviews.

   Rapport is generated by the smoothness (lack of awkwardness, bumbling) with which the counselor opens and conducts the interview. Most students (and counselors) approach their first interview with anxiety and apprehension. Though obviously, the student is there to obtain help, some reluctance to begin is experienced. Recognizing this, the counselor may open the conversation by focusing upon some neutral topic or event known to both to reduce restraint. However, artful judgment based upon cues received from the student is required in any opening statement, since trite conversational leads may result in an increase of strained feelings.

   When a pupil comes to the counselor for help, the counselor may assume that the pupil recognizes he needs help, that he wants to talk about his needs, and that he is motivated to do something about his problems. Other pupils seek the counselor's assistance on the advice and urging of teachers, parents, or friends. Others are called in by the counselor. The opening conversation should take but a very few minutes and focus should be given to the reason for the interview. The counselor might comment "Would you like to tell me what brings you here?" or "What would you like to talk about?" or "I've asked you to come in because I want to discuss. . . ." A natural straightforward tactful approach leads to communication and encourages communality of interest. Versatility, flexibility, and relatability are all essential factors in establishing rapport.

---

[49] Leona E. Tyler, *Work of the Counselor*, p. 61.

2. *Provide some structure.* Since many students will not know what part they are to play in the interview, the counselor should explain very early in the interview the nature of the relationship, the role each plays, the sort of help offered, the task ahead, and the amount of time available. This does not mean that the counselor determines the content of the interview, but, because many students have had little or no experience to draw upon for guides, some definition and clarification of the counselor's and student's responsibilities may be in order. Buchheimer and Balogh remind counselors that:

> The structure of every interview originates in and is guided by the particular self-system of the counselee—the way he constructs reality and the perceptions he has of himself. How the counselor proceeds in the interview is determined largely by the clues to the counselee's self-system that he picks up, as well as by the counselor's own self-system.[50]

Providing some structure for the interview means that the counselor must have clearly in mind his concept of counseling. Structure is also provided in the way the counselor addresses himself to the student. Explanations to the student should be made in broad terms. The kinds of explanations given depend on the understandings the counselor has of the student with whom he is dealing.

3. *Help the counselee to talk.* When the student understands and trusts the counselor, he will discuss those issues with which he is ready to cope. However, the counselee may be unable to express himself readily because of the threatening nature of some of his problems. By leads such as reflection of feeling, reflection of content, silence, acceptance, understanding, and encouragement, the counselor encourages the student to state his perceptions of a situation. The counselor needs a broad repertoire of leads, from which he selects those germane to the situation. A factor in helping the counselee to talk is not only the kind of lead the counselor uses but also the spontaneous tone of voice the counselor uses and the tempo at which he speaks. The counselor should be constantly alert to the importance of pacing leads at a rate that will not overwhelm the student but will sustain and facilitate the conversation.

The astute counselor will not use personal experiences and reactions in an attempt to draw out the student. The student is there to discuss his problems and not to listen to another person's experiences, which he usually does not consider to be relevant to his own. Helping the counselee to talk requires that the counselor say something that enables the counselee to penetrate more deeply into the feeling he is trying to express and to examine it more closely. When the counselor follows the student's train of thought and feeling, his remarks will not divert the student, make him resentful or defensive, or close him up, but keep him on the track and encourage the interview to develop.

---

[50] Buchheimer and Balogh, *Counseling Relationship,* p. 4.

4. *Remain alert to counselee feelings and provide for his needs.* Even in information-imparting interviews the counselor must be alert to the emotional reactions and needs of the student. This calls for close and constant attention not only to what the counselee says but also to how he says it and his nonverbal behavior in saying it.

Counselee needs may include the need for information; the need for making choices and decisions; clarification; planning; support; or a combination of these things as well as others. The counselor has to make judgments of what is needed, based upon sensitive listening and observation and connecting perceptions of the counselee and his situation. If the counselee's needs include help that can be given only by other specialists, readiness for and procedures for referral must be initiated. If the student's needs indicate that information is required, the counselor must decide upon an approach and direction for providing it based upon his understanding of what is appropriate. The point here is that the counselor's goal is to help the counselee use the interview to increase his self-development.

5. *Terminate the interview.* As with the opening of the interview, the counselor has a responsibility to bring the interview to a close smoothly and skillfully. Some verbal preparations are usually needed. Brammer and Shostrom point up "capping techniques" for ending discussion units which consist of shutting off the flow of talk or feeling in such a way that the individual does not stop talking altogether or feel rejected:

Capping techniques consist of *changing the subject* to something less intense yet still propelling the interview forward. The subject can be changed back to a topic previously discussed, the original symptoms, or a new and less-loaded topic. Reducing the *length of counselor lead* and the general *pace* of the interview often reduces client's discomfort, resistance, or undesired feelings toward the counselor. The counselor can help to decelerate the pace by *pausing* longer and more frequently.[51]

Reference to time limitations is one way to remind the student that the time is up. A definite stopping point tends to prevent the development of anxiety which might ensue in the face of an uncertain stopping point. When additional interviews are required, the counselor may express his feeling that they are necessary by indicating the hours that are available. By saying, "When would you like to come back?" the counselor indicates the necessity for maintaining future contacts and gracefully terminates the present interview.

Verbally summarizing the interview is another way of reaching closure. The summarization of important factors can be done by the counselor, the student, or both. A frequent practice is to ask the student to tell what he believes has been accomplished in the interview. Arranging for tests or securing informational materials is another approach to termination.

[51] Brammer and Shostrom, *Therapeutic Psychology*, p. 223.

The counselor normally rises with the counselee and walks to the door with him, since this makes it easier for the counselee to leave. The interview should end positively with the student knowing what he is going to do.

The suggestions contained in these five guidelines do not pretend to take into account all the behaviors that take place in an interview. It is hoped that they outline in brief form some of the essentials upon which interviewing is based. Each interview has its own pattern of movement which is mutually influenced by counselor and counselee behavior.

ANNOTATED BIBLIOGRAPHY

BYRNE, RICHARD HILL. *The School Counselor*. Boston: Houghton Mifflin Company, 1963. Chapter 1, pp. 3–35.

This chapter contains a good discussion of counseling goals. Byrne defines counseling goals, evaluates a number of typical goal statements, and proposes an ultimate statement of goals. He also proposes four specifications of maximum counselor function.

KRUMBOLTZ, JOHN D. "Parable of the Good Counselor," and Patterson, C. H., "Comment," *Personnel and Guidance Journal* Vol. 43 (October 1964), pp. 118–126.

These two stimulating papers are examples of the discussion and debate of two differing approaches to counseling. Krumboltz discusses the similarities and differences between the behavioral and client-centered approaches to counseling, and Patterson's comments provide a thought-provoking response. Taken together, the two papers provide a good example of issues pertaining to the means and ends of counseling approaches.

PEREZ, JOSEPH F. *The Initial Counseling Contact*. Guidance Monograph Series. Boston: Houghton Mifflin Company, 1968, 100 pp.

Perez identifies the major dimensions involved in the initial counseling contact. Through analysis, example, and concrete guides, the author stresses the importance of the first session of interaction between counselor and client. This highly readable volume is helpful in understanding what happens in the initial counseling contact.

SELECTED REFERENCES

ALTEKRUSE, MICHAEL K., AND BROWN, DARINE F. "Counseling Behavior Change Through Self-Analysis," *Counselor Education and Supervision* Vol. 8 (Winter 1969), pp. 108–112.

American Personnel and Guidance Association, Committee on Ethics. "Ethical Standards," *Personnel and Guidance Journal* Vol. 40 (October 1961), pp. 206–209.

ARBUCKLE, DUGALD S. "The Alienated Counselor," *Personnel and Guidance Journal* Vol. 48 (September 1969), pp. 18–23.

BARNARD, MARJORIE, CLARK, ROBERT, AND GELATT, H. B. "Students Who See Counselors the Most," *The School Counselor* Vol. 16 (January 1969), pp. 185–190.

BATES, MARILYN, AND JOHNSON, CLARENCE D. "The Existential Counselor At Work," *Personnel and Guidance Journal* Vol. 16 (March 1969), pp. 245–250.

BRAMMER, LAWRENCE M. "The Counselor is a Psychologist," *Personnel and Guidance Journal* Vol. 47 (September 1968), pp. 4–8.

————. "Eclecticism Revisited," *Personnel and Guidance Journal* Vol. 48 (November 1969), pp. 192–200.

BROWN, O. BRUCE, AND CALIA, VINCENT F. "Two Methods of Initiating Student Interviews: Self-Initiated Versus Required," *Journal of Counseling Psychology* Vol. 15 (September 1968), pp. 402–406.

CHENAULT, JOANN. "Counseling Theory: The Problem of Definition," *Personnel and Guidance Journal* Vol. 47, (October 1968), pp. 110–114.

DAUBNER, EDWARD V., AND DAUBNER, EDITH SCHELL. "The Law, the Counselor and Student Records," *Personnel and Guidance Journal* Vol. 48 (February 1970), pp. 423–432.

DE NEVERS, ANN M. "Counseling the Unwed Mother at School," *The School Counselor* Vol. 17 (September 1969), pp. 30–33.

DILLEY, JOSIAH S. "Counselor Actions that Facilitate Decision Making," *The School Counselor* Vol. 15 (March 1968), pp. 247–252.

FOULDS, MELVIN L. "Self-Actualization and the Communication of Facilitative Conditions During Counseling," *Journal of Counseling Psychology* Vol. 16 (March 1969), pp. 132–136.

GLADSTEIN, GERALD A. "Is Empathy Important in Counseling?" *Personnel and Guidance Journal* Vol. 48 (June 1970), pp. 823–827.

GROSS, EDWARD. "Counselors Under Fire: Youth Opportunity Centers," *Personnel and Guidance Journal* Vol. 47 (January 1969), pp. 404–409.

GUTSCH, KENNETH URIAL. "Counseling: The Impact of Ethics," *Counselor Education and Supervision* Vol. 7 (Spring 1968), pp. 239–243.

HIPPLE, JOHN. "Development of a Personal Philosophy and Theory of Counseling," *The School Counselor* Vol. 16 (November 1968), pp. 86–89.

KNOWLES, RICHARD T., AND BARR, DONALD J. "Pseudo-Subjectivity in Counseling," *Personnel and Guidance Journal* Vol. 46 (February 1968), pp. 572–579.

LOEFFLER, DOROTHY. "Counseling and the Psychology of Communication," *Personnel and Guidance Journal* Vol. 48 (April 1970), pp. 629–636.

LOWE, C. MARSHALL. "The Need of Counseling for a Social Frame of Reference," *Journal of Counseling Psychology* Vol. 15 (November 1968), pp. 485–491.

MAYER, ROY G., AND CODY, JOHN J. "Festinger's Theory of Cognitive Dissonance Applied to School Counseling," *The Personnel and Guidance Journal* Vol. 47 (November 1968), pp. 233–239.

SANFORD, ALPHEUS. "Non-Directive Movements in a Directive World," *Personnel and Guidance Journal* Vol. 48 (September 1969), pp. 29–31.

SHAPIRO, JEFFREY G. "Perception of Therapeutic Conditions from Different Vantage Points," *Journal of Counseling Psychology* Vol. 15 (July 1968), pp. 346–350.

SLINGER, GEORGE E. "Values and the Counseling Relationship in the High School," *The Vocational Guidance Quarterly* Vol. 15 (September 1966), pp. 11–17.

STRONG, STANLEY R. "Counseling: An Interpersonal Influence Process," *Journal of Counseling Psychology* Vol. 15 (May 1968), pp. 215–224.

STUBBINS, JOSEPH. "The Politics of Counseling," *Personnel and Guidance Journal* Vol. 48 (April 1970), pp. 611–618.

THORESEN, CARL E. "The Counselor as an Applied Behavioral Scientist," *Personnel and Guidance Journal* Vol. 47 (May 1969), pp. 841–848.

VONTRESS, CLEMMONT E. "Cultural Barriers in the Counseling Relationship," *Personnel and Guidance Journal* Vol. 48 (September 1969), pp. 11–17.

WOODY, ROBERT H. "Preparation in Behavioral Counseling," *Counselor Education and Supervision* Vol. 7 (Summer 1968), pp. 357–362.

8

COUNSELING IN GROUPS

What are the purposes of group counseling?
What basic terms and concepts are employed in group work?
What are the advantages and limitations of group counseling?
What similarities and differences exist between individual and group counseling?
What is the place of group counseling in the guidance program?

PURPOSES OF GROUP COUNSELING

As an adolescent grows, his emotional needs will urge him to seek a variety of social experiences and interests. There is increasing understanding of the psychological significance group membership has for adolescents. Group participation enables adolescents to develop the capacity for mutual interpersonal interaction. Through group counseling experiences pupils can at times assume the role of leader, and at other times revolt against group members without severe guilt feeling being attached to the revolt. Group counseling experience can provide outlets for such needs as status, security, and mature emotional expression. To channel such needs in fruitful social directions is one of the functions of group counseling experiences. For example, Broedel, Ohlsen, Proff, and Southard[1] conducted group counseling with gifted underachieving adolescents in an effort to improve the students' mental health and academic performance. The researchers believed that group counseling would increase their clients' acceptance of themselves and improve their ability to relate to others. Twenty-nine capable but underachieving ninth graders (top 10 percent on the California Test of

[1] John Broedel, *et al.*, "The Effects of Group Counseling on Gifted Underachieving Adolescents," *Journal of Counseling Psychology* Vol. 7 (Fall 1960), pp. 163–170.

Mental Maturity; ninth decile or below in grade point average) were divided into four counseling groups for an eight-week period. Growth was evaluated by grades earned, achievement test scores, responses to a Picture Story Test, and observations made by clients, their parents, and observer teams. Three of the four groups showed significant growth.

The needs of students may be met by various activities; many are common and universal, however. Numerous studies have demonstrated the importance of the satisfaction of these needs for the adjustment and development of the individual. Each student has a basic need to be accepted and to attain the satisfaction and assurance which group membership provides. Every youth has a desire for some assurance that he is like other young people and is accepted by them. It is often not enough for him to know that he belongs to a group such as a family. He wants to make good with his contemporaries. To do so, students have to develop some competency in dealing with and working with others. Such a competency embodies a series of understandings varying from the relatively simple matter of acceptable manners and courtesy to the more complex one of understanding the behavior of others. Asch has pointed up the complexity of understanding group behavior:

> The paramount fact about human interactions is that they are happenings that are psychologically represented in each of the participants. In our relations to an object, perceiving, thinking, and feeling takes place on one side, whereas in a relation between persons these processes take place on both sides and in dependence upon one another. . . . We interact with others, not as the paramecium does by altering the surrounding medium chemically, nor as the ants do by smell, but via emotions and thoughts that are capable of taking into account the emotions and thoughts of others. Such interaction is to social interactions in general as consciousness is to biology in general.[2]

Group counseling appears to develop members' insights into their problems and feelings and helps them to arrive at some understanding of the causes of their problems. Members of counseling groups talk about themselves, the things that disturb them, and what they can do to improve themselves. Effective group counseling helps each person understand why he feels the way he does, learn what information or skills are needed to master his problems, and develop the capacity to act upon his problems.

Cohn and Sniffen used group counseling with eight seventh grade boys who were underachieving and demonstrating acting-out behavior.[3] Their purpose was to learn more about the pupils and to assist them in school adjustment by changing their attitudes. In group counseling the boys had an opportunity to talk about anything they liked in a way they liked so long as they kept in mind the goals of the group. Cohn and Sniffen termed the

[2] S. E. Asch, *Social Psychology* (New York: Prentice-Hall, Inc., 1952), p. 142.

[3] Benjamin Cohn and A. Mead Sniffen, "A School Report on Group Counseling," *The Personnel and Guidance Journal* Vol. 41 (October 1962), pp. 133–138.

project successful in that group members arrived at a more realistic picture of themselves, became more sensitive to others' feelings, and were less critical toward school and authority figures.

Through group counseling, a pupil learns to express himself in actions, feelings, and attitudes. Initially, communication may be between individual group members and the counselor, but the counselor soon shifts this interaction to the other group members. Pupils learn that they may interact and discuss with group members as well as the counselor and that the group will help each member to draw out his feelings. Alternate ways of behaving may be elicited and tried out through the group's discussion.

Mahler states that

> Students who have completed a group counseling experience appear to be able to transfer their learning to subsequent group interaction. In classes they are more likely than before to speak up and to offer their own ideas and beliefs. Moreover, with increased confidence in their own perceptions, they tend to meet the unexpected with a great deal more zest and less fear.[4]

Although group counseling is not a substitute for individual counseling, many counselors have observed that some students respond better in a group of peers than in an individual counseling relationship. Adolescent needs for conformity and acceptance by their peer group, and for the opportunity to share reactions and ideas, to define meaningful life situations, and to gain independence are all met in part through group counseling. Ohlsen suggests that an adolescent benefits particularly from group counseling in that he learns (1) that his peers have problems too; (2) that, despite his faults, which his peers want to help him correct, they accept him; (3) that at least one adult, the counselor, can understand and accept him; (4) that he is, himself, capable of understanding, accepting, and helping his peers; (5) that he can trust others; and (6) that when he can express his own real feelings about himself and others, as well as about what he believes, it helps him to understand and accept himself.[5]

Another purpose accomplished by group counseling is that it enables counselors to establish contacts with students who may need a different kind of help from that available in individual counseling. Group counseling experience may be indicated when the counselee wants to know how others perceive him, how others react to his proposed actions, and when he needs practice in social skills or help in gaining confidence to act with others. Drawing on clinical experience, Mahler[6] set forth eight statements that describe situations in which individual counseling should be utilized and ten statements that suggest the appropriate conditions for group counseling.

[4] Clarence A. Mahler, *Group Counseling in the Schools* (Boston: Houghton Mifflin Company, 1969), p. 15.

[5] Merle M. Ohlsen, *Guidance Services in the Modern School* (New York: Harcourt, Brace & World, Inc., 1964), p. 148.

[6] Mahler, *Group Counseling in the Schools*, pp. 18–19.

Some of his suggestions are summarized here and presented in parallel form:

INDIVIDUAL COUNSELING INDICATED FOR	GROUP COUNSELING INDICATED FOR
1. Crisis situation complicated by a quest for causes and possible solutions	1. Individual who needs to learn to better understand a variety of people and how others perceive things
2. Situation in which confidentiality is needed to protect client and others	2. Individual who needs to learn deeper respect for others, particularly those who are different
3. Interpretation of test data in respect to self-concept	3. Individual who needs to gain social skills (talking and relating to others)
4. Individual who exhibits extreme fear of talking in a group	4. Individual who needs to share with others (need to experience belongingness)
5. Individual who is so grossly ineffective in relating to peers that he may not be accepted by group members	5. Individual who is free to talk about concerns, problems, values
6. Individual whose self-awareness is limited	6. Individual who needs others' reactions to his problems and concerns
7. Situation in which sexual behavior, particularly of a deviant nature, is involved	7. Individual who finds support from peers helpful
8. Individual who has compulsive need for attention and recognition	8. Individual who prefers to involve himself slowly in counseling and who can withdraw if it becomes threatening

The safety and protection inherent in a group may be what is needed to encourage students to risk relating to another and to discuss their concerns mutually.

Group counseling experience frequently leads to initiating individual counseling. Group members who have started the process of self-exploration may desire opportunities to go further in individual counseling. Woal sought to determine whether or not group counseling could be used successfully to help students (1) reduce failures in subject matter (2) improve work habits (3) improve behavior.[7] Six students who were active indi-

---

[7] Theodore Woal, "A Project in Group Counseling in a Junior High School," *Personnel and Guidance Journal* Vol. 42 (February 1964), pp. 611–613.

vidual counseling cases were selected for group counseling. Throughout the twenty-eight-week period, individual counseling was available upon student request. Group meetings were held weekly for a period of forty-five minutes. The words "counseling" and "guidance" were avoided and the name "club" was given to the group. A 75 percent improvement was obtained in subject-matter performance and work habits, with less improvement noted in behavior. Woal concluded that the students realized that (1) they were not alone; (2) they had an opportunity for a sympathetic and understanding hearing; (3) the counselor was always available for help if needed; and (4) each club member, in some way, helped the others.

In short, the most basic purpose of group counseling is that of helping its members to function effectively and to achieve a satisfactory way of life. Group counseling proposes to give individuals opportunities to recognize their needs and to test ways in which they can find satisfaction. Through group counseling students learn that ability to gratify their needs can only come through responsible behavior. Cartwright, in a summary of research on techniques of achieving change in people, has developed eight principles that provide an excellent statement of the purposes of working with groups:

(1) If the group is to be used effectively as a medium of change, those people who are to be changed and those who are to exert influence for change must have a strong sense of belonging to the same group; (2) The more attractive the group is to its members the greater is the influence that the group can exert on its members; (3) In attempts to change attitudes, values, or behavior, the more relevant they are to the . . . group, the greater will be the influence that the group can exert upon them; (4) The greater the prestige of a group member in the eyes of the other members, the greater the influence he can exert; (5) Efforts to change individuals or subparts of a group which if successful, would have the result of making them deviate from the norms of the group, will encounter strong resistance; (6) Strong pressure for changes in the group can be established by creating a shared perception by members of the need for change, thus making the source of pressure for change . . . within the group; (7) Information relating to the need for change, plans for change, and consequences of change must be shared by all relevant people in the group; (8) Changes in one part of a group produce strain in other related parts which can be reduced only by eliminating the change or by bringing about readjustments in the related parts.[8]

TERMINOLOGY OF GROUP WORK

Much confusion presently exists over the precise meaning of such words as "groups," "group dynamics," "group process," "group guidance," "group counseling," "group therapy," "intensive group experiences," and the like.

[8] Dorwin Cartwright, "Achieving Change in People: Some Applications of Group Dynamics Theory," *Human Relations* Vol. 4, No. 4 (1951), pp. 388–391. Reprinted by permission of Tavistock Publications, Ltd., London.

Yet knowledge of the terminology is essential to beginning guidance students; words and labels are very important to insure clarity of communication. Therefore, some of the terminology and primary concepts that are basic to group work will be presented in brief form in this section.

"Group" Defined

The word "group" has many meanings. Webster's *New World Dictionary* cites six definitions ranging from "a number of persons or things gathered together in a recognizable unit" to its use by the U.S. Air Force to denote a unit of four squadrons of the same kind of aircraft. Three common usages of the term as pointed out by Gibb are summarized here:

1. Objects or persons which are, in some sense, together, for example, in a certain place or in the mind of an observer, are frequently said to be grouped or to constitute a group. Such togetherness is an aggregate or a collection and should be differentiated from a group since the units of an aggregate are characterized by complete independence from one another.
2. A group may be defined as a collection of units having qualities in common. Some aggregates may be homogeneous in some respect and through the perception of this homogeneity they will constitute classes, i.e., a pile of magazines. Social group by this concept would be a collection of individuals who are perceived to have common characteristics, i.e., those who earn less than $3500 a year may be said to constitute an economic class. However, members of such groups do not interact, have contact, or proximity.
3. A group characterized by the interaction of its members in such a way that each unit is changed by its group membership is a third type of group. The important point is that the members have psychological relationship to one another.[9]

Gibb's third usage is that with which we are concerned in this chapter, i.e., groups in which the members interact psychologically with purpose in the pursuit of a common goal. Loeser has cited the characteristics of a group as including (1) dynamic interaction among members; (2) a common goal; (3) a relationship between size and function; (4) volition and consent; and (5) a capacity for self-direction.[10] In summary, a collection of individuals becomes a group when there is reciprocity between and among the members to accomplish a goal and an acceptance of responsibility for each other.

[9] Cecil A. Gibb, "Leadership," Chapter 24 in Gardner Lindzey (ed.), *Handbook of Social Psychology,* Vol. 2 (Reading, Mass.: Addison-Wesley Publishing Company, Inc., 1954), as quoted in C. Gratton Kemp (ed.), *Perspectives on the Group Process: A Foundation for Counseling with Groups,* 2nd Ed. (Boston: Houghton Mifflin Company, 1970), pp. 24–25.

[10] Lewis H. Loeser, "Some Aspects of Group Dynamics," *International Journal of Group Psychotherapy* Vol. 7 (January 1957), pp. 5–19.

Types of Social Groups

That man's life is to a large extent a group life is well recognized. Man not only lives in and creates groups, he develops verbal symbols to identify them. Groups may be classified from a variety of viewpoints: size, nature of social interaction, intimacy of contact among members, range of group interests, duration of interests, organization, or some combination of these. Attention here will be given four types of social groups.

PRIMARY VERSUS SECONDARY GROUPS

Primary groups are those in which the members meet "face to face" for companionship, mutual aid, and the resolution of questions that confront them. Examples of primary groups include the family, the play group, the partnership, and the study group. Such groups are called primary because they are first in time and importance. They are characterized by (1) small size; (2) similarity of members' background; (3) limited self-interest; and (4) intensity of shared interest. Secondary groups are those in which the members are not as intimate and contact is more casual. Examples include large lecture groups or committees.

IN-GROUP VERSUS OUT-GROUP

The group with which the individual identifies, by virtue of his awareness or "consciousness of kind," are his "in-groups"—his family, his sex, his club, his occupation, his religion. The individual's expression of subjective attitudes frequently reveal his in-group memberships. These memberships, in turn, are often related to particular social circumstances.

It follows that the out-group is defined by the individual with relation to the in-group, usually by the expression of contrast between "we" and "they," or "other." Out-group attitudes are marked by expressions of difference, and sometimes, by a varied degree of antagonism, prejudice, hatred or apathy.

PSYCHE- VERSUS SOCIO-GROUPS

Jennings[11] has made the following distinction between psyche- and socio-groups: *Psyche-groups* (e.g., boys' gang, girls' clique) are characterized by informal structure, few regulations, voluntary membership, homogeneity of members' ages and no visualized goal. Their purposes are to satisfy the members' emotional needs. *Socio-groups* (e.g., school dropout committee) are characterized by visualized goals, heterogeneity in age, and status of members; and they are problem-solving or task oriented.

CLOSED VERSUS CONTINUOUS GROUPS

Guidance groups may be *closed* or *continuous*. The closed group consists of only those who were present when the group was started; no one

[11] H. H. Jennings, *Leadership and Isolation,* 2nd Ed. (New York: Longmans, Green & Company, 1950), pp. 278–279.

else may join. This is the most common type. The continuous group, on the other hand, is one that others may join at any stage of progression. This often creates problems of communication, acceptance, and the attainment of readiness by new group members.

Group Dynamics

"Group dynamics" is a term which refers to the interacting forces within groups as they organize and operate to achieve their objectives. Herrold has suggested that the term be reserved to designate processes used by groups organized for problem-solving or action purposes.[12] In such groups the needs of individuals become subservient to the goals of the group. Jenkins uses the term "group dynamics" to indicate group process and group roles.[13] A number of individuals have developed techniques that facilitate group control and group problem solving. One such technique employed by specialists in group dynamics is the utilization of an observer whose task is to keep a running account of the group meeting, in an effort to discover why things go well or why they bog down. Cartwright and Zander state:

> What, then, is group dynamics? The phrase has gained popular familiarity since World War II but, unfortunately, with its increasing circulation, its meaning has become imprecise. According to one rather frequent usage, group dynamics refers to a sort of political ideology concerning the ways in which groups should be organized and managed. This ideology emphasizes the importance of democratic leadership, the participation of members in decisions, and the gains both to society and to individuals to be obtained through cooperative activities in groups. The critics of this view have sometimes caricatured it as making "togetherness" the supreme virtue, advocating that everything be done jointly in groups which have and need no leader because everyone participates fully and equally. A second popular usage of the term group dynamics has it refer to a set of techniques, such as role playing, buzz-sessions, observation and feedback of group process, and group decision, which have been employed widely during the past decade or two in training programs designed to improve skill in human relations and in the management of conferences and committees. These techniques have been identified most closely with the National Training Laboratories whose annual training programs at Bethel, Maine, have become widely known. According to the third usage of the term, group dynamics, it refers to a field of inquiry dedicated to achieving knowledge about the nature of groups, the laws of their development, and their interrelations with individuals, other groups, and larger institutions.[14]

[12] Kenneth F. Herrold, "Evaluation and Research in Group Dynamics," *Educational and Psychological Measurement* Vol. 10 (Autumn 1950), Part II, pp. 492–504.
[13] David H. Jenkins, "What is Group Dynamics?" *Adult Education Journal* Vol. 9, No. 2 (April 1950), pp. 54–60.
[14] Dorwin Cartwright and Alvin Zander, *Group Dynamics,* 3rd Ed. (Evanston, Ill.: Harper & Row, 1968), p. 4.

Group Process

Process was described in Chapter 2 as continuous, dynamic, and directional in movement. Group process refers to two or more people working together on some need or problem toward some end or goal. Group process refers to the actions and interactions used by a group to develop and maintain its identity as a group and its effects upon individuals who compose the group. Hopkins points out that:

> In social behavior the movement is largely from individual to individual, whereas in group behavior there is a tangible qualitative interdependence of each upon others which operates in three ways: individual to individual, individual to whole, and whole to individual. . . .
>
> This quality in the relationship of individuals is the group and the way they work together to produce it is the process. . . . Group process is the way people work together to release an emergent quality, called psychological climate, group morale, esprit de corps, or cooperative units, through which each discovers and develops his inner capacities, realizes better the nature of his self, releases more of his past experience, and learns how to create this emergent quality in all life situations.[15]

Group Guidance

The term "group guidance" is most often used to refer to any part of a guidance program which is conducted with groups of students rather than between an individual pupil and counselor. Lifton places the emphasis in group guidance on the imparting of information,[16] while Caldwell states that "It should also be said at the outset that the common idea of 'group guidance' as an information-giving device is inappropriate to the concept presented here."[17] Caldwell also states that "Group guidance activities are directed, to a large degree, to creating an appropriate setting for subsequent counseling and other teacher relationships with individual students."[18]

Bennett has cited seven common misconceptions about group guidance:

1. That group guidance, group process, and group dynamics are identical.
2. That the major purpose of group guidance is personal development.
3. That group guidance is primarily an information service.
4. That group guidance or counseling may be substituted for individual counseling.

[15] L. Thomas Hopkins, *The Emerging Self in School and Home* (New York: Harper & Brothers, 1954), as quoted in C. Gratton Kemp (ed.), *Perspectives on the Group Process: A Foundation for Counseling with Groups,* 2nd Ed. (Boston: Houghton Mifflin Company, 1970), p. 93.

[16] Walter M. Lifton, *Working With Groups,* 2nd Ed. (New York: John Wiley & Sons, Inc., 1966), pp. 12–18.

[17] Edson Caldwell, *Group Techniques for the Classroom Teacher* (Chicago: Science Research Associates, Inc., 1960), p. 10.

[18] *Ibid.*

5. That group counseling is group therapy.
6. That any member of the school staff can carry on the group guidance function.
7. That group guidance may stifle individuality and creativity.[19]

Bennett has also suggested four purposes of group guidance:

1. To provide opportunities for learning essential for self-direction with respect to educational, vocational, and personal-social aspects of life through:
   a. Assistance in orientation in new school situations and in the best use of school opportunities.
   b. Group study of problems of interpersonal relationships and assistance in choice of group experiences in the school life that may modify both individual and group behavior in socially acceptable ways.
   c. Group study of problems of growing up, establishing adult adjustments, and applying mental hygiene in living.
   d. Group study and application of sound methods of self-appraisal of attitudes, interests, abilities, personality and character trends and traits, and personal-social adjustments.
   e. Group study and application of efficient methods in learning.
   f. Group study about occupational life and problems of occupational adjustment and progress.
   g. Assistance through groups in learning how to project suitable, long-range vocational plans.
   h. Assistance through groups in learning how to project suitable, long-range educational plans.
   i. Assistance in the development of discerning standards of value for making choices of experiences in various areas of living, and the developing of a growing philosophy of life.
2. To provide opportunity for the therapeutic effects of group procedures through:
   a. The perspectives gained from the study of common human problems.
   b. The release of emotional tensions, increased insight into personality dynamics, and creative redirection of energy through group study of these common human problems in a permissive atmosphere.
3. To achieve some of the objectives of guidance more economically—and some more effectively—than would be possible in a completely individualized approach.
4. To implement individual counseling and render it more effective through background study of common aspects of problems and the reduction or elimination of many emotional barriers to the discussion of unique aspects of common human problems.[20]

The distinction between group guidance and group instruction is not always clearcut, nor are the terms used with precision. The thread of distinction that runs through the preceding comments by Bennett regard-

[19] Margaret E. Bennett, *Guidance and Counseling in Groups* (New York: McGraw-Hill Book Co., Inc., 1963), pp. 20–22.

[20] *Ibid.,* p. 8–9. From *Guidance and Counseling in Groups* by Margaret E. Bennett. Copyright 1963. McGraw-Hill Book Co. Used by permission.

ing the purposes of group guidance appears to be related to leadership roles. When the major responsibility for group activities is focused on the adult leader ("teacher") the term "group instruction" seems appropriate. When the focus shifts to the members of the group the term group guidance is applicable.

Group Counseling

Group counseling is a process in which one counselor is involved in a relationship with a number of counselees at the same time. The number of counselees may vary. Six has been recommended by many as the optimum number, while others generally recommend a range of from four to eight members. Gazda, Duncan, and Meadows define group counseling as ". . . a dynamic, interpersonal process focusing on conscious thought and behavior and involving the therapy functions of permissiveness, orientation to reality, catharsis, and mutual trust, caring, understanding, acceptance, and support."[21]

Combs, Cohn, Gibian and Sniffen have also defined group counseling as a social process:

> The persons involved approach problems at their own speed within the safety of a social setting. Here they may explore problems that are important to them within the security of a group of peers who share their problems and with whom they identify. Moreover, they may do this without fear of external direction or the pressure of adult coercion. The adult whom they experience within the group is an adult in a new role—the helpful, non-judgmental, non-threatening adult.[22]

Some have used the term "multiple counseling" rather than group counseling. Boy, Isaksen, and Pine say that multiple counseling ". . . is psychologically a deep relationship between the counselor and the group to the end that group members have the opportunity to explore the causal factors that have influenced the growth of their particular problems."[23] Others have used the words "multiple counseling" to refer to the fact that two or more counselors were used with two or more counselees.

FAMILY GROUP CONSULTATION

The staff of the Division of Continuing Education of the Oregon State System of Higher Education have developed a group counseling process

---

[21] G. M. Gazda, J. A. Duncan, and M. E. Meadows, "Group Counseling and Group Procedure—Report of a Survey," *Counselor Education and Supervision* Vol. 6 (Summer 1967), p. 306.

[22] Charles F. Combs, Benjamin Cohn, Edward J. Gibian, and A. Mead Sniffen, "Group Counseling: Applying the Technique," *The School Counselor* Vol. 11 (October 1963), p. 12.

[23] Angelo V. Boy, Henry L. Isaksen, and Gerald J. Pine, "Multiple Counseling: A Catalyst for Individual Counseling," *The School Counselor* Vol. 11 (October 1963), p. 8.

they call family group consultation.[24] Such a process, reports Grenfell, was initiated to help overcome "the poverty of understanding" which appears in families having some degree of disorganization. Grenfell reports five considerations with which family group consultation is concerned:

1. It is necessary to improve communication and interaction within the family organization.
2. It is necessary to reduce the individual's distortion within situational events.
3. It is necessary to help individuals develop a sense of awareness of their personal impact upon others and the reactions created.
4. It is necessary to clarify for each individual whether the role(s) he plays meets family expectations.
5. It is necessary to determine the effect of individual role expectations upon family interaction.[25]

T Groups

The National Training Laboratories, under the leadership of Kurt Lewin, Ronald Lippitt and Kenneth Benne, originated T Groups (T = training) in 1946. Other terms commonly used as synonyms include "sensitivity training" and "basic encounter" groups. The major purposes of such groups are (1) to facilitate behavioral changes, (2) to enhance the individual's skills in interpersonal relationships, and (3) to develop individuals equipped to provide leadership in changing organizations. The programs conducted by the National Training Laboratories are in constant transition in respect to objectives, designs and methods. Participants in most such group processes are involved in experiences designed so that they learn from their own and others' behaviors. They develop skills of giving and receiving help.

Marathon Groups

Groups which meet in continuous session for longer than two hours are often referred to as marathon groups. Meeting for several continuous hours in saturation sessions, members explore their views of themselves and others, their relationships with significant others, typical ways of reacting to threat, disagreement and prejudice. Presumably, the uninterrupted process lowers the individual's defense mechanisms and enables him to interact truthfully, authentically and transparently. By confronting and challenging, yet accepting each other, members strive to develop open, authentic, self-responsible behavior.

[24] Daniel W. Fullmer and Harold W. Bernard, *Counseling: Content and Process* (Chicago: Science Research Associates, Inc. 1964), pp. 207–226.

[25] John E. Grenfell, "Family Group Consultation: A Description," paper delivered to the American Personnel and Guidance Association in convention, San Francisco, March 24, 1964.

Group Therapy

Group therapy is usually defined as the application of therapeutic principles to two or more individuals simultaneously to clarify their psychological conflicts so that they may live normally. The word "therapy" indicates that a psychiatrist or a clinical psychologist serves as a group leader. Bion believes that group therapy has two meanings: "It can refer to the treatment of a number of individuals assembled for special therapeutic sessions or it can refer to a planned endeavor to develop in a group the forces that lead to smoothly running cooperative activity."[26] As in the case of the distinctions between individual counseling and therapy, group therapy is usually reserved for the more seriously disturbed and treats deeper personality problems. Slavson is reputed to be responsible for introducing the term "group therapy" to meet criticisms regarding the use of the term "group psychotherapy" by persons other than psychiatrists or clinical psychologists.[27] The term "therapy," however, has become practically synonymous with psychotherapy in professional literature.

Hinckley and Hermann identify group therapy by four characteristics: (1) the therapeutic aim of the group, with lack of goal; (2) the alleviation of emotional tensions by sharing experiences—a process involving catharsis, the partial reliving of old experiences, and increasing of self-awareness; (3) the permissive and supportive role of the therapist; and (4) the direct interest in and attack on personal problems in order to foster attitudinal modifications.[28]

Bennett prefers that the term "therapeutic group work" be used in a guidance program so that group therapy may be reserved to those who are trained, licensed, or certified to serve those who are seriously handicapped.[29] Certainly, school guidance personnel must be ever alert in recognizing their limits in dealing with serious maladjustments through group work or individual work.

SPECIAL THERAPY GROUPS

Mowrer refers to special groups and associations which are inspired and operated largely by laymen, and whose main objective is to provide restorative experiences to their members. Alcoholics Anonymous is an example of some 265 such groups. Mowrer believes such groups came into existence because:

> In short, these groups reflect, first of all, a general loss of confidence in professional "treatment," regardless of whether in an individual or group context. Also they reflect the pervasive failure of existing "natural" groups to

[26] W. R. Bion, *Experiences in Groups* (New York: Basic Books, Inc., 1961), p. 11.

[27] As reported in Margaret E. Bennett, *Guidance and Counseling*, p. 21.

[28] Robert C. Hinckley and Lydia Hermann, *Group Treatment in Psychotherapy* (Minneapolis: University of Minnesota Press, 1952), pp. 19–20.

[29] Bennett, *Guidance and Counseling*, p. 21.

perform the ideological and therapeutic functions which they should have been performing. Thus in "inventing" group therapy for themselves, laymen seem to be creating a new social institution—one might almost say a *new culture*—in which a kind of redemptive concern and competence exist which is not otherwise to be found in our time.[30]

ADVANTAGES AND LIMITATIONS OF GROUP WORK

Values

Several writers, including Bennett,[31] Wright,[32] and Warters,[33] have written of the advantages of group counseling. Combs and his associates, who have had much experience in group counseling at the Board of Cooperative Educational Services, Bedford Hills, N.Y., cite the following five advantages:

1. In dealing with several students simultaneously, it (group counseling) spreads the effect of the counselor and at the same time preserves his effectiveness.
2. It seems to be more readily accepted by students in that, since it occurs within a peer group, it is not as "different" or as threatening to them as individual counseling.
3. It makes effective use of the social setting and peer identification.
4. The adult experienced by students in group counseling is unique in that he is accepting of them and facilitating their experiences, rather than imposing an external judgment. He is a resource, a catalyst, and perhaps a new kind of adult.
5. Often, the establishment of counseling groups within the school may facilitate individual counseling and other new opportunities to meet the needs of the students.[34]

Other values may be briefly cited.

1. Participation in group counseling enables adolescents to develop the capacity for mutual interaction. Through counseling groups, pupils experience relationships with others in life experience. Counseling groups provide outlets for such needs as status, security, and mature emotional expression. Through group counseling experiences, such needs may be channeled in fruitful social directions.

[30] O. Hobart Mowrer, *The New Group Therapy* (Princeton, N.J.: D. Van Nostrand Co., Inc., 1964), p. v.

[31] Bennett, *Guidance and Counseling*, p. 138.

[32] E. Wayne Wright, "Multiple Counseling: Why? When? How?" *Personnel and Guidance Journal* Vol. 37 (April 1959), p. 556.

[33] Jane Warters, *Group Guidance* (New York: McGraw-Hill Book Co., Inc., 1960), pp. 189–192.

[34] Charles F. Combs, *et al.,* "Group Counseling: Applying the Technique," *The School Counselor* Vol. 11 (October 1963), p. 18.

2. Reference is frequently made to the efficiency of group counseling in terms of time and money. A more meaningful criterion for efficiency, however, would be a measure of the extent to which group work achieves its counseling goals.

3. Group counseling has a unique contribution to make in providing realistic and life-like social situations, useful for modifying personal habits, attitudes, and judgments of group members. In a safe, less threatening environment, members can learn new, more flexible, and more satisfying ways of relating to others.

4. Members of counseling groups may accept ideas and suggestions proposed by fellow students which they might reject if proposed by adults. Reinforcement provided by other participants often makes decisions more likely to be viewed as commitments rather than acquiescence to an authority figure.

5. Group counseling may provide situations for more adequate problem-solving activities. In groups, collective judgment can be focused on common problems, critical issues can be examined, opinions and judgments can be compared, and new ideas and information not always available in individual situations can be applied.

6. Students working in counseling groups often become deeply involved in social interaction and less expectant of advice or direction from the counselor. Consequently, the counselor can become both a group member and observer. In addition, his role as counselor to individual members of the group will often be facilitated because of the member's experience with the counselor as a group participant.

Limitations

All methods have limitations, and group counseling is no exception. For example, there are students who may experience great difficulty in becoming functioning members of a group. Such students often need to experience a relationship with one individual before they are able to relate and interact with a group. Other interrelated limitations of group work include:

1. Group pressure may be brought to bear upon an individual to engage in self-disclosure before he is ready to do so. If all but one or two group members have revealed themselves to some degree, those who have not done so often feel pressured (and sometimes are confronted directly with their "holding back" or "lack of trust") to reveal, however reluctantly, something of themselves. While groups often establish "ground rules," and properly so, to guard against this pressure, inevitably the individual begins to experience guilt or to have negative feelings about his inability to confide in group members. If the individual experiences this sequence of events as personal failure little positive gain accrues from group involvement.

2. The individual, as a member of the group, is not the exclusive focus of the counselor's helping efforts. As a result, the individual who needs a more intense one-to-one relationship may not be able to make productive use of the multiple relationships found in group experiences. It is inevitable that the counselor's behavior in the group is diffused among many and that his interactions with specific individuals is diluted.

3. The personal problems of a particular member may become secondary to the more general problems of the group or to those of another member. Sufficient opportunity may not be available to an individual to explore, analyze, or discuss his concerns to the degree that he wishes to do so.

4. While the presence of peers undoubtedly is advantageous for most individuals, it seems reasonable to assume that the reverse is sometimes true. This, in part, may be attributed to the individual's inability to disclose (as was discussed above), or it might be related to the homogeneity of problems peculiar to a given age group which are explored in groups, thus contrasting elements which might expedite discussion are not present. One can only speculate about this "limitation." The resolution of questions concerning this limitation depends upon securing greater knowledge about the dynamics of group work.

While other limitations undoubtedly exist, these represent the objections most frequently cited in the literature by those experienced in group work.

GROUP COUNSELING IN THE GUIDANCE PROGRAM

Group counseling is a rather recently developed helping relationship. It is still vigorous in its growth and development and relatively new in public school guidance programs. Careful appraisal needs to be given to the growing body of data being collected on group counseling. With respect to the mounting evidence, Bennett has noted:

> One would *like* to add that this mounting volume of research and practice in the field of group approaches to guidance is clearly pointing the way to next steps ahead in the program. But when one tries to put all the parts together and see the total picture, the fact becomes evident that we are still on the "growing edge," blazing many new trails, and have not yet reached the stage of laying out a broad highway and putting up the signposts with clear directions to the goals ahead. Many of the paths are merging, not only within the field of education, but with those of other professional fields such as psychology in its many divisions, psychiatry, sociology, and social and religious group work. It is becoming evident through cooperative research and coordinated services among all these fields that each has much to share with the others, and that the advancement of our services to improve human life depends upon this concerted effort.[35]

[35] Bennett, *Guidance and Counseling*, p. 23. From *Guidance and Counseling in Groups* by Margaret E. Bennett. Copyright 1963. McGraw-Hill Book Co. Used by permission.

A few observations follow in regard to the authors' perspective of the place of group counseling in a school's guidance program.

First, group counseling is not viewed as a substitute for individual counseling. Group counseling is but one medium through which behavioral change may occur. Although both group and individual counseling may assist individuals in goal setting, decision-making, and educational-vocational planning, one form does not preclude the necessity for the other. Only those students who have developmental problems amenable to group counseling and who express willingness to explore these problems through groups should be included in counseling groups. In short, to the extent that the student's problem involves relating to others and to the extent that he feels secure enough to talk within a group setting, group counseling will be appropriate. A crucial need current in the counseling profession is for a thorough analysis to determine what concerns can best be dealt with in groups, what aspects require individual counseling, and how the two approaches complement each other in the total guidance program.

Second, in well-established programs, counseling groups will be initiated which may serve differing pupil concerns. For example, some counseling groups might be established to (1) provide information needed by certain students and to help them to relate it to themselves, (2) remedy study deficiencies, (3) counter or ameliorate underachievement or scholastic failure, (4) attain skill or insight in coping with others, (5) aid potential dropouts or (6) facilitate personal development. The point here is that group counseling as an effective part of a school's guidance program would not necessarily be restricted to a single task or context. If each counselor (who has the required competencies) devoted a portion of his time to counseling with groups, a diversity of group contexts could be maintained to serve varying pupil needs. Thus, the individual pupil who is a poor risk in one counseling group may readily fit into another group where topics are more nearly compatible with his particular concerns.

Third, group counseling should be conducted by those who are professionally prepared to offer such service. It is only recently that many counselor preparation programs have begun to provide training in group work. Several group counseling specialists have expressed the notion that extensive experience in individual counseling is a necessary prerequisite before a counselor can serve a group effectively. Previously it was indicated that the group counselor's role and function was more difficult because of the diffusion of his attention to the members. Even though he concentrates upon the person speaking, he must observe the responses of the five or six others and help them become involved. Difficult problem cases involving deep personal and cultural conflicts should not be attempted until counselors are prepared to handle such cases. Careful attention and screening should be given so that students selected for groups have concerns such that the counselor can cope with them successfully. The point here is that counseling groups requires certain competencies and skills, which may or may not be present in every school counselor. This is not to assert that group counseling is an art known only to a few, but rather to stress that it is not to be performed by the unskilled, undertrained, uninterested individual. Group counseling will be effective only if the counselor is effective.

Fourth, the school staff must understand the purposes and objectives of group counseling. Mahler and Caldwell have stated the case very well:

> The development of a group counseling program is very much dependent on the support and understanding of the administration. When the people concerned—students, parents, teachers, or administrators—have an opportunity to share in the development of goals and methods, there is a strong likelihood of gaining understanding and support. One of the important steps in implementing a new program is to keep all interested parties informed of its progress. Actual demonstrations or reports to teachers, to parents, and to administrators are effective in helping others understand the guidance program.[36]

School staff members who understand the purposes of group counseling will not just tolerate its functioning in the school, but will actively support it in their contacts with students and parents. School administrators, the director of guidance, and all counselors are responsible for facilitating communications about group counseling, which builds staff receptivity.

Fifth, group counseling programs should be begun slowly and carefully. A commonly accepted educational principle is that one works from the known to the unknown. The speed with which counseling groups are developed must be balanced against the security of the staff and the receptivity of the student body. As insights and experience build, direction and focus will shift. In many guidance programs, the staff is painfully aware of the many activities that need to be started. Two or three exploratory counseling groups can be started in the areas in which the faculty feel immediate need for action or the student population express concern. It must be borne in mind that any guidance service will be effective only if it incorporates the needs of children as children perceive them.

Sixth, provisions should be made for evaluating group counseling. When group counseling is provided, the reasons for its use should lead to a plan for assessing its results. Group counselors should not take for granted that they are achieving their objectives. Although it is not always possible to secure the data needed to make evaluative judgments, in most instances more information can be gathered and used than is presently done. Evaluative results will be important in communicating with colleagues, pupils, and parents. Broedel and his associates have briefly described a content-scoring system used to appraise the growth of gifted underachieving adolescents treated in group counseling.[37] Although evaluation may be time-

[36] Mahler and Caldwell, *Group Counseling,* p. 35. From *Group Counseling in Secondary Schools* by Clarence A. Mahler and Edson Caldwell. Copyright © 1961, Science Research Associates, Inc. All rights reserved. By permission of Science Research Associates, Inc.

[37] John Broedel, *et al., Underachieving Adolescents,* p. 165.

consuming, difficult, and expensive of time and personnel, it is necessary if the needs of youth are to be met.

INDIVIDUAL AND GROUP COUNSELING

In closing, some of the similarities and differences between individual and group counseling will be briefly summarized here.

Similarities

1. The overall objectives in group and individual counseling are frequently quite similar. Both seek to help the counselee achieve self-direction, integration, and self-responsibility. In both approaches, counselees are helped toward self-acceptance and understanding of their motivations.
2. In both individual and group counseling, an accepting, permissive climate must be maintained if the participants are to experience less need for maintaining their defenses. In both, individuals feel free to examine their feelings and experiences because respect has been accorded them. Both approaches strive to engender confidence in the counselee's ability to be responsible for the choices that he himself makes.
3. In both individual and group counseling, the counselor's techniques are important. Clarification of feeling, reflection of feeling, restatement of content, structuring, acceptance, and the like are appropriately used in both situations. In both approaches, the counselor's skills are used to draw out counselees so that they are aware of their feelings and attitudes and can examine and clarify them.
4. The recipients of individual and group counseling are students experiencing normal developmental problems. Both approaches deal with the common needs, interests, concerns, and experiences of the generality of students.
5. For both approaches, individuals need privacy and a confidential relationship in order to develop and to make use of their personal resources.

Differences

Some of the major differences between group and individual counseling are summarized below:

1. The group situation provides immediate opportunities to try out ways of relating to individuals and is an excellent way of providing the experience of intimacy with others. The physical proximity of the members to each other brings emotional satisfactions. A counselee may get his peers' reactions and suggestions concerning alternate ways of behaving with others. Immediate firsthand opportunity is present to test others' perceptions of oneself in relation to others.
2. In group counseling, the counselees not only receive help, but also help others. The more stable and cohesive the group, the more the members

tend to assist each other. The cooperative sharing relationship that is established engenders giving as well as receiving. A group relationship helps the members to feel closer to others, to understand and accept them. The interaction nurtures members and facilitates mutual expression of feelings and interpretation of meanings; it also influences each member's behavior.

3. The counselor's task is more complicated in group counseling. He not only has to understand the speaker's feelings and help him become aware of them, but he also must observe how the speaker's comments influence the other group members. The counselor must not only be aware of the discussion, he must be perceptive of the interplay of relationships among the members.

From the information in this chapter, it is evident that group counseling is becoming established as part of the guidance services. However, even though its popularity is attested to by its growing use in schools, there is still need for careful appraisal because, as a method, it is variable and complex. While in the past group counseling may have been ancillary to individual counseling, in the future it will tend to complement individual counseling.

ANNOTATED BIBLIOGRAPHY

BENNETT, MARGARET E. *Guidance and Counseling in Groups.* New York: McGraw-Hill Book Co., Inc., 1963. Chapters 4, 5, and 6, pp. 79–96, 97–135, and 136–162.

Chapter 4 is devoted to group processes in counseling; Chapter 5, to group techniques; and Chapter 6, to group counseling. These chapters deal with helping individuals understand themselves better through groups. Varieties of techniques are described.

DYE, H. ALLAN. *Fundamental Group Procedures for School Counselors.* Guidance Monograph Series. Boston: Houghton Mifflin Company, 1968, 68 pp.

Dye presents current attitudes toward group work and some of its advantages and disadvantages. He explains and illustrates some of the basic considerations involved in initiating and maintaining a group. Also he deals with the administrative details of engaging in group work in schools.

KEMP, C. GRATTON. *Perspectives on the Group Process: A Foundation for Counseling with Groups.* Second Edition. Boston: Houghton Mifflin Company, 1970. 351 pp.

This is a book of some of the more scholarly and reliable literature in the field of group process. Fifty-seven articles from a variety of sources are brought together in an integrative manner. Several articles present the best available research on the various problems involved in group work.

MAHLER, CLARENCE A. *Group Counseling in the Schools,* Boston: Houghton Mifflin, 1969, 225 pp.

This book presents a clear exposition of group counseling in schools. The nine chapters treat the nature of groups, the psychological framework, formation of groups, different stages of groups, the counselor in the situation, and current research. The author's observations and suggestions are helpful in understanding the helping relationship involved in group counseling.

SELECTED REFERENCES

ANDERSON, ALAN R., AND JOHNSON, DONALD L. "Using Group Procedures to Improve Human Relations in the School Social Setting." *The School Counselor* Vol. 15 (May 1968), pp. 334–342.

BATES, MARILYN. "Themes in Group Counseling with Adolescents." *Personnel and Guidance Journal* Vol. 44 (February 1966), pp. 568–575.

———. "A Test of Group Counseling." *Personnel and Guidance Journal* Vol. 46 (April 1968), pp. 749–753.

BEYMER, LAWRENCE. "Confrontation Groups: Hula Hoops?" *Counselor Education and Supervision* Vol. 9 (Winter 1970), pp. 75–86.

CULBERT, SAMUEL A., CLARK, JAMES V., AND BOBELE, KENNETH H., "Measures of Change Toward Self-Actualization in Two Sensitivity Training Groups." *Journal of Counseling Psychology* Vol. 15 (January 1968), pp. 53–57.

DUNCAN, JACK A., AND GAZDA, GEORGE M. "Significant Content of Group Counseling Sessions with Culturally Deprived Ninth Grade Students." *Personnel and Guidance Journal* Vol. 46 (September 1967), pp. 11–16.

ESPOSITO, JOHN, AND HOPPOCK, ROBERT. "Group Guidance for Prospective Dropouts: An Exchange of Letters." *The Vocational Guidance Quarterly* Vol. 17 (December 1968), pp. 132–133.

GAZDA, GEORGE M.; DUNCAN, JACK A.; AND MEADOWS, M. EUGENE. "Group Counseling and Group Procedures—Report of a Survey." *Counselor Education and Supervision* Vol. 6 (Summer 1967), pp. 305–310.

GILBREATH, STUART H. "Appropriate and Inappropriate Group Counseling with Academic Underachievers." *Journal of Counseling Psychology* Vol. 15 (November 1968), pp. 506–511.

HEWER, VIVIAN H. "Group Counseling." *The Vocational Guidance Quarterly* Vol. 16 (June 1968), pp. 250–257.

HOFFNUNG, ROBERT J., AND MILLS, ROBERT B. "Situational Group Counseling with Disadvantaged Youth." *Personnel and Guidance Journal* Vol. 48 (February 1970), pp. 458–464.

HOWARD, JANE. "Inhibitions Thrown to the Winds." *Life* Vol. 65 (July 12, 1968), pp. 48–65.

INGILS, C. R. "Group Dynamics—Boon or Bane?" *Personnel and Guidance Journal* Vol. 46 (April 1968), pp. 744–748.

JOHNSON, ROBERT L. "Game Theory and Short-Term Group Counseling." *Personnel and Guidance Journal* Vol. 47 (April 1969), pp. 758–761.

KAPLAN, HERBERT H. "A Case Against Multiple Counseling." *The School Counselor* Vol. 17 (March 1970), pp. 247–249.

MALOUF, PHELON J. "Direct Feedback: Helpful or Disruptive in Group Counseling?" *The School Counselor* Vol. 15 (May 1968), pp. 390–393.

McCowan, Richard J. "Group Counseling with Underachievers and Their Parents." *The School Counselor* Vol. 16 (September 1968), pp. 30–35.

Moore, Lorraine. "A Developmental Approach to Group Counseling with Seventh Graders." *The School Counselor* Vol. 16 (March 1969), pp. 272–276.

Ohlsen, Merle M. "Counseling Children in Groups." *The School Counselor* Vol. 15 (May 1968), pp. 343–349.

Pascale, Alfred C. "Enhancing the Counseling Service Through the Utilization of Group Counseling." *The School Counselor* Vol. 16 (November 1968), pp. 136–139.

Shaffer, Marcia. "Group Counseling in a Senior High School." *The School Counselor* Vol. 17 (September 1969), pp. 22–25.

Stetter, Richard, "A Group Guidance Technique for the Classroom Teacher." *The School Counselor* Vol. 16 (January 1969), pp. 179–184.

Thelan, Mark H., and Harris, Charles S. "Personality of College Underachievers Who Improve with Group Psychotherapy." *Personnel and Guidance Journal* Vol. 46 (February 1968), pp. 561–566.

Thompson, Andrew. "The Fairweather Group Program: Implications for Counselor Preparation and Practice." *Counselor Education and Supervision* Vol. 8 (Fall 1968), pp. 55–60.

Truax, Charles B. "Therapist Interpersonal Reinforcement of Client Self-Exploration and Therapeutic Outcome in Group Psychotherapy." *Journal of Counseling Psychology* Vol. 15 (May 1968), pp. 225–231.

Varenhorst, Barbara B. "Innovative Tool for Group Counseling: The Life Career Game." *The School Counselor* Vol. 15 (May 1968), pp. 357–362.

Winder, Alvin E., and Savenko, Nicholai. "Group Counseling with Neighborhood Youth Corps Trainees." *Personnel and Guidance Journal* Vol. 48 (March 1970), pp. 561–567.

Zimpfer, David G. "Expression of Feelings in Group Counseling." *Personnel and Guidance Journal* Vol. 45 (March 1967), pp. 703–708.

————. "Some Conceptual and Research Problems in Group Counseling." *The School Counselor* Vol. 15, (May 1968), pp. 325–333.

9

STUDENT
APPRAISAL: TESTS

Why are tests given?
What types of tests are available?
What are the essential elements of a school testing program?
What general cautions should be observed in administering and using test data?
What principles are involved in the use of test data in the appraisal service?

This chapter and the following one will deal with approaches to the individual inventory or pupil appraisal service. Such a service must be built on a foundation of psychological knowledge and understanding. From school to school, the appraisal service varies both in structure, comprehensiveness, and soundness. A fundamental premise of the individual inventory or pupil appraisal service is that individuals are alike as well as different. Procedures utilized are most concerned with providing data that will highlight the individuality of each pupil.

The appraisal service seeks to gather information about the pupil that will aid him in understanding himself and in making meaningful decisions. The appraisal service is also utilized by the school staff (including teachers, counselors, and administrators) and parents to *know* the pupil so that they will be able to understand and help him.

Basically two types of data are collected and used for these purposes: test and non-test. This chapter discusses test data and Chapter 10 discusses non-test data. In this chapter, the purpose is not to present testing in depth nor is it to describe fully the technical aspects of the vast array of tests available and used in appraisal services. Rather the purpose of the chapter is to acquaint students with the basic general principles of testing as well as the potentialities and limitations of test data in pupil appraisal. This approach is based on the premise that other required training experience as well as many textbooks have as their primary purpose the exhaustive study of testing. Such courses are, of course, almost universally required in counselor preparation programs. The task here is more general, but nevertheless important, i.e., gaining familiarization in the use of test data essential to the pupil appraisal service in the guidance program.

PURPOSES OF TESTING

Much has been said, in the popular and professional literature, about tests and testing and more will be said in the future. Some commentaries are critical, and some replies are defensive, while some are primarily enlightening and informative. What is the object of such comments? What is a test? Considerable agreement exists as to definition. Most authorities define a standardized test as "an objective sample of some aspect of behavior." The term "objective" in the definition refers to the requirement that its administration, scoring, and interpretation are independent of the individual examiner's subjective judgment. Tests are also objective in the scientific sense that their reliability, validity, and item difficulty level are usually experimentally determined before they are used widely.

Standardization in testing terminology refers to uniformity of procedure in administering and scoring. Uniformity of procedure exists with regard to time limits, instructions to subjects, and other details. Standardization also implies that norms—an established normal or average performance on the test—are available. Norms are determined by administering the test to a large representative group of subjects for whom the instrument is designed. From this administration, "average" performance as well as estimates of the degree of deviation above and below average are obtained so that future users may draw conclusions concerning the level of performance of subjects who take the test at a later date.

Underlying Philosophy of Appraisal

Cronbach points out that two prevailing philosophies of testing have influenced contemporary interpretation practice: the *psychometric* and *impressionistic*.[1] The former, chiefly American in origin, obtains numerical estimates of single aspects of performance. The psychometric approach rests upon E. L. Thorndike's dicta: "If a thing exists, it exists in some amount," and "If it exists in some amount, it can be measured." The latter approach, the impressionistic, leads to a comprehensive, descriptive picture of the individual. This approach, mainly German in origin, looks for significant cues to understanding an individual's dynamics by any and all available means and integrates them into a total picture. Such an approach tends to give minimal consideration to "how much" of some characteristic

[1] Lee J. Cronbach, *Essentials of Psychological Testing,* 3rd Ed. (New York: Harper & Row, 1970), pp. 29–35.

is present and maximally seeks to understand how and why it is expressed.

Both approaches have merit as well as limitations. The psychometric approach is definite and structured, while the impressionistic approach seeks "wholeness" or unity and relies upon observation, descriptive data, and self-report. Differences between the two approaches may be found in the (1) definiteness of tasks employed, (2) control of response, (3) recording of basic data, (4) scoring, and (5) interpretation. Counselors commonly use both approaches in their efforts to understand and assist students.

Assumptions Basic to Appraisal

Polmantier has summarized the assumptions underlying the development and use of standardized tests. His eleven assumptions follow:

1. We assume that a sample of achievement, for example, represents the total of achievement in a subject matter area on the level or levels covered by the test.

2. We assume that our tests of intelligence apply generally because they are used with persons with general cultural and educational backgrounds. Many of our current disputes have evolved from this assumption. Where persons do not have these general backgrounds, our tests cannot be interpreted so readily. Nevertheless, if the general backgrounds are necessary for achievement and adjustment in our culture, it is not the tests that are at fault, but rather the failure of our culture to provide the necessary backgrounds for the persons involved in taking the tests. The over-all predictive value of the tests is not lessened by this fact, but rather individual prediction suffers.

3. We assume that the tests are written without author bias and without bias to sub-groups of our population. But this assumption must be studied by each of us. Perhaps we need to look for more precise *timelessness* of the test items — that is, they must not represent a specific era or a specific group of people in time. We know that adults do better on tests designed for their age, vocabularies, and experiences than they do on those designed for children and their age, vocabularies, and experiences. However, there may be times when you want to measure achievement during an era.

4. We assume that norms for tests are based upon samples of the population and that such populations constitute random stratified samples. Here we must find the evidence and also develop local norms that describe our respective school and community populations.

5. We assume that *what* one learns indicates his intelligence. Basically, this is so but a taxonomy of educational objectives must clarify the relationship between learning and intelligence before we go far in considering this assumption.

6. We assume that tests designed to predict training or educational success also predict success in life situations. This is not demonstrated by research. Therefore, we need to look carefully for specific evidence through reports of predictive studies and follow-up studies of a particular test

as well as our own data gathered on previous clients and their later life situations.

7. We assume that academic aptitude or scholastic aptitude tests are better for use in predicting college success than are traditional tests of mental ability. While this is generally shown in research, we need longitudinal studies to determine the significance of the traditional tests for predicting college success.

8. We assume that a general verbal factor is the best single predictor of academic success other than past academic achievement. This has been shown in research, but current emphasis must be placed on a combination of verbal and numerical factors as well as past academic success. Confusing the issue as to the significance of factors other than intelligence that lead to academic success is the fact that the reliability of teachers' marks is seldom higher than a coefficient of .70.

9. We assume that a characteristic that is measured by a test may be an entity in itself. However, it may be part of a complex of characteristics. Thus, some degree of impressionistic testing seems essential in the work of the counselor.

10. We may assume that because a test has its scores reported in the form of some standard score, the psychological characteristic it purports to measure distributes itself in the population in the shape of a normal curve. We should look carefully at a test to determine if the assumptions have been met which make it statistically possible to report scores in terms of derived scores depicted in the form of a standard score. Some studies have revealed that test scores have been forced into a normal distribution. Comparability of scores rests on this foundation; therefore, care must be taken to determine if a base population has been utilized in establishing comparable standard scores.

11. Finally, as we look at the large array of actuarial statistics concerning tests and their predictability, we may be assuming that these data can be applied causally to an individual client. Some persons do not die by actuarial statistics. Expectancy tables and tables of norms for particular settings do have a real place in the counseling process, but one must assume that they apply equally well to all persons who might take the tests.[2]

Harmful Consequences of Testing

Before proceeding further with the purposes of testing, it may be well to indicate a few of the harmful consequences critics have suggested educational testing may cause. Ebel has summarized and cited four such consequences:

It may place an indelible stamp of intellectual status—superior, mediocre or inferior—on a child, and thus predetermine his social status as an adult, and possibly also do irreparable harm to his self esteem and his educational motivation.

[2] Paul C. Polmantier, "Psychological Foundations (Basic Assumptions) of Standardized Testing," in E. G. Kennedy (ed.), *Individual Appraisal in Student Personnel* (Pittsburg, Kans.: Kansas State College of Pittsburg, June 1962), pp. 19–21.

It may lead to a narrow conception of ability, encourage pursuit of this single goal, and thus tend to reduce the diversity of talent available to society.

It may place the testers in a position to control education and determine the destinies of individual human beings, while, incidentally, making the testers themselves rich in the process.

It may encourage impersonal, inflexible, mechanistic processes of evaluation and determination, so that essential human freedoms are limited or lost altogether.[3]

In addition to listing the above social consequences, Ebel also cites the facts that educational testing may unduly emphasize individual competition and success rather than social cooperation; that it may foster conformity rather than creativity; that it may involve cultural bias; that it may make unwarranted invasions of privacy; that it may reward specious test-taking skill or penalize the lack of it; and other important consequences. His analysis of the four basic harmful consequences of educational testing is penetrating and worthy of study by all teachers, counselors, and administrators.

Barclay examined the various kinds of criticisms leveled against testing procedures.[4] Admitting that some charges, particularly that of a psychoanalytic bias in personality test construction, do represent deficiencies, he called for improvements in counselor training programs and the strengthening of professional organizations to counter such charges.

General Purposes of Tests

Although the following discussion of the purposes of testing risks the implication that such data are independent of involvement of the individual, such is not the case for guidance services. School counselors' use of test data is or should be intimately involved with direct assistance to the individual. Only one of the four general purposes stated below appears to be directly applicable to work with the individual, i.e., prediction. However, counselors are frequently called upon to participate in the other applications of test data.

The general purposes for which tests are given are described in detail in Cronbach's *Essentials of Psychological Testing.* Included are the following functions:

1. *Prediction.* Tests are given to obtain a measure of ability, achievement, and/or other characteristics which will offer a solid basis upon which individuals can make decisions. Decisions involve predictions—how well individuals will do at a later time. Prediction based on quantitative data

---

[3] Robert L. Ebel, "The Social Consequences of Educational Testing," in Alexander G. Wesman (chairman), *Proceedings of the 1963 Invitational Conferences on Testing Problems* (Princeton, N.J.: Educational Testing Service, 1964), p. 132.

[4] James R. Barclay, "The Attack on Testing and Counseling: An Examination and Reappraisal," *Personnel and Guidance Journal* Vol. 43 (September 1964), pp. 6–16.

is likely to be more reliable and accurate and provide a balance against wishful thinking.

2. *Selection.* Tests are used by institutions (such as colleges, employers) and organizations to accept some individuals and to reject others. The decision to hire an individual is a selection decision, and the decision to admit a student is a selection decision.

3. *Classification.* Classification is an arrangement according to some systematic division into classes or groups. Classification involves deciding which of the many treatments or groups a person should be assigned to. Examples of classification include diagnosis of mental patients, choice of school or college curriculum, assignment to a military occupational specialty, and the like. Placement should not be confused with classification. Placement tests (assignment of individuals to different *levels* of work within a type of work) differ from classification tests (assignment to different *types* of work) in terms of the kind of validity data available and in terms of providing more individualized descriptions.

4. *Evaluation.* Tests are used to assess and to evaluate programs, methods, treatments, and the like.

Camp, describing the school situation, identifies six purposes of tests, as follows: (1) identification of pupils with superior talents and those with low ability; (2) classification of individual abilities for purposes of grouping students for instruction; (3) selection of pupils for a college or university or industry or positions in the armed forces; (4) evaluation of the instructional program; (5) planning for the future; and (6) adjustment assistance to pupils in school, at work, or at home.[5]

The specific purposes of educational testing may be outlined more clearly by considering separately teachers', counselors', and administrators' use of tests. It should be noted, however, that overlap is to be expected among the uses of tests by these personnel.

Teachers' Use of Tests

Teachers, like other personnel, use tests to aid them in observing more accurately pupil behavior, especially the behavior involved in learning. They use tests to determine the relationship among ability, educational practices, and changes in pupil behavior to better predict and control learning situations. A brief statement of teachers' use of testing includes the following:

1. Teachers use tests to gain an understanding of the achievement and ability levels of individual pupils and classes of pupils so that they can

[5] Dolph Camp, "Uses of Tests," in Kenneth F. McLaughlin (ed.), *Understanding Testing,* Office of Education, Department of Health, Education and Welfare (Washington: Government Printing Office, 1962), pp. 12–13.

predict pupil learning. Understanding is sought of each child's strengths and limitations.

2. Teachers use tests as an aid in determining whether they need to adjust their instructional practices to achieve the expected instructional outcomes.
3. Teachers use tests to diagnose pupil learning difficulties. Diagnostic tests permit the identification of specific learning deficiencies.
4. Teachers use tests to help them make decisions regarding grouping pupils within subject-matter areas.
5. Teachers use tests to help them objectively measure pupil attainment of accepted educational standards. Every conscientious teacher wants to know how well pupils achieve the objectives of instruction.

Chauncey and Dobbin have concisely summarized the particular uses of tests in teaching in six categories: (1) to judge capacity to learn; (2) to guide teaching; (3) to check learning progress; (4) to discover learning difficulties; (5) to improve teaching techniques; and (6) to assess teaching effectiveness. For a more detailed discussion of each of these purposes, the reader is directed to their book.[6]

Counselors' Use of Tests

Among the several competencies demanded of the school counselor is that he be sophisticated in the general field of psychological measurement and understand thoroughly the strengths and weaknesses of tests used most frequently in schools. When well versed in test theory and practice, the counselor can use test scores as significant contributions to the clinical aspects of his work. The use of tests most appropriate to the counselor's function may be outlined as follows:

1. Counselors use tests to secure accurate and reliable information about each student's abilities, aptitudes, interests, and personal characteristics in order to assist the pupil in gaining self-understanding. Lister and Ohlsen, investigating the extent to which test interpretation improved self-understanding of pupils in Grades 5, 7, 9, and 11, reported that at all grade levels interpretation was associated with increasing accuracy of self-estimates of achievement, intelligence, and interests.[7]

    By understanding each pupil—his strengths and limitations—the counselor can provide rational and wise assistance to the individual. Objective comparisons of the individual's characteristics appraised

[6] Henry Chauncey and John E. Dobbin, *Testing: Its Place in Education Today* (New York: Harper & Row, Publishers, 1963), pp. 82–107.

[7] James L. Lister and Merle M. Ohlsen, "The Improvement of Self Understanding Through Test Interpretation," *Personnel and Guidance Journal* Vol. 43 (April 1965), pp. 804–810.

across time as well as matched with the performance of others can contribute to self-understanding and decision-making.

2. Counselors use tests to help predict future performance such as college success, work potential as a secretary or clerk, performance in mechanical occupations, and the like. Tests provide an improved basis for prediction regarding the likelihood of success in those activities in which prospective performance can be measured.

3. Counselors use tests to help students arrive at decisions basic to planning their educational and vocational futures. As the counselor works with each pupil on such personal issues as selection of curriculum, selection of courses within a curriculum, planning further education, vocational development, the counselor depends, at least in part, upon test data which reflect the student's aptitudes, achievement, interests, and personal characteristics. When a student is facing a difficult problem of vocational choice or planning, he may reach a better decision (i.e., one that is facilitating for him) by considering psychological test results that provide some basis for assessing his potentialities in relation to the requirements of an occupation (e.g., interests and characteristics of those in the occupation). At the same time, test data may furnish information regarding limitations of ability, unexpected assets, inappropriate interests or aptitudes, all of which are relevant to counseling. The counselor can then interpret such information to help the student develop insight into his own pattern of assets and liabilities as they relate to various occupational and environmental demands.

4. Counselors use tests to diagnose student problems. Such problems as those related to difficulty or inability of pupils to cope with social environment, problems of student growth and development, or academic deficiencies may be identified and plans for their amelioration may be mutually determined. Accurate diagnosis includes an understanding not only of the indications of maladjustment, but also of dynamic factors related to the maladjustment.

5. Counselors use tests to help them evaluate the outcomes of guidance or counseling. In attempting to assess the worth of their work, many counselors have turned to test data. The usual approach to such efforts involves testing before and after counseling with the use of appropriate control groups. Psychological measures that have been employed include tests in the areas of achievement, social and emotional adjustment, and social attitudes.

Implicit in all that has been said about the use of tests for guidance purposes is the necessity for cumulative records as well as a counselor's personal (confidential) record file in which all test results for each pupil can be entered. Chapter 10 discusses the cumulative record. Continuous application of test results calls for an up-to-date, complete record system so that essential test data are easily available and readily utilized.

Administrators' Use of Tests

The central purpose of educational administration is to provide conditions to facilitate the learning process. Within the formal organization of the school, teaching is commonly defined as the process of changing human behavior in socially desirable directions. Administrators are responsible for and held accountable for an adequate instructional program in the schools. Standardized tests afford an impartial basis for evaluating how well the school meets its objectives. Some of the uses to which tests are put by administrators include the following:

1. Administrators use tests to help them make decisions in overall educational planning. Psychological measurement will be used in making decisions regarding curriculum emphasis, identification of pupil needs, clarification of educational objectives, and the like.
2. Administrators use tests to help them determine the strengths and weaknesses of the instructional program. This does not necessarily mean that tests should be used to reach a decision to hire, promote, or release a teacher, but rather that test data will help administrators to identify strengths and inadequacies in curriculum content and organization.
3. Administrators use tests to help them make decisions regarding the grouping of students for instructional purposes. Information from standardized tests of ability and achievement is useful in determining where pupils may best be placed in subjects and curricular tracks adapted to various levels of instruction.
4. Administrators use tests to identify areas in which supervision is needed. Essentially supervision is given to help teachers develop and secure coordination of instructional efforts. Tests can help identify instructional areas which need modification and to identify needed instructional materials and facilities.
5. Administrators use tests to help determine the overall effectiveness of the school. Administrators are concerned with how well the school achieves its objectives. They seek to determine the changing character of the student body and the appropriateness of school activities. Test results are valuable in discussing with parents the school's effectiveness and the nature of the educational program.

TYPES OF TESTS

Ways of Classifying Tests

Tests have been classified in many ways—by purpose, content, form, procedure, and function, as well as in other ways. A brief explanation of six ways of classifying tests follows:

1. Standardized versus teacher-made tests. Standardized tests are those administered and scored according to specific instructions. Norms based on large samples of students are available to compare a subject's performance with that of others in a similar population category or group. Teacher-made tests are constructed for informal pupil evaluation within the classroom and usually do not have extensive norms available.

2. Individual versus group tests. Individual tests are those administered by a trained examiner to one subject at a time. The examiner observes the subject's responses to oral questions and assigned tasks and, in addition, records the subject's responses. Examples of individual tests include the Stanford-Binet Intelligence Test, Wechsler Intelligence Scales, Rorschach Ink Blot Test and Thematic Apperception Test. Group tests, on the other hand, are those that can be administered to more than one individual at a time.

3. Speed versus power tests. A speed test is one in which the examinee completes as many items as possible within specified time limits. A power test is one in which the examinee demonstrates the extent of his knowledge or scope and depth of his understanding, with the time limit either eliminated or made very generous. Items on a power test usually range from easy to extremely difficult.

4. Performance versus paper-and-pencil tests. Performance tests require the subject to manipulate objects or to assemble parts or actually perform tasks, while paper and pencil tests require the examinee to mark an answer sheet or to provide written responses.

5. Objective versus subjective. Objective tests require little or no judgment on the part of the scorer, while subjective tests require the scorer to exercise judgment in evaluating the examinee's answers.

6. Maximum versus typical performance. Maximum performance tests are those which require the individual to perform at his best, to do the best he can to demonstrate his ability. Typical performance tests are those which seek to determine what the individual usually does or is most likely to do in given situations.

Another way of classifying tests is by the purpose for which they are designed or the aspects of behavior they sample, for example, mental ability, aptitude, achievement, interest and personality. These five types of tests will now be discussed separately and at somewhat greater length.

Mental Ability Tests

Mental ability tests were the first standardized psychological tests to be developed. Various terms (intelligence, academic ability, scholastic aptitude) have been and are still used to designate their purpose, which essentially is to estimate intellectual functioning. Attempts to define what these tests measure have concerned educators and psychologists for over sixty years. Representative of the definitions of intelligence are the following:

The ability to think in terms of abstract ideas.[8]

Intelligence is the aggregate or global capacity of the individual to act purposefully, to think rationally, and to deal effectively with his environment.[9]

The degree of availability of one's experiences for the solution of immediate problems and the anticipation of future ones.[10]

Intelligence is the ability to undertake activities that are characterized by difficulty, complexity, abstractness, economy, adaptiveness to a goal, social value, emergence of originals, and to maintain such activities under conditions that demand a concentration of energy and a resistance to emotional forces.[11]

Examination of these definitions reveals that they are of the *cognitive type,* in which intelligence is seen as the ability to do abstract thinking, to learn. The other form of definition of intelligence is that in which *adaptive processes* of an individual to his total environment are stressed. Guilford points out that most definitions of intelligence are inadequate because they contain undefined and undefinable terms. Guilford has presented a conception of intelligence entitled "Structure-of-intellect model." His three-dimensional conception involves three categories: *content* (figural, symbolic, semantic, behavioral); *operation* (evaluation, convergent production, divergent production, memory, cognition); and *product* (units, classes, relations, systems, transformations, implications).[12]

One thing is certain: ability tests do not measure innate ability. They assess the extent to which the innate potential has been modified by environment—what the individual has learned. It is assumed that everyone being tested has had an equal opportunity to learn—through equal schooling, equal home conditions, and the like. That this assumption has never been confirmed is buttressed by educational research studies of the barren environment of slum children, hill people, and canal-boat children. Ability tests measure the individual's present status, which is the result of the modification of potential brought about by contact with environment. It is further assumed that nothing has interfered with learning, such as emotional disturbance or health problems. This latter assumption is equally untenable since considerable research indicates that emotional disturbance and physical health problems can seriously interfere with learning and therefore with test performance.

[8] L. M. Terman, *The Measurement of Intelligence* (Boston: Houghton Mifflin Company, 1916), p. 42.

[9] D. Wechsler, *The Measurement of Adult Intelligence* (Baltimore: Williams and Wilkins, 1944), p. 3.

[10] H. H. Goddard, "What is Intelligence?" *Journal of Social Psychology* Vol. 24 (1946), p. 68.

[11] G. D. Stoddard, *The Meaning of Intelligence* (New York: The Macmillan Co., 1943), p. 4.

[12] J. P. Guilford, *The Nature of Human Intelligence* (New York: McGraw-Hill Book Company, 1967), pp. 61–65.

HISTORY OF ABILITY TESTING

Wilhelm Max Wundt was among the first to attempt the systematic measurement of man's intelligence. His methods were largely based on physical reaction time. J. McKeen Cattell, after obtaining his Ph.D. at Wundt's laboratory, returned to America and began measuring reaction time, color discrimination, strength of grip, and sensitivity to pain of American college students. Although Cattell was originally interested primarily in the range of individual differences, he later became interested in identifying superior individuals by means of the above procedures.

In 1905, Alfred Binet and Theodore Simon published the first intelligence scale as it is known today. Their instrument, devised at the request of Paris officials, sought to separate the feeble-minded from other children on the basis of thirty short tests. In 1908, Binet published another scale, marking the appearance of the mental-age concept in which each item successfully completed was worth so many months' mental age. In 1911, another revision of his scale was published which extended the age range from three years to adult levels.

Binet's scale was soon brought to America where it was translated and revised. H. H. Goddard, Director of the Vineland, New Jersey, Training School for Mental Defectives, was an early user of the test. The Stanford revision of the Binet-Simon Intelligence Scales was prepared by Terman and was published in 1916. At about this same time, there developed extensive use of the IQ concept, or the ratio of mental age to chronological age, MA/CA. The term IQ reflects a measure of "brightness" that takes into account both the mental-age score on an intelligence test and chronological age. Table V shows the classification of IQs offered by Terman and Merrill for the Stanford-Binet Test, indicating the percent of persons in a normal population who fall into each classification. It is most important to bear in mind that the levels in such a table are arbitrarily determined, for there are no inflexible lines of demarcation between "borderline defective" and "mentally defective" or between "very superior" and "superior" except by convention.

With the advent of World War I, several American psychologists were commissioned to devise a group intelligence test to screen and assign draftees. Led by A. S. Otis and Robert Yerkes, the group constructed the Army Alpha and Army Beta tests. Army Alpha was designed to be used with literate individuals and Army Beta with those who could not read or write. Such tests marked the first time large groups of individuals were tested.

During the 1920's these tests were adopted by industry and education. Research led to refinements. During the 1930's, L. L. Thurstone published the results of his factorial studies which led to the appraisal of ability as more than a single general trait. In 1939, David Wechsler published his individual adult intelligence test, followed in 1949 by his individual intelligence scale for children. World War II marked the emergence of the Army General Classification Test and an increased emphasis upon the factorial approach in the measurement of human ability. Since the War, ex-

TABLE V
Classification of IQs for the Stanford–Binet Test

IQ	PERCENT	CLASSIFICATION
160–169	0.03	
150–159	0.2	Very superior
140–149	1.1	
130–139	3.1	
120–129	8.2	Superior
110–119	18.1	High average
100–109	23.5	
90–99	23.0	Normal or average
80–89	14.5	Low average
70–79	5.6	Borderline defective
60–69	2.0	
50–59	0.4	
40–49	0.2	Mentally defective
30–39	0.03	

From L. M. Terman and Maude A. Merrill, *Stanford-Binet Intelligence Scale* (Boston: Houghton Mifflin Company, 1960), p. 18.

tended efforts have been made to develop "culture-free" tests, but to date the results have not been encouraging.

STANDARDIZED GROUP TESTS OF ABILITY

While individual scales such as the Stanford-Binet and the Wechsler find their application in the clinic, standardized group tests of mental ability are used primarily in industry, education, and the military. Most group mental ability tests give merely a rough estimate of how easily pupils learn from books by requiring the examinee to perform mental activities that are regarded as evidence of intelligence. Such tests emphasize knowledge of vocabulary and ability to reason. Some tests in this category yield a single total score, while others yield separate scores based on both verbal and nonverbal questions. If the purpose of ability testing is to secure an overall measure to group pupils, a single test score on a mental ability test may suffice. However, in most situations, a test which provides both verbal and nonverbal scores is generally preferred for guidance purposes. In this section, some group tests of mental ability that are representative of those in current use will be cited. The entries are taken from *Tests in Print*.

California Test of Mental Maturity, 1957 Edition. Grades kindergarten–1, 1–3, 4–8, 7–9, 9–13, 10–16 and adults; 1936–57; 8 scores: memory, spatial relationships, logical reasoning, numerical reasoning, verbal concepts, language and non-language, total; Elizabeth T. Sullivan, Willis W. Clark, and Ernest W. Tiegs; California Test Bureau. (Revised in 1963).

Cooperative School and College Ability Tests. Grades 4–6, 6–8, 8–10, 10–12, 12–14; 1955–1957; 3 scores: verbal, quantitative, total; Cooperative Test Division.

The Lorge-Thorndike Intelligence Tests. Grades kindergarten–1, 2–3, 4–6, 7–9, 10–12; 1954–59. Irving Lorge and Robert L. Thorndike; Houghton Mifflin Company.

(a) Nonverbal Battery. Grades kindergarten–1, 2–3, 4–6, 7–9, 10–12. (b) Verbal Battery. Grades 4–6, 7–9, 10–12.

Otis Quick-Scoring Mental Ability Tests. Grades 1.5–4, 4–9, 9–16; 1936–54; tests for grades 4 and over are revisions of Otis Self Administering Tests of Mental Ability; Arthur S. Otis; Harcourt Brace and World, Inc. (Revised 1967, now available as Otis-Lennon Mental Ability Test.)[13]

Achievement Tests

Achievement tests are designed to measure the outcomes of instruction, the progress pupils have made in attaining proficiency as a result of training or learning. Cronbach observes that:

> One significant contribution of standardized tests has been to break down the "time-serving" concept of education. A person's standing in school is frequently judged by the number of years he has put in, or the number of courses he has passed through. Time spent is no index of education received. In one study, where thousands of college students took standardized tests of knowledge in various fields, many college seniors knew less than the average high school senior. Since number of units accumulated tells little about proficiency, tests are being given increasing weight as evidence of educational development.[14]

HISTORY OF ACHIEVEMENT TESTING

Examination of the proficiency of students, up to the nineteenth century, was usually by oral methods. Later, compulsory school attendance made individual oral examinations impractical. During the 1840's Horace Mann, secretary of the Massachusetts Board of Education, described written examinations that were being used in Boston. The use of written examinations soon spread and in 1865 the New York State Regents' Examinations were started.

In 1897 Joseph Meyer Rice reported his important study of achievement in spelling as related to amount of time devoted to spelling instruction. In 1900, the *College Entrance Examinations* or "College Boards" were begun. These are still widely used to select students for admission to college. Also during the early 1900's Edward L. Thorndike and his associates began con-

[13] Oscar K. Buros (ed.), *Tests in Print* (Highland Park, N.J.: Gryphon Press, 1961), p. 731 ff.

[14] Lee J. Cronbach, *Essentials of Psychological Testing,* 2nd Ed., p. 363.

structing standardized tests for the different school subject-matter areas. Because of the recognized unreliability and lack of comparability of teacher-constructed tests, standardized achievement tests were quickly accepted during the 1920's and 1930's.

However, the question of whether standardized achievement tests ought to be exclusively concerned with assessing knowledge of facts soon arose. R. W. Tyler, E. B. Green, and others demonstrated by their research that testing knowledge of facts was rather pointless because of the marked "loss of learning" which occurred when they readministered final examinations in September to students who had completed courses in the spring of the year and had taken no further work in the area. Two problems continue to plague educators in the use of standardized achievement tests: (1) How well does the test meet the objectives of the local school or teacher? and (2) What impact does the use or misuse of achievement tests have upon the type of learning that takes place in the classroom?

TYPES OF ACHIEVEMENT TESTS

A special kind of achievement test battery is called a *survey* test. It is used to assess a pupil's growth in broad subject-matter areas. This type of test can be used from the primary grades to the adult level, although its major application has been in the elementary school. Most batteries provide individual profiles of subtest scores in addition to a total score on the entire battery. Survey tests permit horizontal or vertical comparisons, or both, so that a pupil's relative standing in different subject-matter areas can be compared to a uniform normative sample.

Readiness or prognostic tests are used to predict how well the individual may be expected to profit from subsequent training. Foremost among the areas sampled are reading and number skills. Readiness tests are frequently employed for making decisions about entrance into first grade. Special emphasis in such tests is given to the abilities found to be important in learning to read, to do numerical thinking, and to write. Some authors classify readiness tests as ability rather than as achievement tests.

Diagnostic achievement tests are designed to enable teachers and counselors to determine the pupil's performance and yield information on the causes of difficulty in reading, arithmetic, and language. Such tests usually provide several scores and may provide detailed checklists of specific types of errors which may then be related to specific difficulties.

Standardized Group Achievement Tests. Today greater emphasis than ever before is being placed on improving the use of standardized achievement tests. The merit of standardized testing lies in its providing (1) an objective, independent judgment of what has been learned and (2) norms for evaluating performance.

The following is a list illustrating some of the representative standardized tests in use today (see Buros' *Tests in Print*):

California Achievement Tests, 1957 Edition. Grades 1–2, 3–4.5, 4–6, 7–9, 9–14; 1934–59; 11 scores: reading vocabulary, reading comprehension, reading total, arithmetic reasoning, arithmetic fundamentals, arithmetic total, mechanics of English, spelling, language total, handwriting: tests in language, arithmetic, and reading available as separates; Ernest W. Tiegs and Willis W. Clark; California Test Bureau.

Iowa Tests of Basic Skills. Grades 3–9; 1955–56; 15 scores: vocabulary, reading comprehension, language (5 scores), work-study skills (4 scores), arithmetic skills (3 scores), total. E. F. Lindquist, A. N. Hieronymus, and others. Houghton Mifflin Company.

Sequential Tests of Educational Progress. Grades 4–6, 7–9, 10–12, 13–14; 1956–59; 7 tests: essay test, listening, mathematics, reading, science, social studies, writing; Cooperative Test Division.

Stanford Achievement Tests, 1953 Revision. Grades 1.9–3.5, 3–4, 5–6, 7–9; 1923–60; subtests in arithmetic, reading, study skills, science, and social studies available as separates; Truman L. Kelley, Richard Madden, Eric F. Gardner, Lewis M. Terman, Giles M. Kuch; Harcourt, Brace & World, Inc.

Quality achievement tests must be constantly revised to keep pace with the changes in instructional procedures and increased knowledge. A clear example of this is to be found in the necessary revisions of tests in the science area to keep pace with rapidly expanding knowledge.

Aptitude Tests

Warren's *Dictionary of Psychology* defines aptitude as "a condition or set of characteristics regarded as symptomatic of an individual's ability to acquire with training some (usually specified) knowledge, skill, or set of responses, such as the ability to speak a language, to produce music. . . ." Lennon defines aptitude in the following way:

A combination of abilities and other characteristics, whether native or acquired, known or believed to be indicative of an individual's ability to learn in some particular area. Thus, "musical aptitude" would refer broadly to that combination of physical and mental characteristics, motivational factors, and conceivably other characteristics, which is conducive to acquiring proficiency in the musical field.[15]

It should be noted that nothing in these two definitions necessarily assumes that aptitudes are hereditary. Aptitude testing embraces intelligence and achievement, personality and interests, and other skills which predispose to learning. Aptitude, then, is seen as an ability to learn, and aptitude tests assess knowledge, skill, and other characteristics which serve to predict learning success.

[15] Roger T. Lennon, "A Glossary of 100 Measurement Terms," *Test Service Notebook, No. 13* (New York: Harcourt, Brace & World, Inc., n.d.).

History of Aptitude Tests

Since World War II, the development and application of instruments permitting analysis of performance with regard to different aspects of intelligence have moved forward rapidly. Even before the war, it was generally recognized that intelligence testing was limited in the measurement of general abilities. Special aptitude tests to assess factors other than verbal or numerical abilities, such as mechanical and clerical, have been constructed.

Increasing emphasis has been given to the use of multifactor batteries in the measurement of aptitudes. Such batteries were outgrowths of various selection programs set up by the military and civilian organizations. Practically all current-day aptitude tests are constructed by factor-analysis techniques. The principal object of factor analysis is to simplify the description of data by reducing the number of necessary variables or dimensions. Electronic computers made possible the adoption of more refined techniques of analyzing sets of variables. Factor analysis led to the recognition that intelligence itself comprises a number of relatively independent aptitudes, including, for example, verbal comprehension, numerical reasoning, spatial visualization, and memory, as well as a general factor.

Distinctions Between Achievement and Aptitude

In differentiating between achievement and aptitude tests, it is often naïvely assumed that aptitude tests measure innate capacity while achievement tests measure the outcomes of learning. It should be recognized that all tests measure a person's current behavior which inevitably reflects prior learning. Anastasi[16] makes two distinctions between aptitude and achievement tests. One such distinction is the difference in the degree of uniformity of relevant antecedent experience. Achievement tests measure the effects of relatively standardized sets of experience such as a course in solid geometry while aptitude test performance reflects the cumulative influence of a multiplicity of experiences in daily living. The other distinction between aptitude and achievement tests is the difference in their uses. Aptitude tests serve to predict subsequent performance; they are employed to estimate the extent to which the individual will profit from training, or to forecast the quality of his achievement in a new situation. Achievement tests represent a terminal evaluation of the individual's status upon the completion of training.

Types of Aptitude Tests. Aptitude tests cover a wide range of human behavior. Among the areas first tested were sensory acuity, and discrimination (vision and hearing), and motor functions such as speed and coordination. However, five major aptitude areas will be described briefly here.

1. *Mechanical Aptitude.* Mechanical aptitude tests cover a diversity of functions including motor, perception, and spatial and mechanical rea-

[16] Anne Anastasi, *Psychological Testing* (New York: The Macmillan Co., 1961), p. 424.

soning factors. Bennett and Cruikshank believe that research points up three major components in mechanical aptitude: (1) the capacity to understand mechanical relationships, involving complex abilities of spatial perception and imagination; (2) manual and finger dexterity and manipulative ability, the muscular coordination required by most mechanical jobs; (3) motor abilities of strength, speed of movement, and endurance.[17] Mechanical aptitude tests are frequently separated into three groups: tests of mechanical information and experience, tests of spatial ability, tests of manual and finger dexterity.

2. *Musical Aptitude.* From 1900 to 1940 Carl E. Seashore conducted extensive research on the psychology of music. As an outcome of this research, in 1919, he issued the first edition of his Measures of Musical Talent, which was revised in 1938. Currently, this measure consists of six tests, each placed on a separate side of a twelve-inch-record and assessing six aspects of musical aptitude: pitch, loudness, rhythm, time, timbre, and tonal memory. Each item consists of a pair of tones or tonal sequences which the examinee differentiates between in terms of what is being measured. The Seashore tests are applicable from the fourth grade to the adult level. Two other music tests are somewhat similar to the Seashore: the Musical Aptitude Profile and the Drake Musical Memory Test. Many school systems find musical aptitude tests useful in selecting students to be given music lessons to prepare them for playing in school orchestras and bands.

3. *Artistic Aptitude.* Most of the techniques used to assess artistic aptitude are devoted to drawing and painting. Faulkner grouped these techniques into five classes: (1) drawing scales, (2) art judgment tests, (3) art ability tests, (4) achievement tests, and (5) an evaluation of artistic products.[18] Drawing scales consist of a series of scales established to assess drawing ability of children. Such scales are based upon realism rather than expression. A common pattern used to assess art judgment is to have the examinee express his preference of two or more variants of the same object with one usually an original by an eminent artist. In 1930, the Meier–Seashore Art Judgment Test was first issued and later the revised edition, the Meier Art Judgment Test. The general makeup of artistic ability was seen as comprising six factors: manual skill, volitional perseveration, aesthetic intelligence, perceptual facility, creative imagination, and aesthetic judgment. The Meier Art Judgment Test, however, measures only aesthetic judgment. A newer test, similar to the Meier in basic structure, is the Graves Design Judgment.

In art aptitude tests, the examinee is given tasks to perform to see whether or not he can actually draw or paint. Use is made of "work-

---

[17] G. K. Bennett and R. M. Cruikshank, *A Summary of Manual and Mechanical Ability Tests* (New York: The Psychological Corporation, 1942).

[18] R. Faulkner, "Evaluation in Art," *Journal of Educational Research* Vol. 35 (March 1942), pp. 544–552.

sample tests." For example, the examinee in the Knauber Art Ability Test reproduces a drawing from memory, draws specified things, inserts shadows in two compositions, creates borders, monograms and other tasks. The seventeen subtests are scored by comparing the examinee's productions with a scale of standards presented in the manual.

Achievement in art is appraised through tests such as the Fine Arts subtest of the Cooperative General Culture Test, while evaluation of artistic aptitude is appraised by having competent judges pass on the examinee's work.

4. *Clerical Aptitude Tests.* Clerical aptitude comprises a composite of abilities. Tests designed to assess clerical aptitude place emphasis upon perceptual speed and accuracy. Rapid observation of numbers and symbols is an important factor in the work of a clerical worker. One of the most widely used tests of clerical aptitude is the Minnesota Clerical Test (Psychological Corporation) which consists of two parts: number and name checking. In addition, the Psychological Corporation General Clerical Tests consist of nine subtests grouped to yield clerical, numerical, and verbal scores, as well as a total score.

In addition to these general tests there are a few specific tests such as aptitude for shorthand or typing.

5. *Multifactor Batteries.* Reference has already been made to the use of factor analysis in the development of multiple-aptitude batteries. One of the oldest of these is the Differential Aptitude Tests (Psychological Corporation) designed for use in educational and vocational counseling of high school youth. The DAT consists of eight tests: (1) verbal reasoning; (2) numerical ability; (3) abstract reasoning; (4) space relations, including visualization and perception; (5) clerical speed and accuracy; (6) mechanical reasoning; (7) language usage—spelling; and (8) language usage—sentences. The battery can be administered as a series or the subtests administered separately.

A second multifactor battery is the Guilford–Zimmerman Aptitude Survey (Sheridan Supply Company) composed of seven tests. These include verbal comprehension, general reasoning, numerical operations, perceptual speed, spatial orientation, spatial visualization, and mechanical knowledge. A third battery is the General Aptitude Test Battery (United States Employment Service), which was standardized on adults employed in certain occupations. A fourth such battery is the Flanagan Aptitude Classification Tests (Science Research Associates).

In each issue of Volume 35 (1956–57) of the *Personnel and Guidance Journal* there is an article devoted to specific multifactor batteries. Each article is written by at least one of the authors of the battery and each is followed by a "Comments" section by Donald Super. Super's first "comment" is a general discussion of these batteries in which he lists the desirable qualities of tests used in counseling. First, he states what tests should describe: a test should tell about a student's intelligence, his interests, attitudes, special abilities, and overall judgment. Second, a test should predict by telling something about an individual's status, behavior, and attainment in the future. It must reveal not only what an individual will be like but what he will do. Third, a test should be timeless. Finally, a test should be multipotential because people are of a multipotential nature.[19]

Interest Inventories

This section and the next are concerned with self-report inventories, specifically interest and personality. Interests have been described as one of the main factors in the learning situation and as being the motivators of learning. It is a truism that without interest very little learning takes place. A knowledge of the strength and direction of an individual's interests is the key to an important area of his personality.

NATURE OF INTERESTS

Interests are usually defined as the "likes" and "dislikes" of an individual or the feeling of intentness, concern or curiosity about some object. Super gives four interpretations to the term interest, depending upon the way information about them is obtained. These are summarized here:

1. *Expressed interest* is the verbal profession of interest in an object, task, or occupation. The individual states that he likes, dislikes, or is indifferent to the activity in question. Expressed interests are often unstable and usually fail to provide useful data for diagnosis or prognosis, particularly for children.
2. *Manifest interest* is synonymous with participation in an activity or an occupation. Objective manifestations of interest have been studied in order to avoid the subjectivity of expressions or to avoid the implication that interest is static. Manifest interests are embodied in the verb "to be interested," in which both process and activity are involved. Examples of manifest interests are students who are active in dramatic clubs, or the accountant who devotes evenings to operating a model railroad.
3. *Tested interest* refers to interest as measured by objective tests as differentiated from inventories which are based upon subjective self-estimates. It is assumed that interest in a vocation is likely to manifest itself in action and should result in an accumulation of relevant information. For example, individuals interested in mathematics should read about developments in mathematics in journals and newspapers and acquire and retain more information about mathematics than other people.
4. *Inventoried interest* refers to the assessment of one's preference for a large number of activities and occupations. In such inventories each possible response is given an experimentally determined weight, and the weights (corresponding to the answers given by the person completing the inventory) are added in order to yield a score which represents

19 D. E. Super, "The Use of Multifactor Test Batteries in Guidance," *Personnel and Guidance Journal* Vol. 35 (September 1956), pp. 9–15.

not a single subjective estimate as in expressed interests, but a pattern of interests which research has shown to be rather stable.[20]

HISTORY OF INTEREST INVENTORIES

The study of interests has been of major import to counselors in their efforts to understand and assist others. In addition, interest inventories have been used widely to aid in the selection and classification of personnel in industry and business. Early attempts to assess interests were through checklists, questionnaires, and student writings. E. K. Strong, Jr., developed, researched and revised one of the first vocational inventories. His inventory introduced two major procedures in that: (1) the items dealt with the subject's like or dislike for a wide variety of objects, activities, or types of individuals commonly encountered in daily living; (2) the responses were empirically keyed for different occupations, on the premise that persons engaged in different occupations were characterized by common interests that differentiated them from persons in other occupations. As in the case of intelligence testing, progress in the assessment of interests was first made possible by an approach concerned less with the specific nature of that which was being measured than with the fact that it could be measured. Interest factors were first studied by factor analysis by L. L. Thurstone (1931). He applied factor analysis to eighteen occupational scales of the Strong Vocational interests.

VOCATIONAL INTEREST INVENTORIES

The appraisal of vocational interests is usually accomplished by the use of a standardized inventory. Reference has been made to the Strong Vocational Interest Blank (Stanford University Press). The SVIB consists of 399 items, most of which are responded to on a "like," "indifferent to," or "dislike" basis. The items are broken down into groups made up of professional occupations, school subjects, amusements, activities, types and/or peculiarities of people, and a self-rating personality inventory. The SVIB comes in two forms, one for men and one for women. Frequently women at the college level are given the men's form. Strong has recommended that the inventory not be used with individuals below the age of seventeen except in the case of unusually mature fifteen- and sixteen-year-olds. He believes that there is considerable instability of interest between ages fifteen and twenty.[21] However, Darley and Hagenah state that the inventory could be used with ninth- and tenth-grade students who have IQ's of 105 and above.[22]

[20] Abstracted from Donald E. Super, *Appraising Vocational Fitness* (New York: Harper & Brothers, 1949), pp. 377–379.

[21] E. K. Strong, Jr., *Vocational Interest Blank for Men* (Palo Alto, Calif.: Stanford University Press, 1945).

[22] J. G. Darley and T. Hagenah, *Vocational Interest Measurement* (Minneapolis: University of Minnesota Press, 1955).

Strong's inventory was developed by using as subjects mature men (or women in the case of the women's form) known to be successful in their fields. Success was defined by length of employment in occupation, certain minimum annual income, and other relatively objective indices. Their average age was forty years. Items were chosen that distinguished men in a specific profession from men in general. Some fifty keys are currently available for the men's form.

The SVIB (men's form) was revised by Campbell and his associates in 1966. One-fourth of the items were replaced by new items; changes were made in scoring (even with such changes, scoring is still too complex to do efficiently by hand); new scales were added and old ones dropped and other changes were made in certain criterion and reference groups.[23]

The Kuder Preference Record (Science Research Associates) is another popular interest inventory used in the schools. It differs in approach and scoring of items from the Strong. Its major purpose is to indicate relative interest in ten interest areas rather than specific occupations. Its items were originally formulated and grouped on the basis of content validity followed by item analysis of high school and adult groups to attain item groups possessing high internal consistency and low correlations with other groups. The Strong is best scored by an outside agency for a fee, while the Kuder is self-scoring. The Strong is constructed primarily for a more limited occupational group—the professional and semi-professional occupations—while the Kuder covers a wide range of interest areas and is applicable from semi-skilled to professional occupations. The Strong often is limited to seventeen-year-olds and over (except for very mature or bright younger individuals), while the Kuder has recently been revised (Form E) for use at the sixth grade level and above.

The Kuder Preference Record consists of a large number of items arranged in forced-choice triads such as:

Direct an orchestra	( )	( )
Compose music	( )	( )
Repair musical instruments	( )	( )

The examinee is asked to select the one item from the three he would most prefer to do and the one that he would least prefer. Form C and Form E provide ten interest scales plus a verification scale for detecting carelessness and failure to follow directions. The ten scales include such categories as outdoor, mechanical, computational, scientific, persuasive, artistic, literary, musical, social service, and clerical. Separate sex norms are available for junior high school and adult groups. Scores may be plotted on a normal percentile chart or converted to stanine scores.

The Minnesota Vocational Interest Inventory (MVII) is one of the

[23] David P. Campbell, "The 1966 Revision of the Strong Vocational Interest Blank," *Personnel and Guidance Journal* Vol. 44 (March 1966), pp. 744–749.

newer instruments available for the measurement of interests.[24] Appearing in 1965, this inventory made possible the measurement of the interest patterns of nonprofessional occupations. The inventory permits the comparison of an individual's responses to those of persons in a variety of skilled and semiskilled occupations.

Also representative of occupational inventories is the Lee–Thorpe Occupational Interest Inventory (California Test Bureau). The Lee–Thorpe consists of two levels, Intermediate Form for Grades 7–12 and an Advanced Form for Grades 9 through adulthood. The test is divided into three parts: fields of interest (personal-social, natural, mechanical, business, arts and the sciences); types of interests (verbal, manipulative, computational); levels of interest (routine tasks, skilled tasks, expert knowledge, skill and judgment).

USE OF INTEREST INVENTORIES

Interest inventories may be (1) of use in counseling to help obtain information which will aid in educational and vocational decision-making, to verify or confirm choice, or to open up new possibilities and (2) of use as a starting point in teaching or studying the major areas of occupations.

PROBLEMS IN USE OF INTEREST INVENTORIES

In concluding this discussion, the following liabilities of occupational interest inventories should be noted: (1) they can be faked; (2) many employ a vocabulary level beyond the comprehension of many students; and (3) the possibility exists that examinees will respond with socially acceptable choices rather than their own true preferences.

Personality Inventories

Attempts to assess the elusive nonintellective aspects of an individual's psychological makeup have been many and varied. Personality tests are most frequently designed to measure such characteristics as emotional adjustment, social relations, and the motivational aspects of behavior. They cover measures of social traits such as relations with other persons, including, for example, ascendance-submission, introversion-extroversion, and self-sufficiency. The number of available personality tests runs into several hundred and is increasing every year.

THE NATURE AND HISTORY OF PERSONALITY APPRAISAL

Definitions of good mental health usually include both the development of personal qualities and adjustment. Adjustment is a term used to denote a general process in which the individual changes his response patterns as dimensions of his environment change. Adjustments are of two general

---

[24] K. E. Clark and D. P. Campbell, *Minnesota Vocational Interest Inventory* (New York: The Psychological Corporation, 1965).

types, attack and withdrawal. When confronted with an issue, the individual can attack the stimulus causing the issue, or he can attack the barrier between himself and a desired goal, or he can withdraw or do nothing. Generally, psychologists believe that attack is more desirable than withdrawal, in that tension is relieved or eliminated. The nature of the well-adjusted individual has been described by Hountras:

1. He has self-respect, and respect and confidence in others, the essence of a wholesome attitude toward life.
2. He assumes responsibility for his behavior and experiences satisfaction in work and play activities.
3. He demonstrates a sensitivity to the needs of others.
4. He sets realistic goals which are usually capable of attainment.
5. He has goals, interests, and sources of gratification which are within the limits of social approval.
6. He employs a problem-solving approach when confronted by obstacles and uncertainties.
7. He has insight into his own needs as they influence his interaction with others.
8. He develops a philosophy of life which incorporates the values, beliefs, ideals and expectancies that guide his behavior and integrate the various facets of his personality.[25]

It should be noted that what is considered desirable behavior in one culture may be frowned upon or forbidden in another, and what is considered desirable today may be considered undesirable ten years from now. In addition, what is good adjustment for one individual may be exceedingly unhealthy for another.

Theories of personality have usually originated in clinical settings, and the amount of experimental verification supporting each varies. H. A. Murray's manifest need system of personality has stimulated the construction of many inventories.[26] The prototype of personality tests, however, is the Personal Data Sheet developed by Robert Woodworth during World War I. The Personal Data Sheet was devised to be used as a rough screening device for identifying seriously neurotic men who would be unfit for military service. Later personality tests were constructed which divided emotional adjustment into more specific forms, such as home adjustment, school adjustment, and vocational adjustment. Others have concentrated on a narrower focus of behavior.

WAYS OF ASSESSING PERSONALITY

Among the early means for assessing personality was Kraepelin's *free association* test which was used to screen abnormal patients. Kraepelin made use of specially selected stimulus words to which the subject re-

[25] Peter T. Hountras, *Mental Hygiene* (Columbus, Ohio: Charles E. Merrill Books, Inc., 1961), p. 11.

[26] H. A. Murray, *et al., Explorations in Personality* (New York: Oxford University Press, 1938).

sponded with the first word that came to mind. Another approach to assessing personality is that of *performance* or *situational* tests. In such tests, the examinee performs a task (usually everyday situations are simulated) whose purpose is disguised. The examinee's performance is observed without his knowledge. Hartshorne and May utilized situational tests to study children's behavior such as lying and cheating.[27] During World War II, situational tests were used by the Army's Office of Strategic Service to screen for social and emotional problems among its intelligence agents.

A third approach to personality appraisal consists of *projective techniques*. A projective device places an individual in a situation in which he is asked to describe something, relate a story, or respond to words. In responding, the individual unwittingly reveals things about himself. In theory, because the stimulus provided is ambiguous he interjects his own feelings and problems—his characteristic mode of response—into the situation. The subject's responses are evaluated by an individual extensively trained in their interpretation. Projective techniques, like situational tests, are disguised in purpose, which tends to reduce socially desired responses. Among projective devices are the Rorschach Ink Blot, the Thematic Apperception Test, and the Rotter Incomplete Sentence Blank. It should be emphasized that all such instruments are to be used only by individuals who have had special training in their use.

A fourth approach is by the *personality questionnaire*. Personality questionnaires are usually of the paper-and-pencil, self-report variety. Such questionnaires are founded on the assumption that human personality has a certain amount of stability and that over a range of similar situations, the same reactions will be elicited. Different individuals possess varying amounts of each trait. The more responses of a certain nature that an examinee marks, the more likely he is to possess the trait being measured. Representative of the personality inventories used in schools are the Bell Adjustment Inventory (Stanford University Press), California Test of Personality (California Test Bureau), Edwards Personal Preference Schedule (Psychological Corporation), Guilford–Zimmerman Temperament Survey (Sheridan Supply Company), and Mooney Problem Check Lists (Psychological Corporation).

Problems Associated with Personality Appraisal. Downie cites four questions which characterize the complexity of using personality inventories. These include the following: (1) Are the responses of these individuals honest or true? (2) Does the individual understand the questions? (3) How can such inventories be interpreted when actually there is no ideal type of behavior? (4) How has the inventory been validated and what is its reliability?[28] Certainly the possibility of faking and malingering always exists.

[27] H. Hartshorne and M. A. May, *Studies in Deceit* (New York: The Macmillan Co., 1928).

[28] N. M. Downie, *Fundamentals of Measurement,* Second Edition (New York: Oxford University Press, 1967), pp. 359–360.

The behavior measured by personality inventories, as contrasted to other kinds of tests, is more changing and fluid. This leads to complications in determining test reliability and validity. The search for adequate criterion data to establish validity is still present.

Although many authorities question the use of personality instruments in a school's guidance program, data from them can be helpful and useful. Certainly, facilitating the growth and development of an individual's personality is an important educational and guidance objective. As with any other objective, if we wish to ascertain whether students are attaining the goals, evaluation is necessary. It should be recognized that evaluation in this area is more complex. But counselors can use personality inventories or questionnaires to collect objective evidence to test against the many subjective judgments already at hand. That much care should be exercised in their use and in the interpretation of results is taken for granted, since serious damage can be done when inadequately trained people interpret inventory scores. Several points of caution should be emphasized regarding school use of personality inventories. The sale of such tests by reputable companies is rather rigorously controlled, with purchases possible only by qualified users. Despite the value of such test results to qualified personnel, careful consideration should be given to the necessity for such data, the way these data will be used, and who will have access to the information. Many of the tests briefly described above as illustrations of approaches to personality appraisal are restricted to use by qualified psychologists.

ESSENTIALS OF A SCHOOL TESTING PROGRAM

That the quality of a school's testing program depends upon the relevance of the tests chosen to the school's educational objectives has been attested to by many educators. Standardized tests, or schoolwide testing programs, can be useful in (1) evaluating progress toward certain essential outcomes which most schools have in common; (2) instructional practices; (3) counseling and guidance; and (4) administration. The values of standardized tests have become well established and accepted. Even though tests admittedly have limitations, few professional educators or psychologists doubt that a school can perform its functions better for students with the aid of tests than it can without them. Lennon gives the following reasons why tests are inextricably bound to the school:

1. *Tests provide measures of status* in particular skills or content areas for a pupil, a class, or a school. They reveal where the learner or group is at a given time, and thus provide a clue to the level at which instruction must be pitched. If we are to adapt instruction to the particular needs of individual pupils, it follows that we need dependable information as to precisely how they differ in their attainment or mastery — and such information is most easily come by through the use of tests.
2. *Tests provide measures of growth, development, or progress* toward desirable educational goals. Measurement of growth presupposes repeated ad-

ministrations of tests; from these repeated measurements we may infer the extent to which the learner is in fact making progress toward instructional goals and whether his rate of progress compares favorably with what is typical for his peers, or with what may reasonably be expected of him in the light of his ability.

3. *Tests provide measures of differential status,* revealing areas of relative strength and weakness that are of significance for guidance purposes.

4. *Tests provide analytical or diagnostic information,* which permits sharper definition of learning difficulties, and enables instruction to be brought to bear more forcefully on points where it is most needed.

5. *Tests provide inventories of skills,* which serve both as checks on progress and as guides to further instruction.

6. *Tests are one source of data essential for continuing evaluation* of the adequacy of the total instructional program.

It is axiomatic that evaluation is an integral part of the instructional process. Education without evaluation, as someone has put it, is target practice in the dark; without knowledge of the efficacy of our efforts, improvement is impossible. Standardized tests are by no means the whole of evaluation, but they are a rich source of the kind of data on which sound evaluation must depend.

In a word, tests are fact-finding devices; they do nothing but develop in an economical, reliable manner information that helps the teacher, the supervisor, and the administrator to discharge more effectively their instructional responsibilities. Standardized tests are means, not ends; they are a necessary first step in understanding the learner, in keying instruction to his needs, and in evaluation. The prominence that they have come to enjoy in American education is perhaps the best witness to their status as true instructional aids.[29]

A Minimal Testing Program

The question is often asked of the authors, "What is a minimal school testing program?" Inevitably the response is, "Where no test is given." But more seriously, the question is "Given the need to know pupils as much as possible, what, in your opinion, constitutes a minimal school testing program?" It should be recognized that the minimum number of tests to be given varies somewhat from one community to another. But it should also be recognized that because of the developmental, changing nature of children, tests should be systematically administered throughout every stage of their educational experience. For example, Whitten and Kagan reported that 15 to 20 percent of the population of children they were tracking changed their IQ scores by at least 15 points. Further, some children changed their IQ scores by as much as 60 points between ages six and ten. The backgrounds and family experiences of these children

[29] Roger T. Lennon, "Selection and Provision of Testing Materials," *Test Service Bulletin* No. 99 (Yonkers-on-Hudson, N.Y.: Harcourt, Brace & World, Inc., 1962), pp. 1–2.

led these investigators to suggest that the change was due to each child's motivation.[30]

Test programs must be built on the recognition that for different persons various abilities, aptitudes, and skills appear at different ages. If each pupil is to have opportunities to realize the full extent of his educational potential, identification of his strengths (and limitations) as early as possible is desirable. Every test has some degree of inaccuracy as a measure of present status; therefore, repeated sampling is needed to reduce the inaccuracies.

Generally, the authors recommend that at least four measures of ability or intelligence be administered during the elementary and high school years, usually three measures from kindergarten through grade 8, and at least one during grades 9 through 12. In addition, a minimal testing program should include the administration of standardized tests of achievement about every third year. From time to time specialized tests in reading, arithmetic computation, study skills, knowledge and use of resources, and the like should be administered to determine the extent to which these essentials have been mastered.

In addition, nothing has been said of specialized aptitude tests or personality and interest inventories. Such inventories should be administered and the results used by qualified individuals on a "need" basis.

Figure 5 depicts the placement of such tests in a system organized on an 8-4 basis. However, it should be noted that the organization of the school and the purpose and use of test results, rather than any arbitrary judgments, should be the determinants of placement.

Test Selection

Assuming that a school defines its testing needs, knows what kinds of tests are to be given, and at what grade levels at what times of the year, the question arises as to which test to select from among the many available. Discretion is necessary in choosing from among them to select the one that best meets specific testing needs. Since this topic is dealt with extensively in most measurement courses and in many publications,[31] only brief suggestions are cited below:

1. Know precisely the purposes for which the test will be used.
2. Study reference sources (textbooks, catalogs, journal reviews) to learn

[30] Phillip Whitten and Jerome Kagan, "Stimulus/Response," *Psychology Today* Vol. 3 (August 1969), p. 68.

[31] See, for example, Martin Katz, *Selecting an Achievement Test* (Princeton, N.J.: Educational Testing Service, 1961); Roger T. Lennon, "Selection and Provision of Testing Materials," *Test Service Bulletin* No. 99 (Yonkers-on-Hudson, N.Y.: Harcourt, Brace & World, Inc., 1962); John Dobbin, *et al.*, *Large Scale Programs of Testing for Guidance* (Princeton, N.J.: Educational Testing Service, 1958); Walter Durost, *What Constitutes a Minimal Testing Program for Elementary and Junior High School?* (Yonkers-on-Hudson, N.Y.: Harcourt, Brace & World, Inc., 1956).

FIGURE 5
A Minimal Testing Program

Grade	Ability	Achievement	Aptitude	Personality	Interest
K - 1	X				
2		X			
3	X				
4					
5		X	Need Basis	Need Basis	Need Basis
6	X				
7					
8		X			
9					
10	X				
11		X			
12					

what tests are available in the general areas for which they are to be used.

3. Obtain copies or specimen sets of tests (all possible) along with their manuals and descriptive materials.
4. Establish committees to review and criticize each test. Each test should be examined for:
   a. *Its validity*—the extent to which a test measures what it is supposed to measure. Any one or more of three types of validity may be cited: content, criterion related, or construct. The type of validity evidence required depends upon the purpose of the test.
   b. *Its reliability*—the extent to which the test is consistent in measuring what it measures. As with validity, one or more of three types of reliability coefficients may be cited: coefficient of equivalence, coefficient of internal consistency, and/or coefficient of stability. Each type gives a different view of reliability, and judgment as to adequacy again rests upon the use to which the test is to be put.
   c. *Suitability of norms*—a comparison group to which test performance of others may be related and described. The characteristics of a test's norm population should be defined and the adequacy of the sample (basis of sampling) should be examined for their similarity to the population being tested.

    d. *Its standard error of measurement*—the estimate of the size of the error of measurement in a score. All test scores contain error to a certain extent. The standard error of measurement provides an estimate of the amount of error present.

    e. *Practicality*—whether it is suitable or fits into the program because of costs, time limits, ease of marking and scoring, and availability of suitable interpretive aids.

Dobbin and his associates have cited seven criteria to guide test selection. These include the following:

1. A good test for use in a testing-for-guidance program should require that the student demonstrate the possession of basic skills and essential knowledge which are related as directly as possible to future success in study in the area covered by the test.
2. It should be appropriate in difficulty, so that the range of scores obtained from the group tested covers almost all of the possible range of scores.
3. It should be long enough to yield reliable scores, so that it distinguishes clearly between students at different levels of ability. In general, tests requiring less than 40 minutes do not yield scores of sufficient reliability for individual guidance.
4. It should be easy to administer and convenient to score.
5. The provisions for interpretation should be easily understood and used. Test results should be reportable in a form that makes them useful in guidance.
6. The test should be printed legibly and attractively.
7. It should not, ordinarily, place a heavy premium on speed of response. Speed tests are sometimes difficult to administer properly, and they increase student tension considerably. Furthermore, the trait they measure is quite unstable and not highly related to subsequent academic success.[32]

External Testing Programs

Testing programs in schools today consist of two major types: *internal tests,* or those which are controlled, selected, and administered, and whose results are used by personnel within the system, and *external tests,* or those that are basically selected and controlled by personnel in organizations or institutions outside the immediate school system. At present several optional external testing programs are available, particularly to high schools, on a nationwide basis. It should be noted that although the adjective "optional" is used here, few schools resist the many pressures of administering external testing programs. Such testing programs are used (1) to screen students for entrance to college and (2) to determine scholarship awards. Examples of such tests include the National Merit Scholarship Qualifying Test for second-semester juniors, with those pupils scoring high enough permitted to take a second test to be eligible for the final National Merit Scholarship selection; the American College Testing Program; the Scholastic Aptitude

---

[32] Dobbin, *et al., Large Scale Programs of Testing,* p. 17.

Test (College Entrance Examination Board) which determines the qualifications of high school seniors who seek to enter certain colleges (in addition, achievement tests are often required); the Preliminary Scholastic Aptitude Test is available to high school juniors and seniors (1) to provide an aptitude test for guiding college-bound students early in their junior year and (2) to serve as a screening device for certain scholarship sponsors.

Other examples of external tests are those used in employment classifying and placement. Although the federal government does not require or sponsor any kind of a testing program in the schools, it recognizes the usefulness of tests in classifying and placing employees. One such test is the General Aptitude Test Battery, which was designed to be used with adult employment applicants and high school seniors who plan to enter the labor market immediately after high school. The administration, scoring, and interpretation of this battery is handled by local representatives of the United States Employment Security Division. Another example is the Federal Service Entrance Examination, which is administered exclusively by the U.S. Civil Service Commission. Its purpose is to identify candidates for civil service positions.

Another example of an external testing program is the program of statewide tests. Miller briefly traces the history of these in the following account:

> Citywide testing programs were developed in some of the larger cities a number of years ago. Then the idea of statewide testing programs developed and spread. By 1955 Segel (Office of Education, Circular No. 447) found that 29 of the 48 states had one or more statewide testing programs in the elementary grades, in the secondary grades, or in all grades. In 17 of the 29 states one or more programs were sponsored by the State Departments of Education. In 12 of the 29 states the only state programs or services available were those sponsored by colleges and universities.
>
> Three years later, in March 1958, a survey conducted by the Educational Testing Service found that there were 31 testing programs in operation in the 17 states and 2 territories of the 30 states and 2 territories responding.
>
> With the passage of the National Defense Education Act of 1958 (NDEA) public and nonpublic secondary schools in all states and territories may participate in statewide or territorywide testing programs. In those states where state laws permit the testing of pupils in nonpublic schools, tests may be conducted as a part of the overall programs. In states which prohibit the use of state funds for nonpublic schools the U.S. Commissioner of Education is authorized to provide funds for testing by special contract. The eligible nonpublic schools enrolled almost 190,000 secondary school pupils in 1958–59.[33]

Basic Characteristics of A Testing Program

Some general principles serving as guides to school personnel in building a testing program may be stated as follows:

[33] Carroll H. Miller, *Guidance and Programs of Testing: Understanding Tests* (Washington: Government Printing Office, 1962), p. 16.

1. The testing program should be integrated with the school's total program. The general role of testing in a school's program must be considered. Tests should never be thought of as more than a tool to collect the information needed to carry out school functions. They are a means to an end, and the means should be kept in perspective. All staff members should consider the relationship of tests to the goals or purposes of the school if a program is to result in maximum benefits.

2. The testing program should be cooperatively and jointly planned. Because test results are used by counselors, teachers, and administrators, decisions regarding selection, programing, administration, reporting of results, must be made cooperatively by all. Good organizational procedure demands the utmost staff cooperation and close coordination. Involving an optimum number of persons in the planning, selection and use of a testing program does not imply that everybody should be "in the act." A device that many school systems have found effective in giving voice to the many who are concerned with testing is a testing committee. Such a committee is usually a standing committee, with membership representative of the several areas of personnel, charged with the responsibility for planning the testing program and keeping it under continuous review. Persons should be selected for their experience in and knowledge of tests and related problems, their concern for instructional uses of tests, and their competency in guidance activities. Observation of this principle will lead to staff understanding of test purposes, benefits, and limitations.

3. The testing program should be comprehensive. Though spot-testing in one area or another is often necessary and of value, a comprehensive program facilitates evaluation, study, and research. Program comprehension requires (1) assessment in all major areas of human endeavor, (2) provision for makeup testing where pupils have been absent, and (3) provision for retaking tests where errors have occurred in administering or scoring the test.

4. The testing program should be continuous. Occasional testing to serve immediate needs leads to gaps, duplication, and misuse of test results. A continuing program permits measurements of growth and progress leading to a developmental picture of individuals. A continuous program is one in which (1) assessment is conducted at regularly scheduled times and (2) the same or comparable instruments are employed.

5. The testing program's purposes should be communicated to staff members, administrators, and parents. As the purposes of a testing program become clear, those individuals responsible for the program should be given opportunities to discuss the program with faculty and parents. In some school districts parental objections have interfered with the educational use of tests. A curious folklore has grown up about testing and even fairminded and intelligent laymen are often confused by the claims and counterclaims. Many of their objections could be overcome with straightforward presentations to groups such as parent-teacher

organizations regarding the need for particular tests, the way they will be used, their strengths and limitations, etc. There need not be any secrets surrounding a testing program. Faculty and parents are entitled to complete and accurate information. Testing programs will stand or fall as they succeed or fail in contributing to understanding.

6. The testing program should have direction, supervision, and organization. Some one person well prepared and experienced in the field of tests and measurements should be appointed to direct, supervise, and organize the testing program. Such an individual will be responsible for testing and will work with other staff members in planning, administering, and using test results. If the size of the school does not permit the employment of a director or specialist on a full-time basis, the several important duties which he fulfills should be recognized and assigned to a qualified individual as a major area of endeavor.

CAUTIONS TO BE OBSERVED

Mention has already been made of the possible harmful consequences of testing, namely that unwise use of test data may result in permanent status determination, limited concepts of ability, domination by test publishers, and mechanistic decision-making.

Neulinger reports the results of a national sample of 5600 public, 2600 parochial, and 1200 private secondary school students' attitudes toward the use of intelligence tests. These students indicated whether they believed it was fair (or just) to use intelligence tests to *help* make certain educational, vocational, personal, and social decisions. His tabular results are reproduced here as Table VI. Neulinger concluded that anti-test sentiment among adolescents was "neither ubiquitous nor consistent" and that "social backgrounds and individual difference variables interacted with test constructs."[34]

Earlier, Brim had reported these data and had attributed anti-testing sentiment among lay and professional groups as stemming from (1) the inaccessibility of test data, (2) the belief that tests invade the individual's privacy, (3) rigidity in the use of test scores, (4) the narrow types of talent selected by tests, and (5) the belief that tests are unfair to minority groups. Brim discussed each of these issues and analyzed the basic reasons behind opposition to tests and testing. He explains that opposition to testing springs from (1) personal characteristics of certain individuals, (2) one's general system of values, (3) the individual's experiences with intelligence tests, particularly if the individual suffers a loss of self-esteem from poor performance, and (4) restrictions on life's opportunities as a

[34] John Neulinger, "Attitudes of American Secondary School Students Toward the Use of Intelligence Tests," *Personnel and Guidance Journal* Vol. 45 (December 1966), pp. 337–341.

TABLE VI

Percentage Distributions of Responses to the Question: "Given Tests as They Are Now, Do You Think It Is Fair (That Is, Just) To Use Intelligence Tests To Help Make the Following Decisions?" *

| | SECONDARY SCHOOL STUDENTS | | | | | | | | | | | |
| | PUBLIC (N ~ 5273)** | | | PAROCHIAL (N ~ 2621)** | | | PRIVATE (N ~ 1195)** | | | ADULTS (N ~ 1482)** | | |
Decisions	Yes	No	No Opinion	Yes	No	No Opinion	Yes	No	No Opinion	Yes	No	No Opinion
Decide who can go to certain colleges.	32	54	14	40	52	8	41	52	7	55	41	3
Put children into special classes in school.	42	44	14	51	40	9	58	35	7	75	20	5
Find out which children in the family should be given the most education.	12	75	13	12	79	9	10	82	8	37	58	5
Decide who should be hired for a job.	33	53	14	33	58	9	30	61	9	58	37	5
Decide who should be promoted.	24	63	13	21	71	8	15	77	8	46	50	3
Decide who should be allowed to vote.	8	82	10	10	83	7	16	79	5	12	86	2
Decide whom one should marry.	5	86	9	4	90	6	6	89	5	8	88	3
Select leaders in government.	39	45	16	39	50	11	34	57	9			
Select leaders for large corporations.	36	46	19	38	50	12	30	58	12			

* The adult questionnaire included the phrase ". . . or aptitude tests. . . ."
**The total number of cases varies slightly for each item because of a number of no responses.

Source: John Neulinger, "Attitudes of American Secondary School Students Toward the Use of Intelligence Tests," *Personnel and Guidance Journal* Vol. 45 (December 1966), p. 338.

result of poor test performance.[35] The reader is urged to examine the articles by Brim and Neulinger.

The increasing use of internal and external tests has been accompanied by a corresponding flow of critical comment. This situation has led to several investigations and studies of test use by many professional educational and psychological organizations. The American Association of School Administrators, in convention February 8, 1959, adopted Resolution No. 13:

The importance and usefulness of tests in evaluation and teaching cannot be overestimated. There is a great need for improved and more adequate instruments for evaluation of many kinds of educational growth. The misuse of tests and the misinterpretation of test data continue to be a glaring

[35] Orville G. Brim, Jr., "American Attitudes Toward Intelligence Tests," *American Psychologist* Vol. 20 (February 1965), pp. 125–130.

danger to good educational programs. Any test instrument should be selected and used in terms of what a particular school had intended to teach. To judge a school solely on the basis of data derived from any battery of examinations is an invalid and dangerous venture. State or national examination results, used without due regard for the educational objectives of the school and the nature of the student body, are likely to be misleading.

Reasons for Negative Criticism

Reasons for the critical comments, investigations, and resolutions are not hard to identify. *First,* tests in and of themselves, vary in quality and are far from perfect measuring instruments. Each test samples only a portion of the individual's behavior at a given time. No test measures as accurately at the extremes as it does at the middle. *Second,* tests are sometimes improperly administered. Directions for administration must be followed exactly as specified in the test manual. If they are not, the test loses its effectiveness, for valid comparisons with published norms will be out of the question. *Third,* test scores are often misused. Test scores are estimates, not absolutes. Although a score incorporates within a numerical expression some rating of the individual, measurement error is always present. No one should depend upon tests alone in making decisions. They should be used along with other educational, psychological, and sociological data. *Fourth,* test data are sometimes misinterpreted. Too often test interpretations sound like divine judgments rather than *estimates* of behavior. The student or parent is "told" of test results rather than helped to examine the results and their implications in terms of plans, previous data, and the like. Attempts to predict on the basis of test results must be based upon sufficient data. *Fifth,* in many instances tests are improperly safeguarded. Reputable test publishers sell only to qualified users, and they expect local users to safeguard them. Negligence in handling tests, such as permitting students to study them in advance, lessens their measuring value. *Finally,* testing is sometimes purposeless. A test should be given only because it (1) describes, within reasonable limits of accuracy some behavioral aspect of an individual; (2) extracts information obtainable in no other way; (3) provides information more efficiently than other methods, and (4) implements the purposes of the educational process. In short, tests should be given for the purpose of advancing a student's understanding of himself and others' understanding of him. Two popular books that describe at great length the effect of misuse and abuse of tests are those by Black[36] and Gross.[37]

Some Guides

Traxler has summarized some suggestions to be observed in the use of tests as follows:

[36] H. Black, *They Shall Not Pass* (New York: Random House, 1962).

[37] Martin L. Gross, *The Brain Watchers* (New York: Random House, 1962).

1. Make sure that all tests are administered under favorable working conditions and with faithful attention to the manual of directions. The best tests will give useless results if they are not administered well.
2. Carefully plan and carry out the scoring procedure, or utilize outside professional scoring services, to insure accuracy and reasonable dispatch.
3. Report the results promptly, with appropriate interpretations, to guidance personnel and teacher, and have the scores and percentiles recorded on cumulative records.
4. Make the test results available to parents who are willing to come to the school for interviews. Do not release the scores to parents in routine fashion by mail.
5. Express the results of scholastic aptitude tests in percentiles or other easily understood terms. Except in rare instances, avoid the use of IQ's.
6. Disregard small differences between pupils in score on a test and for the same pupil on different kinds of tests.
7. Relate test results to other kinds of information about the pupil. Do not depend exclusively on test scores and never regard the results of just one test as final.
8. Make sure that you understand the data yielded by a test before you try to interpret them for yourself or others.
9. Pay attention to the past test results for an individual pupil; that is, to his cumulative record. Growth is often more important than status.
10. See that the teachers in your school have continuous opportunity to become well informed concerning the meaning and interpretation of the results of tests.[38]

Sources of Information About Tests

Those who use tests have an obligation not only to secure appropriate training, but also to keep up to date in their training and with new developments in testing. The increasing proliferation and rapid revisions of tests makes the task of locating pertinent material a difficult one. Consequently, many sources of information have been developed for those interested in tests. Familiarity with these major resources is a necessity for those working as teachers, counselors and administrators.

A major source is the series entitled *The Mental Measurements Yearbook,* edited by Oscar K. Buros.[39] At present it consists of six volumes covering almost all commercially available educational, psychological, and vocational tests published in the English-speaking countries. The third to sixth yearbooks include critical reviews of most of the tests by one or more test experts. In addition, each yearbook lists the publisher, date of publication, price, forms, age levels, and other data.

[38] Arthur E. Traxler, "Fundamentals of Testing," *Test Service Notebook* No. 27 (New York: Harcourt, Brace & World, Inc., 1962), p. 4.

[39] See Oscar K. Buros (ed.), *The Sixth Mental Measurements Yearbook* (Highland Park, N.J.: Gryphon Press, 1965).

Another publication edited by Buros is *Tests in Print*,[40] which presents a comprehensive bibliography of tests and serves as a classified index and supplement to the six volumes of *The Mental Measurements Yearbook*. It contains a comprehensive listing of tests available and also a listing of out-of-print tests. It does not, however, contain reviews of the tests.

Other sources of information for those who use tests include the reviews of newly published tests in educational and psychological journals. Among the journals which either contain a special section or give some attention to tests are *Psychological Abstracts, Educational and Psychological Measurement, Measurement and Evaluation in Guidance, Journal of Consulting Psychology, Journal of Counseling Psychology* and the *Personnel and Guidance Journal*. A comprehensive critical survey of all types of psychological and educational tests is published every three years in the February issue of the *Review of Educational Research*.

Additional information about tests may be found in the catalogs and manuals provided by test publishers. Certainly each test manual should detail all essential information required for administering, scoring, interpreting, and evaluating a particular test. Data on norms, validity, and reliability should be reported. It should be kept in mind that some test manuals fall short of this desired goal, but more and more reputable test publishers are giving increasing attention to this important objective.

Finally, guides for the evaluation and use of tests are to be found in the *Standards for Educational and Psychological Tests and Manuals*.[41] Such recommendations represent a summary of desirable practices in test construction and use. In addition, the American Psychological Association[42] and the American Personnel and Guidance Association[43] have addressed themselves to the ethical considerations of test use. Each association has adopted and published a statement of ethical standards that contains general guides relevant to the use and publication of tests.

To conclude this section, the remarks of Barry and Wolf seem particularly pertinent:

> Essentially, the use of tests imposes three responsibilities upon the counselor. First, he needs to be well acquainted with the test he proposes to use in order to know the purposes for which it was designed. Second, he must know the purposes for which he and the other members of the school want to use the test. If these two sets of purposes conflict, the test is being misused. And finally, the counselor has to insure that the test results are used in a manner consonant with the purposes. The basic consideration for

---

[40] Buros (ed.) *Tests in Print.*

[41] American Psychological Association, *Standards for Educational and Psychological Tests and Manuals* (Washington: The Association, 1966).

[42] American Psychological Association, *Ethical Standards for Psychologists* (Washington: The Association, 1960).

[43] American Personnel and Guidance Association, *Ethical Standards* (Washington: The Association, 1961).

the counselor should be: would he like his own test scores to be handled in the manner in which he contemplates handling those of his students.[44]

TEST DATA IN THE APPRAISAL SERVICE

The basic need for individual appraisal in schools is based upon the belief in the right of each child to an education uniquely suited to his needs, interests, and abilities. Although educators have always known that children differ from one another, their acknowledgment of the desirability of differences is a more recent phenomenon. This recent emphasis upon individuality and the right of a child to an education uniquely appropriate for him forced the school to seek ways of identifying the direction and extent of pupil differences. In addition, ways were sought to identify not only interindividual differences, but also intraindividual differences. Traditionally, appraisal services have been concerned with nomothetic (group) data, but recent trends have emphasized idiographic (individual) data. In short, the individual's pattern of variability has become a source of study.

In developing an appraisal service in the guidance program, several questions need to be examined and constantly reviewed: (1) How much test and non-test data on each pupil are really needed to help him reach attainable goals? (2) To what extent should test data be directed toward remedial as opposed to developmental goals? (3) What provisions should be made for transmitting certain aspects of appraisal data to all concerned and to all other professional staff members?

Many appraisal services are built primarily for the purpose of predicting student behavior. In such programs standardized tests have been utilized to compare students with reference to such basic questions of "how well?" or "how much?" From such test data certain aspects of the pupil's future were predicted and were used in guidance to communicate to the student the basic essentials of the prediction to help him in decision-making processes. Other schools have developed appraisal services to classify students. This is essentially an administrative use of appraisal data. Many present-day school counselors, however, are routinely using appraisal data to schedule and section the student population. A third and more legitimate reason for developing appraisal service is that of increasing staff understanding of pupils and pupil self-understanding. Here is where most test and non-test appraisal devices find their greatest utility.

Hoyt has presented eight operational principles around which programs of student appraisal should be built. It is hoped that some of the basic ideas presented in the material in this chapter are reflected in Hoyt's statement of principles, which follows:

> *Principle I:* There is no single best appraisal method or procedure to be universally recommended.

---

[44] Ruth Barry and Beverly Wolf, *An Epitaph for Vocational Guidance* (New York: Bureau of Publications, Teachers College, Columbia University, 1962), p. 52.

Principle II: The effectiveness of student appraisal programs is directly related to the extent to which all professional staff members accept active roles in the program.

Principle III: To aim for complete understanding of students is both futile and foolish.

Principle IV: Understanding and helping students should be concurrent and not sequential operations.

Principle V: Student appraisal procedures involve both the study of students and the study of their environments.

Principle VI: The potential value of using appraisal procedures in combination is greater than the simple additive value of their respective potentialities.

Principle VII: Student appraisal procedures are not required in the same amount or to the same degree or necessarily for all students at the same time.

Principle VIII: The ultimate purpose of student appraisal procedures is increased student self-understanding leading to wiser student decisions.[45]

In addition, Hoyt raises six questions that are useful in determining the adequacy of student appraisal programs:

First, how much have you learned about the wide variety of student appraisal procedures suitable for use in school settings?

Second, how much are you willing to seek understanding from data collected in your student appraisal program?

Third, to what extent are you willing to treat students differently based on your understandings?

Fourth, how much do you worship the idols of reliability and validity?

Fifth, to what extent is your program of student appraisal procedures school-system-wide in scope?

Finally, what are you really doing in your school to improve student self-understanding.[46]

ANNOTATED BIBLIOGRAPHY

American Psychologist, Vol. 20, No. 2 (February 1965) and No. 11 (November 1965).

These issues contain worthwhile articles dealing with professional responsibility and testing, and public policy and testing.

KENNEDY, E. G. (ed.) *Individual Appraisal in Student Personnel.* Pittsburg, Kans: Kansas State College of Pittsburg, 1962, 46 pp.

This bulletin is a report of the keynote speeches given by Kenneth B. Hoyt and Paul C. Polmantier at a conference of city school superintendents, principals, directors of guidance, and counselors. It contains an excellent treatment of the psychological foundations of individual appraisal, basic as-

---

[45] Kenneth B. Hoyt, "Methods of Individual Appraisal," in E. G. Kennedy (ed.), *Individual Appraisal in Student Personnel* (Pittsburg, Kans.: Kansas State College of Pittsburg, June 1962), pp. 26–28.

[46] *Ibid.,* pp. 28–32.

sumptions of testing, methods of individual appraisal, and general principles for developing testing programs.

LINDEN, JAMES D., AND LINDEN, KATHRYN W. *Modern Mental Measurement: A Historical Perspective.* Guidance Monograph Series. Boston: Houghton Mifflin Company, 1968, 114 pp.

These two authors present a contemporary history of ability measurement. Study of the monograph will provide readers with background information essential to understanding the effort to measure and assess mental ability.

WOMER, FRANK B. *Basic Concepts of Tests.* Guidance Monograph Series. Boston: Houghton Mifflin Company, 1968, 93 pp.

Womer's monograph presents in a highly readable way some of the basic concepts utilized in testing. Particularly valuable are the applications of these concepts which the author includes.

SELECTED REFERENCES

BARRETT, ROGER L. "Changes in Accuracy of Self Estimates." *Personnel and Guidance Journal* Vol. 47 (December 1968), pp. 353–357.

BOTT, MARGARET M. "Measuring the Mystique." *Personnel and Guidance Journal* Vol. 46 (June 1968), pp. 967–970.

BRAZZIEL, WILLIAM F. "Beyond the Sound and the Fury." *Measurement and Evaluation in Guidance* Vol. 3 (Spring 1970), pp. 7–9.

CAREY, ALBERT. "Test Interpretation: Verbal versus Written Summaries." *The School Counselor* Vol. 16 (November 1968), pp. 120–124.

————. "Take a Look at Your Testing Program." *The School Counselor* Vol. 16 (January 1969), pp. 205–207.

DROEGE, ROBERT C. "Validity of USES Aptitude Test Batteries for Predicting MDTA Training Success." *Personnel and Guidance Journal* Vol. 46 (June 1968), pp. 984–989.

ELLIS, JOSEPH R. "Should Students Be Told Their I.Q.—An Old Question Studied from a New Dimension." *The School Counselor* Vol. 15 (November 1967), pp. 118–124.

ELTON, CHARLES F. "Patterns of Change in Personality Test Scores." *Journal of Counseling Psychology* Vol. 16 (March 1969), pp. 95–99.

ELTON, CHARLES F., AND ROSE, HARRIET A. "Personality Assessments Compared with Personality Inferred from Occupational Choices." *Journal of Counseling Psychology* Vol. 16 (July 1969), pp. 329–334.

ENGER, HAROLD B., AND MILLER, LEONARD A. "The Development of an SVIB Interest Scale for School Counselors." *Personnel and Guidance Journal* Vol. 47 (April 1969), pp. 767–772.

HALE, PETER P., AND BEAL, LANCE E. "MVII Occupational Interest Profile for Hospital Housekeeping Aides." *Vocational Guidance Quarterly* Vol. 17 (March 1969), pp. 218–220.

HIERONYMUS, A. N. "Comparability of IQ Scores on Five Widely Used Intelligence Tests." *Measurement and Evaluation in Guidance* Vol. 2 (Fall 1969), pp. 135–140.

KEHAS, CHRIS D. "Grouping for Instruction and Self Definition." *Measurement and Evaluation of Guidance* Vol. 2 (Winter 1970), pp. 205–213.

KOEPPE, RICHARD P. "National Assessment: An Analysis." *The School Counselor* Vol. 16 (September 1968), pp. 24–29.

KOHLAN, RICHARD G. "Relationships Between Inventoried Interests and Inventoried Needs." *Personnel and Guidance Journal* Vol. 46 (February 1968), pp. 592–598.

KRANZLER, GERALD D. "Some Effects of Reporting Scholastic Aptitude Test Scores to High School Sophomores." *The School Counselor* Vol. 17 (January 1970), pp. 219–227.

KUNCE, JOSEPH T., AND CALLIS, ROBERT. "Vocational Interest and Personality." *Vocational Guidance Quarterly* Vol. 18 (September 1969), pp. 34–40.

MATHIS, HAROLD I. "The Disadvantaged and the Aptitude Barrier." *Personnel and Guidance Journal* Vol. 47 (January 1969), pp. 467–472.

MUNDAY, LEO A., BRASKAMP, LARRY A., AND BRANDT, JAMES E. "The Meaning of Unpatterned Vocational Interests." *Personnel and Guidance Journal* Vol. 47, (November 1968), pp. 249–256.

OSIPOW, SAMUEL H., AND ASHBY, JEFFERSON D. "Vocational Preference Inventory High Point Codes and Educational Preferences." *Personnel and Guidance Journal* Vol. 47 (October 1968), pp. 126–129.

PECKENS, RUSSELL G., AND BENNETT, LLOYD M. "A Study of the Effectiveness of the Secondary School Counselor in Test Interpretation." *The School Counselor* Vol. 15 (January 1968), pp. 203–208.

ROTHNEY, JOHN W. M. "Some Not-So-Sacred Cows." *Personnel and Guidance Journal* Vol. 48 (June 1970), pp. 803–808.

TAYLOR, RONALD G., AND CAMPBELL, DAVID P. "A Comparison of the SVIB Basic Interest Scales with the Regular Occupational Scales." *Personnel and Guidance Journal* Vol. 47 (January 1969), pp. 450–455.

THORESON, RICHARD W., AND KUNCE, JOSEPH T. "Client Assessment Issues: A Perspective." *Personnel and Guidance Journal* Vol. 47 (November 1968), pp. 271–276.

VAUGHN, RICHARD P. "Academic Achievement, Ability, and the MMPI Scales." *Personnel and Guidance Journal* Vol. 46 (October 1967), pp. 156–159.

WHITELEY, JOHN M. "Intellectual Assessment of the Culturally Deprived: Implications for the School Counselor." *The School Counselor* Vol. 15 (November 1967), pp. 97–102.

10

STUDENT APPRAISAL: NON-TEST TECHNIQUES

What non-test appraisal techniques are useful?
What criteria should non-test appraisal techniques meet?
When can the different techniques best be used?
What are the major limitations of the different techniques?
What are the major advantages of the different techniques?

Effective teachers and counselors often become known to others because they possess and communicate an understanding of students to a degree not attained by their colleagues. Those who attain excellence know their pupils as individuals. They are knowledgeable about each pupil's interests, values, achievements, abilities, and aspirations. Knowing pupils well is a time-consuming, complex process demanding the utilization of many techniques and skills. But that such a process must and can be learned is attested to by the fact that teachers and counselors are often named as the most "influential persons" in the lives of many eminent men and women.

Analysis of the individual has always been of paramount importance in guidance services. It has been and will continue to be stressed for two fundamental reasons: (1) systematic analysis of pupil information permits teachers and counselors to help pupils, and (2) analysis aids pupils to better understand themselves, which is a basic objective of guidance. These two purposes can be realized only through sound techniques of collecting, organizing, and using relevant pupil information. In Chapters 9 and 10 a variety of testing and non-testing data-gathering devices are discussed. As pointed out in Chapter 9, testing instruments have made significant contributions to education by emphasizing the quantitative dimension of studying pupil behavior. However, the limitations and imperfections of tests make it desirable that in studying individuals non-testing techniques also be utilized. The purpose of this chapter is to examine the ways the major non-testing techniques can be used advantageously to appraise student behavior.

OBSERVATION

Observation is the base for most of the various non-testing appraisal techniques and is intimately bound with the development of the objective testing techniques described in Chapter 9. Observing and recording descriptions of pupils in action have a number of important purposes for those who work with pupils. Prescott has summarized these purposes as follows:

> It supplies facts which ultimately may refute certain tentative hypotheses and confirm others, thus yielding deeper insight into the dynamics that shape the child's behavior and development. It provides the most practical way of testing the validity of all the hypotheses that have been made about him. And, most important, it provides the means of evaluating the effectiveness of the steps that are being taken to facilitate his learning, his development, and his adjustment. Finally, it records changes which are occurring in the dynamic constellation of forces playing within and upon him and demonstrates that the individual is growing, changing, and fulfilling his potentialities to the degree made possible by the factors in his private world.[1]

Observation is not magical, intuitive, nor dependent upon an "x-ray eye" that enables one to peer into the individual's innermost self. Effective observation involves grasping clearly, concisely, and as completely as possible the essential behavior of individuals within given situations. No observer is ever able to perceive completely a given situation—the meaning a critical incident has for an individual, the facts underlying actions on the part of the observed, the attitudes and emotions associated with responses. But careful, trained observation can supply meaning to a particular sample of behavior which can be put into words for further clarification and study. Of particular importance in observation is the ability to determine the factors that initiate behavior and to describe accurately the way the person observed reacts to a given situation. Human behavior has been compared by many to a complex, blurred, ambiguous tapestry. Observers of student behavior try to see this tapestry as clearly as possible. This cannot be done quickly, haphazardly, or without effort. Observation may need to be carried on for a considerable time to determine how each of several small details fits into the larger design. It should be remembered that the analogy used here is faulty, since a tapestry is a static thing, while human behavior is viable, changing, and constantly in the process of development.

[1] From *The Child in the Educative Process* by Daniel A. Prescott. Copyright 1957. McGraw-Hill Book Co. Used by permission. P. 212.

Difficulties in Observing Pupils

There is no easy route to mastering the skill of observation. Some of the difficulties involved in observation can be described, however. Unconscious biases in observation sometimes occur because the observer fails to admit to his own feelings and limitations or because he is unaware of them. The biased observer tends to attribute his own behavioral tendencies to others. For example, an authoritarian teacher may see a pupil's frankness as impudence, or he may view a student who disagrees with him as domineering. Accurate observations demand an ability to evaluate objectively what is being perceived as well as an awareness of one's own feelings and behavior. If the observer lacks the objectivity to report behavior as it really occurs, then his observations may be useless, since they tend to describe the observer more accurately than the individual being observed.

Another difficulty confronting observers is that of adequate sampling. A pupil observed as withdrawn in a history class may be a discussion leader in a chemistry class. To ensure that the behavior observed is representative of the individual, a number of observations should be made in a variety of situations and at different times. By so doing, the observer not only collects more data but also is able to synthesize a more accurate, representative, and meaningful picture of the pupil.

Misinterpretation of observed behavior and inaccuracy in reporting are other problems that can destroy the usefulness of observations. Mental sets, interests, or expectancies often alter our perceptions of behavior or situations, because each of us tends to see the other's world as we have experienced our world. Experience in observing will enable teachers and counselors to be less likely to perceive events at great variance with reality unless the cues are insufficient or the mental stress is very great. Teachers and counselors should remember that for rapid observation to function efficiently it must be developed into a habit reaction. This comes through repeated practice in diverse situations. Even after relatively high levels of observational skills are acquired, practice and use are necessary for their maintenance.

Improving Observations

Practice will help pupil personnel workers to observe accurately. Practice in which two or more individuals observe simultaneously and compare results will be most beneficial. Other considerations which help control the observer's techniques should be followed. Such considerations, based on research, are outlined briefly below:

1. Before observation takes place, determine what is to be observed. The purpose of the observation should be known in advance. What dimensions of behavior are to be looked for? What traits are to be investigated?

Knowing these things will add meaning and purpose to observation periods.

2. Observe only one pupil at a time. Few well-trained observers can watch with any degree of accuracy two or more pupils at one time. When group behavior is studied, film and recording equipment should be used to obtain a record of the multitude of happenings that take place simultaneously.

3. Watch for significant behavior. Just what is significant may not be entirely clear at the time it occurs just as many of the things a pupil does are trivial and reveal nothing about him.

4. Spread observations over the school day. Time sampling of behavior, i.e., observing a pupil at 8:00, 10:30, 12:00, 1:00, etc., for brief periods of time often gives a truer, more comprehensive description of his behavior than does a description obtained from a few prolonged observations.

5. Learn to observe without resorting to writing notes during the observation period. The presence of a pad and pencil often cues children regarding what is occurring and results in behavior different from what might be obtained if these were absent. Significant behavior will probably be remembered anyway.

6. If possible, record and summarize the observation immediately after it is completed. Techniques for doing so will be discussed below.

ANECDOTAL RECORDS

There are two basic types of observations made by teachers and counselors—recorded and unrecorded observations. Treatment here is given to recorded observations, which are called anecdotes or anecdotal records. Anecdotal records, one of the many techniques used by guidance workers to assist them to better understand individual students, have been defined as follows:

> An anecdotal record consists of an objective description of pupil behavior in a particular environmental setting, an interpretation of the behavior by the observer writing the description, and a recommendation for future action based on the incident and its interpretation.[2]

> The anecdotal record is a record of some significant item of conduct, a record of an episode in the life of a student; a word picture of the student in action; the teacher's best effort at taking a word snapshot at the moment of the incident; any narrative of events in which the student takes a part so as to reveal something which may be significant about his personality.[3]

[2] From *Guidance Testing* by Clifford Froehlich and Kenneth Hoyt. Copyright © 1959, Science Research Associates, Inc. All rights reserved. By permission of Science Research Associates, Inc. P. 235.

[3] Jane E. Warters, *High School Personnel Work Today* (New York: McGraw-Hill Book Co., Inc., 1956), p. 9.

The anecdotal record is a specialized form of incidental observation. It is a description of the child's conduct and personality in terms of frequent, brief concrete observations of pupils made and recorded by the teacher.[4]

Study of the definitions of anecdotal records reveals that the following characteristics seem to be inherent in all of them: (1) anecdotal records are objective, factual, recorded accounts of observed behavior; (2) they are concise and describe only one incident at a time; (3) they are continuous and cumulative; and (4) they are descriptive.

The major difference in the definitions cited above is whether interpretation should be a part of the anecdotal report. Among the authors quoted, only Froehlich and Hoyt indicated that an interpretation of the behavior should be given. For practical purposes, anecdotal records can be of value if the observation is recorded without an interpretation, since a particular response, if typical, will probably recur. It may be of more value to hold interpretation in abeyance until several anecdotes have been obtained. This would provide the guidance worker with an opportunity to study and determine patterns of behavior and to base interpretation on a larger sample of data.

Characteristics of a Good Anecdote

A good anecdote is one that has been recorded. Beyond this point, a good anecdote must possess the characteristics listed in the preceding definitions. Prescott summarizes the characteristics of a good anecdote:

1. It gives the date, the place, and the situation in which the action occurred. We call this the setting.
2. It describes the actions of the child, the reactions of the other people involved, and the response of the child to these reactions.
3. It quotes what is said to the child and by the child during the action.
4. It supplies "mood cues"—postures, gestures, voice qualities, and facial expressions—that give cues to how the child felt. It does not provide interpretations of his feelings, but only the cues by which a reader may judge what they were.
5. The description is extensive enough to cover the episode. The action or conversation is not left incomplete and unfinished but is followed through to the point where a little vignette of a behavioral moment in the life of the child is supplied.[5]

A teacher's first reaction upon reviewing the characteristics of a good anecdote would be, "Where will I get the time to write anecdotes?" The

[4] Ruth Strang, *Counseling Techniques in College and Secondary School* (New York: Harper & Brothers, 1949), p. 84.

[5] Prescott, *The Child*, pp. 153–154. From *The Child in the Educative Process* by D. A. Prescott. Copyright, 1957. McGraw-Hill Book Co. Used by permission.

busy teacher will not take lightly the idea of spending a great deal of time writing observations unless he understands the purpose and values of records. Hence, one of the first steps the counselor must take is to enlist the cooperation of the staff. When a reasonable amount of acceptance has been assured, the counselor and the staff must decide: what should be expected of the observers, how are the records to be maintained, how should the reports be writt:n, what types of incidents should be recorded, when should the reports be written, and what use will be made of the anecdotal record? The decisions arrived at after a consideration of these questions will follow general patterns but will vary in accordance with local school policies and philosophies.

What Should Be Expected of Observers?

The observer should set aside a portion of time each day for the writing of anecdotes. A problem inherent in this is that the teacher may forget the incident or inject bias into the observation if a long period of time has elapsed before recording anecdotes. A question often arises concerning the advantages of spontaneous versus planned observations. This will vary with the teacher. Some teachers may be more at ease in recording spontaneous incidents immediately after they happen, while other teachers might schedule time for observation and recording.

How Are Records to Be Maintained?

Records should be maintained by the teacher with the assistance and continual supervision of the counselor. This provides an opportunity for the counselor and teacher to share information. At the end of the school year the information obtained in the anecdotal records becomes a vital part of the cumulative record, assisting future teachers and guidance workers.

How Are Anecdotes Written?

There are many different forms for writing anecdotes. In some schools, the incident is recorded on a piece of paper and placed in the cumulative file. In other schools, forms are provided for the writing of anecdotes. Figures 6, 7, and 8 present examples of the type of forms used.

Whatever type of form is used, the following information should be included: name of the student, grade, date, description of the setting, description of the incident, and the observer's name. Some forms include a space for the observer to place a comment, recommendation or interpretation. This is optional, but it may add information concerning the feelings of the observer at the time of the recording. However, it is important on any form to distinguish clearly between the observer's description of the behavior and his interpretation of the behavior.

What Incidents Should be Recorded?

Any incident that seems important and significant to the observer should be recorded. The anecdotal records should cover a wide sampling of pupil behavior; i.e., class, playground, cafeteria, gym, free time, bus, picnic, field trip, auditorium, etc.

When an anecdotal record program is inaugurated, the guidance worker must caution the teacher about picking out the student who causes the

FIGURE 6
Anecdotal Record Form (3″ x 5″ Cards)

Name_____	Date_____
Class_____	Place_____
	Anecdote

Observer_____

FIGURE 7
Anecdotal Record Form (3″ x 5″ Cards)

Student_____   Class_____

Date	Incident	Comment

Observer_____

FIGURE 8
Anecdotal Record Form (8½″ × 11″ Forms)

| Pupil _____ | Class _____ | |
| From _____ | To _____ | |

Date	Observer	Anecdote

most difficulty and writing all the anecdotes about him. It might be more beneficial to have several anecdotes about all the children than to have many about one child who is a problem.

According to Prescott, the following should be incorporated in an anecdotal record:

> In general, the description should give a cross section of the pupil's life at school and show how he acts in a variety of situations. Some children behave so differently in different classes and with different teachers that one would hardly recognize them as the same individuals; a proper distribution of anecdotal material should demonstrate this. It is as important to see what bores a child as to see what excites his interests, and a good case record would reveal how he acts under both circumstances. It would show him in action when things are going well and when they are not going well; interacting with his teacher, the principal, other adults, his peers, and younger and older children; studying, loafing, creating, sulking, or pursuing an interest alone; interacting with his parents, siblings, and near-neighbor children; informal situations such as eating lunch or playing. In short, samplings from the whole range of his life experience in and around the school are needed.[6]

When Should the Reports be Written?

It has been suggested that reports should be written daily; either after school or at a specific time set aside by the teacher. The time will vary according to the type of school in which the teacher is working.

In a large high school, where the teacher has many students, it would be impossible for the teacher to write anecdotes about all of the students,

[6] *Ibid.,* p. 155. From *The Child in the Educative Process* by Daniel A. Prescott. Copyright, 1957. McGraw-Hill Book Co. Used by permission.

but records could be maintained for selected students. These could be written after school, during a free period, or possibly between classes. In an elementary school, where the teacher is with a group of students most of the day, comprehensive records of observations can be kept for all students in the class, using free time available during or after school.

What Are the Purposes of the Anecdotal Record?

Traxler has listed the following values and uses of anecdotal records:

1. Anecdotal records provide a variety of descriptions concerning the unconstrained behavior of pupils in diverse situations and thus contribute to an understanding of the core or basic personality pattern of each individual and of the changes in pattern.
2. They substitute specific and exact descriptions of personality for vague generalizations.
3. They direct the attention of teachers away from subject matter and class groups and toward individual pupils.
4. They stimulate teachers to use records and to contribute to them.
5. They relieve individual teachers of the responsibility of making trait ratings and provide a basis for composite ratings. Moreover, they provide a continuous record, while trait ratings are usually made only at certain points in a pupil's school experience.
6. They encourage teacher interest in and understanding of the larger school problems that are indicated by an accumulation of anecdotes.
7. They provide the information which the counselor needs to control the conferences with individual pupils. An appropriate starting point for each conference can be found in the data and the discussion can be kept close to the pupil's needs.
8. They provide data for pupils to use in self-appraisal. While in some cases the anecdotes should not be shown to the pupils, each pupil can profitably study the indications in many of the anecdotes about him in order to decide what he needs to do to improve.
9. Personal relationships between the pupil and the counselor are improved by anecdotal records, for these records show the pupil that the counselor is acquainted with his problems.
10. Anecdotal records aid in the formulation of individual help programs and encourage active pupil participation in remedial work.
11. They show needs for the formation of better work and study habits.
12. Curriculum construction, modification, and emphasis may be improved through reference to the whole volume of anecdotal record material collected by a school. The anecdotes indicate where there should be general presentation of material in character development to satisfy the needs of the whole school community.
13. An appropriate summary of anecdotes is valuable for forwarding with a pupil when he is promoted to another school.
14. Anecdotal records may be used by new members of the staff in acquainting themselves with the student body.

15. The qualitative statements contained in anecdotal records supplement and assist in the interpretation of quantitative data.
16. Collections of anecdotal records may provide the necessary validating of evidence for various evaluating instruments.
17. Anecdotal records aid in clinical service. When pupils are referred to clinical workers for special study of their problems, there is great advantage in having anecdotal records available.[7]

Consideration of the usefulness of anecdotal records indicates that the counselor, teacher, administrator, and student all benefit from a systematic program of observation with its resultant anecdotal records: (1) Both counselor and teacher gain more information about an individual's cumulative pattern of development; (2) the teacher becomes a better observer and interpreter of student behavior; (3) the administrator has a more understanding staff; and (4) the student, who realizes that the school and staff are interested in him, benefits from such understanding.

Limitations of Anecdotal Records

Anecdotal records, like any other instrument or tool, have limitations. The limitations of anecdotal records have been listed by Traxler as follows:

1. It is apparent, of course, that an anecdotal record can be valuable only if the original observation is accurate and is correctly recorded; otherwise, it may be worse than useless.
2. Many persons find it extremely difficult to write with complete objectivity, but practice will do a great deal to overcome the tendency to intersperse the report of behavior with statements of opinion.
3. A pernicious but fortunately rare use of anecdotal records is the employment of them for defense purposes.
4. It is evident that there is danger in lifting a behavior incident out of the social setting in which it occurred and reporting it in isolation.
5. At best, only a small proportion of the total number of significant behavior incidents for any pupil will find their way into anecdotal records.
6. Some persons fear that anecdotes, through preserving a record of unfortunate behavior incidents on the part of certain pupils, may prejudice their success long afterward, when the behavior is no longer typical of them.
7. It cannot be too strongly emphasized that the adoption of a system of anecdotal records is no small commitment and that it will inevitably add to the load of the entire staff, particularly the counselors and the clerical staff.
8. There is some danger that anecdotal records will throw the need for better adjustment of certain pupils into such high relief that too marked an effort will be made to short-cut the adjustment process.

[7] Arthur E. Traxler, *The Nature and Use of Anecdotal Records* (New York: Harper & Brothers, 1949), pp. 21–22. Reprinted by permission of Harper & Row, Publishers.

9. Undesirable behavior, because of its nuisance aspect, is likely to make a stronger impression on teachers than desirable behavior.
10. Occasionally teachers will observe incidents that are not at all typical of the behavior of the pupil concerned.[8]

The limitations of anecdotal records, and the amount of work required of the counselor and staff may make it hard to decide if such records are worth the investment of staff effort. If anecdotal records assist students in better understanding themselves and provide information that will assist the staff in better understanding individuals, then the work is well worth the effort.

RATING SCALES

Rating scales are also used by school personnel to implement observations. This type of measurement device was first used in the early 1800's by the British navy to describe weather conditions. More extensive use was made of rating scales in America during World War I to rate the efficiency of military officers, and during and following World War II they came into greater use by military, industrial, and educational personnel.

The rating scale form presents a list of descriptive words or phrases which are checked by the rater. Teachers, counselors, and principals are frequently asked to rate pupils on such characteristics as dependability, honesty, cooperativeness, self-reliance, leadership, industriousness, and the like. Note that these examples are indices of personal qualities that usually are quantified and dealt with statistically.

Use of Rating Scales

The greatest use of rating scales in schools is to obtain personality ratings on students (see Figure 9, pp. 281–282). Some schools secure annual ratings of specific classes, such as all students in grades 9 and 12. At the present time, rating scales are not as widely used as they were thirty years ago. Sociometric and inventory techniques have, in part, replaced them. College admission officers and employers still use them quite extensively, however.

Most studies of the reliability of ratings have produced coefficients ranging from the high 40's into the 60's. In general, reliability of ratings increases with the number of judges. The nature of the factor to be rated influences reliability, however. If the factor is not readily observable, reliability decreases. Validity coefficients usually tend to be relatively low, but vary with the nature and quality of the criterion being rated.

---

[8] Traxler, *Anecdotal Records,* pp. 17–20. Reprinted by permission of Harper & Row, Publishers.

Guiding Principles for Constructing Rating Scales

As guidance personnel prepare or select rating scales for use, they should ask themselves the following questions regarding the scales' characteristics:

1. Is each factor or characteristic clearly defined? The specific behavior to be rated should convey the same meaning to each person who uses the rating scale. It is considered desirable to train raters in the use of scales with such training focusing on the meaning of the specific labels applied to the behavior being rated, for unless such traits as "cooperativeness" or "promptness" are defined precisely, each rater may

FIGURE 9
Personality Rating Form

NAME_____   Fresh.____Soph.____Jr.____Sr.____
                                  Other_____

DIRECTIONS: Place a check at the point which most nearly describes the student's behavior. Check * if you have had no opportunity to observe.

1. Does he or she present a good general appearance—   COMMENTS
   clean and well groomed?
   ⌞__|____|____|____|____⌟
   Always   Seldom

2. How would you rate his or her health?
   ⌞__|____|____|____|____⌟
   Excellent   Poor

3. Have you had reason to question his or her character?
   Underline if specifically applies: Sincerity, honesty, morals
   ⌞__|____|____|____|____⌟
   Never   Frequently

4. Does he or she accept authority and cooperate with regulations?
   ⌞__|____|____|____|____⌟
   Supports and cooperates willingly   Rebels

5. How well adjusted is he or she to group living?
   ⌞__|____|____|____|____⌟
   Very Well   Anti-social

6. How concerned is he or she for others?
   ⌞__|____|____|____|____⌟
   Deeply concerned   Only thinks of self

7. a. How emotionally stable is he or she?
   ⌞__|____|____|____|____⌟
   Very stable   Unstable

   b. If you marked unstable underline individual's usual reaction:
   Excitable   Hyperemotional   Unresponsive   **Apathetic**

FIGURE 9, Continued
Personality Rating Form

---

8. a. Which role does he or she most often take:
   _____Leader   _____Follower
           If it is leader: _____Positive _____Negative

   b. How well does he or she accept and carry out re-
      sponsibilities related to offices and activities?

   | | | | | |

   Enthusi- Willing,   Varies Unreliable Never
   astic,   dependable with   participates
   ambitious,   activity
   has
   initiative

9. Does he or she exhibit poise and manners in social
   situations?

   | | | | | |

   Outstanding   Improving Shy Definitely
                                         lacking

10. How well liked is he or she by others?

    | | | | | |

    Friendly and well liked   Tolerated Avoided

11. In a situation where group pressure is exerted, what
    role would he or she be most apt to take? (Positive
    influence—best interest of group; negative influence—
    not in best interest of group)

    | | | | | |

    A positive Follows   Easily   Follows   A negative
    influence positive swayed negative influence
               group   group

    COMMENTS:

    Signed _____   Date _____
                    Title:_____

---

give it a different meaning. For example, one rater may think of
"cooperativeness" as the ability to get along with others, while another
rater considers it faithful adherence to classroom or school regulations.

2. Is each factor or characteristic observable? Traits which are not readily
   apparent to all observers should be avoided. For school ratings,
   characteristics which are observable during the normal school routine
   should be used. Froehlich and Darley noted that one school rating
   scale asked teachers to evaluate the following: "If teacher left study
   hall or class, extent to which student could be trusted." Asking a
   teacher to make such a rating demands that he judge a student's behavior without observing it.[9]

[9] Clifford P. Froehlich and John G. Darley, *Studying Students* (Chicago: Science
Research Associates, Inc., 1952), p. 108.

3. Are the degrees of the characteristic defined? The degrees or different levels for each factor to be rated should be established. These gradations usually range from low to high, simple to complex, unacceptable to acceptable, and the like. The consensus is that at least five gradations for most characteristics are preferable. Too few gradations, i.e., two or three, produce ratings that are too gross; while too many gradations, such as ten or twelve, call for the rater to discriminate too finely. In general, such words as "very," "some," "average," and "large," which convey different meanings to different individuals, should be avoided as descriptive statements of degrees or levels.

Types of Rating Scales

There are many types of rating scales. Four types of scales widely used by school personnel are described briefly below:

NUMERICAL SCALES

Numerical scales employ numbers for denoting gradations and the meaning of each number is defined. For example, an item on a scale might ask: "How would you rate his enthusiasm?" Numerical scales could be set up as follows: "1. apathetic, 2. rarely enthusiastic, 3. sometimes enthusiastic, 4. usually enthusiastic, 5. intensely enthusiastic." The rater would then write in the blank provided the number of the degree that best describes the individual he has observed.

DESCRIPTIVE SCALES

Scales are sometimes constructed which employ a series of phrases describing various degrees of the characteristic rated. These phrases are usually arranged in order, with instructions to the rater to check the phrase that comes closest to describing the characteristic being considered.

Example:

How would you rate his industriousness?
_____Indolent, expends little effort.
_____Frequently does not complete work.
_____Gets required work done, but no more.
_____Steady worker and occasionally does more than required.
_____Eager, usually does more than required.

PAIRED COMPARISONS

Using this method, the rater compares each person rated with respect to the trait to every other individual rated in general terms of "equal," "better," or "worse." Such a method tends to be somewhat cumbersome for large groups. However, paired comparisons do force the rater to compare each individual to every other individual in the group, which may be advantageous.

GRAPHIC RATING SCALES

In graphic rating scales, the units or degrees are indicated on a continuum, with descriptive phrases placed appropriately under the line. Each rater indicates his observation by checking the point which best describes the degree of the trait which applies.

Example:

LEADERSHIP				
Actively avoids leadership	Prefers not to lead	Accepts leadership if asked	Occasionally prefers not to lead	Actively seeks out leader's role

When setting up the degrees to be used to rate a characteristic, the poor and good responses may be scattered in random fashion to discourage the rater from checking the individual on each characteristic at the same point on each scale. Graphic scales are the commonest type in current school use. They are easily administered and easily understood. If well constructed, and if they employ words with as precise a meaning as possible, they can be of considerable value.

Advantages of Rating Scales

The advantages usually cited for rating scales are that they are a means of quantifying observations and that they also are a means by which several observers can rate the same individual. This latter procedure usually increases the reliability of ratings by combining several raters' evaluations. Equivalent ratings from several judges, providing, of course, that they have equal knowledge of the individual being rated, are usually superior to one judge's opinion.

Limitations of Rating Scales

Rating scales, like all forms of observations, are subject to error. Errors peculiar to rating scales have been described by many as errors of personal bias, halo effect, central tendency, and logical error. Because rating scales have been in widespread use for many years these characteristic errors are well known to those who construct and use such scales. It should be noted, however, that these types of errors may be present in all forms of data collection based on observation of the individual.

Personal bias error is introduced when the observer makes sweeping generalizations about certain groups; e.g., minority groups. Because of his own generalizations, the observer may rate all such individuals either too high or too low. Known also as the error of leniency or severity, this error can be reduced by statistically scaling each observer's ratings to an arbitrary mean and standard deviation. Inservice education for those who make this type of error might consist of discussion sessions about their problems in making sound ratings.

Errors of central tendency are committed when a rater avoids the extremes of any rating scale. In other words, he usually assigns ratings near the midpoints of each scale. Such an individual finds it difficult to make extreme judgments, and his easiest solution is to give everyone a "break" by marking all near the middle of the continuum.

Halo effect errors occur when the rater permits the influence of one or two outstanding characteristics, whether good or bad, to color all judgments about an individual. The observer rates the individual the same on all traits. For example, if Suzie R. is academically outstanding, a rater's mental set about her might cause him to rate her outstanding in social adjustment, promptness, or virtually anything else. Such errors may be reduced by rating all individuals on one characteristic and then all individuals on the next characteristic until the entire scale is completed. This technique is similar to having the classroom teacher score each essay question for an entire class rather than all essay questions for a single individual.

Logical error occurs when the rater does not understand the trait to be rated. This happens when not enough time has been spent in clearly defining the trait on the form or in training the judges so that agreement on its meaning is understood by all raters.

CUMULATIVE RECORDS

Ideally, cumulative records present an organized, progressive record of information about the individual student which distinguishes him from all other students. A cumulative record must be organized so that it can be readily interpreted by teachers, counselors, and administrators. Objective information is sought which will portray significant and representative characteristics of the individual. Likewise, cumulative records are progressive, showing trends and growth patterns. The cumulative record, a composite of data collected by teachers, counselors, administrators, and health personnel, can provide a comprehensive picture of the student and his background when it is obtained over a period of time. This information is then used by counselors and teachers to help the student make effective adjustments to school situations. In addition, the cumulative record may be useful in helping the student understand himself—his physical, academic, emotional, and social progress. If it is effectively used, the cumulative record could indicate to the school staff the degree to which the school is meeting the child's needs. Data collected in counseling sessions should not be placed in the cumulative record, however. Such data have been obtained in a confidential setting and should remain confidential.

The cumulative record represents a storehouse for data about a pupil, yielding a maximum of information in a minimum of space. Ideally and practically, the record should require minimum clerical work. Usually included in the cumulative folder are the following: (1) personal data and family background information; (2) medical and health information; (3) date of school entry; (4) school grades; (5) transcripts from previous schools attended; (6) schoolwide test results; (7) personality and behavior trait ratings; (8) school activities; (9) anecdotal records; and (10) auto-biographies written in class settings.

All the data in the cumulative folder should be carefully kept up to date. By all means, the cumulative folder should not be used as a place for odds and ends. Rather, it should be a valuable source for those kinds of information that will create an understanding of the child and will tend to promote realistic planning with him. It is important that all entries be dated, as this helps the reader to form a clearer picture of the scheme and development of information. Entries should be initialed, thus making it possible for the teacher or counselor to seek any needed clarification and to locate additional resources. The folder and record card format should be such that it facilitates the forwarding of full information to other schools or organizations when authorized requests are made.

Types of Cumulative Records

During the 1920's and 1930's some schools began using a cumulative record that was kept by the student. The idea originated during World War I with the Soldier's Classification Card. Student-kept cumulative records were fashioned so that such a record would contribute significantly to a pupil's understanding of himself. Though the idea was not without merit, the student-kept record had obvious shortcomings and therefore never caught on and was soon abandoned.

Three of the most common types of cumulative records are the packet type, the single-card or folder, and the combination. The packet type, which is a plain manila folder in which materials can be inserted, is the easiest to construct. Its value lies in its flexibility and inexpensiveness. Single-card or folder records are published commercially by several school supply companies, and many states have adopted uniform records of this type. The major disadvantage of commercially published records is that they lack flexibility. Published folders or cards do not have the space needed for certain items nor the items arranged as some schools prefer them. Their advantage is that a uniform record is more easily understood when students move from school to school. The combination form usually incorporates a commercially printed folder with locally developed supplemental records.

Criteria for Cumulative Records

In the selection or construction of a cumulative form, Humphreys and his associates advise a school staff to keep in mind such important points as the following:

1. The cumulative record form for a student should agree with the objectives of the local school.
2. The forms should be the result of the group thinking of a faculty committee.

3. The forms should provide for a continuous record of the development of the student from the first grade to the end of his formal education; for this purpose a series of forms may be used.

4. The form should be organized according to the customary sequence of academic years; for each year the source of similar kinds of information should be recorded for a student.

5. The form should contain carefully planned spaces in which to record the results of standardized tests including date of test, title of test, student's score, his standing in terms of norms, and the like.

6. The form should provide for the annual recording of the personality ratings or behavior descriptions that represent the consensus of the student's counselor and teachers.

7. The form should be as comprehensive as possible, but it should not overburden the clerical or teaching staff of the school.

8. The form should be accessible to the teachers as well as to the principal and counselors. If a counselor has recorded highly confidential information about the student, this information should be filed outside the regular form.

9. The form should be re-evaluated periodically; it should be revised as needed to take account of educational developments.[10]

It is important to remember that only through the cooperation of the total educational team can good, effective cumulative records be achieved. In fact, the very nature of the recording function is one which makes for cooperation among school workers.

Use of Cumulative Records

Use of records will depend a great deal upon the relevance of the data contained within them. All teachers, if they have adopted the attitude of considering the "whole pupil," will use the file as needed. To prevent loss of records, a simple notation should be made at the time the folder is used. Such information may include date, person responsible, identification of folder, and date of return.

It is important that teachers be instructed in the use and formation of cumulative records. If the cumulative record has been forced upon them, they may not be willing to accept its use and maintenance. Therefore, teachers should be given the opportunity to suggest forms and information to be collected and procedures for recording it. Unified effort is best achieved through conferences or committees.

Information in properly constructed cumulative records becomes the basis for most guidance services. Mortensen and Schmuller have outlined the uses of the cumulative record as follows:

[10] From *Guidance Services* by J. Anthony Humphreys, Arthur Traxler, and Robert D. North. Copyright © 1960, Science Research Associates, Inc. All rights reserved. By permission of Science Research Associates, Inc. P. 151.

1. In revealing information concerning the previous experiences of the pupils as individuals.
2. In providing information about group activities.
3. In the organization of needed curriculum or guidance experiences.
4. In the evaluation of pupils.
5. In the evaluation of different curricula.
6. In the working out of certain administrative procedures—district-wide, inter-district, county, or state-wide.
7. In recording the present experiences of pupils.
8. In carrying out research on the adequacy or results of education, or research on such important considerations as personality variables.
9. In grouping pupils within classes for more effective use of time and effort.
10. In assigning students to particular classes, that is, the placement service.[11]

Careful planning and organization are necessary unless the cumulative record folder is to become a catch-all for useless and possibly harmful information. Certainly, it is necessary that all folder and record-card entries be valid. For example, if a counselor should for any reason believe that a test result is not valid, it either should not be entered at all or a notation should be placed with the result, and retesting performed to verify results.

Since it is possible to misinterpret information recorded on cumulative records, and since this misinterpretation can be harmful to the student, it is wise to develop a complete explanation for their use and to identify any codes used in the cumulative record system. This information can be then used for inservice teacher training and for new school personnel.

There is always a question of how much confidential information should be placed in the cumulative record, for in no case should a pupil's confidence be betrayed by any member of the school faculty. It is advisable to record confidential information on a separate form which can be placed in the counselor's private file. A notation can be entered in the folder that additional information may be available from the counselor on a need-to-know basis. When and to whom such information is available represents a highly complex issue involving professional ethics. Potentially harmful information concerning extreme behavior should be carefully controlled and placed in the counselor's confidential file.

Essentially a cumulative folder should include only those kinds of information that will, in a positive way, foster understanding of the child and tend to promote sound and realistic planning with him. Information which may operate against a pupil frequently needs specialized interpretation to school staff. Special interpretation helps to place deviant behavior in perspective and assists in identifying each staff member's role in helping the individual student.

[11] Donald G. Mortensen and Allen M. Schmuller, *Guidance in Today's Schools,* Second Edition (New York: John Wiley & Sons, 1966), pp. 231–232.

Parental Concern over Records

Tennyson, Blocher, and Johnson have commented upon the fact that parents are concerned and worry about student personnel records. They believe that the source of parental concern can be traced to (1) the laxness of school personnel in communicating why certain kinds of information are needed, (2) appraisal services which are conducted for administrative expedience, and (3) unprofessional handling of appraisal data by the school staff. In short, these authors bring into question whether records are used for the benefit of students. Are they primarily to serve students or are they to serve the school? Can they do both?

If records are to be used to serve students, the following five statements of principles may be used as guides to action in collecting and using pupil data:

1. In collecting appraisal information, I can justify an invasion of another's privacy only if the information will be used by the *school* in a way that is helpful to the student.
2. When I ask the student or parent to reveal personal information in the course of interviewing, testing, or other inventory, or when I allow him to divulge such information of his own accord, I shall do so only after making certain that he is aware of the purpose of this information and the way it will be used.
3. I must distinguish between appraisal data that describes student academic performance and that which describes student behavior or personality. This latter kind of information will be shared by the school only with the student, his parents, and those persons who will use the information for the professional purpose of helping the student.
4. Where students specifically request that certain information be kept in confidence, or where such intent may reasonably be interpreted from the content of the counseling interview or the context of the relationship, I shall reveal such information only under exceptional circumstances such as imminent danger of life.
5. All other information revealed in the course of a counseling relationship is considered confidential, and I shall reveal such information to other professional workers in the school only when there is a specific reason for doing so and where the purpose is clearly to help the student. I shall exercise judgment in determining the extent to which I am able to communicate to others "a feeling for the student" without revealing specifics.[12]

PUPIL-DATA QUESTIONNAIRES

Schools have long used the pupil-data questionnaire to obtain vital information about their students. Usually such questionnaires consist of items regarding the student's home, family, health, educational and vocational

[12] W. Wesley Tennyson, Donald H. Blocher, and Ralph H. Johnson, "Student Personnel Records: A Vital Tool But a Concern of the Public," *Personnel and Guidance Journal* Vol. 42 (May 1964), pp. 888–893.

plans, out-of-school and in-school activities, study habits, and the like. Although these data are also located in the cumulative record, the pupil-data questionnaire represents a cross-sectional approach to such information, while the cumulative record is basically a longitudinal record. Pupil-data questionnaires give school personnel information that enables them to see the student as he is now and provide extensive data dealing with the present life situation of the student.

Use of Pupil-Data Questionnaires

Pupil-data questionnaires provide information regarding students whose records are incomplete or who are new to the school. They are also used by many counselors to obtain background information needed for counseling pupils. Such a form has been used by the Purdue Guidance Clinic. Figure 10 presents the Purdue form, which has been revised a number of times to obtain the specific kinds of information useful to counselors in helping high school pupils who come to the Clinic. Such questionnaires also serve as a means of providing an organized system by which pupils can think about themselves.

A pupil-data questionnaire is often administered by counselors to all entering freshmen students in a high school. In using such questionnaires, the school faculty needs to determine: (1) For what purpose is this questionnaire administered? (2) At what time or grade level is this questionnaire to be used? (3) Who is to administer it? (4) Who is to analyze the data obtained? Normative data collected by such questionnaires permit examination of differences between and among individuals. Froehlich and Hoyt urge the use of open-ended types of items so that more idiographic data can be obtained.[13] Used longitudinally, idiographic data help to identify changes that occur in a particular person. They suggest use of such items as the following:

My hobbies are—	My school work—
I enjoy reading about—	A real friend—
My greatest weakness is—	I'd be happy if—
The people I like best—	I am considered—
I am at my best—	

In administering pupil data questionnaires, pupils should be told why such forms are important. The extent of confidentiality of the data obtained should also be discussed with them.

Advantages and Limitations

The main advantages of the pupil-data questionnaire have been cited in the previous discussion, including such things as a means to obtain: (1)

[13] Froehlich and Hoyt, *Guidance Testing*, pp. 327–328.

FIGURE 10
Purdue Guidance Clinic Personal Data Inventory

Case No._____

Date_____

Counselor_____

Please complete this inventory as carefully as you can. The purpose of collecting this information is to be of assistance to you in making choices and decisions. All information which you provide about yourself will be treated confidentially.

Name_____

Last   First   Middle

Address_____

School_____   Grade_____

Age_____   Birthdate_____   Phone_____   Sex_____

School Information:

	Name of School	Grades Attended	Years Attended	Course of Study
Elementary				
Jr. High				
Sr. High				
College				
Other				

Best Liked Subjects_____   Easiest Subjects_____

Least Liked Subjects_____   Hardest Subjects_____

Out-of-school leisure time activities and hobbies_____

What magazines do you read regularly?_____

What types of books do you enjoy?_____

Activities and Hobbies:

School Activity	Number of Years of Participation	Offices Held	Kind of Activity

Class offices held_____

Work Experience:

Job Held	When	What did you like best about it?
1. _____	_____	_____
2. _____	_____	_____
3. _____	_____	_____
4 _____	_____	_____

Family and Home:

Last-name — First name	Live at Home	Age	Occupation	Years of Schooling Completed
Father _____	_____	____	_____	_____
Mother _____	_____	____	_____	_____
Bro/Sis_____	_____	____	_____	_____
_____	_____	____	_____	_____
_____	_____	____	_____	_____
_____	_____	____	_____	_____
_____	_____	____	_____	_____

Health:

Do you have normal eyesight?_____   Normal hearing?_____

Briefly summarize important factors in your health history_____

_____

_____

_____

Underline any of the following words which seem to describe you fairly well:

Active, ambitious, self-confident, persistent, hard working, nervous, impatient, impulsive, quick-tempered, excitable, imaginative, original, witty, calm, easily discouraged, serious, easy-going, good-natured, unemotional, shy, submissive, absent-minded, methodical, timid, lazy, frequently gloomy, hard-boiled, dependable, reliable, cheerful, sarcastic, jittery, likeable, leader, sociable, quiet, retiring, self-conscious, often feel lonely.

Plans:

What are your plans for the future?_____

_____

What occupations have you seriously considered as possible goals? Why?

_____

_____

What topics would you like to discuss with the counselor? _____

_____

_____

_____

Comments:

comprehensive information; (2) information dealing with the student as he is now; (3) idiographic and normative data; (4) missing or incomplete information about students; and (5) collection of data in an efficient manner.

The limitations of pupil-data questionnaires include such issues as whether the school has a right to obtain personal information about students or members of their families. Data collected by this means may also be difficult to organize and interpret, since conflicting information is sometimes obtained.

AUTOBIOGRAPHIES

Little research attention has been given to autobiographies, owing, probably, to the informal and unstructured character of this particular technique. The autobiography as a tool for understanding individuals not only reveals behavior, but, perhaps even more important, personal attitudes and emotions behind the behavior of an individual. The autobiography is a person's own written report of his life and, as such, may provide insight into the "inner person"—the individual's experiences and knowledge about himself. Caution should be exercised in interpreting autobiographies because interpretation is heavily dependent upon experienced, clinical judgment.

By way of terminology, most authorities agree that there are two basic types of autobiographies—structured and unstructured. It is possible to combine the two basic types or to vary the degree of structure present. Some call the two types controlled and uncontrolled while others refer to them as structured and free essay, or comprehensive and topical. The unstructured autobiography is perhaps the most fruitful for counseling purposes and may reveal many hidden facets of the personality which may not be brought to the surface by any other techniques of guidance short of extensive, skilled interviewing. It is often difficult to interpret, however, particularly if the individual does not present material in an organized way. The unstructured autobiography is basically an account of the individual's life as he presents it without regard to specific questions. It is freely written and does not force any answer or the inclusion of any particular topic. It is the student's choice to write what he thinks has been important to him and the experiences that have had a bearing on his life to the present time.

The structured autobiography is written according to an outline or in response to specific questions or topics. It may be more useful for work with pupils who are not very verbal. Even by following a set form and giving short answers, however, many students reveal items that are significant to the alert counselor.

Danielson and Rothney compared structured (following an outline) and unstructured (freely written) forms of student autobiographies written by seventy-eight eleventh grade students in an English class.[14] Their analysis

---

[14] Paul J. Danielson and John Rothney, "The Student Autobiography: Structured or Unstructured?" *Personnel and Guidance Journal* Vol. 23 (September 1954), pp. 30–33.

dealt with the effectiveness of these two approaches in their ability to elicit student problems in six areas. No significant difference was found between them regarding the number of problems elicited in four of the six areas. Significantly greater numbers of problems were expressed in the area, "Family Relationships," in unstructured autobiographies; and significantly greater numbers of problems in the area, "Education," were elicited by the structured approach. Grouping all problems together, a significantly greater number of problems was expressed in the structured autobiography. Danielson and Rothney concluded that the form of the autobiography should be a function of the problem areas in which the counselor is interested.

Mueller, Schmieding, and Schultz have also sought to determine the kind of autobiographical form which elicited the most useful student responses. The subjects were 203 ninth graders who were divided into four groups. The students in Group I wrote a structured autobiography in the first person; those in Group II wrote a structured autobiography in the third person; those in Group III wrote a semistructured autobiography in the first person; and those in Group IV wrote a semistructured autobiography in the third person. Three judges, using agreed-upon criteria (references to peer problem, school problem, home problem, personal values, vocational problems, pleasurable incidents, and positive, negative, or ambivalent self-evaluations) read and rated all autobiographies. The authors concluded that (1) differences exist in self-report data elicited by the four autobiographical forms; (2) semistructured, first person, is the most effective form; (3) structured, third person, is the least effective; (4) either form of semistructured is superior to a structured form; and (5) differences are clearly less between the first- and third-person forms than between the semistructured and structured forms.[15]

The autobiography as a guidance technique is usable by classroom teachers as well as counselors. Some school personnel have used it for purposes of theme writing in English classes and for providing personal information for use by the counselor. However, most guidance authorities believe that grading the autobiography renders it useless as a means of gathering personal information about an individual, since autobiographies written for a course grade may emphasize grammar, writing style, spelling, etc., at the expense of meaningful personal content. Analyzing autobiographies can frequently provide counseling leads for use with pupils in need of special help with personal problems. At least one autobiography should become a part of each pupil's cumulative record. It will be a valuable aid in learning about planning and in understanding pupil adjustment. Autobiographies collected in conjunction with case studies are useful instruments for revealing subjective feelings, hopes, and aspirations.

---

[15] Richard J. Mueller, O. A. Schmieding, and John L. Schultz, "Four Approaches to Writing Autobiographies," *The School Counselor* Vol. 11 (March 1964), pp. 160–164.

Outline of the Structured Autobiography

The structured autobiography follows an organized outline. The pupil is asked to answer questions that deal with his family background, his personality, his relationships with other individuals, his interests, his likes and dislikes, his future plans and aspirations, significant people in his life, and the like. Cromwell has suggested a structured student autobiography that included topics designed to get at the student's past, present, and future. His suggested topics were as follows:

1. My family (optional).
2. My first years before school.
3. My years in the elementary school.
4. Places I have lived.
5. Vacations I have spent.
6. Trips I have taken.
7. The way I usually spend the afternoon when school is out.
8. The way I spend my evening after supper.
9. The way I spend a typical Saturday or Sunday.
10. Studies I liked the most; the least.
11. Some subjects and activities I wish our school would provide.
12. Things I do well; things I could do well; things I should like to do well.
13. The work I hope to do (three choices) and reasons for the choices.
14. Kinds of magazines and books I like to read; kinds of radio programs I like to listen to; kinds of movies [and TV programs] I like to see.
15. If I could have all the things I wanted by asking for them, I would ask for these things.[16]

The purpose of structuring is to stimulate the pupil to self-expression in specific, important areas. On the other hand, the structured autobiography may sometimes hinder the student because it forces him to consider what he is writing rather than respond with complete freedom. He may feel limited to answering only the questions that are outlined for him. All autobiographies, whether structured or unstructured, are limited by the individual's (1) willingness to reveal himself frankly, (2) self-insight and self-understanding, (3) ability to understand the content of the topic, and (4) ability to communicate in writing. The autobiography is a very intimate technique since it involves the direct expression of the individual. It is an extremely personal affair with the weaknesses inherent in any subjective technique: many people are prone to overlook their limitations and build up real or imagined strengths when judging themselves, and many tend to understate their good points and dwell only on their shortcomings and weaknesses.

[16] R. Floyd Cromwell, "Also, the Autobiography," *The School Guidance Worker* Vol. 3 (March 1942), p. 85.

Interpreting Autobiographies

No quick and easy route can be drawn that will result in foolproof analysis and interpretation of student autobiographies. Interpretation takes time, careful attention to detail, and some background knowledge about the individual. As autobiographies are read, the following questions can help guide the interpretation.

What general impression does the paper convey? Note the variations in tone as the writer touches upon things that are of vital concern to him. Does the writer give an impression of happiness, depression, good mental health, etc.? Observe the use of emotionally charged words: "love," "hate," "mother," "father," and the like. The appearance of the paper, whether neatly or carelessly done, usually has little correlation with behavior patterns of the individual.

From your knowledge of the individual's history, has he omitted significant experiences or persons? Do not expect an autobiography to be complete in every detail, but significant omissions may be cues worthy of followup in an interview situation. If the student has avoided mentioning members of his family or a known event or experience, such omissions should be studied carefully. This does not mean that the counselor should expect a week-by-week, year-by-year, or blow-by-blow account. Normally, individuals tend to write briefly about peaceful, pleasant periods in their lives and to concentrate more heavily upon incidents of major importance to them.

What is the length of the autobiography? The length of an autobiography is dependent upon many things, including (1) student motivation to write; (2) the form of the paper—whether an outline is followed; (3) the facility with which a person expresses himself; and (4) the degree to which a student believes he needs help with his problems. Suggestions have been given as to the ideal length and these range from 200 to 5,000 words.

How is the paper organized? If students are given an outline to follow, few cues for interpretation can be obtained from this guideline. However, any changes in the prepared outline should be noted. The most common organization for unstructured autobiographies is chronological. Are there gaps or omissions in the material? What has the author chosen to emphasize?

What is the level of expression? If the student believes no value will result from the autobiography, he may write in a very superficial manner. Students, particularly in upper elementary and junior high school, are apt to report fairly superficial events and experiences. Also extremely defensive individuals may resort to shallowness in writing about their development. Lack of depth or evasiveness characterizes the papers of students who are attempting to hide, or who do not wish to disclose, their concerns or anxieties.

Are there inaccuracies in the paper? Inaccuracies as used here refers both to attempts to deliberately falsify experiences or events and to unconscious errors in reporting. Relatively few autobiographies are deliberately distorted; the distortions occur when the individual is not convinced of the value of writing the autobiography. The ability to detect inaccuracies increases with experience in reading autobiographies as well as from previous knowledge of the individual.

Problems in Using Autobiographies

No technique is of value unless it is put to use. Shaffer reported in 1954 that the autobiography was used by only one-fourth of the counselors in large school systems and that only one-half of them had ever seen an autobiography. Ratings obtained from sixty-eight of the counselors placed the autobiography next to last in a list of ten sources of data. The rank order was as follows: (1) interview; (2) achievement tests; (3) intelligence tests; (4) anecdotal records; (5) oral teacher reports; (6) grades; (7) written teacher reports; (8) personality tests; (9) autobiographies; and (10) questionnaires. In studying five hundred autobiographies from pupils in these schools, Shaffer reported that the technique was extremely useful in gaining an understanding of high school pupils. Most autobiographies appeared to be honest and accurate.[17]

The problems encountered in using autobiographies to elicit facts are primarily those of communication. When questions are carefully formulated in printed form and answers are written down, misunderstanding may occur either in the respondent's interpretation of the question or in the counselor's interpretation of the pupil's response. If there is no personal interaction, these misunderstandings cannot be cleared up through oral questioning or further probing into the area of uncertainty. Herein lies the importance of counseling sessions with the individuals subsequent to the collection of autobiographical data.

SOCIOMETRIC TECHNIQUES

Sociometry is concerned with the measurement of interpersonal preferences among the members of a group in reference to a stated criterion. In its broad sense, however, the field of sociometry is multidimensional in that it includes not only measurement techniques but also methods and principles followed in making groups more effective in pursuing their goals and more personally satisfying to their members.

The purpose of sociometric methods is to measure each individual's social stimulus value, or, in other words, his social worth or personal value as viewed by his associates. In a more general sense what is measured is primarily overt group adjustment or acceptability. It cannot be assumed, however, that a sociometric test merely measures popularity, since much depends upon the particular choice-criterion utilized.

[17] Evan E. Shaffer, Jr., "The Autobiography in Secondary School Counseling," *Personnel and Guidance Journal* Vol. 32 (March 1954), pp. 395–398.

Purposes of Sociometric Techniques

Bonney and Hampleman state the rationale upon which sociometric measurement is based, summarized as follows:

> Within any formal organization there is an informal organization based on interpersonal attractions and repulsions. These informal relationships greatly affect the official functioning of the group and have important personality consequences for each person in the group. Interpersonal bonds between the members of a group are necessary to good morale and to the normal personality growth of each individual. If this rationale is accepted, it naturally follows that an adequate program of personality evaluation of pupils must include data on interpersonal relationships.[18]

Barclay defines sociometry as a method of discovering and analyzing patterns of friendship within a group setting. His view is that sociometry may be used as a screening device to detect children whose behavior in social settings is incongruent. Further, he notes that sociometric test choices have been found to be related to mental health, to teacher ratings, and to achievement and that they have been used as predictors of school dropouts.[19]

Terminology

For an adequate understanding and use of the sociometric technique, some explanation of terms is necessary. The following list has been condensed from Gronlund, whose book the reader should consult for a more comprehensive understanding of terminology in this area:

> *Sociometric Question or Sociometric Criterion:* Provides the basis of the choice which the student must make.
>
> *Sociometric Status, Social Status, or Group Status:* Refers to the number of choices each individual receives from the other members of the group. In other words, it is the number of times an individual is chosen by other students on the basis of the sociometric question.
>
> *Sociometric Structure, Social Structure, or Group Structure:* Refers to the pattern of choices to and from individuals, revealing the network of interpersonal relations among group members.
>
> *Sociogram:* The term applied to the diagram which shows visually this sociometric structure.
>
> *Sociometric Test:* The method used to evaluate group structure.

[18] Summarized from Merle E. Bonney and Richard S. Hampleman, *Personal–Social Evaluation Techniques* (Washington: The Center for Applied Research in Education, Inc., 1962), pp. 60–61.

[19] James R. Barclay "Sociometry: Rationale and Technique for Effecting Behavior Change in the Elementary School," *Personnel and Guidance Journal* Vol. 44 (June 1966), pp. 1067–1076.

Star: An individual who receives a large number of choices on a socio-metric test. The number of choices received in order to be designated a star varies with the number of choices permitted in the sociometric test and the number of pupils taking the test. (A complete table for the purpose of dis-tinguishing the stars is found in Gronlund, p. 67.)

Isolate: A physical member of the group who is psychologically isolated from the other group members. He receives no choice on the test. Outsider or social island are other designations for the isolate.

Neglectee: The individual who receives relatively few choices on the socio-metric test. Negative choices result when the sociometric question requests students to indicate those whom they least prefer for a specified activity.

Rejectee: The individual who receives negative choices on a sociometric test. Rejected choices result when the sociometric question requests students to indicate those whom they do not prefer for a specified activity.

Mutual Choice, Reciprocated Choice, or Pair: Two individuals who have chosen each other on the same sociometric criterion.

Sociometric Clique: A situation in which a number of individuals choose each other on the same sociometric criterion, but give relatively few choices to individuals outside their group.

Sociometric Cleavage: The lack of sociometric choices between two or more subgroups.[20]

Kinds of Sociometric Measurements

Sociometric testing falls into two major categories which may be described as: (1) the use of choices or specific criteria to serve a particular purpose at a particular time; and (2) questionnaires or rating instruments which measure interpersonal attitudes and feelings but not in respect to a specific, functional type of criterion.

Specific Criteria

The first category is the one most often used as a sociometric measurement in the school setting. Here the investigator asks the pupils to respond to a question which is pertinent to a need in a particular situation, i.e., "Which other pupils in this group would you most like to sit by?" It should be noted that pupils are not asked to list the names of other children with whom they now associate, work, or play with, but rather the ones whom they would like or prefer to have as an associate or partner. What is measured here is not necessarily social facts but social aspirations. This, then, indicates that one of the major values of sociometric data lies in their use in changing interpersonal alignments to bring about more satisfying relationships. This should be of distinct value for the teacher and counselor because they need to know not only what is happening to the student now but also what the student would like to have happen so that he can better realize his personal aspirations.

[20] Abstracted from Norman E. Gronlund, *Sociometry in the Classroom* (New York: Harper & Brothers, 1960), pp. 3–6.

There are certain qualifications concerning the use of this category of sociometric tests. Moreno,[21] called the Father of the Sociometric Technique, insists that sociometric choices should be based on a criterion which reflects an actual situation or activity in which group members have a real opportunity for participation. Requesting pupils to choose associates on criteria related to living in close proximity, working in close proximity, and spending leisure time together would meet this requirement. In order to be valid, the test should use situations or activities which are meaningful to the students so that they can see the consequences of their choices. The examiner should also follow through and arrange or rearrange the groups in accordance with the sociometric choices. This becomes very important if the technique is to be used more than once. Rearrangement should be employed in a continuing program of evaluation so that changes can be noted and taken into consideration in the on-going program of the institution. Rearrangements build the confidence of the students in the technique so that their choices will remain valid.

In relation to the limitations mentioned above, asking pupils such questions as, "Whom do you like best?" or "Who are your best friends?" could not be considered sociometric questions. Tests using questions such as these are called "near-sociometric." Such tests may be useful in certain research settings but they are not usually of immediate practical value because it is hard to provide the special motivational techniques that will assure sincere and accurate responses.

In order to use the sociometric test effectively, every group member should be familiar with the choice situation or activity and be free to participate in it. This then means that the question should be applicable to the group involved. Also, no limit should be placed on the pupils in the group who may be chosen. It is, of course, important to define the group involved, for example, all of the students in the tenth grade or all of the students in a particular homeroom.

Group members should have had sufficient opportunity to become acquainted with each other before the test is administered. An equally important aspect of sociometric testing is that of assuring the group members that their choices will remain anonymous. Students may be naturally reluctant to record the names of preferred associates if they suspect that their choices will be revealed. By making this information confidential, feelings and attitudes may be directed toward individuals who are unavailable for actual association. For a more thorough discussion of criteria for using the sociometric test, the reader should see Gronlund,[22] Jennings,[23] and Taba *et al.*[24]

21 J. Moreno *et al., The Sociometry Reader* (Glencoe, Ill. The Free Press, 1960).

22 Gronlund, *Sociometry in the Classroom*, pp. 7–10.

23 Helen Hall Jennings, *Sociometry in Group Relations* (Washington: American Council on Education, 1959), pp. 13–20.

24 Hilda Taba, *et al., Diagnosing Human Relations Needs* (Washington: American Council on Education, 1951), pp. 75–77.

Space does not permit instructions on the administration of a sociometric test and the construction of the sociogram, nor for the interpretation of the results and the followup interview which is an indispensable part of the technique. This information is readily available in numerous books and articles, however. Perhaps one of the most concise references is the booklet, *How to Construct a Sociogram,* published by Teachers College, Columbia University.[25] Other good sources are Gronlund,[26] Cronbach,[27] Jennings,[28] and Taba, *et al.*[29]

QUESTIONNAIRES

The second broad category of sociometric measurement—questionnaires or rating instruments—measures interpersonal attitudes and feelings but not with respect to a specific, functional type of criterion. Such a technique includes a number of instruments which will merely be mentioned here. For a better discussion of these instruments the reader is directed to Bonney and Hampleman.[30]

Questionnaires and rating instruments ask the members of a group to indicate their feelings toward each other, but not in reference to a specific criterion. Further, there is not necessarily an expectation that some group changes will result from the testing. These questionnaires are concerned primarily with measuring interpersonal feelings as opposed to leadership qualities or desirability as a work associate.

One such questionnaire, The Ohio Social Acceptance Scale,[31] consists of six headings: (1) "My very, very best friends," (2) "My other friends," (3) "Not friends, but okay," (4) "Don't know them," (5) "Don't care for them," and (6) "Dislike them." Every pupil is given a list of the names of all the students in his group and asked to place each of his classmates in one of the above categories.

The Syracuse Scales of Social Relations[32] is also essentially a sociometric questionnaire. The purpose of these scales is to arrive at scores which are indicative of the degree to which each pupil in a class regards all his classmates as sources of satisfaction for his personal-social needs. These scales

---

[25] Horace-Mann–Lincoln Institute of School Experimentation, *How to Construct a Sociogram* (New York: Bureau of Publications, Teachers College, Columbia University, 1947).

[26] Gronlund, *Sociometry in the Classroom,* pp. 57–113.

[27] Lee J. Cronbach, *Essentials of Psychological Testing,* Third Edition (New York: Harper & Row, 1970), pp. 589–594.

[28] Jennings, *Sociometry in Group Relations,* pp. 62–67.

[29] Taba, *et al., Diagnosing Human Relations Needs,* pp. 71–97.

[30] Bonney and Hampleman, *Evaluation Techniques,* pp. 62–67.

[31] Ohio State Department of Education, *The Ohio Social Acceptance Scale* (Columbus, Ohio: The Department, 1944).

[32] Eric F. Gardner and George Thompson, *The Syracuse Scales of Social Relations* (New York: Harcourt, Brace & World, Inc., 1958).

have been standardized; reliability coefficients of .67 and .78 are reported, as well as a mean validity coefficient of .74, between social relations indexes obtained from the scales and the relative degree of *esprit de corps* of fraternities on a large university campus.

Measurement of reputation as found in the Ohio Social Acceptance Scale, while not strictly speaking a sociometric test, holds promise for use by the counselor. Here each member of a group renders judgments in regard to the personal traits or behavior characteristics of his group associates.

The scales and questionnaires mentioned above can be purchased commercially. It is possible, of course, for the teacher or counselor to construct such instruments for himself, if he has the necessary background in sociometry.

Sociometric tests, whether of the first or second category, are relatively simple to administer and interpret, and can be used by most teachers and counselors if they are willing to take the time to familiarize themselves with the field of sociometry. An overall text in this area which might be used for the purpose is Gronlund's book, *Sociometry in the Classroom.*[33]

Advantages and Limitations

Sociometric tests have certain limitations and certain advantages, just as all testing devices do. First of all, it should be recognized that sociometric tests, like the better known psychological tests, do not give a final or exact answer. They can merely give the examiner indications or direction in his study of the individual. Just as scholastic aptitude tests give an indication of ability, so the sociometric tests give an indication of the social structure at one point in time. Secondly, the whole body of sociometric theory has not been developed, nor its postulates tested to the point that it is infallible. This is a relatively recently developed body of knowledge, and a great deal more research is needed in order for it to fulfill its potential. It should also be pointed out that no standardized methods of administration or of formulation of the criteria of choice have yet been developed. This, to some degree, limits comparisons of results from test to test administered and constructed by the same person—and certainly it limits comparisons of results of tests administered and constructed by different persons. The results are, of course, no better than the choice criteria used and the adequacy of administration.

There are also limitations in interpreting and applying the results of these tests. For example, one should avoid assuming that a "star" is a leader and has good personal adjustment. The recipient of a large number of choices on a sociometric test merely has been frequently chosen by his associates for certain activities. The number of choices received will probably vary from test to test as the sociometric criterion differs. The test tells nothing of a "star's" emotional stability or his power as a leader. Further investi-

[33] Gronlund, *Sociometry in the Classroom.*

gation is needed before drawing conclusions concerning these matters. Conversely, one should avoid assuming that because an individual is shown to be an isolate by the test he is maladjusted. Again, more investigation is necessary before such a conclusion can be drawn. Likewise, characterization of the highly rejected individual as a person of doubtful character or undesirable personal qualities is completely unjustified. Here again, the test merely gives an indication of a possible difficulty. The counselor should investigate the case further to determine why this student is rejected by his peers. Many of these questions can be answered at least in part by use of the sociometric interview. A good discussion and illustration of this interview is given by Taba, *et al.*[34]

Perhaps the greatest advantage of the sociometric techniques is that they provide objective information about the functioning of individuals within their groups which is available from no other source. These techniques provide valuable information about how children are perceived by their peers, which supplements information gained from other sources. The knowledge gained helps to give a complete picture of the individual when it is viewed along with information obtained from the other tools of the counselor.

In closing this section, a quote from Tolbert seems appropriate:

> The technique itself (sociometric tests) could not be used in the counseling process. The counselor might request that someone obtain the data or he might obtain them himself if he had the counselee in a group or class. The primary use of the data would be to combine them with other sorts of information to learn about and understand the counselee's behavior, and to identify clues for further exploration. It would seem quite unwise to use the results of the study directly with the counselee or to let him know that such a study had been made.[35]

CASE STUDIES

The case study, a commonly used method of summarizing data about an individual, is the most comprehensive of analytical techniques. It seeks to present a cumulative picture of the total personality by giving a full-length study of an individual that shows his development and the interrelations of the factors governing his current status. The information employed in it is gathered from all available reliable sources: cumulative records, observations, interviews, autobiographies, self-reports, tests, teacher reactions, and other school records. It contains interpretations, recommendations for action, and provisions for a followup to check development and adjustment. Generally, case studies conducted by school personnel are of pupils who have called attention to themselves because of learning difficulties, social relationships, or other evidence of behavior needing special attention, es-

[34] Taba, *et al.*, *Diagnosing Human Relations Needs*, pp. 88–94.

[35] From *Introduction to Counseling* by E. L. Tolbert. Copyright 1959. McGraw-Hill Book Co. Used by permission. P. 198.

pecially those cases requiring a diagnostic approach beyond the usual routine investigations. The intent of the case study is to provide increased understanding of the child. The school counselor usually is the person who writes it. In the case of serious maladjustment, the school refers the child to outside agencies where complete data are gathered in a joint effort by medical, social work, and education personnel, and parents, clergy, and court officials. The data are then interpreted and therapy established by a psychiatrist, psychologist, or staff in a guidance clinic or hospital.

Many contend that the task of writing a case study is a job for a specialist. They maintain that the case-study technique represents a clinical approach to a serious problem of adjustment which goes beyond the training and experience of most school guidance personnel. According to this view, the school counselor would be confined to writing a case history. Those who feel that the counselor is qualified to do a case study present a strong argument for their position too. They do concede, however, that the skill needed for perceiving diagnostic significance in data that others might ignore is simply the factor that differentiates the effective counselor from the amateur.

Definitions

Before proceeding, it might be best to differentiate between two terms frequently employed synonymously—the case history and the case study. The term "case history" has been defined by Rosecrance and Hayden as follows:

> A case history is a detailed itemization of data relating to a given individual and usually covering a span of years. It includes (1) identifying facts, (2) family history, (3) early childhood experiences, (4) educational history, (5) health history, (6) experience in social development, (7) test results, (8) vocational experiences, (9) hobbies, interests, goals and ambitions, (10) previous referrals.[36]

A case study is an analysis and writeup of the data collected in a case history, including an analysis of the interrelationships in the data.

According to Hadley,[37] a case history is information gathered about a client, including that pertaining to family development, physical development, educational, social, and vocational history. "Case history" is a more specific term than is "case study." A frequent synonym for a case history is "anamnesis," used in its commonly accepted but not precise form. In its technical sense, anamnesis refers to only that data secured directly from the individual being studied, i.e., data based on his memory. Hadley defines a case study as all information gathered about an individual. In addition to

---

[36] Francis C. Rosecrance and Velma D. Hayden, *School Guidance and Personnel Services* (Boston: Allyn & Bacon, Inc., 1960), p. 72.

[37] John Hadley, *Clinical and Counseling Psychology* (New York: Alfred A. Knopf, Inc., 1958), pp. 300–308.

historical data, the case study includes test data, interview data, and the results of examinations and observations. Hadley says the difference between the case history and the case study is that the history includes only the past, but the study includes past and present and often even projects into the future. A case study begins with a clarification of the present problem and a definition of factors leading up to the current situation.

Another definition of the case study is available in a totally different context. It may be viewed as a study in which real or assumed situations are presented for discussion as a way of arriving at basic principles in a given field or to encourage examination of an individual's or a group's understanding of principles. This is the case-study method of instruction.

Although the majority of guidance personnel and psychologists agree to the value of case studies, some counselors are opposed to the taking of a formal case history. These counselors contend that diagnosis by the counselor is unnecessary and that any solution not emanating from the counselee is valueless. This view might be best illustrated by the following criticism from Rogers:

When the counselor says in effect, "I would like to have you tell me about your problems and yourself, your background and your development, your education and your medical history, your family experiences and your social environment," he also implies the additional assurance, "and then I can tell you how to solve your problems."[38]

Format

The format of a case study and its specific content varies somewhat, depending upon the setting and function of the institution. Some agencies employ standardized forms. However, most of these forms cover the same basic information and elaborate on the following outline:

Name: School:
Date of birth: Date:
Parents: Siblings:
Referral source:
Reason for referral (specific problem including observable symptoms):
Family background (family relationships, home environment, socio-economic status):
Physical history (disabilities, speech defects, vision, height, weight):
Scholastic achievement:
Aptitudes (test data—including mental ability, reading level):
Personality and social adjustment (general behavior patterns):
Interests, hobbies, and experience:
Plans (vocational or educational):
General appraisal, interpretation, and hypotheses:
Recommendations:

[38] Carl R. Rogers, *Counseling and Psychotherapy* (Boston: Houghton Mifflin Company, 1942), p. 81.

There is no set method of writing up a case study. Like the format and the specific areas stressed, the writeup will vary with the purpose, setting, and prior training of the person conducting the study. Again, considerable variation exists in the treatment given certain topics. The major task is to present the most important facts in an orderly fashion and to formulate a plan for using them in understanding and helping the pupil.

Use of Case-Study Technique

The obvious use of a case study is as a thorough source of information. This seems particularly significant because there are many theories regarding the cause of behavior disorders and present knowledge is still inadequate. Case studies help to summarize and clarify the large amount of information needed for the understanding of a particular pattern of behavior. No set criteria exist to determine specifically which data may or may not be important.

Many counselors use the case history and case study to facilitate their approach to understanding a student so that they can respond to him more intelligently. The case study permits the counselor to provide information and to interpret the individual to others who are concerned about him in a comprehensive manner. Thus it includes all of the known factors which may have a bearing on making the child what he is.

Criteria for Evaluating a Case Study

In order to be valuable, the case study must be written clearly, accurately, and objectively with a minimum of personal bias in the interpretation. Irrelevant items, technical terms, and generalizations unsupported by specific data are to be avoided. General statements become more convincing when they are reinforced by definite data. Finally the case study should be as concise as possible.

Advantages

The case-study approach, in which all data are obtained, recorded, and integrated before diagnosis and treatment, permits the person to be understood and treated as an individual. It also provides a basis for more complete understanding and gives a more accurate evaluation of events, thus preventing superficiality and quick judgments. Precisely, it can reduce the number of errors in diagnosis by ensuring that the counselor thoroughly studies the facts the client presents. The case study can be very useful in isolating key factors in situations in which conflicting accounts confuse the case. In interpreting data, multiple causation and constellation of contributing factors can be identified. A frequently ignored use of the case study is that of prediction, in which past behavior may indicate what might be expected of the individual in similar future situations.

Disadvantages

One factor that discourages more extensive use of the case history is the time required for gathering extensive data. Sometimes taking a case history results in delaying aid to the person. The time factor may be a very realistic limitation, particularly in a school setting. Counseling, however, need not necessarily be delayed until all information is accumulated, for hypotheses are frequently made and tested continuously until the counselor is reasonably certain as to the problem and its treatment.

In some cases, past information is difficult to obtain and can also be grossly inadequate and questionable. It is also true that case histories and studies written by different people at different times may vary significantly. To combat this type of problem, there frequently is a tendency to follow a rigid style of reporting, which may detract from the client's individuality. An important limitation of the case history is that it may not always be sufficient as a basis for arriving at conclusions concerning the individual and thus for formulating a diagnosis. As suggested earlier, this may be a limitation stemming either from the method or from the person using it. Either case study or history, when unskillfully used, can be a meaningless chronology or a confusion of fact and fiction, of guesswork and interpretation. On the other hand, case-study techniques can be the most revealing method of all non-testing appraisal techniques. This is the reason for the debatable question, "Is the school counselor qualified to diagnose?" Many believe that counselors are prone to jump to conclusions based on available data and to attempt to force everything neatly into a pattern. There is also the fear that diagnosis will be made on the basis of objective data alone and not take into account the feelings and attitudes of the counselee. Some writers believe the information in a complete case study goes beyond the scope of a school and that the school is not able to gather all the information needed for an adequate case study. After serious problems are diagnosed, the followup practices of some schools are often inadequate except when the problem pertains to academic matters.

SUMMARY

The appraisal service is a major activity engaged in by school counselors. Both test and non-test appraisal techniques may be utilized to the advantage of students. The most legitimate purposes for which student appraisal data are collected and used include helping the student to understand himself better and helping others to better understand the student. A weakness in far too many guidance programs is that once test and non-test data are collected, they are not used to facilitate the student's understanding of himself. For students in such schools, test and non-test data may appear to be the means schools use to build up cases against them. Appraisal, then, becomes threatening and restrictive rather than enlightening and useful in projecting what the individual is like and what he can do.

Finally, a long-standing and recently re-emphasized concern in appraisal is that of who has access to student data. School policies and practices in respect to releasing personal information—test data, psychological reports, personality ratings, grades, attendance—are varied, often haphazard, and too often formulated on the spot. Often ignored or overlooked is the primary responsibility to protect the student against harm from those who would misuse or misinterpret the information. Guidelines (ethical codes) have, of course, been formulated as to the release of pupil data. But Heayn and Jacobs[39] point out that schools should develop written policies and procedures regarding who should have access to pupil data. Such policies would be based upon (1) the professional code of ethics, (2) protecting the decision-making responsibility of the counselor from overly restrictive procedures, and (3) consideration of the needs of the student, the school, and the individual or agency seeking the information. Heayn and Jacobs classified pupil information into two major categories: *matters of judgment* (data which are descriptive and evaluative of the individual and which require interpretation) and *matters of record* (data which are descriptive in nature). The latter category was further classified as to whether the data were "unrestricted" or "restricted." Unrestricted data would be information judged to be in the public domain (name, sex, nationality, subjects taken, graduation) while restricted data would include disciplinary records, health records, and the like.

These two authors have specified some guidelines from which a decision can be made as to whether information about a student can be released. Basically the decision depends upon who makes the request, how the request is made, and above all, the kind of information sought by the inquirer. Heayn and Jacobs have further identified some general regulations as to how types of requests for information (by telephone, written, personal requests) are to be handled, and whether certain sources who request information (parents, family members, staff, peers, agencies) should be given access to the data. Their article is a highly important source of information and could be utilized by counselors as a model for formulating policies regarding the accessibility and use of pupil data.

ANNOTATED BIBLIOGRAPHY

DOWNIE, N. M. *Fundamentals of Measurement: Techniques and Practices.* Second Edition. New York: Oxford University Press, 1967. Chapter 14, pp. 331–371.

In this chapter, Downie discusses non-test appraisals of personality, including the use of observation, anecdotal records, rating scales, autobiographies, and sociometric techniques. This discussion is presented concisely and clearly.

---

[39] Maurice H. Heayn and Howard L. Jacobs, "Safeguarding Student Records," *Personnel and Guidance Journal* Vol. 46 (September 1967), pp. 63–67.

FROEHLICH, CLIFFORD P., AND HOYT, KENNETH B. *Guidance Testing.* Chicago: Science Research Associates, Inc., 1959. Pp. 222–395.

These pages present a most comprehensive treatment of the non-test appraisal techniques used most often by school personnel. The different appraisal devices are well defined and illustrated.

GIBSON, ROBERT L., AND HIGGINS, ROBERT E. *Techniques of Guidance: An Approach to Pupil Analysis.* Chicago: Science Research Associates, 1966, 264 pp.

Chapter 5 (pp. 104–131) discusses observational techniques including anecdotal records, rating scales, and check lists. Chapter 6 (pp. 132–147) concentrates upon sociometric approaches, and Chapter 7 (pp. 148–169) deals with pupil questionnaires, autobiographies, and other self-report techniques.

TOLLEFSON, NONA F. *Counseling Case Management.* Guidance Monograph Series, Boston: Houghton Mifflin Company, 1968, 75 pp.

This monograph focuses upon the case study, the case conference, and counseling records. An illustrative case is presented, stressing the use of the case-study technique in the school.

SELECTED REFERENCES

ANNIS, ARTHUR P. "The Autobiography: Its Uses and Value in Professional Psychology." *Journal of Counseling Psychology* Vol. 14 (January 1967), pp. 9–17.

BARCLAY, JAMES R. "Sociometry: Rationale and Technique for Effecting Behavioral Change in the Elementary School." *Personnel and Guidance Journal* Vol. 44 (June 1966), pp. 1067–1076.

BARRETT, ROGER L. "Changes in Accuracy of Self-Estimates." *Personnel and Guidance Journal.* Vol. 47 (December 1968), pp. 353–357.

BITTER, JAMES A. "Bias Effect on Validity and Reliability of a Rating Scale." *Measurement and Evaluation in Guidance.* Vol. 3 (Summer 1970), pp. 70–75.

DUGGAN, BESSIE. "English Themes: Clues for Better Guidance." *The School Counselor* Vol. 12 (December 1964), pp. 101–104.

FELDHUSEN, JOHN F., THURSTON, JOHN R., AND BENNING, JAMES J. "Sentence Completion Responses and Classroom Social Behavior." *Personnel and Guidance Journal* Vol. 45 (October 1966), pp. 165–170.

FOLEY, WALTER J. "It's Time to Re-examine Confidentiality of Pupil Records." *The School Counselor* Vol. 15 (November 1967), pp. 92–96.

HANSEN, LORRAINE S. "How Can We Use Appraisal Data for Students' Welfare?" *The School Counselor* Vol. 14 (May 1967), pp. 281–286.

HEAYN, MAURICE H., AND JACOBS, HOWARD L. "Safeguarding Student Records." *Personnel and Guidance Journal* Vol. 46 (September 1967), pp. 63–67.

HEISEY, MARION. "A Case Study of Behavior Change." *The School Counselor* Vol. 16 (September 1968), pp. 60–64.

NUGENT, FRANK A. "Confidentiality in College Counseling Centers." *Personnel and Guidance Journal* Vol. 47 (May 1969), pp. 862–877.

RICCIO, ANTHONY C. "The Status of the Autobiography." *Peabody Journal of Education* Vol. 36 (July 1958), pp. 33–36.

RILEY, JOHN E., AND STANDLEY, FRED L. "Literature and Counseling: The Experience of Encounter." *Counselor Education and Supervision* Vol. 7 (Summer 1968), pp. 328–334.

RUCH, CHARLES. "The Development of an Attitude Toward Learning Scale." *The School Counselor* Vol. 15 (March 1968), pp. 290–292.

SHERTZER, BRUCE, AND FESLER, PATRICIA. "Teacher Comments about Pupils— Relevant or Self-Revealing?" *Elementary School Journal* Vol. 62 (April 1962), pp. 371–374.

TENNYSON, W. WESLEY, BLOCHER, DONALD H., AND JOHNSON, RALPH H. "Student Personnel Records: A Vital Tool, but a Concern of the Public." *Personnel and Guidance Journal* Vol. 42 (May 1964), pp. 888–893.

WALKER, ROBERT C. "Let's Set the Records Straight." *The School Counselor* Vol. 17 (September 1969), pp. 11–13.

WARNKEN, ROBERT G., AND SIESS, THOMAS F. "The Use of the Cumulative Record in the Prediction of Behavior." *Personnel and Guidance Journal* Vol. 44 (November 1965), pp. 231–237.

WILLIAMS, ROBERT L., AND COLE, SPURGEON. "Self-Concept and School Adjustment." *Personnel and Guidance Journal* Vol. 46 (January 1968), pp. 478–481.

11

THE
INFORMATIONAL
SERVICE

What are the purposes of the informational service?
What kinds of data are involved?
What informational materials exist and what criteria are used to select them?
How are informational materials put to use?
What general principles should be followed in the informational service?

A brief explanation of the aims and purposes of the appraisal service in guidance was given in Chapter 2. In essence, this explanation stated that the appraisal service was designed to provide pupils with appropriate educational, vocational, and personal-social data needed to understand themselves and their environment. That such a service is needed by secondary school pupils has long been recognized. More recently educational and guidance organizations have begun to develop informational materials appropriate for use with elementary pupils. This chapter concentrates upon the informational service *per se,* and the next chapter outlines theories or approaches to career development.

PURPOSES OF THE INFORMATIONAL SERVICE

The forces at work in a rapidly changing American society need to be understood by all individuals. Automation, space exploration, advances in the sciences, struggles for civil rights, increased technology, increasing specialization, manpower shortages, the changing nature of jobs all point up the increasingly complex and changing world in which we live. Such forces greatly add to the complexity of choice, decision-making, and planning that confront the individual. The margin of personal error or failure for leading an individually satisfying life seems to become smaller. These forces continue to put greater rather than diminished demands upon the individual. To succeed in what he attempts, the individual will have to demonstrate progressively higher levels of competence and responsibility. Personal growth is a highly integrated process, each level blending imperceptibly into the next. It does not occur in isolated episodes; the various levels are articulated. Guidance programs which fail to provide youth with the basic knowledge and opportunity for learning more about their environment and themselves shortchange youth. A good informational service helps young people to meet the challenges of today and tomorrow.

In December 1968, the Purdue Opinion Poll, using responses given by 12,000 high school students who constituted a nationwide representative sample, reported that only 21 percent of these high school students believed that they were receiving enough information and help in vocational decision-making. Those who believed that they were receiving enough help and information were students whose parents had high incomes. Further, they were 12th grade students who earned better than average grades. This same poll asked students how many times they had seen a counselor last year. The results (1968 compared to 1966) were as follows:

	Poll 78 *1966*	*Poll 85* *1968*
Never	34%	22%
Once or twice	40	45
Three or four times	16	22
Five times or more	9	9

More students who resided in the southern part of the United States reported that they had never seen a counselor during the 1968 year than students in other geographic areas. When asked who they thought could best help them with vocational decisions, they reported: parents (28 percent); teachers (9 percent); counselors (36 percent); close friend (9 percent); none or no one (19 percent).[1]

There are at least three major reasons why an informational service is a vital part of an organized school guidance program. First, an informational service is fundamental if students are to be equipped with the basic knowledge needed to think through important personal issues—extent of education, choice of occupation, maintenance of individuality—with which they are confronted. Growing up in a complex and competitive world, going further in education, and undertaking autonomous responsibility impose great demands upon youth. The goal of the informational service is not only to impart information, but also to stimulate the student to critically appraise ideas, conditions, and trends in order to derive personal meanings and implications for the present and the future. Becoming a functioning member of society requires that the individual seek out, recognize, and use

[1] Purdue Opinion Poll, *Counseling Needs of High School Students* (Lafayette, Ind.: Measurement and Research Center, Purdue University, December 1968), pp. 1–8.

all relevant information necessary for his development. The informational service, appropriately designed and staffed, will enable more individuals to realize their potentialities by becoming aware of their opportunities.

Second, an informational service is fundamental if students are to become, or be, self-regulatory. Present-day youth are expected to assume more autonomous responsibility than their predecessors. An essential condition of self-regulation is that the individual plan and know what he is doing as he does it and act correctively on the basis of known data. In other words, mature (planned) behavior is based upon accurate information. It is stable but flexible. An active, vigorously conducted informational service must have (1) excellent resources and devices for quickly gathering relevant, current information, and (2) the facilities for providing such information to students so that they can understand and use it.

Third, an informational service is fundamental if students are to explore and become aware of the contingencies of stability and change that mark their development. Pupils need to explore the positions which they are likely to occupy as they move through one or more possible pathways. They must understand their choices and the consequences and sequences of choice. Lack of knowledge about self-development frequently leads to failure, rejection, and defeat. Knowledge of self-development leads to positive images and encourages individuality.

Norris, Zeran, and Hatch have stated that certain objectives of the informational services receive emphasis at one school level more than at other levels. They cite the following as appropriate informational service objectives for elementary schools:

1. To help youngsters to explore job fields and to assess their strengths and their interests in which they can develop their abilities.
2. To provide abundant experiences which will acquaint children with many different types of workers, particularly community helpers in their own locality.
3. To assist pupils to see the interrelationships among various fields of work.
4. To assist pupils in building good work habits and learning how to work with all kinds of people.
5. To aid pupils in developing proper attitudes toward all types of socially useful work.
6. To acquaint pupils with some of the problems encountered in choosing a vocation.
7. To acquaint pupils with certain problems related to educational planning and educational facilities available so that they can be helped to select the high school or its one curriculum most appropriate to future educational plans.
8. To assist those students who do not continue in high school to seek employment on the basis of valid information.[2]

[2] Willa Norris, Franklin R. Zeran, and Raymond N. Hatch, *The Informational Service in Guidance,* Second Edition (Chicago: Rand McNally and Company, 1966), p. 26.

Norris, Zeran, and Hatch also cite five additional objectives of the informational service at the secondary school level:

1. To present understanding of broad fields of work.
2. To develop means for aiding students to study intensively a few selected occupations or educational training facilities.
3. To become fully acquainted with occupational and educational plans based upon thorough self-study.
4. To develop tentative educational and occupational plans based upon thorough self-study.
5. To present specific techniques to aid in meeting immediate needs confronting school leavers, such as obtaining employment, continuing an educational program, or establishing a home.[3]

Baer and Roeber,[4] Brayfield,[5] Hoppock,[6] Brammer and Shostrom,[7] and others have pointed out some ways information may be used by counselors. Although their discussion of the purposes to which informational materials may be put is often based upon its use within a one-to-one counselor–counselee relationship, some of the uses cited are equally appropriate to groups of students. A brief summary of these uses follows:

1. *Assurance Use.* Counselors use informational data to inspire student confidence in the appropriateness of decisions.
2. *Evaluative Use.* Counselors can use informational data to check the accuracy or adequacy of students' knowledge and understanding of a decision.
3. *Exploratory Use.* Information may be used to help students explore and study all alternatives of possible choices or decisions.
4. *Information Use.* Data are used to add to students' knowledge of occupations, choices, changing conditions, and the like.
5. *Holding or Motivational Use.* Informational materials and knowledge may be used to retain the counselee in the counseling situation until he gains insight into his "real" needs.
6. *Readjustive Use.* For students who have markedly inappropriate goals, informational data may be used to reorient them to different levels of goals or objectives.

[3] *Ibid.,* p. 27.

[4] Max F. Baer and Edward C. Roeber, *Occupational Information,* Third Edition (Chicago: Science Research Associates, 1964), pp. 430–452.

[5] Arthur Brayfield, "Putting Occupational Information Across," *Educational and Psychological Measurement* Vol. 8 (Autumn 1948), pp. 485–495.

[6] Robert Hoppock, *Occupational Information,* Third Edition (New York: McGraw-Hill Book Co., Inc., 1967), pp. 131–164.

[7] Lawrence M. Brammer and Everett L. Shostrom, *Therapeutic Psychology,* Second Edition (Englewood Cliffs, N.J.: Prentice-Hall, Inc., 1968), pp. 407–411.

7. *Startle Use.* Counselors may ascertain if counselees are anxious or uncertain about their choices through questioning the extent of their knowledge of information relevant to choice.
8. *Synthesis Use.* Informational data may be related to other personal data such as tests. This encourages the synthesis of a pattern of behavior.
9. *Verification Use.* Informational materials may be used by students to verify and clarify choices, opportunities, and decisions.

Although it seems self-evident that the informational service is a necessary part of guidance programs, several have questioned the necessity for such a service. For example, Barry and Wolf maintain that the informational area has been founded on several myths and that much time and money has been wasted preserving these myths. They believe that the assumptions underlying the informational service—that formal information is authentic and factual, that specific information about the work world is valid and applicable to the future, that such information meets student needs and produces important learnings, that such information furnishes the basis for reasoned decisions—are false, and only tradition and usage make them seem inviolate.[8] An examination of their criticisms of the informational service leads to the conclusion that it is better to do "just what comes naturally" or to "accept whatever fate may bring." The authors of this book believe, however, that individuals (pupils) do want to grow and to make something of themselves, to exercise freedom of choice, and to be responsible for their decisions. Consequently, information about the individual and his current and future environment is needed for planning, for looking ahead, and for broadening student perspective.

One caution that cannot be overemphasized relates to the timeliness of available occupational materials. As was previously pointed out, society's occupational structure and demands are constantly in flux as a result of innovations in technology. New jobs are created yearly, old jobs disappear, and what superficially appear to be stable types of work constantly undergo modification in specific characteristics. If the information service is not flexible and constantly updated, Barry and Wolf's accusations about "myths" are shown to be valid.

TYPES OF INFORMATION

Data used in the informational service are frequently categorized into three major divisions—educational information, occupational information, and personal-social information. Other writers sometimes refer to educational and occupational data as career information.

---

[8] Ruth Barry and Beverly Wolf, *Epitaph for Vocational Guidance* (New York: Bureau of Publications, Teachers College, Columbia University, 1962), pp. 74–89.

Educational Information

Educational information has been defined in an acceptable way by Norris, Zeran, and Hatch:

Educational information is valid and usable data about all types of present and probable future educational or training opportunities and requirements, including curricular and co-curricular offerings, requirements for entrance, and conditions and problems of student life.[9]

This definition implies that data would be collected by guidance personnel and would be used by students to learn more about educational programs and opportunities. More specifically, such data would acquaint students, counselors, teachers, and parents with the following:

1. School hours and regulations.
2. Available curricular offerings and subjects.
3. School clubs and social activities.
4. Values of education.
5. High school units, credits, majors, minors.
6. Existing post–high school educational programs.
7. The subjects required to go to college or other post–high school educational institutions.
8. Requirements for entering post–high school educational institutions.
9. The costs of going to college or to any type of post–high school training.
10. The education or training required for different occupations.
11. The characteristics of different colleges and other educational programs.
12. Study habits and skills.
13. Scholarships, student loans, ways of financing post–high school education.
14. Accreditation of educational programs.
15. Correspondence schools.
16. On-the-job training opportunities and programs.
17. Student social life and cultural opportunities in post–high school educational programs.

Occupational Information

Norris, Zeran, and Hatch define occupational information as follows:

Occupational information is valid and usable data about positions, jobs, and occupations, including duties, requirements for entrance, conditions of work, rewards offered, advancement pattern, existing and predicted supply of and demand for workers, and sources for further information.[10]

[9] Norris, Zeran, and Hatch, *Informational Service*, p. 24.
[10] *Ibid.*, p. 23.

It seems clear from that definition that occupational information would include data relevant to the following items:

1. The labor force: size, composition, geographic factors, sex, racial, age distribution, major industrial groups.
2. The occupational structure and major occupational groups.
3. Work trends including labor supply, population changes, public demand for goods, technological changes.
4. Labor legislation.
5. Sources of information for studying occupations.
6. Classification of occupations and occupational information.
7. Essential and critical occupations.
8. Duties of certain occupations, nature of work.
9. Qualifications necessary for employment in various occupations.
10. Preparation needed for various occupations.
11. Methods of entering occupations and methods of advancement.
12. Earnings and other rewards of various occupations.
13. Conditions of work in various occupations.
14. Criteria for evaluating occupational informational materials.
15. Typical places of employment.
16. Meaning of work.

Personal-Social Information

Personal-social information deals with self-understanding and the understanding of others. Norris, Zeran, and Hatch cite the following definition:

> Social information is valid and usable data about the opportunities and influences of the human and physical environment which bear on personal and interpersonal relations. It is that information about human beings which will help a student to understand himself better and to improve his relations with others. Included, but not constituting the whole, are such broad areas of information as "understanding self" and "getting along with others," as well as such specific areas as boy-girl relations, manners and etiquette, leisure-time activities, personal appearance, social skills, home and family relationships, financial planning, and healthful living.[11]

This definition indicates that the personal-social information service is concerned with the securing of materials and the use of information which deals with such conditions and factors as the following:

1. Achieving self-insight and understanding.
2. Achieving mature relationships with the same and the opposite sex.
3. Understanding masculine and feminine roles.

[11] *Ibid.*, pp. 24–25.

4. Developing healthy personalities.
5. Understanding one's behavior and one's characteristics.
6. Understanding how one differs from others and in what ways one is like others.
7. Understanding others' behaviors and their needs.
8. Adjusting, accepting, and understanding home conditions, family members, and parental expectations.
9. Knowledge of dating practices, sex information, marriage responsibilities.
10. Physical and mental health developments.
11. Personal appearance, manners and etiquette.
12. Social skills, financial planning, and leisure-time activities.

INFORMATIONAL MATERIALS: SOURCES AND THEIR EVALUATION

Informational materials available for youth are increasing in number and scope. The informational service in schools will succeed to the extent that its staff accumulates materials which present information and to the extent students are assisted in relating the information to themselves. This section discusses the sources for such materials, the criteria by which they may be evaluated, and the informational material library.

Sources of Informational Materials

Informational materials may be secured from a variety of sources. The sources of published materials are usually broken down into three major areas: local, state or regional, and national.

Local Sources. Local sources include the materials, such as community surveys and job analyses published by industries, businesses, fraternal and civic clubs, professional organizations, chambers of commerce, and the like.

State or Regional Sources. Such sources include the state employment security divisions, departments of education, mental health organizations, state governmental agencies, state organizations, manufacturing and industrial organizations, etc.

National Sources. Such sources include commercial publishers, governmental agencies, professional organizations, popular magazines, film distributors, and the like.

There are also published materials which are excellent sources of informational data. A brief explanation of these follows.

1. *Job Descriptions.* These are statements of the duties, qualifications, and other important items relating to various jobs. When they are used

as interview guides for employing workers, they are usually called *job specifications*.

2. *Occupational Descriptions.* These are statements which give composite descriptions of occupations in a number of establishments. The United States Employment Service Agency prepares a number of such statements.

3. *Occupational Briefs and Guides.* These are brief statements (three to five thousand words) about an occupation, describing its history, the work performed, hours, requirements, wages, working conditions, and methods of entry; they usually supply other reference sources. Briefs are the most popular type of published occupational materials.

4. *Occupational Monographs.* These are longer, more detailed statements (six to ten thousand words). Since they are longer, they usually are more expensive and require longer periods of time to prepare and/or revise.

5. *Books, Bulletins, and Articles.* Descriptions of occupations, educational opportunities, and personal-social information appear in numerous books, bulletins, and articles. For example, the *Dictionary of Occupational Titles*[12] classifies and codes occupations. For every job listed, the *D.O.T.* gives an industrial designation, an occupational code number, alternate job titles, and a definition of the job. Other examples are articles published in journals and magazines such as *Changing Times, Charm, Mademoiselle, Seventeen, Vocational Guidance Quarterly*.

6. *College Catalogs and Educational Directories.* Educational information needed by students can be found in the catalogs distributed by colleges. Though college catalogs vary considerably in their manner of presentation of material, they usually describe admission requirements, fees and tuition, scholarships and loans, housing facilities, degrees and curricula, and faculty and staff.

An increasing number of college directories are available. They present, usually in abbreviated, tabular form, information on admissions, scholarships, accreditation, costs, enrollment, etc. Examples of standard directories are *American Universities and Colleges,*[13] *Lovejoy's College Guide,*[14] *The College Blue Book,*[15] *Barron's Profiles of American Colleges,*[16] Cohen's *Vocational Training Directory of the United States,*[17]

---

[12] United States Employment Service, *Dictionary of Occupational Titles,* Vols. I and II, Third Edition (Washington: Government Printing Office, 1965).

[13] Otis A. Singletary (ed.), *American Universities and Colleges,* Tenth Edition (Washington: American Council on Education, 1968).

[14] Clarence E. Lovejoy, *Lovejoy's College Guide* (New York: Simon and Schuster, Inc., revised periodically).

[15] *The College Blue Book,* Volumes I–III (Yonkers, N.Y.: Christian E. Burckel, revised periodically).

[16] Benjamin Fine, *Barron's Profiles of American Colleges* (Woodbury, N.Y.: Barron's Educational Series, 1968).

[17] Nathan M. Cohen, *Vocational Training Directory of the United States* (Arlington, Va.: Potomac Press, revised periodically).

the *Directory of Technical Institute Courses,*[18] and the *Home Study Blue Book.*[19]

7. *Military Service Materials.* Since many of today's young men are subject to a period of active military service, full information about the armed services, specific service branches, training opportunities, ways of meeting military obligations, and kinds of adjustment problems encountered should be made available to youth. The branches of the military services have devoted considerable resources to the development of materials for prospective personnel. Some examples are *Your Life Plans and the Armed Forces*[20] and *Army Occupations and You.*[21] Also an excellent source of information in the military services is the local recruiting office personnel.

8. *Visual and Auditory Aids.* Although many printed informational materials are available, visual aids can also be useful. Films, charts, tape recordings, records, filmstrips, and films are available from commercial companies, audiovisual rental centers, organizations, and professional societies. Such visual and auditory aids may be found in all three areas —educational, occupational, and personal-social information.

9. *Financial Aid Information.* An increasing flood of printed materials are available covering scholarships, student loans, student employment, and work-study plans. Examples include *Scholarships, Fellowships, and Loans*[22] and *Financial Aid for College Students: Undergraduate.*[23]

10. *College Entrance Examinations and Scholarship Examinations.* Such materials are designed to help students prepare for tests required for admissions and scholarships. Examples of such materials include *How to Prepare for College Entrance Examinations,*[24] and *You Can Win a Scholarship.*[25]

11. *Study Aids.* Educational aids have been prepared to help junior and senior high school students increase their studying effectiveness. Such

---

[18] National Council on Technical Schools, *Directory of Technical Institute Courses* (Washington: The Council, revised yearly).

[19] H. H. Kempfer (ed.), *Home Study Blue Book* (Washington: National Home Study Council, revised yearly).

[20] North Central Association of Colleges and Secondary Schools, *Your Life Plans and the Armed Forces* (Washington: American Council on Education, 1955).

[21] *Army Occupations and You* (Washington: Office of Personnel Operations, Department of the Army, revised periodically).

[22] S. Norman Feingold, *Scholarships, Fellowships, and Loans,* Vols. I, II, III, IV (Cambridge, Mass.: Bellman Publishing Co., Supplement periodically).

[23] Theresa Welking, *Financial Aid for College Students: Undergraduate,* U.S. Office of Education Bulletin No. 18, 1957 (Washington: Government Printing Office, revised annually).

[24] Samuel C. Brownstein and Mitchel Weiner, *How to Prepare for College Entrance Examinations* (Great Neck, N.Y.: Barron's Educational Series, revised annually).

[25] Samuel C. Brownstein, *et al., You Can Win a Scholarship* (Great Neck, N.Y.: Barron's Educational Series, revised annually).

aids range from textbooks to workbooks and pamphlets. Some examples are *Studying Effectively*[26] and *Make Your Study Hours Count.*[27]

12. *Personal and Social Information Books, Booklets, and Pamphlets.* Many commercial publishing companies, professional organizations, and foundations have prepared an extensive array of materials which are valuable sources for personal-social information. For example, Science Research Associates has prepared a series of "Better Living Booklets" and "Life Adjustment Booklets" which discuss issues such as dating, interpersonal relations, manners, religion, and a wide variety of other topics.

13. *Annotated Materials.* Comprehensive listings of annotated materials available in various areas are published commercially. Examples include *Occupational Literature: An Annotated Bibliography*[28] and *Educators Guide to Free Guidance Materials.*[29]

Furthermore, extensive detailing of the preceding thirteen classifications of personal-social, occupational, and educational information materials may be found in Shartle,[30] Baer and Roeber,[31] Hoppock,[32] and Norris, Zeran, and Hatch.[33]

Evaluation of Materials

Because change is a marked characteristic of today's world, there is a danger that informational materials may be out-of-date, contain unreliable information, and present misinformation. There are several statements of criteria against which informational materials may be compared. According to Ohlsen, materials should be evaluated in the following terms:

1. Who published the materials? Are they reputable publishers?
2. Who wrote the materials? Is the author qualified in this field?
3. What was his motive in preparing the material? Was he obligated in any way to present a point of view or to recruit for his sponsoring organization?
4. When was the material published? Is it still up-to-date?

[26] Frank Robinson, *Studying Effectively* (New York: Harper & Row, Publishers, revised periodically).

[27] C. d'A. Gerken and Alica Kemp, *Make Your Study Hours Count* (Chicago: Science Research Associates, Inc., 1956).

[28] Gertrude Forrester, *Occupational Literature: An Annotated Bibliography* (New York: H. W. Wilson Company, revised periodically).

[29] Mary S. Saterstrom and Joe A. Steph, *Educators Guide to Free Guidance Materials* (Randolph, Wisc.: Educational Progress Service, revised annually).

[30] Carroll L. Shartle, *Occupational Information,* Third Edition (Englewood Cliffs, N.J.: Prentice-Hall, Inc., 1959), pp. 169–192.

[31] Baer and Roeber, *Occupational Information,* pp. 136–144.

[32] Hoppock, *Occupational Information,* pp. 27–43.

[33] Norris, Zeran, and Hatch, *Informational Service,* pp. 117–238.

5. Is the material well written? Is it on the reading level of those who should read it?
6. Is the material well illustrated? Will it appeal to pupils who should read it?[34]

An examination of the criteria cited by Ohlsen reveals the necessity for up-to-date informational material. This criterion cannot be overstressed, yet the informational service that attempts to meet it is confronted with some very real problems. First, some publication lag (usually two to five years) in commercial materials is inevitable. Second, labor trends are extremely complex and require considerable effort to incorporate into usable information. Governmental publications such as those available from the Department of Labor probably reflect changes more quickly than other sources. The *Occupational Outlook Quarterly* and the *Occupational Outlook Handbook* are examples of highly current information.

Conscious of the necessity for quality informational materials, the National Vocational Guidance Association has published and consistently refined its "Standards for Use in Preparing and Evaluating Occupational Literature." Such standards assist those who write, publish, or evaluate descriptive materials. The "Standards" are divided into three major areas: "Basic Concepts," "Guidelines for Content," and "Criteria for Style and Format." The five standards presented under "Basic Concepts" are as follows:

1. A basic standard for any occupational publication should be the inclusion of a clear statement as to its purpose and the group to whom it is directed.
2. Occupational information should be related to developmental levels which will vary with age, educational attainment, social and economic backgrounds.
3. Consideration should be given to the implications of the material for all groups in our society.
4. The description of an occupation should be an accurate and balanced appraisal of opportunities and working conditions which should not be influenced by recruiting, advertising, or other special interests.
5. Occupational information should include the nature of personal satisfactions provided, the kinds of demands made and the possible effects on an individual's way of life.[35]

The "Standards" specify as guidelines for content the history of the occupation, the nature of the work, requirements, methods of entering, opportunities for experience and exploration in the occupation, lines of advancement, employment outlook, and the like. Criteria for style and format are also specified.

[34] Merle Ohlsen, *Guidance Services in the Modern School* (New York: Harcourt, Brace & World, Inc., 1964), p. 306.

[35] National Vocational Guidance Association, "Standards for Use in Preparing and Evaluating Occupational Literature," *Vocational Guidance Quarterly* Vol. 12 (Spring 1964), pp. 221–222.

The Informational Library

Essential to the informational service is the collection, housing, and use of materials. Most school guidance programs attempt to have educational, vocational, and personal-social informational materials available in the guidance suite as well as in the school's library. Each year one counselor is generally charged with the responsibility of securing and housing the informational materials. This counselor works with the librarian in obtaining and organizing materials, since a meaningful organization is necessary if students are to make use of them. An orderly method of cataloging, filing and housing bound and unbound materials should be worked out. Filing plans can be purchased from commercial companies or a filing system can be individually constructed. Filing systems for occupational materials are often based on the *D.O.T.* classification codes, others are based on the U.S. Census, and still others, on the Standard Industrial Classification System. Some follow an alphabetical arrangement while others are grouped by occupational interest inventory areas.

Simplicity in filing and maximum accessibility to such materials are two major criteria for filing and housing. Each year all materials should be examined and the out-of-date materials updated or removed. The primary purpose of constant reappraisal of the contents of an informational file is to prevent the inclusion of misleading and incorrect information.

PUTTING INFORMATIONAL MATERIALS TO USE

The acquisition of informational materials is only one aspect of the informational service. The major responsibility of teachers and counselors is that of encouraging students to use such materials. A school's guidance program attempts to encourage student use of the information through individual and group approaches. Each of these approaches will be discussed briefly here.

Using Information with Individuals

Students often have vague, erroneous, and limited perceptions of the work world, educational opportunities, and personal-social relationships. Unless encouraged to use available materials, many students will leave to chance any clarification of directions, goals, or problems. During interviews with students, counselors often need to give information about occupations, educational opportunities, and personal-social relationships, since such information may be vital to self-exploration. Though some counselors believe that giving information during counseling interferes with the dynamics of counseling because it places the counselor in an authoritarian role, it seems more likely that this possibility depends upon the way the information is offered. The mishandling of any aspect of the counseling relationship can lead to a breakdown in the relationship. If information is correctly handled by the counselor, assuming that it has relevance, the helping role will not necessarily be impaired. Such information can lead the student to test roles, project himself, and explore the meanings the information possesses for him. Arbuckle states that:

> Even though in the actual counseling relationship information will play a minor role, the school counselor will periodically be called upon to supply information. There would seem to be no reason why he could not do so and at the same time maintain his counseling relationship with the client. Generally speaking, however, he should not be seen as the giver of information, but rather as the individual who will help a person to get to the point where he can make sensible use of sensible information.[36]

Educational, occupational, and personal-social information has been treated in previous discussions as if it were independent of the counseling process. But we should recognize that informational data received by students do not fall into such neat divisions. All data become highly integrated when the individual student attempts to assimilate, analyze, project, and discuss their meanings in terms of personal decisions or future plans. Information to which the individual student has been exposed will be accepted if it fits into his self-perceptions. If it does not, it will be perceived as unrealistic or appropriate only for others. Information about occupations, education, or personal-social situations may help the adolescent formulate realistic plans or make decisions acceptable to him. Hoppock points out that it is not the purpose of counseling to recruit for particular occupations or to direct students away from certain occupations, or to select students for college. Information is used in counseling "to help the client to clarify the goal that he wants to reach and to move in the direction in which he wants to go, so long as the goal and the means of obtaining it are not injurious to others."[37]

Goldman identified two reasons why information is sometimes viewed as disrupting the counseling process. The first reason is that factual information may direct the client's attention away from his feelings, values and his inner life; and the second is that counselors may tend to become less accepting of a client's perceptions and/or values of the external information. Further the counselor sometimes acts as though he must defend test data or occupational information brought into the interview. Goldman stated that one solution to this situation was to separate the two processes, but he preferred for the counselor to combine functions of assessment and information-giving with counseling. He believed that the two functions could be united (1) if the counselor maintained the same attitude about appraisal and environmental information that he did regarding all other information and (2) if the counselor remained up-to-date in respect to

---

[36] Dugald S. Arbuckle, *Counseling: Philosophy, Theory and Practice,* Second Edition (Boston: Allyn & Bacon, Inc., 1970), p. 312.

[37] Hoppock, *Occupational Information,* p. 148.

information. Finally, Goldman interpreted the counselor's role with reference to information as that of an "... *interpreter of probabilities*."[38]

Using information in counseling interviews often raises questions about timing, the approach to be used, the amount of counselor assistance needed, and the like. Patterson, in discussing occupational information, cites the following guidelines in response to such questions:

1. Occupational information is introduced into the counseling process where there is a recognized need for it on the part of the client.
2. Occupational information is not used to influence or manipulate the client.
3. The most objective way to provide occupational information, and a way which maximizes client initiative and responsibility, is to encourage the client to obtain the information from original sources, that is, publications, employers, and persons engaged in the occupations.
4. The clients' attitudes and feeling about occupations and jobs must be allowed expression and dealt with therapeutically.[39]

In a study of the occupational goals of students, Speer and Jasker reported that undirected reading of information by the students was significantly less valuable than directed reading that had been suggested by the counselor and discussed with him after it had been read.[40] This suggests that the counselor not only should provide information to the student, but must provide assistance in how to use it. Several years ago Brayfield theorized that self-study should precede exploration of occupational information on the basis that understanding of one's strengths and limitations is necessary before career planning can legitimately take place.[41] But in many instances it may be advantageous for the student to pursue career planning at the time he expresses interest in doing so. Counselors would not accomplish anything if they insisted upon student self-study first. Perhaps information about education, occupations, and personal-social situations may well constitute the framework for self-study.

Baer and Roeber have indicated that students who read materials aloud to a counselor react to them more adequately than if they read them alone.[42] Rundquist[43] reported the use of tape-recorded interviews of men and

[38] Leo Goldman, "Information and Counseling: A Dilemma," *Personnel and Guidance Journal* Vol. 46 (September 1967), pp. 42–46.

[39] Cecil H. Patterson, "Counseling: Self Clarification and the Helping Relationship," in Henry Borow (ed.), *Man in a World at Work* (Boston: Houghton Mifflin Co., 1964), pp. 453–455.

[40] George S. Speer and Leslie Jasker, "The Influence of Occupational Goals," *Occupations* Vol. 28 (October 1949), pp. 15–17.

[41] Arthur H. Brayfield, "Dissemination of Occupational Information," *Occupations* Vol. 1 (March 1951), pp. 411–413.

[42] Baer and Roeber, *Occupational Information,* p. 429.

[43] Richard M. Rundquist, "Tape Recorded Interviews Vitalize Occupational Information," *Vocational Guidance Quarterly* Vol. 4 (Winter 1955–56), p. 62.

women in different occupations to present occupational information to students. If the counselor and student listened to such tapes together, many cues could be followed up in respect to the student's perceptions of the occupation. Counselors have also found that students who personally interview adults in different occupations obtain perceptions which may need further exploration in the counseling interview. In summary, dealing with information in counseling requires skillful, sensitive work on the part of the counselor if students are to be helped to study, interpret, evaluate, and utilize information for their development.

Using Information with Groups

Group approaches which incorporate the use of information materials are usually organized in three ways: (1) a semester or year course, (2) special units within a school subject or within homerooms, and (3) special conferences or events. Such approaches are built upon providing experiences for students which give them data about (1) themselves (abilities, interests, values, personality), and (2) vocational and educational opportunities and trends.

Some of the more frequently stated advantages of using group approaches to informational data include the following:

1. Group approaches are economical in terms of time, personnel, and facilities.
2. Group approaches utilized to present certain kinds of information (i.e., how to apply for a job) may be more effective than other approaches, since discussion with peers makes the information more meaningful.
3. Group approaches to informational materials encourage positive relationships among students. Some students may find it easier to discuss their concerns with a group of peers.
4. Group approaches to informational materials may pave the way for better student-counselor relationships and further utilization of guidance services.

Some of the more frequently stated disadvantages of using group approaches to informational data are as follows:

1. Many individual concerns of pupils about such data cannot be given consideration in a group approach.
2. The heterogeneity of a group (interests, maturity level) makes it difficult to organize materials and discussions to secure any impact above a superficial level.
3. Securing teachers or counselors with group competencies is difficult.
4. Finding time within crowded, demanding, school schedules and curriculum for such activities is difficult.

GUIDANCE INFORMATIONAL COURSES

Various titles are given to courses designed to provide guidance information to students: "occupations," "guidance," "orientation," "careers," "group guidance," and the like. Such courses vary widely in purposes, grade placement, duration, frequency of meetings, and whether school credit is given. Some time ago, Jones and Miller reported that some 92,000 secondary school students were enrolled in group guidance courses, some 158,000 in occupation courses, and 115,000 in orientation courses.[44] Recently, Mezzano surveyed the 326 school districts in the state of Wisconsin. Of the 298 districts that returned his questionnaire, three-fourths reported that occupations were taught in some form. Some 203 of the schools taught occupations as a unit in a regular academic subject while only seven percent reported that occupations were taught as a separate course. Ninth and twelfth grades were the grades most often assigned the unit.[45]

Such courses typically focus upon either (1) a general coverage of such topics as self-study, vocations, educational opportunities, career planning, school orientation, military service, marriage, and the future, or (2) a special area such as the study of occupations. The organization of the school, the content to be covered, the student attrition rate, and other factors are important considerations with respect to which grade levels such courses are suitable for. Surveys by Hoppock and his associates[46] show that the ninth and twelfth grades were most favored for occupations courses. Inclusion in the ninth grade curriculum enables students to have information helpful in planning future courses. In addition, potential dropouts can be reached. Placement in the twelfth grade course of study is valuable because senior students are more ready to utilize such information since they are more aware of the immediacy of leaving school.

GUIDANCE INFORMATIONAL UNITS WITHIN COURSES AND HOMEROOMS

Informational material presented as a unit within a school subject demands careful organization. Such units are generally exploratory in nature. The topics covered are similar to those cited above where such information was presented as separate courses. The time given to the unit and

[44] Arthur J. Jones and Leonard M. Miller, "The National Picture of Pupil Personnel and Guidance Services in 1953," *The Bulletin of the National Association of Secondary School Principals* Vol. 38 (February 1954), pp. 153–159.

[45] Joseph Mezzano, "A Survey of the Teaching of Occupations," *Vocational Guidance Quarterly* Vol. 17 (June 1969), pp. 275–277.

[46] See Norman Lowenstein and Robert Hoppock, "Teaching of Occupations in 1952," *Personnel and Guidance Journal* Vol. 31 (April 1953), pp. 441–444; and Robert Hoppock and Nancy D. Stevens, "High School Courses in Occupations," *Personnel and Guidance Journal* Vol. 32 (May 1954), pp. 540–543; and Daniel Sinick, William E. Gorman, and Robert Hoppock, "Research on the Teaching of Occupations 1963–64," *Personnel and Guidance Journal* Vol. 44 (February 1966), pp. 591–610.

the interest and background of the teacher determine the coverage and character of such units. An important objective for the teacher is to focus on student reaction to such information presented in the unit rather than simply to disseminate the information.

SPECIAL CONFERENCES

Large numbers of schools employ special conferences to present educational, occupational and personal-social information to students. Some examples of these are cited briefly below.

1. *Career Conferences.* Career conferences are organized to provide vocational guidance information of a supplementary or preliminary nature. At such meetings representatives of various occupations give presentations of their impressions of their occupations, such as what they do, the advantages and disadvantages of the occupations, methods of entry, salaries, and the like. A wide variety of plans and programs have been employed, including those organized for a school class or for a group of schools and those organized for a single day or for several days or weeks.

   Some frequent criticisms of career conferences include the following: (1) students are often not prepared for participation in conferences; (2) such conferences are often viewed as the entire guidance program or as a substitute for it; (3) career representatives speak mostly for the professions while the greater proportion of students actually enter blue-collar occupations; (4) career representatives may or may not give valid pictures of their occupations and students may receive and proceed on highly inaccurate impressions; (5) career conferences may restrict rather than broaden students' goals, perspectives, and plans; and (6) career conferences take too much time and attention which could better be given over to individual counseling.

   Despite these limitations, career conferences are popular and continue to be used extensively. Those who use them cite the following advantages: (1) students gain information firsthand from people actually employed in the occupation; (2) career conferences are a means of presenting basic information to large numbers of students; (3) the conferences introduce students to occupations found in the local community, and students have an opportunity to meet business and industrial leaders who may eventually be their employers; (4) the conferences cause students to think more about career possibilities and encourage further self- and career-study; (5) the conferences often serve as a means for expanding a guidance program, since they encourage students to seek additional counseling and other services; (6) the conferences have a high public-relations value because publicity about the conferences is easily secured and teachers, counselors, and administrators become better acquainted with community leaders.

   Given their limitations and advantages, career conferences should not be viewed as substitutes for properly staffed and organized guidance services. Any values that they possess can be voided by poor management, while able leadership can overcome some of their known limitations.

2. *School and College Conferences.* At such conferences, which may be called "college day," "college night," "further education conferences," and the like, representatives of colleges, trade schools, business schools, and technical institutes present information concerning the admissions requirements, housing facilities, costs, types of programs, scholarships, work opportunities, etc., of their respective institutions. More and more schools are finding it advantageous to conduct such programs at night so that parents may also attend. The advantages and limitations cited above with regard to career conferences apply about equally to school and college conferences.

3. *Assemblies, Clubs, and Field Trips.* Opportunities for providing information through assemblies and school clubs can be used advantageously. Through such activities, speakers, films, and dramatizations may be wisely used. Field trips to plants, industries, and businesses can be useful to students at any grade level if students are briefed before the trips and discussions are held following them.

INNOVATIVE INFORMATIONAL SERVICES

Changes in the methods and processes available to provide youth with career information have advanced rapidly in the past few years. The hope is that these innovations will enable youth to explore information relevant to decision-making and will free the counselor to engage the client in matters meaningful to his concerns as well as the longer range implications of his choice. Many of the innovations that are being developed and tried are ambitious in aim and scope, sophisticated in their use of technology, and firmly anchored in decision and vocational development theory. These innovations, it should be noted, come at a time when the school's informational systems are being challenged as irrelevant, out-of-date and unattractive to students. In truth, challenges coupled with a growing technology stimulated the development of new informational systems.

Currently, innovations in informational services have drawn heavily upon the use of computers and simulation techniques. Bohn and Super point out three ways that computers are used in guidance programs: (1) to provide the counselor with information about the student which the counselor then shares with the student, (2) to deal directly with the student (the student requests the information directly from the machine), and (3) to provide for student and computer interaction.[47] Two computer-

[47] Martin J. Bohn, Jr., and Donald E. Super, "The Computer in Counseling and Guidance Programs," *Educational Technology* Vol. 9 (March 1969), pp. 29–30.

based information programs will be outlined which are representative of the use of the computer in guidance programs.

Computer-Based Programs

EDUCATIONAL AND CAREER EXPLORATION SYSTEM (ECES)

ECES is an experimental computer-based system being developed by the International Business Machines Corporation (See Bohn and Super). Frank J. Minor of that corporation directs the project and Donald Super and Roger Myers of Teachers College, Columbia University, serve as consultants. The conceptional framework of ECES reflects Super's vocational development theory; i.e., that vocational development is a continuing process which may be divided into life stages including growth, exploration, establishment, maintenance and decline (see Chapter 12 of this book). The ECES system has undergone field tests with students (ages 12–19) who, according to Super's classification, fall into late growth and exploration stages.

Three phases are involved in the ECES model, with each phase utilizing a computer-based information bank. Phase I, orientation to the work world, consists of occupational information that the student explores to clarify what the work world is like, the nature of careers, and the occupations that interest him. Phase II, educational information, involves exploration of training programs and different types of education and their relationship to the student's vocational goals. Phase III, training and job search, covers post–high school educational and training opportunities to be utilized in formulating career plans. A school data profile (grades, courses, vocational interests) and a self-concept profile (estimate of learning ability and interests) are stored in the computer for each student.

Counselors help students decide their starting point (Phase I, II, or III) in the system. The student sits at the IBM computer terminal that has a typewriter-like keyboard console above which is located a visual screen. The student types in his questions or responses at the computer terminal and they, as well as the computer's responses, appear on the screen. Simultaneously, a second console types a printout of the complete interaction with the computer system (the student can take the printout home and refer to it in future explorations). A film image projector is connected with the computer terminal and the student can view films selected from an occupational film library. The computer also prepares an interpretative report which checks the logic and progress of the student's interaction with the machine.

INFORMATION SYSTEM FOR VOCATIONAL DECISIONS (ISVD)

The ISVD originated in 1966, founded by a grant from the U.S. Office of Education to Harvard College (David Tiedeman and Robert O'Hara). Essentially ISVD was designed to link together the student, the computer, and the counselor in such a manner that the student could first interact with the computer and then interact with the counselor for an interpretation and evaluation of the student's dialogue with the computer. The computer is used primarily to identify, evaluate, and classify data and to process this information at appropriate times for the individual. Decision-making is sorted into two steps: (1) preparing for the decision and (2) implementing the decision. Three ISVD routines are directed toward: (1) exploration—awareness that a decision must be reached, (2) clarification—improving self-understanding, and (3) reviewing—systematic consideration of the decision in light of available information.

Three primary data files are incorporated in the ISVD system: educational data, military data, and vocational opportunities data. Each file is subdivided in several ways. "Scripts" tell the computer what to do through a set of directions or rules. Scripts determine the text to be presented to the student by either video devices or printers, by activating tape recorders, motion pictures or 35 mm slides, and they provide instructions on how to process the student's responses. The student sits at the terminal console with the keyboard before him and the video screen above. He interacts with the system through an introductory script that provides instruction on how to use the system. At certain strategic points in his interaction with the system, the student is urged to consult with his counselor. Typed printouts of the computer dialogue are provided the student.

The counselor helps students use the facts and information acquired through the system. Tiedeman and O'Hara have sought to incorporate a "sense of agency" into the system. That is, they have attempted to ensure that the student will be aware that he is the active agent in determining his career.

Other computer-assisted informational systems include the Computerized Vocational Information System (CVIS) at Willowbrook High School (Ill.); the System of Interactive Guidance and Information (SIGI) being developed by Martin Katz at Educational Testing Service (Princeton, N.J.); and the Computer-Assisted Career Exploration System (CACE) being developed by Joseph T. Impellitteri at Pennsylvania State University. These and other models have been described more fully by Joyce Chick.[48] Chick also details the principal advantages and disadvantages of computer-based informational systems.

Simulation and Gaming Techniques

Other innovations in informational services depend upon the use of simulation and gaming techniques.

THE LIFE CAREER GAME

Developed at Johns Hopkins University by Sarane S. Boocock, the "Life Career Game" involves both simulation and gaming. It simulates features of the education, labor, and marriage "markets" as these presently operate

---

[48] Joyce Chick. *Innovations in the Use of Career Information.* Guidance Monographs. Boston: Houghton Mifflin, 1970.

in the United States and are projected to operate in the future. The major objective is to assist youth to acquire a better understanding of these markets and to provide them with preplanning experiences believed beneficial to their future development. Teams (each with two to four players) participate in game rounds (discussion periods) during which they make decisions about the alternatives available to a fictitious person whom the teams represent. Each game round is used to depict a year in the life of the person represented. The game requires players to complete job application and college admission forms. Each of four areas—education, occupation, family life and leisure—is scored. Varenhorst reports using the *Life Career Game* in California school settings, and she has adapted it for use with both junior and senior high school students.[49]

OCCUPATIONAL SIMULATION KITS

Krumboltz and Bergland[50] have constructed lifelike problem-solving job experiences for seven occupations, such as accounting, appliance service and repair, electronics technician, and the like. Each simulated experience is contained in a self-administering kit. The format employed includes an introduction to the occupation, a statement of the problem and the information needed to solve it. Results from evaluative studies of the effectiveness of the simulated occupational experience were that (1) students from lower socioeconomic schools reacted more positively than their middle-class school counterparts, (2) the problem-solving booklet generated interest in the occupation it presents, and (3) students who personally choose their own kits sought further occupational information and tended to predict more favorable estimates of job satisfaction than equivalent students who had not personally selected their kits.

Multimedia Techniques

An example of the simultaneous application of several types of media to the information services is the Vocational Information for Education and Work project (VIEW) developed by the San Diego County Department of Education. Project VIEW is a regional center for the collection, synthesis and dissemination of career information. Phase I of the center, according to Gerstein and Hoover,[51] was designed to assess the types of career information needed by students, counselors, and teachers and to devise a useful and appropriate method for disseminating such information to local schools. Phase II was designed to develop an operational model-system for the 100,000 students in the 70 school districts located

[49] Barbara B. Varrenhorst. "Innovative Tool for Group Counseling: The Life Career Game," *The School Counselor* Vol. 15 (May 1968), pp. 357–362.

[50] John D. Krumboltz and Bruce Bergland. "Experiencing Work Almost Like It Is," *Educational Technology* Vol. 9 (March 1969), pp. 47–49.

[51] Martin Gerstein and Richard Hoover. "VIEW—Vocational Information for Education and Work," *Personnel and Guidance Journal* Vol. 45 (February 1967), pp. 593–596.

in San Diego County. The label "VIEW" seems highly appropriate to the materials utilized because microfilm and electronic data-processing cards are used for collecting, storing, and disseminating information. This information is processed into an occupational brief entitled a "Viewscript." The Viewscript consists of an aperture card (electronic data-processing card) which contains a rectangular 35 mm microfilm frame. Completed aperture cards, by means of a microfilm processor-camera, can be prepared quickly (35 copies per hour can be made for distribution to schools). The material used can be translated into Spanish or any language. Schools using the system are equipped with a microfilm reader-printer and reader and a flash-filing aperture card storage tray. Students use a microfilm reader to view the occupational briefs and a reader-printer if they want a printed copy of the brief.

Summary

The systems described above, as well as many other innovative practices, represent the future of informational services. Presumably technological advances will enable counselors not only to do better but to do more efficiently that which they strive for in the informational service. Constant experimentation and testing of ideas in this area, leading to more knowledgeable and ingenious programs, extend great hope for the future of meaningful development and refinement of the information service within the total constellation of guidance services.

PRINCIPLES OF THE INFORMATIONAL SERVICE

From the previous discussion of the informational service, certain principles may be summarized.

1. *The information service* is an essential part of the school's guidance program. Elementary and secondary school youth have problems to cope with, academic and social decisions to make, and careers to plan which demand information. They need as much information about themselves and about their world as they can acquire. Enlargement of awareness of their opportunities is a task accepted by every school. Students need assistance in acquiring, evaluating and using educational, vocational, and personal–social information for their own developing purposes. The informational service helps more students to increase their chance of managing their futures by providing meaningful data at strategic times.
2. *The focus of the informational service is upon self-study and future trends and change.* Change is ever present. Trends in the labor force, shifts in the nature of occupations, and new directions in educational programs not only occur rapidly, but are sometimes subtle and deceptive. Change cannot be held back. For example, some have esti-

mated that automation will effect 60,000,000 jobs within the next generation. The informational service deals with change as an inherent, meaningful condition in student planning. Although informational materials may deal with facts and conditions as they *were,* counselors must work with students in terms of what conditions *may be like* or what situations *may become.*

The nature of the informational service is also focused upon encouraging student self-study. One's personality and need structure are examined. Projections into different roles are encouraged. Educational, vocational, and personal-social information will be meaningful to the student only as it is related to him and his environment. Students are helped to appraise their interests, their abilities, their aptitudes, their attitudes, and their personal characteristics. Tentative educational and vocational plans result from thorough self-study and study of change. Erich Fromm has written that "There is no meaning to life except the meaning man gives his life by the unfolding of his powers, by living productively."[52] The realization of a productive life in a complex society frequently rests on wise, informed decisions made as early as possible.

3. *Both group and individual techniques are used to convey informational data to students and to assist them in interpreting and using such data.* Both approaches encourage self-analytic and diagnostic methods. Both call for the student to relate impressions about himself to environmental findings.

Group approaches represent a medium through which information about the work world and educational decisions may lead to personality change, goal-setting, decision-making, and planning. Peer reaction and influence significantly affect an individual's goals, decisions, and achievement. Group approaches build upon inherent attitudinal and motivational factors.

Individual approaches are designed to assist the individual to relate information to himself as a unique individual. The realities of work and education for an individual can be considered as he is helped to become aware of his development and progression by sharing counselor understandings.

4. *The informational service is more than information-giving.* The informational service is clearly more than securing educational, vocational, and personal-social data and handing materials to students to read. Such a service implies that attention will be given to the individual's attitudes and emotional reactions to the information. The presentation of information must be planned in terms of students' needs. Opportunities for the student to react to what is presented must be provided, and time must be given over to the assimilation of information if it is to be related to one's self and one's plans. Rusalem states:

[52] Erich Fromm, *Man for Himself* (New York: Rinehart & Company, Inc., 1947), p. 45.

The process of imparting occupational information will become interwoven with the problem of meanings. A movie on the profession of nursing will not necessarily result in similar understandings of the profession on the part of a group of students. One may perceive the contact with sick individuals as the whole nursing job and find it consistent with her self concept. Another student may select the aspect of making beds and providing physical comfort as the essence of the job and may reject it as unsuitable for her.[53]

Rusalem's statement points up the fact that the individual's perceptions based upon selective attention to material must be taken into account. The meanings counselors assign certain information may or may not be the same as those that students assign to it. Informational data have to be sought, weighed, and assessed in relation to each pupil.

5. *Qualified personnel to staff the informational service is essential.* The quality of the staff will be reflected in the quality of the service. Upgrading of staff and reassignment are responsibilities that guidance administrators must accept and carry out.

6. *The informational service must contain provisions for its evaluation.* Checks must be undertaken to determine how effective it is. Techniques used in the service should be evaluated. Pupil, teacher, and counselor reactions to the service should be examined to determine if better ways can be found to achieve the objectives of the informational service.

ANNOTATED BIBLIOGRAPHY

BOROW, HENRY (ed.). *Man In a World at Work.* Boston: Houghton Mifflin Company, 1964. Chapters 18 and 20, pp. 411–433 and 460–486.

In Chapter 18, "Occupational Exploration in Counseling: A Proposed Reorientation," Joseph Samler presents seven proposals for occupational exploration through counseling. Margaret Bennett, in Chapter 20, "Strategies of Vocational Guidance in Groups," points up the interrelations of group and individual services, the objectives of group services, and the contributions of the group setting; she also cites some specific group techniques.

CHICK, JOYCE M. *Innovations in the Use of Career Materials.* Guidance Monographs. Boston: Houghton Mifflin Company, 1970, 80 pp.

Chick describes many of the innovative approaches being tried out in the informational service. She identifies and discusses the merits and disadvantages of these approaches.

Computer-based Vocational Guidance Systems. Washington, D.C.: Office of Education, 1969, 168 pp.

Nine papers are devoted to theoretical discussions in developing informational services, seven papers to problems of implementing systems, and 10 papers to describing systems presently under development.

ISAACSON, LEE E. *Career Information in Counseling and Teaching.* Boston: Allyn and Bacon, 1966, 430 pp.

Part I introduces career information and outlines theories of vocational

---

[53] Herbert Rusalem, "New Insights on the Role of Occupational Information in Counseling," *Journal of Counseling Psychology* Vol. 1 (Summer 1954), p. 85.

choice; Part II presents systems of classifying occupations; Part III discusses the factors that influence workers and their careers; Part IV discusses the preparation needed for different types of work; Part V suggests useful materials that describe work; and Part VI concentrates upon utilizing career information with groups and individuals. The book is well written and is highly useful to teachers and counselors.

VRIEND, JOHN, *et al.* "Counseling Technology," *Educational Technology.* Vol. 9 (March 1969), 76 pp.

The authors—Vriend, Blocher, Geis, Super, Impellitteri, Van Hoose and others—seek either to conceptualize counseling as a technology or to describe how computers are being used in informational services.

SELECTED REFERENCES

ANDERSON, LEORA, AND STAHL, EARL. "Employability Changes of the High School Dropout Over a Two-Year Period," *Vocational Guidance Quarterly* Vol. 18 (June 1970), pp. 289–293.

ARBUCKLE, DUGALD S. "Occupational Information in the Elementary School," *Vocational Guidance Quarterly* Vol. 12 (Winter 1963–64), pp. 77–84.

———. "Counselors, Admissions Officers, and Information," *The School Counselor* Vol. 16 (January 1969), pp. 164–169.

ASBURY, FRANK A. "Vocational Development of Rural Disadvantaged Eighth-Grade Boys," *Vocational Guidance Quarterly* Vol. 17 (December 1968), pp. 109–113.

BAILEY, JOHN A. "Career Development Concepts: Significance and Utility," *Personnel and Guidance Journal* Vol. 47 (September 1968), pp. 24–28.

BANK, IRA M. "Children Explore Careerland Through Vocational Role-Models," *Vocational Guidance Quarterly* Vol. 17 (June 1969), pp. 284–289.

BERGLAND, BRUCE W., AND KRUMBOLTZ, JOHN D. "An Optimal Grade Level for Career Exploration," *Vocational Guidance Quarterly* Vol. 18 (September 1969), pp. 29–33.

BIDWELL, GLORIA P. "Ego Strength, Self-Knowledge, and Vocational Planning of Schizophrenics," *Journal of Counseling Psychology* Vol. 16 (January 1969), pp. 45–49.

ENGLISH, URMA. "An Eighth Grade Group Guidance Unit In Educational Planning," *The School Counselor* Vol. 15 (November 1967), pp. 137–140.

FIBKINS, WILLIAM. "A Different Approach to Sharing Occupational Information," *The School Counselor* Vol. 16 (May 1969), pp. 390–393.

FINE, SIDNEY A. "The 1965 Edition of the Dictionary of Occupational Titles: Content, Contrasts, and Critique," *Vocational Guidance Quarterly* Vol. 17 (March 1969), pp. 162–172.

GOLDMAN, LEO. "Information and Counseling: A Dilemma," *Personnel and Guidance Journal* Vol. 46 (September 1967), pp. 42–46.

GOODSON, SYLVIA, "Occupational Information Materials in Selected Elementary and Middle Schools," *Vocational Guidance Quarterly* Vol. 17 (December 1968), pp. 128–131.

GREEN, ROBERT L. "The Black Quest for Higher Education: An Admissions Dilemma," *Personnel and Guidance Journal* Vol. 47 (May 1969), pp. 905–911.

HALPERN, GERALD, AND NORRIS, LILA. "Student Curriculum Decisions," *Personnel and Guidance Journal* Vol. 47 (November 1968), pp. 240–243.

HARRIS, JO ANN. "The Computerization of Vocational Information," *Vocational Guidance Quarterly* Vol. 17 (September 1968), pp. 12–20.

HERR, EDWIN L. "Guidance and Vocational Aspects of Education: Some Considerations," *Vocational Guidance Quarterly* Vol. 17 (March 1969), pp. 178–184.

HERSHENSON, DAVID B. "Techniques for Assisting Life-State Vocational Development," *Personnel and Guidance Journal* Vol. 47 (April 1969), pp. 776–780.

HIGGINS, EDWARD L., AND BROWN, DUANE, "Motion Pictures: A Source of Vocational Information," *Vocational Guidance Quarterly* Vol. 12 (Autumn 1963), pp. 68–71.

HOPPOCK, ROBERT. "Some Do's for the Use of Occupational Information," *The School Counselor* Vol. 15 (November 1969), p. 134.

IMPELLITTERI, JOSEPH T. "A Computerized Occupational Information System," *Vocational Guidance Quarterly* Vol. 15 (June 1967), pp. 262–264.

IVEY, ALLEN E., AND MORRILL, WESTON H. "Career Process: A New Concept for Vocational Behavior," *Personnel and Guidance Journal* Vol. 46 (March 1968), pp. 644–649.

JOHNSON, R. PAUL. "Job Corps: Information for School Counselors," *The School Counselor* Vol. 16 (March 1969), pp. 291–295.

JUOLA, ARVO E., WINBURNE, JOHN W., AND WHITMORE, ANNE. "Computer-Assisted Academic Advising," *Personnel and Guidance Journal* Vol. 47 (October 1968), pp. 146–150.

KABACH, GOLDIE RUTH. "Occupational Information in Elementary Education: What Counselors Do—What Counselors Would Like to Do," *Vocational Guidance Quarterly* Vol. 16 (March 1968), pp. 203–206.

KALDOR, DONALD R., AND ZYTOWSKI, DONALD G. "A Maximizing Model for Occupational Decision-Making," *Personnel and Guidance Journal* Vol. 47 (April 1969), pp. 781–788.

KRASNOW, BERNARD S. "Occupational Information As a Factor in the High School Curriculum Chosen by Ninth Grade Boys," *The School Counselor* Vol. 15 (March 1968), pp. 275–280.

LAIR, GEORGE SCOTT, "Educational Counseling: Concern of the School Counselor," *Personnel and Guidance Journal* Vol. 46 (May 1968), pp. 858–861.

LOCKWOOD, OZELMA, SMITH, DAVID B., AND TREZISE, ROBERT. "Four Worlds: An Approach to Occupational Guidance," *Personnel and Guidance Journal* Vol. 46 (March 1968), pp. 641–643.

MARUSIC, SVETO S. "Use of Occupational Drawings to Enhance Vocational Development," *Personnel and Guidance Journal* Vol. 47 (February 1969), pp. 518–520.

McDaniels, Carl. "Youth: Too Young to Choose?" *Vocational Guidance Quarterly* Vol. 16 (June 1968), pp. 242–249.

Miller, Adam W. "Learning Theory and Vocational Decisions," *Personnel and Guidance Journal* Vol. 47 (September 1968), pp. 18–23.

Minor, Frank J., Myers, Roger A., and Super, Donald E. "An Experimental Computer-Based Educational and Career Exploration System," *Personnel and Guidance Journal* Vol. 47 (February 1969), pp. 564–569.

Norman, Russell P. "The Use of Preliminary Information In Vocational Counseling," *Personnel and Guidance Journal* Vol. 47 (March 1969), pp. 693–697.

O'Hara, Robert P. "A Theoretical Foundation for the Use of Occupational Information in Guidance," *Personnel and Guidance Journal* Vol. 46 (March 1968), pp. 636–640.

Ohlsen, Merle M. "Vocational Counseling for Girls and Women," *Vocational Guidance Quarterly* Vol. 17 (December 1968), pp. 124–127.

Perrone, Philip A., and Thrush, Randolph S. "Vocational Information Processing Systems: A Survey," *Vocational Guidance Quarterly* Vol. 17 (June 1969), pp. 255–266.

Pruitt, Anne S. "Teacher Involvement in the Curriculum and Career Guidance," *Vocational Guidance Quarterly* Vol. 17 (March 1969), pp. 189–194.

Quey, Richard L. "Toward a Definition of Work," *Personnel and Guidance Journal* Vol. 47 (November 1968), pp. 223–227.

Samler, Joseph. "Vocational Counseling: A Pattern and a Projection," *Vocational Guidance Quarterly* Vol. 17 (September 1968), pp. 2–11.

———. "The Vocational Counselor and Social Action," *Vocational Guidance Quarterly,* Special Supplement, Vol. 18 (June 1970), 23 pp.

Sinick, Daniel. "Using Occupational Information with the Handicapped," *Vocational Guidance Quarterly* Vol. 12 (Summer 1964), pp. 275–277.

Thompson, Jack M. "Career Development in the Elementary School: Rationale and Implications for Elementary School Counselors," *The School Counselor* Vol. 16 (January 1969), pp. 208–209.

Thoresen, Carl E., and Mehrens, William A. "Decision Theory and Vocational Counseling: Important Concepts and Questions," *Personnel and Guidance Journal* Vol. 46 (October 1967), pp. 165–172.

Unger, Myron B., and Karlin, Muriel. "A Vocational Resources Conference," *Vocational Guidance Quarterly* Vol. 17 (June 1969), pp. 300–301.

Watley, Donivan J. "Career Progress: A Longitudinal Study of Gifted Students," *Journal of Counseling Psychology* Vol. 16 (March 1969), pp. 100–108.

Whitfield, Edwin A. "Vocational Guidance in the Elementary School—Integration or Fragmentation?" *The School Counselor* Vol. 16 (November 1968), pp. 90–93.

Whitfield, Edwin A., and Glaeser, George A. "The Microfilm Approach to Disseminating Vocational Information: An Evaluation," *Vocational Guidance Quarterly* Vol. 18 (December 1969), pp. 82–86.

Zytowski, Donald G. "Toward a Theory of Career Development for Women," *Personnel and Guidance Journal* Vol. 47 (March 1969), pp. 660–664.

12

DYNAMIC FACTORS
AND THEORIES
OF CAREER
DEVELOPMENT

What factors are involved in career development?
What is the value of theories of career development?
What theories can be used to understand career development?

DYNAMIC FACTORS IN CAREER PLANNING

Certain factors are generally accepted as being influential in planning and in placement of students. In the past, planning has often been ineffectual because it was based upon simply matching intellectual ability or interest with a choice, without considering other important factors. Career planning and placement cannot ignore the total range of factors involved in choice. These factors will be discussed briefly in this chapter, and Chapter 13 will present the service aspects of planning and placement.

Intellectual Ability

Although a wide range of intelligence is represented in nearly every occupation and the distribution of intelligence scores in one occupation overlaps that in another to some extent, intellectual ability remains a significant factor in educational and occupational choice. A study of the relationship between civilian occupations and Army General Classification Test (AGCT) scores indicated that (1) there was a clear occupational hierarchy with respect to AGCT scores; (2) occupations were not equally spaced along the hierarchy; (3) median AGCT scores for all occupations tended toward a normal rather than a rectilinear distribution; (4) differences in median scores for occupations were much larger at the extremes of

339

the range; and (5) there was a tendency for entrance into certain occupations to be contingent on the possession of some minimum abilities as measured by the AGCT or similar tests, but there was no upper limit of ability for membership in an occupation.[1] By itself, a test like the AGCT cannot furnish an unquestioned answer regarding the choice of one specific occupation or even a narrow range of occupations. But if properly interpreted, the results of such tests can be of considerable usefulness in planning and placement. Usually, the more restricted the range of ability scores for a given occupation, the more important is the part ability plays. Lower limits of ability can indicate the likelihood of probable failure in some of the higher level occupations. At best, the individual who enters an occupation in which the majority of workers have a higher degree of intelligence than he possesses will find himself at a competitive disadvantage. And if he enters an occupation in which the majority of workers have intelligence ratings definitely below his, he may find that neither the work nor his associations are satisfying to him.

Intellectual ability is an important consideration, since the individual may find his entry into occupations which require considerable educational preparation completely barred. College training is universally required by the professions, demanded by the bulk of occupations classed as semiprofessional, and considered highly desirable for managerial positions. College graduates average well above the total population in intellectual ability. Although there is much overlapping from one specialized field to another, the margin of superiority is not the same for all fields. The results of a study comparing college students in sixteen specialized fields with other students at the same educational level, regardless of their field of specialization, showed that (1) students in some fields are more highly select with regard to intelligence test scores than are students in other fields; (2) some fields attract or admit students of a higher intelligence level than are attracted or admitted to other fields; (3) the differences among fields appeared to be about the same, regardless of the educational level at which the students were studied.[2] Finally, it should be noted that measured ability scores typically correlate more highly with success in training than with success in work performance. Presumably the latter is based upon a wider range of expectations and criteria than the former.

Aptitudes

It appears quite probable that further research will confirm the present indication that many occupations differ quantitatively from each other in

---

[1] Naomi Stewart, "AGCT Scores of Army Personnel Grouped by Occupation," *Occupations* Vol. 26 (October 1947), pp. 5–41.

[2] Dael Wolfle, *America's Resources of Specialized Talent* (New York: Harper & Brothers, 1954).

the specific competencies demanded, i.e., require differing amounts of specialized abilities. The qualitative differences in competencies demanded are fully as impressive as the quantitative differences. Any one occupation usually demands only a few abilities as prerequisite to entrance into its work, but when several thousand occupations are examined, the variety of skills, talents, and aptitudes demanded becomes so great as to defy a manageable system of classification.

Personality

It is generally accepted that certain people are genuinely unsuited to some types of occupations, and that personality factors are of major importance in determining this. A particular occupation may demand from its workers personality traits quite different from those demanded by another occupation. Empirical studies of occupational demands testify, virtually without exception, to the primary importance of personality traits over all other types of occupational information. A study by Teevan was concerned with whether or not correlations between personality and vocation could be demonstrated before the individual became actively engaged in the vocation or if it was the vocation itself which tended to fit its members into a common mold. In summarizing the results of the study, Teevan concluded that correlations between personality and vocation previously found by Roe for professional groups can also be demonstrated during the period preceding entrance into a profession.[3]

Research into the reasons behind vocational choice strongly suggest that an individual's choice of occupation may be definitely related to his basic personality needs.[4] The importance of the individual's self-concept is pointed out by Combs and Snygg, who postulate that the basic human need is the protection and improvement of one's unique perception of oneself or one's self-concept.[5] Thus, it is possible to view occupational decision-making as a further attempt on the part of the individual to enhance or defend his self-concept.

In a study of the value assigned to nine different aspects of work by high school freshmen and seniors, Dipboye and Anderson[6] found that all groups ranked the value of "interesting work" first. Even though there were significant mean sex differences, the authors felt that interesting work was the prime motivating factor in the selection of an occupation. The high rank given to the value of "security" led the authors to conclude that this

---

[3] Richard C. Teevan, "Personality Correlates of Undergraduate Fields of Specialization," *Journal of Consulting Psychology* Vol. 18 (June 1954), pp. 212–214.

[4] Edward C. Glanz and Ernest B. Walston, *An Introduction to Personal Adjustment* (Boston: Allyn and Bacon, Inc., 1958), p. 145.

[5] Arthur Combs and Donald Snygg, *Individual Behavior* (New York: Harper & Brothers, 1949).

[6] W. J. Dipboye and W. F. Anderson, "The Ordering of Occupational Values by High School Freshmen and Seniors," *Personnel and Guidance Journal* Vol. 38 (October 1959), pp. 121–124.

is another of the most important factors in the career-planning process of high school students. Dipboye and Anderson believe that the occupational values held by an individual constitute an essential and important element of his motivational structure and, if understood, can provide invaluable insights into the decision-making process.

Bell[7] views ego-involvement as a factor in occupational choice. According to Bell, one must consider that when a youth is confronted with the problem of what he is going to be when he reaches adulthood, he is forced to come out with "I" projections, which become imbedded in his self-structure. Where there is consistency in the reactions of others to his projections, his self-picture in this area of his experience becomes stabilized and capable of considerable resistance to outside forces. Moreover, he may become aroused emotionally when his self-picture is threatened. In effect, his vocational decision becomes ego-involved.

Cautela[8] postulates that the symbolic value of an occupation may affect the individual's occupational choice. He further indicates that psychoanalysts have stressed the symbolic values of occupations for some time, but that counselors have paid only lip service to this idea. From the cases he had studied, Cautela concluded that the student's behavior concerning occupational choice became more realistic after hypotheses concerning symbolic gratification were used as a basis of counseling. He adds this further word of caution: ". . . even if the individual is attempting to achieve symbolic gratification by his occupational choice, it does not mean he is making a 'wrong' choice. The choice, because of other factors, could be an adaptive one."[9]

The relationship of personality characteristics to occupational choice continues to be a topic of considerable research interest. Holland's theory building, in particular, has been based upon the assumptions that the choice of an occupation is an expression of personality and that members of an occupation share similar personality characteristics. Six types of orientations and/or environments—realistic, intellectual, social, conventional, enterprising and artistic—were proposed by Holland. The process of choice was viewed as a search for an environment congruent with the individual's coping orientation.[10]

Counselors using adjustment inventories need to be aware of the general lack of agreement regarding what is being measured before glib interpretations are made of scores derived from such instruments. It might also be pointed out that validity studies of a large number of the adjustment inven-

[7] Hugh M. Bell, "Ego-Involvement in Vocational Decision," *Personnel and Guidance Journal* Vol. 38 (May 1960), pp. 723–736.

[8] Joseph R. Cautela, "The Factor of Psychological Need in Occupational Choice," *Personnel and Guidance Journal* Vol. 38 (September 1959), pp. 46–48.

[9] *Ibid.,* p. 48.

[10] John L. Holland, *The Psychology of Vocational Choice* (Waltham, Mass.: Blaisdell Publishing Company, 1966).

tories made during the last few years have also failed to show empirical support for their validity. The problem of faking also becomes an issue with this type of test, although several include lie or faking estimates as a part of the data derived from the instruments. Too, the counselor must always remember that values and attitudes in different subgroups may make norms derived from other groups with different backgrounds inappropriate. Thus, the user of personality inventories frequently has to be prepared to develop his own normative data for the specific group with which he is working.

Interests

Bordin[11] presents a theory of the nature of vocational interests based on the individual's responses to the Strong Vocational Interest Blank. It is his contention that theories of vocational interest can and have taken one of three directions: (1) the static point of view, in which vocational interests are believed to be fixed after the individual has reached maturity; (2) the dynamic view, in which vocational interest is seen as a product of psychological influences and, as such, subject to change with shifts in the psychological equilibrium; and (3) the empirical view, in which there are merely sets of preferences that can be shown to distinguish successful men in various occupations from men in general. Bordin believes that the static point of view is presented by Darley; that the empirical view is taken by Strong; and that his own formulations represent an attempt to develop a dynamic view.

The basic assumption of Bordin's theory is that an individual's answers on a vocational interest inventory express his acceptance of a particular view or concept of himself in relation to occupational stereotypes. Bordin offers two corollaries to further clarify the implications of his basic assumption: (1) the degree of clarity of an interest type will vary positively with the degree of acceptance of the occupational stereotype as self-descriptive, and (2) the degree of clarity of an interest type will vary positively with the degree of knowledge of the true occupational stereotype. The second corollary necessitates the assumption that the occupational stereotypes used in interest tests are true stereotypes of the occupations involved, and that all occupations can be stereotyped. Bordin's attempt to present a dynamic point of view can be seen in the following comment:

> If personality is assumed to include the long- and short-term goal-directed strivings of the individual . . . , one must recognize that these strivings are in a state of flux, changing to meet the fluctuations in the situation. When the concept of the self becomes incompatible with the present goal, a state of disequilibruim is created which can only be resolved by some reconciliation between these two factors.[12]

[11] Edward S. Bordin, "A Theory of Vocational Interests as Dynamic Phenomena," *Educational and Psychological Measurement* Vol. 3 (Spring 1943), pp. 49–65.

[12] *Ibid.,* p. 54.

Bordin has offered the most rigidly designed theory of vocational interests. Interests, to Bordin, are strictly inventoried. In his theory, they are considered to be a byproduct of personality and are subject to change whenever the self-concept changes or when there is a change in knowledge of the occupational stereotype.

The volume *Vocational Interest Measurement* by Darley and Hagenah presents a thorough review up to 1955 of the development and use of the Strong Vocational Interest Blank. These authors have also reported the literature on interest measurement.[13]

Interests are of importance for vocational planning because it has been found that men in particular occupations have characteristic sets of likes and dislikes which differentiate them from men in other occupations and from men in general. The principal research in this area has been done by E. K. Strong.[14] Concentration has been focused on relatively high-level occupations; i.e., principally those at the professional, semiprofessional, and managerial levels. It has not been determined whether men engaged in work at all occupational levels can be distinguished on the basis of characteristic interest patterns. The psychological measurement of interests has tended to be concerned primarily with the area of prediction; there has been less research in the area of vocational interest development. Research on the Strong Vocational Interest Blank has permitted the prediction, with a rather high degree of accuracy, of the stability of individuals' interest patterns. According to Strong, people's interests change considerably between the ages of 15 and 20, are more stable from age 20 to 25, and change very little from age 25 to 55. Also, most changes that take place with maturity are completed by age 20, and are more systematic and predictable on the basis of interest-inventory data. The Strong, with its empirical keying, provides no information regarding the development of interests or the relationship between interest patterns and occupational success or job satisfaction. Inventories having a logical or factor-analytic key offer limited information of a theoretical nature, but in the case of many such inventories, sufficient research data are not available. The bulk of research done with the use of the Strong has considered the differences between interest patterns of men in different occupations. Super calls attention to the communality of interests:

> People's interests are far more similar than different, regardless of sex, age, or occupational status. The likes of college men and women are very similar ($r = .74$); those of 15-year-old boys and 55-year-old men are no less similar ($r = .73$); and those of unskilled workers and professional-managerial men resemble each other even more closely ($r = .84$).[15]

[13] John G. Darley and Theda Hagenah, *Vocational Interest Measurement: Theory and Practice* (Minneapolis: University of Minnesota Press, 1955).

[14] E. K. Strong, Sr., *Manual for Vocational Interest Blank for Men* (Palo Alto, Calif.: Stanford University Press, 1943).

[15] Donald E. Super, *Appraising Vocational Fitness* (New York: Harper & Brothers, 1949), p. 393. Reprinted by permission of Harper & Row, Publishers.

The relationship of vocational interests to sex differences, personality, intelligence, and aptitude has been studied, and the research tends to yield some conflicting findings. Men tend to be more interested in physical activity, mechanical and scientific matters, politics, and selling. Interest in art, music, literature, people, clerical work, teaching, and social work is more characteristic of women. Sex differences in attitudes that have vocational significance appear very early. Tyler found them, both in specific items and in organization of interests, among first graders.[16] Growing research evidence indicates correlations among vocational interest scores and the measured personality traits of defined occupational groups. Some studies investigated personality traits in relation to interests; others studied the personality traits of persons in various occupations. Significant relationships have been discovered between personality and interest in a sizable number of these studies.

Research evidence would further seem to indicate that there is at best only a moderate relationship between interests and aptitudes or abilities. The few studies of the relationship between special aptitudes and interests have yielded generally inconclusive results. In general, studies of the relationship between intelligence and interests have shown the higher positive correlations occurring between scientific and linguistic interests and intelligence, and negative correlations between intelligence and interests in social welfare, business contact, and business detail. Research studies in which intelligence test results have been correlated with occupational scales on the Strong, show that only scientific interests are related to intelligence to a degree that approaches practical significance. This relationship is so low, however, that it should probably not be given weight in counseling. Presumably, such special aptitudes as musical and artistic ability might show closer relationships with appropriate interest scales, but these have not been investigated. Though no definite correlation has, at present, been established between the two, research as well as common sense seems to indicate that ability without interest is more likely to succeed than interest without ability.

Many researchers have attempted to come up with specific interest factors through the use of the specialized statistical techniques of factor analysis. Cottle's findings will be quoted in this respect, as they appear to be closely related to personality needs. Five categorized bi-polar interest factors were revealed by his study: "(1) 'Things versus people' factor; (2) business contact versus scientific interest; (3) interest in business detail versus abstract and creative interest; (4) social welfare interest versus nonsocial interest; (5) prestige interest versus tangible, productive interest."[17]

These factors were named by Cottle after he derived intercorrelations

---

[16] Cited in Anne Roe, *The Psychology of Occupations* (New York: John Wiley & Sons, Inc., 1956), p. 87.

[17] William C. Cottle, "A Factorial Study of the Multiphasic, Strong, Kuder, and Bell Inventories Using a Population of Adult Males," *Psychometrika* Vol. 15 (March 1950), pp. 25–47.

among the Minnesota Multiphasic Personality Inventory, the Strong Vocational Interest Blank, the Kuder Preference Record, and the Bell Adjustment Inventory.

Realism as a Factor in Occupational Choice

There is a vast array of data which shows that the obvious approach of using answers to direct questions about interests is often unreliable, superficial, and unrealistic. Research seems to indicate that the expressed interests of children and adolescents are unstable and do not provide useful data for diagnosis or prognosis. There are several factors which partially explain this situation. First, most persons have insufficient information about different jobs, courses of study, and other activities. They are thus unable to judge whether they would really like all that their choice actually involves. A second related factor is the prevalence of glamorized stereotypes regarding certain vocations. The problem, therefore, is that individuals are rarely in a position to know their own interests in various fields before they actually participate in those fields; but by the time they have had the benefit of such direct occupational experience, it is often too late to profit from the experience. A third factor might be that expressed interests are frequently the outcome of an awareness of social pressures. Expressed interests are stated because they are often demanded by or approved of by the society or environment in which the individual is reared.

Stephenson draws the following generalizations regarding the realism of vocational choice from a review of the literature on this topic: (1) A large percentage of every pre-work age group has made no occupational choice whatsoever; (2) for those making a choice, there is a strong tendency to select from a narrow range of occupations; (3) occupational choices are largely in the upper range of the occupational hierarchy, with a higher percentage in the professions; (4) the distribution of occupational choices has very little correspondence either to the national or local distribution of job opportunities or to the father's occupation.[18]

Most studies have shown that as children progress from childhood through adolescence, their vocational choices become more realistic—realistic in the sense of being more in line with the individual's capacities, interests, or opportunities for placement, or with the occupational distribution found in the community, state or nation. (Strong's research has also shown that inventoried interests of adults remain quite constant.) There seems to be greater realism in expressed occupational choice when students are asked about their expectancy choice (what they *expect* to do). Clack[19] reported that very low (and nonsignificant) correlations exist between stu-

---

[18] Richard M. Stephenson, "Realism of Vocational Choice: A Critique and An Example," *Personnel and Guidance Journal* Vol. 35 (April 1957), pp. 482–488.

[19] Ronald J. Clack, "Occupational Prestige and Vocational Choice," *Vocational Guidance Quarterly* Vol. 16 (June 1968), pp. 282–286.

dents' "reality" choices and their "prestige" rankings of occupations. "Fantasy" choices correlated highly with students' prestige rankings of occupations. Presumably, students desire high-prestige occupations but barriers prevent them from attaining their fantasy choices. Aware that their interests, abilities, skills are not adequate to enable them to fill prestigeful occupations, they settle for something less (more realistic?) than the occupations they most desire.

Stephenson studied the occupational aspirations and occupational plans of one thousand ninth graders and found (1) a significant difference between the student's occupational plans and aspirations (it was noted that a number of students lowered their aspirations when considering plans and that their plans were more realistic in relation to the occupational structure); (2) males approached planning more realistically than females; and (3) the lowering of aspirations was not a random phenomenon, but took place primarily among students in the lower socioeconomic levels. The study concluded that "a specific occupational choice is very probably an indication of a youth's general orientation to the occupational hierarchy when expressed as an aspiration, and a judgment of his general expectation and life chances when expressed as a plan."[20]

From Small's research with the occupational choices of adolescent boys (fifty better adjusted boys and fifty disturbed boys between the ages of fifteen and nineteen) it was found that: (1) the better adjusted boys were consistently more realistic in their vocational choices than were the disturbed boys; (2) the better adjusted boys showed more of the needs that are associated with environment-involvement, the forming of relationships with people, and the exercise of skills and talents, while the disturbed boys showed more of the needs associated with environment-avoidance and the restriction of both relationships with people and the exercise of talents; (3) the second vocational choice of the better adjusted boys was less realistic than their first choice, whereas the second choice of the disturbed boys tended to be more realistic than their first choice; and (4) within the age group studied, no evidence was found to support Ginzberg's theory that occupational choice is a developmental process leading chronologically to increasing realism as a determinant of choice.[21]

According to Patterson,

Clinical experience indicates that emotionally disturbed persons frequently express interests in certain occupations and fields of work more often than the normal person. Their interests seem to be in areas requiring a high degree of special talent or ability for success. Some of the frequently chosen fields require skill in interpersonal relationships, which would appear to be an area of deficiency in the emotionally disturbed. For these reasons, the occupational or vocational interests of the emotionally disturbed are more likely

---

[20] Stephenson, "Realism of Vocational Choice," p. 488.

[21] Leonard Small, "Personality Determinants of Vocational Choice," *Psychological Monographs* Vol. 67, No. 1 (1953), p. 1.

to be inappropriate or not vocationally significant than is the case for the non-emotionally disturbed client. There is also evidence to the effect that emotionally disturbed clients are different from normal persons in tending to be more unrealistic in terms of appraising aptitude and ability requirements of the occupations in which they express interest. While the counselor should be aware of these factors, he should also be aware that the client cannot be forced into an "appropriate" type of work. If he is, he is not likely to succeed; interest and motivation as well as aptitude and ability are important in success.[22]

Thomas, in summarizing studies of the vocational ambitions of youth, noted that in recent years the percentage of high school youth intending to qualify for employment in the professions appears to be running two to three times the percentage of the labor force currently working in these categories. He further contends that although the occupational aspirations of youth are unrealistic in terms of factors of supply and demand, they are realistic in terms of responding accurately to the primary values ascribed to occupations in our culture—the values of prestige and remuneration.[23]

Probably no study of vocational choice has been accomplished with the thoroughness and objectivity of the Super and Overstreet study of ninth-grade boys.[24] They believe the ninth grade is the most crucial point for the individual in planning his occupation. The results of this study suggest, as have others before it, that taking the student's occupational aspirations at face value is often a mistake, that seeking to help him formulate a *specific* occupational objective at the ninth grade level may be a strategic error.

Super and Overstreet caution counselors always to assess the vocational maturity of the boy while appraising his development and his vocational prospects. They further assert that the task of planning in the ninth grade is essentially a matter of furthering vocational development rather than of fostering specific vocational choice. Looking at planning in the ninth grade realistically, the major value of planning at this level is that it encourages students to start thinking early about vocational plans.

Self-Concept

Previously it was stated that when a youth is confronted by adults and others about what he is going to be when he "grows up," he is forced to voice "I" projections that tend to become imbedded in his self-structure. When others express approval of his projections, his self-picture in this area

[22] C. H. Patterson, "Interest Tests and the Emotionally Disturbed Client," *Educational and Psychological Measurement* Vol. 17 (Summer 1957), pp. 264–280.

[23] Lawrence G. Thomas, *The Occupational Structure and Education* (Englewood Cliffs, N.J.: Prentice-Hall, Inc., 1956), p. 252.

[24] Donald Super and Phoebe Overstreet, *The Vocational Maturity of Ninth-Grade Boys* (New York: Bureau of Publications, Teachers College, Columbia University, 1960), p. 155.

of his experience becomes stabilized and capable of considerable resistance to outside forces. On the other hand, he may become threatened emotionally when his self-picture is questioned. Briefly, then, his vocational decision becomes highly ego involved (it becomes an integral part of his self-concept.)

Role performance may be defined as the effectiveness with which an individual performs a given role. Interpersonal adjustment, however, is defined as the ability to perform roles recognized to be situationally and socially appropriate. Successful criminals and successful businessmen might have equal role-performance ability, but, judged by conventional social standards, they would differ in interpersonal adjustment. Until recently, it was unnecessary to consider the relationship between role-performance ability and interpersonal adjustment, but now there are numerous studies demonstrating that role-performance ability is intimately related to interpersonal adjustment. From the standpoint of planning, it would seem significant when work is viewed as performing a role that conflict in role performance would produce conflict in the one's self-concept, indicating that individuals need to develop and choose roles that correctly fit their self-concepts.

Sex Differences

Although physical sex differences appear to be somewhat less important as factors in occupational choice than in the past, the psychological and social aspects of sex differences require special consideration. Sex differences in attitudes, interests, and intellectual patterning are of considerable importance to planning and placement. Psychological masculinity or femininity refers to whether the individual has interests, acts more like, and is more easily understood by men or women. Differences in relative masculinity or femininity are related in many ways to occupational interests and occupational choice.

The social aspects of sex differences tend to become as important as the physical aspects. Although a much larger percentage of women are working today than ever before, except during wartime, and the trend is steadily increasing, there is still resistance to the entrance of women into the labor force. Such resistance is expressed subtly but effectively by encouraging women to enter only certain occupational fields such as clerical work, stenography, teaching, etc., while discouraging them from entering occupations in which men traditionally dominate. Resistance is also expressed in wage and salary schedules in which women are paid less than men for the same or very similar work in the same occupation, although this form of discrimination now runs counter to existing federal legislation.

Certain fields have tended to develop as men's and women's fields. Perhaps in no case is one sex completely excluded, but in a few fields the ratio of males to females runs higher than ninety-nine to one. In contrast, many fields which have recently undergone rapid expansion tend to include a larger proportion of women. In general, the more recently a field has expanded as a source of employment for college graduates, the more likely it is to include a sizable number of women.

A study by Singer and Stefflre was addressed to the question of whether sex roles influence adolescent desires in the fields of occupational selection and adjustment. Singer and Stefflre compared the job values and desires of seventeen- and eighteen-year-old male and female high school seniors. The boys were found to desire a job offering power, profit, and independence more often than the girls, who were found to be more inclined to select or value jobs characterized by interesting experiences and social service.[25]

Environmental Influences

A child's particular socioeconomic inheritance may have a more direct and important effect on the occupations open or attractive to him than does his physical inheritance. The economic and occupational level of the home affects the vocational goals of youth by influencing a greater proportion of aspirations to the parental level than would be expected by chance and by discouraging aspirations to levels much above or below the parental occupational status.

The total cultural milieu may greatly limit the avenues of expression open to its members. This may be fairly direct, through failure to support entry into some occupation or at times even through the social ostracism of those who seek to enter the occupation. One of the most important general cultural factors influencing occupational choice is the degree of conformity required by the society, either in the degree of rigidity with which particular patterns of behavior must be adhered to, or in the number of different acceptable stereotypes.

Lyman presented a review of the findings of studies concerned with differences between socioeconomic groups with respect to the value attached to various aspects of work. She found a larger proportion of respondents in the higher income categories mentioned congeniality and a smaller proportion mentioned economic benefits when asked: "What do you think is the most important single thing to consider when one chooses his life work?"[26] In a nationwide study of job satisfaction, Centers found that a larger proportion of business, professional, and other white-collar respondents than manual workers mentioned a feature of the work itself as a reason for liking the job, and a smaller proportion mentioned economic rewards. The major finding of the latter study was that middle-class persons desired a job

[25] Stanley L. Singer and Buford Stefflre, "Sex Differences in Job Values and Desires," *Personnel and Guidance Journal* Vol. 32 (April 1954), pp. 483–484.

[26] Elizabeth L. Lyman, "Occupational Differences in the Value Attached to Work," *American Journal of Sociology* Vol. 61 (September 1955), pp. 138–144.

offering self-expression, and the working class preferred a job offering security.[27]

Although socioeconomic studies vary in the validity of their methodological approaches, they all agree that persons at the lower end of the socioeconomic scale are more likely to emphasize the economic aspects of work than are persons at the upper end of the scale, who tend more typically to stress the satisfaction intrinsic in the work itself. Lyman's study indicated that white-collar workers usually tend to emphasize the nature of the work and freedom; blue-collar workers emphasize the physical ease of the work, economic rewards, working conditions, and cleanliness. It is well for counselors to keep in mind that some individuals enter an occupation primarily because of intrinsic interest in the work, while others engage in work that has only minimal interest for them except for the fact that it provides money or other benefits which they are desirous of obtaining. It is assumed that semiskilled and unskilled occupations provide more extrinsic than intrinsic interest to workers.

Berdie studied a group of 136 male college students in an attempt to determine the factors that are associated with vocational interests. The study indicated the importance of factors in the individual's background and value factors, the latter of which will be reviewed here. The term "value factors" refers to situations, objects, and experiences that the individual uses as points of reference in answering questions. Berdie suggests the following value factors as possibly related to vocational interests: (1) The people who possess "value" for a student may be related to his vocational interests, and many occupational choices are influenced by hero worship; (2) interest in an occupation may be related to the financial rewards offered by the occupation; (3) family attitudes and influences are value factors in an individual's occupational choice; and (4) individuals who value intellectual pursuits may select an occupation which they feel will offer intellectual stimulation.[28]

Prestige is generally recognized as an important feature in occupational choice, and consequently, it has a decided effect on the occupational aspirations of youth. It is generally accepted that the vocational preferences of boys and girls are determined to a considerable degree by the social prestige attached to certain occupations.

The general appeal of an occupation may involve its remuneration in relation to other occupations, its social prestige, the regularity of employment, and its opportunities for advancement. Some students tend to choose an industry rather than an occupation, and some of the reasons for this appear to be that: (1) the industry has been surrounded with unusual glamour

[27] R. Centers, "Motivational Aspects of Occupational Stratification," *Journal of Social Psychology* Vol. 28 (November 1948), pp. 187–217.

[28] Ralph F. Berdie, "Factors Associated with Vocational Interests," *The Journal of Educational Psychology* Vol. 34 (May 1943), pp. 257–277.

and publicity; (2) a parent, relative, or friend has had a satisfactory working experience in the industry; (3) a labor market is dominated by a single industry; and (4) the individual is unable or unwilling to pursue lengthy training and wishes to enter the labor market as quickly as possible.

Ability to Acquire a College Education

The ability to acquire a college education or secure further training is an important factor in planning and placement. The "ability" required to attain a college education is multifaceted, involving such diverse elements as geographic location, finances, family background, social status, prejudicial discrimination, and personal talent. Though previous academic records and financial considerations are factors which strongly determine who goes to college, the student's desire to attend college is also very important. Studies show that parental attitudes are an extremely influential variable in a student's desire to attend college. Family background becomes one of the most effective factors in determining not only whether a person continues his schooling, but whether he has the desire to do so. There are at least two major ways in which family background can act as a barrier to further education. One is the family's inability to finance extensive schooling. The second is psychological rather than economic and rests on the valuing of schooling by families at different socioeconomic levels. Family traditions and neighborhood expectations are also powerful influences. The disadvantaging effect of family background appreciably influences school enrollment at about the ninth grade. From this point onward increasingly disproportionate percentages of the children from the lower economic groups are eliminated from school. The occupation of a high school student's father is a relatively good predictor of whether or not the student will enter college.

It is clear that a wide variety of factors interact to influence the career plans of students. A number of individuals have devoted considerable effort to bringing together many of these factors into unified theories of career development.

THE VALUE OF CAREER DEVELOPMENT THEORIES

Comments in previous chapters (e.g., see Chapter 8) have been directed to the value of theory for the counselor. It was pointed out that theory is a way of organizing and systematizing what is known about a phenomenon. In effect a theory serves as a model which is used to know what to look for, what to expect, and where to go. The model leads to a statement of the relationships believed to prevail in a comprehensive body of facts. Theory is more solidly supported by evidence than is hypothesis but less established than law.

Increasing speculation and research have been devoted to the factors that underlie choice and progress in an occupation. Psychologists, sociologists, psychiatrists, and economists have formulated approaches, if not theories, to vocational choice and development. Carkhuff and his associates present a schematic representation of the inductive and deductive functions of theory and then employ the schema to evaluate the works of Roe, Super, Holland, Tiedeman and O'Hara, and others. <u>These investigators concluded that, at present, no vocational choice approach merits the descriptive term, "theory."</u>[29] These approaches will be reviewed briefly in the next section of this chapter.

One theory may seemingly conflict with another. Stefflre has aptly commented on this conflict with these words:

> Conflicting theories also may be somewhat traumatizing to the student. Closer examination, however, may in some cases indicate that theories complement each other rather than contradict. . . . The use of more than one theory may point to the same facts and give clarity where previously we had confusion. The analogy might be made of the use of a variety of stage lights in a theatrical production. Sometimes the overhead light will give us the view we want; sometimes the red spotlight or blue will illuminate what we are looking for.[30]

Teachers and counselors need to seek constantly for insight into the reasons why students are motivated to make certain career choices. Only by doing so will they be able to understand and help them. Vocational-choice theory building is a continuous process, since new knowledge adds new clarity to an event, behavior, etc.

Hewer[31] has written of the meanings vocational-choice theories have for a practicing counselor. She believes that from sociologists she has learned that (1) attention should be paid to clients' social class since it may indicate the range of occupations they are willing to consider, and (2) counselors need to be sensitive to the effect that vertical mobility may have on client anxiety. From economists she has learned that labor market demands are such that individuals may not exercise the privilege of choosing a vocation because only certain ways of earning their livings may be available.

Hewer believes that trait-and-factor theorists have been helpful to her in the following ways:

1. They have developed good tools for the assessment of aptitudes and abilities.
2. They have given me good interest tests so that I can understand the goals and motivations of the individual.

---

[29] Robert R. Carkhuff, Mae Alexik, and Susan Anderson, "Do We Have a Theory of Vocational Choice?" *Personnel and Guidance Journal* Vol. 46 (December 1967), pp. 335–345.

[30] From *Theories of Counseling* by Buford Stefflre (ed.). Copyright 1965. McGraw-Hill Book Co. Used by permission. P. 11.

[31] Vivian H. Hewer, "What Do Theories of Vocational Choice Mean to a Counselor?" *Journal of Counseling Psychology* Vol. 10 (Summer 1963), pp. 118–125.

3. They have helped me understand jobs and their requirements in relation to the person.
4. They are increasingly helping me understand the impact of the style of the individual's interpersonal relations on his vocational choice.[32]

CHOICE AND CAREER DEVELOPMENT THEORIES

Today there is a growing realization that the planning, placement, and followup service is not solely an intellectual process. An increasing effort is being made to understand the dynamic rationale of career planning and development. The following section of this chapter will discuss some of the theories of choice-making, particularly those pertaining to career choice.

Ginzberg and Associates

Ginzberg and his associates[33] present a theory representing a basic disagreement with "accident" and "impulse" theories of occupational choice. The "accident" theory (accident of birth which establishes family, race, nationality, social class) of occupational choice holds that individuals make decisions about the future accidentally and that therefore it is not possible to evaluate the decisive factors in their choices. The "impulse" theory explains the individual's behavior and occupational choice in terms of unconscious forces. According to Ginzberg, the "accident" and "impulse" theories each tend to overstress a single factor or set of factors. Both theories assume the individual is largely passive and impotent with respect to the choice process.

Ginzberg and his associates were concerned with the developmental process of making a vocational choice. Their theory is based on the belief that each individual selects a particular occupation not through chance but through developing patterns of activities that are largely irreversible and take place throughout all the formative years of a child's life. They advocate a development approach to the question of occupational choice and see the process of occupational decision-making as being divided into three distinct phases: the period of fantasy choice; the period of tentative choice; and the period of realistic choice.

The first phase coincides with the latency period, between the ages of six and eleven; the second, with early and late adolescence; and the third, with early adulthood. The period of tentative choices is thought to progress through four stages: (1) the *interest stage,* in which the preadolescent makes choices primarily in relation to his interests; (2) the *capacity stage,* in which the individual becomes more aware of the necessity for introducing realistic elements into his considerations; (3) the *value stage,* characterized by the adolescent's attempts to find a place for himself in society; and (4)

---

[32] *Ibid.,* p. 124.

[33] Eli Ginzberg, S. W. Ginsburg, S. Axelrad, and J. L. Herman, *Occupational Choice: An Approach to a General Theory* (New York: Columbia University Press, 1951).

the *transition stage* in which the individual approaches the end of high school and must look forward either to work or additional education. The period of realistic choices can be divided into three distinct stages: (1) *exploration,* in which the individual tries to acquire the experience he needs to resolve his occupational choice; (2) *crystallization,* covering the time when the individual is able to assess the multitude of factors influencing the occupational choice he has had under consideration and is finally able to commit himself; and (3) *specification,* in which the alternatives are reviewed with respect to a field of specialization and to particular career objectives.

There are three fundamental considerations in this theory. First, occupational choice is a process which takes place over a minimum of six or seven years, and more typically, over ten years or more. Second, since each decision during adolescence is related to one's experience up to that point, and in turn has an influence on the future, the process of decision-making is basically irreversible. Finally, since occupational choice involves the balancing of a series of subjective elements with the opportunities and limitations of reality, the crystallization of occupational choice inevitably has the quality of a compromise.

In comparison to the theories which follow, little research evidence exists to document the major premises of Ginzberg's theory.

Hoppock

Hoppock's theory[34] includes ten basic propositions, four of which will be abstracted to provide a general indication of his rationale: (1) Occupations are chosen to meet emotional needs and particular values, which are often unconscious, such as a need to remain in a familiar environment or a need to play a dominant role (the self-concept, in Hoppock's theory, is considered essentially a constellation of needs); (2) the occupation the individual chooses is the one he feels will best meet his needs; (3) needs may be intellectually perceived, or they may be only vaguely felt as attractions which draw the individual in certain directions, but in either case influence his choice; and (4) occupational choice is always subject to change; choices may change as frequently as a person's awareness of his needs changes or as frequently as he discovers that another occupation might better meet his needs. This theory has basis in many psychological studies, all reflecting the following assertions by Hoppock:

> Most human action is caused by feelings, by our desire to be more comfortable or less uncomfortable, more satisfied or less frustrated; in short, by our desire to feel better than we do. Human action is affected by intellect only after feelings have indicated that some kind of action is desirable and only to the extent that our intellect can convince us that a particular course of

[34] Robert Hoppock, *Occupational Information,* Third Edition (New York: Harper & Row, Publishers, 1967), pp. 111–112.

action will improve or relieve our feeling tone. Intellect gives direction to our actions when factual information or logical reasoning indicates that one course of action is more likely than another to bring us the satisfactions that we seek.

It may appear that human action is sometimes caused, not by a desire to feel better than we do, but by a desire to maintain the comfortable state that we have already attained. Certainly the latter desire can provide motivation for action, but only when we feel some concern that our comfortable state may deteriorate if we do not act. We then act to relieve our concern. In relieving our concern, we feel better. Thus we act in order to feel better.

. . .

Psychological factors influence occupational choice by helping to determine the extent to which one perceives his own needs, accepts or suppresses them, faces the realities of employment opportunities and of his own abilities and limitations, and thinks rationally about all these facts.[35]

Roe

In her speculations concerning the determinants of vocational choice, Anne Roe[36] emphasizes the importance of early satisfactions in the development of interests and the primarily unconscious needs that determine the nature of these interests. She has presented a schema which includes the child's pattern of early experiences with parents, the relationship between parental attitudes and need satisfaction, and the style of parental handling of the child. This schema leads to the prediction of the broad and general vocational orientation that develops in the individual. Roe has also developed an occupational classification scheme based on groups and levels (see Table VII, p. 359).

As a working formula for needs, Roe employs Maslow's hierarchical or graduated classification of needs, stated as follows:

1. Physiological needs.
2. Safety needs.
3. Need for belongingness and love.
4. Need for importance, respect, self-esteem, independence.
5. Need for information.
6. Need for understanding.
7. Need for beauty.
8. Need for self-actualization.[37]

In connection with Maslow's needs, Roe has expressed seven basic hypotheses. The four most relevant are as follows:

[35] *Ibid.*, pp. 112–113. Reprinted by permission of Harper & Row, Publishers.

[36] Anne Roe, "Early Determinants of Vocational Choice," *Journal of Counseling Psychology* Vol. 4 (Fall 1957), pp. 212–217.

[37] A. H. Maslow, *Motivation and Personality* (New York: Harper & Brothers, 1954).

1. The intensity of these (primarily) unconscious needs, as well as their organization, is the major determinant of the degree of motivation as expressed in accomplishment.
2. Needs satisfied routinely as they appear do not develop into unconscious motivators.
3. Needs for which even minimum satisfaction is rarely achieved will, if higher order, become in effect expunged, or will, if lower order, prevent the appearance of higher order needs, and will become dominant and restricting motivators.
4. Needs, the satisfaction of which are delayed but eventually accomplished, will become unconscious motivators, depending largely upon the degree of satisfaction felt.[38]

It is well to remember here that Maslow's theory states that higher order needs cannot appear until lower order needs are at least relatively well satisfied. High-level needs show great variability. Lower order needs, on the other hand, are essential for the maintenance of life and permit much less variability in their strength.

Roe claims these needs develop to a great extent from the attitudes of the parents toward the child during the child's early formative experiences. Three basic divisions of attitudes are outlined as follows:

A. Emotional concentration on the child:
    1. Overprotecton.
    2. Overdemanding.
B. Avoidance of the child:
    1. Emotional rejection of the child.
    2. Neglect of the child.
C. Acceptance of the child:
    1. Casual acceptance of the child.
    2. Loving acceptance.

Before this outline can assume any significance, a relationship between the divisions and needs must be determined. Homes in which children are the center of attention provide satisfaction of physiological and safety needs, and attention to needs for love, but gratification is usually not routine. The overprotecting home places great emphasis upon gratification, which keeps lower level need satisfaction in the foreground. Love is conditional on dependency, and genuine self-actualization may be discouraged, although there is likely to be encouragement of special capacities.

In the case of overdemanding parents, satisfaction of needs for love and esteem is made conditional upon conformity and achievement, which is frequently oriented to status. Need gratification is extremely lacking in the next division (avoidance of child). Rejecting parents provide gratification of physiological and safety needs, but refrain from love and esteem grati-

<hr>

[38] Roe, "Early Determinants," pp. 212–214.

fication. Neglect of physiological and safety needs, but not beyond necessary minimal gratification, is much more tolerable than personal depreciation and deliberate withholding of love. Reasonable gratification of all needs is offered by accepting parents, the difference in the subgroups being the degree of deliberate encouragement and gratification.

Probable relationships between these orientations and parent-child interaction are shown graphically by Roe (see Figure 11), using a system of concentric circles. The next-to-the-outer segment of the circle indicates the probable orientation of the child in terms of persons or nonpersons. The division is suggested by jagged lines, since it is uncertain.

Later on in a child's life, this orientation unifies into patterns of special interests and abilities. The degree of social interests is clearly related, and it is likely that verbal abilities are associated with this, since personal interactions are largely mediated through words. Scientific and mechanical in-

FIGURE 11
Early Determinants of Vocational Choice

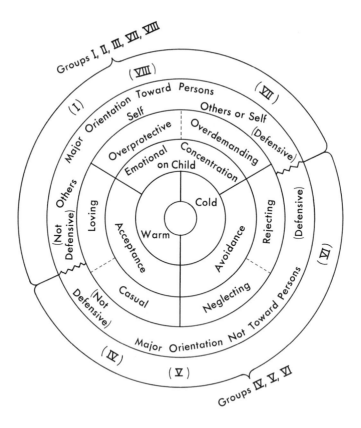

From Anne Roe and Marvin Siegelman, *The Origin of Interests* (Washington: American Personnel and Guidance Association, 1964), p. 6.

terests reach their fullest development in those who are concerned with nonpersons.

According to Roe,

> Depending upon which of the home situations is experienced, there will be developed basic attitudes, interests and capacities which will be given expression in the general pattern of the adult's life, in his personal relations, in his emotional reactions, in his activities, and in his vocational choice.[39]

Those from child-centered families who do not develop primary self-concentration will still be constantly aware of the opinions and attitudes of other persons toward themselves and of the need to maintain self-position in relation to others. Persons reared in rejecting homes may develop intense defensive awareness of others; if so, they will probably have aggressive tendencies which may find socially acceptable expression in occupational terms. Otherwise, they may strongly reject persons and turn defensively to nonperson-related pursuits. Persons from accepting homes may have primary interests in persons or in nonpersons, but they will not be defensive in either case.

TABLE VII
Categories in Roe's Classification of Occupations

GROUPS	LEVELS
I. Service	1. Professional and managerial
II. Business contact	2. Professional and managerial
III. Organizations	3. Semi-professional, small business
IV. Technology	4. Unskilled
V. Outdoor	5. Semi-skilled
VI. Science	6. Unskilled
VII. General cultural	
VIII. Arts and entertainment	

From Anne Roe, *The Psychology of Occupations* (New York: John Wiley & Sons, Inc., 1956), pp. 143–152.

Holland

John L. Holland[40] describes his theory as a heuristic theory of personality types and environmental data in that its pervasive character suggests ideas

[39] Roe, *The Psychology of Occupations,* p. 217.

[40] John L. Holland, "A Theory of Vocational Choice," *Journal of Counseling Psychology* Vol. 6 (Spring 1959), 35–44; "A Theory of Vocational Choice, Part I: Vocational Images and Choice," *Vocational Guidance Quarterly* Vol. 11 (Summer 1963), pp. 232–239; "A Theory of Vocational Choice, Part II: Self Descriptions and Vocational Preferences," *Vocational Guidance Journal* Vol. 12 (Autumn 1963), pp. 17–24; "A Theory of Vocational Choice, Part IV: Vocational Daydreams,"

for research. Six personality types were used: realistic, intellectual, social, conventional, enterprising, and artistic. Holland believes that individuals who are in the process of making a vocational choice "search" for situations which satisfy their "adjustive orientations." Stereotypes of occupations guide the individual's decisions. Vocational preferences are correlated with the individual's ways of coping with stress and frustration and his ways of utilizing outstanding abilities. Thus, preferences are associated with self-conceptions. Stability in vocational choice is greater when the individual's choice is appropriate to his sex role, that is, when the individual selects vocations in which he or she may engage in attractive roles and activities and avoid those viewed as distasteful.

Holland's theory has been researched more thoroughly than many other career-choice theories.

Super

Donald E. Super and his associates[41, 42, 43] have actively sought to develop and test a theory of vocational development. The key to understanding their formulations lies in the following statement:

> In expressing a vocational preference, a person puts into occupational terminology his idea of the kind of person he is; that in entering an occupation, he seeks to implement a concept of himself; that in getting established in an occupation he achieves self actualization. The occupation thus makes possible the playing of a role appropriate to the self concept.[44]

Super sees vocational development as a continuous process and views occupational choice as a synthesizing process: the synthesizing of an individual's personal needs and resources on one side and the economic and social demands of the culture on the other. This synthesizing process is a learning process, with learning taking place in role-playing and role-taking. What is learned is a function of the interests, values, attitudes, and behavior patterns that are valued and rewarded by the individual's peers and adult models. Super further contends that vocational development implies interaction which is both intra-individual, stimulated by environmental pro-

---

Vocational Guidance Quarterly Vol. 12 (Winter 1963–64), pp. 93–97; *The Psychology of Vocational Choice* (Waltham, Mass.: Blaisdell Publishing Company, 1966), 132 pp.

[41] Donald E. Super, "A Theory of Vocational Development," *American Psychologist* Vol. 8 (May 1953), pp. 185–190; "Career Patterns as a Basis for Vocational Counseling," *Journal of Counseling Psychology* Vol. 1 (Winter 1954), pp. 12–20; and *The Psychology of Careers* (New York: Harper & Brothers, 1957).

[42] Super and Overstreet, *Ninth-Grade Boys.*

[43] Donald E. Super, *et al., Career Development: Self-Concept Theory* (New York: College Entrance Examination Board, 1963).

[44] *Ibid.*, p. 22.

cesses, and individual-environmental, complicated by simultaneous interaction in the individual and in the environment. This interaction is not always at the level of consciousness, so lack of verbalization does not imply that it is not occurring. The individual's career pattern is determined by his parental socioeconomic level, mental ability, and personality characteristics, and by the opportunities to which he is exposed. Super's theory of vocational development takes the form of ten propositions which are summarized here:

1. People differ in abilities, interests, personalities.
2. Because of the above, they are qualified for many occupations.
3. Each occupation requires a characteristic pattern with tolerances wide enough to allow some variety of individuals in each occupation.
4. Vocational preferences change with time and experience, although self-concepts are generally fairly stable from late adolescence until late maturity.
5. The process may be summed up in a series of life stages characterized as those of growth, exploration, establishment, maintenance and decline, and these stages may in turn be subdivided into (a) fantasy, tentative and realistic phases of the exploratory stage, and (b) trial and stable phases of the establishment stages.
6. The nature of career pattern is determined by the individual's parental socioeconomic level, mental ability, personality and opportunities.
7. Development is guided by the maturation of ability, interest, reality testing and the self-concept.
8. The process of vocational development is essentially that of developing and implementing a self-concept: it is a compromise process in which the self-concept is a product of the interaction of inherited aptitudes, neural and endocrine make-up, opportunity to play various roles, and evaluations of the extent to which results of role playing meet with the approval of superiors and fellows.
9. The process of compromise between individual and social factors, between self-concept and reality, is one of role playing, whether the role is played in fantasy, in the counseling interview, or in real life activities.
10. Work satisfactions and life satisfactions depend upon the extent to which the individual finds adequate outlets for his abilities, interests, personality traits and values.[45]

During the period of the early development of the self-concept theory it appeared that only vocational guidance personnel and counseling psychologists were recognizing the relevance of self-development to vocational development. More recently both personality theorists and counselors have shown concern and interest in self theory—especially concerning occupational choice as a means of implementing the individual's self-concept. Yet some occupational choice and personality theorists have criticized Super's

[45] Donald E. Super, "A Theory of Vocational Development," *American Psychologist* Vol. 8 (May 1953), pp. 185–190.

propositions as being too general and vague to provide a sound basis for deriving testable hypotheses and to generate significant research effort. However, there have been empirical studies to show the relationships between the self-concept and criteria of vocational development, such as occupational preferences, success, satisfaction, level of occupational attainment, and stages of personality development. Such research has tended to indicate that the propositions do generate tenable hypotheses, which may be useful to counselors.

The basic elements in self-concept approaches to vocational development are self-concept formation, exploration, self-differentiation, identification, role-playing, reality testing, translation of self-concepts into occupational terms, and implementation of the self-concepts.

In order for a theory to provide a basis for sound research, its constructs must be defined operationally. For this reason, the terms and constructs of the self-concept theory have been defined, and possible means for formulating and testing related hypotheses presented. Self-concept is developed by observations and impressions of oneself, called "self-percepts," which are related, organized, and meaningfully interpreted. The "self-concept system" is defined as "the constellation, more or less well organized, of all the self-concepts," and when this constellation is considered in the occupational context or made relevant to occupational choice, it is referred to as the "vocational self-concept."[46] Since self-concept is defined as an object within the individual's awareness, its assessment is usually through self-report. Although such self-reports do not always appear to be consistent, they are still important and relevant to an understanding of how the individual perceives himself.

One aspect of vocational choice and development which has previously received little attention and effort from counselors and psychologists has been the nature and process of the individual's exploratory behavior. Preliminary investigations in this area have indicated that exploratory behavior can occur in any life stage, but most especially during periods of developmental change and periods of change of status, e.g., entry into high school, graduation from high school, etc. Uncertainty and perplexity, usually originated by ambiguity, lack of information, lack of understanding of role requirements, and biosocial changes, are important determinants of exploratory behavior.

Purposeful activity directed toward gaining information about oneself or one's environment to arrive at a decision is considered exploration. This activity is characterized by searching, experimenting, investigating, trying, and hypothesis-testing. Such activities have vocational relevance if the exploration aids in choice, preparation, entrance, adjustment, or progress in an occupation. The results of exploration will be an increased knowledge and understanding of self, environment, and the world of work. In brief, exploration provides a source of information for the formation and modi-

[46] Super, *et al., Career Development,* p. 19.

fication of self-concepts and occupational concepts. Super and his associates suggest that ". . . counselors can facilitate this type of exploration by helping the subject to formulate relevant hypotheses about himself and the world of work; to become aware of appropriate ways of testing these hypotheses both against past and new experiences; and to see the vocational relevance of what he already knows, or has been helped to discover, about himself and the world of work."[47]

The stages of adolescence and adulthood become of particular concern, since these are the primary exploration and establishment stages when the concept of development through life stages is applied to vocational development. The exploration stage is further subdivided into tentative, transition, and trial (little commitment) stages. The establishment stage is subdivided into trial (commitment) and stabilization, and advancement stages. The vocational tasks corresponding to these stages of development include crystallizing a vocational preference in the early middle-adolescent years (14 to 18), specification of a vocational preference in the middle- and late-adolescent years (18 to 21), implementation of a vocational preference in late adolescence and early adulthood (18 to 25), stabilization in a vocation in late adolescence and particularly in early adulthood (18 to 30 or beyond), and consolidating of status and advancement in a vocation in young adulthood (30 to the mid-40's). Attitudes and behaviors are associated with each of these vocational tasks. The life stages, vocational tasks, attitudes, and behavior provide a basis for assessing vocational maturity by comparison of one's vocational maturity to that of others in the same life stage or by longitudinally comparing one's vocational maturity to that of an earlier stage in one's own development.

Tiedeman and O'Hara

Tiedeman and O'Hara[48] view a career as affording an opportunity for the expression of hope and desire as well as limitation upon life. Their monograph explores the relationship of personality to career development. Believing that Super's career development propositions do not portray the relationship of personality and career as it is "forged within the process of choosing," Tiedeman and O'Hara deal with this dimension in terms of (1) purpose; (2) authority; (3) responsibility; and (4) acceptance of the position one has evolved in life.

They conceptualize career development ". . . as the process of fashioning a vocational identity through differentiation and integration of the personality as one confronts the problem of work in living."[49] Throughout, they stress the fact that it is the total personality that develops and later ac-

---

[47] *Ibid.,* p. 77.

[48] David V. Tiedeman and Robert P. O'Hara, *Career Development: Choice and Adjustment* (New York: College Entrance Examination Board, 1963), 108 pp.

[49] *Ibid.,* p. v.

commodates to the career. They consider a career as the "pursuit of intent at work." Careers are viewed as an advantage, an expectation of society, and a necessity of psychological freedom.

Tiedeman and O'Hara define career development as "those aspects of the continuous, unbroken flow of a person's experience that are of relevance to his fashioning of an identity 'at work.' "[50] These experiences are important only as they become a part of the individual's awareness. The same experience for two different individuals is perceived differently according to the unique personality and attitudes of each. The individual's thoughts and attitudes not only modify present experience but precondition future experience.

Making a living may require only that one satisfy his own desires and the desires of those he supports. A goal such as merely making a living, when pursued for an extended period, can cause the loss of perspective, balance, and growth in life. Therefore, making a living needs to become not a single pursuit but a part of a larger endeavor, that of "making a life."

Personality or ego-identity is the combination of meaning, values, and attitudes which the individual develops as he strives for identification with members of increasingly larger social collectivities. Ego-identity involves the person's biological constitution, psychological makeup, and society or subculture as it serves as a source of identification for the person. "A basic assumption is that, while differentiation and integration are proceeding in the realm that is specifically concerned with career choice, there is also a process of differentiation and integration in the realm of personality development that is related to career development."[51]

Differentiation and integration are the mechanisms of career development. Differentiation is the separation of an aspect from larger considerations (part from whole). It comes through (1) visual perceptions; (2) thoughts; (3) feelings; and (4) experiences. Stimulation for differentiation originates both internally (physiologically or psychologically) and externally. External stimulation for differentiation may be either haphazard or planned.

Integration is the combination of differentiated parts into an appropriate context. Integration is not achieved without prior differentiation. Failure to achieve integration occasions further differentiation. Differentiation and integration occur in rational solutions to the problem of the individual's vocational situation.

Tiedeman and O'Hara present a paradigm of the process of differentiation and integration.[52] This model graphically portrays how rational differentiation occurs when a problem is experienced and a decision must be made. The problem of deciding is divided into two aspects, which are summarized briefly here:

[50] *Ibid.,* p. 2.

[51] *Ibid.,* p. 5.

[52] *Ibid.,* p. 40.

I. *The Aspect of Anticipation or Preoccupation.* Preoccupation with a problem can be subdivided into four steps. Despite the fact that these steps may be relatively inseparable, they may be artificially separated and summarized here as follows:

Step I-A, Exploration, or the introduction of a previously absent distinction between two things. Different alternates or possible goals are considered. Goals are affected by the person's past experiences, the degree of investment in himself in modifying or continuing his present state, and the help he seeks or is given.

Step I-B, Crystallization, or the stabilization of thought. After considering the advantages, disadvantages, cost, and value of each alternative, crystallization emerges. Definiteness, clarity, and complexity develop and are advanced.

Step I-C, Choice, or decision, follows crystallization. A relevant goal orients the individual to his problem.

Step I-D, Clarification, or the elaboration and perfection of the image of the future ensues. The making of a decision readies a person for action.

II. *The Aspect of Implementation or Adjustment.* Interaction is a necessary part of implementing choice. An individual enters a social system, is accepted, begins to assert himself, and attain equilibrium. Three steps are involved in implementation:

Step II-A, Induction, or the initiation of experience. He gains acceptance of others in the field.

Step II-B, Reformation, or the acknowledgment that the person is accepted and successful, leads to immersion in the field. He asserts his convictions of his role on society.

Step II-C, Integration, or the synthesis of the older group members' convictions and the individual's convictions into a compromise.

It should be noted that during each step the individual may return to a previous step or take additional steps to alter any prior decision. "Because rational decisions can bear upon one another," say Tiedeman and O'Hara, "we must recognize that higher order oganizations of attitude toward self-in-situation can arise during the process of sequential choosing."[53]

Tiedeman and O'Hara point out that differentiation and integration are repeated many times in the course of life. Career development is self-development related to choice, entry, and progress in educational and vocational pursuits. Further, they see career development as an evolving conception of self-in-situation which occurs over *time.* It occurs not in just one decision but within the context of several decisions.

Tiedeman and O'Hara relate the personality dimensions set forth by Erikson[54] to career development through the "crises" experienced by the

[53] *Ibid.,* p. 45.

[54] Erik H. Erikson, *Childhood and Society* (New York: W. W. Norton, Inc., 1950).

psychologically healthy person. One such crisis is that of *trust versus mistrust.* They develop the hypothesis that "those people for whom the world of work has the greatest meaning consonant with their own previously developed meaning system will find the greatest satisfaction and success in their work."[55] Vocational guidance, they say, is the catalytic agent for the fusion of the unique world of the individual and the unique world of work.

The individual's sense of *autonomy* (self-direction) prevents premature effort and creates opportunity for choice. The degree of autonomy granted in career development varies along a continuum from letting the individual fend for himself to dependence upon others as well as environmental restrictions. Autonomous effort on the part of the individual may be encouraged by environmental support.

The sense of *initiative* indicates that after an individual discovers that he *is* a person, he will strive to find out *what kind* of person he is. Finding out continues throughout life. They believe that "for the average boy or girl to achieve a sense of unbroken initiative as a basis for a high and yet realistic sense of ambition and independence, a program of extracurricular activities would be required."[56]

In career development, the locus of the crisis, *industry versus inferiority,* is the school. In this stage of personality development which highlights the fact that "I am what I learn," a single mode of activity should not be fostered. Rather, several types of programs should be available, else a sense of inferiority may result.

One's *identity* is attained in a career. Successful adjustment to the job necessitates the preliminary formation of an ego-identity. In career development the sense of *intimacy* and *distantiation* (readiness to repudiate, to isolate or to destroy forces or people whose essence are dangerous to one's own) is evidenced in the horizontal mobility involving several job changes. *Generativity versus stagnation* (establishing and guiding the next generation) in a career is evident when work takes on more meaning than money and status. Creativity and productivity come from generativity. *Integrity versus despair* in a career may be seen in the individual's total life style.

Tiedeman and O'Hara give attention to *time* and *occupation.* People are prone to speak of work as if time were boundless. Biological and sociocultural requirements both demand time. They discuss the "work history" of man and methods for assessing career development. Man is not required to stick to one occupation throughout his life. Many things can occur; new goals can be decided upon, new occupations may arise, jobs may be abolished, and time may permit the holding of more than one position at a time.

[55] Tiedeman and O'Hara, *Career Development,* p. 51.
[56] *Ibid.,* p. 53.

Bordin and His Associates

Bordin, Nachmann, and Segal[57] present an analytical scheme of vocational choice based upon identifying the gratifications that varieties of work offer individuals. They emphasize the importance of early experiences to occupational pursuits. Their theory is designed to cover the life span of an individual but excludes individuals whose occupational motivation is constrained by external economic, cultural, and geographic forces. Bordin, Nachmann, and Segal make the following assumptions:

1. A continuity in development [exists] which links the earliest work of the organism in food-getting and mastery of the body and coping with the stimulations of the environment, to the most highly abstract and complex of intellectual and physical activities.
2. The complex adult activities retain the same instinctual sources of gratification as the simple infantile ones.
3. Although the relative strengths and configurations of needs are subject to continual modification throughout the life span, their essential pattern is determined in the first six years of life. The seeking out of occupational outlets of increasingly precise appropriateness is the work of the school years, but the needs which will be the driving forces are largely set before that time.[58]

These authors establish a series of dimensions (needs, motivations, impulses, and activities) that account for the major gratifications which work offers. Occupations are then described in terms of the relative strengths and modifications of the component dimensions. Achievement of these dimensions comes through ". . . repeated weaving back and forth between job analysis, personality traits and assumptions regarding childhood experiences which generate . . . traits."[59]

These authors present the basic need-gratifying activities of the accounting, social work, and plumbing occupations in tabular form. These have been mapped into the ten major dimensions for illustrative purposes. The ten major dimensions include nurturant, oral, manipulative, sensual, anal, genital, exploratory, flowing-quenching, exhibiting, and rhythmic. Space does not permit an explanation of each dimension, but perhaps the authors' comments upon one will be helpful:

. . . By the first pair of dimensions, the nurturant ones, we mean those activities that involve the care of living things—feeding, protecting and promoting the growth of people, animals, plants, both literally with food and

[57] Edward S. Bordin, Barbara Nachmann, and Stanley J. Segal, "An Articulated Framework for Vocational Development," *Journal of Counseling Psychology* Vol. 10 (Summer 1963), pp. 107–117.

[58] *Ibid.,* p. 110.

[59] *Ibid.,* p. 112.

shelter and symbolically with words. We would see the interest in feeding activities as stemming from the infantile experiences of being fed. Special delight, pain or anxiety about the taking in of nourishment develop into concerns that food be plentiful, that others not want and, more remotely, to interest in words. By fostering we mean those activities that involve either literally or figuratively shielding, comforting, protecting the young or the helpless—giving warmth and shelter as first one was warmed and sheltered. Their physical prototype is seen in the need to burrow into the warmth of mother, bed, home, and in the tactile and temperature sensitivity of the skin.[60]

The authors emphasize that confirmation of their scheme is dependent upon the development of measures for the dimensions in terms of personality organization and job analysis which identifies the workers' modes of expressing and controlling impulses.

Stefflre

Stefflre[61] has set forth ten propositions that explore various psychological factors capable of influencing vocational development. These propositions are considered by many to be especially helpful in summarizing the present state of vocational development theory building. The ten propositions are given below in Stefflre's words:

1. An occupation permits an expression of the individual's public personality which is a special instance of differentiation of function.
2. The occupational persona [work role] represents the individual's choice among those masks he would like to wear and those that society will permit him to wear.
3. An occupational role may represent avoidance reaction as well as, or instead of, approach reaction.
4. The importance of the work aspect of the public personality—the occupational persona—varies from being psychologically peripheral to being central.
5. The societally limiting forces that determine the occupational persona of any individual vary from the accidental to the essential.
6. The expression of the public personality through an occupation—the selection of an occupation—must be made on incomplete information.
7. The stability of the choice of an occupation after additional information about the work role becomes available varies directly with the psychological commitment to the occupation on the part of the chooser.
8. As further information about the self comes to light, it is more apt to lead to change within the occupation for those who are psychologically

---

[60] *Ibid.,* p. 113.

[61] Buford Stefflre, "Vocational Development: Ten Propositions in Search of a Theory," *Personnel and Guidance Journal* Vol. 46 (February 1966), pp. 611–616.

committed to the occupation as opposed to change to a different occupation for others.

9. The occupational persona and the self concept have a symbiotic relationship that moves toward congruence.
10. The selection of an occupational persona may express any of four relationships between the self and society. [The four relationships are "fitting," "permitting," "transforming," and "binding."]

According to Stefflre, the implications of these propositions include (1) that the choices moving the individual toward an occupation are of variable importance depending upon his age, sex, social class, nationality and other conditions; (2) that for some, occupational choice may be very central and ego-involving while for others it may be very peripheral to their personal identity; (3) that the counselor should search for the hidden meaning that lies behind choice; and (4) that counselors should aim at helping students to understand themselves rather than being concerned with making wise choices.

All of these theories are complex statements that attempt to make sense of complex processes. As in any theory, their value lies in the degree to which practitioners can utilize them in understanding the complexity of the career development process. They have the additional value of providing bases for generative research hypotheses in the area of the dynamics of career choice.

No one doubts that much remains to be done in career development theory building. Super has identified four areas that he believes warrant extended study and research. His descriptions are summarized as follows:

1. To formulate a career model with appropriate methods and data.
2. To attain greater understanding of exploratory behavior and its relevance to vocational development.
3. To construct practical measures of vocational maturity.
4. To refine self-concept theory, including methods of assessing self-concept.[62]

ANNOTATED BIBLIOGRAPHY

HOLLAND, JOHN L. *The Psychology of Vocational Choice.* Waltham, Mass.: Blaisdell Publishing Company, 1966, 132 pp.
    The author presents his theory of vocational choice and behavior. The last chapter summarizes the research and practical applications that are needed.

KATZ, MARTIN. *Decisions and Values.* New York: College Entrance Examination Board, 1963. 67 pp.

[62] Donald E. Super, "Vocational Development Theory in 1988: How Will It Come About?" *Counseling Psychologist* Vol. 1 (1969), pp. 9–10.

Katz defines guidance as assistance in career decision-making. He presents a theory of occupational choice and provides a rationale for the nature of guidance intervention at certain choice-points.

OSIPOW, SAMUEL H. *Theories of Career Development.* New York: Appleton-Century-Crofts, 1968, 259 pp.

The author examines and evaluates the major theories of vocational choice. The similarities and differences among theories are presented. Chapter 9 (pp. 234–249) is devoted to synthesizing theory and projecting future trends in vocational development.

SELECTED REFERENCES

BAILEY, JOHN A. "Career Development Concepts: Signficance and Utility," *Personnel and Guidance Journal* Vol. 47 (September 1968), pp. 24–28.

BELL, ALAN P. "Role Models in Young Adulthood: Their Relationship to Occupational Behaviors," *Vocational Guidance Quarterly* Vol. 18 (June 1970), pp. 280–285.

BORDIN, EDWARD S., NACHMANN, BARBARA, AND SEGAL, STANLEY J. "An Articulated Framework for Vocational Development," *Journal of Counseling Psychology* Vol. 10 (Summer 1963), pp. 107–117.

BYERS, ALVAH P., FORREST, GARY G., AND ZACCARIA, JOSEPH S. "Recalled Early Parent-Child Relations, Adult Needs and Occupational Choice: A Test of Roe's Theory," *Journal of Counseling Psychology* Vol. 15 (July 1968), pp. 324–328.

CLACK, RONALD J. "Occupational Prestige and Vocational Choice," *Vocational Guidance Quarterly* Vol. 16 (June 1968), pp. 282–286.

FLORES, THOMAS R., AND OLSEN, LEROY C. "Stability and Realism of Occupational Aspiration in Eighth and Twelfth Grade Males," *Vocational Guidance Quarterly* Vol. 16 (December 1967), pp. 104–112.

FOLSOM, CLYDE H., JR. "An Investigation of Holland's Theory of Vocational Choice," *Journal of Counseling Psychology* Vol. 16 (May 1969), pp. 260–266.

HOLLAND, JOHN, AND LUTZ, DAVID P. "The Predictive Value of a Student's Choice of Vocation," *Personnel and Guidance Journal* Vol. 46 (January 1968), pp. 428–433.

HOLLANDER, MELVYN A., AND PARKER, HARRY J. "Occupational Stereotypes and Needs: Their Relationship to Vocational Choice," *Vocational Guidance Quarterly* Vol. 18 (December 1969), pp. 91–98.

LEWIS, CHARLES A., BRADLEY, RICHARD L., AND ROTHNEY, JOHN W. M. "Assessment of Accomplishments of College Students Four Years After High School Graduation," *Personnel and Guidance Journal* Vol. 47 (April 1969), pp. 745–752.

LOCASCIO, RALPH. "Delayed and Impaired Vocational Development: A Neglected Aspect of Vocational Development Theory," *Personnel and Guidance Journal* Vol. 42 (May 1964), pp. 885–887.

LUNNEBORG, PATRICIA W., AND LUNNEBORG, CLIFFORD E. "Roe's Classification of Occupations in Predicting Academic Achievement," *Journal of Counseling Psychology* Vol. 15 (January 1968), pp. 8–16.

MALNIG, LAWRENCE R. "Fear of Paternal Competition: A Factor in Vocational Choice," *Personnel and Guidance Journal* Vol. 46 (November 1967), pp. 235–239.

MARR, EVELYN, "Vocational Maturity and Specification of a Preference," *Vocational Guidance Quarterly* Vol. 18 (September 1969), pp. 45–48.

MASIH, LALIT. "Career Saliency for Teachers and Other Occupational Groups." *Personnel and Guidance Journal* Vol. 47 (April 1969), pp. 773–775.

MILLER, ADAM W., JR. "Learning Theory and Vocational Decisions," *Personnel and Guidance Journal* Vol. 47 (September 1968), pp. 18–23.

MINTZ, RITA S., AND PATTERSON, C. H. "Marriage and Career Attitudes of Women in Selected College Curricula," *Vocational Guidance Quarterly* Vol. 17 (March 1969), pp. 213–217.

MUNDAY, LEO A., BRASKAMP, LARRY A., AND BRANDT, JAMES E. "The Meaning of Unpatterned Vocational Interests," *Personnel and Guidance Journal* Vol. 47 (November 1968), pp. 249–256.

OSIPOW, SAMUEL H., AND GOLD, JAMES A. "Personal Adjustment and Career Development," *Journal of Counseling Psychology* Vol. 15 (September 1968), pp. 439–443.

SLOCUM, WALTER L., AND BOWLES, ROY T. "Attractiveness of Occupations to High School Students," *Personnel and Guidance Journal* Vol. 46 (April 1968), pp. 754–761.

STEFFLRE, BUFORD. "Vocational Development: Ten Propositions In Search of a Theory," *Personnel and Guidance Journal* Vol. 44 (February 1966), pp. 611–616.

STEFFLRE, BUFORD, RESNIKOFF, ARTHUR, AND LEZOTTE, LAWRENCE. "The Relationship of Sex to Occupational Prestige," *Personnel and Guidance Journal* Vol. 46 (April 1968), pp. 765–772.

STEWART, JAMES A. "Vocational Choice Theories—Helps and Hazards for Practitioners," *The School Counselor* Vol. 16 (November 1968), pp. 103–107.

SUPER, DONALD E. "Vocational Development: The Process of Compromise or Synthesis," *Journal of Counseling Psychology* Vol. 3 (Winter 1956), pp. 249–253.

———. "A Developmental Approach to Vocational Guidance: Recent Theory and Results," *Vocational Guidance Quarterly* Vol. 13 (Autumn 1964), pp. 1–10.

———. "Vocational Development Theory in 1988: How Will it Come About?" *Counseling Psychologist* Vol. 1 (Spring 1969), pp. 9–14.

———. "Vocational Development Theory: Persons, Positions, and Processes," *Counseling Psychologist* Vol. 1 (Spring 1969), pp. 2–9.

"A Symposium on Clinical Appraisal in Vocational Counseling," *Personnel and Guidance Journal* Vol. 43 (May 1965), pp. 867–885.

WAGMAN, MORTON. "Perceived Similarities in Occupational Value Structure," *Vocational Guidance Quarterly* Vol. 16 (June 1968), pp. 275–281.

WALSH, W. BRUCE, AND LACEY, DAVID W. "Perceived Change and Holland's Theory," *Journal of Counseling Psychology* Vol. 16 (July 1969), pp. 348–352.

WHITNEY, DOUGLAS R. "Predicting from Expressed Vocational Choice: A Review," *Personnel and Guidance Journal* Vol. 48 (December 1969), pp. 279–286.

ZYTOWSKI, DONALD G. "Toward a Theory of Career Development for Women," *Personnel and Guidance Journal* Vol. 47 (March 1969), pp. 660–664.

13

CAREER PLANNING AND PLACEMENT SERVICE

Why are planning and placement so critically needed?
Through what activities are planning and placement conducted?
What characteristics distinguish an effective planning and placement service?

Chapter 12 focused on the dynamic factors and theories of career development, while this Chapter concentrates on the career planning, placement, and followup service, with emphasis on the need, activities, and characteristics of this guidance function.

THE NECESSITY FOR PLANNING AND PLACEMENT

In a broad sense, the function of the school is to provide ways for students to learn. More specifically, the purpose of the school is to provide selected learning experiences which enable students to attain educational objectives that facilitate their development as individuals. It has frequently been pointed out by educational psychologists that the learning process is a goal-seeking process. This means that a student learns more readily if he is directing his efforts toward attaining objectives which he is cognizant of and has helped select. Learning is also selective in that individuals, faced with the desire to satisfy more than one need simultaneously, choose the needs to be acted upon most immediately from among the other needs they have. There is little disagreement that learning processes are enhanced through thoughtful planning by students.

Planning, Placement, and Followup

The planning, placement and followup service is the systematic assistance given pupils in developing goals and choices related to their educational and vocational futures. This service is concerned with obtaining information about opportunities, helping students determine if the opportunities fit them, and helping them take suitable steps to achieve goals. The primary emphasis of the service is upon (1) creating understanding of the many problems that confront students in their immediate and long-range planning and (2) determining how to do something about them.

For the student, career planning consists of thinking through short-range as well as long-range goals. The attainment of short-range goals often, but not always, contributes to the achievement of long-range goals. Many individuals give little thought to long-range goals, but are preoccupied with day-to-day or short-range objectives.

Planning is predicated on the premise that all individuals, at some time or other, need help in clarifying and discussing long-range goals and in deciding which of their short-range goals will best serve their long-range objectives. The purpose of planning is to minimize the possibility of error in choosing among the multitude of career paths and alternatives. In clarifying objectives, a student must take stock of his abilities, resources, and motivations. Goals established through planning will probably be unrealistic if they are not in harmony with the factors that determine whether or not the student can be successful in the pursuit of his goals.

Planning will be unsuccessful if it is something done *for* a student. The focus of planning is the student: *his* career, *his* goals, *his* abilities, *his* interests. For each student it is a process of self-examination in an attempt to determine: What is there to be done? What do I want to do? What can I do?

The end product of planning is choice or decision, which, in turn, determines placement. Choices that need to be planned in the junior and senior high school years include (1) part-time employment; (2) subjects in junior high school; (3) curriculum or program of study in high school; (4) extracurricular activities; (5) subjects within a curriculum; (6) military service; (7) specialty in military service; (8) job; (9) college selection; (10) program of study in college; (11) graduate school; and (12) program of study in graduate school. Although some of these choices appear to be far advanced in a student's future, inappropriate early plans can make the attainment of later goals difficult, if not impossible.

Placement must be student oriented, or conducted in the interest of the individual, rather than institution oriented. It involves both in-school (curriculum, subjects, school activities) and out-of-school (part-time and full-time work) activities. Good placement results in opportunities for the individual to develop and achieve consonant with his objectives.

Followup is the procedure conducted to determine whether the individual is developing in his placement. It is in reality an integral part of placement, since it is a natural outgrowth of the planning and placement processes. The student is helped both to understand what is required in the situation and to evaluate his personal development within the situation with regard to his short- and long-range objectives.

Time studies of school counselor activities show that a substantial portion of time and energy is devoted to pupil planning and placement and followup. Admittedly, the first two frequently overshadow followup activities. It is also true that the planning, placement, and followup service often falls short of its mark by failing to base its activities upon study of the individual student: his physical condition, his capacity for learning, his school record, his social adjustment, his aptitudes and interests.

Complexity of Career Planning and Placement

First and foremost, the complexity of planning and placement needs to be recognized. Planning behavior, like behavior in any situation, is a function of the transactional relationships between the individual pupil and his environment. For purposes of discussion, a student may be described as composed of three major systems—a system of drives, an internalized system of rewards and punishments, and a system of adaptive mechanisms. Each student has his own unique constellation of these three systems. As counselors work with individuals in planning and placement, they must take into account differences in individuals and in situations. The foundation for planning and placement lies in the individual's values and goals, which enable him to order his current undertakings with reference to his future. Although it is recognized that the future can never be predicted with a great degree of accuracy, it is equally true that it cannot be ignored. Many critical problems confound such planning, and simple, sovereign solutions are not readily available.

The Necessity for Career Planning and Placement

A variety of social, economic, educational, and vocational factors underscore the critical need for pupil planning, placement, and followup. An increasingly complex society demands of the individual a continuous process of lifelong learning, planning, and assessment. Automation, space developments, and advances in science and technology require that individuals be better educated and more highly skilled than ever before. It is through careful planning that reconciliation of individual needs and society's needs can be examined and dealt with. Following is a brief summary of some of the factors that place in bold relief the necessity for a carefully operated program of planning, placement, and followup.

1. *Accelerated Increase in Knowledge.* Although no factual source is available, the dramatic statement that man's knowledge has accelerated at an ever-increasing rate is often heard. One such estimate is that man's

knowledge doubled from A.D. 1 to 1750, doubled again by 1900, again by 1950, and still again by 1960. Areas of human knowledge expand latitudinally, longitudinally, and unequally. The acceleration of knowledge requires lifelong attention. Of particular significance to guidance is the development of newer fields of specialization. If the goal of education is not simply to impart information but to stimulate critical appraisal of ideas and develop original thoughts and ways of behaving, and if each individual is to leave the educational system prepared to use his learning potential, planning is essential.

2. *Lack of Educational Opportunity.* The significance of planning and placement is apparent in the fact that lack of adequate education and lack of opportunity for education are major contributing factors to America's present high rate of unemployment, poverty, delinquency, and crime. In science and medicine, engineering and agriculture, in education itself, and in a host of other occupations that require special or advanced training, manpower shortages are major barriers to social and economic progress. American educators are confronted with the possibility that educational opportunity may be denied many young men and women because the supply of college teachers, classrooms, and facilities has failed to keep pace with the demand. From predictions based on previous trends, it is estimated that of every 10 youngsters now in grade schools, 3 will not finish high school; that of the 7 who earn a diploma, 3 will go to work and 4 will continue their education; and that even though college enrollments doubled during the 1960's, 6 out of 10 college-bound youths did not complete college. To this may be added the sad fact that lack of schooling is clearly associated with lower earning capacity, higher rates of unemployment, and more dependence on public aid.

3. *Culturally Disadvantaged Youth.* Planning and placement are needed to aid the culturally disadvantaged youth in order to remove some of the obstacles to their economic and social betterment. Poverty imposes handicaps upon the achievement potential of young people as do discriminatory barriers. Merely opening educational doors to the culturally deprived and those discriminated against will not be enough. Education will have to be made meaningful for them in new and more effective ways. Unless such youth are helped by planning and placement, many will continue to remain alienated from education and society. By engaging in planning, such youth learn to manage their problems, mobilize their resources, and gain the capacity to continue on their own. Because of motivational factors related to previous generations who lacked opportunity, such youth need to be involved early in career planning. Early planning can be preventive if it is designed to identify and help such young people *before* they are lost to a life of aimlessness. Planning is needed that emphasizes a basic, meaningful commitment in order to develop to the fullest possible extent the potentialities each person possesses.

4. *Changing Role of Women.* A careful planning, placement, and followup service is needed if the educational and vocational needs of women are to be met. Eight of ten American women will be working for pay outside the home at sometime during their lives. Special attention must be given to their planning, especially to the discontinuous sequential pattern of employment, marriage, child rearing, and re-employment. From infancy, socially approved roles for girls often deflect talents into relatively narrow channels. Through planning, however, girls can be encouraged to develop broader ranges of skills and to raise their aspirations beyond those influenced by the stubbornly persistent assumptions regarding "women's roles" and "women's interests." The capacities of many women are not being developed to their full potential. Many able girls who graduate from high school do not attend college. Currently one worker in three is a woman, and women will make up 36 percent of the 92 million persons in the labor force forecast for 1975. Approximately three of five women workers are married. One-third of the women in the current work force are employed part time. Often those who go on to college specialize within a relatively restricted range of occupational fields: education, the social sciences, and journalism. The President's Commission on the Status of Women urged that "Individuals should be helped to find out what alternatives exist, aided to reach judgments about them, and encouraged to make plans and take appropriate action."[1]

Should counseling for girls be different from that for boys? Havighurst[2] finds the answer in the affirmative for two reasons: "The pathways to adulthood for girls are different from those for boys," and "The problem of identity achievement for girls is different from that of boys." He believes that during the age period from fifteen to twenty most girls take the steps and make the decisions that determine their career patterns. Four basic patterns were identified: (1) Pattern A leads from school or college directly into marriage (about 46 percent of all girls); (2) Pattern B leads from school or college into employment and then into marriage (about 31 percent fit this pattern); (3) Pattern C leads from school or college into employment and stays there (some 7 percent follow this pattern); and (4) Pattern D leads from school into a "waiting" period of several months or even years (such girls, while waiting for marriage, may turn to employment).

5. *Manpower Changes.* How well human skills are developed and employed is a fundamental factor influencing the eventual attainments of the nation. The change in population between 1960 and 1970 is reflected in

[1] The President's Commission on the Status of Women, *American Women* (Washington: Government Printing Office, 1963), pp. 13–14.

[2] Robert J. Havighurst, "Counseling Adolescent Girls in the 1960's," *Vocational Guidance Quarterly* Vol. 13 (Spring 1965), pp. 153–160.

demands made upon the labor force. Consequently, major shifts in the occupational and industrial structure have important implications for guidance planning and placement. Such changes include (1) the diminishing need for unskilled labor; (2) geographic shifts of industries; (3) job insecurities due to accelerated technology; (4) the decline in goods-producing industries; (5) the decline in agricultural occupations; (6) the increase in service occupations; (7) increasing jobs which demand more education and/or training (see Table VIII), (8) the continued rise of youth unemployment; and (9) more youth entering the labor force (see Figure 12).

TABLE VIII
Median Years of Schooling for Various Occupational Fields

OCCUPATIONAL GROUP	MEDIAN YEARS OF SCHOOLING
Professional, Technical, and Kindred Workers	16.2
Managers, Officials, and Proprietors, Except Farm	12.5
Clerical and Kindred Workers	12.5
Salesworkers	12.5
Craftsmen, Foremen, and Kindred Workers	11.2
Operatives and Kindred Workers	10.1
Private Household Workers	8.7
Other Service Workers	10.8
Laborers, Except Farm and Mine	8.9
Farmers and Farm Managers	8.8
Farm Laborers and Foremen	8.5

Sources: From U.S. Department of Labor, *Manpower Report of the President* (Washington: Government Printing Office, 1963), p. 13 and *Occupational Outlook Handbook* (Washington: U.S. Government Printing Office, 1968–1969), p. 26.

Pupils in school now must plan for a work world that calls for more education and training. More and more employers will require high school diplomas for increasingly complex jobs, and planning will be needed to keep abreast of the rapidly changing occupations and industries (see Figure 13). The over-riding need of young people is to learn to cope with change.

6. *Automation.* Automation, the revolutionary techniques for mechanizing industrial processes of many kinds, has tremendous implications for youth planning. In broad terms, automation will result in (1) the requirement of less human effort for monotonous work, (2) fewer and fewer unskilled and semiskilled factory workers, and (3) shorter work weeks with longer periods of leisure. Citing numerous data to show the increase in automation that is taking place in government alone, Donovan points up the fact that machines are drastically changing society:

FIGURE 12
Major Changes in the Labor Force

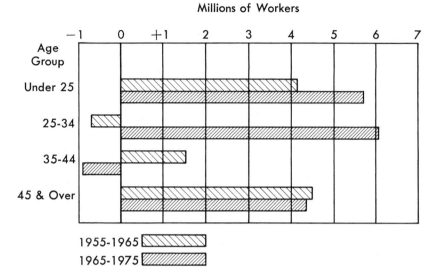

Source: *Occupational Outlook Handbook* (Washington: U.S. Government Printing Office, 1967–1968), p. 26.

FIGURE 13
Percent Changes in Employment, 1960–1970

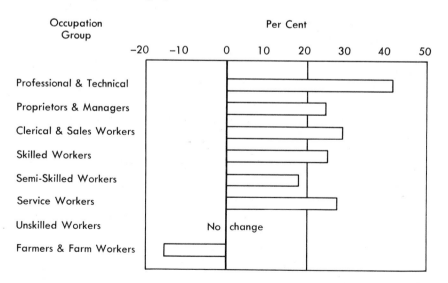

Source: U.S. Department of Labor, *Manpower: Challenge of the 1960's* (Washington: U.S. Government Printing Office, 1961), p. 13.

One last figure giving some notion of the fantastic increase in the use of computers is to be found in a recent statement of a Senate Government Operations Committee. This says that in 1959 some $251 million was spent in annual operating costs for automatic data processing equipment. The current budget for fiscal 1965 provides over $1 billion for the care and feeding of these machines, their appetites being utterly voracious.[3]

Many persons have been displaced or have had to be retrained for other jobs because of automation. On the other hand, large numbers of new jobs have been created by automation. Youth in their planning can no longer rely on the certainty that the choice of one career will be a lifetime pursuit. Basic capabilities will need to be developed for acquiring new skills as old ones become obsolete. Automation creates a dual problem: there are too few highly educated and skilled personnel and a surplus of individuals lacking specialized skills and education. Planning in an age of automation must take into account the interpretation of today's developments as well as attempt to forecast the trend of future developments.

7. *Military Obligations.* The facts of military service point up the necessity of intelligent planning and placement. The various military options must be taken into account as high school students, particularly boys, plan their future. While it is anticipated that the 1970 Executive decree in respect to military conscription will eliminate some of the uncertainty about an individual's military obligation, many male 18-year-olds are confused and uncertain as they plan, knowing that unless the international situation undergoes a marked change for the better, some will be called upon to serve a period of active duty in the armed forces. Planning must take into account the reality of this responsibility. The long-range personal, educational, and vocational implications of military service must be incorporated into personal planning.

8. *Society Under Threat.* Recent generations of Americans have been labeled "lost," "beat," "twisted," and the times have been called "The Age of Turmoil," "The Age of Anxiety," and the like. In 1964, President Johnson sought to create "The Great Society," in which productivity, happiness, security, and a better existence could be attained by all. Although actual widespread famine has disappeared from "The Great Society," there remains the constant possibility of uncontrollable depressions, hunger, and the fear of war. These impending crises generate a deep anxiety over whether each of us individually, as well as society collectively, is proceeding in the right direction. Though it is clear that positive successes have been achieved in many areas of human endeavor, certain basic causes of unhappiness obviously remain.

The threat of an uncertain future dramatically underscores the necessity for planning and placement. Planning that focuses on individual

[3] James A. Donovan, "The Automation of Government," *Saturday Review* (December 12, 1964), p. 23.

initiative and responsibility to self and society, and work that brings enthusiasm and extends the individual, will help alleviate feelings of indifference, pessimism, and aimlessness.

9. *The Quest for Excellence.* Excellence has become a goal, a rebuke, a challenge and a watchword for Americans today. John W. Gardner, former Secretary of Health, Education and Welfare, wrote a book which he titled simply, *Excellence.* It was about what Gardner refers to as "toning up a whole society, bringing a whole people to that fine edge of morale and conviction that makes for greatness."[4] Gardner's thesis is that the search for excellence takes place at all levels of life. It is a quality that exists and should be encouraged. The cultivation of excellence remains the task of all. Planning can bring about understanding of the need for originality, experimentation, initiative, and openness to experience.

Most of the nine forces cited above which point up the necessity for planning have been with us for some time. As is true of other forces and problems, they confound the process of planning. They will not be removed by Congress or by governmental directives. They must be taken into account by counselors and students who think about them, discuss them, and gradually incorporate their personal impact into their intellects, their imaginations, and their aspirations.

PLANNING, PLACEMENT, AND FOLLOWUP ACTIVITIES

Career planning is not solely an intellectual process. Equally important are the many motivational influences that have bearing on the direction taken. Career development is a process, not an event—a process that unfolds at varying rates and different times for different people. The emphasis in planning and placement should be on this lifelong process aspect rather than on the making of an isolated decision now for a lifetime. Career planning must be directed toward the realization that, in the last analysis, the student has freedom of choice that is accompanied by the concomitant implication of individual responsibility for the choice made. Individuals involved in planning and placement activities must recognize that choice and adjustment are part of the individual's total development, and that career planning is a special aspect of life planning involving patterns of living and expectations that relate to the individual's overall adjustment to other life situations.

Counselors and teachers serve a most useful function if they do not encourage students to form static, highly specific plans, but rather encourage them to consider a range of general occupational areas. This function might be realized better if the counselor assists students in formulating a network

[4] John W. Gardner, *Excellence: Can We Be Equal and Excellent Too?* (New York: Harper & Row, Publishers, 1962), p. xiii.

of vocational goals including both vertical and horizontal occupational mobility, and if the counselor can group occupations in occupational families so as to facilitate consideration of a range of related occupations. In vocational counseling, as in all learning activities, the counselor must keep in mind that individuals differ markedly with respect to their readiness for certain types of planning activities and that planning and the need for it does not necessarily cease at the termination of formal education.

Baer and Roeber caution counselors against four fallacies common to career planning: (1) a person can find one, and only one, occupation that will meet his personal need; (2) as soon as possible, a student should make a final vocational choice; (3) a student who is unable to choose a final goal is maladjusted; and (4) a person can find only one correct way of attaining his vocational goal.[5]

According to Glanz and Walston, the "myth" of success and the "myth" of an occupational niche are disadvantageous to occupational planning. They see the "myth" of success as leading many people to believe that they can attain success by dint of sheer drive and perseverance and that, often as not, the degree of success is measured by financial income. They further contend that it is definitely wrong for anyone to believe that there is a special occupational niche for every person and that the task is only to seek and to find this mythical round or square hole.[6]

Ohlsen offers these cautions for teachers and counselors in planning and placement activities: (1) Counselors and teachers should be cautious about making dogmatic statements concerning a student's chances for achieving success; rather they should recognize the student's right to determine whether he wants to gamble on the odds for success reflected in the data; (2) A great danger in planning is that a pupil will do whatever is suggested without understanding the significance of the choice made.[7]

Super, noting that little empirical investigation has been devoted to identifying the characteristics of the planning process, speculates that certain behaviors are involved. His description of these behaviors is paraphrased here:

1. *Surveying alternatives.* This includes such activities as listing alternative plans, trying out appealing plans, and/or re-examining the possiblities to determine whether other alternatives may be used to reach one's goal.
2. *Choice.* This means deciding between or among alternatives. It includes choice of *route* (e.g., going to school full time, versus earning while learning); choice of *steps* in a plan (e.g., if the decision is to go to college, one step for the student is to make a list of suitable colleges, a second

[5] Max Baer and Edward Roeber, *Occupational Information* (Chicago: Science Research Associates, Inc., 1964), pp. 402–407.

[6] Edward C. Glanz and Ernest B. Walston, *An Introduction to Personal Adjustment* (Boston: Allyn and Bacon, Inc., 1958), p. 218.

[7] Merle Ohlsen, *Guidance Services in the Modern School* (New York: Harcourt, Brace & World, Inc., 1964), p. 314.

step is to obtain catalogues, another is to complete an application, and so on); and forseeing *contingencies*—assessing the probability of contingencies having an impact upon that which is undertaken and deciding whether certain contingencies ought to be incorporated in the planning.
3. *Identifying and using resources.* The resources that are available to the individual should be identified and he should be helped in learning how to use them.[8]

Information Needed for Planning Activities

Successful planning is a continuous process carried on throughout the pupil's stay in school. For the counselor and the teacher it means learning about the individual and helping him learn about himself. It means that a great deal of educational and vocational information must be provided to the student and that counseling services must be available so that planning can be carefully and skillfully done.

Those who serve students in planning and placement activities must learn about students and must be alert so as to collect and record significant information. A cumulative record card is one of the best sources for such purposes and analyses of such records will help identify goals to be met in planning activities. Those concerned with planning will need information such as the following: (1) the student's interests, including the general types or major kinds of interests he has shown, the strength and stability of these interests; (2) the relationship of the individual's interests to his abilities and attitudes; (3) the extent to which the individual's interests are supported in the educational program; (4) the student's aptitudes and abilities, his general ability (both potential and demonstrated) to do school work; (5) his special subject abilities, his reading abilities, and his working efficiency as related to his level of achievement; (6) the student's physical and emotional health level; and (7) his social and personal characteristics and background of family traditions, economic resources, and personal contacts.

Essentially teachers and counselors who help students plan their high school work should be aware of (1) the content and requirements of the courses and curricula offered in the school; (2) local and state requirements for graduation; (3) the training necessary for entrance into selected occupations; and (4) entrance requirements for college and the educational opportunities offered by universities, colleges, and other institutions of advanced training; and (5) the student's own interests, abilities, and limitations. Those working in planning activities with a pupil must have certain broad goals: to make his world meaningful to him; to make sense from the known data appropriate to possible choices and situations; to make the

[8] Donald E. Super, "Basic Functions of Guidance and Counseling: Planning Personal Career Development," in *Computer-based Vocational Guidance Systems* (Washington, D.C.: Office of Education, 1969), pp. 3–9.

stresses of inadequacy more tolerable; to stimulate constructively; to enhance self-respect; to give recognition to self through planning which can be interpreted by the pupil as a step toward adequacy.

Planning activities should be so directed that they enable teachers and counselors to (1) permit early identification and interpretation of the general and specific abilities of each student; (2) provide each child with educational experiences through curricular and extracurricular activities that will produce the maximum practical development of his potentialities; and (3) provide services that will assist pupils and their parents in making adjustments and plans to secure full realization of the experiences provided. Some of the individual and group activities through which the planning, placement, and followup service is conducted are presented briefly in the following pages.

Parent Conferences

Planning and placement activities often require that parents be involved. Parents are being consulted more frequently in more and more schools. Certainly at those strategic periods when pupils are making long-term plans, parents should be included in the planning process. Whenever possible, planning should be a cooperative responsibility with parents at every grade level. Parents differ greatly in their degree of involvement in the achievements and interests of their children, but most of them want and need to know as much about their children as possible. The acquisition of such information helps them to know the quality and quantity of schoolwork their children are capable of performing and to make educational plans for the future.

The degree of parent involvement in planning has been reported in a recent survey. Eugene Gilbert, president of Gilbert Youth Research, Inc., has reported in a syndicated newspaper column that a crosscountry survey of 1,072 young people showed that 46 percent of the sample talked to their parents and received their advice in educational and vocational planning, and that 75 percent of this group asserted that parents encouraged them in their choices, while 11 percent reported that parents discouraged them.[9]

There are times when the counselor's judgment of the appropriateness of educational plans for the student runs counter to parents' ambitions and dreams. Many parents are firmly convinced that a boy who plays the violin at the age of twelve will be a great musician when he is twenty-five; that a girl who plays "school" will surely develop into a good teacher. In such situations, the counselor's task is to help the parents realize that educational-vocational predictions cannot be made on the basis of a single event, but rather take form during a long-term developmental process.

[9] As reported in *Guidance Newsletter* (Chicago: Science Research Associates, Inc., November, 1961), p. 3.

In many guidance programs there are group meetings for parents at the eighth grade level to acquaint them with the course offerings of the school and to enable them to meet teachers and become acquainted with the school. At such meetings counselors can discuss the policies and processes of student educational planning. This general meeting usually sets the stage for individual conferences with parents. Because parents find it difficult to come to the school during working hours, many schools have established evening hours for parent and child conferences.

Planning with Individual Students

For planning and placement to be effective, individual planning sessions are needed. The educational plans of the ninth grader are frequently tentative, and rightly so. His ideas of what he desires to do often reflect a failure to analyze correctly his abilities and aptitudes and inadequate knowledge about various occupational opportunities. Often his plans reflect the ambitions of his parents. Cognizance must be taken of these hidden motivations in working out an educational program.

Individual planning sessions are strongly indicated in conflict situations engendered by parental ambitions, the prestige implications of college selection, the student's interests and abilities, his past achievements, his maturity level, and his vocational goals. In order to provide assistance to the student making educational plans, many schools establish a guidance policy which encourages each pupil to confer individually with the counselor at least twice yearly. With the counselor, a program is developed which corresponds to the pupil's abilities, interests, and performances. Individual conferences are a means of working out an individualized educational program for the student. Many guidance personnel make use of a four-year planning sheet (see Figure 14) as a way to help the pupil and the school staff to think in developmental terms and to prepare for the future.

Planning Through Groups

Before guidance personnel can assist students in ascertaining what educational opportunities are open to them, they must make available a considerable body of information. Students should be thoroughly familiar with the curricular and extracurricular offerings of their own school and other schools in their city or vicinity to which they might transfer. This is especially important if vocational and technical schools are available as separate institutions. The information provided may be stored in folders or found in school handbooks in descriptions of programs and specific courses.

For students who will not be changing schools, group guidance classes, units presented within courses, or small-group sessions may be used to provide students with information and give them an opportunity to discuss their plans. Students should be given a chance to discuss what they wish

FIGURE 14
Four-Year Plan Sheet

Name _____

Address _____

Telephone _____

Record of Conference

Curriculum _____
Majors _____ Minors _____

Vocational Preferences _____

S.S. _____

Test Data
Reading _____
Ability _____
Interest
Areas _____
Achievement _____

College Plans _____

1st Sem., Fall, 19___	GR.	CR.	2nd Sem., Spring, 19___	GR.	CR.
English 1			English 2		

7th Sem., Fall, 19___	GR.	CR.	8th Sem., Spring, 19___	GR.	CR.

to do, what they logically can do with reasonable expectations of success, and how the school can help them. When students are properly informed about educational opportunities and their own interests and capacities, they are in a better position to outline their educational plans intelligently and effectively.

ORIENTATION

Orientation activities are group approaches through which youth are given assistance in making plans and adjustments to school and post–high school situations. The purpose of orientation is to help the pupil feel emotionally secure in a new setting and to provide him with the information needed to be successful in that setting. Orientation programs typically feature visits to new schools, visits by counselors and teachers to those leaving old schools, printed materials, and conferences with parents and students. Some of the limitations of orientation programs are that they (1) tend to be directed toward problems pupils have yet to meet and which currently may have little meaning for them; (2) frequently are not based upon what pupils believe they need to know; and (3) are not continuous over a period of time.

HOMEROOMS

Homeroom periods (not administrative units of ten to fifteen minutes) can be used advantageously for planning and placement activities. Homerooms which are successful (and so very few are!) feature students' discovery of themselves, discussion of their experiences, and a meaningful examination of their values and attitudes.

OTHER ACTIVITIES

Other activities through which planning is conducted have been discussed in Chapter 11. These include occupations classes, career conferences, guidance courses, and the like.

Placement Activities

In-school and out-of-school placement means that each pupil and those who assist him must understand his interests, abilities, and plans and be familiar with the opportunities available to him. Both the student and those who assist him must be able to relate placement opportunities to the student's perception of himself and to his projected life goals. Without adequate placement services, students may enter whatever activities exist without considering the cost in relation to eventual goals.

IN-SCHOOL PLACEMENT

In-school placement consists of helping students select an appropriate curriculum, the subjects within a curriculum, extracurricular activities, special groupings or special classes, and the like. In most American schools, the eighth or ninth grade marks a transition from following a single prescribed curriculum to placement in one of several alternative curricula. In large complex school districts, placement may also involve selecting among different secondary schools—commercial, academic, vocational. Placement within a curriculum at the eighth or ninth grade level is extremely important because of its eventual influence on careers, particularly for those occupations requiring a college education. Stice, in a stratified national sample, found that 15 percent of "very high ability" boys and 30 percent of "very high ability" girls, who were presumed to be capable of success at selective colleges, were pursuing vocational and commercial curricula. The relative "irreversibility" of choosing a noncollege course was evident; i.e., it was difficult to "step up" from an alternative curriculum to a college-preparatory course, while "stepping down" was comparatively easy.[10]

In-school placement is also concerned with placing students in school activities that will aid their development as individuals. Placement in such activities helps youth to meet their needs for social development, civic participation, and personal growth. It helps in their selection of activities that contribute to their development in line with their interests, and helps them engage in more activities or in fewer, as warranted.

In-school placement helps pupils select the special classes that are suitable for them. More and more schools are providing classes grouped according to ability—some for the more able, others for the large group whose members' abilities are about average, and others for the less able. Placement in such classes often involves helping pupils avoid tendencies to elect easy classes or it involves helping those with limited academic ability to deal with overambitious parents who wish to force them into advanced mathematics, foreign languages, and the like.

OUT-OF-SCHOOL PLACEMENT

Out-of-school placement includes assisting youth to secure part-time and summer employment, full-time employment after their school career is terminated, and placement in post–high school educational and training situations. The United States Employment Service, which has offices in each state and in many communities, can render assistance by providing information on the labor market for local, state, and national conditions; local job openings, including part-time and summer employment; opportunities for on-the-job training in business and industry; and, apprenticeship programs. It also provides a placement service, particularly for those just entering the labor market. Local schools should arrange for a USES representative to register students and to test and place them.

[10] G. Stice, "Talent Losses Before High School Graduation," *Research Bulletin 60–1* (Princeton, N.J.: Educational Testing Service, 1960).

Followup Surveys

Followup of students is needed to (1) obtain information as to how well students do after completing school; (2) help students realize the problems that lie ahead; (3) gain an appraisal of school programs and services; and (4) obtain ideas for improving school services. Followup studies need to be planned with care. Before initiating such studies, attention needs to be given to the purposes of such studies, the data to be obtained, the use of such data, the instrument to be used to obtain the data, the management of nonrespondents, the processing of the data, and the method of reporting the results.

Followup studies are frequently made of school dropouts, graduates, progress in college, jobs held by students, and the like. Students can be helpful in conducting such studies and should be involved early in the planning in order to assure their cooperation.

THE CHARACTER OF THE SERVICE

The nature and character of the planning, placement, and followup service may be expressed in five basic requirements:

1. *The planning, placement, and followup service must be current in outlook and dynamic in practice.* Care must be taken to recognize the inevitability of change, to guard against a too narrow and rigid conception of the individual and his possibilities. Planning for individuals consists of more than considering alternatives for earning a living; it is concerned with opening the doors of opportunity. The purpose of the planning, placement, and followup service is to help the individual to understand and to live in harmony with his total environment, to develop a sense of responsibility for using his skills for his own and society's betterment. The recognition of change as a definite characteristic of life implies that teachers and counselors accept responsibility for studying trends and knowing how to relate them to pupils in meaningful ways.

2. *The planning, placement, and followup service provides for equality of opportunity in accord with potentiality so that no individual will be deprived of educational and vocational opportunities because of race, religion, physical, social or economic conditions.* This principle is not romantic or sentimental but thoroughly realistic. Planning is primarily concerned with the need for individual development. This concern means that losses which accrue to society through neglect to provide for the highest potentialities of every individual can be reduced. Planning implies a differentiated service adjusted to the individual, for every youth deserves his democratic birthright—opportunity. If economic maladjustments have produced severe restrictions, then planning must

help the individual to seek opportunities to cut through these restricting conditions.

3. *All school personnel contribute to and participate in the planning, placement, and followup service.* Both teachers and counselors consult with pupils and their parents to help individuals make use of opportunities. This means that the service will be coordinated across grades in addition to being comprehensive and continuous. The service pivots around the counselor, who is assigned pupils to work with. In order to have an essential focus or consequence for individual pupils, teachers and counselors will have to work directly with pupils to help them evaluate individual progress. While overlapping may be both inevitable and desirable, a delineation of responsibilities can do much to provide an effective way of handling the problems that arise in borderline areas.

4. *Every pupil shall have the benefit of the planning, placement and followup service.* All pupils have choices to make. Therefore, all pupils will need essential information concerning educational and vocational opportunities, and all pupils will need to think through the alternatives available to them. Some will need more assistance than others. Awareness of educational and vocational potentialities, limitations, and opportunities is essential to self-development.

5. *The individual's right and freedom of choice shall be respected.* Freedom of thought and action for the student is essential in the planning, placement, and followup service. The student's choices and plans must be based upon his values, needs, and interests, and not those of the teacher, counselor, or parent. His right and freedom of choice may require the exercise of patience, vision, and flexibility. Respect for and faith in the individual imply that he should formulate the ends he shall serve as well as the means he shall employ to obtain his goals. The capacity for self-direction is best developed by seeking goals to which the individual is committed because he learns to think for himself, to be self-dependent, and to weigh and use knowledge instrumentally.

The discussion in this chapter reflects the fact that the planning, placement, and followup service is a vital part of the school's guidance program. Career planning progresses from level to level in the educational system, and its pattern of development is guided by and reflects many factors. Parents and pupils alike are concerned with the choices that are made as school progresses. Individual and group activities can help resolve many issues that need examination as choices are made.

ANNOTATED BIBLIOGRAPHY

BOROW, HENRY (ed.). *Man in a World at Work.* Boston: Houghton Mifflin Company, 1964. 606 pp.

This volume represents a series of papers by outstanding professionals on the history of vocational guidance, the meaning of work experience, and research and practices in vocational guidance. See especially Chapter 21 (pp. 487–509) for Albert S. Thompson's discussion of school settings for vocational guidance.

CALVERT, ROBERT, JR., and STEELE, JOHN E. *Planning Your Career.* New York: McGraw-Hill Book Company, 1963, 152 pp.

This book was designed as a career planning guide for college students. Part One presents goal selection, Part Two, the ways of securing employment, and Part Three, an evaluation of progress.

MOREHEAD, CHARLES G., and FULLER, FRANK G. (eds.) *Career Planning and Development.* Raleigh, N.C.: State Department of Public Instruction, 1965, 95 pp.

The editors report the content of two workshops conducted for counselors. The psychological bases of career planning are discussed by Albert S. Thompson and the sociological bases by Sigmund Nosow. Morehead presents a developmental approach to career planning and Edward C. Roeber identifies some concepts in career planning.

SELECTED REFERENCES

ASTIN, HELEN S. "Stability and Change in the Career Plans of Ninth Grade Girls," *Personnel and Guidance Journal* Vol. 46 (June 1968), pp. 961–966.

BELL, ALAN. "Role Models in Young Adulthood: Their Relationship to Occupational Endeavors," *Vocational Guidance Quarterly* Vol. 18 (June 1970), pp. 280–284.

BETZ, ELLEN L. "Need-Reinforcer Correspondence as a Predictor of Job Satisfaction," *Personnel and Guidance Journal* Vol. 47 (May 1969), pp. 878–883.

BIRNBAUM, ROBERT. "Influencing College Attendance Plans," *Personnel and Guidance Journal* Vol. 46 (April 1968), pp. 786–789.

BOTT, MARGARET M. "Measuring the Mystique," *Personnel and Guidance Journal* Vol. 46 (June 1968), pp. 967–970.

D'COSTA, AYRES, AND WINEFORDNER, DAVID. "A Cubist Model of Vocational Interests," *Vocational Guidance Quarterly* Vol. 17 (June 1969), pp. 242–249.

EDWARDS, CARL N. "Cultural Values and Role Decisions: A Study of Educated Women," *Journal of Counseling Psychology* Vol. 16 (January 1969), pp. 36–40.

FORTNER, MILDRED L. "Vocational Choices of High School Girls: Can They Be Predicted?" *Vocational Guidance Quarterly* Vol. 18 (March 1970), pp. 203–206.

HENDERSON, GEORGE. "Role Models for Lower Class Negro Boys," *Personnel and Guidance Journal* Vol. 46 (September 1967), pp. 6–10.

HERSHENSON, DAVID B. "Life-Stage Vocational Development System," *Journal of Counseling Psychology* Vol. 15 (January 1968), pp. 23–30.

————. "Techniques for Assisting Life-Stage Vocational Development," *Personnel and Guidance Journal* Vol. 47 (April 1969), pp. 776–780.

KALACHEK, EDWARD D. "Automation and Full Employment," *Vocational Guidance Quarterly* Vol. 15 (June 1967), pp. 242–247.

LARAMORE, DARYL. "Career Experiences Appropriate to Elementary School Grades," *The School Counselor* Vol. 17 (March 1970), pp. 262–263.

MISKIMINS, R. W., WILSON, L. T., BERRY, K. L., OETTING, E. R., AND COLE, C. W. "Person-Placement Congruence: A Framework for Vocational Counselors," *Personnel and Guidance Journal* Vol. 47 (April 1969), pp. 789–793.

MITCHELL, JOYCE S. "Girls Need Vocational Counseling Too," *The School Counselor* Vol. 16 (November 1968), pp. 143–145.

REED, HAROLD J. "Educational Changes for Manpower Development," *Vocational Guidance Quarterly* Vol. 17 (December 1968), pp. 82–86.

REITZ, JOHN R. "The Anatomy of College Admissions," *The School Counselor* Vol. 16 (September 1968), pp. 66–68.

ROSSMAN, JACK E., and PREBONICH, ELAINE M. "School Counselor-Employment Service Relations: The Minnesota Report," *Vocational Guidance Quarterly* Vol. 16 (June 1968), pp. 258–263.

WITCZAK, LOIS A., AND EHLERS, DOROTHY. "Project: Occupational Information," *The School Counselor* Vol. 17 (May 1970), pp. 362–363.

PART THREE
GUIDANCE
RESPONSIBILITIES
AND
RELATIONSHIPS

WHO IS responsible for guidance? How is guidance related to other school programs? These questions serve as the basis for the discussion that follows.

Part Three consists of two chapters. Chapter 14 discusses the guidance responsibilities held by certain school personnel because of their positions, training, and contact with students. This statement of these responsibilities takes into account not just existing practice, but the expectations of others, and existing trends, and other reality factors. The responsibility for guidance is broadly based, but at the same time it is recognized that certain individuals are in more potent, strategic positions to assist pupils.

Treatment is given in Chapter 15 to the major relationships that exist between guidance and the curriculum, administration, discipline, and the home. What part do counselors play in these areas? How do these areas contribute to guidance? As schools increase in size, there is a corresponding need to understand what each area contributes to other school areas and how each is related.

14

RESPONSIBILITIES FOR THE GUIDANCE PROGRAM

Who are the primary guidance personnel and what are their responsibilities and/or functions?
What are the guidance responsibilities of the administrative staff?
What are the guidance responsibilities of pupil personnel specialists?
What factors are involved in utilizing guidance personnel?

This chapter presents a discussion of the levels of guidance that can reasonably be expected from the many individuals who share its responsibility. The guidance services previously described in Part Two function best when appropriate, reasonable clarification of responsibilities among the staff has been attained. Essentially, the goal is to define clearly who is to do what, so that overlaps or gaps are minimized. At the same time, it should be recognized that clear or entirely pure distinctions between and among functions are not always possible or particularly desirable, since the helping relationship is implicit in the role and function of all educational personnel.

The position taken in the discussion is that counselors and teachers are the primary guidance agents in a school program. It is recognized that parents have and fulfill many guidance responsibilities for their children. However, this chapter concerns itself with what can be and is legitimately expected of school personnel. It may appear that descriptions of who has primary responsibility is an academic issue rather than a real one, but some few years of school experience leads to the conclusion that considerable confusion exists in the area now as in the past. The use of the word, *primary,* is based on its usual meaning; i.e., first in time or order of development. It is hoped that the comments that follow will make more explicit why counselors and teachers, in that order, are considered the *primary* guidance personnel in a school program.

RESPONSIBILITIES OF PRIMARY GUIDANCE PERSONNEL

School Counselors

Although many, many books, articles, and speeches have emphasized that the teacher is *the* key person in guidance, the position here is that the personally committed and professionally prepared counselor is the key person in a guidance program. There is no desire to deprecate the guidance responsibilities of teachers. It is expected that teachers will make many contributions and it is recognized that they do so because they are sensitive and understand the developmental needs of children. But the teacher's first, major, and all-consuming responsibility is to teach—to manage a learning climate for as many as five or six groups, each composed of twenty-five to thirty-five students—to impart and develop knowledge, skills, and attitudes. According to Harold Taylor,

> The aim of the teacher and of true education must be to peel away the layers of custom and to give nourishment and strength to the individual consciousness which lies beneath. Otherwise, the educational effects of the rewards and punishments which society provides will train each person to be exactly alike and to perpetuate exactly its own kind. We need to remember that each generation of young people, as it comes into the world, develops its own style and its own truth, having lived through a particular expanse of time which belongs to it and to no other. Each member of each generation reflects some part of the character of his own time and starts almost imperceptibly to transform this character into something else.[1]

The impetus of the learning climate is to ". . . draw students into the traditions of society and invite their membership in it," rather than to ". . . move *particular* children in *distinctive* directions on the basis of their special characteristics and potentialities."[2] The primary function of the classroom teacher is to transmit the culture of one generation to the next. Teachers are not counselors; their central role is to implement the learning process in the classroom, recognizing that learning is a personal and emotional experience as well as an intellectual experience. Their knowledge, energies, and efforts during each class period necessarily will be focused upon the needs that they perceive are possessed by the twenty-five to thirty-five class members as a group. If one individual in the group has certain needs not exhibited by the other members, the teacher appropriately must give preference in his or her classroom behavior to the needs of the group rather than the individual. His professional preparation has been designed so that he can instruct youth in a particular area of knowledge deemed vitally important by society. Arbuckle cites nine reasons why teachers are not

[1] Harold Taylor, "The World of the Individual," *Educational Leadership* Vol. 22 (October 1964), p. 9.

[2] Edward Shoben, "Guidance: Remedial Function or Social Development?" *Harvard Educational Review* Vol. 32 (Fall 1962), p. 432.

counselors, four of which are abstracted here: (1) the teacher's basic responsibility is to society or the school rather than to an individual child; (2) the overt teaching role of the instructor is contrary to the quiet, listening, clarifying counseling role; (3) problems arise in class situations if a child is given full rein in the expression of his feelings, particularly negative ones; and (4) an oft-heard complaint is that many teachers do not have enough professional training to be effective as counselors.[3]

The nature of the teacher's function, the demands it makes, and the direction of training all lead to the conclusion that the teacher should not and, indeed, cannot be expected to be *the* key guidance person. The school counselor, whose competencies include counseling, pupil appraisal, group work, planning and placement, referral, and consulting work with parents and school staff, is the primary guidance person. Even with the ideal conditions of a dedicated and enlightened teaching staff, it is probable that schools would need counselors because of the kind of problems that students cope with today. Mammarella and Crescimbeni[4] have categorized these problems as being cultural and cosmic. Cultural problems are those of meeting academic requirements, learning a vocation, earning a living, marrying and rearing a family, accepting community responsibility, finding a social identity, attaining ego satisfaction through financial and social rewards, and the like. Cosmic problems were identified as those that come as a result of man's inescapable fate of suffering, old age, and death. Because man is man, he is anxious and worries over the significance of his existence, the meaning of his life, and his eventual destiny.

Extensive treatment will not be given to the school counselor's responsibilities, since they have been discussed in greater detail in Chapters 6 and 7. To review these functions and to point up the commonalities and differences in counselor functions in elementary and secondary schools, Arbuckle's ten points seem applicable here: (1) The counselor in both schools helps emotionally disturbed children to come to a happier and more satisfying solution of their problems; (2) the counselor in both schools helps children with their academic difficulties, although the elementary school counselor is more involved in the academic experiences of the children than is his secondary school colleague; (3) counselors in both schools are concerned with the preventive and the remedial, but in the elementary school there is particular stress on the preventive and developmental so that there may be less need for the remedial later on; (4) both counselors work with teachers to help them come to a greater understanding of the children in their classes and of themselves; (5) both counselors help parents to come to a greater understanding and appreciation of their children, although most elementary school counselors are probably more involved in the problems

---

[3] Dugald S. Arbuckle, *Pupil Personnel Services in American Schools* (Boston: Allyn and Bacon, Inc., 1962), pp. 108–121.

[4] Raymond Mammarella and Joseph Crescimbeni, "Guidance Problems: Cultural or Cosmic," *Saturday Review* (November 21, 1964), p. 67.

of the home; (6) both counselors develop testing batteries for diagnosis and counseling purposes; (7) both counselors maintain extensive and up-to-date records on the children for whom they are responsible; (8) secondary school counselors spend much of their time helping students to make wise college or job decisions; (9) the secondary school counselor aids needy students to get part-time jobs; and (10) all school counselors work closely with other specialized personnel.[5] The nature of the school counselor's responsibilities suggests two major roles: counseling and consulting.

COUNSELING ROLE

The counseling role consists of the well-understood and traditional activities of the individual who counsels in school settings. Since this role has been broadened somewhat and is progressing toward clearer definition, especially within recent years, there seems little point in belaboring the nature of the counseling function. In his counseling role, the counselor works directly with students on such matters as emotional concerns, self-understanding, decision-making, educational and vocational planning; and, when appropriate, he prepares them for referral to other specialists. He performs this role in both individual (see Chapter 7) and small-group counseling relationships (see Chapter 8).

CONSULTING ROLE

The counselor's consulting role includes performing such functions as working with teachers, parents, educational specialists, and administrators on matters involving student understanding and student management. His knowledge of student body characteristics will be utilized by curriculum committees, study groups, department heads and other supervisors. Consultation, broadly interpreted, is a major function of counselors and undoubtedly will become even more significant in the future. Yet little material in professional publications deals directly with the counselor's consultative functions.

CONSULTING WITH TEACHERS

Many guidance authorities have pointed up the counselor's difficulties in relating to or establishing effective communications with teachers. Frequently this is seen as a major roadblock in a great number of school guidance programs. Counselors and teachers need a mutually productive relationship if they are to improve the conditions for learning in the school. There is no merit in pointing the finger of blame at either group. What is needed is a mutuality of consent to engage in efforts to define problems and areas that are amenable to attack by both groups. This requires improved communications. The effective school counselor develops techniques for establishing a satisfactory relationship with teachers.

Though consulting with teachers often erroneously seems to indicate a

[5] Arbuckle, *Pupil Personnel Services,* pp. 105–107.

one-way process with the counselor in a superior advisory position, emphasis should be placed upon the development of a working relationship between teachers and counselors which is based upon the mutually understood and accepted goal and purpose of helping children to achieve productive lives. Teachers seek answers to what can be done immediately with "Joe," "Sally," and "Tom" because they have them in class today and tomorrow. Counselors who succumb to pressures to act as experts with readymade solutions for all classroom ills will find their consultant role short lived. The counselor's consulting role with teachers is not envisioned as that of telling them how to teach, what to teach, or the techniques to be used in classroom management. Rather, the focus of the consultation is upon helping teachers to better understand pupils and their behavior. Through discussion of pupils the counselor and teacher may work out recommendations as to what specifically can be done in the classroom for certain pupils.

The counselor can, however, work with teachers in many ways. One such way is by interpreting children's behavior in terms of the teacher's background and understanding. Through joint observation, the counselor and teacher can pool insights and perceptions of the child and discuss their composite knowledge of him. Another situation in which the counselor and teacher can collaborate is that of securing assistance for pupils whose needs require special help and/or facilities; e.g., children with severe reading disabilities. The counselor should be instrumental in securing the kind of actions he needs to take.

Caplan suggests that another type of consultation with teachers is the ". . . professional context, so their professional strengths may be more effectively mobilized for the mental health of their pupils, and so that their unresolved emotional problems may not interfere with the utilization of their existing professional knowledge and skill."[6] Consultation in some situations is required because the teacher is unable to function with a given child. Caplan recommends two major techniques to be used in such a situation. The first is referred to as "segmental tension reduction," in which the consultant approaches the problem by focusing upon the child in the expectation that this will reduce the teacher's tension. The second technique, "dissipation of the stereotype," is an attempt to help the teacher focus upon the child's behavior realistically rather than through the stereotyped perceptions that frequently typify the teacher's crisis view of the child.[7]

In other matters—test interpretation, collecting and using career information, securing sociometric measures, assisting in interpreting the child to his parents—the counselor can be helpful to teachers. In turn, the teacher can be a consultant to the counselor on such matters as reporting children's

[6] G. Caplan, "Mental Health Consultation in the Schools," in *The Elements of a Community Mental Hygiene Program* (New York: Milbank Memorial Fund, 1956), p. 77.

[7] G. Caplan, *Concepts of Mental Health and Consultation* (Washington: Children's Bureau, 1959), pp. 129–130.

reactions in group situations, their approach to learning tasks, their response to directions and class controls, and the like.

CONSULTING WITH PARENTS

Parental contacts with the school may occur for a variety of reasons and under many circumstances. The circumstances often set the tone of the contact. Counselor contacts with parents are often initiated by the counselor to (1) interpret test results; (2) discuss pupil planning and placement; (3) interpret a child's behavior in school; (4) discuss college selections, applications, and finances; (5) discuss a child's achievement and development; and (6) facilitate referral to other individuals or agencies. Parents may initiate conferences for these and many other reasons. They may view the counselor as a threatening figure and if so, the counselor must cope with and attempt to change such views as quickly as possible by being thoroughly familiar with the pupil's school experience, and by explaining his behavior in the school. Mutual exploration of the reason why parents and counselors are meeting can then proceed.

Parents can often supply counselors with information concerning the pupil's behavior at home, his relationships with siblings and friends, the methods used to discipline the pupil at home, possible home difficulties, the child's physical health, childhood habits, and the like. Often parents seek practical advice about career planning for their children. At other times their contact with the counselor is to gain reassurance about their handling of specific situations with their children. Parents frequently have high expectations for a child whose resources cannot measure up to them. In such circumstances a factual description of their child's abilities and potentialities is useful. Such an approach may help parents to modify their views of the child and to attain a more realistic, beneficial outlook.

CONSULTING WITH CURRICULUM SPECIALISTS

The school counselor's responsibility for knowing the characteristics of the student body places him in a position in which he can be extremely helpful to curriculum specialists and committees. His knowledge of the range and distribution of abilities, vocational aspirations and plans, pupil readiness and maturation, interests, changing college requirements, and changing economic, social, and scientific conditions can be of great value to curriculum planners. The counselor's interest in curriculum development lies in his fundamental concern with individuals in the learning situation and in assisting pupils so that their performance will be optimally effective.

Since a major premise of curriculum planning is that materials and experiences should be related to youth needs, the counselor's efforts to obtain precise information concerning such needs will be invaluable to those concerned with curriculum development. Through interviews, questionnaires, surveys, behavioral case studies, and tests, these factors can be identified and curricular experiences planned that will provide opportunities to meet needs that are often overlooked or neglected.

Further discussion of guidance and the curriculum is presented in Chapter 15. It is sufficient here to indicate that only by a concerted action in unifying youth programs can the school hope to achieve more fully its youth-serving function. Regardless of how skillfully guidance activities may be conducted, their value will be greatly minimized if the pupil is left in classes in which his needs and interests are neglected or ignored.

CONSULTING WITH REFERRAL AND COMMUNITY AGENCIES

Although most pupils can be helped within the school, a sizable number may need referral or assistance from community agencies and nonschool specialists. The counselor will need to consult with individuals and representatives of agencies about referral procedures and necessary followup. Chapter 17 discusses the ways of identifying and using such agencies.

The counselor's consulting role is complex and multidimensional, requiring constant alertness to the contributions he can make to others. Wrenn warns that the culturally encapsulated counselor will not make effective contributions to students, teachers, or parents. Encapsulation—self-protection from change by a pretended reality based upon the past and the known—comes through (1) being surprised or unbelieving about changes in truth; (2) becoming cushioned in an academic cocoon that has little reference to the total culture; and (3) assuming that in counseling one may safely draw upon his own educational and vocational experience. To avoid encapsulation, Wrenn recommends that the counselor (1) persist in a regime of "unlearning" something each day; (2) encourage those who think differently, and (3) suppress his tendencies to be self-righteous.[8]

CONSULTING WITH ADMINISTRATORS

Many of the consultant activities cited above apply equally to the counselor's consultative function with school administrators. A case could be made that the counselor's consultative functions are of even greater value to administrators than to teachers since administrators, by virtue of their responsibilities, may become isolated from pupils. Basically the counselor is an invaluable source of knowledge concerning the student body—its characteristics, needs, attitudes, morale, and the like. Frequently the counselor must serve as a buffer between the pupil and other adults in the pupil's environment, including administrators. The counselor's specialized role in the discipline function is discussed in greater detail in Chapter 15.

Teachers

Relatively speaking, the counselor is the newcomer to the school scene as compared with teachers and principals. Because he is a late arrival he has striven to define and establish his role within the school setting. Because

[8] C. Gilbert Wrenn, "The Culturally Encapsulated Counselor," in Ralph L. Moser, Richard F. Carle, and Chris D. Kehas (eds.), *Guidance: An Examination* (New York: Harcourt, Brace & World, Inc., 1965), pp. 214–224.

of this and also because of a dire shortage of school psychologists, the counselor probably comes closer to being a psychological expert than anyone else in the typical school. Also, because of his special training, there are activities which only he should perform, since he has had specialized training. These activities, for the most part, are not part of the traditional teacher or principal roles.

During the past few years there has been considerable research effort expended in the direction of defining the counseling function in guidance services. This research has often been conducted as though the counselor operates alone with no help from other school personnel. Consequently, little consideration has been given to teaching members of the school staff working in the guidance area. Few educators would doubt that the teacher has a substantial responsibility for student guidance, but precisely what the teacher's function should be is still open to considerable debate.

The teacher is the official of the school having historical seniority so far as his place in the school is concerned. In his training he has learned that he is the facilitator of learning, the leader in maintaining mental health, and the parent surrogate. Conceptualizing his position in such a manner may lead him to perceive his role in guidance quite differently than would counselors or principals.

Authors of various guidance textbooks—Mathewson,[9] Roeber, Smith, and Erickson[10] and Humphreys, Traxler and North,[11] to name but a few —have included sections describing the teacher's role. In these texts the major theme is that teachers are expected to perform guidance responsibilities commensurate with their training and ability. Within this context considerable latitude and many discrepancies exist regarding the guidance expectations that are held for the teacher. For example, Humphreys, Traxler, and North have listed eleven functions of the teacher within the guidance program, all of which are conducted in the classroom.[12] Writing on this same subject, Mathewson has said:

> It is true that all teachers engage in appraisal of pupil characteristics, adjustment of behavior, evaluation of individual performance, etc., and may even undertake some individual counseling. To the extent that these functions are performed professionally, teachers are participating in guidance practice. But at best, these can be only a restricted set of functions on the part of teachers.[13]

[9] Robert H. Mathewson, *Guidance Policy and Practice* (New York: Harper & Brothers, 1962), p. 142.

[10] Edward C. Roeber, Glenn E. Smith, and Clifford E. Erickson, *Organization and Administration of Guidance Services* (New York: McGraw-Hill Book Co., Inc., 1955), p. 31.

[11] J. Anthony Humphreys, Arthur E. Traxler, and Robert D. North, *Guidance Services* (Chicago: Science Research Associates, Inc., 1960), pp. 381–384.

[12] *Ibid.,* pp. 383–384.

[13] Mathewson, *Guidance Policy,* p. 142.

Teachers and professors have also written about the necessity for teachers to provide guidance for their pupils. Many articles (for example, Leonard,[14] Long,[15] and Mathis[16]), based largely upon opinion and practical experience, have been written on this subject, but though these writings generate reaction, very little clarification results. The basic problem still remains: What is the teacher's role in guidance? Examination of the literature dealing with the topic leads to the conclusion that teachers and those who prepare them do not fully agree with counselors and counselor educators concerning the nature of the teacher's role in guidance. For example, Davis has written:

> Today, for example, many teachers as part of their regular assignments are holding interviews with individual pupils, doing group guidance, working out scattergrams of their classes, and doing many other things usually considered to be guidance.[17]

This statement and many others which could be cited make it clear that there are conflicting views of the teacher's guidance role. Even among teachers there may be differences in conceptualizing their guidance tasks. Teachers instructing in academic subject areas usually are concerned with imparting sufficient knowledge of their subject-matter specialty to carry the student successfully through college. Consequently, they may believe that this will take care of the student's total development. Teachers who instruct in vocationally oriented subjects, more aware that training of their students is often terminal, frequently are more interested in getting the student ready to adjust to the work world after high school. It is known that the antecedents of guidance were in the vocational movement and the fact that the vocational information-giving service is still important is witnessed by the large number of articles written by vocationally oriented teachers, counselors, and others. In addition, teachers' perceptions of their guidance functions may be tempered by years of school experience, age, sex, contacts with counselors, and involvement in guidance work. Some time ago, Grambs and Iverson pointed out the essential differences between the "Teacher-Academician" and the "Teacher-Counselor:"[18]

---

[14] Dorothy V. Leonard, "A Classroom Teacher Looks at Guidance," *Education* Vol. 57 (March 1955), pp. 446–449.

[15] Viona E. Long, "Guidance and Classroom Teachers," *The Clearing House* Vol. 32 (March 1958), pp. 419–421.

[16] G. K. Mathis, "Guidance: It's Our Work," *Illinois Education* Vol. 50 (May 1962), pp. 398–399.

[17] Frank G. Davis, "Why Call It Guidance?" *Education* Vol. 75 (March 1955), pp. 439–440.

[18] Jean D. Grambs and William J. Iverson, *Modern Methods in Secondary Education* (New York: The Dryden Press, 1952), p. 413.

TEACHER–ACADEMICIAN	TEACHER–COUNSELOR
Subject matter has priority.	Personality is of first concern.
Test results determine levels of potential achievement in subject matter.	Test results point out areas of personal need and barriers to successful adjustment.
Grades are a function of subject matter learning only.	Grades reveal many kinds of achievement other than subject matter alone—social, psychological, aesthetic.
Only students who can learn the subject are able to succeed to a high degree.	Avenues of success for a variety of talents are vitally important.
Few personal interviews are held with students except about academic problems.	Many individual interviews are held about personal as well as academic problems.
The student's counselor or other teachers are seldom consulted about the progress of an individual.	Student problems are often discussed with counselors and other teachers.
Few home visits are made and parent conferences at school are avoided.	A number of home visits are made and special invitations to individual parents to come to school for conferences are issued.
The role of emotion in learning is discounted.	Sensitivity to emotional tone in the classroom and with individual students is maintained.

Grambs and Iverson's statement of differences presents an interesting contrast between two types of teacher orientations. It should be noted, however, that it appears to be somewhat outdated, since the current trend is toward full-time commitment to the counseling role rather than occupancy of a dual role. Considerable agreement currently exists that the roles of teacher and counselor are not compatible, since the teacher's prime responsibility is for cognitive development. A teacher in a normal professional career spends over a million child hours (40 hours × 40 weeks × 30 children × 30 years) in the classroom. No other professional individual working with children comes even close to this amount of direct contact. The teacher's impact on the child—for good or for ill—is tremendous. In some ways the typical classroom may be viewed as the source and site of conflict between teachers and students. It is there that the details for carrying out the school's intellective objectives through instruction are brought to bear upon the student. Granted that teachers do have some flexibility regarding how their courses will be taught, almost all struggle to impose their authority over a class for they know that students are quick to seize the initiative and that the quickest way to be criticized by administrators and colleagues is to lose control of a class. The evaluation of student performance also involves teachers in conflict situations. Norms require that they treat students equally and fairly. But few teachers limit their assessment to only objective measures of skills and knowledge acquisition. Rather, students are judged by such criteria as whether and how they participated in class discussions, the attitudes they exhibited toward work assigned to them and how courteously they behaved. Subtle, powerful pressures are exerted upon students to accommodate themselves to teachers. Some resist openly but most who rebel do so in covert ways.

Johnson, Stefflre, and Edelfelt urge teachers to be alert and to capitalize on opportunities in the classroom which help pupils to: (1) develop realistic self-concepts; (2) recognize and deal with their strengths and weaknesses effectively and intelligently; (3) begin to recognize and understand emotional responses and to learn to deal with them; (4) face some of the problems and processes of social development and learn how to get along better with peers, adults, and younger people; (5) learn good study habits and skills; (6) discover and gain some perspective concerning the educational opportunities open to them and some notion of various fields of knowledge; and (7) discover and gain some perspective regarding occupational possibilities.[19]

More and more teachers are learning to provide for individual differences and to help pupils participate in cooperative teacher-pupil planning. Teachers put considerable effort into organizing their classwork in a way that centers attention on students and their problems. This approach not only makes classwork highly meaningful but also helps pupils learn to meet their own problems in socially acceptable and personally satisfying ways.

Teachers have a responsibility to define and enforce behavioral limits in the classroom. How they enforce these limits makes a difference as to how a child learns to understand and live within boundaries. Ohlsen has suggested fourteen questions a teacher should ask himself when a child misbehaves:

1. What did the child do the last time he misbehaved in my presence?
2. Outside of the incidents in which discipline problems arise, how do I feel about this child?
3. What did I do when he misbehaved in my presence the last time?
4. What unsatisfied needs are suggested by the child's behavior?
5. Do I have any reason for believing this child is not well?
6. Do I know of anything worrying him?
7. How do the members of his family feel about one another?
8. Is there anything unusual about the child's family life that may account for his unacceptable school behavior?
9. How is the child disciplined at home?
10. Did the child know what I expected from him and his peers?
11. How does this pupil "rate" with his classmates? Who are his friends?
12. How has the composition of the group contributed to this discipline problem?

[19] Walter F. Johnson, Buford Stefflre, and Roy A. Edelfelt, *Pupil Personnel and Guidance Services* (New York: McGraw-Hill Book Company, Inc., 1961), pp. 124–125.

13. What are the working conditions of my classroom?
14. What is the quality of the child's schoolwork?[20]

Even a brief observation of instructional behavior reveals a great diversity of teacher activities. Teachers ask questions; listen and appraise responses; listen and respond to students' questions; reprimand, approve, or react neutrally to students. They tell how something is done or show how it is done. They listen to pupils tell how to do something or observe their efforts to do it. How these numerous activities are performed is important to the kind of mental health established in the classroom. Withall, in studying interpersonal interaction in the classroom as a function of the manner in which teachers communicate with and relate to learners, comments:

> If our experience during this research has any validity, it seems clear that when teachers, regardless of the level at which they teach, demonstrate to learners that they care about *what* they are teaching and *whom* they are teaching the quality and quantity of learning apparently is enhanced.[21]

Withall also stresses that teachers must know and consistently keep in mind *why* they are teaching, what their goals are, and how they hope to attain them.

In recent years much attention has been given to the fact that an increasing number of people, both youth and adults, do not enjoy good mental health. One cause of emotional stress may lie in unfortunate classroom experiences, i.e., requiring children to meet achievement standards beyond their capabilities. Teachers have responsibilities for carefully evaluating pupil achievement and progress in their classes. Such evaluations will be useful in pupil planning and guidance.

Specifically, what guidance responsibilities lie within the domain of teachers? In citing the five areas below, it is assumed that all teachers recognize and accept the individual worth of each student; that they know the guidance services available in the school; that they realize that each pupil has different potentialities in relation to subject matter; that they are cognizant that pupils need to know how well they are doing and in which areas they need to improve, and that they provide a wholesome learning climate. In addition to these very important contributions, teachers are expected to assist in the guidance services in the following ways.

1. *Teachers engage in child study and diagnosis.* They study pupils to understand their backgrounds, abilities, and needs. A thorough knowl-

[20] Merle M. Ohlsen, *Guidance Services in the Modern School* (New York: Harcourt, Brace & World, Inc., 1964), pp. 395–401.

[21] John Withall, "Mental Health—Teacher Education Research Project," *Journal of Teacher Education* Vol. 14 (September 1963), p. 323.

edge of pupils requires time and comes gradually as a result of the continuous study and observation of pupils' appearances, attitudes, and behavior. Alert teachers develop a sensitivity to differences in pupil behavior and unusual conduct.

2. *Teachers identify and refer pupils who have special needs.* Teachers are in a position to spot early symptoms that suggest a specialist is needed. They have a most important responsibility to identify children who are prone, vulnerable, or exposed to the development of undesirable behavior patterns before such patterns become serious. A large proportion of children who eventually come into contact with child-welfare agencies, police, courts, and other institutions can be identified early and screened for help and assistance. Teachers can be sensitive to such characteristics as emotional lability, extreme restlessness, lack of self-control, defiance, defensive attitudes, submissiveness, marked assertiveness, fears, emotional conflicts, inferiority feelings, and many other behaviors which may indicate the necessity for special help. DeHaan and Kough[22] cite a number of checklists of characteristics which are helpful to teachers in identifying pupils with special needs.

3. *Teachers contribute to and make use of guidance records.* Teachers record their observations of some pupils. Anecdotal records of observations are used to secure a developmental picture of the child. Such records are submitted to counselors to facilitate child study. Sociometric studies of pupils in class activities are made and reported to counselors. To understand and help pupils, the teacher examines and studies the data—tests, school marks, health, vocational goals, activities, and the like—available in cumulative records.

4. *Teachers help pupils develop effective study habits.* The teacher periodically reviews procedures appropriate for studying materials and processes involved in assigned units of work. Specific study devices and methods of studying various phases of classwork are presented. Periodic attention is given to discussing study problems and study conditions.

5. *Teachers contribute to educational and vocational planning and placement.* Every teacher contributes something to pupil planning. By relating his subject matter to future courses, by discussing career opportunities which depend upon the mastering of present and future subject matter, by discussing in individual conferences with pupils their potentialities for certain opportunities, the teacher aids in pupil planning.

Teachers and counselors must find ways to cooperate to increase their effectiveness, since neither can operate effectively alone. The success or failure of any guidance program is dependent upon their cooperation, initiative, and skills.

[22] Robert F. DeHaan and Jack Kough, *Identifying Students with Special Needs* (Chicago: Science Research Associates, 1956), 94 pp.

RESPONSIBILITIES OF ADMINISTRATIVE STAFF

An administrator's training greatly influences his view of the guidance function. Administrators in training are imbued with the idea that theirs is the responsibility for the school and that although they must delegate some of this responsibility, the final decisions concerning the school ultimately rest with them. Some administrators may view the counselor as infringing on their traditional rights because some of the things the counselor does were once considered to be administrative responsibilities. In some cases, an administrator may feel more comfortable if the teacher has charge of all guidance responsibilities, for he is much surer of the teacher's traditional role, that is, one subordinate to his own. In this section attention will be given to the guidance responsibilities of directors of guidance, deans, principals, and superintendents.

Directors of Guidance

Director of Guidance is the title usually given to an individual who supervises school counselors and is responsible for the administration and coordination of guidance services in a school or school district. MacDonnell found that over 65 percent of the two hundred directors of guidance in forty states surveyed reported spending from one-half to three-quarters of their time coordinating guidance activities.[23] Directors of guidance are responsible for (1) assisting in the selection and placement of school counselors; (2) supervising counselors; (3) communicating budgetary needs to administrative officers; (4) providing physical facilities; (5) establishing and maintaining cooperative working relationships with community agencies for referral purposes; (6) apprising the staff, parents, and administration of guidance needs and program development; and (7) conducting evaluative studies of the guidance program.

Assistant Principals

Assistant principals often have responsibility for attendance and for administering discipline. They frequently are responsible for scheduling classes and assigning students to various classes, and in many cases are in charge of student club activities.

Principals

The specific guidance responsibilities carried out by principals will be dependent upon the size of the administrative unit. If the school unit is large enough to employ a director of guidance, technical leadership will

[23] John F. MacDonnell, "City-Wide Directors of Guidance," *Personnel and Guidance Journal* Vol. 35 (November 1956), p. 162.

be delegated to the director. In most schools, however, some guidance leadership is expected from principals and superintendents.

Principals have a responsibility to recognize the need for and the importance of a comprehensive guidance program. If they do not support such a program, little support will come from teachers, pupils, or parents. Principals must be active in studying the values, purposes, and limitations of the guidance program in their school. A comprehensive listing of the guidance functions of the school principal has been reported by the 1959 Kent State University NDEA Study Work Guidance Conference. These include (1) securing staff for counseling that is professionally prepared and numerically adequate; (2) seeing that the roles of various staff members in the guidance program are defined and that staff members are able to function in their roles; (3) delegating the responsibility for the actual operation of the program to well-trained guidance specialists; (4) providing adequate facilities and materials; (5) making clear to the staff what the guidance program is, and providing active encouragement and support; (6) providing class time for group guidance; (7) organizing a school guidance committee and encouraging its development as an advisory and policy-recommending body; (8) promoting inservice education in guidance for the entire school staff; (9) encouraging constant evaluation and improvement of the building program; (10) coordinating guidance planning with other phases of educational planning; (11) providing for the interpretation of guidance services to the community; and (12) consulting with teachers and counselors regarding specific pupil needs and problems.[24]

Superintendents

The superintendent sets the pace and tone for guidance services, as he does for all school services. Commonly, he is the agent through which the community is kept informed of the guidance services. The superintendent, through his leadership and service to the school board and the community, provides essential personnel, budgets, and facilities. He interprets guidance and its value to the board of education. He supports school personnel in developing a balanced program of guidance services and encourages adequate evaluation of these services.

RESPONSIBILITIES OF RELATED SPECIALISTS

The point has been made previously that all personnel associated with school have opportunities and responsibilities for guidance. Some of the guidance responsibilities of the psychometrist, psychologist, social worker, and health officials will be cited briefly here.

[24] Division of Guidance and Testing, *Guidance in Grades Seven, Eight, and Nine: A Report of a Study Work Conference Conducted at Kent State University* (Columbus, Ohio: State Department of Education, 1960), pp. 43–44.

School Psychometrist

The school psychometrist is specially trained in mental measurement and testing. He administers some types of individual psychological examinations, makes diagnoses, and writes reports. The psychometrist consults and works closely with counselors, teachers, and other student personnel workers with regard to test data and their interpretation and use.

The psychometrist's functions overlap that of the school psychologist. Cases involving detailed personality investigations, short-term therapy, and community referral and contact are most often reserved as the domain of the school psychologist. Since the school psychologist is able to perform more specialized functions in testing and test interpretation, the position of school psychometrist seems unnecessary except in large school districts in which specialization and division of duties may be justified.

School Psychologist

The school psychologist is an individual especially well trained in counseling and in clinical and educational psychology. He spends a substantial portion of his time on individual learning problems, followup consultation and recommendations to teachers, counselors, and others. Lockman's description of the subfields of psychology reflects the school psychologist's emphasis on performing individual diagnosis, on therapy and on working with continued learning problems.[25] Special concerns such as mental retardation, slow learning, severe behavior deviations, giftedness, emotional disturbance, and physical handicaps such as blindness and neurological disabilities constitute many referrals to the school psychologist.

White and Harris cite four major services of school psychologists, which are summarized here:

1. *Educational Diagnosis.* The school psychologist defines the educational status of pupils, including assets and difficulties, and identifies the factors related to their difficulties and successes.
2. *Educational Remediation.* The school psychologist outlines a program aimed at improving the educational program of pupils studied. These programs may include selected teaching, tutoring, placement in special classes, counseling, therapy, and the like.
3. *Personality Diagnosis.* Through personality tests, diagnostic interviewing, observation of pupil, compiling a personality and social history, the school psychologist pinpoints the factors associated with a pupil's adaptation and maladaptation.
4. *Personality Remediation.* After making a personality diagnosis, the school psychologist outlines a program of personality remediation which may include individual or group therapy, counseling techniques, and other reparative measures.[26]

[25] Robert F. Lockman, "An Empirical Description of the Subfields of Psychology," *American Psychologist* Vol. 19 (August 1964), pp. 645–653.

[26] Abstracted from Mary Alice White and Myron W. Harris, *The School Psychologist* (New York: Harper & Row, Publishers, 1961), pp. 5–6.

School psychology as a profession is growing, and its functions are currently being redefined, clarified, and expanded. In 1955, the American Psychological Association reported that the school psychologist serves in an advisory capacity to school personnel in performing the following functions: (1) measuring and interpreting the intellectual, social, and emotional development of children; (2) identifying exceptional children and collaborating in the planning of appropriate educational and social placement and programs; (3) developing ways to facilitate the learning and adjustment of children; (4) encouraging and initiating research, and helping to utilize research findings for the solution of school problems; and (5) diagnosing educational and personal disabilities, and collaborating on the planning of re-educational programs.[27]

School Social Workers

Social work has also developed rapidly within recent years. The Department of Labor estimated that in 1961 some 2400 visiting teachers or school social workers were employed. Social workers in the schools have often been designated as home and/or visiting teachers but they are now a recognized subspecialty as are psychiatric social workers and social group workers. Some, but not all, school social workers are graduates of two-year programs accredited by the Council on Social Work Education.

Social workers may work in a central-school child-study clinic doing intake interviews and performing casework and group work functions. Often social workers coordinate the services of attendance workers, child-welfare workers, and the like, all of which are concerned with such problems as child neglect, financial, and welfare needs, child-labor laws, attendance, and other school adjustment situations. Often, especially in large school systems, they are the chief contact between home and school.

Specific guidance functions include (1) providing information relevant to developing plans and programs for meeting certain children's needs in the school, (2) assisting in the referral of children and their families to other agencies, and (3) casework with certain children.

Special-Education Personnel

Special-education teachers, speech and hearing specialists, and other similar personnel who staff programs for retarded, emotionally disturbed, physically handicapped, and gifted children, have commitments to youth which are intimately related to guidance responsibilities. They are concerned with securing for the child the best placement in available courses or remedial programs. Close cooperation between them and guidance personnel is a necessity.

---

[27] Norma E. Cutts (ed.), *School Psychologists at Mid-Century—A Report of the Thayer Conference on the Functions, Qualifications, and Training of School Psychologists* (Washington: American Psychological Association, 1955), pp. 30–31.

Health Personnel

School nurses, physicians, dentists, and psychiatrists frequently work within the educational setting. Few schools have the full-time services of these personnel, with the exception of school nurses. Nurses are often involved in the processing of students referred for psychological assistance. They screen the child's health history and note health factors such as operations, accidents, impaired hearing, poor eyesight or developmental difficulties.

FACTORS IN UTILIZING GUIDANCE PERSONNEL

It seems clear that guidance is not a one-person undertaking, that counselors do not "do guidance" by themselves. The change from sole responsibility (if indeed it ever existed) to the recognition that many personnel are involved in guidance has been dictated by the growing awareness of the requirements for program effectiveness. Guidance as conceived today is a complex undertaking, and its programs reach out in many directions. The counselor is to a high degree dependent upon the good will and support of his teaching colleagues, the parents, and other professionals. Building and conducting a comprehensive guidance program is a task beyond a single individual's capacity and intellectual resources. Counselors are expected to take the initiative in advancing proposals, in stimulating others to do so, and in being prepared to pool their ideas with others.

Staffing guidance programs cannot at any time be considered complete; it should never be frozen. Guidance personnel must always be flexible and able to change as the need for change becomes evident. New circumstances crop up, unanticipated complications develop, certain responsibilities prove in the course of experience to be impracticable. These and other happenings make difficult or undesirable an unvaried adherence to the details of previously planned assignments. Wise assignment of guidance responsibilities does not include rigid adherence to a prior assumption and doctrinaire principles which do not work in practice. This is not to urge that sound objectives and principles of staffing should be abandoned in favor of opportunistic practices. Rather, assignment of guidance responsibilities must at all times be done with cognizance of the complexity of effecting guidance improvement. Guidance personnel, if they are to be effective, must be adaptable to new conditions and pressures as they arise. Responsibility for guidance is a shared responsibility in which many participate. It is the restricted one-person program, already an anachronism in modern guidance, which will frustrate rather than foster the needs of youth.

Surveying the content and outlook of this chapter, three factors stand out in terms of the guidance responsibilities of a school staff. These are summarized below.

First, all personnel must have a clear understanding of fundamental guidance goals or objectives. Guidance is fundamentally concerned with increasing each pupil's personal development. The first essential for guidance personnel is to make this a living reality in the school rather than educational jargon. The more specific and clear the vision of what guidance can do, the more important the function of guidance will be and the more definitely it can be planned. What should be the objectives of guidance for this school is a question that underlies each comprehensive guidance program. Only by answering this question to their mutual satisfaction can a staff decide who does what. For these authors, the major objective of guidance is advancing self-development of students so that they can utilize their potentialities in productive ways for themselves and society.

Second, all personnel must be aware of what guidance is and what it can do. Improved guidance is every counselor's chief concern, and ultimately every plan of guidance services must concern itself with helping all personnel grow in effectiveness. It is mandatory that counselors, teachers, and administrators know the principles of guidance and that they constantly add to their knowledge by practice, reading, and observation of themselves and others. Any vision of what guidance is will provide the staff with some direction in which to move. As the vision develops and broadens, it will become more facilitating. As more and more staff members share in this understanding and participate in its practice, they will become increasingly emancipated from the deadening drudgery of traditional routine practice.

Third, all personnel must share their knowledge of possible guidance experiences for pupils. Each staff member has some insight into the possible guidance experiences that will enable pupils to grow and to develop toward intelligent and wholesome maturity. Counselors not only must be receptive to but must solicit suggestions of novel experiences from teachers and other school staff of desirable guidance experiences for pupils which can be introduced in the life of the school. Both suggestions and proposals should always be evaluated in relation to guidance objectives which have been deemed desirable and acceptable. Planning guidance experiences for pupils cannot be done without thorough knowledge of pupils and the community in which they live.

Finally, the effective use of personnel in the guidance program is not a short-term affair. Sound principles and practices in use today have been a long time in the making. Better distribution of professional assignments, correcting faults in the use of certain personnel, evaluation of how well things are being done, require time and thought.

ANNOTATED BIBLIOGRAPHY

HUMMEL, DEAN L., AND BONHAM, S. J., JR. *Pupil Personnel Services in Schools.* Chicago: Rand McNally and Company, 1967, 331 pp.
Chapter 3 (pp. 37–63) identifies the components of balanced pupil personnel programs. Brief descriptions are given of the functions of counselors and other personnel.

MILLER, FRANK W. *Guidance: Principles and Services. Second Edition.* Columbus, Ohio: Charles E. Merrill Books, Inc. 1968, 536 pp.

Part II (pp. 53–147) discusses the responsibilities of teachers and counselors in the guidance program. Brief treatment is given to the role of counselors in elementary schools as well as in secondary schools.

ROEBER, EDWARD C., WALZ, GARRY R., and SMITH, GLENN E. *A Strategy for Guidance.* London: Collier-Macmillan Limited, 1969, 293 pp.

Chapter 6 (pp. 133–156) and Chapter 9 (pp. 205–224) focus upon consultation and developing the school guidance staff. Seven guidelines are given as recommendations for developing a guidance program. These authors discuss various staff members' roles in guidance.

SELECTED REFERENCES

ARBUCKLE, DUGALD S. "Does the School Really Need Counselors?" *The School Counselor* Vol. 17 (May 1970), pp. 325–330.

———. "A Question of Counselor Function and Responsibility," *Personnel and Guidance Journal* Vol. 47 (December 1968), pp. 341–345.

CAMP, WILLIAM L., AND ROTHNEY, JOHN W. M. "Parental Response to Counselors' Suggestions," *The School Counselor* Vol. 17 (January 1970), pp. 200–203.

DUNCAN, L. WENDELL, AND FITZGERALD, PAUL W. "Increasing the Parent–Child Communication Through Counselor–Parent Conferences," *Personnel and Guidance Journal* Vol. 47 (February 1969), pp. 514–517.

ELLISON, MARTHA. "The Counselor as Seen by a Curriculum Development Specialist," *Counselor Education and Supervision* Vol. 8 (Fall 1968), pp. 66–72.

FRIEDLAND, STANLEY H. "Teacher–Counselor Friction: An Analysis," *The School Counselor* Vol. 16 (March 1969), pp. 263–267.

HAETTENSCHWILLER, DUNSTAN L. "Style of Role Enactment Expected of Parent, Teacher and Counselor," *Personnel and Guidance Journal* Vol. 47 (June 1969), pp. 963–969.

JONES, JOHN E. "Components of the High School Environment," *Personnel and Guidance Journal* Vol. 47 (September 1968), pp. 40–43.

LORIMER, JOHN, AND HADDAD, JOSEPH. "Pupil Personnel Services in the Elementary School," *Personnel and Guidance Journal* Vol. 47 (June 1969), pp. 975–978.

MACHT, LEE B. "Education and Mental Health: New Directions for Interaction," *Personnel and Guidance Journal* Vol. 47 (May 1969), pp. 855–858.

McGEHEARTY, LOYCE. "The Case for Consultation," *Personnel and Guidance Journal* Vol. 47 (November 1968), pp. 257–262.

MILLING, MARGARET. "An Elementary School Teacher and Group Guidance? You Bet!" *The School Counselor* Vol. 17 (September 1969), pp. 26–28.

PATTERSON, C. H. "The Counselor in the Elementary School," *Personnel and Guidance Journal* Vol. 47 (June 1969), pp. 979–986.

PERRONE, PHILIP A., AND GILBERTSON, CARLYLE W. "Case Study: A Research Approach to Establishing Pupil Services," *Personnel and Guidance Journal* Vol. 46 (June 1968), pp. 990–996.

QUINN, PAUL F. "Rapprochement—The Teacher and Counselor," *The School Counselor* Vol. 16 (January 1969), pp. 170–173.

WHITLEY, A. DAN, AND SULZER, BETH. "Reducing Disruptive Behavior Through Consultation," *Personnel and Guidance Journal* Vol. 48 (June 1970), pp. 836–841.

ZIMMER, JULES M. "Content Analysis of Counselor and Teacher Responses," *Personnel and Guidance Journal* Vol. 46 (January 1968), pp. 456–461.

15

GUIDANCE RELATIONSHIPS

What is the relationship of guidance to the curriculum?
What is the nature of the relationship between guidance and administration?
How is guidance related to discipline?
What relationship exists between school guidance and the home?

GUIDANCE AND CURRICULUM

School curricula change, sometimes slowly and imperceptibly, as society changes. Profound societal change upsets much that exists in the school's curricula and requires that careful attention be given to its purpose and content. Advances in sciences and technology call for extensive curriculum reconstruction if major youth maladjustments and discontinuities and certain nonrelevant skills and knowledges are to be avoided.

Curriculum Defined

In its broadest sense the curriculum includes the complete school environment, including courses, activities, and readings with which pupils come into contact in the school. But in a more limited and probably more realistic sense, the school curriculum is a systematic arrangement of courses of study designed to advance students' knowledge and competencies. Various types of curricula are commonly designated, such as college preparatory, general, business or commercial, home economics, vocational, industrial arts, and the like.

While considerable disagreement exists as to what specific experiences should be provided youth in the school, all individuals agree that the curriculum is the means by which a school achieves its aims and purposes.

There are some who are quite sure that certain academic subjects should be stressed, such as mathematics, science, grammar and languages; others stress vocational subjects and skills, while others (like the founders of the academy of old) urge the school to include everything that is both "useful and ornamental."

Some years ago, Smith, Stanley, and Shores pointed out that the curriculum is a reflection of what people think, feel, believe, and do. The school, charged with the responsibility for teaching certain things, sets up "A sequence of potential experiences . . . for the purpose of disciplining children and youth in group ways and acting."[1] The curriculum, then, is the planned learning activities engaged in by pupils to induct them into society. The basic purpose of such activities is to foster the intellectual development of the individual. Wrenn points out that while the schools in this generation are clearly concerned with intellectual growth, universal education has brought an increasing range of intellectual ability and academic motivation into the school. Consequently, social and emotional growth cannot be separated from intellectual growth.[2] To see that each pupil receives maximum benefit from the available curricular experiences is a responsibility shared by teachers, counselors, and administrators.

Relationship Between Guidance and Curriculum

Previously (see Chapter 2), guidance was defined as the process of helping pupils to know and understand themselves and their world. This does not mean that guidance has no concern or responsibility for the individual's intellectual development. Rather, its primary concern is with the individual's emotional and social development. Guidance activities and curricular activities are related in that both share the goal of helping an individual achieve his maximum potentiality and become capable of self-direction. However, guidance and curriculum are separated in their operational activities. One reason why they remain separate is the degree of complexity attached to the activities of each. Specialists are required in each field to provide the kinds of experiences demanded in a changing society. A second reason why guidance and curriculum are separated is that the learning activities provided through the curriculum are those common to groups of students rather than specific to individual students. The learnings provided by guidance services are highly individualized and tend to emphasize each individual's unique characteristics rather than the common needs of groups. Guidance focuses on the individual's need to learn about himself, his abilities, his interests, his values, and his aspirations. Guidance and curriculum are differentiated in terms of the major responsibility for

[1] B. Othanel Smith, William O. Stanley, and J. Harlan Shores, *Fundamentals of Curriculum Development* (New York: Harcourt, Brace & World, Inc., 1950), p. 4.

[2] C. Gilbert Wrenn, *The Counselor in a Changing World* (Washington: American Personnel and Guidance Association, 1962), p. 75.

their implementation in the schools; i.e., by counselors as contrasted to teachers. Miller states that it ". . . serves no useful purpose to try to make curriculum and guidance services identical. In practice, at least, their starting points are different."[3] But more important than whether guidance is separated or integrated operationally with curriculum, a clear need exists for reciprocal reinforcement. Counselors and teachers can only reinforce each other's efforts by being aware of what each tries to do and what each needs from the other.

Curricular Contributions to Guidance

Current developments in the schools are having an impact upon the curriculum. Morse,[4] Russell[5] and Trump[6] have vividly presented the developments that signal advances in curriculum development. Trump suggests that pupils will be exposed to three types of teaching and learning in the future: (1) large-group instruction may occupy 40 percent of student time; (2) independent study will comprise about 40 percent of their time; and (3) small groups will take the remainder of the time.[7]

Hutson has cited three basic principles of curriculum development which have implications for guidance. These include the following: (1) breadth of opportunity must be present, i.e., curricula should be available for pupils of different levels and kinds of ability; (2) flexibility is required so that pupils may have opportunities for self-discovery through exploration and experimentation without penalty; and (3) vertical and horizontal articulation must be present to enable pupils to plan meaningfully from one grade level to another, and to shift horizontally as situations require.[8]

Although a well-planned school curriculum, including the activities program, contributes in many ways to the development of the individual, three major contributions will be noted here. *First,* systematic curricular opportunities assist the developing pupil by offering experiences that contribute to feelings of adequacy and belonging. *Second,* curricular activities provide exploratory avenues through which pupils develop their interests and abilities. Curricular experiences, as part of the total activities experienced by the individual, provide situations in which pupils may learn what sort of individuals they are and begin to formulate and test an ideal self-concept of the sort of person they would like to be. *Third,* curricular ex-

---

[3] Carroll H. Miller, *Guidance Services* (New York: Harper & Row, Publishers, 1965), p. 49.

[4] Arthur D. Morse, *Schools of Tomorrow—Today* (Albany, N.Y.: The State Education Department, 1960).

[5] James E. Russell, *Change and Challenge in American Education* (Boston: Houghton Mifflin Company, 1965).

[6] J. Lloyd Trump, *Images of the Future* (Urbana, Ill.: Commission on the Experimental Study of the Utilization of Staff in the Secondary School, 1959).

[7] *Ibid.*

[8] Percival W. Hutson, *The Guidance Function in Education* Second Edition. (New York: Appleton-Century-Crofts, Inc., 1968), pp. 211–213.

periences contribute to guidance by providing youth with the knowledge needed for educational and vocational planning. Classes or units planned for such purposes provide needed environmental information on such matters as the meanings an occupation has for life and the satisfactions derived from engaging in certain occupations.

Guidance Contributions to Curriculum Development

The Association for Supervision and Curriculum Development, in its 1955 yearbook, suggests several ways in which guidance personnel can contribute to curriculum development in both the elementary and secondary school. Some of these suggestions are summarized here:

1. Counselors can help plan and supervise the gathering of facts essential to understanding each pupil so that teachers can individualize instruction and provide satisfying experiences for individual pupils.
2. Counselors can help teachers interpret and use these facts in contacts with parents and pupils.
3. Counselors can help school administrators, teachers, and parents with the implications and applications of what is known about child growth and development in such ways as placement of the child in curricular areas.
4. Counselors can help teachers use guidance tools more effectively, i.e., interpreting tests, referring pupils, pupil planning, and the like.[9]

But more directly related to the purposes of the present discussion are two major ways that guidance contributes to curriculum development. In the first instance, the needs of individuals and groups for curricular extensions and activities may become visible through counseling, testing, planning, followup, and other guidance activities. Counselors can be instrumental in providing curriculum specialists with data that describe the student body's ability range, achievements, strengths and deficiencies, interests, problems, socioeconomic backgrounds, educational objectives and other characteristics that are essential to curriculum development. To suggest modifications or extensions to curriculum committees based upon such data is part of the counselor's consultative functions (see Chapter 14). While it is true that few, if any, schools are able to operate on an ideal level of serving all the needs of all pupils, in practical curriculum planning, knowledge of pupil needs helps to establish priorities and suggests where major efforts should be placed to meet the most important needs.

In the second instance, counselors help the student to understand and choose curricular offerings best suited to develop social and vocational competencies necessary for effective living in a complex society. If the curriculum pursued by the individual is to be meaningful, decisions as to what he pursues must be individualized, balanced in respect to his skills, knowledges, and purposes, with unlimited opportunity for expressing initiative and creative capacities.

[9] Abstracted from Association for Supervision and Curriculum Development, National Education Association, *Guidance in the Curriculum,* 1955 Yearbook (Washington: The Association, 1955), pp. 104–126.

In summary, if guidance and curriculum development are to function as integral parts of the school and be concerned with the developmental needs of all youth, personnel in both specialities must exercise cooperative leadership. Both groups must experiment with ways to mobilize the school's resources to promote pupil development. Through cooperative research efforts, data will be secured for revising curricular and guidance services so that each becomes a positive continuing force designed to facilitate student development and growth. Individuals in both groups can supplement, emphasize, intensify, and support each other's work with individuals and groups.

GUIDANCE AND ADMINISTRATION

The purpose of this discussion is to clarify the relationships between guidance and administration. Several studies have indicated the need for clarification because many counselors perform administrative functions.

Administrative Functions

As the purposes of the school have encompassed the total development of the child, an increasing number of responsibilities have devolved upon it. Not only has the curriculum been broadened to teach students the many skills they need to take their place in society, but services have increased in number and kind. These services exist to create conditions in which learning can best take place.

The sheer weight and number of these responsibilities and enlarging services bring into sharp focus the necessity for professional administrative leadership. The central purpose of administration is to coordinate the efforts of people to achieve the goals of the organization. In education this means that administrative functions are those centering on enhancing teaching and learning.

Educational organization and administration are two interrelated phases in the processes of facilitating teaching and learning. *Organization* is basically concerned with making arrangements to enable the school to realize its purpose. Organization and/or reorganization is necessary because imperfections appear in existing arrangements, original purposes become modified or extended, conditions change, and/or new techniques are discovered. *Administration* is concerned with the conduct, operation, and management of the school. Administration implies authority and responsibility. As a process it seeks to manage situations by which people of differing skills, interests, and abilities focus their efforts to achieve the goals of an enterprise. Vested authority gives school administrators the privilege to act in the best interests of the citizens of the community. Responsibility is attached to authority, which means that an accounting may be requested regarding the success or failure of the organization.

Campbell, Corbally, and Ramseyer cite three primary types of activities school administrators are required to perform to advance teaching and learning: (1) to discern and influence the development of goals and policies basic to teaching and learning; (2) to stimulate and to facilitate the planning and operation of appropriate programs for teaching and learning; and (3) to procure and to manage personnel and material to implement the programs of teaching and learning.[10]

The suggestion by Campbell and his associates that administrators not only discern but also *influence* goals and policies is a departure from typical formulations. Their point is that the division between policy-making and administration is not a clear one and that administrators necessarily influence policy as they discern and clarify it.

Guidance as Related to Administration

The administrative functions cited above, though generally stated and perhaps somewhat theoretical in nature, place in bold relief the differences between guidance and administration. Administration exists to move the school toward fulfillment of its goals; it is appropriately institution centered and exists to facilitate the institution as a whole. The school administrator is concerned about the efficiency of the school system. He makes certain that a sufficient number of staff members have been recruited to perform each task assigned. He sees that buildings are constructed and maintained near where students live. He is responsible for students' being fed, kept warm and comfortable, and transported to and from school. He is concerned that the end product of a 12-year sequence resembles what the community wants.

Guidance is responsible for protecting and preserving the interests of the individual; it is structured to help the individual attain his goals.

In a research article, Filbeck clearly differentiates between counselors and principals:

> The typical school principal studied in this investigation, in situations where the individual student is in conflict with the policies or practices of the school or with the larger social order, favors an approach by the counselor that: (1) is supportive of the school's policies, (2) is reinforcing for student conformity to social standards or norms of behavior, (3) is reinforcing of student acceptance of status quo, (4) promises to reduce the likelihood that students will overtly challenge or threaten the authority of the school.
>
> The counselors, on the other hand, tended to stress an approach that emphasized student decision-making based on individual values and factors.[11]

[10] Roald F. Campbell, John E. Corbally, Jr., and John A. Ramseyer, *Introduction to Educational Administration* (Boston: Allyn and Bacon, Inc., 1962), p. 76.

[11] Robert W. Filbeck, "Perceptions of Appropriateness of Counselor Behavior: A Comparison of Counselors and Principals," *Personnel and Guidance Journal* Vol. 43 (May 1965), p. 895.

Kehas has charged that the way authority has been defined and distributed in schools works against the development of a distinctive guidance function. Pointing out that his argument is not to ask administrators to "understand counselors better" but rather to call for a functional allocation of authority based on competence and expertise instead of "ultimate" authority, Kehas states:

> Serious examination and study should be given to the question of authority in school systems, and primarily to the notion of the "autonomy of the principal in *his* school." Such examination and study is necessary because of the central importance of this notion in the actual administration and organization of the schools. Further, I would argue that a redistribution of authority as regards the guidance function must come about—that authority for guidance in a system must reside with the chief guidance officer of that system, and that the involvement of others with the *basic* decisions regarding guidance must be circumscribed.[12]

Kehas envisions counselors as being primarily responsible to the director of guidance for some things and to the principal for others, depending on whether the activities involve institutional responsibilities or involvement with students.

It is recognized that the discussion here tends to place guidance (emphasis upon the individual) in opposition to administration (emphasis upon the institution). However, it cannot be overlooked that individual needs and institutional needs are often fused and not separated. Institutions are populated by people, and individuals find satisfaction in the company of others. But the purpose here is to make clear that guidance is not administration and must not be so construed. Administrative functions serve to provide machinery and direction to the organization so that its goals can be achieved with efficiency and adequacy. Probably some conflict between guidance functions and administrative functions is inevitable because of basic differences in philosophy, role, and responsibility. This does not mean, however, that administration should be construed as inimical to guidance. Dichotomizing the two services—guidance as an agent for the individual and administration as an agent for society—exaggerates the issue and does an injustice to the goals of both. Administration at its best provides a climate for learning which includes learning about one's self as well as one's world. Theoretically, both services encourage freedom of inquiry, exploration, and action, along with sensitivity to and responsiveness to individuality. The realities of a school society encourage both freedom and responsible action. Guidance and administration seek to secure for the individual pupil a sense that he is an individual functioning in a society.

To say that guidance and administration are both central parts of the total educational effort is not to imply that the two are identical or are substitutes for the other. Each has an identity of its own. Each provides spe-

[12] Chris D. Kehas, "Administrative Structure and Guidance Theory," *Counselor Education and Supervision* Vol. 4 (Spring 1965), pp. 147–148.

cialized services to pupils and teachers. Each must operate within the broad philosophy of a school society.

Administrative Deterrents to Guidance

There is no desire here to make administrators scapegoats for ineffective guidance programs. But it seems important to note some of the chief administrative deterrents that may impair the operations of a guidance program. Though lack of staff, leadership, facilities, and money are often cited as major deterrents, other equally serious impediments may exist, with the factors mentioned being symptoms rather than causes.

Perhaps the most critical deterrent is one noted by Landy:

> Unfortunately many administrators, who recognize their limitations in various areas of subject matter and methods of teaching, and who are quite willing to allow specialists in those fields to take on leadership roles, assume an expertness in the field of guidance that they do not possess.
>
> Of course "experts" or specialists in a particular field need to be under the overall supervision and policy control of the general administrator. And he can provide good ideas or a useful healthful skepticism.[13]

Peters cites nine factors that interfere with guidance program development. Although these are not just administrative in nature, they do have relevant implications for the management of the guidance program. The nine include the facts that (1) guidance workers and school counselors have tended to avoid theory development; (2) discrepancies exist between stated program premises and program practices; (3) guidance workers have assumed that their publics understand the nature and purpose of guidance, which they do not; (4) differences may exist in basic value orientations held by school counselors and their principals; (5) custom and self-interest are rationalizations for omission of needed leadership; (6) counselors and staff members resist either overtly or covertly change and new experiences; (7) the counselor's broad role commitment to and security in his former teacher role induces a marginal professional commitment to guidance; (8) lack of depth in counseling; and (9) inattention to the changing adolescent.[14]

Shertzer and Stone cite the following as detrimental actions by school administrators: (1) inadequate programing of guidance by emphasizing large-group services rather than services to the individual; (2) appealing to the public and justifying guidance services on nonlogical terms such as the superiority of "our school" over "their school"; (3) assigning administrative duties to counselors after justifying the hiring of counselors with the

[13] Edward Landy, "Who Does What in the Guidance Program?" *The School Counselor* Vol. 10 (March 1963), p. 115.

[14] Herman J. Peters, "Interferences to Guidance Program Development," *Personnel and Guidance Journal"* Vol. 42 (October 1963), pp. 119–124.

argument that they are needed to provide individual counseling relationships with students; (4) postponing guidance program development on the basis that controversies in the field ought to be clarified before proceeding with the program; (5) providing inadequate physical facilities and budgets; (6) fostering the notion that the existence of guidance services in the schools is a cure-all for every educational difficulty.[15]

Although it is true that vigorous professional administrative leadership alone cannot overcome some of these impediments imposed by problems outside its sphere of influence, administrators can and should address themselves to important, immediate and long-range problems which can be resolved. Though some changes may not suffice to produce the whole of needed reform, they will serve to effect many needed guidance improvements.

What Guidance Personnel Expect from Administrators

What can guidance personnel legitimately expect from administrative personnel? The discussion in Chapter 14 cited some of the major guidance responsibilities of school administrators, including exercising executive leadership for the program, securing physical facilities, providing adequate budgets and qualified personnel, and interpreting the program to the public. Aside from these fundamental tangible elements, what kind of working relationships can guidance personnel legitimately expect from school administrators?

First, guidance personnel can legitimately expect school administrators to provide challenge and vitality in their executive leadership. Though alternating patterns of inactivity and dynamic movement tend to be characteristic of leadership, positive direction and support calculated to evoke creative variations in program development can be supplied. Ideal leadership stimulates personnel to move forward from one program achievement to fresh struggles, from the solution of one problem to the confrontation of another. Such leadership is marked by an *elan* which projects its personnel from challenge through response to further challenge and ultimately toward both outward and inward growth. External growth manifests itself through an extension of services based upon student needs, while inward growth expresses itself in the progressive improvements in existing services.

Second, guidance personnel can legitimately expect school administrators to insist upon guidance services that are integrated and bound together by common purpose and relationship. Unrelated services do not constitute a program. By definition, a program has purpose and organization, with its component services interrelated and pointing toward defined consistent objectives. Counselors and teachers can expect the school administrator to insist that they be clear as to what they are trying to achieve in guidance

[15] Bruce Shertzer and Shelley C. Stone, "Administrative Deterrents to Guidance Program Development," *Theory Into Practice* Vol. 2 (February 1961), pp. 24–32.

and that the means employed be appropriate to the total school purposes.

Third, guidance personnel can legitimately expect administrators to utilize them as a planning group for future guidance program developments. Although administrators are expected to initiate planning, guide it, and coordinate contributions to it, ready-made, dictated plans rarely fit situations or produce sound educational policy. Cooperative guidance planning, in which proposals from counselors and teachers are weighed and tested, should be the approach of every administrator. Having personnel feel a sense of responsibility and participation in planning and policy formulation is an effective way of achieving high morale as well as program objectives.

Fourth, guidance personnel should expect school administrators to maintain an evaluative attitude toward the program. Since responsibility accompanies authority, a close review of the progress of any program is necessary. Administrators are expected to ask for evidence showing how the program is operating, as well as for facts regarding the extent to which expressed outcomes have been achieved. By so doing, the program can be expected to operate more smoothly and effectively. Modifications and adjustments, when and where needed, can be made intelligently.

Fifth, guidance personnel should expect school administrators to insist upon program continuity, integration, and balance. This book has repeatedly emphasized that an effective guidance program cannot be developed in isolation from other educational, social, and psychological forces. Continuity in the sense of being linked to other educational activities, and in terms of being linked to prior and expected program developments, must be assured. Administrators are responsible for providing balance in the total program.

Sixth, guidance personnel expect administrators to reduce the burden of routine clerical and administrative duties and to free them for productive professional responsibilities. Guidance personnel whose energies are largely expended in doing minor clerical and administrative activities are unlikely to accomplish guidance functions. Those personnel who are unsuited to the work or are professionally incompetent should be discharged by the administrator. Conversely, guidance personnel whose work reflects superiority should be recognized and rewarded.

What Administrators Expect from Guidance Personnel

First and foremost, administrators can expect guidance personnel to champion the individual, to "care" for the pupil. They can expect counselors to stress ways in which pupils can gain help in understanding themselves and other people, in trying out their understandings, getting the most out of school, and exploring their interests and abilities. By so doing, counselors facilitate the accomplishment of school goals.

Administrators can expect guidance personnel to supply them with research evidence of student achievement, interests, and progress in school and post-school activities. This permits administrators to study ways in which the school is accomplishing its goals.

Administrators can expect guidance personnel to help the school's staff see more clearly the problems and needs of students and to help provide for these needs. Although many pupil problems stem from the maturation process, others flow from social and economic forces and pressures. Counselors can aid teachers in becoming more aware of and sensitive to the needs of pupils at various stages of development.

Administrators can expect guidance personnel to act responsibly and professionally. Without question, they want guidance personnel who are professionally prepared, who understand the nature of society and the part that schools play in it. They expect guidance personnel to grow in their positions, to constantly analyze their duties with regard to what they do well and what needs improvement. They expect them to read systematically the professional literature and to participate in professional groups, activities, and organizations.

GUIDANCE AND DISCIPLINE

Everyone seems to have his own idea of what discipline is. It is indeed an elusive concept. Combining the terms, "guidance" and "discipline," tends to create disagreement and produces additional confusion. Balance needs to be found in the relationship between the two terms.

Concepts of Discipline

The term "discipline" is most commonly restricted to situations involving the handling of misbehavior by imposing punishment. Lee clearly states this view:

> . . . disciplinary role implies a *punitive power*. This power is of necessity external, exclusively directive, and threatening. It is external because it is imposed upon the student by the administrative authorities. It is exclusively directive because it spells out in precise terms what these authorities wish the student to do or undo. It is threatening because of its essence, punishment must be threatening to a person.[16]

This concept of discipline requires that social control, based upon imposing conformity, or obedience to authority, will be maintained by external restraining authorities such as parents, teachers, principals or representatives of the law.

A second view of discipline emphasizes its rehabilitative function for those who commit errors. Discipline is seen as a reconstructive effort so that errant individuals may find substitute channels for unacceptable actions that result from feelings of frustration and disappointment.

[16] James Michael Lee, "Counseling Versus Discipline: Another View," *The Catholic Counselor* Vol. 7 (Spring 1963), pp. 114–119.

A third conception of discipline is that it is a preventive force. Optimum development of individuals comes through providing an emotional climate and environment that encourages, assists, and permits positive healthy attitudes and feelings. The school or home environment should be minimally repressive so that little motivation for misbehaving exists. This type of environment encourages the discovery of satisfactions that conform to healthy, acceptable social standards. This view of discipline is focused upon training to develop self-control.

A fourth concept of discipline is that it is a process designed to help individuals accept the reality of external authority. Advocates of this concept of discipline believe that students who misbehave need help in perceiving and accepting authority as it impinges upon their inner life and overt behavior. The disciplinary process stresses the fact that misbehaving individuals need to learn to understand and accept emotionally the necessity and wisdom of authority as it affects responsible self-direction in society.

From the guidance point of view, discipline is most often conceived as a means of correcting the fault-lines in the individual's personality, rather than as the external maintenance of social control. Discipline as punishment alone, or as a means of encouraging conformity, is less apt to be corrective or growth-producing. Active rehabilitative procedures are needed to transform misbehavior into enlightened self-directed behavior.

Factors Influencing School Discipline

Factors often pointed out as causing school discipline problems are arbitrarily imposed authoritarian methods; lack of planning, preparation, and purpose in the school; disorderly classrooms; and indecisiveness or favoritism and unfairness on the part of school staff members. On the other hand, discipline problems tend to be minimized in schools where there is curriculum improvement and revision directed toward serving students; where there is an extracurricular program that stimulates and satisfies student interests; where there is counseling for students that helps them toward maximum development; and where there are administrators who are willing to allow participation in the solution of school problems by teachers, counselors, and students themselves. From a consideration of these factors, it seems evident that good school discipline depends on something more fundamental than the administration of restraints. The student learns self-discipline through experiences that help him recognize the rights of others and balance these with his own needs for independence. Young people can best learn both responsibilities and rights in a democratically organized school system where they have an opportunity to participate in solving problems and a voice in determining their own regulation.

The causes of misbehavior are legion. Fundamentally, individuals who misbehave have unsatisfied emotional needs. Resentment and rejection in the home, school, and/or community frequently induce deviations in behavior toward oneself and others. Misconduct is symptomatic behavior, and symptoms disappear when the underlying pressures are relieved. Students who become problems in the classroom are usually students who have some individual difficulty. Some of them may have an unhappy home life, and others may have no close friends in school. There may be some who cannot do the work of the class, or some who find the work unchallenging. Some may have physical problems that interfere with their school adjustment. Many other examples could be given, but fundamentally, the problem is that the emotional needs of individuals are not being met.

Students such as these may express their feelings of inadequacy or frustration in a variety of negativistic ways. They may break rules, hurt other people, "talk back," destroy property, refuse to do their schoolwork, be truant, be insolent to teachers, swear, etc. Any behavior that interferes with learning and cooperative living in the classroom and school must be dealt with firmly, and the student who is responsible must be disciplined. However, disciplinary action or penalty that is not followed up with a well-organized plan to remove the causes of misbehavior tends to create even more serious problems. A student can grow toward self-discipline only as he understands his behavior and the way it affects himself and others. Thus, discipline as punishment is no real corrective of misbehavior.

Today's Shifting Standards[17]

In a discipline program, the school administrator has problems peculiar to his times, his school, his generation. These problems may not be any more difficult, pressing, or numerous than those of other schools or generations; they are merely different, which means that he probably cannot rely on techniques, ideologies, pressures or solutions that have been developed at other times and places.

Every school administrator involved in the area of discipline has the problem of establishing school standards in both morals and manners according to conventional folkways or ideologies that prevail in the society of his time. To be sure, every student, faculty member, and administrator has a share in this process. No one person or group can do it alone, nor is it the total responsibility of only one individual or group. It cannot be done independently of the world outside the school.

It is perhaps becoming trite and platitudinous to state that society is shifting rapidly from absolute to relative standards, or even to reiterate with the modern sociologist that individuals are tending to be less and less "inner-directed" and more and more "other-directed" in their values and behavior patterns. Translated into everyday behavior problems, this means that students do not hold to an absolute standard of "right" and "wrong" according to a traditional, "revealed" formula, which they know to be generally accepted by the society in which they live. This does not mean, however, that students today are any "better" or any "worse" in their general

[17] Abstracted from Kate Hevner Mueller, *Student Personnel Work in Higher Education* (Boston: Houghton Mifflin Company, 1961), pp. 360–362.

behavior than children who lived in another age or under a different system of ethical standards.

The relativity and variety of today's standards does mean that the administrator has an added problem in the field of discipline, which the administrator in previous times may not have had. He must help the school community decide which of many current ethical systems is most acceptable and how it can best be strengthened. His difficulty is all the greater because of the common knowledge that values, religious beliefs, ethics have changed, are currently in transition, and probably will continue to change. In earlier centuries when technological and conceptual changes evolved more slowly, when mass communication proceeded slowly, awareness of change and the concomitant uncertainties of mind and spirit that accompany such awareness were much less disruptive.

Pupils bring with them from the world outside the school the weaknesses and strengths in current morality. However, they seem to assimilate the weaknesses more readily than the strengths, perhaps because the immaturity of youth make them the more vulnerable—especially to attractive weaknesses. The common acceptance of statements about the "idealism" of youth is perhaps misleading. Such "idealism" may prove to be merely a set of beliefs that remains intact because it is untried and untested in the harsh outside world.

The school administrator often feels uncertain in his role of disciplinarian, and this uncertainty leads to vulnerability. When he is not clear regarding the positions he must take on issues, it is difficult for him to know when and where to compromise, negotiate, or persuade. Effective discipline frequently requires compromise, middle courses, half measures, arbitration, conciliation, and postponement. The quality and effectiveness of a disciplinarian's compromises derive from (1) a knowledge of students; (2) an understanding of both social problems and techniques of social control; (3) the educational and preventive programs of the school; (4) an ability to dramatize the positive aspects of discipline and morale-building projects.

Guidance and/or Discipline?

Should the counselor be asked to administer disciplinary measures? Should he be placed in a position that requires him to make direct judgments on a student's behavior? These and other similar questions have been debated for some thirty years. Figure 15 summarizes some arguments of those who believe that counselors should be free of the disciplinary process and some arguments of those who believe that counselors *should* handle discipline.

The Counselor's Role in Discipline

A widely held view which this text supports is that the counselor must be involved in the disciplinary *process*. The involvement is of a particular kind, however, i.e., as counselor to the student who has misbehaved; the

FIGURE 15
Guidance and Discipline

Counselors Should be Involved in Discipline	Counselors Should be Free of Discipline
1. Those who misbehave are most in need of counseling to clarify their emotions and actions.	1. Supervision and enforcement of regulations for the common good are a responsibility of the administration.
2. If counselors are not involved in disciplinary cases, guidance is limited in its usefulness, since it would be only for the good, conforming pupil.	2. Counselors involved in discipline become identified as authority figures which threatens their acceptive, non-judgmental role as counselors.
3. Counselors are needed to diagnose and treat the correctable causes of misbehavior.	3. Each discipline case requires exhaustive investigation which would mean that counselors would have little time left to use their counseling skills as they should be used.
4. Disciplinary work at its best is preventative, the counselor's skills and attitudes are attuned to preventative work.	4. Counseling requires a permissive, self-initiated relationship rather than the compelled relationship that characterizes discipline.
5. The goal of discipline—self-discipline, self-direction, self-growth, and self-development—is the goal of guidance.	5. Discipline—enforcing conformity—is a public process; guidance is private and confidential.
6. Rehabilitation requires the use of guidance principles, psychological diagnosis and skills possessed only by counselors in schools.	6. Discipline is centered on the community, school or group while guidance is centered on the individual.
	7. Williamson has characterized discipline with such words as repressive, regulatory, forced conformity, law abiding, orderliness, imposed, forced control; while counseling is described as growth producing, ego strengthening, self-regulating, affecting integration, confidence development, self-initiated, self-centered.

From E. G. Williamson, "The Fusion of Discipline and Counseling in the Educative Process," *Personnel and Guidance Journal* Vol. 34 (October 1955), p. 74.

counselor has the responsibility of helping him explore, sort out, understand, and correct the motivations underlying his misbehavior. The actual meting out of punishment is an administrative function. Unfortunately, this view places principals and deans in the role of "bad guys"—as harsh, demanding, threatening, authoritative figures.

According to this view of the counselor's role in discipline, teachers would refer pupils who are in need of counseling before a situation develops that calls for overt punishment. Such referral requires exceptional care and skill, otherwise the pupil is merely *sentenced* to counseling. According to this view, counseling is directed toward a preventive function by helping individuals to (1) achieve an understanding of their behavior and (2) develop self-control before more serious problems develop. Mueller comments:

The counselor's job is not to search and pin-point any one cause, nor to indulge in superficial philosophizing about life's dilemmas. His job is to bring the particular behavior in question into a different perspective for his client, to give him a useful way of looking at this behavior and at himself, to help him adopt an attitude with the proper balance between responsibility and irresponsibility—neither that of the victim nor of dictator, but rather an attitude which suggests: "I did it, and the reason is myself."

It is not exceedingly difficult for the counselor to ascertain whether he is dealing with a disciplinary case or a case requiring therapeutic counseling, and it is as ridiculous to treat the normal but erring student with elaborate therapy as it is to treat the common cold with a complete physical examination and a two-week hospitalization.[18]

For those students whose misbehavior is serious enough to require referral to the principal, the principal should notify the counselor so that arrangements can be made with the student for an interview aimed at determining the causes of the misbehavior. Both the principal and the counselor are concerned with what is best for the pupil, but they do not perform the same functions. The disciplinarian, or principal, must act to enforce the rules of the school and curb the activities of those who have not been able to discipline themselves. Thus, he is forced into a judgmental role and required to take punitive action of some kind.

The counselor can best serve the student's needs when he is not required to pass judgment on a student's actions or to punish infringements of school rules. It should be emphasized that this does not mean that the counselor condones a student's misbehavior or refrains from discussing it in a counseling interview. The counseling relationship requires that the student feel a sense of trust in the counselor as an individual with whom he can discuss his problems freely, without fear of punishment or violation of confidence, even when some problems may concern conflicts with other members of the school staff. In this process, the counselor does not perform the function of disciplinary officer, but he does have a clearly defined, constructive responsibility in good school discipline.

OTHER RESPONSIBILITIES

Other ways in which counselors can use their specialized skills and training to help students solve problems and help the school staff achieve better school discipline are briefly summarized here. Such practices include (1) clarifying for teachers classroom activities that will help students who misbehave; (2) helping teachers to identify as early as possible students who may need help; (3) establishing regular procedures for automatic referrals which encourage teachers and administrators to notify counselors of potential or actual disciplinary cases; and (4) helping students, teachers, parents, and administrators to establish codes of student conduct that are workable and acceptable to all.

---

[18] Mueller, *Student Personnel Work*, p. 355. Reprinted by permission.

RESEARCH STUDIES

Although few research studies can be cited to support the view that guidance functions should be separated from administrative functions, or vice versa, Jensen obtained reactions from a random sample of 20 percent of eight thousand Phoenix, Arizona, high school students, grades 9–12, as to whom they would approach for assistance with problems. From this data, Jensen concluded that deans of boys and girls (known by the students to be responsible for school discipline) were avoided because of their authoritative roles.[19]

Gilbert studied students' perceptions of ideal and actual student-counselor relationships in three different school districts. The degree of responsibility for discipline in the districts varied from none to total responsibility. Students agreed that ideally the counselor's role should not be linked with discipline or authority. In the school in which counselors had no discipline responsibility pupils described the student-counselor relationship as closer to the ideal than did students in the other two schools.[20]

Discipline Programs

Policies for handling discipline should be formulated through the combined efforts of the faculty, administration, and teachers. The effectiveness of programs so formulated in schools in which they exist indicates that the effort is worthwhile. For example, the Alfred Vail Junior High School, Morris Township, Morris Plains, N.J., has such a program. Lynch has reported that school personnel there believe that (1) there is a relationship between discipline and problems and the kind of job teachers and other school people do in planning; (2) classroom control can be exercised equally well by men and women teachers, and by old and young teachers, provided they are willing to learn and use sound principles of guidance and human relations; (3) it is possible to organize both a school and an individual classroom in such a way as to avoid many situations that cause trouble; and (4) a friendly pupil-teacher relationship is the most important factor in avoiding disciplinary problems, since students exhibit better behavior when they can participate in determining classroom and school policies and help determine their own behavior. Lynch reports that the school had the familiar problems, ranging from disorder on the school bus to faulty personality adjustments. Measures taken to solve these problems included (1) dispensing with uniformity of punishment for all problems; only two offenses were subject to immediate and prescribed punishment—smoking on the school grounds and leaving the grounds without permission; (2) achieving good school morale and an understanding of school policy through

---

[19] Ralph E. Jensen, "Students' Feelings About Counseling Help," *Personnel and Guidance Journal* Vol. 33 (May 1955), pp. 498–503.

[20] Norman S. Gilbert, "When the Counselor Is a Disciplinarian," *Personnel and Guidance Journal* Vol. 43 (January 1965), pp. 485–491.

an inservice program for new teachers in the techniques and methods that seem to work in the particular school environment, and a review of the fundamental principles of human relations and mental hygiene by the experienced teachers; (3) having a faculty meeting once a year to discuss the subject of discipline; there were also additional conferences for new teachers involving the use of school services and an analysis of and methods for handling situations of various kinds.

According to Lynch, the results of the program were gratifying. Of 232 students counseled and assisted on various matters, long-term adjustment was made in approximately 75 percent of the cases. Of the remaining 25 percent, cooperation with the parents was sought, and efforts on the part of the school continued.[21]

Williamson and Foley, who view discipline as fused with counseling, have schematically outlined the following sequence of procedures for college personnel programs:

1. Identification of alleged disciplinary situations.
2. Identification of student or students allegedly involved.
3. Report of situation to the counselor.
4. Charges made against student.
5. Case investigation made.
6. Student interviewed for counseling purposes.
7. Appraisal of causes of incident-behavior.
8. Assessment of potentialities for rehabilitation.
9. Tentative formulation of needed rehabilitation steps.
10. Comprehensive report to committee.
11. Review and deliberation by committee (or official).
12. Consultation and review by committee with student.
13. Action by committee (or official).
14. Enforcement of committee action.
15. Rehabilitation counseling as long as needed.[22]

Gometz and Parker stated that the procedures cited above need to be modified because of certain changes in educational practice since 1949. They note, *first,* that the American Civil Liberties Union has crusaded for the protection of students' rights on campus. These rights are theirs by virtue of being citizens. For example, "due process" has been interjected into the disciplinary process. *Second,* Gometz and Parker believe that very few students who are seen by the "Disciplinary Counseling Office" actually go through these steps because (a) much of what they do is minor and can be treated simply, and (b) many students gain insight and achieve behavioral change so that extensive administrative procedures are unnecessary.[23]

[21] James M. Lynch, Jr., "For Good Discipline, You Must Plan," *Bulletin of the National Association of Secondary School Principals* Vol. 38 (March 1954), pp. 56–59.

[22] E. G. Williamson and J. D. Foley, *Counseling and Discipline* (New York: McGraw-Hill Book Co., Inc., 1949), pp. 61–62.

[23] Lynn Gometz and Clyde A. Parker, "Disciplinary Counseling: A Contradiction?" *Personnel and Guidance Journal* Vol. 46 (January 1968), pp. 441–442.

Currently, school officials are seeking ways to incorporate "due process" within disciplinary procedures. Without due process, the mere accusation of rule violations convicts the student for there is no presumption of innocence until evidence is heard. Due process means that the student is given an opportunity to defend himself against accusations.

In a report of their use of group counseling with underachieving, "acting-out" junior high school boys, Gibian and his associates say that although such students "harbored hostile feelings toward others and seemed externally to be very sure of themselves, they were actually very insecure and had very basic needs for warmth, understanding and acceptance from the very people they tried to punish: parents, teachers, and peers." These authors urge school personnel to become more sensitive to such pupils' needs, to look beyond their overt behavior, to realize that their aggressive behavior is not aimed at school personnel personally, and to be consistently acceptant of them.[24]

GUIDANCE AND THE HOME

Mechanical inventions, scientific discoveries, new ideas, and economic changes have all deeply affected the form and character of home life. These processes are still in progress today. Increasingly, many of the home's functions are being taken over by social agencies, as larger and larger numbers of mothers are gainfully employed and families become more mobile. Sociologists have sometimes claimed that the home is no longer the inclusive focus of its members' interests. Because of this, the home's common interests are increasingly being restricted to limited functions, and the breakdown or disappearance of the family as a social unit is pessimistically seen as inevitable. Other sociologists see the instability of the modern home (as measured by divorce rates, separations, domestic discord) as the byproducts of man's attempt to evolve new patterns of human relationships. If such new patterns are in the process of evolving, instability of home life probably will persist.

School-Home Cooperation

Research findings reported in *Elmtown's Youth*[25] and in *The Psychology of Character Development*[26] strikingly reveal the multiplicity of effects of the home environment upon the individual. The inculcation of values and attitudes, the conditioning of daily habits of living, the shaping of outlooks on life, the value of and commitment to education all testify to the impact

[24] Edward J. Gibian, Benjamin Cohn, Charles F. Combs, and A. Mead Sniffen, "The Acting-Out Underachiever," *The School Counselor* Vol. 11 (May 1964), pp. 200–205.

[25] A. B. Hollingshead, *Elmtown's Youth* (New York: John Wiley & Sons, Inc., 1949).

[26] Robert F. Peck and Robert J. Havighurst, *The Psychology of Character Development* (New York: John Wiley & Sons, Inc, 1960).

of the home. Though education is sometimes accused of assuming more and more of the home's responsibilities for youth development, more perceptive judgments indicate that the schools are a reflection only of what the members of society expect and demand of them.

There is mutual advantage to home and school when close contacts are maintained. The pupil is the one who benefits if the school and home reinforce each other in their reciprocal task of educating and socializing him. Parents often need help in understanding their children and in appreciating fully the emotional and social factors that bear upon his development. Parents should be encouraged to visit schools frequently, made to feel welcome, and urged to confer with members of the school staff. Such efforts strengthen both the school and the home.

Guidance Services and the Home

Some forward-looking guidance staffs are conducting parent study groups directed toward learning more about children's problems. As a result, the child's ego-ideals in the home and school tend to be mutually reinforcing. Arony reports that such study groups result in (1) better parental understanding of adolescents; (2) a greater awareness of the guidance process; (3) a sharper awareness of the social needs and educational aspirations of youth; and (4) more efficient parent-counselor guidance conferences.[27] Other staffs are encouraging frequent home visitations by counselors and teachers and providing some training for this through professional improvement programs. In addition, many school staffs conduct continuous parent-education programs and, as always, fight the continual problem of trying to reach those parents who most need help. Such courses attempt to relate directly to the problems met in everyday family living, personal relations, and homemaking. Other guidance staffs are offering counseling services to parents, since many parents, at one time or another, face critical problems and need the help of trained professional workers. Two questions immediately arise in connection with such services. The first concerns the legitimacy of the school's providing such a service when other agencies exist for that purpose. The second is that of getting the service to the right home at the right time without having the home become dependent upon the school in meeting future problems of living.

The school and home are, of course, two of the strongest forces in the lives of children. The strength of these two can be markedly increased if effective schools work cooperatively with homes to reduce the factors that disrupt youth and to rehabilitate children who already show undesirable behavior. The schools occupy a central position in providing guidance to youth. They have close and continued contacts with every child over a period of time. They receive him early in life and have as their central

[27] Edward R. Arony, "Helping Parents Understand Adolescence," *Bulletin of the National Association of Secondary School Principals* Vol. 45 (May 1961), pp. 27–31.

objective assisting him directly to become a well-integrated, useful citizen. Because the schools enroll virtually all children, and because counselors are trained to deal with youth and their problems, they have a tactical advantage enjoyed by no other social agency concerned with youth guidance and development. It should also be recognized, however, that the school is only one of many agencies dealing with young people.

Since parents and the school are concerned with guidance, neither should expect to blueprint an effective plan for guidance independently. An effective program will emerge only in situations in which cooperative planning and actions are undertaken. Cooperative participation processes may necessarily be slow, but they will lead to more real and permanent gains.

Mathewson cites four points in connection with school-home collaboration in guidance:

1. Where school guidance services and community agencies exist, the family need not "go it alone" in dealing with knotty problems of child adjustment, orientation, or development, but may make whatever use of such services as seems advisable.
2. Home and school may cooperate effectively, not only in dealing with problems of child guidance but discussions of college choice, vocational development and educational planning.
3. The home may learn to place responsibility for certain problems of guidance, such as the behavioral adjustment in school, upon professional personnel just as professional medical assistance is utilized in health problems.
4. Recognizing the strong advisability of guidance for their children, parents may join other citizens in extended support of improved guidance processes and services in both school and community.[28]

Guidance services can provide parents with vocational information which will make them better informed in their planning situations with children and result in sounder expectations and decisions. Counselors can assist parents in obtaining the assistance of private and community agencies and organizations which help children who need such attention because of physical and emotional problems. Through consultation with parents, the counselor can help them gain a greater understanding and appreciation of the parental relationship and its effect on children. Counselors may serve as a liaison between teachers and parents. Certainly the counselor's interpretation of modern schools and their concern for individuality hold the promise of improving school-home relationships.

In summary the furtherance of the relationship between the parents, the school, and the community is an extremely important outcome of the guidance process. Quality in their cooperation depends upon clarity in communicating the ways in which they can pool their resources for improving the guidance program. That there is need to develop better mutual understanding and support of what each can do is not an issue.

[28] Robert Mathewson, *Guidance Policy and Practice* (New York: Harper & Row, Publishers, 1962), p. 47.

ANNOTATED BIBLIOGRAPHY

BOY, ANGELO V., AND PINE, GERALD J. *The Counselor in the Schools.* Boston: Houghton Mifflin Company, 1968, 406 pp.

Chapter One (pp. 3–15) identifies and compares the goals of education and counseling. Boy and Pine identify some common elements in teaching and counseling.

FULLMER, DANIEL W., AND BERNARD, HAROLD W. *Counseling: Content and Process.* Chicago: Science Research Associates, Inc., 1964. Chapter 10, pp. 207–226.

This chapter describes in detail the process and content of family group consultation as conducted at the Portland (Oregon) Counseling Institute.

GLANZ, EDWARD C. *Foundations and Principles of Guidance.* Boston: Allyn and Bacon, Inc., 1964. Chapter 15, pp. 340–357.

Glanz cites the contributions of guidance services to administration and of administration to guidance, calling for integration of effort between the two.

MUELLER, KATE HEVNER. *Student Personnel Work in Higher Education.* Boston: Houghton Mifflin Company, 1961. Chapters 14 and 15, pp. 349–394.

Though these chapters are directed to discipline on the college campus, the author's comprehensive treatment and analysis of the topic has meaningful implications for all schools. The sociological and psychological aspects of discipline, the sources of misbehavior, discipline, and the counselor and administrative structures are all illuminated.

SELECTED REFERENCES

BRAKEL, EUGENE. "Parents: The Neglected Party in Pre-College Counseling," *The School Counselor* Vol. 16 (January 1969), pp. 216–217.

DARTER, RICHARD LEE. "Counselors, Principals, and Philosophy," *The School Counselor* Vol. 15 (March 1968), pp. 305–307.

DEMBSKI, MINNA, AND DIBNER, ANDREW S. "Let's Do More Work With Parents!" *The School Counselor* Vol. 15 (January 1968), pp. 180–185.

DONNAN, HUGH H., AND HARLAN, GRADY. "Personality of Counselors and Administrators," *Personnel and Guidance Journal* Vol. 47 (November 1968), pp. 228–232.

ELLISON, MARTHA. "The Counselor As Seen by a Curriculum Development Specialist," *Counselor Education and Supervision* Vol. 8 (Fall 1968), pp. 73–76.

GIFFORD, ROBERT, AND SOMMER, ROBERT. "The Desk or the Bed?" *Personnel and Guidance Journal* Vol. 46 (May 1968), pp. 876–878.

GOMETZ, LYNN, AND PARKER, CLYDE A. "Disciplinary Counseling: A Contradiction?" *Personnel and Guidance Journal* Vol. 46 (January 1968), pp. 437–443.

HENJUM, RAYMOND J., AND ROTHNEY, JOHN W. M. "Parental Action on Counselor's Suggestions," *Vocational Guidance Quarterly* Vol. 18 (September 1969), pp. 54–58.

HILLIARD, THOMAS, AND ROTH, ROBERT M. "Maternal Attitudes and the Non-Achievement Syndrome," *Personnel and Guidance Journal* Vol. 47 (January 1969), pp. 424–428.

LITTLE, DONALD F., AND WALKER, BASIL S. "Tutor–Pupil Relationship and Academic Progress," *Personnel and Guidance Journal,* Vol. 47 (December 1968), pp. 324–329.

MALLORS, PATRICIA B. "Thinking About Group Counseling for Parents?" *The School Counselor* Vol. 15 (May 1968), pp. 374–376.

NUGENT, FRANK A. "A Framework for Appropriate Referrals of Disciplinary Problems to Counselors," *The School Counselor,* Vol. 16 (January 1969), pp. 199–201.

PECKENS, RUSSELL G. "Counseling Parents of Special Education Students," *The School Counselor* Vol. 15 (September 1967), pp. 22–25.

PETERSON, BARBARA G. "Parent Effectiveness Training," *The School Counselor* Vol. 16 (May 1969), pp. 367–369.

PRUITT, ANNE S. "Teacher Involvement in the Curriculum and Career Guidance," *Vocational Guidance Quarterly* Vol. 17 (March 1969), pp. 189–193.

SOMMER, ROBERT. "The Social Psychology of Cramming," *Personnel and Guidance Journal* Vol. 47 (October 1968), pp. 104–109.

SPITHALL, ALMA C. "The Valuable Allies," *Personnel and Guidance Journal* Vol. 46 (May 1968), pp. 879–883.

STANNARD, EDITH. "Family Life Education Series: A Program for Teenagers," *Personnel and Guidance Journal* Vol. 42 (March 1964), pp. 706–707.

WALZ, GARRY, AND MILLER, JULIET. "School Climates and Student Behavior," *Personnel and Guidance Journal* Vol. 47 (May 1969), pp. 859–867.

WRENN, C. GILBERT. Chapter 2, "The Changing Family," in *The Counselor in a Changing World* (Washington: American Personnel and Guidance Association, 1962), pp. 28–33.

PART FOUR
EVALUATION, REFERRAL, AND COMMUNITY RESOURCES

EVALUATION OF guidance is a complex but essential undertaking. It is complex because many factors both within and outside the school produce change in the individual. To separate the influence of school guidance services from that of other factors and then to assess this influence constitute the core of guidance evaluation. Evaluation of guidance is essential if its future is to be meaningful. As guidance becomes more and more visible, demands from within and without the field will increase for an objective accounting of its "goodness." Evaluation of guidance is treated in Chapter 16, with attention given to the need for, difficulties in, and methods for conducting evaluation.

Chapter 17 describes the referral function and the use of community resources in guidance. The school counselor is expected to know when and how to refer, and which referral source should be used. Caring for students' psychological, social, health, and other needs requires a vast array of school and community resources. The intelligent use of these resources will come closer to realization if close working relationships among all personnel are established.

16

EVALUATION OF GUIDANCE PROGRAMS

What are the characteristics of an effective guidance program?
Why is program evaluation necessary?
What approaches have been used in program evaluation?
What criteria have been suggested for program evaluation?
How may appraisal data be used to secure program improvements?

CHARACTERISTICS OF EFFECTIVE GUIDANCE PROGRAMS

It is not uncommon to hear a teacher, counselor, or administrator remark, "School X has a better guidance program than School Y" or "That school has a good guidance service." What are the bases for such remarks? What characteristics distinguish one program from another? Is it personnel, organizational structure, unity in program purposes and practices? Inquiry focused on the criteria that influence such judgmental remarks indicate that both external and internal characteristics influence such statements. It is a truism that the criteria against which programs are judged often tend to be ambiguous, hidden, and complex. At the same time, it is clear that poor, marginal, and good guidance programs exist across the country. An attempt will be made to present what can be termed external, readily quantifiable characteristics followed by internal characteristics of a more qualitative nature.

Attention to the more specific, tangible characteristics of highly reputed guidance programs must be paired with the awareness that such indexes are all based upon acceptance of the value and validity of present practices. There also is an implied satisfaction with the direction these characteristics indicate. The point here is that all such external indexes need to be examined critically if "what is" is to move toward "what should be" or "what might be." It should also be noted that external indexes do not, in and of themselves, guarantee effectiveness but merely provide convenient preliminary checks on the way to a qualitative judgment. One further note is in order. Both external and internal characteristics are, in reality, subjective in nature, and are derived from personal judgments. Some, primarily external characteristics, are accepted by consensus, however. Because they are more readily observable, external characteristics tend to appear highly objective and tend to become fixed standards with little attention given to their derivation and meaningfulness. In truth, many external indexes have highly arbitrary origins and have become "gospel" through repetitious usage and easy quantification. Although many of the nine characteristics cited below are useful, they should not be accepted unquestioningly.

External Evaluative Characteristics

1. A counselor-student ratio of one full-time counselor for 250 to 300 students has become one of the most obvious and well-known external criteria of judging a good system. Although a few schools have attained such an ideal staff-student ratio, many schools are just now beginning their efforts to attain this "standard," and most are probably at twice or three times this ratio. Perhaps the general professional acceptance given to this ratio has obscured the fact that little actual research exists to support it, and even more importantly, that 250 to 300 students per counselor may be too high a ratio in some schools. Nevertheless, the fact remains that schools recognized by others as possessing distinguished guidance programs have a counselor-pupil ratio that permits them to meet the student body's educational and developmental needs rather than an external, arbitrary standard. A caseload of approximately this magnitude is probably a maximum if counselors are to have the time to counsel students individually and in small groups, as well as to spend time consulting with the school faculty and with parents. It should also be noted that personnel in schools meeting this criterion are usually full-time counselors with a strong sense of professional commitment.

2. Counselors are qualified for their positions at least to the minimum required for state certification, or by holding a graduate degree in counseling. Clearly, the practices of awarding counseling positions to those who experience difficulty managing classrooms, appointing "deserving" individuals who are ill prepared for counseling, and using counseling positions as a testing ground for future administrators do not characterize high-quality programs. Rather, counselors in highly rated programs are both personally inclined and educationally prepared to be counselors. They want to be counselors because they desire intensive, intimate professional contact with pupils and are productive in their relationships with them. They take pride in their particular kind of work, they consider it important, and they communicate their enthusiasm to students as well as to others who are interested.

3. Appropriate, usable records are maintained which reflect a body of information about each pupil, enabling teachers and counselors to understand and help students. These records are used, not only for a demographic study of the student population, but also to (1) help students grow in self-understanding which in turn enables them to make appropriate decisions, and (2) facilitate understanding of students by counselors, teachers, and parents, so that educational programs can be adapted to meet students' individual needs and enhance the students' unique development.

   Record systems in good guidance programs reflect the monumental amount of work needed to abstract adequately the individuality of the student, to preserve the essence of who the student is, and to reflect his continuous, cumulative development. Data collection does not occur be-behind a cloud of secrecy, for purely administrative purposes, for labeling or categorizing students, or for ". . . subtle, benevolent manipulation of the student." [1] Provison is made, not only for the interpretation of appraisal data to parents and pupils, but also for the interpretation of the value and necessity of records and how they are used.

4. Informational materials are present and accessible. Essentially, this means that up-to-date materials are available which describe the changing character of educational and vocational opportunities and requirements. Provisions are built into such programs to keep career materials current, to interpret them to pupils, and to maintain them in condition for use by students and staff. Schools judged to be effective maintain materials in a manner that incorporates changes anticipated by educational and occupational authorities. The flow of change data is implemented by use of computers, current audiovisual aids, including educational television and radio presentations. Use of such aids dramatically portrays the nature of change and enriches the student's understandings of the psychological and sociological implications of changes in education and work.

5. Appraisal data are available and used by school personnel to help pupils with individual concerns relating to adjustment, planning, and development. Schools that have good reputations do not glorify the mere collection of facts about pupils but see these data as a means to an end: the identification of strengths and weaknesses within and among individuals and the maximization of insight and understanding by the student. The predictive power and the diagnostic clues available from pupil appraisal data are not misused. "Appraisal of the student" is not for deterministic or directive ends but is pursued because it can provide the basis for student self-understanding. It is not intended to imply that students come to counselors merely for prescriptive answers. They come to gain under-

---

[1] W. Wesley Tennyson, Donald H. Blocher, and Ralph H. Johnson, "Student Personnel Records: A Vital Tool but a Concern of the Public," *Personnel and Guidance Journal* Vol. 42 (May 1964), p. 890.

standing of how their behavior interacts with life situations and demands.

Appraisal data, then, will be used by the student and counselor for vocational planning, educational planning, self-exploration and understanding of personal development. The counseling interview is the primary vehicle by which appraisal data are transmitted to students. When a student is involved in a difficult but relatively common problem, such as vocational planning, he may reach a better decision by considering appraisal data relating to his previous development and achievement. These data provide a basis for determining probabilities and stimulating insight into his personal assets, liabilities, and interests. Personnel in well-regarded guidance programs also know that there are certain student problems involving conflicts of motives, ambivalence of feelings, and emotional factors in which, admittedly, the usual school appraisal data are of minimal value.

6. Personnel are self-evaluative and research oriented. Quality programs have specified their guidance objectives and appraised their progress toward mutually determined goals. They do more than routine accounting and surveying of the year's activities. The staff is committed to testing one method against another and feels obligated and free to use imaginative approaches and take the risks involved in efforts to improve their services. They know that steady improvement of the school's guidance service will come through objective and scientific evaluation.

7. Effective guidance programs are not confined to one grade or one school level, but operate throughout the entire span of the pupil's school career. Such schools do not risk curtailing the effectiveness of their guidance efforts by locating services at the high school level only. They know that a high-quality guidance program is continuous as well as comprehensive, with coordinating efforts made at all grade levels.

8. Physical facilities are available for guidance. This characteristic is a readily observable one, and often leads to the belief that a school has a good guidance program. Planned, functional physical facilities which adequately provide for space, privacy, accessibility, and the like, are a hallmark of quality guidance programs.

9. Another major external characteristic is the existence of adequate financial support. Current estimates (and they are just that) indicate that good guidance programs cost approximately 40 to 50 dollars per pupil annually. Over-budgeted programs are as unjustifiable as inadequately financed programs. Though costs may vary considerably among schools, personnel in successful settings know that the public will review the services provided in relation to costs. Are the program outcomes worth the cost? But how is a dollar estimate put on one youngster who understands himself better? Someone, by some means, will be responsible for judging whether costs are commensurate with results. Costs of highly regarded guidance programs are not buried in instructional and administrative expenditures. They are clearly stated and defendable on their own merits by the staff.

Does the mere presence of these nine quantitative characteristics guarantee effectiveness for a guidance program? Are not these characteristics simply descriptive of what is external to the program, while an understanding of what is internal to the program is more crucial? A criticism of external characteristics, which should not be overlooked, is that their mere presence guarantees nothing regarding program effectiveness. The critical issue is whether a demonstrable relationship exists between the above characteristics and their meaningful impact upon the various facets of the school and the personnel and students within the school.

Other attributes of a qualitative nature are stamped into successful programs and give them a particular strength. The argument here is not for mystical evaluation but rather for a beam of light upon the shadows of an effective guidance program in the hope of providing a deeper understanding of what makes one program qualitatively better than another. Perhaps in this endeavor only glimpses and guesses can be identified.

Internal Evaluation Characteristics

1. Guidance programs praised by others are based on pupil needs. How many times is this statement heard? It has been rendered almost meaningless by hollow repetition. If we say that guidance programs fail or succeed principally by virtue of the degree to which they are geared to meet pupil needs, what does this mean? What is meant by needs, anyway? The term "need" in educational usage has become jargon; its meaning has been destroyed by loose overusage.

   Needs may be seen as personal inadequacies in particular situations. Need has been defined as "a lack of something which if present would tend to further the welfare of the organism . . . or facilitate its usual behavior."[2] It is in this sense that "need" is used in the jargon of education. It implies that "meeting pupils' needs" requires the contrivance and arrangement of situations, experiences, and surroundings that further the educational welfare of students and facilitate desirable behavior.

   Student needs are always present and evolving. The counselor's approach to the task of ascertaining needs does not assume they are fixed for all time. Some needs stem principally from the maturation process and necessitate continuous personal, social, and environmental adjustment. Other needs are attributable to complex social, psychological, and economic forces and pressures. Some needs are relatively general among youth of a given age, and others specific to certain individuals in particular localities or schools. Given the axiom that guidance programs attempt to meet the needs of young people, how is this done in successful programs? First, teachers and counselors listen

[2] Horace B. English and Ava C. English, *A Comprehensive Dictionary of Psychological and Psychoanalytic Terms* (New York: Longmans, Green & Co., Inc., 1958), p. 338.

closely to what youth say and write because they know they are expressing either personal or situational inadequacies when they say:

> I'm going to quit school.
> I don't seem to have any life goals.
> I want to help people.
> How can I make the mo⌣ of myself?
> I don't seem to get anything out of school.
> I want to stay with my friends.
> I should do better in school.
> It seems like I'm nothing—a zero.
> What can I really do after finishing school?
> How can school help me to become a brick layer?

These are expressions of needs to understand oneself, needs to know personal characteristics, needs to understand environmental conditions, needs for orientation to present and future conditions, and needs to develop personal potentialities. Second, recognizing these needs, successful school administrators build appraisal, planning, informational, and counseling services to care for them. They do not make the serious error of losing the individual by gearing the program to a mythical "average" or statistically "typical" pupil, for they know that to establish a program which ignores the individual student places the program in jeopardy and destroys in large part the very reason for its emergence as a special school service.

2. Guidance programs of real merit balance corrective, preventive, and developmental functions. Personnel in such programs know when youth require assistance in extricating themselves from potentially harmful difficulties that inevitably confront them. Yet without unduly deprecating this important corrective function, greater efforts are made to *anticipate* pupil difficulties, to reduce threat, and to strengthen the child so that he can cope with his problems successfully. Guidance personnel do this by providing cumulative learning experiences for pupils in which they can test and try themselves in exploratory situations rather than by providing ready-made solutions which too often do not fit unique future conditions. Guidance in such schools is focused upon assisting students "to reason about human behavior,"[3] and to regard conflict as a problem to be met intelligently.

This characteristic requires that schools do not confine their efforts merely to program planning or to vocational guidance. It carries with it the view that guidance is not just for the classroom misbehavior case who irritates the teacher or for those who underachieve or fail or are chronic absentees. It requires that guidance practice be designed

---

[3] Robert Hendry Mathewson, *Guidance Policy and Practice* (New York: Harper & Row, Publishers, 1962), p. 37.

to develop the capability of school personnel to understand the individual and provide the kind of assistance necessary for his maximum development.

3. Quality programs are purposeful. A guidance activity such as counseling is not an end in itself, but is merely one important service for accomplishing definite purposes. Career information, routinely presented to pupils, will be no more than routine unless it is supported by the recognition that it is related to program purpose. Schools in which the personnel have gone through the process of clearly deciding what they hope to achieve and can realistically accomplish find that the practices they employ are more appropriately chosen to achieve desired objectives.

4. Balance is an essential quality of good organization. A balanced guidance program is one in which the various services have been developed strictly in accordance with the relative importance of their contributions to student needs. In actual practice, perfectly balanced organizations are seldom found because some services, e.g., counseling or placement, are stressed because of the "pet interests" of personnel. The point is that certain services may be more highly developed, but should not be developed at the expense of other necessary services. If imbalance exists, it should exist because it is appropriate to the particular requirements of the school setting. Effective guidance programs guard against the lack of balance often found in ineffective programs and caused by (1) personnel who are more interested in one aspect of the program and exaggerate its importance, (2) personnel who attempt to advance themselves, regardless of the program's well-being, and (3) quick growth of the program.

5. Program stability—the quality or ability to adjust to loss of personnel without serious loss of effectiveness—is directly related to program quality. Stability demands that the system is able to fill positions quickly and satisfactorily. Good guidance programs are concerned about stability, and personnel in such programs work hard at recruiting from both within and without the system.

6. Another characteristic of effective program organization is flexibility. Flexibility in the sense of adaptability to future growth is the quality that enables the program, or an element of it, to expand or contract, without serious loss of effectiveness. Flexibility frequently demands modification in the load a service must carry. Effective programs provide for future growth and realignment of services, both of which require the foresight to recognize the need for changes in services and personnel that are required by altered objectives, functions, or the modified character of the student population. Good programs avoid the dangers of inflexibility, destruction of organizational balance, and overloading of counselors.

7. The staff of guidance programs that have achieved recognition and praise have high morale and work cooperatively. Good morale is a quality that leads individuals and groups willingly to subordinate their personal objectives, temporarily and within reason, to further the success of the program. It is the quality that induces personnel willingly to accept and execute directions, to adapt cheerfully to reasonable requirements, and to give their best efforts without undue pressure from authority.

Cooperation among personnel marks the good guidance program. Cooperation is a condition of working together effectively. In its negative form, it may result wholly from compulsion based on fear; in such cases personnel, in a prompt, mechanical way, do merely what they are told to do, but little more. In its positive form, cooperation develops from individual volition and serves as a basis for collective accomplishment.

Cooperation in guidance programs is manifested in the degree of mutual help and collaboration between counselors and teachers. In positive programs of guidance, teachers and counselors relate meaningfully to each other. The schism that may separate them in less effective programs—jealousy, defensiveness, misunderstanding—is replaced by loyalty, confidence in each other's professional integrity, and willingness to share success. Cooperation between teachers and counselors occurs voluntarily when the professional integrity and ethical practices of both are mutually respected; it cannot necessarily be purchased through elaborate, forced, inservice training schedules.

Cooperation among teachers, counselors, and administrators will not and probably should not prevent some conflict of interest and attitudes. Professional commitment on the part of all in discovering, analyzing, and ameliorating legitimate frictions promptly is more apt to be present in cooperative programs. In high-quality programs, active participation and active interest in guidance services are exhibited by teachers and administrators. Successful guidance programs are characterized by teachers who understand and support what counselors do, who respect the process by which students are referred to counselors, and who consult with counselors about individual pupils who may need further attention.

8. Personnel in high-quality programs avoid the search for quick answers and face the reality that guidance in its broadest sense has many dimensions. Though counselors bring to the helping situation skill in counseling, appraisal, and a knowledge of educational and work opportunities, they simultaneously recognize that (1) pupils need help from a variety of sources, and (2) these sources may represent many different levels of competence. Pierson points out that the task of assisting pupils without weakening their initiative and self-reliance is difficult, complex and fraught with danger:

[The counselor] . . . struggles constantly, therefore, to discover the kind of help students really need and to perfect the art of administering that help constructively. He does not subscribe to the myth that a simple "scientific" solution can be discovered for all human relations problems.[4]

Counselors in such programs marshal the resources of the school and the community for the use of students and faculty. They are aware of referral resources and will use them without hesitation when they are appropriate.

9. In guidance programs praised by others, counselors have thought through and arrived at an understanding of their role and function which they are able to communicate to others. Statements of school counselor role and function have appeared with increasing frequency within the past five years.[5] Among the conceptualizations is that of the late C. Harold McCully[6] who viewed the counselor as an agent for change. He cited four shortcomings in our social processes and two in the schools which may well serve as the mandate needed for counselors to become professionals rather than technicians. These social needs or lacks are (1) loss of effectiveness in the methods of inducting large numbers of youth into full, participating membership in the adult society; (2) work instability resulting from the accelerated change of a rapidly advancing technology; (3) an "overdeveloped" society which needs increasing numbers of trained workers at the highest levels of intellectual ability and a constantly decreasing number of workers at the lower reaches of mental ability; (4) an increasingly corporate society which depresses individualism; (5) the school's failure to deal with individual differences, and (6) the school's failure to expect and obtain excellence from all pupils. McCully believed that these forces threaten cumulative loss of individuality and self-definition and result in an increasing sense of meaninglessness and alienation. Because of these needs or lacks, he called for intervention by the counselor to combat and arrest these trends. Such intervention in student's lives and in their learning process is justified if it enables them to experience the meaning of freedom and responsibility. The process of becoming free and responsible starts with awareness of self, and self-definition comes largely through choice-making.

McCully's view of the counselor as an agent of change means that the counselor would not only be an expert in learning theory—the barriers that prevent, and the conditions that facilitate learning—but

[4] George A. Pierson, "Results and Achievements to Date: The Failures and Successes of Current Guidance Practices," *Transactions of the New York Academy of Sciences* Series II, Vol. 24 (November 1961), p. 55.

[5] John W. Loughary, *et al.* (eds.), *Counseling, A Growing Profession* (Washington: American Personnel and Guidance Association, 1965), pp. 94–106.

[6] C. Harold McCully, "The Counselor—Instrument of Change," *Teachers College Record* Vol. 66 (February 1965), pp. 405–412.

that he would be able to communicate this knowledge meaningfully to teachers and others. He would be sophisticated in the features and consequences of social change and would be able to introduce change in the school.

Whether the counselor accepts McCully's definition of the counselor's role and function or some other definition, the important point is that he knows who he is as a counselor and can communicate this identity in meaningful terms to others. He has a purpose for being in the school which provides focus for the activities in which he engages.

10. A tenth characteristic is that the students who are a part of good guidance programs are not nameless and faceless to the guidance personnel. Effective guidance programs are concerned both with process and with product. The questions, "How well is the program operating?" and "What are its outcomes?" must both be answered. It has often been said that a guidance program should produce change in the behavior of students. The question here is what pupil behavior changes may legitimately be expected. In other words, what behavioral manifestations should be apparent in students as a result of an effective guidance program?

First, and obviously at a superficial level, students should know of the existence of counselors in the school. They should know their counselor because they have had personal contact with him. They are aware of what a counselor does and why his presence in a school is needed. When asked, they do not describe him as another teacher or as an assistant to the principal. Second, students have some grasp of the intent and eventual outcomes of the curriculum which they are pursuing because they have actively participated in its choice. Third, students have a good grasp of the nature of planning through their own experience. They are conscious that they have choices to make both now and in the future, because they are able to relate these choices meaningfully to knowledge of their own self-development. This is not to argue that all students have developed a specific, detailed blueprint for the future from which no deviation is expected. Rather, they exhibit a cognitive awareness of the forces affecting choice and a tolerance for the relatively tentative nature of decisions. Fourth, students not only know that counselors are in the school but they avail themselves of the guidance service for specific types of assistance.

11. Finally, a characteristic of highly praised programs is that leadership is exercised by individuals formally prepared by a study of guidance and experienced in the counseling of students. What is qualitatively apparent is that the leader exhibits imagination in approaches to guidance, courage in confronting manifold problems, and intelligence in working with his colleagues. Good programs are marked by directors of guidance who are not afraid to lead and who are willing to risk failure and disapproval. They are not afraid to assert themselves because they have a clear conception of what is possible for the program and can communicate this meaningfully to others.

In summary, there is no doubt that these nine quantitative and eleven qualitative internal characteristics could be supplemented by additional ones. But the preceding characteristics are general and apply to all programs. To some degree each program, however, is unique to its particular setting and consequently would either (1) add other characteristics or (2) stress those cited in varying degrees.

THE NECESSITY FOR PROGRAM EVALUATION

What Is Evaluation?

Simply defined, evaluation consists of making systematic judgments of the relative effectiveness with which goals are attained in relation to specified standards. As was implied throughout the above description of characteristics of quality guidance programs, evaluative criteria vary widely in specificity, objectivity, and ease of application.

Value of Evaluation

Systematic program evaluation results in several values to individuals associated with a service and often results in improvement of the program itself. Certainly the future of guidance is dependent upon providing concrete data regarding its benefits and limitations. Although guidance currently enjoys public favor and is generally accepted on faith alone, sooner or later the public will ask for documentation of its values. Evidence that guidance services do produce desirable benefits—demonstrable behavioral change in students—will be demanded, but only through research and evaluation can such evidence be secured.

Evaluation of guidance programs is mandatory if the effectiveness of its services is to be known or its services improved. Though it is probably true that informal evaluation is continually underway since decisions are constantly made about personnel, time, activities, etc., systematic study is urgently needed as a basis for program improvement. Kefauver and Hand point out that through systematic analysis and appraisal of guidance services, "More data would be secured in such a stock-taking than is ordinarily possible in the normal operation of the program."[7] The fundamental nature of evaluation consists in judging the worth "of an experience, idea, or process."[8] The evaluation of guidance programs enables school personnel to judge how well they are doing and results in bases for deciding the nature of improvements if they are needed. Dressel and his associates have aptly stated that "failure to engage systematically in evaluation in reaching the

[7] Grayson N. Kefauver and Harold C. Hand, *Appraising Guidance Services in Secondary Schools* (New York: The Macmillan Co., 1941), p. 21.

[8] Paul Dressel and Associates, *Evaluation in Higher Education* (Boston: Houghton Mifflin Company, 1961), p. 6.

many decisions necessary in education means that decision by prejudice, by tradition, or by rationalization is paramount. . . ."[9]

Evaluative data are urgently needed to assist school personnel in interpreting the guidance programs to the community. Parents need to be informed of the present status of a program if they are to participate intelligently in its support and assist in defining its direction and objectives.

Finally, pursuing evaluative activities constitutes a learning experience for the staff. The process of evaluation leads to unity of thinking among staff members and mutuality of commitment by them.

Difficulties Inherent in Evaluation

Although the literature on guidance is extensive, little of it deals directly with the evaluation of services. Many reasons for this state of affairs have been advanced.

1. Many school counseling practitioners state that they do not have time for evaluation. They claim that the great amount of time and energy demanded for the conduct of programs does not permit them to evaluate, except informally. Perhaps what they most need is to convince themselves and school administrators of the eventual values of evaluation.

2. Many school counselors legitimately insist that they do not have the training to conduct either research or evaluative studies. It is the exceptional staff member who has had the specialized training to plan and conduct an extensive research project. This shortcoming in the preparation of guidance personnel sorely needs rectifying.

3. By their nature, guidance programs are dynamic, unique, and complex. The modification of human behavior is not easily assessed through observation or other tools of measurement. The crude nature of present measuring instruments and methods, particularly in the areas of personality, attitudes, motivation, and environment, presents severe obstacles. Until better techniques and tools are forthcoming, most schools will have to depend heavily upon subjective approaches to determine the adequacy of their guidance efforts. Controlling the numerous variables that influence human behavior is essential to adequate evaluation.

4. From a pure research point of view, available school data tend to be incomplete and fragmentary. The original reason for gathering such data is inevitably different from the research uses that often evolve at a later date. Unless evaluative purposes are conceived in advance and meticulous collection of all pertinent data is accomplished, it is difficult to conduct reliable and valid evaluation.

5. Evaluation costs time and money. There is no doubt that initially evaluation appears costly. In the long run, however, it represents the most

[9] *Ibid.*

economical route to more appropriate and effective guidance services. Without evaluation, the school guidance program will be marked by wasteful, trial-and-error methods. Too often, boards of education consider funds for research as a luxury item that can be expunged. School administrators often do not have sufficient conviction regarding the value of evaluative results to push such costs past the board opposition.

6. Employing a suitable control group (a group used for comparison purposes but not used experimentally) is a difficult problem. The control group must be similar in all relevant respects to the experimental group. Although some studies have matched the control group to the experimental group on factors such as ability, age, grade, achievement, socioeconomic background, sex, and other readily classified dimensions, motivation for counseling is a variable that is often overlooked or, when used, inadequately assessed. Further, Rothney and Lewis caution against ignoring the developmental history of subjects. Because control and experimental group subjects are similar at the time that groups are established does not necessarily mean that the development of members up to that time had been similar or that they would continue to be so as long as there was no special intervention. They argue that attributing differences between the experimental and control groups to the experimental treatment may be erroneous because such differences may, in fact, be related to patterns of development not observed (perhaps not even present) in the original data. These two authors acknowledge that gathering such longitudinal data on subjects would be costly in terms of time and money but they believe this caution should be heeded if control group investigations are to be used.[10]

7. Formulating appropriate, assessable criteria is a difficult problem in evaluation and research in guidance. A research criterion is a standard selected for comparison purposes to determine if change has occurred. Many criteria such as those discussed in the earlier section of this chapter have been proposed for use, but most have been found wanting or of questionable value for a specific situation or purpose.

APPROACHES TO EVALUATION

The evaluation of guidance has been approached in various ways. Whatever approach is utilized, however, three component elements are inherent in any comprehensive evaluative process. *First,* the objectives of the program, service, or activity must be stated in observable behavioral terms. The anticipated outcomes of whatever is being done must be formulated in such a manner that they can be observed and verified. *Second,* the activities or methods that are used to attain the objectives must be established. As an example, one school stated that a guidance objective was to help the

[10] John W. M. Rothney and Charles W. Lewis, "Use of Control Groups in Studies of Guidance," *Personnel and Guidance Journal* Vol. 47 (January 1969), pp. 446–449.

student develop an awareness of educational opportunities following high school graduation. In line with this objective, the school conducted such activities as (1) college conferences, (2) interviews with students concerning their college plans, and (3) supervised use of college materials to help students attain this objective. *Third,* procedures must be developed to collect evidence as to whether the activities or methods result in the attainment of objectives. This involves giving consideration to the kind of observable evidence, the situations in which it may be found, its collection and organization, and its appraisal and significance.

Although three approaches to guidance evaluation will be briefly described, many of the evaluative efforts cut across approaches and involve a mixture of methods.

Survey Approach

The survey approach is probably the most frequently used appraisal method in the school setting. Basically the survey method (1) selects predetermined criteria to inventory, (2) collects evidence of the services being offered, and (3) makes judgments regarding the degree to which these services are provided in reference to the predetermined criteria. The survey approach is often used in self-study by schools to appraise the assumed impact of the entire guidance program upon the lives of pupils.

Survey approaches usually focus upon the intent and presence of certain services, the number of staff personnel, their qualifications and use of time, physical facilities, and other external factors. Though survey approaches involve both objective and subjective judgments, they supply little evidence as to whether student behavior is significantly affected by the services. A more rigorous and specific kind of evaluation is required to gain the latter evidence. The survey approach tends to emphasize the availability of activities, staff, facilities, and programs. While some effort is made to provide at least a subjective judgment as to the quality of these services, such judgments frequently are questionable in that the mere presence of certain characteristics in a program does not guarantee quality.

Illustrations of the kinds of instruments used and the characteristics commonly included may be found in the following sources:

Cooperative Study of the Secondary-School Standards. *Evaluative Criteria, Section G, Guidance Services.* Washington: Cooperative Study of the Secondary-School Standards. 1950. Pp. 219–233.

Arthur L. Benson. *Criteria for Evaluating Guidance Programs in Secondary Schools,* Form B, U.S. Department of Health, Education and Welfare, Office of Education. Washington: Government Printing Office, April 1961. 33 pp.

Colorado Criteria for Evaluative Study of Programs of Guidance Services, Parts I, II, and III. Denver, Colo.: Colorado State Department of Education, 1956.

Frank Wellman and Don D. Twiford. *Guidance, Counseling and Testing*

Program Evaluation, U.S. Department of Health, Education and Welfare, Office of Education. Washington: Government Printing Office, 1961. 37 pp.

George E. Hill. *Evaluating the School's Testing Program.* Athens, Ohio: Ohio University, 1959. 28 pp.

Rolla F. Pruett and Duane Brown. *Guidance Evaluation Form.* Indianapolis, Ind.: State Department of Public Instruction, 1963. 18 pp.

The limitations of survey approaches—lack of experimental validation, difficulty in inferring causal relationships, sampling errors which bias survey data—have led school personnel to be increasingly critical of a simple survey approach to program evaluation.

Experimental Approach

Experimental methods require carefully planned steps to study one or more groups of individuals in terms of one or more variables. Experimental studies require the application of scientific methods which involves a predetermined sequence such as: (1) the determination of objectives and methods of attaining these objectives; (2) the development of ways to measure the attainment of these objectives; (3) the selection of one or more groups for control and experimentation; (4) the process of carrying out necessary steps for the objectives; and (5) a measurement of the outcomes of experimentation.

The most appropriate form of this method requires control and experimental groups. Experimental control is employed in order to ascertain whether change or gain by the experimental group can be attributed to the method of treatment rather than to chance alone. Much ingenuity and many technical means are employed in conducting experimental research.

Case-study Approach

The case-study approach, as the term applies, is designed to assess the changes that take place in an individual as a result of introducing a variable, such as counseling. Goals appropriate to the individual are formulated, counseling takes place, data are collected on progress toward goals. These steps are followed by review and assessment of changes in the individual which are attributable to the procedures employed.

The case-study approach is time consuming, but it has certain advantages. It emphasizes the individual and his growth. It avoids the massing effects of many other evaluative approaches by which much may be learned of the effect on the group but little is known of what happens to single individuals.

Some twenty years ago, Dressel criticized evaluative studies because they (1) lacked clear, acceptable statements of objectives; (2) failed to relate student personnel objectives to all-institutional educational objectives; (3) used immediate and easily available criteria and failed to validate such criteria against long-term goals; (4) regarded certain goals as equally desirable for all individuals, thereby ignoring individual differences; (5) confused means with ends or processes with outcomes; (6) made excessive use of subjective reactions, and (7) paid little attention to satisfactory experimental designs.[11] It is distressing but nevertheless true that many of Dressel's criticisms are still valid today, no matter which approach is used.

THE CRITERION PROBLEM

At the outset of this chapter certain characteristics were suggested as indicative of effective guidance programs. The implication was that the existence of such characteristics provides one type of evidence of a high-quality program. Rigorous evaluation of program effectiveness even when such characteristics are present demands a much more specific base for adequate judgment. This base is commonly referred to as a criterion.

The major difficulty besetting any evaluator of guidance or, for that matter, any researcher is the criterion problem. The selection of a criterion is crucial, for the degree of confidence placed in the evaluation depends upon the appropriateness of the criterion. Some of the more common criteria that have been employed in guidance programs are (1) later success in college; (2) salary in later life; (3) job satisfaction ratings; (4) expression of fewer personal problems; and (5) realistic level of aspiration.

An analysis of some of the advantages and limitations of these and other criteria is given in Figure 16. The criticism is made, for example, that reduction in the number of problems checked by students on a problem questionnaire immediately after counseling leads researchers to conclude that counseling was very effective. But information collected later may indicate that such changes were of short duration. Some years ago, Jensen, Coles, and Nestor concluded that criteria should be (1) defined in such a way that they can be understood by research consumers; (2) stable; (3) relevant; and (4) variable with regard to measurement in the population.[12]

SECURING PROGRAM IMPROVEMENT

Program evaluation is basically the assessment of the existing status. It can do no more than provide quantitative and qualitative descriptions of current program conditions. The basic fallacy of descriptions of evaluative procedures is that they often stop short, leaving the impression that the process is an end in itself. Ending the process of collection, analysis, and description of findings is justifiable only when final judgments indicate

[11] Paul L. Dressel, "Personnel Services in High School and College," *Occupations* Vol. 29 (February 1951), p. 331.

[12] Barry T. Jensen, George Coles, and Beatrice Nestor, "The Criterion Problem in Guidance Research," *Journal of Counseling Psychology* Vol. 2 (Spring 1955), pp. 58–61.

FIGURE 16
Analysis of Guidance Evaluative Criteria

SUGGESTED CRITERIA	ADVANTAGES	LIMITATIONS
1. Reduction in scholastic failure.	1.1. Guidance services should enable students to select learning experiences commensurate with their abilities.	1.1. School marks involve not only student achievement but school and teacher philosophy.
	1.2. Guidance services should help students cope with academic difficulties.	1.2. Students may simply learn to avoid difficult courses.
		1.3. Experiencing failures may lead to personal growth.
2. Reduction in discipline problems.	2.1. Guidance should lead to an appropriate understanding and acceptance of authority, thereby eliminating most disciplinary problems.	2.1. It is difficult to clearly define "discipline problems."
	2.2. Preventive guidance services should provide a climate in which the student is in a good working relationship with the administration and accepts his responsibility as a member of society.	2.2. Teachers may simply learn that fewer discipline problems referred to the administration implies better teaching ability.
		2.3. Reduction may result from *teacher change,* a valuable criterion only if it in turn effects student behavior change.
3. Greater utilization of the counseling service with a concomitant number of self-referrals.	3.1. At least superficially this implies greater acceptance of the guidance point of view and of the counselor's capacity to help.	3.1. Mere numbers do not indicate the kinds of situations treated (Value of an increase in treating routine educational problems vs. rare use for treating personal problems).

satisfaction with existing conditions. Though termination at this point may be justified in rare instances, it is highly unlikely that many programs conform to or can meet professional standards in all respects. At least implicit in undertaking an evaluation are three factors: (1) a suspicion, however

FIGURE 16, Continued
Analysis of Guidance Evaluative Criteria

SUGGESTED CRITERIA	ADVANTAGES	LIMITATIONS
	3.2. Guidance should help students to have sufficient insight into their problems to recognize when help is needed.	3.2. An increase in the quantity of counseling services may only indicate a decrease in their quality.
4. Reduction in program changes.	4.1. Guidance should enable students to have a systematic plan for their work.	4.1. Schools may merely be so authoritarian there is little curriculum choice.
	4.2. Guidance influences should make students less prone to whimsical changes.	4.2. Changes may be so difficult that requests are seldom made and almost certainly denied.
		4.3. Recognition of the real need for a program change may show greater student maturity.
5. Choice of "suitable" vocational goals.	5.1. Guidance should effect better student self-knowledge, and consequently vocational choices consistent with student ability and interests.	5.1. It is difficult to determine if "suitability" from the counselor's viewpoint is a really "suitable" vocational goal for the student.
	5.2. Guidance should eliminate both a wastage of talent and unrealistic goals.	5.2. "Suitable" vocational goals are often influenced by social status norms and may therefore produce socially acceptable but maladjusted workers.

Abstracted in part from Raymond N. Hatch and Buford Steffire, *Administration of Guidance Services* Second Edition (Englewood Cliffs, N.J.: Prentice-Hall, Inc., 1965), pp. 270–275.

vague, that some change(s) may be in order, (2) a commitment to make any needed changes, and (3) recognition that program modifications involve some degree of risk.

It is one thing to conduct a program evaluation to identify strengths and limitations but quite another to use the results to bring about change. The question of concern here may be simply put: "If program evaluation has been conducted and change is indicated, how may it be secured?" Reforms in guidance programs, as in other educational endeavors, are not a simple matter, since presumably each segment of the total school program is interrelated with all other segments.

Until recently it was thought that changes in guidance program development consisted largely of incorporating "new" techniques, practices, or materials. It is now recognized that program modification is a highly complex process, involving technical innovations, shifts in school population composition, and staff personalities. It is a complex process because the functions of a guidance program are enmeshed in a web of educational expectations and relationships.

Rate of Change in Education

Several authorities have commented upon the difficulty of effecting change in the educational enterprise. Mort and Cornell, in their classical studies during the 1940's of the diffusion rates of new adaptations, found that it took seven times as long for the first 10 percent acceptance as for the next 10 percent.[13] Ross and others,[14] some ten years later, summarized the substantive findings of seventy studies of change. On the average, it took fifty years from the recognition of a need for change in educational systems to the time when something was first done about it, and another fifty years to approach complete adoption of the change. A 3 percent adoption often took fifteen years or more, while the next 3 percent was obtained in about three more years. We now have reason to believe that future change will proceed much more rapidly than that depicted by Ross and his group. For example, Carlson showed the year-by-year cumulative percentages of adopters of a modern math program from the time of its introduction into a county in 1958 until the program was 88 percent accepted within the county in 1963.[15]

Miles believes that the educational establishment tends to obstruct change and innovation. He states that many promising innovations gasp and expire because we have not ". . . focused upon the features and consequences of change process."[16] We recognize that it is easier to talk about program change than it is to take the actions needed to secure improvements. It is easier and safer to discuss gadgets and gimmicks that falsely promise change than it is to honestly accept the fundamental reasons why change is difficult, and, possibly, how it may be secured.

It is true that every teacher, every counselor, and every administrator would say that he wished to make the guidance program responsive to individual and social needs, and there have been changes for the better, but these have been slow and sporadic. The fact remains that many in-

[13] P. R. Mort and R. G. Cornell, *American Schools in Transition: How Our Schools Adapt Their Practices to Changing Needs—A Study of Pennsylvania* (New York: Bureau of Publications, Teachers College, Columbia University, 1941).

[14] D. H. Ross, *et al.* (eds.), *Administration of Adaptability* Vol. 11 (New York: Bureau of Publications, Teachers College, Columbia University, 1951).

[15] R. O. Carlson, "School Superintendents and Adoption of Modern Math: A Social Structure Profile," unpublished study, Institute for Community Studies, University of Oregon, September 1963.

[16] Matthew B. Miles, *Innovation in Education* (New York: Bureau of Publications, Teachers College, Columbia University, 1964).

dividuals oppose change and balk at instituting new directions in guidance programs. This reluctance to change is not confined to schools, however. Many of those engaged in counselor education are equally guilty; witness the delaying tactics in implementing counselor education standards.

In recent times no problem has been more puzzling to thoughtful people than why, in a troubled, complex world, educators are reluctant to change programs when such change is clearly needed. The lack of educational statesmanship has sometimes been assumed. But it is clear that the trouble goes much deeper. It is a reflection of our attitudes toward and desire to avoid disruption and will persist as long as these attitudes and this desire remain unchallenged and unexamined.

Attitudes Restricting Change

Those who seek the improvement of guidance programs must understand the attitudes and forces that work to counteract change. Two such attitudes will be briefly described. They must be recognized and dealt with by guidance personnel who seek to introduce change.

The first attitude that impedes change is the tendency among educational personnel to wait and see if the problem will disappear. In part, this attitude is justified, since probably no social institution is to such a great degree at the mercy of public whim as the school. The history of public education is one of the recurrent attacks by "critics" whose expertise frequently consists of unhappy personal experience in their education or concern with specific segments of the school population. It should be quickly added that some of this criticism is inevitable in a publicly supported enterprise. It should also be made clear that some criticism is justified and can produce positive change. The difficulty lies in the unevenness of the flow of criticism—it tends to occur in waves—and in the overgeneralization of criticisms to the entire educational program. Also, special-interest groups periodically gain ascendancy in their demands. The past decade has witnessed the emergence of demands for programs for the retarded, concern for the gifted, general stress on academics, and most recently, pleas for vocational programs. Some gain may accrue to the schools as a result of such demands—at least one hopes so.

Second, an attitude of defensiveness prevents program improvement. Teachers, counselors, and administrators who have grown accustomed to the relationships by which their status is defined and maintained are often upset and defensive about change, especially if these changes involve modifications of pet theories and routine ways of doing things. But, from whatever vantage point the matter of program improvement is viewed, there will be opposition by defenders of the status quo. Their personal commitment to habitual ways of thinking and acting goes counter to their interest in the necessity for program modification. Solidly entrenched teachers, counselors, and administrators will not submit readily or meekly to demands for change. They want to retain the comfortable and the familiar while the world moves on. Any change tending to alter their activities, especially if it is perceived as an adverse or threatening alteration, will be viewed with alarm and met with resistance.

There is no doubt that these two attitudes will be encountered by those who wish to advance guidance programs, but the question remains, Given these and other attitudes, can changes be made?

The Concept of Equilibrium

The concept of equilibrium is a useful one for the task at hand. It has been estimated that it takes fifty years for a new idea to become operative nationwide in educational practices. As stated above, part of the explanation is that educators tend to be conservative and make changes only when they have to. But perhaps this is an oversimplification of the situation, an assumption that all resistance stems from obdurate school personnel. What is probably more correct is the fact that several forces, pushing for change in one direction or another, simultaneously come to bear on the school. Some forces urge change in one direction, and others act in the opposite direction. When the two balance each other so as to create a dilemma in which satisfaction of one demand requires denial of the other, equilibrium is reached.

From this viewpoint, change in the guidance program could be made only by upsetting the old equilibrium and establishing a new equilibrium at another level. This means that those who seek change in guidance programs will have to assess the total constellation of forces accurately and know the realities with which they are working.

Perhaps a simple illustration based on an actual experience will give meaning to the abstraction. School X had conducted a "career day" for about ten years. A newly employed school counselor noted that twenty-nine of the thirty-five scheduled careers represented were professional or managerial. He also noted that currently only 25 percent of the student body attended either a two-year or four-year college following high school, whereas a decade before, over 50 percent had gone to college. The segment of the community served had markedly shifted from middle- to working-class families. Armed with this information, the counselor sought administrative support for modification in the ratio of professional careers represented at the forthcoming career day program. The school principal and director of guidance defended the retention of past practices on the bases that (1) students had indicated on the "sign-up" form that these were the careers in which they were interested, and (2) any change in the representatives might be embarrassing since they were influential individuals from the local or surrounding towns who had always participated. Early in the next year the counselor was able to get the principal and director of guidance to appoint an advisory committee which included some of the more influential representatives of previous career days. Then the counselor obtained students' first- and second-stated occupational preferences from their four-year plan sheets, which had been completed individually with counselors. These statements of *actual* (as opposed to aspirational) occupational preferences indicated that over half of the students were interested in nonprofessional occupations. The advisory committee recommended inviting career representatives who could talk about the occupations in which the students had shown the greatest interest on their four-year plan sheets; this was carried through for the current and later career days. Perhaps this illustration points up Lewin's statement that "A successful change includes . . . three aspects: unfreezing (if necessary) the present level, moving to the new level, and freezing group life on the new level."[17]

Steps to Secure Change

Change may be in one of two directions—atrophy or improvement—and its direction is determined by a variety of factors embedded in the school. Some of the steps that may be taken to initiate changes to improve guidance services are outlined here. These steps would be undertaken to change the equilibrium by either removing or reducing the strength of restraining forces or adding or strengthening the driving forces in a school. Hopefully, these steps indicate that there is no easy way to secure change. There is no "best" way, for there is no substitute for thinking through and deciding how change can be accomplished at the local level.

Perhaps an example of how one school managed to secure change will add meaning to the discussion. The three counselors and the director of guidance at "Able High School" conducted a survey of the needs of its student body of about fifteen hundred and an evaluation of its guidance services. Able High School is a single comprehensive high school in a town of thirty thousand. While a complete evaluation of student needs, staff, and facilities had been undertaken, the most striking outcome was that 30 percent of its students were college bound, 50 percent entered the labor market immediately after high school, and the remainder failed to complete high school. The survey of guidance services revealed that the college-bound students received approximately 80 percent of the guidance time and services, with two-thirds of that time devoted to program planning. This simple set of data will be used as a basis to outline the steps taken to secure change.

1. *Establish a commitment to change.* Although change for the sake of change is not advocated, Able High School counselors, in conducting an evaluation, were committed to some degree to the process of change if the evaluation indicated that change was warranted. The director of guidance at Able High School had suggested the evaluation, and the staff

---

[17] Kurt Lewin, "Group Decision and Social Change," in T. Newcomb and E. L. Hartley (eds.), *Readings in Social Psychology* (New York: Holt, Rinehart & Winston, Inc., 1947), p. 344.

had somewhat reluctantly agreed that a reasonable effort would be made to incorporate the changes. Though some reluctance did exist, the general attitude toward the process appeared promising.

2. *Determine most pressing needs.* The problem of "where to begin" to secure change may involve a choice of moving the total school program forward or concentrating on a single service or one aspect of a single service. Usually it is best to approach improvement in areas in which the evaluation shows the most pressing need for change. This emphasizes again the need for an appraisal that is thoroughly and carefully conducted. Budget, space, and personnel considerations may dictate which changes can be more quickly realized and which ones will have to be delayed. Able High School counselors were struck by the fact that the college-bound 30 percent of their school population received the bulk of their time and services. They decided that one of their most pressing needs was to provide more guidance services to the 50 percent of the population that entered the labor market immediately after high school and the 20 percent who failed to graduate.

3. *Study the school situation to determine the constellation of forces at work to maintain present practices.* The suggestion here is that guidance personnel will use their diagnostic skills to determine the concentration of forces with which they are dealing. They will seek to determine which individuals are most complacent with regard to present practices and why.

Able High School counselors noted that even though the bulk of their time was spent with college-bound students, it was centered primarily upon program planning. In their deliberations, some of the counselors defended such arrangements on the grounds that this constituted their major responsibility as counselors. Other Able High School counselors were equally adamant that those who saw the counselor's responsibility as being primarily one of program planning had failed to keep pace with current trends in counselor role and function. They reasoned that counselors who wished to restrict their functions to this activity did so because they were uncomfortable in performing other functions, since their training had been secured some years ago.

4. *Clarify present status and present the ideal.* It may be that the potentiality for change in a school system is analogous to the potentiality for change in an individual in that the degree of change needed may be estimated by the degree of discrepancy between the self-concept and the ideal concept. Guidance personnel who wish to introduce change must perform three functions: (1) clarify present status (self-concept) by evaluation, (2) describe the desired program (ideal concept), and (3) point out discrepancies and introduce the aspects of needed innovations. The critical tasks of identifying the ideal can be accomplished, at least in part, by seeking out and acquainting the staff with the most promising practices in guidance throughout the country. Knowledge of what is being tried constructively in other localities relevant to the specific situa-

tion for which change is demanded helps reduce complacency and induce the desire for productive change. To accomplish this step, Able High School counselors secured published statements of counselor role and function from the professional journals, circulated them among the counseling staff, administrators, and teachers, and conducted a series of study discussion sessions on the topic.

5. _Gain administrative support._ Change to improve guidance services is dependent upon and cannot be secured without administrative support. Without administrative support, far-reaching improvements are unlikely to be made or, if instituted, they will have no lasting or pervasive effect. To move for change without administrative support is usually unprofitable. This means that guidance personnel, primarily the director of guidance, has the responsibility to present to principals and superintendents what conditions are like at present and what conditions are possible. Without this information, administrators cannot make decisions with any degree of perspective. Administrative support will come as a result of knowledge that is clearly and persuasively transmitted to them. To gain administrative support for change does not imply that change must necessarily emanate from administrators, however.

Knowing that administrative support would have profound effect on the willingness of the school staff and community to incorporate the changes that were being suggested, Able's director of guidance conducted a campaign to interpret the reasons for program modifications to the principal and superintendent. They were presented the data from the evaluation and the suggested changes in program operation. Suggested changes included: (1) counselor time spent with students should be prorated on the basis of college versus non-college percentage; (2) specialization in counseling functions should be undertaken by permitting those counselors who see program planning as their major responsibility to assume the greatest amount of work in this area, while delegating to the other counselors the major responsibility for counseling students on vocational and personal concerns; and (3) combining the efforts of faculty and teachers to identify potential dropouts and to develop special programs for them.

6. _Involve the staff in change._ Any change or steps taken to improve the program is dependent upon the good will of the staff, including teachers. Change involves human values and human relationships which always defy categorization and standardization. How to obtain staff involvement is a crucial problem. But, only by sharing responsively in the process will change ever be pervasive and lasting. A school staff is often heterogeneous and looks with veiled hostility, or at best, with apathy, at efforts to manipulate them in directions they may not willingly take. But other social sanctions and psychological factors lead teachers to have a desire to participate in policy formation, and they will respond positively to respected and trusted leadership. If those who wish to secure change do

not enlist the energies of the staff, they will fail. When teachers are unable to identify with modifications and accept responsibility to make use of them, there is little likelihood that improvements will last.

Able High School counselors approached staff involvement to secure change with a certain amount of timidity, but they reasoned that leadership is exercised rather than achieved automatically. They expected some conflict, ideological tensions, and they were not disappointed. A healthy degree of autonomy makes for a desirable attitude toward change. Through faculty meetings, committees, and study groups, Able High School counselors worked to develop staff insight into the reasons why changes were needed, the meanings for their need of such changes, and the services to students that would be the result of such changes. They stressed in their interactions with teachers that they were open to suggestions as to how to identify school dropouts and what changes might be made to better accommodate them.

7. *Acquaint the community with the reasons and necessity for change.* Too often it is believed that the utility of an innovation is sufficient to gain its acceptance. Utility is a highly relative matter. Innovations somewhat congruous with pre-existing practices are always accepted more readily than those which are not. This principle may serve as a guideline when alerting the community and staff to change.

Every community has certain expectations with respect to the school program. Some communities are fervently demanding expansion and improvement of their guidance programs. Admittedly, some communities may have too high and quite unrealistic expectations as to what a guidance program can legitimately accomplish. Nevertheless, a staff has to acquaint parents with the nature, scope, present state and anticipated changes in guidance services. Parents seek to understand, accept, and contribute to a school's program.

Administrators and counselors of Able High School used to good advantage advisory groups made up of nonprofessionals in the community. Such groups become sources of informal support when changes were introduced. They offered advice and experience in awakening the community to the necessity for program innovations to care adequately for the pupils being served by the school.

8. *Plan for future evaluation.* It has been said many times that evaluation is continuous as well as periodic. Those who are interested in improving programs must build into their programs provisions for surveys and analysis of the "needs" of the student body, including the making of decisions about the breadth of responsibility that the school will assume. They will build in surveys to appraise the program in order to acertain areas that need extension or strengthening. Simultaneous with, or subsequent to these steps, they will provide growth experiences for the staff so that their repertoire of suggestions for improvement will be broadened.

In summary, processes of change fall into definite sequence. Modifications of guidance programs are dependent upon a well-prepared, alert, flexible staff who can pool their ingenuity to reduce the barriers to change. Social psychologists have repeatedly emphasized that modifications appear at the time that institutions need them. Periods of advance are often followed by low tides of change during which sorting and integrating may be carried on.

Any school staff which pursues program improvement can expect to experience disharmony. As disharmony becomes more pronounced, more and more of the school's efforts will go into makeshift efforts until the changes gradually are incorporated. Our society is experiencing this at the present time in its tremendous and still accelerating science and technology which has outstripped development in social, economic, and political patterns.

It seems safe to predict that one hundred years from now, changes currently being undertaken in guidance programs will be regarded as primitive experiments. It can also be noted with equal safety that the total school climate does indeed set broad limits on the kinds of modifications that can be undertaken. Finally, in spite of education's innumerable deficiencies, school history as a whole shows certain outcomes of change. Each new stage is usually a little better than the one before it.

ANNOTATED BIBLIOGRAPHY

BOY, ANGELO V., AND PINE, GERALD J. *The Counselor In the Schools: A Reconceptualization.* Boston: Houghton Mifflin Company, 1968, 406 pp.
Chapter 11 (pp. 245–282) presents some diverse topics related to evaluation: the client, the counselor, and counseling service. The authors provide several checklists for evaluating the effectiveness of counseling.

HUTSON, PERCIVAL W. *The Guidance Function in Education.* Second Edition. New York: Appleton-Century-Crofts, 1968, 786 pp.
Chapter 19 (pp. 757–775) reviews the literature that describes guidance appraisal. The author presents investigations relating to such topics as students' familiarity with educational and vocational opportunities, self-knowledge, emotional and social adjustment, and the like.

MILLER, FRANK W. *Guidance Principles and Services.* Second Edition. Charles E. Merrill Publishing Company, 1968.
Chapter 11 (pp. 262–279) presents research in and evaluation of guidance. Attention is given to school surveys, followup studies, and methods of evaluation. The author gives some suggestions for evaluating guidance services.

SELECTED REFERENCES

BARKER, DONALD G. "Development of a Scale of Attitudes Toward School Guidance," *Personnel and Guidance Journal* Vol. 44 (June 1966), pp. 1077–1083.

BROUGH, JAMES R. "A Comparison of Self-Referred Counselees and Non-Counseled Junior High School Students," *Personnel and Guidance Journal* Vol. 47 (December 1968), pp. 329–332.

GRAFF, ROBERT W., AND MACLEAN, G. DONALD. "Evaluating Educational-Vocational Counseling: A Model for Change," *Personnel and Guidance Journal* Vol. 48 (March 1970), pp. 568–574.

GRANDE, PETER P. "Attitudes of Counselors and Disadvantaged Students Toward School Guidance," *Personnel and Guidance Journal* Vol. 46 (May 1968), pp. 889–892.

KENNEDY, JOHN J., AND FREDRICKSON, RONALD H. "Student Assessment of Counselor Assistance in Selected Problem Areas," *Counselor Education and Supervision* Vol. 8 (Spring 1969), pp. 206–212.

KETTERMAN, CLARK S. "The Opinion of Selected Publics Concerning The School Counselor's Function," *The School Counselor* Vol. 16 (September 1968), pp. 41–45.

LEE, WALTER S. "The Evaluation of School Guidance Programs," *The School Counselor* Vol. 17 (November 1969), pp. 84–88.

MILLER, C. DEAN, AND IVEY, ALLEN E. "Student Response to Three Types of Orientation Programs," *Personnel and Guidance Journal,* Vol. 45 (June 1967), pp. 1025–1029.

MURO, JAMES J., AND REVELLO, EDWARD A. "Counselor-Student Perceptions of the Extent of Performance of Guidance Services," *The School Counselor* Vol. 17 (January 1970), pp. 193–199.

PERRONE, PHILIP A., AND GILBERTSON, CARLYLE W. "Case Study: A Research Approach to Establishing Pupil Services," *Personnel and Guidance Journal* Vol. 46 (June 1968), pp. 990–996.

ROTHNEY, JOHN W. M., AND LEWIS, CHARLES W. "Use of Control Groups in Studies of Guidance," *Personnel and Guidance Journal* Vol. 47 (January 1969), pp. 446–449.

SKAGER, RODNEY, AND WEINBERG, CARL. "Relationships Between Selected Social Factors and Extent of High School Counseling," *Personnel and Guidance Journal* Vol. 45 (May 1967), pp. 901–906.

TRUAX, CHARLES, AND LISTER, JAMES L. "Effectiveness of Counselors and Counselor Aides," *Journal of Counseling Psychology* Vol. 17 (July 1970), pp. 331–334.

WALTON, FRANCIS X., AND SWEENEY, THOMAS J. "Useful Predictors of Counseling Effectiveness," *Personnel and Guidance Journal* Vol. 48 (September 1969), pp. 32–38.

WALZ, GARRY R., AND LEE, JAMES L. "Funded Personnel Services Research: Patterns and Trends," *Personnel and Guidance Journal* Vol. 47 (June 1969), pp. 970–974.

WITTMER, JOE, "The Effects of Counseling and Tutoring on the Attitudes and Achievement of Seventh Grade Underachievers," *The School Counselor* Vol. 16 (March 1969), pp. 287–290.

ZIMPFER, DAVID G. "Some Conceptual and Research Problems in Group Counseling," *The School Counselor* Vol. 15 (May 1968), pp. 326–333.

17

REFERRAL PROCEDURES AND COMMUNITY GUIDANCE RESOURCES

What is the nature of guidance referrals?
What factors are involved in the counselor's referral decision?
What administrative and coordinative functions are involved in school and community referrals?
What types of referral services are required?
How may community guidance resources be identified?

THE NATURE OF GUIDANCE REFERRALS

Referral is simply defined as the act of transferring an individual to another person or agency either within or outside the school. Personnel or agencies outside of school are utilized because they provide some form of specialized assistance not available from the original counselor or within the school setting. It is important to emphasize that referrals are made for the purpose of specialized assistance, but that referral does not necessarily mean that the individual referred has a serious problem, for such a view is narrow and misleading. Many referrals occur simply because the problem is beyond the scope of the services provided. Many other referrals are made because the person or agency makes a cooperative decision with the counselor that the service available in the school is inappropriate. For example, a school counselor may refer a student to an employment agency because that agency is better equipped to assist the student in getting a job. Or the school counselor whose counselee presents a problem complicated by his parents' marital difficulties may work with the parents in an effort to refer them to a

The authors acknowledge with gratitude the assistance of H. Allan Dye, Assistant Professor of Education, Counseling and Personnel Services, Purdue University, in the initial preparation of this chapter.

marriage counseling service. The point to be emphasized is that referral involves the transfer of an individual to a person or agency providing a *different* kind of assistance.

The ability to recognize when the needs of a particular student are not within the scope of one's personal resources or those of the school is a professional necessity for the counselor. The foregoing statement is vulnerable to three inaccurate inferences, all of which have been widely drawn and acted upon. In order of importance, the most serious misinterpretation accrues from viewing referral as simply a technique. Within a consistent rationale and philosophy of guidance, providing needed specialized services for even a relatively small proportion of the student body is of major importance. The second fallacy concerns the notion that referral decisions are expected to occur only in times of emergency. If guidance is continuous and developmental and consists of a systematic, orderly structure, few genuine emergency (unexpected) situations will materialize. The final misconception derives from the scope of one's personal resources. Counselors sometimes tend to either unnecessarily prolong or too quickly terminate a relationship, rather than lose face by referring when their personal resources are inappropriate to the client's need. Other counselors see nearly all clients as being in need of others' help. Arbuckle has described this as characterizing "a referral technician rather than a professional counselor."[1] Shertzer and Stone have also commented on the critical matter of terminating the relationship too quickly.

> Some counselors are so timid about working with emotional issues at a level appropriate to their competencies that they are completely unwilling to discuss substantive personal issues with students. In part, this timidity has been encouraged by counselor educators and school administrators who stress that the counselor should not overextend himself or overstep the bounds of his competencies in the area of "personal problems." Forgotten and/or ignored in this situation is the fact that normal students have emotions which are not necessarily equated to serious emotional problems but do come into play materially in their daily lives. Counselors who refuse to deal with emotions frequently find it impossible to cope effectively with students who have more serious emotional disturbances when they are inevitably confronted with them. For students with disabling emotional problems, the counselor's refusal to work toward even enough understanding to permit appropriate referral, is tantamount to negligence. At a safer and less critical level, the counselor's refusal to cope with feeling components forces students to focus upon purely informational factors rather than permitting the motivations and feelings which crucially influence human decisions to come into play.[2]

[1] Dugald S. Arbuckle, *Counseling: Philosophy, Theory and Practice* Second Edition (Boston: Allyn and Bacon, Inc., 1970), p. 353.

[2] Bruce Shertzer and Shelley C. Stone, "Challenges Confronting Counselors," *The School Counselor* Vol. 12 (May 1965), p. 238.

From Stepchild to Major Service

Referral has been looked upon as an unclassified task, typically invoked as a last resort in situations requiring great expediency and performed by counselors who, in so doing, have "capitulated" to ·forces beyond their control. Historically, the referral process has been a guidance stepchild. In the light of an emerging unified guidance rationale, the referral services deserve full family membership.

The underlying assumption has been that all referrals are for remedial action:

> The member shall decline to initiate or shall terminate a counseling rela- tionship when he cannot be of professional assistance to the counselee or client either because of lack of competence or personal limitation. In such instances the member shall refer his counselee or client to an appropriate specialist. In the event the counselee or his client declines the suggested referral, the member is not obligated to continue the counseling relation- ship.[3]

Although remedial service of either a psychological or medical nature is often the objective, planned utilization of various intraschool services and community agencies may serve to realize certain preventive and develop- mental goals as well.

Intraschool services which are often not fully developed and utilized as sources of assistance for individual students are, for example, teachers, health and medical staff, administrators, psychometrists, psychologists, and social workers. Community agencies whose services frequently extend be- yond those of a remedial nature include social service and mental health agencies, civic organizations, churches, police youth activities, organiza- tions of business and industrial leaders, physicians, and lawyers. When gui- dance personnel are familiar with these sources of special assistance, com- municate with them, and establish a common goal of personal growth for all the children of the community, an important and contributing service will have been added to the guidance program.

Attitude and Manner

Making a referral does not necessarily indicate a departure from a "pro- found faith in the worth, dignity and great potentiality of the individual human being."[4] Patterson has called attention to the necessity for main- taining "a fundamental respect for the individual and a fundamental belief that it is best for him to work out his own problems in his own way."[5]

[3] "Ethical Standards," *Personnel and Guidance Journal* Vol. 40 (October 1961), p. 207.

[4] Preamble to "Ethical Standards," *ibid.,* p. 206.

[5] C. H. Patterson, *Counseling and Guidance in Schools* (New York: Harper & Row, Publishers, 1962), p. 331.

Students who are referred, particularly for remedial or preventive attention, are likely to be apprehensive, anxious, and somewhat fearful. These attitudinal and behavioral cues require that the counselor clearly exhibit acceptance, understanding, and concern, as communicated in his willingness to help. An attitude of reassurance born of confidence that appropriate steps are being taken is a critical ingredient. This is a matter of realistically facing the facts and the related available alternatives. Feelings of remorse for having failed to act sooner on the basis of previous evidence can result in hasty and ill-advised decisions. Naturally, the earliest possible detection and action increase the likelihood of rational and desirable counselor functioning. Appropriate and consistent counselor behavior and specialized assistance can be best provided by conceptualizing and organizing the referral process as a cumulative and comprehensive program involving the coordinated planning and services of the total school staff and the community.

Identification of Students in Need of Specialized Services

An effective referral system is less a matter of devising new forms than it is one of utilizing existing identification and reporting media. The cumulative record, anecdotal record, observational report, and other appraisal techniques are tools that serve no purpose unless used. In describing a unique team approach in guidance, Mattick and Nickolas point out that the sophisticated reports and recommendations that fill personnel records often fail to have any impact on the child in the classroom.[6] These media are more valuable in the evaluation of a potential referral than they are necessary for identification purposes.

Guidance personnel, teachers, and administrators are typically aware of students with special needs. The critical questions are, What kind of special service does each student require? Is the needed service available, and if so, where? It is the answer to these questions which those responsible for the referral process must determine. The identification procedure must be planned to include all who are in contact with students and must be coordinated in order to provide direction for the combined effort.

Provision should be made in new staff orientation and in faculty meetings for direct notification and action in the case of extreme student behavior. The faculty should be contacted each semester for lists of the names of students whose records should be reviewed or who should be given special attention. These lists should be reviewed for possible action by a referral committee that represents the administrative, instructional, and guidance staffs. In this way early indications of unique needs can be planned for by school or community services. Implicit in the foregoing is that the staff (1) recognizes when students' needs cannot be met in the classroom, (2) is

[6] William E. Mattick and N. A. Nickolas, "A Team Approach in Guidance," *Personnel and Guidance Journal* Vol. 42 (May 1964), pp. 922–924.

aware of the availability of many types of special services, and (3) is as concerned with developmental goals as it is with factors of expediency.

Following preliminary identification and screening with suggested recommendations by the referral committee, the stage is set for careful consideration of each student's situation. Since referral decisions are complex, each should be the subject of a case conference. Much valuable time can be conserved by scheduling case conferences so that the staff involved may consider at any one time the cases of several students with whom they share a common contact. For example, a group of ten staff members may be called together for a conference at which the cases of four students are to be considered. Although each staff member might be directly concerned with one or more of the students, perhaps none except the director of guidance and/or the principal is concerned with all of the cases. Further, the conference can be arranged so that some of the staff need not be on hand at the start and that others may leave before the session ends. There are potentially many alternatives, and careful planning can result in case conferences that are less tedious and time consuming, more productive, and utilized more frequently to meet a variety of objectives.

THE REFERRAL DECISION

Effective referral requires (1) judgment in determining the need and the type of service required, (2) knowledge of available specialists and services, and (3) skill in assisting students and their families to make use of referral services. Of these requirements, the first and third are the least specific and most difficult to attain. It is in meeting the needs of the minority proportion for remedial and preventive psychological and social care and attention that school counselors most often experience apprehension concerning the adequacy of their professional skills and abilities.

Primary Considerations

The counselor's primary considerations are as follows: (1) What information do I have about the needs of this student? (2) How valid is the information? (3) Are there other staff members who may be able to provide additional information? (4) Based on all the available information about the student and his situation, what remedial or preventive treatment is indicated? (5) What sources of treatment are available? (6) How soon should treatment begin? The answers to these questions are largely a matter of judgment and degree; hence, counselor training and preparation programs are designed to increase one's proficiency in achieving appropriate solutions. In this situation as in many others, however, experience provides the most useful discriminating criterion for complex decisions regarding behavior.

With regard to the first and second questions above, Shertzer and Stone's earlier comments concerning the need to develop an adequate understanding of the problem before considering referral are appropriate.[7] What this suggests is that one or two interviews devoted to superficial content may not provide a sufficient basis for a referral consideration. Further contact with the individual is necessary to ascertain whether referral is needed. It is important to know the context or life situation within which the problem exists. That is, how does a particular problem or need relate to other aspects of the student's life? The quest for additional information is a likely setting for contacts with other staff members who know the student. The purpose of these contacts is basically to provide a means of evaluating all available information. Decision-making need not be the sole objective in preliminary contacts. The referral decision is ultimately the responsibility of a single individual, either the director of guidance or his appointee. Following the counselor's preliminary evaluation and case conference, it may also be worthwhile to consult with professional colleagues, as Tyler suggests:

> Besides these decisions as to whether to continue a case and what kind of help the person needs most, the counselor will often have to decide at this early stage whether or not to seek some kind of consultation with regard to it. It is in accord with generally accepted ethical principles for him to talk the case over with other professional persons on the staff of the agency in which he works. In many agencies it is customary to hold staff meetings at which group decisions can be made with regard to a case one counselor is handling. Such consultation constitutes a real resource for a counselor, even if he is a person with considerable experience, and it is wise for him to arrange for it if he has any doubts about his own decisions.[8]

Several possibilities may be identified as a result of a consultation; referral is only one of these. School counselors are likely to work with less emotionally laden cases, and consultation may provide the needed consensus and support from colleagues that a decision to continue working with a specific student is justified and perhaps advisable.

Contacts with the Student and His Parents

When the preliminary considerations suggest referral as the appropriate course of action, discussion with the student and his parents is the next step in the process. It is imperative that the counselor be fully familiar with potential referral sources before suggesting this possibility to the student. Inclusion of parents as soon as possible without violating ethical responsibilities to the student is essential. With regard to referral agencies, students, and parents, Patterson's reminders, as adapted from a Michigan State University publication, *How to Make Referrals*, are timely:

[7] Shertzer and Stone, "Challenges."

[8] Leona E. Tyler, *The Work of the Counselor* (New York: Appleton-Century-Crofts, Inc., 1961), p. 78.

It is unwise and impractical to refer a student to community agencies without the knowledge, consent, and cooperation of his parents. Many child-guidance agencies will not accept students for treatment unless parents cooperate fully and are willing to present themselves for help, too. Check on the policy of your local agencies in this regard.[9]

Further,

When telling students or parents about available services, in the school or in the community, explain both the functions and the limitations of these services. Do not give the impression that any specialist or agency has all the answers and can work wonders.[10]

Successful referral is more likely to be accomplished by offering to arrange for the special services than by dwelling on the counselor's inability to continue and the uncommon problem represented. Suggesting referral to students requires a positive, helpful approach with no strings attached. Circumstances can arise occasionally which necessitate direct action, but these usually require administrative action that should not be confused with the counselor's efforts.

The actual presentation should be straightforward and tactful; labels and diagnoses should be avoided. The fact that another service is available which may provide the needed assistance should be included. Whatever is needed in the way of making contacts and arrangements should be offered by the counselor. Having provided this information, identified the referral service, and discussed what acceptance of the referral involves, the counselor's task is to assist the student and his family in deciding what action to take.

The Necessity for Family Cooperation

Obtaining family cooperation is necessary if the services of persons or agencies outside the school are to be utilized. The procedures to be followed in discussing referral with parents are similar to those followed in discussions with the student. Some additional considerations, however, have been pointed out by Warters:

Probably the most difficult type of referral is the one involving an emotional problem, such as problems of family relations and of personality disorder. The counselor needs to be able to work slowly and carefully. Hence, everything possible should be done to avoid making the referral an emergency or a crisis situation. Never should it be made an ultimatum situation where the student must accept referral or withdraw from school. If it is, the agency accepting referral may be so seriously handicapped at the start that it has little chance of success. A parent may docilely accept the ultimatum in the school office. In the agency office, however, he may be strongly resistant

[9] Patterson, *Counseling and Guidance,* p. 330.
[10] *Ibid.,* p. 330.

and even explosive. Moreover, parents may vent the resentment and ire provoked by such an ultimatum upon the student, thus worsening his problem.[11]

Each referral case contains unique characteristics, and, for this reason, only a few of the common elements have been discussed here. Counseling principles and ethical codes constitute other references for the exceptional case. Rejection of the referral suggestion need not always be interpreted as failure on the counselor's part. The very fact that the student and his family are now confronted by the problem may contribute materially to a more satisfactory resolution. Resistance, doubts, fears, guilt and defensiveness are factors with which the counselor must be prepared to cope in discussing referral with students and their parents. The conscientious application of his skills in these difficult situations may result ultimately in further development of both the counselor and the student.

ADMINISTRATIVE AND COORDINATING FUNCTIONS

Provision for the observance of legal considerations, the maintenance of ethical standards, clear and direct communication among the school services and community agencies, ease of client access, and mutual regard for the competencies of all service organizations which facilitate the sustaining of a common clientele are conditions that characterize a community well equipped to deal effectively with the development of its youth. Moreover, these conditions indicate attractive professional circumstances suggestive of a community with vital and progressive attitudes.

Legal and Ethical Considerations

With regard to legal and ethical factors, the school guidance staff should operate within the framework of a carefully prepared statement for the information of other members of the faculty and the community. Legal provisions for privileged communication and confidentiality of student records, for example, vary widely among the states. Even among communities within a given state these conditions vary as a result of precedent or tradition. For a more detailed treatment of this subject, the reader is referred to McGowan and Schmidt,[12] Peters and Shertzer,[13] and Gauerke.[14] Ethical de-

[11] From *Techniques of Counseling* by Jane Warters. Copyright 1964. McGraw-Hill Book Co. Used by permission, Pp. 372–373.

[12] John F. McGowan and Lyle D. Schmidt, *Counseling: Readings in Theory and Practice* (New York: Holt, Rinehart & Winston, Inc., 1962), Chapter 15.

[13] Herman Peters and Bruce Shertzer, *Guidance: Program Development and Management* Second Edition (Columbus, Ohio: Charles E. Merrill Books, Inc., 1969), Chapter 14.

[14] Warren E. Gauerke, *Legal and Ethical Responsibilities of School Personnel* (Englewood Cliffs, N.J.: Prentice-Hall, Inc., 1959).

cisions almost invariably accompany referral situations. Observance of ethical considerations minimizes difficulties which might develop. It should be a matter of policy to obtain from the student and his family written permission to furnish other agencies any information that they might request. After referral, measures that insure the confidentiality of the fact that a student is under the care of an outside person or agency should be taken. Such information should be available to school personnel only on a need-to-know basis.

Communications Necessary

Communications with other school services and community agencies must be established in the referral system so that information can travel both ways with as little indirect handling as possible. Timing and confidentiality are basic concerns, of course, but exclusive of this are the matters of administrative cost and efficiency. As communications media, written reports tend to be slow, indirect, and sometimes difficult to obtain. Direct verbal contact, either in person or by telephone, is a rapid method that requires simply knowing whom to contact. Familiarity with a new agency should include this information. The school and its representatives should also identify themselves for any future reference by the agency.

The term "reciprocity," as used in the context of the referral process concerns the amount and kind of feedback to be expected from another agency. It will suffice to point out that a given agency is probably governed by an established general policy covering this subject which may allow for either fairly comprehensive reports, on the one hand, or none at all, on the other. The central consideration always reflects the need for information rather than the satisfaction of curiosity or administrative routine. Any general policy should be identified in the initial informational contact with the agency, and in specific cases the request for a report should be based on clearly defined need. It is common practice for agencies to acknowledge acceptance of a referral. Beyond this, most agencies restrict their requests to suggestions for structuring the student's school experience. Counselors, in making a referral, may not be asked by the agency for a professional opinion. This is not a discourtesy. Such a request would be incongruent, since it is not usually necessary, and might contribute to a biased view of the student. The acceptance of a referral by an agency will usually be accompanied by a request for objective data about performance and behavior in school. Since the school and its staff maintain their interest and concern in students during the time they are being seen by others, it is important that the arrangements for reciprocity be understood in the beginning by all persons involved. To learn subsequently that an agency's policy is contrary to the school's expectation can result in unnecessary misunderstanding and ill will.

Most referral agencies do not lack for clients. Providing for ease of client access to special services is the responsibility of the school and its staff. As in the case of reports, this is fundamentally a matter of becoming acquainted in advance with the procedures to be followed in placing the student in contact with the service. Agency representatives are typically quite cooperative in explaining their organization and routine to those who take the time to inquire. They may be willing to describe their organization and its services in addresses to professional groups who have a need for or an interest in such information. The counselor's particular responsibility in this regard is to be able to provide the student and his family with accurate instructions and to assist as needed in completing the referral. This may be a matter of making telephone calls, obtaining and forwarding request or consent forms, applications, etc., and even occasionally accompanying the student and his family to the agency.

Working Relationships

Schools and agencies from time to time share a common clientele. That is, the agency may suggest that the student continue seeing a school counselor during part or all of the time the agency is working with the student. In such cases the agency specialist will discuss with the counselor the purpose of maintaining the school counselor relationship and will usually suggest what its orientation should be. The student may require support for the periods between visits to the agency; the counselor's work with the student may be of an entirely different sort from that of the agency's, so that both may continue without conflict; it may be an active part of therapy or rehabilitation involving assistance in completing school tasks assigned by the agency. Two precautions to be observed are the maintenance of confidentiality and staying within one's own realm of responsibility. The fact that a student is working with two or more professionally qualified persons, all parties being aware of the fact, does not constitute a circumstance that justifies exception to the ordinary standards of confidentiality. By the same token, counselors and others are obliged to avoid the possibility of overlapping service. Students may precipitate this, either intentionally or unintentionally, by discussing their agency experience with their school counselor.

Responsibility for Referral

The responsibility for coordinating the referral service is a logical assignment of the director of guidance, since he is most likely to be in communication with all school services and may also be most concerned with those in the community. The school administrator will often maintain an active liaison with the community and is also intimately familiar with the school's various operations, but he may lack the required special interest and/or preparation for coordinating the referral service; also, he may not have enough time. Whoever assumes this responsibility must have sufficient time available and a schedule flexible enough to allow for satisfactory performance. Thus, the principal, the director of guidance, or an appointee may administer the referral service.

The referral coordinator is essentially responsible for all the components described in this chapter: consultations with counselors who have identified students with special needs, a knowledge of all services available, the arrangement for and conduct of case conferences, and the establishment and maintenance of communication and access between the school and community services. A frequently overlooked facet of referral coordination involves responsibility for the status and disposition of referred students. It is essential that the coordinator have a knowledge of whether the referral was followed through by those involved. This is especially important when several referral sources are involved in a single case.

Familiarization with Resources

The coordinator has unique and distinct obligations for familiarity with possible referral resources. Among the methods that may be employed are personal interviews and visits, written requests for information, telephone calls, and attendance at professional meetings. With regard to the latter, some local chapters of the American Personnel and Guidance Association have found that familiarization with referral sources can be a worthwhile and challenging project involving all staff members, and improved relations with mental and physical health agencies and civic organizations have resulted.

Records

Records containing descriptive information about each referral source and its prior use by students are also maintained by the coordinator. A periodic review may indicate the desirability of developing new sources, discontinuing others, reducing the amount of service duplication or using the service in a new or different way.

TYPES OF SERVICES REQUIRED

Several classification systems have been suggested that are designed to offer administrative flexibility, autonomy, and expediency. These are valid considerations that ought not overshadow the recognition of student need as the basic criterion in determining which services are provided. Referrals may be made for either remedial or preventive reasons. Remedial referrals are defined as those that become necessary as a result of an inability to meet the daily demands of school living. Some assert that the school's concern extends to life in general. This issue need not be discussed here, however, for school is such an integral part of the total life situation that distinguishing between the two serves no useful purpose. Preventive referrals are those made when there is preliminary evidence available that a difficulty may be anticipated that would later interfere with acceptable school performance.

Types of student needs have been identified in a variety of contexts by Remmers and Hackett,[15] Havighurst,[16] Coleman,[17] Williamson,[18] Conant,[19] and Wrenn,[20] to name but a few; a summary of these needs furnishes a classification of needs which includes the following: (1) psychological; (2) physiological or health; (3) social; (4) financial; (5) educational–vocational; and (6) growth and actualization. An observation relevant to the organization of referral sources is that needs are subject to stages of development, each suggesting different action. Examples of each type of need and of intraschool and community referral sources are discussed below.

Resources for Students with Special Psychological Needs

Examples of psychological needs requiring attention are represented by excessive anxiety, depression, fear, hostility, aggression, passivity, indecisiveness, irresponsibility, inadequate and/or distorted self-concepts, retardation, etc. It is useful to bear in mind that although the origin of needs may be familial, social, or biological, it is the effect of these factors upon the individual's psychological processes with which the referral service is concerned. When students are faced with emotional difficulties that preclude satisfactory academic performance, remedial action must be taken. Emotional disturbance has pervasive effects, so that much more is involved than school achievement. The counselor's or student's failure to act when remedial steps are taken may jeopardize a student's ultimate psychological welfare and may even involve the physical welfare of the student and others.

Relatively few schools are properly staffed to serve this type of need, for it usually requires the services of those with advanced training and experience in clinical psychology or psychiatry. When the service of a psychologist or psychiatrist is available within the school organization, referral to him is a relatively easy matter. In some cases the student's condition may necessitate removal from school and perhaps hospitalization. If school psychological specialists are available they will ordinarily initiate the appropriate action. Otherwise the director of guidance and/or a school ad-

[15] R. H. Remmers and C. C. Hackett, *Let's Listen to Youth* (Chicago: Science Research Associates, Inc., 1950).

[16] Robert J. Havighurst, *Developmental Tasks and Education* (New York: Longmans, Green & Co., Inc., 1951).

[17] James S. Coleman, *The Adolescent Society* (New York: The Free Press of Glencoe, 1961).

[18] E. G. Williamson, *Counseling Adolescents* (New York: McGraw-Hill Book Co., Inc., 1950).

[19] James B. Conant, *Slums and Suburbs* (New York: McGraw-Hill Book Co., Inc., 1961).

[20] C. Gilbert Wrenn, *The Counselor in a Changing World* (Washington: American Personnel and Guidance Association, 1962).

ministrator is responsible for seeking needed assistance from persons or organizations in the community. Parents or other adults responsible for the child must always, for legal purposes and other obvious reasons, be consulted for their consent. In the event of a clearly defined emergency situation in which the physical welfare of any person is threatened, direct and immediate action to remove the student is required, even if time does not allow for prior notification.

In the usual case of remedial psychological care outside the school, the student will be absent from school for only a relatively brief period or perhaps not at all. Students under nonschool remedial care often continue in a helping relationship with a member of the school counseling staff. The nature of this relationship may be only supportive; nevertheless, it can and does constitute a critical ingredient in the rehabilitative process. Depending upon circumstances, teachers, social workers, administrators, and occasionally even other students play important roles in remedial programs.

The direct source of care for those experiencing severe forms of emotional difficulty is likely to be an individual, institution or agency outside the school. Psychiatrists, psychologists, hospitals, mental health clinics, and physicians in general practice are common referral sources. Because of their specialized nature these services tend to be clustered in metropolitan areas and the guidance staff should be familiar with the many agencies and the nature of their programs. In rural areas and small communities the guidance staff faces a different problem, that of developing sources of assistance. Physicians in general practice are the most logical referral source wh n specialized psychological care is unavailable. Other persons and organizations are sometimes used but the fact remains and should be acknowledged that there seldom is a satisfactory substitute for professional remedial care; modern transportation makes it unnecessary to settle for less.

Though psychological needs requiring referral for preventive treatment are less dramatic than those of a remedial nature, they are more amenable to the services of the school staff. Further, they are more closely aligned with traditional educational practice so that more is known about identification and treatment methodology. The distinction between remedial and preventive referral cannot be made clearly except that in the latter case either prior knowledge or early identification of impending difficulty can prevent the development of overwhelming circumstances. For example, high school students whose previous behavior in the elementary and junior high grades has been hostile and aggressive can be expected to continue to be so unless efforts are made to resolve the underlying conflict and/or provide for adequate releases of tension. The situation is analogous for other forms of psychological need, such as inhibition, anxiety over grades, need for approval, etc.

Counseling has been demonstrated as an effective preventive procedure. To rely exclusively on counseling, however, is to fail in fully utilizing the services of the entire school staff and to be overly confident of the counseling process. Teachers who are informed of the special psychological needs of students often are able to provide valuable assistance in the form of modified instructional and personal relationships. Consulting with teachers in this way does not constitute a complete referral in the usual sense, but this variety of semi-referral is a rich source of preventive attention.

Community referral sources for preventive attention include those useful in remedial care. Agencies may be used in supplemental and consultative ways based on only limited contact with students. In addition, these specialists represent a logical source of assistance for inservice education and evaluation of mental health conditions in the school. Psychological growth and development are objectives of counseling and guidance shared with others in the school and community. Other referral sources in the community include all those persons and organizations in contact with students with whom the counseling staff can communicate on a professional level. Examples are the Boy Scouts, Girl Scouts, Boys' Clubs, Police Athletic League, churches, community centers, and many other organizations providing service to youth.

Communities offer psychological services through such organizations as the child guidance clinics, marriage counseling centers, welfare agencies, and family aid societies. More and more, churches are extending pastoral counseling services.

Although small communities do not generally have the services of a psychiatrist, the number of psychiatrists in private practice is increasing. School guidance personnel will need to know those who practice in their communities as well as others in surrounding cities so that appropriate referrals can be made.

Most families know little about the counseling services available in the community. The information they possess concerning sources of help is seldom complete or accurate and is often shrouded in negative attitudes. Even if a member of the family needs counseling services, it is unrealistic to expect families to seek out and learn what assistance is available completely on their own.

MENTAL HEALTH AGENCIES

Mental health agencies are making their appearance in more and more communities. The term "orthopsychiatry" designates the fusion of psychiatry, medicine, psychology, and social work as applied to problems of adjustment. The core of orthopsychiatry is not the separate activities of the disciplines represented, but the interaction of several approaches to the individual. Mental health agencies that offer services primarily to children are usually termed "child guidance clinics" or "child guidance centers." Mental health agencies usually offer a group of specialists who cooperate in attacking problems of conduct and adjustment. Such specialists usually include a psychologist, a psychiatrist, psychiatric social workers, and sometimes a pediatrician. In general, children between the ages of three and sixteen are treated. Intellectual retardation and pathological states of long standing, such as epilepsy, childhood schizophrenia, and the like, are not usually treated routinely in child guidance clinics.

The trend in the work of personnel associated with mental health clinics is to direct efforts toward the family rather than the individual as the unit to be treated. Relationships between parents and children are significant in determining the mental health of the latter. Parents' techniques of managing their children often stem from their own emotional states. Naturally, the scope of therapeutic help given to the family varies with the need and also with the facilities available.

Tremendous impetus is currently being given to the creation of comprehensive community mental health services. Public Law 88–164, the Community Mental Health Centers Act, authorizes the financing of up to two-thirds of construction costs for such centers. The intent of the Act was to stimulate treatment of the mentally ill in the community and by the community. Though the program is just now under way, ultimately it will provide comprehensive mental health services for restricted geographical areas. Further information about psychological community resources may be obtained from local, state, and national mental health agencies and associations, state psychological associations, and family and children's agencies.

Referral Resources for Health Purposes

Physiological or health factors such as vision, hearing, diet, the effects of crippling and chronic disease, personal hygiene, including dental habits—all these and other matters frequently become the concern of school personnel. Many students are provided maximum care in this area by their families. Because medical care is expensive, other families of limited means rely heavily on aid obtained directly through the auspices of school or community services.

The primary school resources for remedial treatment of health needs are the school physician and nurse. The amount and quality of health service provided varies considerably from community to community. Although the amount made available is an administrative matter, it is an area of vital concern for the student personnel staff. Other school sources of remedial assistance would normally include speech and hearing therapists and teachers of physical education and special education. Well-trained personnel in these areas are capable of conducting certain types of treatment programs without consulting nonschool specialists. Community resources for remedial care are physicians in general practice, hospitals, clinics, physical therapists, rehabilitation agencies (governmental and community) and physicians whose practice is limited to a specialty area.

Preventive attention to physiological or health needs may also be obtained from school health services. The first principle of good health care emphasizes early detection and treatment. Consequently, it is at the preventive stage of health need development that school services are centered.

While all students are entitled to instruction concerning preventive health practices, teachers and counselors in particular should be sensitive to the symptoms associated with the existence of any special health needs so that referrals can be made promptly. Health needs require attention at the earliest possible moment. In addition to the professional medical and health personnel and agencies described in connection with remedial treatment, several additional referral sources are often available. Medical and dental associations occasionally conduct free examinations and informational programs. Mobile chest x-ray units and blood-typing services may be utilized by all students, since usually no cost is involved. Service organizations in some cities provide medical examinations and treatment for students unable to pay. Organizations such as the Scouts, Boys' Clubs, YMCA, and YWCA provide some diagnostic service and programs designed to encourage resistance to illness and injury.

The relationship between physical well-being and other phases of living has been underestimated by many in education. The term "developmental medicine," for example, has been introduced recently in the medical literature. It is becoming increasingly clear that prevention is not enough, that increased attention on the part of schools to the need for physiological development will be required. As life in America becomes increasingly sedentary, the needs of students for developmental physical activities will increase. Counselors and teachers regularly encounter students who appear to be without medical symptoms, whose school work is satisfactory, but who may be nonetheless characterized as listless or suppressed. Zest and stamina resulting from vigorous play can produce significant improvement. Athletic and intramural programs available to all students in a variety of sports and games are developmental services which can be used with good effect. Community recreational programs, too, such as those sponsored by youth service organizations may be called up, particularly when school programs are incomplete.

Referral Resources for Social Needs

The social needs of students, at least as they occur during school life, have been the legitimate concern of education from its beginning. The scope and nature of this problem area have grown apace with the economic, social, and moral fluctuations of our society so that today issues exist for which there are few, if any, precedents. Several of the more important issues are included in the dilemma of the acquisition of values, a subject reviewed by Stone.[21] All levels of social behavior have undergone modification, however, so that the everyday tasks of teachers relative to classroom control are quite different in many respects from those of previous periods. Most of

[21] Shelley C. Stone, "The Acquisition of Values: An Educational Dilemma," *SPATE (Student Personnel Association for Teacher Education)* Vol. 4 (December 1964), pp. 3–9.

the attention devoted to this area by educators has been directed toward developing and maintaining programs of social development. With the current realization that necessary antecedent conditions for social development are frequently missing, there is a need for the expansion of remedial and preventive measures.

Characteristic of the need for remedial attention are malnutrition, unsatisfactory hygiene habits, disrespectful attitudes toward the property of others, evidence of physical punishment and abuse, and the lack of such basic necessities as clothes and books. As the need for remedial social service has increased, both public and private agencies have been created. Referral sources now found in some schools are the social worker and legal counsel. Counselors whose preparation has included sociology and social casework are found in increasing numbers and their qualifications are well suited for accepting referrals of this nature. Certain teachers and administrators, too, have backgrounds in home visitation and consultation so that their assistance may be of value.

Basically, however, the school lacks authority for implementing needed changes in home and family situations. In the case of cruelty or neglect, often the school's only recourse is to notify the appropriate legal or law enforcement agency, while attempting to sustain the student. Community referral resources for social needs would include agencies of law enforcement, child welfare, social work, legal aid, family counseling services, and mental health. The social needs of students take many forms, one of the more notable being lack of skill in interpersonal relations. Although personality factors are often involved, many students are socially inept and underdeveloped primarily as a result of lack of experience. Family customs and mores that differ markedly from those of the student's peer group can subject the student to dual standards which also interfere with adequate social development.

SOCIAL WORK RESOURCES

Social work agencies provide services that supplement home care and school programs. This is particularly true of public welfare departments. Social work is an inclusive concept that defies categorical delimitation. Some think of social work as equivalent to the totality of community services. Historically, social welfare efforts have moved from providing for relief of the destitute to multifaceted services to individuals, families, and groups, including educational, guidance, and counseling functions in addition to economic assistance.

Most social welfare services are now supported by public funds. The federal government provides funds to assist states under certain conditions in giving financial help to three categories of people: the aged, the blind, and dependent children. In addition, federal assistance is given in the form of old-age and survivor's insurance, vocational rehabilitation, and unemployment insurance.

Private and voluntary social work agencies have had a prolific growth, especially in cities. Many are under religious or denominational auspices. Private agencies have often been pioneers in that they demonstrate the needs for and benefits of certain services that later have become accepted as governmental responsibilities.

Three principal methods used in social work include: casework, group work, and social welfare organization. Casework is just what the name implies: individualized service to persons or families. Group work in the past emphasized leisure-time activities for young people but is moving to the use of counseling groups. Social welfare organization involves efforts to obtain cooperation among county agencies and groups interested in similar objectives. This includes formation of councils and other groups to coordinate planning and financing.

The conditions with which social work agencies deal are largely problems of behavioral adjustment. In some areas of social work, such as child welfare, this can be seen very clearly. Mistreatment of children by their parents does not result primarily from ignorance, nor can it be regarded moralistically. To readjust the family situation requires a reconstructive approach. The most radical of environmental treatments for a child or adolescent is to take him from his family and home and place him in a different environment. However, this method is used only when it is felt that no other procedure will be effective. Placement can usually be carried out only when parents consent to the separation, when economic and psychological poverty exists, when the youngster has made himself subject to court action because of delinquency, or when home conditions are so poor that legal intervention is possible. Placement of the child may have to be done for varying periods of time, but work is usually continued with the parents in the hope of reconstituting the family.

Financial assistance through county and city welfare departments may be obtained for children who are in need. Further information with respect to social work agencies may be obtained from county departments of welfare, children's aid societies, family service associations, the Council of Social Agencies, the Child Welfare League of America, and the like.

Planning and Placement Needs

Most local offices of the United States Employment Service offer testing and placement assistance to youth entering the labor market. Through the state office and local branches of these agencies, the director of guidance or counseling staff members may arrange for students to take the General Aptitude Test Battery. The results are interpreted to students and used by the agency in its job placement of students, without cost to the school or student. In addition, the Employment Service gathers and dispenses information about the local, state, and national job markets. Analysis of current labor market conditions are distributed monthly by many state employment services. Through such information, the local school can keep up to date on the jobs available within the state.

Another planning and referral resource is the local branch of the State Division of Vocational Rehabilitation. This agency exists to provide rehabilitation services for physically and mentally handicapped persons and to bridge the gap between rehabilitation and gainful employment. Agency personnel provide counseling, rehabilitation, and training in school or industry for a job fitted to the client's disability. They strive to either remove or correct the disability so as to fit the client for gainful employment. Men and women of working age (sixteen years or older) who have handicaps resulting from physical or mental impairments are eligible for vocational rehabilitation services.

School guidance personnel need to identify individuals within the community who are able to serve as representatives of career areas. Many such individuals are willing to take time from their busy schedules to consult with students individually and in groups with respect to vocational planning and placement.

Service and fraternal clubs are interested in vocational guidance. These clubs frequently have standing committees which provide personnel and financial aid for special guidance projects such as career conferences, occupational materials, and field trips to businesses and industries. Their members often provide scholarships, student loan funds, and part-time jobs for students in the community.

Referral Resources for Students with Financial Needs

The financial needs of students present the school with a problem that is at once both a major stumbling block and a means of achieving significant gains. As in the case of some social needs, no direct control can be exerted by the school over the contributory factors related to financial distress. In addition, the effects are usually manifested in the social, psychological, and perhaps even physiological behavior of students. The basic problem of financial need is easily identified, but is frequently formidable.

Remedial assistance for financial need is available through: part-time employment secured through the school's placement service; special-needs funds that are frequently maintained by administrators; school lunch programs; and informal sponsorships consisting of donations of food, clothing, eyeglasses and money for loan funds. The dollar value of these remedial services does not usually approach that of the total need. Nonetheless, enterprising counselors, teachers, and administrators, through judicious management of such admittedly meager resources, have enabled many financially handicapped students to complete their high school education. The community referral sources available are employers and employment agencies, welfare agencies, and civic and professional groups.

At the preventive level there are instructional programs and individual attention by teachers of commercial subjects and home economics concerning the management of personal finances. Part-time employment obtained through the placement service is another referral source that may be used advantageously in assisting students to avert acute needs and attain financial responsibility. Representatives of banks, savings and loan institutions and accounting services offer assembly and convocation programs and talks to classes for the purpose of illustrating the principles of money management.

IDENTIFYING COMMUNITY RESOURCES

Community guidance referral resources consist of those services available from individuals, agencies, and organizations which through study and analysis of each individual attempt to provide formal and informal experiences to encourage growth toward the individual's highest potential developmental level. In some communities there is a dearth of services, while in others, particularly large cities, the problem is one of integrating the many and varied resources of numerous specialized agencies.

The size and composition of a community, its wealth, its values and leadership affect the resources which the community makes available to youth. That many forces in the community affect the growth, development, and behavior of children has long been known. Negative forces may include unhealthy family situations, inadequate housing, inconsistent or conflicting value systems. Positive constructive forces are stable family life, neighborhood clubs, playgrounds, health and welfare services and church organizations. Guidance is not the exclusive domain of the school; the home and church have concern for every youth. Any endeavor directed toward ensuring optimal youth development can succeed only to the extent to which all community agencies and organizations join forces. The use of such facilities will only come through identifying possible facilities, studying their services systematically, and organizing and implementing the ways of using their services. Knowing community agencies that provide guidance services to youth and drawing them into partnership with the school will have positive values for improving guidance services.

Every counselor, at one time or another, will be called upon to refer a child to a community agency. Every counselor will need to know the referral agencies and the individuals available in the community who can be of help. Though the nature and extent of community resources for guidance may vary, it is difficult to believe that there is a guidance program that could not profit from actively identifying and using community resources.

Community resources for guidance often vary markedly in their degree of effectiveness. Too many are undermanned, with their personnel often carrying such heavy caseloads that their effectiveness is seriously curtailed. The training and experience of professional personnel in community agencies range widely. Many persons may want to cooperate and participate in improving services to youth, but they often lack the know-how to do so. In any event, the impetus for increased use of community guidance resources by the school should originate with school personnel. This requires special time and effort. New demands will be made upon counselors and teachers as they confer with representatives of community agencies and associations and gather information about their services to youth, their staffs, and their referral procedures. After such information is gathered, it must be organized and briefed in some readily understandable form.

Surveying Community Resources

It is surprising how often local ability and talent that desires to work with youth goes unrecognized and unused by the schools. In a survey by Hoyt and Loughary of the work of 118 Iowa school counselors in non-metropolitan secondary schools, 58 percent were acquainted with possible referral sources but only 12 percent made use of them. Hoyt and Loughary concluded that school counselors were not familiar enough to know how to use the referral sources available to them.[22] To counteract this tendency, school guidance personnel need to survey periodically all the youth-serving organizations in their community.

Most state-operated youth agencies provide communities officially requesting such help with a comprehensive survey of youth services. This information generally includes all local associations and agencies concerned with child health and welfare, such as schools, church organizations, law enforcement agencies, recreation, youth welfare, juvenile courts. The survey is often conducted by representatives from the state youth commission, the state department of education, and the Public Health Service, who work with local community leaders. A state agency survey of a local community avoids certain dangers of local bias and competition.

In other situations school guidance personnel have conducted their own surveys of available community resources through the use of questionnaires assigned to elicit information concerning the names of the individuals or agencies or organizations, the types of services provided, the types of clientele that can be referred, procedures for referral, staff, resources, and the like.

Organizing Information Concerning Community Guidance Resources

Once the resources have been surveyed, the information collected is assembled for use by the staff. A card file for such purposes is often established (See Figure 17). The file identifies the individual or agency, the type of services provided, the clientele served, procedures for referral, charges or fees, the name and telephone number of the contact person, the address of the agency, its office hours, and so on.

[22] K. B. Hoyt and J. W. Loughary, "Acquaintance With and Use of Referral Resources by Iowa Secondary School Counselors," *Personnel and Guidance Journal* Vol. 36 (February 1958), pp. 388–391.

FIGURE 17
Community Resources Card File

UNION COUNTY MENTAL HEALTH CENTER

2316 South Street   SH 2-4059

Director: _____ SH 2-4059

Function: Diagnosis and out-patient treatment of emotional disorders in adults and children.

Services: 1. Personal interviews by staff.
    2. Prescribing of medication.
    3. Consultation with other agencies.

Staff: Psychiatrist (M.D.), psychologist (Ph.D.), two psychiatric social workers.
   Contact person in agency:_____

Fees: Sliding scale according to ability to pay. No one is denied service because of inability to pay. No financial or material assistance is given.

Eligibility: 1. Resident of Union, Montgomery, White, Carroll, Fountain, or Warren County.

     2. Private psychiatric care unavailable for financial or other reasons.

Main Sources of Income: 1. United Fund.
           2. State Division of Mental Health.
           3. Fees.

Cards of this type can easily be grouped and filed in one or several useful ways: by the type of service, the kinds of problems dealt with, or alphabetically by agency name. Every community resource of whatever type should be investigated insofar as possible before referrals are sent to the agency. In any referral situation, the individual referred relies heavily on the professional judgment of the person who suggests referral. The mere existence of an agency does not necessarily insure high-quality service. Evidence of staff qualifications can be obtained through knowledge of their training and professional membership. For example, information on psychologists may be secured from the state psychological association, while information on physicians may be obtained from the county medical association. Professional directories are available in almost all fields, and accrediting agencies exist in some cases.

ANNOTATED BIBLIOGRAPHY

OHLSEN, MERLE M. *Guidance: An Introduction.* New York: Harcourt, Brace and World, Inc., 1955, Chapter 17, pp. 357–394.
  This chapter is devoted to the identification of community guidance services. Ohlsen discusses pupils who may need special help and the types of community resources that can best assist them.

PATTERSON, C. H. *Counseling and Guidance in Schools.* New York: Harper and Brothers, 1962, pp. 327–333.
  In these pages Patterson discusses some of the procedures used in making referrals.

PETERS, HERMAN J. AND FARWELL, GAIL F. *Guidance: A Developmental Approach.* Chicago: Rand McNally and Company, 1967, 606 pp.
  Chapter 14 (pp. 447–474) discusses referral procedures and resources. the authors present some guidelines for making referrals and identify some behaviors of teachers useful in making referrals to counselors and others.

SELECTED REFERENCES

ALLEN, GEORGE H. "Aspirations and Expectations of Physically Impaired High School Seniors," *Personnel and Guidance Journal* Vol. 46 (September 1967), pp. 59–62.

BERLIN, I. N. "The School Counselor: His Unique Mental Health Function," *Personnel and Guidance Journal* Vol. 41 (January 1963), pp. 409–414.

CARSON, GARY L. "The Self-Concept of Welfare Recipients," *Personnel and Guidance Journal* Vol. 45 (January 1967), pp. 424–428.

DUNCAN, C. W. "Counselors in Private Practice," *Personnel and Guidance Journal* Vol. 47 (December 1968), pp. 337–340.

ELDER, LAWRENCE A. "An Inservice Community Occupational Survey," *Vocational Guidance Quarterly* Vol. 17 (March 1969), pp. 185–188.

FAUNCE, R. W. "When Is a Counselor. . . ?" *Personnel and Guidance Journal* Vol. 48 (March 1970), pp. 542–545.

HOLT, IRVING. "The School Counselor and Drugs," *The School Counselor* Vol. 17 (September 1969), pp. 14–16.

KRANZLER, GERALD D. "Providing for the Mental Health Needs of Children," *The School Counselor* Vol. 17 (September 1969), pp. 47–54.

LEVANTHAL, ALLAN M. "Characteristics of Clients Judged to Require Long-Term Counseling," *Personnel and Guidance Journal* Vol. 45 (April 1967), pp. 828–833.

MOSES, HAROLD. "Referring Handicapped Students to Appropriate Agencies," *The School Counselor* Vol. 16 (September 1968), pp. 55–57.

NUGENT, FRANK A. "A Framework for Appropriate Referrals of Disciplinary Problems to Counselors," *The School Counselor* Vol. 16 (January 1969), pp. 199–201.

PATTERSON, C. H. "Rehabilitation Counseling: A Profession or a Trade?" *Personnel and Guidance Journal* Vol. 46 (February 1968), pp. 567–571.

RAMSEY, GLENN V. "The Referral Task in Counseling," *Personnel and Guidance Journal* Vol. 40 (January 1962), pp. 443–447.

RYDEN, ARTHUR H. "Diamonds at Your Doorstep," *Vocational Guidance Quarterly* Vol. 13 (Winter 1964–65), pp. 131–133.

———. "Referral Resources Needed? Roll Up Your Sleeves," *The School Counselor* Vol. 12 (October 1964), pp. 14–17.

VASSOS, SONYA T., AND TAYLOR, VAUGHN K. "Militancy and Counselor Relationships Between School and Community," *The School Counselor* Vol. 17 (May 1970), pp. 350–356.

WINDER, ALVIN E., AND SAVENKO, NICHOLAI. "Group Counseling with Neighborhood Youth Corps Trainees," *Personnel and Guidance Journal* Vol. 48 (March 1970), pp. 561–567.

PART FIVE
ISSUES
AND TRENDS

R EFLECTION UPON what has been said in Parts One through Four leads to the need to present and amplify the issues and trends in guidance. Despite the uneven course of the development of guidance, its history attests that steady growth marks its progress.

There are issues in guidance that are challenges to counselors, teachers, and administrators. A discussion of some of them is presented in Chapter 18. An examination of these major issues should make it quite clear that guidance is dynamic, that its direction is not always clear, and that many ideological battles still lie ahead.

Chapter 19 focuses upon some of the trends that are occurring in guidance. Change is anticipated, but when viewed in perspective it becomes a natural transition from one stage of development to another. What has been done in guidance is history. What will be done to make it a more powerful force lies with those who accept responsibility for its form and direction.

18

ISSUES IN COUNSELING AND GUIDANCE

What are some of the major issues in counseling and guidance?
What are the bases for disputed matters?

The issues—matters of disagreement to be resolved—set forth in this chapter are presented to furnish students with a way to organize and analyze their opinions on these matters. The issues presented here will be wasted if they do not provoke active discussion aimed at more accurate and adequate understanding of the position individuals assume in regard to their resolution, since resolution of issues can come only through analysis, discussion, understanding, and choice.

The twenty issues are grouped into three general categories: Counselor Role and Function, Preparation and Certification, and Guidance Practices and Program Policies. The issues overlap somewhat from category to category.

The discussion of most issues is presented in three parts: (1) the identification or statement of each issue, (2) summary statements of the pros and cons of each issue, and (3) some discussion pertinent to the issue which probably reveals the authors' biases. It is doubtful whether there will be any final resolution of many of the issues, and in some cases it would not be healthy for the field if inflexible solutions were to be reached.

To some degree the issues are directed more to counselors and the counseling function. Since counseling is viewed as the core of guidance services, no effort is made to separate the two in the presentation and discussion of the issues. What affects the specific service of counseling also affects the entire guidance program and vice versa.

Reflection will suggest that the past has shaped the issues of the present. No doubt these issues will soon be lost in the torrent of events to come. The content of the arguments surrounding each issue is certain to be blurred with the passage of time.

COUNSELOR ROLE AND FUNCTIONS

Issue I:
Is teaching experience and/or prior teaching preparation necessary for entry into school counseling and successful functioning as a school counselor?

Teaching experience and/or teacher preparation is necessary because:

1. Teaching experience provides counselors with the necessary insight into the school as a social institution.
2. Teaching experience gives counselors an understanding and appreciation of teachers, their point of view, and issues and problems involved in classroom instruction.
3. Teaching experience has enabled counselors to observe pupils in a classroom setting, to be aware of their needs in such settings, and to understand the conditions that facilitate and inhibit learning.
4. It serves as a common facilitating experience between counselors and teachers. Counselors who have had teaching experience and teacher preparation are more likely to be accepted by teachers and will be better able to relate to them. Without this common background, counselors may be viewed suspiciously and distrustfully by teachers.
5. Requiring teaching experience gives the individual the perspective needed to decide the area of specialization (teaching, counseling, administration) he wishes to enter in graduate work.
6. Most school administrators will not employ counselors who do not have teaching experience.
7. If teacher preparation were not required, individuals from other disciplines would rush into the field. Advisers to students in other disciplines might use school counseling as a dumping ground for inferior, marginal candidates.
8. Teacher preparation and teaching experience is, in reality, an expression of the individual's prior commitment to public-school education.

Teaching experience and teacher preparation is unnecessary because:

1. Counseling and teaching are fundamentally different activities. Little that is learned in teaching transfers meaningfully to the counseling relationship.
2. Extended teaching experience frequently results in undesirable, authoritarian and patronizing attitudes and outlooks toward children that conflict with the basic attitudes essential in counseling.

3. Present-day counselors (with teaching experience) have generally failed to establish a satisfactory relationship with teachers; consequently, such a relationship is most likely dependent upon variables other than teaching experience per se.

4. An increasing number of counselors must be sought in the years ahead. The nation-wide shortage of school counselors reflects the fact that the teaching profession as a source of supply for counselors is inadequate. The availability of recruits for the teaching profession in light of population increase is itself questionable.

5. Since teaching as a profession has failed to attract the best minds and the most able individuals, opening school counseling to other disciplines provides a better source of supply for able and capable candidates.

6. A more effective way to provide the counselor with an understanding of the school environment, the wide range of student and teacher problems, and the understanding needed to relate to school personnel is through a guidance internship experience, which is uniquely structured and carefully directed, supervised, and evaluated.

7. The practice of mandating four years of undergraduate teacher preparation; two, three, or more years of teaching experience; and two years of counselor preparation before actual admission to school counseling is unrealistic, considering the financial rewards received by practicing school counselors. Ways to shorten preservice time must be found if able counselors are to be attracted and retained in the field.

DISCUSSION

With regard to the above sampling of statements cited for and against prerequisite teacher preparation and experience, the arguments appear to be related to two basic factors. The first of these is the matter of the appropriateness of prior experience to later counselor functioning and the second is that of the supply and demand of counseling personnel. Though these two factors can be separated for discussion, in reality they are highly interdependent.

Little argument can be made against the point that familiarity with the school setting and experience with students, *if they lead to functional knowledge,* are appropriate and desirable. To the degree that knowledge of students and the institutional setting facilitates the counselor's adequacy in performing counseling functions, prerequisite teaching experience should be supported. In the past, there has been a tendency to accept this position at face value rather than permitting or encouraging any deviation that would allow this traditional position to be tested.

The position of other occupational groups that require prolonged training appears to argue against demanding prior training and experience in a different occupation. Occupational groups such as physicians, attorneys, psychologists, and social workers do not insist upon preparation and service in related but distinctly different fields. This does not mean that they deny the value of prior experience but that they recognize the extended nature of their own required professional preparation and utilize broad general education as the basis for later preparation rather than experience in other fields. Most of the aforementioned occupations stress the quality and breadth of general education rather than the specific content. Because of this, they are able to induct individuals into their respective professions through graduate preparation. This is accomplished through educational experiences uniquely structured and carefully directed toward knowledge of the clientele and the institutional setting in which the students will eventually work.

The sequence outlined above appears directly applicable to the preparation of school counselors. Those who stubbornly argue for teacher training and teacher experience as mandatory prerequisites may be blindly insisting upon wasteful initiation rites of dubious value to the actual functions of the school counselor.

Supply and demand is a persistent problem in all highly skilled occupational groups. Quantity alone presents serious problems. Demands for quality further complicate the issue of supply and demand. Active recruitment by all professions minimizes the opportunities of each group to secure the best raw material, since all tend to compete for a relatively small proportion of the population. It is quite likely that one of the defenses employed by various groups will be to strive for increased holding power. This may mean that the day may come when desirable personnel from the teaching field are actively discouraged from shifting to another occupation—even if it is within the educational setting, e.g., counseling. If this becomes the case, obviously other sources of counselor supply will be needed.

For further discussion of this issue, see the following references at the end of this chapter: Cohen (1961), Fredrickson and Pippert (1964), Hudson (1961), Hutson (1962a), Peterson and Brown (1968), Ricker (1969), Rossberg (1963), and Wrenn (1962).

Issue II:
Is the counselor a generalist or a specialist?

The counselor is a generalist:

1. Historically, the guidance function evolved at least in part as an effort to overcome specialization and impersonality in mass education. Therefore, it is a paradox to conceive of the counselor as a specialist simultaneously charged with the task of counteracting the harmful effects of specialization.
2. The counselor's primary task is to facilitate individual learning, personal planning, and decision-making, and be the prime advocate of individual differences. This calls for a generalist who can coordinate and administer services and resources to accomplish these goals.
3. The major portion of the counselor's time should be devoted to individual inventory, orientation services, group guidance activities, and planning, placement, and followup activities. To function as a generalist,

the counselor needs to be able to conduct effective counseling sessions but this skill is only one of many needed within the guidance service.

4. The counselor's skills and attitudes are best directed to the improvement of the relationships existing among teachers, administrators, parents, and community resource personnel and students rather than to individual counselees. The counselor is only one member of a team of pupil personnel workers. He performs a coordinative function directed toward the establishment of optimal conditions in the school.

5. The counselor's preparation is not of sufficient depth to provide the thorough-going remedial role which a specialization would require. As a generalist, he performs a health-giving function by fostering a preventive, developmental guidance program.

6. Teachers and administrators expect counselors to do more than counseling. There are clerical, disciplinary and administrative duties that teachers and administrators rightfully may expect the counselor to perform.

7. A semantic accident is responsible for introducing and perpetuating the title of "counselor" for school guidance personnel. This created an unintended narrow conception of what counselors are expected to do, despite the fact that their training often inadequately prepares them for actually meeting this expectation.

The counselor is a specialist:

1. The counselor was historically brought into public schools as a specialist in vocational guidance. Although his area of specialization has broadened far beyond vocational guidance, his primary obligation remains that of counseling students.

2. The generalist function "spreads" the counselor so thinly that he can make little or no impact upon students or the schools as an institution.

3. Teachers and other school staff can conduct many of the informational services counselors perform so that his skills can be devoted entirely to counseling students.

4. The low status and poor regard currently attributed to counselors by other members of the school staff prevents the counselor from being a truly effective coordinator of services. If a generalist is to have impact, his coordination responsibilities require high status, authority, and leadership which are recognized by others in the school. Therefore, given existing circumstances surrounding counselor status, he should be a specialist who concentrates upon counseling.

5. Many students need more intensive, centralized remedial and therapeutic counseling services if they are to remain in school and benefit from their educational experiences.

DISCUSSION

The evolution of all occupations has inevitably involved a mixture of modification and upgrading of skills, which has incorporated advanced technology and led eventually to specialization. Because the school counselor's occupation is of relatively recent vintage, current arguments may reflect the initial phases of this evolutionary process.

Though many authors have seized upon the specialist-generalist dichotomy, a basic issue has apparently been overlooked by some. The negative aspects of specialization have tended to be stressed, and the positive aspects of the generalist position emphasized. The kind and purpose of specialization have all too often been overlooked, and criticism has been predicated upon the fact that extreme subject-matter specialization among teachers has led to neglect of the individual student for the sake of the subject matter. But there appears to be little disagreement that the fundamental reason for the counselor's existence lies in fostering the individual's development. Therefore, the true purpose of specialization for the counselor is to orient him quite strongly toward understanding and helping the individual. Thus, the very argument against specialization becomes a strong point in its favor.

How much can legitimately be expected of the school counselor? Effective discharge of the responsibilities frequently attributed to the generalist would indeed demand a social scientist possessing uncommon background and preparation. In effect, his responsibilities would overlap with those of an even larger number of school personnel than at present. By definition, he would not only pre-empt responsibilities held by teachers and mental hygiene workers, but also duplicate the efforts of curriculum specialists, principals, and perhaps even superintendents. Many believe that a narrower range of highly specific and appropriate functions done well by counselors would be more suitable to the existing school situation.

For further discussion of this issue, see Arbuckle (1961), Beymer (1961), Blocher, *et al.* (1963), Brammer (1968), Heilfron (1964), Hoyt (1961 and 1962), Knowles and Shertzer (1965), Krumboltz (1964), Patterson (1969), Pierson (1965), Sherman (1962), Thoresen (1969), and Wrenn (1962).

Issue III:
Is the school counselor a technician or a professional?

The school counselor is a technician because:[1]

1. Teachers or those concerned solely with instruction determine the direction and scope of guidance efforts, which means guidance practitioners are not expected to play and do not play a professional role in determining the goals of their efforts.
2. Counselors are in the school to aid teachers. Teachers traditionally and necessarily are in a superior position to that of counselors. ". . . the current practice of guidance stems from the traditional desires of educa-

[1] Most of the arguments cited here are from David V. Tiedeman and Frank L. Field, "Guidance: The Science of Purposeful Action Applied Through Education," *Harvard Educational Review* Vol. 32 (Fall 1962), pp. 481–501.

tional authorities and practitioners to make teaching more powerful without limiting the authority of teachers."[2]

3. Current guidance practice takes place "beside" rather than "within" education. Therefore, counselors lack a valid professional identity which is an integral part of the educational enterprise and are not expected to contribute creatively to education.

4. Those who achieve professional status do so as psychologists, scientists, or professors rather than as school guidance personnel.

5. Counselors apply principles borrowed from current behavioral sciences to assist teachers in the pursuit of their own established educational goals; the diversity of interests, techniques, and goals among school counselors prevents the establishment of an integrated science of guidance.

6. Criteria have not been developed for determining the relevance of available knowledge regarding the desired future of guidance services.

7. A social mandate has not been given to the functions performed by counselors.

The school counselor is a professional because:

1. The nature of the responsibilities assumed by the practitioner, and the judgments he makes with respect to his clients, are too broad to fit into the limited and restricted activities implied by the label "technician."

2. His behavior is guided by a code of ethical behavior accepted by practicing members of the profession.

3. His role and function have been relatively well formulated, and reasonably well accepted by the members of his occupational group. Information regarding role and function has been disseminated to and is known by the public.

4. Admission to the occupation is regulated by criteria established by counselor-training institutions, which are guided by standards recently accepted by the national professional organization. Also, consent to practice, or certification, is regulated by state departments of education.

DISCUSSION

Among the three groups involved—counselors, teachers, and administrators—this issue above all others arouses great emotional response, since it can easily become the focus of professional jealousy and ill will. At a superficial level, each of the three groups involved tends to support professionalization among school counselors. Members of all three groups know the ideally correct responses regarding discharge of the counselor's responsibilities. If on-the-job activities matched ideal statements of counselor functions, there would be little argument that school counseling has attained the status of a profession, but the gap between the ideal and the real is sometimes broad indeed. The apparent consensus among the three groups seems

---

[2] *Ibid.,* p. 484.

to dissipate rapidly whenever one probes into a specific counselor's activities within a particular setting. Somehow, job descriptions and statements by counselors regarding why they do what they do lead to the conclusion that in most school situations their operational behavior is that of a technician.

Ideal statements of counselor functions have filtered down from counselor educators. The filtration of these ideals has been slow and selective at best. The recent literature would suggest relatively full acceptance of the ideal by school counselors, particularly by those who have recently entered the field, but relatively little true acceptance by other school personnel. Understanding and encouragement of the activities stated in descriptions of the ideal professional image as well as exclusion of extraneous duties and nonprofessional pursuits will undoubtedly require additional time. It is to be hoped that acceptance of the ideal will be achieved because of its inherent value as demonstrated through actual practice.

The discussion should not be construed to mean that full acceptance of school counseling as a profession has taken place among all guidance service practitioners. The "professional view" is relatively recent in origin. Consequently, its greatest acceptance, as well as the greatest preoccupation with the whole issue of technician versus professional, is to be found among counselors who have recently participated in counselor-education programs.

For further discussion of this issue, see Dunsmoor (1964), Loughary, *et al.* (1965), McCully (1962, 1963, 1965, 1969a, 1969b), Stefflre (1964), and Wrenn (1962).

Issue IV:
Can the school counselor differentiate his services to students from those which are provided by other specialized noninstructional personnel?

No, because:

1. Commonality of preparation among all school personnel and mutuality of purpose in the educational system discourages separatism of services regardless of specialty.
2. The ultimate goal of all pupil contacts demands highly similar activities by noninstructional specialists.

Yes, because:

1. Considerable differentiation occurs by virtue of differences in prior training and its attendant variation in approaches to problems and clientele.
2. The school counselor's focus is on typical students and typical problems rather than the atypical.
3. The "treatment" alternatives available to the school counselor both limit and define his activities.

DISCUSSION
Each counselor individually (and all counselors within a given school system) retains the responsibility for functionally differentiating his services

from those offered to students by other personnel. All counselors do not function in the same fashion. A given counselor's function differs from that of other counselors according to the setting in which he works, the availability of other counselors in his school, and the nature of his training, skills and interests. Despite diversity in individual functioning, commonalities do exist in counselor activities, and they permit a generally accepted definition of function. Counselors themselves are primarily responsible for this definition; otherwise, by default, the counselor's role would be defined by school administrators or others. This definition must be firm enough to provide counselors with a basis for their activities, but at the same time it must be sufficiently flexible to allow for growth and change within the profession.

Professional counselors tend to be aligned with either of two broad student service functions: (1) the organization and administration of programs, and (2) counseling per se, wherein a one-to-one and/or small-group relationship with students is emphasized. In situations in which student needs are evident and staff resources permit, further specialization by some counselors may facilitate work with specific groups of students in a school, e.g., the gifted, potential dropouts, students oriented toward trade or business education, etc. Formal training programs for counselors first need to focus upon the general body of knowledge and skills common to all counselors. More advanced graduate training may emphasize the specialized work of the guidance administrator or master counselor, but programs more specialized than these would likely prove to be uneconomical. The individual counselor who finds himself with highly restricted responsibilities may best prepare for such service through continued advanced study designed on an individual basis.

School counselors must work cooperatively with administrators and others who are not directly related to instruction but who do serve students, such as psychiatrists, school psychologists, psychometrists, social workers, medical personnel, and the like. The differentiation of the counselor's function from that of administrators with responsibility for pupil accounting, scheduling, and decisions pertinent to discipline, as well as the distinction necessary between counseling and psychiatric treatment, psychological evaluation, and social casework, are necessary prerequisites to the establishment of any cooperative working relationship among personnel.

A case in point is illustrated by the fact that there is a considerable demand for trained psychometrists to evaluate children for assignment to special education. Counselors are frequently encouraged to obtain training in individual intelligence-test administration so that they might be utilized as psychometrists in the schools. Because of the need in this area the counselor may find himself increasingly called upon to function as a psychometrist rather than as a counselor. Unless a counselor obtains specialized psychological preparation, however, he will function as a testing technician who lacks the professional competence to provide truly adequate evaluations of the children he tests. Such a condition obscures the professional image of the counselor and encourages interdisciplinary misunderstanding.

To avoid duplication, the coordination of the contributions made by the several professional groups who provide services to students is essential. Such coordination is the responsibility of school administrators, but should be undertaken only by those who have training and experience in providing noninstructional services to students. A likely candidate for such an assignment is the experienced guidance administrator, who should possess sufficient professional sophistication to appreciate the potentialities of special-service resources and should be able to communicate with members of other professional disciplines to foster planning and expedite the provision of all services for students.

For further discussion of this issue, see Arbuckle (1961, 1965), Loughary, *et al.* (1965), Mathewson (1964), Peterson and Featherstone (1962), McCully, (1969a, 1969b), Pierson (1965), Riccio (1964), and Wrenn (1962).

Issue V:
The school counselor's skills should be restricted solely to the educational-vocational decision-making concerns of youth.

Yes, because:

1. Generally, the preparation of school counselors is most centrally directed toward educational-vocational decision-making activities.
2. Expectations of the counselor's publics—pupils, teachers, administrators, parents—are that he will assist youth with curriculum problems and educational-vocational planning and placement.
3. Analysis of what counselors do—information-giving, test interpretation, parent consultations, educational-vocational planning, pupil appraisal —are best described within the narrow framework of educational-vocational decision-making.
4. The school's responsibility is confined to educational-vocational concerns of pupils; to go beyond this area is to invade the responsibilities of the home and community.
5. Only a small proportion of youth need assistance other than help with educational-vocational decision-making. To concentrate upon this minority would be to neglect the educational-vocational counseling of the majority of students.

No because:

1. Counseling involves the whole person. To separate pupil problems into educational-vocational and social-emotional categories is both artificial and superficial and blocks their full solution. Educational problems involve emotional states, and to neglect emotional issues as they manifest themselves would be detrimental.
2. Students who seek help in educational and/or vocational planning are, in reality, seeking self-realization and help in achieving personal identity.

3. Restricting the school counselor's responsibility to educational-vocational concerns requires a reduction of the counselor's role to primarily that of an "information-giver."

DISCUSSION

This is a long-standing issue, but one that appears relatively well resolved. Given the current status of knowledge about the learner and the general acceptance of learning-theory approaches to counseling, few would dispute the statements made in support of refusing to restrict the counselor's role in the manner implied. A direct analogy exists in the classroom situation in which an enlightened teacher would not ignore the role of emotional factors as they bear upon learning.

With respect to the invasion of home and community responsibilities, it is commonly accepted that schools can merely reflect the desires of the population they serve. Although in extreme cases the charge of invasion of family responsibility might be legitimately made, in most instances the trend appears to be in the opposite direction, with the school being asked to assume increasingly diverse obligations. In any case, the schools have tended to provide leadership in stimulating awareness of a variety of concerns unrecognized or ignored in the recent past. Perhaps there is no clearer evidence of public acceptance of noninstructional pursuits than the relatively easy entry and support of a wide range of student personnel specialists into the schools.

For further discussion of this issue, see Collins (1965), Herr (1968), Hoyt (1962), Hutson (1962a, 1962b), Lair (1968), Loughary, *et al.* (1965), McCully (1965), Salyer (1964), Stern (1965), and Wrenn (1962).

Issue VI:
Is the elementary school counselor to serve primarily as a counselor to children or primarily as a consultant to adults who influence the lives of children?

Primarily as a counselor because:

1. Counseling is most needed in the schools.
2. Direct intervention with children will yield better returns than indirect approaches.
3. It is the individual who has to change; therefore effort should be focused on the child.

Primarily as a consultant because:

1. A greater number of children can be served by consulting with those— teachers, principals, parents—who are influential with them.
2. Effort should be directed toward changing the environment rather than changing the individual.

3. Since research on counseling outcomes with elementary school children shows relatively few positive results, consulting should be the main activity of elementary school counselors.

DISCUSSION

Few, if any, question that a need for elementary school guidance service exists. It exists at several levels. Elementary school teachers and administrators increasingly demand a variety of specialized services to cope with pressing problems. Secondary school counselors bemoan the lack of earlier preventive efforts that could minimize long-standing pupil problems. Parents are increasingly aware that the early school years are important to the later school and nonschool development of their children. Various mental health authorities stress the contributions to good mental health of early identification, prevention, and treatment of problems. The elementary school becomes the natural focal point of these demands and expectations.

Clearly the need for this type of service not only exists, but cries for fulfillment. The demand for individuals to meet this need is so great that guidance-trained personnel may be stampeded into attempting to meet it at the expense of appropriate, professional considerations.

The difficulty is that the demands have produced many conflicting and often unrealistic expectations for elementary school guidance personnel. Without question, neither of the two alternatives—counseling or consulting —could exist in its pure form in most school settings. Some situations will demand aggressive environmental modification while others will require direct help to individual students. Probably, the vast majority of school settings will require a judicious balance of both approaches.

There appear to be two approaches to deciding the question of the elementary school counselor's primary activity. One approach involves trial-and-error methodology while the other involves a logical theoretical approach. Both will require the passage of time before any decision can be made.

Trial-and-error would involve placing reasonably well-qualified individuals in elementary schools. During a trial period such individuals would attempt to provide the services requested of them within the limitations of their competencies. Actual practice would produce a definition of the activities demanded for the elementary school situation. It is highly probable that different school situations would require somewhat different kinds of functions. In light of the pressing demand for elementary school counselors, the trial-and-error approach will undoubtedly be the approach most commonly pursued.

The logical, theoretical approach would require exhaustive analysis of the basis for the claimed needs and thorough study of the expectations for elementary counselor service. Following these procedures, decisions would be made concerning their legitimacy, and a model would be developed to meet the needs and expectations deemed appropriate to the setting.

It seems unlikely that the logical, theoretical approach will be followed because it inevitably involves postponement of the placement of personnel in the schools. The history of the development of guidance services suggests that this would be a somewhat foreign procedure. Past efforts have tended to evolve in response to immediate demand rather than deliberate, logical design.

Delay would probably also result from the nature of existing preparation programs. This is especially true if an analysis of a school setting revealed a high degree of emphasis upon consulting activities. This relatively new function for the counselor would require considerable modification in existing preparation programs. Much greater emphasis would have to be placed upon the skills involved in analyzing social systems and in conferring with responsible adults regarding school program changes and modification of their behavior.

For further discussion of this issue, see Aubrey (1967), Faust (1968), Hill (1967a and 1967b), Hutson (1962a, 1962b), Koeppe (1964), Kranzler (1969), McNassor (1967), Meeks (1963), Muro and Oelke (1968), Nelson (1967), Patterson (1969), and Perrone and Evans (1964).

GUIDANCE PREPARATION AND CERTIFICATION

Issue VII:
Can better, more scientific methods be employed for the selection and retention of students in counselor education?

Yes, by:

1. Raising the undergraduate academic performance level required for admission to counselor education programs.
2. Utilizing nonintellective criteria such as personality characteristics believed essential to successful functioning in counseling.
3. Encouraging administrators to identify and nominate counselor candidates through the use of characteristics needed by successful school counselors.
4. Practicing selective retention as a process during didactic courses, during practicum and internship courses, and in placement of counselors in school situations.

No, because:

1. The personal characteristics of successful counselors vary so widely that no one pattern can be used in the identification or selection process.
2. The academic prerequisites upon which present counselor selection procedures are so heavily based serve only to screen out those who may be unsuccessful in the didactic portion of the counselor education program.
3. Contact work with students is dependent upon personal characteristics and values that cannot readily or accurately be identified.

DISCUSSION

There seems to be general agreement that the academic requirements in and of themselves are not enough to ensure good counselor selection; they are a necessary but not a sufficient requirement. Most high-quality counselor preparation programs require demonstration of academic ability and/or a satisfactory record of academic performance to assure that this type of criterion is met. For many years it has been the fond hope of counselor educators that nonintellective criteria could be successfully employed to raise the quality of counselors produced. A tremendous amount of effort and energy has been devoted to research in this area. The results to date are mixed, and no doubt disappointing to many. No clearcut personality pattern has emerged that could be used with assurance in the selection of counselor candidates. This is not to say that the results have been entirely negative, since much more is now known regarding the characteristics of counselors as a total group and of those who seek entry to training programs.

Some have suggested the use of school administrators to identify potential counselors. However, the use of school administrators in this way needs careful attention because it appears that some individuals now encouraged by school administrators to seek counselor education are not the most desirable candidates. The practice of nominating or encouraging classroom teachers who appear to deserve opportunity merely because they may return to their old school setting should be discouraged. Because it might simplify staff acquisition and reduce turnover, this is an understandable hope of the administrator. However, it will not necessarily lead to quality guidance programs, nor does it constitute a responsible administrator contribution to counselor selection.

Better selection probably would occur if enough time and effort were devoted to thorough screening procedures. However, such efforts might well require that each candidate be subjected to a lengthy assessment procedure involving extensive testing, interviewing, evaluation of performance in situational tasks, and the like. Many institutions practice these procedures quite informally as part of the retention process. Obviously, the expense required for such admission practices might make them prohibitive.

It could be argued that better selection and retention procedures would undoubtedly result from formalizing and standardizing these efforts. However, it should be noted that although such efforts are admirable, the procedure is wasteful in terms of both individual candidates and programs, since each candidate eliminated in the process represents wasted time and effort for the candidate and the institution. In addition, each failure case represents a lost opportunity to a potentially successful candidate. This loss is particularly hurtful when it occurs late in the training sequence, i.e., during practicum and internship. Despite these shortcomings, initial selection and selective retention remain an essential obligation of counselor education.

For further discussion of this issue, see Arbuckle (1965), Hill (1961),

Johnson (1963), Loughary, *et al.* (1965), Patterson (1968), Pierson (1965), Walton and Sweeney (1969), and Wrenn (1962).

Issue VIII:
Should interdisciplinary study be included in counselor education programs?

Yes, because:

1. School counselors are concerned with human behavior within culture, not with human behavior as an abstraction. Therefore, the classroom use of sociologists, anthropologists, psychologists, and the like will provide counselors with a better basis for understanding individuals in their culture.
2. Interdisciplinary study gives counselors breadth and depth in understanding upon which to base perceptions of human behavior.
3. Counselor education programs are often isolated islands in professional education. The base of counselor preparation needs broadening if counselor practitioners are to work within a highly fluid society.

No, because:

1. Instructors in other disciplines have had little contact with the school, and are far removed from it. Because such experts would not understand the school counselor's functions, their contributions would be abstract and impractical.
2. The introduction of adequate amounts of interdisciplinary work would lengthen the training program unrealistically, especially since present programs are geared to meet state certification requirements.
3. No one has specified clearly the actual contributions such disciplines could provide. Therefore, requiring counselors to take sufficient coursework in supporting disciplines—history, law, economics, anthropology, sociology, psychology—is beyond reason. As yet, no acceptable approach has been made available to organize and integrate the contributions of supporting disciplines.
4. The undergraduate preparation program is the time and place to secure a broad liberal education in other disciplines. Graduate preparation is by tradition and definition specialist preparation.

DISCUSSION

The question of interdisciplinary broadening of counselor preparation has been present to some degree for many years. However, it has only been within the past ten years that it has assumed major importance in the deliberations concerning counselor training and certification. Arguments on both sides seem relatively clearcut, pitting the practical considerations of those who oppose an interdisciplinary approach against the more idealistic view of those who urge its adoption but have difficulty demonstrating its utility.

If one equates the interdisciplinary approach with quality or academic respectability of program, it becomes extremely difficult to argue against such an approach. Stated in these terms, opposition to broad cross-discipline training is tantamount to opposing motherhood or virtue! The real resolution of the issue will lie in the demonstration that the content of other disciplines has value to the counselor, that it can be organized for inclusion in programs of reasonable length, and that it does, in fact, contribute directly or at least indirectly to counselor effectiveness.

For further discussion of this issue, see Boy and Pine (1964), Lloyd-Jones and Rosenau (1968), Loughary, *et al.* (1965), McCully (1965), Pierson (1965), Smith and Mink (1969), and Wrenn (1962).

Issue IX:
Are two years of full-time study needed to prepare school counselors?

Two years are needed, because:

1. The complexity of the school counselor's job demands that he have extended, high-quality preparation if he is to work effectively with youth.
2. Counselors report that one year of training is not sufficient for counseling youth. They frequently seek additional training because their functions demand greater skill development.
3. Most current state certification requirements specify a minimum of one year of training. Graduate institutions have an obligation to hold standards and length of preparation substantially above minimal levels required by states for counselor certification.
4. An extended period of counseling practicum and a guidance internship are needed if counselors are to be adequately prepared. The didactic background courses needed for counseling, coupled with more practice and internship experience, cannot be provided within a single academic year or on a part-time basis.
5. Part-time summer and evening study leads to inadequate, fractionated knowledge and, for the individual, fails to result in an identity as a professional counselor.

Only one year is needed, because:

1. The nationwide shortage of school counselors demands that the supply be increased; requiring a second year of preparation would seriously curtail the number of counselors available.
2. Requiring the second year represents "empire building" by counselor educators who are striving to hold on to students and secure physical facilities simply to increase their own stature in universities.
3. The nature of the school counselor's present assignment does not require an additional year of preparation. The additional year will isolate him from teachers and administrators, who will view him with suspicion because he has had more education than they have.

4. Part-time study is a practical necessity for most since sufficient financial support is unavailable for counselor trainees.

DISCUSSION

By almost any index, a shortage of counselors exists. Where the most serious shortage exists, why it exists, and its actual magnitude is a complicated matter. The over-riding question behind the issue is whether quality can be sacrificed for quantity and whether merely filling job vacancies will achieve the goals of guidance services.

There seems little doubt that the trend is toward an extended training period. It will be incumbent upon counselor education programs to make certain that the extension produces significant results. Such results would probably be best achieved through modification of the internal design of programs coupled with the lengthened preparation. If the extended program deteriorates into a repetition of the courses which preceded it, no material gain can be expected. The standards for the professional preparation of secondary school counselors include general specifications of content which, if followed, should, to some degree, ensure desirable outcomes.[3]

For further discussion of this issue, see Hansen and Moore (1968), Hill (1967a, 1967b), Loughary, *et al.* (1965), Noble (1965), Pierson (1965), Richardson (1968), and Wrenn (1962).

Issue X:
Should counselor preparation be based on an analysis of present counselor duties?

Yes, because:

1. Training program content that is structured and focused upon what counselors actually do prepares them thoroughly and competently for effective service in the schools.
2. Concentration of preparation on what counselors actually do would reduce much of the irrelevancy in preparation and lead directly to qualitative improvement of present practices.

No, because:

1. Duties of counselors are most often determined by situational expediency, by the variable expectations of school administrators, teachers, and parents, and by pressures of routine clerical and quasi-administrative chores. Basing training programs on present duties would simply reinforce undesirable practices and consequently lead to no positive gain.
2. The range of activities reflected by surveys of counselor activities is so broad that, taken in the aggregate, no one could perform them all.

[3] Association for Counselor Education and Supervision, "Standards for the Preparation of Secondary School Counselors—1967," *Personnel and Guidance Journal* Vol. 46 (September 1967), pp. 96–106.

3. Training based on present activities would be training that looks to the past rather than to the future.

DISCUSSION

Again, the arguments on both sides seem clearcut. Candidates frequently make the accusation of impracticality of content in their training. There is little doubt that some of these accusations spring from the student's anxiety over his adequacy in coping with future job demands. Above all, he desires tailor-made solutions to practical problems he anticipates facing on the job. Student accusations also frequently stem from comparisons of the ideal presented in training with the specifics of known school situations. What appears impractical in one school situation may appear highly practical in a different situation, and vice versa. This condition often leads to contradictory views by students regarding what is and what is not practical. Counselor educators have little recourse but to present that which, in their professional judgment, is the ideal. Efforts at application of the ideal in real situations will temper any completely impractical aspects of the ideal. Though they are certainly not infallible, counselor educators should be equipped by preparation, experience, and inclination to function as experts with regard to these matters.

For further discussion of this issue, see Blocher, *et al* (1963), Chenault (1968), Guese (1968), Hutson (1962a, 1962b), Lister (1967), Loughary, *et al.* (1965), McCully (1962), and Strickland (1969).

Issue XI:
Do the NDEA or EPDA counseling and guidance institutes constitute an adverse influence in counselor education?

Yes, because:[4]

1. Institute participants are taught in isolated groups and do not mix with other students or identify with the university. This inevitably leads to restriction and narrowness in their education.
2. Instructors in institutes tend to be younger, less experienced, and perhaps less competent than regular staff members. Because instructor appointments are temporary, i.e., one-year appointments only, better qualified and more experienced counselor educators accept only regular positions, with the result that institute staffs are drawn from an increasingly less desirable pool of candidates.
3. Institutions conducting institutes must maintain two parallel counselor education programs, a practice that is costly and artificial. Efforts to maintain and extend the regular counselor education program are negated, since institute temporary appointments decrease the need for permanent staff openings. Rather than continuing institute programs, federal support might better take the form of stipends or fellowships to

[4] See C. H. Patterson, "The NDEA and Counselor Education," *Counselor Education and Supervision* Vol. 3 (Fall 1963), pp. 4–7.

individual students who would enroll in regular counselor education programs.

4. Since federal monies are involved, federal control is exercised over counselor education. The U.S. Office of Education selects those institutions that provide counselor preparation incorporating content, direction, and practices which Office of Education personnel wish to impose on the profession.

5. Many students who attend counseling institutes do so for questionable purposes. It is the availability of subsidized training that they can use to their own ends which attracts them, and not a sincere commitment to school counseling. They are not really interested in the educational experiences provided or in becoming school counselors.

6. Universities merely use institute programs as a way to recruit doctoral candidates.

No, because:

1. The NDEA and EPDA institute programs have stimulated needed innovations in counselor education. These innovations carry over and have positive results in regular counselor education programs.

2. NDEA and EPDA institutes not only have increased the quantity of counselors available to the nation's school, but also have provided the schools with an unparalleled example of quality.

3. The institute program has upgraded the skills of practicing school counselors who were and might have remained only partially trained.

4. The institute program is voluntary; only institutions which choose to do so submit proposals. The proposals originate from the educational institution. Also, panels of counselor educators and experts from other disciplines are drawn from outside the U.S. Office of Education to rate the proposals. The U.S. Office then selects institutions with which to contract.

5. Selection of students is an institutional reponsibility. The overwhelming evidence indicates that high-quality students are selected and that a great proportion of these students return to schools as counselors. In addition, the full-time study in residence afforded by institute programs has helped to counteract the fractionated preparation of part-time students who are hard put to integrate their educational experience.

6. The institute program has led to improved facilities, materials, program coordination, planning, and evaluation, as well as to increased supervised training experiences of all kinds.[5]

7. Stipends to individual students who would then enroll in a regular program of their own choice are out of the question until a way is found to evaluate counselor education programs. The range of quality in existing counselor education programs is extremely broad. The U.S. Office

[5] Gordan Klopf and Nancy C. Cohen, "The Impact of NDEA Counseling and Guidance Institutes on the Professional Education of School Counselors," *Counselor Education and Supervision* Vol. 1 (Spring 1962), pp. 151–161.

has an obligation to Congress and to the American people to ensure that its money is wisely spent on quality programs.

DISCUSSION

The Counseling and Guidance Institute program (conducted under Title 5B, NDEA of 1958, as amended) and Education Professions Development Act program basically represent a response to a recognized nationwide shortage of school guidance personnel. Viewed in this light, the overall impact of these programs appears to have been positive, especially when one considers that "crash programs" frequently appear to earn this rather colorful label because of their downfall rather than their useful impact. Reviewing the outcomes of counseling institute programs, one is forced to agree that they have materially increased the number of counselors in the field, while favorably influencing counselor education.

It is equally true that some problems are associated with institute programs. One of these is the year-to-year contractual arrangements with institutions. This has resulted into two related difficulties. The first of these might best be described as a "rags-to-riches" phenomenon. Alternating loss and gain of financial support creates obvious problems in the planning and management of programs. The second related problem is in the area of staffing. The short-term nature of institute contract arrangements creates severe hiring problems, since many employment arrangements are one-year temporary assignments. This type of arrangement may predispose the institution to employ individuals who at best lack merely experience and at worst, competency.

The question of federal control over counselor education often reduces to the emotional reactions of an individual to federal influence. Some control appears inevitable, at least in the accounting of funds, attainment of minimal standards regarding facilities, and sufficient staff. Perhaps what appears to some as federal control may in actuality represent efforts at subtle leadership by the U.S. Office of Education.

In respect to the students selected for participation in the institute programs, followup surveys by the U.S. Office show that the vast majority (up to 90 percent) do return to schools as counselors. Almost universally, the experience of universities has been that the students are capable persons. No doubt some errors in selection are made, but probably with less frequency than in regular counselor education programs.

A fellowship program consisting of program support over a period of three to five years would do much to alleviate the problems encountered in the year-to-year contractual arrangement. This, of course, would leave little room for "pump priming" efforts to stimulate fledgling counselor education programs, since presumably they could not qualify for such support.

For further discussion of this issue, see Dettloff (1964), Foley and Proff (1965), Jones (1963), Klopf and Cohen (1964), McDaniels (1967), Patterson (1963), Pierson (1965) and Stripling (1967).

Issue XII:
What is the best way to integrate didactic instruction and practicum?

1. Practicum experience must be preceded by sufficient didactic work to ensure adequate performance.
2. Practicum experience should be spread across the entire sequence of training with the increasing responsibility assumed by the student counselor.

DISCUSSION

Basically at issue here is the meaning given to the word "practicum." Used broadly, it can include role-playing activity, critiques of mock and actual counseling sessions, and a variety of laboratory experiences. In this sense, such experiences can and should begin early in the training sequence. Used in a more restricted sense, the student counselor assumes major responsibility, under supervision, for the management of counseling cases. Here, counseling practicum refers to a training course in which counselor candidates conduct critiqued counseling sessions with actual clients under observed, supervised conditions. Counseling practicum experience is viewed as the focal point for the integration and synthesis of prior didactic and laboratory experience. Didactic preparation leads directly to application of basic course work in counseling contact as experienced in practicum by the novice counselor. The sequential nature of most existing programs consists of prior didactic preparation culminating in practicum experience. Preparatory work, particularly in the areas of occupational and educational information, testing and appraisal techniques, and counseling theory and technique, is requisite to adequate practicum performance. Synthesis of prior learnings as well as increments of new learnings appear to occur best when an adequate basic knowledge in such essential content areas is available to the candidate for application in the counseling setting.

There seems little doubt that practicum experience has increasingly come to be viewed as the major vehicle for counselor training. Although there is no definitive information regarding the proportion of total training time that should be devoted to this activity, it would probably be advantageous to devote approximately one-quarter to one-third of the program to practicum-type activities, including supervised field practice. However, it remains essential that careful consideration be given to adequate prerequisite preparation to ensure reasonable professional competency on the part of counselor candidates. Even with close supervision, the introduction of candidates with inadequate skills and knowledge to a counseling relationship would be unprofessional, unethical, and potentially dangerous to the counselee.

Some argue that the practicum should begin early in the preparation of counselors, because by its very nature, practicum experience is potentially self-analytical and self-evaluative. Indeed, it is generally agreed that the whole of counselor preparation inevitably contains the seeds of these two crucial elements. Thus, the basic issue in counselor education is one of *implementation* of the personal evaluative process. On the premise that self-evaluation occurs for all candidates to some extent and at various points throughout the training sequence, the central need in training is to know the optimal way of encouraging, fostering, and, if possible, systematically enhancing the process. Emphasis upon self-evaluation by counselor candidates cannot replace staff responsibility for consistent, continuing evaluation of each candidate's progress.

For further discussion of this issue, see Boy and Pine (1964), Gysbers and Johnston (1965), Hansen (1965), Lister (1966), (Patterson (1967), Seaman and Wurtz (1968), and Strickland (1969).

Issue XIII:
Do state certification requirements for school counselors constitute sufficient means to establish quality control and reciprocity between states?

Yes, because:

1. Certification is an official verdict that a person possesses a minimal level of competence to perform a specified service.
2. Although variation in certification requirements exists among the several states, a common core ensures qualification.

No, because:

1. Present certification requirements represent poor minimal, rather than highly desirable, standards.
2. Variability in state certification is so wide that reciprocity is an impossibility until entry-level requirements are agreed upon nationwide.
3. Not all states have established certification requirements for counselors.

DISCUSSION

Up to the present time, counselor education programs have tended to function relatively independently. Counselor education standards may, in the near future, exert a desirable influence if they become a means for accrediting counselor education programs. The rapid rise in accrediting agencies, such as the National Council for Accreditation of Teacher Education, is an example of an independent agency that provides criteria for states to employ in deciding questions of reciprocity in teacher licensing.

Currently, state certification requirements for school counselors are somewhat haphazard and by no means can they resolve questions of quality of training. At best they describe course titles required for certification. Though this requirement may be a poor substitute for responsible accreditation by a professional agency, they are currently the only official means available to ensure that the beginning counselor has completed minimal coursework. Even a cursory examination of the requirements for certifying guidance workers clearly demonstrates the range of requirements among the fifty states.[6]

For further discussion of this issue, see Arbuckle (1968a), Dickey (1968), Dudley and Ruff (1970), Dugan (1960), Lloyd (1962), Loughary, *et al.* (1965), Stefflre (1964), and Wrenn (1962).

GUIDANCE PRACTICES AND PROGRAM POLICIES

Issue XIV:
Should and can counseling and guidance be separated from teaching activities?

For integration of guidance and teaching activities:

1. "Every teacher a counselor" has long been urged, on grounds that the teacher's day-to-day contact with pupils gives him an understanding of them that is possessed by no one else.
2. Guidance is an inherent part of teaching with one achieved best through the other.
3. The purpose of elementary and secondary education is to promote the "intellectual development" of youth. A structure for guidance (separate from that inherent in instructional activities) is not a proper domain of the school. In short, guidance is an ancillary service that could and probably should be dispensed with.
4. Specialized guidance services are unnecessary. They came into being as a result of expediency. Rather than employing counselors, the schools should reduce the teacher-pupil ratio to manageable proportions.
5. Separation of the two activities implies that the counselor treats the emotional life of the child while the teacher deals with his cognitive activities. This violates a cardinal educational principle of treating the child as a totality.

For separation of teaching and guidance activities:

1. Teachers are most essentially concerned with the transmission and inculcation of knowledge, skills, and attitudes. As specialists in subject matter, teachers have little time to fulfill the individual pupil's guidance needs even if they were disposed to do so.
2. Expanding enrollments, double sessions, and subject-matter specialization, coupled with the problems of automation, increasing college enrollments, changing manpower demands, dropouts, delinquency, and the need for individual career planning all militate against the teacher adequately serving all pupils.

[6] Hubert W. Houghton, *Certification Requirements for School Pupil Personnel Workers,* U.S. Department of Health, Education and Welfare, Office of Education (Washington: Government Printing Office, 1967).

3. Youth problems cannot be alleviated by information alone but require specialized professional knowledge, attitudes, and competencies which teachers do not possess because their preparation has not stressed them.

4. The teacher understands and is concerned primarily with the student as a learner of subject matter. This understanding and concern is not enough to achieve the goals of counseling and guidance.

5. Integrating teaching and guidance means that the guidance relationship would become incidental. Guidance as everybody's business becomes, in practice, no one's responsibility.

6. The evaluative and disciplinary activities inherent in teaching preclude the establishment and maintenance of the permissive, understanding, intimate relationship necessary for guidance.

7. Theoretically, guidance can be separated from teaching because teaching is the communication of other peoples' experiences, data, and conclusions, while guidance is the examination of the individual student's experiences.[7] The counselor, in contrast to the teacher, furnishes the information, the recommendations, and the impetus needed to move particular children in distinctive directions on the basis of their special characteristics and potentialities.[8]

DISCUSSION

Guidance should be separated from teaching activities. Although each individual member of the educational enterprise has certain guidance responsibilities that he is expected to perform, counseling and guidance activities are too complex and too important in today's world to leave the school's obligation to chance in this respect. The authors' respect for good teachers—what they do and what they mean to youth—is unlimited. But the hard fact remains that efforts to do all and to be all things to all pupils are not fruitful. Specialization in every area of life, including education, inescapably and inevitably has occurred. As has been stated in this book, it is anticipated and expected that teachers will conduct certain guidance functions. But to expect them to provide this service by themselves, in addition to their primary activity of teaching, is to ask the impossible. The more widely the responsibility is spread, the less likely is the guidance program to achieve its purposes and objectives. Both teaching and guidance activities are necessary for education, but neither is sufficient alone. Partial combinations of the two are of extremely doubtful value.

The responsibility for instruction belongs to the teacher, and the primary responsibility for guidance services lies with the guidance counselor. A program of organized guidance services under the direction of the counselor

---

[7] David V. Tiedeman and Frank L. Field, "Guidance: The Science of Purposeful Action Applied Through Education," *Harvard Educational Review* Vol. 32 (Fall 1962), p. 495.

[8] Shoben, "Guidance: Remedial or Reconstruction?" p. 432.

provides for better organization of services, a reduction of overlapping services, and an increase in effectiveness. Teachers are responsible for providing a curriculum-based learning situation for the child, usually in a group situation, and ordinarily for the period of a school year. Counselors are usually responsible for the individual child longitudinally in the educational process. From background information concerning the developmental growth of the child, the counselor provides information and suggestions about him to the teacher. The counselor assumes responsibility for the educational-vocational guidance of the counselee because he is the primary person in the educational setting who assists students in developing self-understanding for decision-making. The counselor assists the child in understanding himself in relation to his unique needs, interests, and goals. The·teacher is responsible for presenting subject-matter content, but the focus of the counselor is the self-development of the individual. Each is an indispensable part of the educational process with unique contributions to the full development of the individual.

For further discussion of this issue, see Arbuckle (1961), Blocher, *et al.* (1963), Cohen (1961), Cottingham (1962), Hill (1961), Kehas (1966, 1970), Pierson (1965), Sherman (1962), Shoben (1962), and Tiedeman and Field (1962).

Issue XV:
Should special subgroups within the school have priority for counseling services?

Counseling priorities should be established, with the major focus on these special subgroups:

1. The bright students, because in large measure counseling depends upon the individual's ability to perceive relationships in life as a result of perceptive thinking prompted by the interaction process between the individual and the counselor.
2. Children with emotional problems, because there is no one else in the school who is especially prepared to deal with the emotional conflicts of students.
3. Underachievers, because the purpose of school is to promote the intellectual development of children; therefore, every effort should be made to help those who are capable and yet underachieve or fail in school.
4. Those who misbehave or "act out" in classroom situations for the dual reason that they are (a) asking for help and (b) interfering with others' learning and limiting the teacher's effectiveness.
5. Those who seek counseling help voluntarily because an essential element in counseling is that the student possess the internal motivation to take action to resolve his problem. Counseling should be directed toward those who will profit from it most.

Predetermined priorities should not be established regarding the availability of counseling services because:

1. All students should have access to counseling service in the public schools, subject only to their own rejection of the service in those counseling activities that go beyond routine program planning.
2. The provision of counseling for only the gifted, disturbed, underachieving, or misbehaving students deprives the majority of students in the school of a necessary service.

DISCUSSION

Many argue that focusing attention on certain groups would be wise because of its obvious value to the school and to the special groups concerned. All guidance personnel are faced with the temptation to restrict their services to special groups such as those described above. This type of approach would be defensible only if sufficient time and personnel are available to serve the remainder of the school population.

If one accepts the premise that guidance programs are established for *all* students, it would seem to follow that the availability of service probably cannot be on a strictly volunteer basis. Students fail to seek assistance for many reasons: lack of knowledge of services available, difficulty of counselor accessibility, lack of freedom of choice of counselor, the reputation that a school's counseling service is for special groups only, and the like. Factors such as these may make it difficult for even the motivated students to utilize counseling services. It is also true that assistance cannot be forced on the individual. Assistance should be available and understood by all members of the student body. Its utilization should be encouraged by the school's policies and staff members. Probably if this were always the case, guidance services would be sought by students themselves.

For further discussion of this issue, see Arbuckle (1965), Brough (1968), Flanagan (1963), Grande (1968), Gross (1969), Havighurst (1965), Heilfron (1964), Holleman (1961), Loughary, *et al.* (1965), Mathewson (1964), Patterson (1969), and Wrenn (1962).

Issue XVI:

Can school counselors establish and maintain effective counseling relationships with poor or minority-group clients?

No, because:

1. A language barrier exists between middle-class adults and individuals from the lower classes.
2. Counselors who have assimilated middle-class values cannot understand the values, the psychological imperatives and the attitudes of economically disadvantaged or minority-group individuals.

3. Many poor children as well as some minority-group children have had little or no experience with professionals or counseling and will not voluntarily come to counselors.
4. Many of the poor and minority-group children have been "taught" not to disclose themselves to others and/or that it is a form of weakness to seek help.
5. Minority-group and poor children are generally distrustful and suspicious of adults who are in positions of authority.

Yes, because:

1. The counselor's expertise lies in communicating with others and in understanding human behavior.
2. The counselor does not have to experience directly every hurt or engage in every type of human existence to initiate, establish and maintain helping relationships.

DISCUSSION

The initiative for resolving this issue appears to lie in the lap of the profession itself. Enlightened efforts to carry service to such groups must be made if there is to be progress. The need cannot be questioned and neither can the necessity for the profession to extend its services to these groups. If there are communication barriers, the counselor must at least learn to understand what is said to him, even though he does not necessarily need to use the same language. If distrust of professionals is part of the problem, it is the professional's responsibility to build trusting relationships, at least initially. If the client's prejudice makes skin color a problem, an effort still must be initiated by the counselor.

Direct personal experience with poverty or minority-group membership, while often helpful to the counselor, can also work to his detriment. While on the surface it appears that direct experience could make it easier for the counselor to assist an individual from a similar background, overidentification with the client's problems can be a drawback.

Occasionally the counselor may be seen by the client as one who has attained an impossible goal or who has sold out to the system to become successful. These views can retard rather than enhance a meaningful relationship. The difficulties of working with these individuals are similar to those of working with mandatory referrals or those who view counseling as part of the disciplinary process. One is confronted with negative attitudes that must be resolved and worked through before proper use can be made of the counseling experience.

For further discussion of this issue, see Arbuckle (1969), Hoffnung and Mills (1970), Leacock (1968), Smith (1970), Vontress (1967, 1969), and Warner and Hansen (1970).

Issue XVII:
Should school counselors administer and score schoolwide tests?

Yes, because:

1. Among school personnel, counselors are the best trained to conduct testing.
2. If counselors do not perform the function, then it devolves upon teachers who are ill-equipped to conduct complex, standardized testing operations.

No, because:

1. The function of administering and scoring most group tests is largely a routine task that does not require extensive specialized training.
2. Such a function would consume too much of the counselor's time; his skills are better used in test interpretation and counseling.

DISCUSSION

Three major factors—test selection, collection of test data, use of test results—are involved in this issue.

The selection of tests to be given schoolwide should be a committee function. A representative from the guidance services will probably be the committee's chief resource person regarding the technical characteristics of tests. The selection of achievement tests is a good example of an area in which the counselor's influence would be restricted to consultation concerning the technical characteristics of tests. The validity of achievement tests is intimately dependent upon the content and objectives of the instructional program. For this reason, instructional personnel must be involved in the choice of achievement tests. Although there is much to be said in favor of schoolwide involvement in the selection of other kinds of tests, guidance personnel probably would assume major responsibility in the choice of ability, aptitude, and interest measures.

Most test publishers have devoted tremendous effort to producing instruments that can be simply and economically administered and scored. At issue in the administration and scoring of tests given schoolwide is the appropriate use of counselor time. It would seem more appropriate for the counselor to use his time in making full use of test results—compilation of local norms, summarization and report of test results that can aid the instructional program, inservice training in the meaning of test results, and test interpretation to students and their parents—than in administering the tests.

Perhaps the most efficient means of test-scoring is to be found in the scoring services offered by test publishers or independent concerns. Though at first glance such scoring services seem expensive, a frequently overlooked fact is that school staff time involved in test scoring is equally, if not more, expensive. There is little information available regarding the relative accuracy of hand-scored tests, but there is little doubt that tests scored by machines are more accurate than those scored by disgruntled, unhappy school personnel.

For further discussion of this issue, see Arbuckle (1970), Lundy and Shertzer (1963), Shoben (1962), and Tiedeman and Field (1962).

Issue XVIII:
Should pupils be informed of their test results?

Test data should not be interpreted because:

1. Interpretation develops class consciousness, increasing snobbishness among highly able students, and feelings of inferiority among less capable students. As Ebel says, "It may place an indelible stamp of intellectual status—superior, mediocre or inferior—on a child, and thus predetermine his social status as an adult, and possibly also do irreparable harm to his self-esteem and his educational motivation."[9]
2. "It may lead to a narrow conception of ability, encourage pursuit of this single goal, and thus tend to reduce the diversity of talent available to society."[10]
3. Test data are complex. Limitations in validity, reliability, and the like may lead to misunderstanding and subsequent misuse of data by students.
4. A fully satisfactory way of reporting test results that will ensure understanding by all consumers has yet to be worked out.

Pupils should be informed of test results, because:

1. Knowledge of test scores is vital to sound educational and vocational planning since test results supply valuable estimations of probable success.
2. There is no use in trying to conceal from pupils the facts concerning their capabilities, however limited or promising. If they show strengths or limitations in some area or in a variety of areas, the counselor's responsibility is to make these conditions known to them and to help pupils cope with them effectively.
3. Testing is not conducted just because it is the thing to do; it is conducted to yield information that can contribute to wise decision-making, and students should enter into such decision-making.
4. Taking a test requires the individual to invest himself in a situation. Therefore, he has a right to a knowledge of the outcome.
5. Not informing pupils of their strengths and limitations is contrary to democratic principles which emphasize individuality, self-reliance, and individual attainment.

[9] Robert L. Ebel, "The Social Consequences of Educational Testing," in *Proceedings of the 1963 Invitational Conference on Testing Problems* (Princeton, N.J.: Educational Testing Service, 1964), p. 132.

[10] *Ibid.*

DISCUSSION

This issue revolves around the social implications involved in testing and the accurate understanding of results reported to individuals. Ebel's article presents very succinctly the social implications. The reader is urged to examine this source for a better understanding of this complex and value-laden topic.[11]

The discussion here, however, will be restricted to the kind and amount of test information provided individuals, though it is recognized that this facet of the problem is not entirely free of social implications. This in itself is an extremely important topic. Some states have legislative regulations regarding the kinds of tests that may be used, and many school districts have an established administrative policy regarding test use and interpretation. However, most states and school districts either by design or omission permit counselors full latitude in test use and interpretation procedures.

The counselor's responsibility for accurate, thorough, and meaningful interpretation is always subject to counteraction by what the counselee perceives and the way in which he may act upon the information given. It is perfectly clear that the mere reporting of scores without relatively extensive counseling effort is inappropriate. It is only through patient, detailed interpretation, coupled with extensive discussion of the individual's reactions, that truly meaningful use can be made of test results.

For further discussion of this issue, see Barclay (1964), Brim (1965), Ebel (1964), Lister and Ohlsen (1965), Needham, Stodola and Brown (1963–64), Neulinger (1966), Riccio (1964), and Wesman (1968).

Issue XIX:

In legal and ethical conflict situations between the welfare of the individual pupil and the welfare of the school, does the counselor champion the individual or is his primary loyalty to the school?

The counselor's basic responsibility is to the individual:

1. The counselor's primary obligation is to respect the integrity and promote the welfare of the counselee.
2. Confidentiality is essential in a counseling relationship; if the counselor cannot provide this to his clientele, his effectiveness is severely and perhaps irreparably curtailed.

The counselor's basic responsibility is to the school:

1. As a member of the school faculty, the counselor's basic loyalty is to the employing institution.
2. Privileged communications for school counselors has not been given legal status in most states.

[11] *Ibid.*

DISCUSSION

Rarely, in an ultimate sense, are there conflicts between the counselor's responsibilities to the individual and to the school or society. Most often, when the counselor is helping one, he is also helping the others. In most instances, if the counselor decides that he must break the client's confidence, he is usually convinced that to remain silent would have a disastrously harmful effect on the client or on society. Perhaps the basic problem to individual counselors is in determining what constitutes the circumstances of such disaster. The usual generalizations concerning harm to self or to others require fairly simple decisions for most counselors.

But, within the school setting, where the counselor deals with minors' sexual behavior, delinquent acts, and the like, there are no easy solutions. Each situation must be considered on its own merits, and each decision must be based upon the client's welfare and not upon the counselor's welfare. In most, if not all, counseling relationships it is important that the counselor realize that when he is forced to break confidence, he destroys the counseling relationship probably for all time to come.

For a good presentation of the various levels of responsibility counselors face, the reader is urged to examine Patterson's discussion of ethics.[12] In addition, all counselors should be thoroughly familiar with the American Personnel and Guidance Association and with the American Psychological Association ethical codes referenced at the end of Chapter 7.

For further discussion of this issue, see Arbuckle (1968b), Barclay (1964), Cox (1965), Livingston (1965), Miller and Simpson (1961), Nugent (1969), Phillips and Margoshes (1966), Riccio (1964), Schmid (1967), Tennyson, Blocher and Johnson (1964), and Wiener (1964).

Issue XX:
What is the nature of the educational-vocational choice-making process?

Choice is an illusion because man's present and future states are determined by his past state.

Choice is possible because man directs his own destiny.

DISCUSSION

The educational-vocational choice-making process cannot be construed as a problem isolated from the day-to-day development of the individual. Rather, decision-making is properly viewed as a developmental process. Educational and vocational choices interact with and are influenced by all aspects of a student's life. They cannot be made by considering only a narrow set of seemingly relevant characteristics over a limited time span. In spite of the obvious scientific and technical revolutions and the more subtle changes in the social and cultural characteristics of our civilization, the pos-

[12] C. H. Patterson, *Counseling and Psychotherapy: Theory and Practice* (New York: Harper & Brothers, 1959), pp. 31–52.

sibility and the necessity of making appropriate career choices remain a reality for adolescents.

In practice, the counselor's approach may be seen as partly deterministic in that it is affected by such client characteristics as health, ability, financial resources, and other social, cultural and environmental forces that are a reality for the individual. But beyond these factors, it is generally accepted that there exists a great potentiality for autonomous, actualizing behavior and that free will and choice are more than illusory concepts.

The vocational choice process is a longitudinal and cumulative process during which adolescents pass through several critical periods. The nature and number of these periods, each of which contains a range of opportunities, are variable and often a function of environmental conditions, e.g., social milieu, financial circumstances, educational opportunity, etc. Adolescents frequently pass through critical periods unaware of the variety of opportunities for choice available to them. In retrospect, as adults, they may recall having made only one, or at best a few, educational and vocational decisions. Yet the mere failure to recognize and act upon such opportunities constitutes making a choice by default. The counselor's first responsibility in the choice process, therefore, lies in being sensitive to the existence of critical periods and of apprising students of the available opportunities for choice. In addition, through application of appraisal and counseling skills, the counselor assists students in understanding themselves and their life situations with regard to social, educational, and vocational problems and opportunities.

Through conscious efforts, counselors assist students to understand both themselves and the opportunities available to them. Inevitably, counselors transmit to students their personal values and those of the institution and society, which emphasize achievement, maximum development, and the worth and dignity of the individual. Potentially, counselors not only exert great influence upon the educational-vocational choice process, but also strive to recognize clearly their own values and needs so that they can consciously separate them from those of their clients.

For further discussion of this issue, see Chenault (1968), Collins (1965), Lair (1968), Maes (1968), O'Hara (1968), Pierson (1965), Schell and Daubner (1969), and Shoben (1961).

CONCLUSION

It is hoped that the preceding pages shed some light on the persistent issues confronting guidance personnel. Many look wistfully back to the time when the problems seemed fewer in number and simpler. However, the past is often idealized. Undoubtedly, the "good old days" were not an unmixed blessing; nor were the issues then as clearcut and simple as they now seem to have been. To the men who met them, they probably were as complex and confusing as contemporary issues are to us today. But whether or not the good old days were better, escape into the past provides no solution for present issues. The issues facing guidance personnel should not be minimized nor looked upon gloomily since fear that all is lost will inhibit action. No issue can be resolved by a refusal to confront it. That guidance is flourishing in America and that we have somehow muddled through presents no guarantee that it will continue to flourish. Neither extreme pessimism nor extreme optimism (which represent moods, not actions)—neither ignoring the issues nor being overwhelmed by them—is the answer.

It would be easy to turn over the solution of these issues to the "authorities" and expect neat, tidy explanations. This is similar to the response of children who look to their parents for assurances and protection against the complexities and cruelties of a world they cannot understand and refuse to face. Reliance upon "authority" is a tempting appeal to the guidance practitioner who must cope with pressure, frequently from conflicting forces, while feeling that he is caught in the grip of dilemmas not of his making and beyond his control. But if the forty thousand or more school counselors in this country are to remain professionally alive, it will be because of their zest in meeting and resolving these issues. That the issues can be met and mastered is taken as an article of faith. Guidance leaders of vision and courage are essential, but it is from the individual guidance practitioner that future leaders are recruited and issues will be resolved.

With regard to issues, other facts should be stated. In any viable profession, issues will always be present, and they serve to stimulate additional growth. Fundamental issues frequently appear to be resolved but they have the habit of cropping up in new forms. The very existence of controversial issues is desirable. It indicates professional awareness, which presumably is a characteristic of professional strength.

ANNOTATED BIBLIOGRAPHY

BARRY, RUTH, AND WOLF, BEVERLY. *Modern Issues in Guidance-Personnel Work.* New York: Bureau of Publications, Teachers College, Columbia University, 1963. 256 pp.

Barry and Wolf trace the historical background of issues in guidance and personnel work, analyze the pros and cons of each issue, and arrive at certain conclusions for each issue. This book is well worth a student's time and study.

LITWACK, LAWRENCE; HOLMES, JUNE; AND O'HERN, JANE S. *Critical Issues in Student Personnel Work.* Chicago: Rand McNally and Company, 1964. 105 pp.

The case-study method is used to dramatize student personnel issues evolving from such contexts as the community, the school, and the individual. Questions are posed for each case, which help to evaluate approaches and conflicts.

WRENN, C. GILBERT. *The Counselor in a Changing World.* Washington: American Personnel and Guidance Association, 1962. 195 pp.

Wrenn and his committee's monumental report not only treated a number of issues, but brought up issues that have involved the profession in serious discussion since the release of the publication.

SELECTED REFERENCES

ARBUCKLE, DUGALD S. "The Conflicting Functions of the School Counselor," *Counselor Education and Supervision* Vol. 1 (Winter 1961), pp. 54–59.

————. (a) "Current Issues in Counselor Education," *Counselor Education and Supervision* Vol. 7 (Spring 1968), pp. 244–251.

————. (b) "A Question of Counselor Function and Responsibility," *Personnel and Guidance Journal* Vol. 47 (December 1968), pp. 341–345.

————. "The Alienated Counselor," *Personnel and Guidance Journal* Vol. 48 (September 1969), pp. 18–23.

————. *Counseling: Philosophy Theory and Practice* 2nd Ed. (Boston: Allyn and Bacon, Inc., 1970), pp. 320–327.

AUBREY, ROGER F. "The Legitimacy of Elementary School Counseling: Some Unresolved Issues and Conflicts," *Personnel and Guidance Journal* Vol. 46 (December 1967), pp. 355–359.

BARCLAY, JAMES R. "The Attack on Testing and Counseling: An Examination and Reappraisal." *Personnel and Guidance Journal* Vol. 53 (September 1964), pp. 6–16.

BEYMER, LAWRENCE. "The Procrustean Counselor: Myth or Reality?" *Vocational Guidance Quarterly* Vol. 10 (Autumn 1961), pp. 19–23.

BLOCHER, DONALD H., TENNYSON, W. WESLEY, AND JOHNSON, RALPH H. "The Dilemma of Counselor Identity," *Journal of Counseling Psychology* Vol. 10 (Winter 1963), pp. 344–349.

BOY, ANGELO V., AND PINE, GERALD J. "A Recommendation to Counselor Educators," *The School Counselor* Vol. 12 (December 1964), pp. 80–84.

BRAMMER, LAWRENCE M. "The Counselor Is a Psychologist," *Personnel and Guidance Journal* Vol. 47 (September 1968), pp. 4–8.

BRIM, ORVILLE G., JR. "American Attitudes Toward Intelligence Tests," *American Psychologist* Vol. 20 (February 1965), pp. 125–130.

BROUGH, JAMES R. "A Comparison of Self-Referred Counselees and Non-Counseled Junior High School Students," *Personnel and Guidance Journal* Vol. 47 (December 1968), pp. 329–332.

CHENAULT, JOANN. "A Proposed Model for a Humanistic Counselor Education Program," *Counselor Education and Supervision* Vol. 8 (Fall 1968), pp. 4–11.

COHEN, NANCY C. "Must Teaching Be a Prerequisite for Guidance?" *Counselor Education and Supervision* Vol. 1 (Winter 1961), pp. 69–71.

COLLINS, CHARLES C. "Junior College Counseling: A Critical View," *Personnel and Guidance Journal* Vol. 43 (February 1965), pp. 546–550.

COTTINGHAM, HAROLD F. "Implementing Two Vital Teacher Functions," *Counselor Education and Supervision* Vol. 1 (Spring 1962), pp. 166–169.

Cox, Robert I. "Confidentiality—Where Is Our First Obligation?" *The School Counselor* Vol. 12 (March 1965), pp. 153–161.

Dettloff, E. G. "Attitudes Toward Guidance Institutions," *Counselor Education and Supervision* Vol. 4 (Fall 1964), pp. 32–36.

Dickey, Frank G. "What is Accrediting and Why is it Important for Professional Organizations?" *Counselor Education and Supervision* Vol. 7 (Spring 1968), pp. 194–199.

Dudley, Gerald, and Ruff, Eldon. "School Counselor Certification: A Study of Current Requirements," *The School Counselor* Vol. 17 (March 1970), pp. 304–311.

Dugan, Willis E. "The Impact of NDEA Upon Counselor Preparation," *Personnel and Guidance Journal* Vol. 39 (September 1960), pp. 37–40.

Dunsmoor, C. C. "Counselor—Or What?" *Personnel and Guidance Journal* Vol. 43 (October 1964), pp. 135–138.

Ebel, Robert L. "The Social Consequences of Educational Testing," in *Proceedings of the 1963 Institutional Conference on Testing Problems* (Princeton, N.J.: Educational Testing Service, 1964), pp. 130–143.

Faust, Vernon. *History of Elementary School Counseling: Overview and Critique* (Boston: Houghton Mifflin Company, 1968), 162 pp.

Flanagan, John C. "The Effective Use of Manpower Resources," *Personnel and Guidance Journal* Vol. 42 (October 1963), pp. 114–118.

Foley, Walter J., and Proff, Fred C. "NDEA Institute Trainees and Vocational Rehabilitation Counselors: A Comparison of Characteristics," *Counselor Education and Supervision* Vol. 4 (Spring 1965), pp. 154–159.

Fredrickson, Ronald H., and Pippert, Ralph R. "Teaching Experience in the Employment of School Counselors," *Counselor Education and Supervision* Vol. 4 (Fall 1964), pp. 24–27.

Gilbert, Norman S. "When the School Counselor is a Disciplinarian." *Personnel and Guidance Journal* Vol. 43 (January 1965), pp. 485–491.

Grande, Peter P. "Attitudes of Counselors and Disadvantaged Students Toward School Guidance," *Personnel and Guidance Journal* Vol. 46 (May 1968), pp. 889–892.

Gross, Edward. "Counselors Under Fire: Youth Opportunity Centers," *Personnel and Guidance Journal* Vol. 47 (January 1969) pp. 404–409.

Guese, L. E. "A Neglected Need in Counselor Education," *Counselor Education and Supervision* Vol. 7 (Winter 1968), pp. 114–118.

Gysbers, Norman C., and Johnston, Joseph A. "Expectations of a Practicum Supervisor's Role," *Counselor Education and Supervision* Vol. 4 (Winter 1965), pp. 68–74.

Hansen, James C. "Trainee's Expectations of Supervision in the Counseling Practicum," *Counselor Education and Supervision* Vol. 4 (Winter 1965), pp. 75–80.

————, and Moore, Gilbert D. "The Full-Time—Part-Time Debate: A Research Contribution," *Counselor Education and Supervision* Vol. 8 (Fall 1968), pp. 18–22.

HAVIGHURST, ROBERT J. "Counseling Adolescent Girls in the 1960's," *Vocational Guidance Quarterly* Vol. 13 (Spring 1965), pp. 153–160.

HEILFRON, MARILYN. "Changing Students' Perceptions of the Counselor's Role," *The School Counselor* Vol. 11 (May 1964), pp. 221–225.

HERR, EDWIN L. "Comment," *Personnel and Guidance Journal* Vol. 46 (May 1968), pp. 862–863.

HILL, GEORGE E. "The Selection of School Counselors," *Personnel and Guidance Journal* Vol. 39 (January 1961), pp. 355–360.

————. (a) "Agreements in the Practice of Guidance in the Elementary School," *Elementary School Guidance and Counseling* Vol. 1 (June 1967), pp. 188–195.

————. (b) "The Profession and Standards for Counselor Education," *Counselor Education and Supervision* Vol. 6 (Winter 1967), pp. 130–136.

HOFFNUNG, ROBERT J., AND MILLS, ROBERT B. "Situational Group Counseling with Disadvantaged Youth," *Personnel and Guidance Journal* Vol. 48 (February 1970), pp. 458–464.

HOLLEMAN, JERRY R. "National Needs and Individual Liberty," *Vocational Guidance Journal* Vol. 9 (Spring 1961), pp. 147–151.

HOYT, KENNETH. "What the School Has a Right to Expect of Its Counselor," *Personnel and Guidance Journal* Vol. 40 (October 1961), pp. 129–133.

————. "Guidance: A Constellation of Services," *Personnel and Guidance Journal* Vol. 40 (April 1962), pp. 690–697.

HUDSON, GEORGE R. "Counselors Need Teaching Experience," *Counselor Education and Supervision* Vol. O (Spring 1961), pp. 24–27.

HUTSON, P. W. (a) "Deriving Counselor Education from Activity Analysis," *Counselor Education and Supervision* Vol. 1 (Spring 1962), pp. 132–140.

————. (b) "Another 'Position' Paper," *Counselor Education and Supervision* Vol. 2 (Fall 1962), pp. 40–44.

JOHNSON, RALPH H. "Selection of School Counselors: An Example," *Counselor Education and Supervision* Vol. 2 (Winter 1963), pp. 66–68.

JONES, VERNON. "Attitude Changes in an NDEA Institute," *Personnel and Guidance Journal* Vol. 42 (December 1963), pp. 387–392.

KEHAS, CHRIS D. "Toward a Redefinition of Education: A First Step Toward a Framework for Counseling," in B. Shertzer and S. C. Stone (eds). *Introduction to Guidance: Selected Readings* (Boston: Houghton Mifflin, 1970), pp. 59–71.

————. "Theoretical Formulations and Related Research," *Review of Educational Research* Vol. 36 (April 1966), pp. 207–218.

KLOPF, GORDON, AND COHEN, NANCY. "The Impact of the NDEA Counseling and Guidance Institutes on the Professional Education of School Counselors," *Counselor Education and Supervision* Vol. 1 (Spring 1964), pp. 151–161.

KNOWLES, RICHARD, AND SHERTZER, BRUCE. "Attitudes Toward the School Counselor's Role. *Counselor Education and Supervision* Vol. 5 (Fall 1965), pp. 9–20.

KOEPPE, RICHARD P. "The Elementary School Counselor—What Is He?" *The School Counselor* Vol. 12 (October 1964), pp. 11–13.

KRANZLER, GERALD D. "The Elementary School Counselor as Consultant: An Evaluation," *Elementary School Guidance and Counseling,* Vol. 3 (May 1969), pp. 285–288.

KRUMBOLTZ, JOHN D. "Parable of the Good Counselor," *Personnel and Guidance Journal* Vol 43. (October 1964), pp. 118–124.

LAIR, GEORGE SCOTT. "Educational Counseling: Concern of the School Counselor," *Personnel and Guidance Journal* Vol. 46 (May 1968), pp. 858–861.

LANDSMAN, TED. "Existentialism in Counseling: The Scientific View," *Personnel and Guidance Journal* Vol. 43 (February 1965), pp. 568–573.

LEACOCK, ELEANOR. "The Concept of Culture and its Significance for School Counselors," *Personnel and Guidance Journal* Vol. 46 (May 1968), pp. 844–851.

LISTER, JAMES L. "Supervised Counseling Experiences: Some Comments," *Counselor Education and Supervision* Vol. 6 (Fall 1966), pp. 69–72.

————. "Theory Aversion in Counselor Education," *Counselor Education and Supervision* Vol. 6 (Winter 1967), pp. 91–96.

————, AND OHLSEN, MERLE M. "The Improvement of Self-Understanding Through Test Interpretation," *Personnel and Guidance Journal* Vol. 43 (April 1965), pp. 804–810.

LIVINGSTON, INEZ B. "Is the Personnel Worker Liable?" *Personnel and Guidance Journal* Vol. 43 (January 1965), pp. 471–474.

LLOYD, DAVID O. "Counselor and Counselor Trainer Attitudes Toward Counselor Certification in the United States," *Personnel and Guidance Journal* Vol. 40 (May 1962), pp. 791–798.

LLOYD–JONES, ESTHER M., AND ROSENAU, NORAH (eds.). *Social and Cultural Foundations of Guidance* (New York: Holt, Rinehart and Winston, Inc., 1968), 641 pp.

LOUGHARY, JOHN W., *et al.* (eds.). *Counseling, A Growing Profession* (Washington: American Personnel and Guidance Association, 1965).

LUNDY, CHARLES T., AND SHERTZER, BRUCE. "Making Test Data Useful," *Personnel and Guidance Journal* Vol. 42 (September 1963), pp. 62–63.

MAES, WAYNE R. "Human Freedom and the Counselor," *Personnel and Guidance Journal* Vol. 46 (April 1968), pp. 777–781.

MATHEWSON, ROBERT H. "Manpower or Persons: A Critical Issue," *Personnel and Guidance Journal* Vol. 43 (December 1964), pp. 338–342.

McCULLY, C. HAROLD. "The School Counselor: "Strategy for Professionalization," *Personnel and Guidance Journal* Vol. 40 (April 1962), pp. 681–689.

————. "Professionalization: Symbol or Substance?" *Counselor Education and Supervision* Vol. 2 (Spring 1963), pp. 106–111.

————. "The Counselor—Instrument of Change," *Teachers College Record* Vol. 65 (February 1965), pp. 405–412.

————. (a) "Memorandum To An Emerging Profession," in Lyle L. Miller (Compiler) *Challenge for Change in Counselor Education* (Minneapolis: Burgess Publishing Company, 1969), pp. 35–44.

————. (b) "The School Counselor and His Unique Contribution," In Lyle L. Miller (Compiler) *Challenge for Change in Counselor Education* (Minneapolis: Burgess Publishing Company, 1969), pp. 35–43.

McDANIELS, CARL. "The Impact of Federal Aid on Counselor Education," *Counselor Education and Supervision* Vol. 6 (Spring 1967), pp. 263–274.

McNASSOR, DONALD, "High Priority Roles for Elementary School Counselors," *Elementary School Guidance and Counseling* Vol. 2 (December 1967), pp. 83–92.

MEEKS, ANNA R. "Elementary School Counseling," *The School Counselor* Vol. 10 (March 1963), pp. 108–111.

MILLER, FRANK W., AND SIMPSON, RICHARD J. "Some Legal Aspects of the Counselor-Client Relationship," *Counselor Education and Supervision* Vol. 1 (Fall 1961), pp. 19–30.

MURO, JAMES J., AND OELKE, MERRITT C. "The Elementary School Guidance Specialist as Perceived by Elementary School Principals and Teachers," *Elementary School Guidance and Counseling* Vol. 2 (March 1968), pp. 195–201.

NEEDHAM, JOHN, STODOLA, QUENTIN, AND BROWN, DARINE F. "Improving Test Interpretation Through Films," *Vocational Guidance Quarterly* Vol. 12 (Winter 1963–64), pp. 141–144.

NELSON, RICHARD C. "Issues and Dialogue," *Elementary School Guidance and Counseling* Vol. 1 (March 1967), pp. 146–151.

NEULINGER, JOHN. "Attitudes of American Secondary School Students Toward the Use of Intelligence Tests," *Personnel and Guidance Journal* Vol. 45 (December 1966), pp. 337–341.

NOBLE, F. C. "The Two-Year Graduate Program in Counselor Education: A Reexamination," *Counselor Education and Supervision* Vol. 4 (Spring 1965), pp. 160–162.

NUGENT, FRANK A. "Confidentiality in College Counseling Centers," *Personnel and Guidance Journal* Vol. 47 (May 1969), pp. 872–877.

O'HARA, ROBERT P. "A Theoretical Foundation for the Use of Occupational Information in Guidance," *Personnel and Guidance Journal* Vol. 46 (March 1968), pp. 636–640.

OLDRIDGE, BUFF. "Two Roles for Elementary School Guidance Personnel," *Personnel and Guidance Journal* Vol. 43 (December 1964), pp. 367–370.

PATTERSON, C. H. "The NDEA and Counselor Education," *Counselor Education and Supervision* Vol. 3 (Fall 1963), pp. 4–7.

————. "The Practicum Requirements in 'Standards'—1967 Edition," *Counselor Education and Supervision* Vol. 6 (Summer 1967), pp. 352–353.

————. "The Selection of Counselors," in John M. Whiteley (ed.). *Research in Counseling: Evaluation and Refocus* (Columbus, Ohio: Charles E. Merrill Publishing Company, 1968), pp. 69–101.

————. "The Counselor in the Elementary School," *Personnel and Guidance Journal* Vol. 47 (June 1969), pp. 979–986.

PERRONE, PHILIP A., AND EVANS, DAVID L. "The Elementary School Counselor: Coordinator? Or What?" *Counselor Education and Supervision* Vol. 4 (Fall 1964), pp. 28–31.

PETERSON, BETTIE H., AND BROWN, DUANE. "Does Teaching Experience Matter?" *Personnel and Guidance Journal* Vol. 46 (May 1968), pp. 893–897.

PETERSON, RON, AND FEATHERSTONE, FRED. "Occupations of Counseling Psychologists," *Journal of Counseling Psychology* Vol. 9 (Fall 1962), pp. 221–224.

PHILLIPS, JOHN L., JR., AND MARGOSHES, ADAM. "Confidence and Confidentiality," *The School Counselor* Vol. 13 (May 1966), pp. 235–238.

PIERSON, GEORGE A. *An Evaluation: Counselor Education in Regular Session Institutes* (Washington: U.S. Department of Health, Education and Welfare, Office of Education, 1965).

RICCIO, ANTHONY C. "Rationale and Irrational Criticism of the Guidance Movement," *The School Counselor* Vol. 11 (May 1964), pp. 226–232.

RICHARDSON, H. D. "Preparation for Counseling as a Profession," *Counselor Education and Supervision* Vol. 7 (Winter 1968), pp. 124–131.

RICKER, GEORGE A. "Must Counselors Have Taught?" *The School Counselor* Vol. 17 (September 1969), pp. 40–46.

ROSSBERG, ROBERT. "To Teach or Not to Teach: Is that the Question?" *Counselor Education and Supervision* Vol. 2 (Spring 1963), pp. 121–125.

SALYER, RUFUS C. "In Defense of Vocational Guidance," *Vocational Guidance Quarterly* Vol. 13 (Autumn 1964), pp. 66–68.

SCHELL, EDITH, AND DAUBNER, EDWARD. "Epistemology and School Counseling," *Personnel and Guidance Journal* Vol. 47 (February 1969), pp. 506–513.

SCHMID, KURT. "Code of Ethics for Counselors," *The School Counselor* Vol. 15 (September 1967), pp. 64–66.

SEAMAN, EARL H., AND WURTZ, ROBERT E. "Evaluating the Practicum: Whether and Whither?" *Counselor Education and Supervision* Vol. 7 (Spring 1968), pp. 282–285.

SHERMAN, ROBERT. "The School Counselor: Generalist or Specialist," *Counselor Education and Supervision* Vol. 1 (Summer 1962), pp. 203–211.

SHOBEN, EDWARD J., JR. "Personal Responsibility, Determinism, and the Burden of Understanding," *Personnel and Guidance Journal* Vol. 39 (January 1961), pp. 342–348.

———. "Guidance: Remedial Function or Social Reconstruction?" *Harvard Educational Review* Vol. 32 (Fall 1962), pp. 430–443.

SMITH, C. E., AND MINK, O. G. (eds.). *Foundations of Guidance and Counseling* (New York: J. B. Lippincott and Company, 1969), 514 pp.

SMITH, PAUL M., JR., Guest Editor. "What Guidance for Blacks?" *Personnel and Guidance Journal* Vol. 48 (May 1970), pp. 707–766 (complete issue).

SORENSON, GARTH. "Pterodactyls, Passenger Pigeons, and Personnel Workers," *Personnel and Guidance Journal* Vol. 43 (January 1965), pp. 430–437.

STEFFLRE, BUFORD. "What Price Professionalization?" *Personnel and Guidance Journal* Vol. 42 (March 1964), pp. 654–659.

————, AND LEAFGREN, FRED. "Value Differences Between Counselors and Administrators," *Vocational Guidance Quarterly* Vol. 10 (Summer 1962), pp. 226–228.

STERN, HERBERT J. "The Immediate Task of School Counselors," *Counselor Education and Supervision* Vol. 4 (Winter 1965), pp. 93–96.

STRICKLAND, BEN. "The Philosophy–Theory–Practice Continuum: A Point of View," *Counselor Education and Supervision* Vol. 8 (Spring 1969), pp. 165–175.

STRIPLING, ROBERT O. "Federal Legislation for Counseling and Guidance Services," *Counselor Education and Supervision* Vol. 6 (Winter 1967), pp. 137–140.

TENNYSON, W. WESLEY; BLOCHER, DONALD; AND JOHNSON, RALPH. "Student Personnel Records: A Vital Tool but a Concern of the Public," *Personnel and Guidance Journal* Vol. 42 (May 1964), pp. 888–893.

THORESEN, CARL E. "The Counselor as an Applied Behavioral Scientist," *Personnel and Guidance Journal* Vol. 47 (May 1969), pp. 841–848.

TIEDEMAN, DAVID V., AND FIELD, FRANK L. "Guidance: The Science of Purposeful Action Applied Through Education," *Harvard Educational Review* Vol. 32 (Fall 1962), pp. 481–501.

VONTRESS, CLEMMENT E. "Counseling Negro Adolescents," *The School Counselor* Vol. 15 (November 1967), pp. 86–91.

————. "Cultural Barriers in the Counseling Relationship," *Personnel and Guidance Journal* Vol. 48 (September 1969), pp. 11–17.

WALTON, FRANCIS X., AND SWEENEY, THOMAS J. "Using Predictors of Counseling Effectiveness," *Personnel and Guidance Journal* Vol. 48 (September 1969), pp. 32–38.

WARNER, RICHARD W., JR., AND HANSEN, JAMES C. "Alienated Youth: The Counselor's Task, "*Personnel and Guidance Journal* Vol. 48 (February 1970), pp. 443–448.

WESMAN, ALEXANDER G. "Intelligent Testing," *American Psychologist* Vol. 23 (April 1968), pp. 267–274.

WIENER, FREDERICK. "The Role of the Vocational Counselor as an Expert Witness," *Personnel and Guidance Journal* Vol. 43 (December 1964), pp. 348–354.

WRENN, C. GILBERT. *The Counselor in a Changing World* (Washington, D.C.: American Personnel and Guidance Association, 1962).

19

TRENDS IN GUIDANCE

What are some of the major trends in defining the counselor's role and functions?
What are the trends in preparation programs for guidance personnel?
What are the trends in guidance practices and program development?

The purpose of this final chapter is to picture trends in the field as moving, dynamic processes, and to describe them fully without becoming bogged down in minutiae. It would be idle to pretend that these trends—extensions in specific directions—are clearcut and simple. Trends in any field are highly complex affairs. They involve clusters of ideas, interests, institutions, and individuals all intricately interrelated, often tangled and untidy.

The trends discussed are those that we believe are most appropriate to the student in a first course in guidance. Concentration is frankly centered on what seemed to be a few main areas of concern. Reference notations are used sparingly. How does one document a trend? Like blind men feeling an elephant, most individuals "see" guidance and the direction in which it is moving from their own narrow viewpoints, and the authors are no exception.

The trends presented in this final chapter are grouped into three major categories: counselor role and function; preparation and certification; and, practices and programs. To some extent, separation of trends into these categories is for ease of presentation. Some of the trends could fit one category as well as another, just as some overlap with another.

TRENDS IN COUNSELOR ROLE AND FUNCTION

Trend I:
Practicing school counselors, as individuals and as a group, will increasingly assume initiative and leadership in determining counselor role and function.

Every counselor, by acts of omission and commission, contributes to the expectations others have for school counselors. Each contributes to the success or failure of a role definition acceptable to present and future school counselors. Defining what is and what should be the counselor's role is a personal responsibility that cannot be avoided. Those who, because of ignorance or indifference, try to stay on the sidelines, inevitably influence the course of events, even though their influence is due to lack of involvement.

In the last few years, activities such as the study of counselor role and function conducted by the American School Counselors Association[1] have given evidence that practicing school counselors are increasingly providing leadership in defining the school counselor's role and function. Within this group, positions vary from those who would prefer to return to a time when the counselor's functions were simple to those who want to move ahead toward specialization at an unrealistically rapid rate. Despite these curiously conflicting attitudes and positions, most working school counselors appear to approach the question of counselor role and function on a practical, matter-of-fact basis.

Defining counselor role and function is the object of pressure from various groups and individuals—counselor educators, school administrators, psychologists, sociologists, school patrons, the U.S. Office of Education, etc. Pressures from these groups are not surprising; on the contrary they are both unavoidable and desirable. Each of these groups has a stake, in one way or another and to one degree or another, in what is finally requested of the school counselor. The important point is that school counselors have become more and more organized and sophisticated in sifting out and deciding for themselves what is relevant in defining the job of the school counselor. They have become increasingly concerned that they and not others are responsible for their role definition and job functions.

Trend II:
The counselor, at both elementary and secondary school levels, is emerging as (1) a counselor to students, and (2) a consultant to teachers, parents, and administrators.

Counselors today operate amid a complex web of expectations. Although this has always been so, in the early 1970's the consensus of what coun-

[1] John W. Loughary, Robert O. Stripling, and Paul Fitzgerald, *Counseling, A Growing Profession* (Washington: American Personnel and Guidance Association, 1965).

selors can and should do is beginning to consolidate. That which emerges, however, is not unanimously supported. Some individuals want to maintain a variety of counselor functions. Others insist upon a single or at least minimal set of functions. The problem of bringing all who claim membership in the school counseling profession to some agreement regarding counselor role and functions is formidable and perhaps unachievable. But some clarification of the general expectations held for counselors now seems to be emerging. It is highly probable that the specifics will always vary to some degree, depending upon the setting and the individual.

The authors' assessment of the many conflicting perceptions of the school counselor's role is that it is emerging as a broad role that includes the art of counseling pupils, individually and in small groups, and the function of consulting with teachers, administrators, and parents. This definition implies a relatively high degree of specialization by individuals. It is a definition that emphasizes the use of interpersonal skills in a counseling relationship that helps pupils achieve appropriate, self-selected goals. It emphasizes the counselor's consultative capacity in order to facilitate change in the basic social and learning environment of the school and encourages the individual's facility in utilizing the available conditions for his optimal development.

Change in counselor functions must incorporate two factors—change in individual staff members and institutional change. Counselors' conceptions of what are legitimate counseling concerns and how they may be met must evolve from orderly program changes. Program changes will emanate increasingly from changes in individual counselors; i.e., depending largely upon their understandings of the meanings of and rationale behind what they do.

This definition of the school counselor requires that he is both a generalist and a specialist. In reality he is "both/and" not "either/or." He is a generalist in the sense that he is available to all students and in the sense that he possesses knowledge of the total school program. He is a specialist in the dynamics of human behavior and in counseling and consulting relationships as well as an expert in his knowledge of counseling theory and practice and career development. He is also a specialist in securing changes in the school to better accommodate all pupils, while facilitating the development of individual pupils.

Trend III:
School counseling is becoming a lifetime career field.

At one time—and no doubt even today—school counseling was viewed as simply a way-station for a career in administration. Many individuals entered the counseling field for negative rather than positive reasons. Some entered to take refuge from the rigors of classroom teaching. Because they had difficulty in working with students in a class setting and never acquired the skills that would make classroom work interesting and rewarding for pupils, they decided to enter counseling as a means of entrance to administrative positions. Therefore, their choice of counseling was not a positive discovery, but rather an expediency. Many have commented on the curious career pattern—teacher-coach, counselor, principal, superintendent—characterizing the transient career pattern of many school counselors. But who can deny the persuasive power of the human need for more financial remuneration to care for growing families and the individual psychological need for status and prestige?

Today, counselors are speaking not only of having a counseling job, but also of being members of a profession. Their professional preparation, if it truly succeeds, leads to psychological identification of person and function so that the individual achieves a meaningful occupational identity. Counselors will increasingly identify with what they do in counseling, they will derive satisfaction in doing it, and will achieve meaning from the status which their function will afford them in the school community. Increasingly, committed counselors are finding it difficult to think in terms of occupational change, even if greater economic security is offered in other endeavors. Their deepest satisfactions stem from carrying on activities that are rewarding. The sense of a lifetime commitment to the field is an indispensable attribute of a profession.

It seems certain that school counseling now and in the future will be a lifetime profession with much to offer the person who brings something to it. Certainly the counselor's need for recognition and prestige is increasingly being met without the necessity of turning to the route of general school administration. Some will find their satisfactions in the establishment and maintenance of the helping relationship, while others will find their satisfaction in providing professional leadership in guidance program development and management. While the school counselor undoubtedly will be confronted for some time with obstacles in the achievement of a consolidated, lifetime professional identity, he will find it correspondingly easier in the future to move toward a clearly defined role that he himself helps to develop.

TRENDS IN THE PREPARATION AND CERTIFICATION OF GUIDANCE PERSONNEL

Although the various points developed in this section could legitimately be treated as separate factors, the authors have chosen to group them under two major trends. The first of them pertains to changes already underway in counselor preparation programs which have direct impact upon individuals seeking training. This impact will be found in the educational activities they experience. The second major trend includes several influences more external to the individual pursuing training, yet of considerable import to counselor preparation programs and certification procedures.

Trend IV:
Major changes will continue to occur in counselor preparation programs.

Full-time, integrated, two-year graduate school programs of preparation for guidance practitioners are now available in high-quality training programs. Although it is true that counselors with one year's preparation are urgently needed in schools and that a nationwide shortage of counselors exists, the demand for two years of preparation is increasingly recognized. Counselor preparation will move from one year to two years, not because counselor educators or professional standards have stated that such a program is necessary before counselors are qualified for school placement, but because of a more pressing consideration. School counselors, when confronted by the harsh realities of coping with the counseling relationship and other guidance activities, feel ill prepared. Their common reaction is to seek additional training or to point out how their previous training had been inadequate for specific situational demands. In further training, they seek not more of the same, but differentiated advanced training accommodated to identifiable needs of a personal and professional nature.

Many have commented upon a two-year training program, but few have clarified the perplexing questions that nag those who attempt to offer such a program. For example, in areas other than academic performance, how may potential candidates best be selected? Should a degree be awarded, in addition to the usual master's degree, for successful completion of a two-year program? Not only must these and many other even more fundamental questions relating to course offerings, content, and nature of program be dealt with, but pragmatic tests must be made of the speculations that are offered as answers to such questions.

Extensive study and research will be devoted to improving selection criteria for admission and retention in preparation programs for guidance personnel. Reflection upon the competencies needed for performance as a school counselor makes it clear that most programs place a disproportionate emphasis upon academic performance for admission and retention. However, it should be noted that there is some justification for this practice, since much of the current content of counselor preparation programs demands academic proficiency. But it is almost universally agreed that academic excellence should not be the sole criterion, even though it is expected of all candidates in quality programs. Given this quality, research efforts will turn increasingly to identifying the constellation of personality factors needed for successful counselor performance.

The content of programs will increasingly reflect an interdisciplinary approach in the preparation of guidance personnel. More attention will be given to the essential psychosocial foundations of human behavior and interaction. Present practices in high-quality programs include child and adolescent psychology, personality and learning theory, measurement and research principles as undergirdings for the development of counseling competencies and attitudes. Increasing interaction with other disciplines such as sociology, economics, philosophy, anthropology, and political science is rapidly becoming the hallmark of quality preparation. More seminars in counselor education programs will be devoted to integrative explorations across a variety of related disciplines. Counselor educators, with the help of experts from other disciplines, will move in the direction of selecting and organizing pertinent content necessary to true interdisciplinary study.

Preparation will increasingly incorporate heavy utilization of simulated materials because of problems inherent in providing "live" experiences at an early level of training. Both ethical and practical considerations demand the use of suitable substitutes for live clients at that period of preparation when the trainee is considered a novice. Simulated materials provide a natural and safe solution to the dilemma involved in extending early practical experiences to counselor trainees. Additionally, these simulations possess great promise for structuring varied experiences that are often not available through didactic instruction but which are considered highly desirable.

Emphasis in counselor preparation will increasingly be placed upon self-understanding and knowledge of how the individual's self-structure contributes to counseling effectiveness. Though techniques and "how to do it" methods will continue to dominate the focus of counselor education for some time, greater stress upon the unique, the personal, the distinctively human character of the counselor's work will emerge.

Up to the present time, many, if not all, counselor education programs have "just grown." If they are to become individualistic and oriented to achieving student personal growth, a reorganization of the total program, not just the addition of single courses, will be necessary to achieve the goal of self-examination and self-growth. Supervised practica, guidance internships, and small-group experiences are presently being used to foster individual growth. The amount of time devoted to individual and group counseling experience, internship, and process-group experiences will undoubtedly increase in preparation programs. Professional standards for preparing secondary school counselors currently call for one-quarter of the preparation program to be given over to supervised practice and internship experience. Most programs do not currently meet this standard, but many are moving in this direction, and more will do so.

Trend V:
A variety of external forces will increasingly influence counselor preparation and certification.

State certification requirements will undergo upgrading, and more uniformity among the fifty state patterns will evolve. State certification for guidance personnel undergoes constant change as a result of developments and changes in counselor preparation. This will continue in the future. Change will occur in several respects: (1) the number of years of teaching experience will be reduced substantially (to one year or to the substitution of a guidance internship in lieu of teaching experience); (2) reciprocity procedures will be initiated so that personnel prepared in one state at a nationally accredited counselor education institution will be able to practice in the schools of any state; (3) the practice of certifying personnel, or waiving certification, for those who spend half-time or less in counseling will disappear; and (4) the determination of candidate eligibility for employment in school guidance positions will increasingly rest with counselor education institutions rather than with the state education departments.

Preparation programs and state certification requirements for elementary school counselors will achieve separate status. An increasing number of counselor education institutions will establish programs for preparing elementary school counselors. In such programs, overlap with secondary school preparation and certification requirements will continue to exist because all counselors share common goals and a common basis of occupational identity. However, delineation of the distinctive qualities of elementary school guidance programs and functions will lead to recognizably separate programs and certification requirements.

Governmental support and financial aid for the preparation of guidance personnel will increase. In view of the shortage of counselors that exists at the elementary, secondary, junior college, and college levels, the amount of federal government financial support for counselor preparation programs will, of necessity, increase to help alleviate the shortage. This financial support is needed to attract promising candidates to the field, as well as to strengthen the quality of counselor preparation programs.

Governmental support to counselor education programs will increasingly be given on a longer term basis than the one year that exists at present. Though many individuals involved in counselor education hope that the nature of the support given would be changed from contract programs with institutions to stipends or fellowships to individual students, it appears unlikely that this will become the pattern.

A national organization will be used to accredit institutions that provide guidance preparation programs. The "Standards for Counselor Education in the Preparation of Secondary School Counselors"[2] will be used as evaluative criteria for judging counselor education programs to ensure adequate professional preparation. The responsibility for implementing the "Standards" will be placed on some type of national accrediting organization. This national organization will either be (1) the Association for Counselor Education and Supervision (ACES) division, or another American Personnel and Guidance Association agency; (2) a presently constituted accrediting organization such as the National Council for Accreditation of Teacher Education (NCATE); (3) a voluntary organization of counselor education institutions that have gone through the process of internal or self-evaluation and external evaluation conducted by other professionals; or

[2] *Ibid.*

(4) some combination of the preceding approaches, possibly involving ACES-appointed members to NCATE evaluation teams.

If a national accrediting organization for counselor education does come into existence, several events are likely to occur. First, a gradual reduction in numbers will take place among the some four hundred institutions purporting to offer counselor education programs. Second, graduates of nationally accredited counselor education programs will automatically meet state certification requirements in all fifty states. Third, full-time, two-year programs of study in counselor education will become the rule rather than the exception.

GUIDANCE PROGRAMS AND PRACTICES

Trend VI:
A variety of factors will increasingly influence the development of guidance programs.

The number of guidance personnel employed in elementary, secondary, junior college, and collegiate institutions will increase. It takes little vision to recognize that expanding enrollments at all school levels will necessitate the employment of more and more guidance personnel. The public's acceptance of, and demand for, such personnel does not seem to be waning. High expectations and public support continue to favor counseling services and increasing numbers of counselors in the schools. The impetus provided by federal governmental financial support for counselor preparation and for local school program extension will continue to stimulate the employment of greater numbers of guidance personnel.

A related trend is the increased tendency for more and more guidance personnel to be employed on a full-time basis. Although many school administrators have in the past preferred part-time guidance personnel, the trend has been, and continues to be, toward full-time responsibilities. In addition, an expanding number of schools will employ counselors during the summer months. It may be anticipated that more schools will provide full-time guidance services to students on a year-round basis. Good salary increments are being paid to counselors and this trend will continue for many reasons, not the least of which is the short supply of counselors.

Federal financial support for elementary and secondary school guidance programs will continue. More and more federal funds will be earmarked for elementary school guidance programs for those states participating in federally supported educational programs. To administer these funds at the state level, the number of guidance personnel in the state departments of education will be increased. State department of education personnel will increase their consultative and supervisory services to elementary and secondary schools.

Guidance programs will become more centrally organized and administered. While teachers will continue to be counted upon to fulfill their guidance responsibilities, more and more schools will make use of full-time counselors. Guidance as a recognizable, clearly definable service conducted by specialists will be identified as indispensable to the schools. Responsibility for administration and coordination of the program will be assigned to individuals who are personally inclined and professionally prepared to give it leadership and direction. The ratio of students to counselors will continue to be reduced so that counselors can (1) provide individual and small-group counseling to students and (2) consult with parents, teachers, administrators, and other school staff members. School systems will provide integrated guidance programs from kindergarten through Grade 12. Further, clarification of the guidance duties and responsibilities of teachers, counselors, administrators and related pupil personnel workers will emerge.

An increasing number of other specialized pupil personnel workers will be sought for employment. Efforts to secure the services of psychologists, psychiatrists, social workers, and psychometrists will meet persistent shortages and the competition that other employment settings pose. When schools are successful in acquiring these personnel, however, they will work in much closer relationship to counselors, teachers, and administrators than they have in the past. The services provided by each of these specialists will need to be more clearly delineated if duplication among them is to be avoided.

Trend VII:
Continued program modification will result from two important influences.

Greater use will be made of automated equipment for the storage and retrieval of pupil appraisal data and other information about the school and community. Wrenn states:

> The school system of the near future will have information centers where three kinds of information are electronically collated, analyzed, and transmitted for use by various members of the staff—centers for educational information, for vocational information, and for information about student characteristics.[3]

Automated equipment will of necessity be used if demographic studies of the changing student population and ecological studies of the changing communities are to be conducted efficiently. Self-teaching devices—computers, teaching machines and programed textbooks—will be used to impart educational and vocational information.

Grossman and Howe advance the following reasons why automated data-processing equipment is used minimally in schools: "(1) The equipment has been designed primarily for use by business and industry; (2) school

[3] C. Gilbert Wrenn, *The Counselor in a Changing World* (Washington: American Personnel and Guidance Association, 1962), p. 145.

budgets are restricted by law to the extent that it is difficult to finance data processing machinery needed for a complete job; (3) school operations are fixed by tradition more than those of business and industry."[4] But the necessity to handle records more adequately and quickly will lead to greater use of data-processing machinery.

Research and evaluative studies of guidance programs and practices will increase. Because more and more school and lay personnel will ask "Of what value is guidance?" greater efforts will be expended for research activities. Service studies dealing with data descriptive of pupils, the situations in which students operate, and the factors bearing on the process of counseling will be conducted more extensively and with greater intensity in the schools.

Trend VIII:
Counselor practices will increasingly undergo modifications.

Specialization will occur in the functions assigned local school guidance personnel. As smaller schools are consolidated and the number of counselors employed in each school increases, specialization will occur in the assignments given counselors. For example, one counselor may be assigned primary responsibility for testing operations, another will be responsible for college counseling and placement, and a third will have the primary responsibility for personal counseling. Some schools have already so defined their assignments on this or some other basis of specialization, and others will do so increasingly in the future.

Greater use will be made of small-group counseling and group guidance practices and procedures. Whether the use of group procedures is justified in the name of economy of time and effort, whether it is merely fashionable, or whether such procedures best accommodate need, more and more guidance practitioners will use them in an increasing number of school situations. Acceleration of the use of group work will in part stem from the increasing numbers of counselor education programs that offer training in the area. Greater research efforts will be expended to identify situations and conditions in which group procedures are valuable.

More selective and discriminatory use of standardized tests will be practiced. Criticism of tests—their construction, selection, interpretation and use—will probably continue, but the criticism will wane with an increase in the appropriate usage of tests. The present practice of indiscriminate administration of test after test will slowly be curtailed. While the proportionate number of tests administered will be reduced, more appropriate use will be made of the results of those administered. Expectancy tables will be constructed covering the differential probabilities of success in different high school curricula, the chances of success in different colleges and among the

---

[4] Alvin Grossman and Robert Howe, "Human Economy and Data Processing," *Personnel and Guidance Journal* Vol. 43 (December 1964), p. 343.

different departments and schools within colleges. More schools will establish policies requiring that if tests are administered, their results must be interpreted to students and their parents. In short, guidance personnel will become much more sophisticated in the selection, use, and interpretation of tests.

Finally, the recent increased stress in counselor preparation programs upon behavioral approaches will result in greater use of these techniques in counseling settings. Techniques such as reinforcement, modeling, role playing, simulation, and the like, will be incorporated in some counselors' practices.

ANNOTATED BIBLIOGRAPHY

SHERTZER, BRUCE, AND STONE, SHELLEY C. (eds.). *Introduction to Guidance: Selected Readings.* Boston: Houghton Mifflin Company, 1970, 459 pp.

Treatment in Part Eight (pp. 421–443) is given to trends in guidance. Philip Harris presents some ideas as to what guidance may be like in 2000, Robert Crary discusses specialization as a trend in counseling; Joseph Johnston, the challenge of data processing; and Buford Stefflre, the direction of future research in guidance.

TRAXLER, ARTHUR E. "Trends in Guidance," *School Review,* Vol. 58 (Spring 1950), pp. 14–23.

Back in 1950, Traxler described ten trends that were emerging in the then-current theory and practice of guidance. A review of them to determine how many have "emerged" to date provides fascinating reading in light of the past twenty years.

ZERAN, FRANKLIN N., LALLAS, JOHN E., AND WEGNER, KENNETH W. *Guidance: Theory and Practice.* New York: American Book Company, 1964. Chapter 14, pp. 281–296.

The authors structure their "look into the future" of guidance around seven broad themes. They expect changes in guidance to accelerate considerably in the near future.

SELECTED REFERENCES

COTTINGHAM, HAROLD F. "National-Level Projection for Elementary School Guidance," *Personnel and Guidance Journal* Vol. 44, (January 1966), pp. 499–502.

CRARY, ROBERT W. "Specialized Counseling—A New Trend," *Personnel and Guidance Journal* Vol. 44 (June 1966), pp. 1056–1061.

DELANEY, DANIEL J. "Simulation Techniques in Counselor Education: Proposal of a Unique Approach," *Counselor Education and Supervision* Vol. 8 (Spring 1969), pp. 183–188.

DUNLOP, RICHARD S. "Employment and Compensation Practices for Counselors," *Personnel and Guidance Journal* Vol. 47 (June 1969), pp. 944–950.

HANSEN, JAMES C. "Job Satisfactions and Job Activities of School Counselors," *Personnel and Guidance Journal* Vol. 45 (April 1967), pp. 790–794.

HARRIS, PHILIP R. "Guidance and Counseling in the Year 2000," *Counselor Education and Supervision* Vol. 7 (Spring 1968), pp. 262–266.

HASCALL, EDWARD O. "Campus Unrest: Worldwide Challenge for Student Affairs," *Personnel and Guidance Journal* Vol. 48 (April 1970), pp. 619–628.

HOPPOCK, ROBERT. "Guidance Fifty Years Ago," *Vocational Guidance Quarterly* Vol. 16 (December 1967), pp. 130–133.

HOYT, KENNETH B. "Attaining the Promise of Guidance for All," *Personnel and Guidance Journal* Vol. 45 (February 1967), pp. 624–630.

ISAKSEN, HENRY L. "Emerging Models of Secondary School Counseling as Viewed from the Context of Practice," *The School Counselor* Vol. 14 (May 1967), pp. 273–280.

IVEY, ALLAN E. "The Association for Human Development: A Revitalization for APGA," *Personnel and Guidance Journal* Vol. 48 (April 1970), pp. 527–532.

JOHNSON, BEVERLEY B. "Into the Seventies," *Counselor Education and Supervision* Vol. 8 (Fall 1968), pp. 73–76.

LISTER, JAMES L. "The Consultant to Counselors: A New Professional Role," *The School Counselor* Vol. 16 (May 1969), pp. 349–354.

MACHT, LEE B. "Education and Mental Health: New Directions for Interaction," *Personnel and Guidance Journal* Vol. 47 (May 1969), pp. 855–858.

MILLER, LYLE L. (compiler). *Challenge for Change in Counselor Education* (Minneapolis: Burgess Publishing Company, 1969), 181 pp.

PATTERSON, C. H. "What is Counseling Psychology?" *Journal of Counseling Psychology* Vol. 16 (January 1969), pp. 23–29.

RICCIO, ANTHONY C., AND WALZ, GARRY R. (eds.). "Forces for Change," *Counselor Education and Supervision* Vol. 6, No. 3SP (Spring 1967), pp. 213–284.

SAMLER, JOSEPH. "Vocational Counseling: A Pattern and A Projection," *Vocational Guidance Quarterly* Vol. 17 (September 1968), pp. 2–11.

WALZ, GARRY R., AND LEE, JAMES L. "Funded Personnel Services Research: Patterns and Trends," *Personnel and Guidance Journal* Vol. 47 (June 1969), pp. 970–974.

WINBORN, BOB B., AND MARTINSON, WILLIAM D. "Innovation in Guidance: A Mobile Counseling Center," *Personnel and Guidance Journal* Vol. 45 (April 1967), pp. 818–820.

APPENDIX

PROFILE OF A GUIDANCE PROGRAM

DOROTHY JOHNSON
Associate Professor of Education
Purdue University
Calumet Campus
Hammond, Indiana

The development of these profile sheets for use in the introductory course in guidance grew from the realization that students need some firsthand knowledge of a functioning program in order to comprehend the course content adequately. It is not enough to wander into the guidance office now and then or to lunch occasionally with a counselor, though both of these activities should be encouraged. Some method of organized investigation is necessary. Completion of the profile sheets on the following pages provides a procedure by which students in a beginning guidance course may systematically acquaint themselves with at least one guidance program, preferably the one in operation in their own school.

The forms were designed to be useful to the following groups of people:

1. Students who are preparing to become counselors. The profile sheets may help these students gain some insight into the work of the school counselor in his actual setting, which may help them to decide whether or not to pursue the counselor preparation program.
2. Teachers who have felt the need to learn more about guidance and counseling. The profile sheets may serve to acquaint teachers with the guidance program and with the work of the counselors in their own schools; thus, the teachers may more clearly understand and more effectively assume their role in the guidance effort in their schools.
3. Administrators who want to know more about the principles and purposes of guidance and counseling. The profile sheets may be applied to inventory services, facilities, and staff in their own schools and to help them to plan future guidance programs.
4. Working counselors who have enrolled in the introductory guidance course for any of a number of reasons. The profile sheets may be employed to assess the facilities and functioning of the programs in their own schools and to provide a basis for evaluating themselves as counselors. They may further be used as a guide for inservice training work of administrators, teachers, and other pupil personnel.

Actually, the objectives served by the profile sheets are the same as those served by the course itself. These profile sheets merely extend course content and objectives to application within the school setting.

It is suggested that students complete the profile sheets one area at a time periodically during the semester, and not attempt to cover all areas in one visit with the counselor. Practice indicates that benefits are greater if students complete the appropriate profile sheets at the time a particular area or service is being discussed in class.

PROFILE OF A SCHOOL GUIDANCE PROGRAM

Part 1:   Background Data

Kind of school:

Enrollment:

Brief description of community:

Average class size:

Staff (administrative; instructional personnel; pupil service personnel; services, including library, audio-visual, etc.; clerical) :

Special classes or groups:

Curricula:

Extracurricular offerings:

Percentage of students who
   a. Enter the job market upon graduation:
   b. Enter post–high school training other than four-year college:
   c. Enter four-year colleges:
   d. Enter armed forces:

e. Drop out:

f. Other:

Brief general statement of school philosophy:

Additional information:

Comments:

Part II: Guidance Staff

No. of counselors

Total:

Full-time:	Male:	Female:
Part-time:	Male:	Female:

Number certified:

For part-time assignments:
   a. Number of periods per day for counseling:
   b. Other assignments:

Pupil-counselor ratio:

Assignment of students to counselors:

If counselors are not employed by your school, who is charged with counseling and guidance functions?

Clerical assistance:

Location and description of guidance offices:

Additional information:

Comments:

Part III: Cumulative Records

Location:

Accessibility:

Information recorded:

Recorder(s) of information:

Disposition of records:

Additional information:

Comments (including your attitude toward the cumulative records in your schools, their usefulness, the extent to which you use them, etc.):

Part IV: Appraisal Instruments

1. Standardized tests:

    Philosophy concerning standardized tests:

    Purpose of testing in this school:

    Group Tests   *Individual Tests*

    Testing program:

    Developed by:

    Instruments Used   *Testing Schedule*   *Administered by*

Scored by:

Results recorded by:

Procedure for interpretation of results

    a. To students:

    b. To teachers:

    c. To parents:

Counselor use of test results:

Teacher use of test results:

Administrator use of test results:

Student use of test results:

Additional information:

Comments:

Part V: Interviewing and Counseling

If the counselor were to classify himself as operating from a particular theoretical orientation, how would he identify himself?

Approximately what percentage of the counselor's time is spent in:

  a. Counseling individual students?
  b. Working with small groups of students?
  c. Working with large groups of students?
  d. Interviewing parents?
  e. Working with teachers?
  f. Working with other school personnel?
  g. Working with outside agencies?
  h. Doing clerical tasks?

Approximately what percentage of students:

  a. Are called in by the counselor for interviewing or counseling?
  b. Are self-referred?
  c. Are referred by teachers?
  d. Are referred by others?

Does the counselor routinely call students into his office?
  Circle one: YES   NO

If YES, how many times a year?
What order of precedence, if any, does he follow (e.g., seniors first)?
What (mechanical) procedure does the counselor use for getting students into his office for counseling?

Is group counseling employed? Circle one: YES   NO
If YES, what kinds of topics are discussed?

How are group members chosen?

What is the counselor's opinion of the effectiveness of group counseling as compared with individual counseling?

Describe briefly group guidance activities in the school:

Additional information:

Comments:

Part VI: Using the Information Service

Briefly list the kinds of occupational material available:

Where is the material kept?
What filing system is used?

Briefly list the kinds of educational material available:

Where is the material kept?
How is it filed?

Briefly list the kinds of social-personal material available:

Where is the material kept?
How is it filed?

Who is responsible for gathering informational material?

Who is responsible for filing informational material?

To what extent do the following people use the material?
(Rate this item by indicating *very much, much, average, little, none.*)

  a. Students:
  b. Teachers for class units:
  c. Counselors working with students:
  d. Other (specify):

Additional information:

Comments:

Part VII: Integrating the Guidance Program

Briefly describe the organizational pattern of the school guidance program. (If it is part of the pupil personnel organizational pattern, show it as related to the whole program. Use the reverse side of this sheet if necessary to draw an organizational chart.)

What do teachers and guidance personnel understand the teacher's role in guidance to be?

What do the administrator and guidance personnel understand the administrator's role in guidance to be?

What does the counselor understand his own role to be?

Describe briefly the counselor's role in working with parents:

Describe briefly the counselor's role in cooperating with other school personnel:

List the community agencies with which the counselor works:

Additional information:

Comments:

Part VIII: Research and Evaluation

What research has the counselor been involved in within the past two years?

How were the results used?

What plans does he have for future research activities?

Has the school guidance program or any part of it undergone an evaluative study within the past two years?

within the past five years?

If so, briefly describe purpose, procedures, and results:

What revisions, if any, are being considered as a consequence of the outcome of the study?

What problem does the counselor see in terms of conducting research and evaluation studies involving guidance and counseling activities?

In the counselor's opinion, what are the particular strengths of the guidance program in this school?

In the counselor's opinion, what improvements are needed?

Additional information:

Comments:

INDEX OF NAMES

INDEX OF SUBJECTS

DATE DUE			